The History and Nature of Sociological Theory

The History and Nature of Sociological Theory

Daniel W. Rossides
BOWDOIN COLLEGE

Houghton Mifflin Company   Boston
Dallas   Geneva, Illinois
Hopewell, New Jersey   Palo Alto   London

To Anna Rossides,
who is also my mother

Portraits by Ben Black

Library of Congress Catalog Card Number: 77–074382

ISBN: 0-395-25059-5

Contents

Preface

The purpose of this text is to introduce students to the distinctive methods and concepts of sociological theory. By necessity, it is also an introduction to social theory—and, to a considerable extent, to philosophy and the history of natural science. Though it is primarily intended for students taking courses in sociological theory (both the history of theory and current theory), it should also be useful for theory courses in political science, anthropology, and philosophy. Its heavy emphasis on the epistemological problems of social science also recommends it for courses in disciplines that deal with how humans acquire and validate knowledge about themselves and nature.

Social theory is the most abstract aspect of social science, so I have given considerable attention to its special pedogogical problems. I have assumed that few undergraduates have much background in intellectual history or social theory and that a first course in sociological, political, or social theory is the student's first exposure even to modern thinking about society. Accordingly, the text provides considerable background material—especially on ancient, medieval, and early modern thought—to introduce students to the rudiments of social analysis. Throughout, I have defined terms as they appear and have provided bibliographic footnotes with the textual material. A classification scheme (which is explained in Chapter 1) is provided to structure the incredible richness of Western social theory. In addition, I have made an effort to select representative theorists to ensure that all the main ideas, positions, themes, and problems in sociology (and, in considerable measure, social science) are covered. In-depth analyses of individual theorists, organized around a number of themes, offer students the full range of sociological theory while permitting them to keep the main tradition and themes of sociology in sight. Given this framework, instructors should find it easy to expand any of these discussions or to follow their own bent in choosing additional or alternate theorists, themes, and emphases.

Part I introduces liberal (or capitalist) civilization, which spawned sociological theory. It depicts the salient aspects of liberal thought as it emerged in the seventeenth century and reached fruition in the French and Scottish Enlightenments, concentrating on the work of Hobbes, Locke, and the *philosophes*. Sociological theory, the special type of social thought that is peculiar to liberal/capitalist society, is delineated by contrasting it with the general current of social theory (by definition, Western in nature). The ideas of theorists representing the salient concerns of ancient, medieval, and early modern social theory—for example, Plato, Aristotle, the Stoics, Saint Thomas, Marsileo of Padua, Machiavelli, and Bodin—provide a comprehensive introduction to the main body of the text, the extended analysis of sociological theory.

In the West, concern about society took the unusual form of theory or rational analysis and synthesis; indeed, the only distinctive feature of diverse periods of Western history is the continuous commitment to a rational world view. To understand Western thinking about society, therefore, is also to understand its rational or scientific orientation (constantly challenged and hampered, of course, by nonrational and irrational forces). One of this study's basic organizing assumptions is that no understanding of Western social theory, including sociological theory, is possible without relating it to general currents of thought in philosophy and science (epistemology, moral philosophy, and natural philosophy). Thus I have provided considerable background in currents of thought in philosophy and science and their relation to social theory.

Despite its commitment to rationalism, Western society has undergone deep transformations in its concept of reason and in the results derived from its use. Part I is also devoted to exploring these transformations, primarily to bringing the conscious and unconscious assumptions behind the modern views of nature and human nature into relief. However, the emphasis on basic transformations in the Western world view is balanced by a stress on continuities.

The most important organizing idea of this study is that symbolic culture is not understandable independent of its social context. Accordingly, there is considerable background material about the social contexts in which social and sociological theory developed and about the social functions that theories perform. Social theory prior to the seventeenth century met the needs of a complex agrarian society. The rise of capitalism produced a distinctive mode of thought called *liberalism*, which in its various forms has helped to legitimate and direct liberal (capitalist) society. Throughout the text sociology is assumed to be the scientific wing of liberal social theory; its development is related to stages of social development within various societies. Accordingly, there are extensive discussions of and contrasts among the specific national contexts (England, France, Germany, Italy, and the United States) in which sociology grew. Thus, this study is also an analysis and interpretation of liberal society.

The heart of the study is a close examination of sixteen representative sociologists selected on the basis of some or most of the following criteria: originality, influence, basic ideas and values, and temporal and national context. The thought of these seminal thinkers is thematically linked, and overall stages of development in sociological theory are introduced by chapters providing background material on intellectual and scientific developments (for example, conservative social theory, romanticism, socialist social theory, nineteenth- and twentieth-century science, and pragmatism). There are brief discussions of various personages, including Burke, Maistre, Bonald, Laplace, Fourier, LePlay, Maurras, Kautsky, Bernstein, Luxemburg, Lenin, and Mao. There are also lengthier treatments of some key figures such as Hobbes, Quetelet, and Marx. (However, as a leading figure in socialist, as opposed to liberal, thought, Marx is not treated as a sociologist.) A concluding chapter indicates the range of current sociology by showing deviations from a main tradition. Since there is considerable diversity along several lines in the dominant empirical mode of thought, I develop three typologies to bring current sociology into relief.

It is an extremely revealing fact about the discipline of sociology that no genuine historical treatment of the development of its main methods and ideas exists. Many of the "histories" and "commentaries" are based, either implicitly or explicitly, on the assumption that the history of sociology is a steady and cumulative emancipation from superstition and error. Much of what passes for the history of sociology is based on the teleologically inspired assumption that a progressive enlightenment through science is rooted in the nature of things; this is an intellectual relic of early evolutionary positivism. The various historians of sociology have accepted (sometimes consciously, often not) a number of corollaries of this assumption. The first is the belief that the theorists of the past, especially those of the eighteenth and nineteenth centuries, were well-intentioned but inadvertent contributors to the march of sociology and that, therefore, a short digest of their thought adequately accounts for their place in history. A second corollary is the view that the major purpose of examining the past is to extract from thinkers the permanent insights contained in their thought (insights which these thinkers did not always appreciate) and thereby to speed the process of synthesizing knowledge about human behavior. In other words, the assumption at the root of most surveys of sociological theory has a deeply ahistorical bias. The overriding interest of historians of sociology has been to describe what sociology has established about human behavior—and thereby to establish sociology as a science. However, it is just as important to ask, How is sociology possible? It is unscientific, in short, to neglect questions concerning the origins of sociology and the social functions that, wittingly or unwittingly, it performs.

Only by asking such questions can sociology (and social science) free itself from the distortions to which it is subject by virtue of its dependence on historical and social conditions. Its failure to develop a historical perspective about its development also has its roots in the nature of the discipline itself. As a fledgling science, sociology set itself a daring goal, the attainment of a unified scientific theory of human behavior. In formulating this goal, the founders of sociology gave the discipline a static, metaphysical cast that it has never been able to shed.

One of the great ironies of intellectual history is that the devastating analysis of natural law and traditional metaphysics in the positivist philosophy of David Hume never seriously affected the metaphysical pretensions of sociological positivism. This history of sociological theory explores a number of errors and deadends, but none rival sociology's failure to face up to the momentous implications of Hume's insistence that the realms of reason, fact, and value are intrinsically different and that their unification is beyond the power of history, philosophy, and science alike. Needless to say, in writing this history, I also rely on Hume's emphasis on the controlling force of experience in human life, a force that is as influential in sociological theory as it is in any other form of behavior. More precisely, the major interpretive idea underlying this study of sociological theory is that ideas have their source in social experience, an idea that is derived from sociology itself. Therefore, the use of the sociology of knowledge, the more formal term for this mode of analysis, means that sociology will study itself and write its own history. It also means that those who study this history will be doing sociology, not merely reading about it.

The teleological approach to the history and development of sociology, in which each generation engages in the conceit of assuming that all previous intellectual endeavor is a preparation for its synthesizing genius, is the most dangerous pitfall that sociology faces. The effect is to evade or mask the serious philosophical dilemma that has plagued sociology ever since the teleological view was refurbished by the Enlightenment and smuggled back into both normative and scientific social theory: to the extent that the various studies of the development of sociological theory distort our view of the past by their failure to recognize the metaphysical and ideological nature of much of that theory, they also distort our view of the present. This study, therefore, will have achieved its purpose if, in making it easier for students to acquaint themselves with some of the great theorists of sociology, it also helps them avoid the metaphysical craving that underlies much of those theorists' thought. However, in achieving this goal, it will have failed its full purpose if it creates the impression that there exists outside of science a better means of ensuring human survival and well-being.

D. R.

The History and Nature of Sociological Theory

Chapter 1
The Interpretive Frame: Sociology
and Liberalism

Human thought reflects time and circumstance, and this is as true for social theorists as it is for business leaders, carpenters, and homemakers. One of the main dangers in analyzing thought is the rationalist conceit that thinking is an ahistorical, asocial natural process rather than a natural process evolving from time-bound, sociocultural ingredients and forces. This analysis of sociological theory will be based on the latter view. Throughout this book, I shall assume that human symbolic achievements are related to the type of society in which people live, especially to the society's economy. My major assumption is that the stages of development in sociological theory follow the stages of capitalist development within given national and international contexts.

The advent of a capitalist economy, around 1500, was a momentous event in human history, comparable in importance to the Neolithic revolution or the domestication of agriculture, approximately ten thousand years ago. The social philosophy that emerged with capitalism was liberalism, or the form of thought expressing the values and beliefs of the middle class.[1] The transformation of the capitalist economy, predominantly agricultural and commercial until the eighteenth century, into an industrial economy was and is the most revolutionary aspect of the capitalist era; it spawned unique benefits and miseries, first in the West and then gradually in other parts of the world. My major assumption, to repeat, is that for more than two centuries, a fundamental affinity has existed between the thought structure of

---

[1] The meaning of the term *liberalism* will unfold gradually. Essentially, it refers to the acceptance of private property, private economic motives and actions, and political and legal equality as central social institutions. Thus, both Democrats and Republicans in the United States are liberals; that is, both accept the validity and superiority of capitalist/liberal society while disagreeing on how to run it. For a fuller discussion of historical, European developments in liberal social thought, see George H. Sabine's classic commentary, *A History of Political Theory*, 4th ed. (Hinsdale, Ill.: Dryden Press, 1973); *The Encyclopedia of the Social Sciences* (New York: Macmillan, 1930–1935; or its successor, *The International Encyclopedia of the Social Sciences* (New York: Macmillan and Free Press, 1968).

sociology—and social science in general—and the intellectual and moral needs of liberal/capitalist society.

Sociologists have been interested in the evolution of their specialty since the time of Condorcet, Saint-Simon, and Comte. However, in seeking an explanation of sociology's origins and development, sociologists have failed to subject the discipline to its own scientific canons. As a consequence, sociology still accepts uncritically the essentially teleological explanation of its origin and nature put forth by early sociologists. In an attempt to correct this view, my study will assume that sociological theory is not a mysterious or spontaneous emanation of human creativity or rationality but an understandable process of historical development. It will shed useful light on sociological theory by examining it in relation to liberal society.

THE SOCIOLOGY OF KNOWLEDGE

The sociology of knowledge holds that thinking is not an autonomous mental activity explicable only in terms of categories like mind or reason, but an activity that takes place under determinate social and cultural conditions. In applying this idea to the development of sociology, I shall not be writing conventional intellectual history. The primary objective of intellectual history is to trace the development of ideas. Intellectual historians are not unaware of the sociological basis of thought—witness, for example, the work of John Herman Randall, George Sabine, or Richard Hofstadter—but their major task is to show the congeniality, clash, or causation among ideas.

This study does something quite different. In addition to analyzing the development of the methodological and substantive ideas of sociology, I wish to impart an understanding of the origins of these ideas and their functions in a liberal society. I hope, in other words, to show how liberal society has influenced the assumptions, methods, conclusions, and problems of sociological theory.

By necessity many of the peripheral intellectual currents that have figured in the development of sociology and of modern social science must be either omitted or treated in a cursory fashion. However, to achieve historical perspective, our analysis must take into account some movements and individuals outside sociology. Thus, attention will be paid to the relations among sociological theory, moral philosophy, epistemology, and the general current of natural science. Attention will also be directed at the important role played by conservatism (monarchical-theocratic traditionalism) in the development of French sociology; romanticism in the development of both science and sociology; German idealism and historicism in the development of German sociology; pragmatism, institutional economics, and Freudian and Watsonian psychology in the development of American sociology; and socialist thought, especially Marxism, in the development of sociology in general.

I shall also discuss individual thinkers—for example, Kant, Hegel, Maistre, Marx, William James, Veblen, and Dewey. However, since this is not a history of social science, even these important figures cannot be treated exhaustively despite their large contributions to social science or to sociology. Some of them, like Kant, Hegel, Veblen, and Dewey, are liberals but not sociologists; some, like Maistre and Marx, stand outside the tradition of both liberalism and sociology.

Because of Marx's enormous contribution to social science and because of the considerable overlap between his thought and the ideas of sociology, his omission as a representative sociologist requires a word of explanation.[2] Despite the similarity between Marxian and sociological thought, Marx worked outside the main assumptions and methods of both liberalism/ capitalism and sociology. The similarities exist because Marx accepted liberalism as a valid and progressive historical movement; he sought not to deny but to perfect its main bent toward the rational mastery of the world. Thus, partly by definition and partly on the basis of the ensuing argument, I shall assume at the outset that Marx is not a sociologist. However, Marx (and Marxism) played a large role in the development of sociology, especially from the late nineteenth century on; by then, the general current of sociology had turned from an attempt to justify the liberal revolt against feudalism and monarchy to a defense of liberalism, not only against Marx but against socialism in general. Although as a pioneer contributor to the sociology of knowledge and to the idea of economic causation, Marx will be represented on every page of this study, I do not include him in the universe of representative sociologists.

Sociological theory is subjected to the sociology of knowledge not to discredit it, but to portray it as human activity taking place through a social medium. Most of the contributors to the sociology of knowledge did not regard the social origin of thought as incompatible with truth or with scientific objectivity. Only by displaying the competing methods and ideas of sociology against the backdrop of the social structure(s) that gave them birth can one hope to scrape away the historical dross, expose the hidden presuppositions that either nourish or contaminate scientific social thought, lay to rest outmoded disputes and differences, and avoid the unscientific waste involved in the replication of ideas and methods already in the storehouse of science.

The variables involved in such an enterprise are many and complex and cannot be treated adequately in any one study. Thus, very little will be said

[2] Marx's social theory, as well as a general discussion of Marxism and socialist social theory, may be found in Chapter 13.

about the personal lives of the theorists, and only brief references will be made to their class, education, or occupational background.[3] The main emphasis will be on the relation between the theories of sociologists and the general sociocultural experiences to which they were exposed in their respective temporal and national contexts. It is hoped that this study will establish a comprehensive framework for a scientific understanding of sociological theory and stimulate others to fill in the gaps that remain.

THE CONCEPT OF LIBERALISM

Liberalism Defined

To use the term *liberalism* in sociology is apt to cause misunderstanding, and it is best to define it at the outset. As used conventionally in the field of political science, liberalism refers to the symbols of capitalism, or, more precisely, to the political, legal, economic, and social values and doctrines of the middle class. On the theoretical spectrum of complex social systems, liberalism occupies a position between feudalism and feudal-absolutism, on the one hand, and socialism on the other. Translated into its sociological synonyms, it is equivalent to such terms as *positive, industrial, Gesellschaft, rational-legal, urban, or associational* society. Since this type of society has been the main concern of modern sociology, a fuller analysis of it will emerge in due course. However, it would be helpful, paying due regard to the caution that is necessary when dealing with high-order abstractions, to give some of its salient characteristics now.

The logic underlying liberal society is that human beings, functioning in large part individually, can achieve both a theoretical and a practical mastery of the natural and social universes. From the Middle Ages on, mostly as a consequence of economic expansion, there arose a new confidence in the ability of human beings to understand and to control the forces in both nature and human nature. The achievements in natural science of Copernicus (1473–1543), Galileo (1564–1642), and Newton (1642–1727) were matched during the seventeenth century by an attempt by two of liberalism's major early theorists, Thomas Hobbes (1588–1679) and John Locke (1632–1704), to make comparable discoveries about human nature. This double-barreled surge of confidence in human reason reached full tide during the French Enlightenment, when the belief in the power of reason to penetrate every reach of the phenomenal world characterized the modal intellectual climate of Western society.

The attempt to embody this new view of human reason in social institutions emerged unevenly during the seventeenth, eighteenth, and nineteenth

---

[3] Useful material along these lines about a number of major figures in modern social science may be found in Lewis A. Coser, *Masters of Sociological Thought: Ideas in Historical and Social Context,* 2nd ed. (New York: Harcourt Brace Jovanovich, 1977).

centuries. Once established, however, the institutionalization of bourgeois rationality led to private property, economic individualism, intellectual freedom, and political and legal equality. Fundamentally, the image of society was based on the idea of the free individual, the market economy, and the centralized rational-legal state. With the emergence of the new social system, the norms of social control lost their organic congruity and closure and became less structured and more open-ended. Despite the diversity and the conflict produced by this new social system, the early liberal theorists were certain that the natural order on which these norms rested would eventually ensure social harmony and progress. The later disenchantment of liberals with the idea of a natural order marks a new phase in the development of liberalism, and we must therefore distinguish between early and late liberalism.

Early and Late Liberalism

The social development of capitalism can be divided into two general phases, something political science does on the level of political philosophy by referring to early and late liberalism. Each phase, though continuous in fundamentals, has a distinctive economic, political, moral, and intellectual flavor. The first period, from the late Middle Ages to the middle of the nineteenth century, marks the evolutionary surge of the European middle class, a surge that effected the most profound social transformation in human history. The fact that this social upheaval reached a series of well-defined and well-known climaxes in 1688 and in 1789 should not obscure the less apparent fact that its origins reach back to medieval, Roman, and Greek natural and social philosophy, the Judaic-Christian tradition, Eastern technology, known and unknown merchant adventurers, and the complex consequences of ecclesiastical and dynastic rivalry. The first phase of liberalism, which reached its climax in the late eighteenth and early nineteenth centuries, had an intellectual and institutional unity based on Newtonian cosmology. The social theory of early liberalism redefined the medieval tradition of natural law in the light of Newtonian physics and the needs of a business civilization. By the middle of the nineteenth century, ideas of individual liberty, political-legal equality, private property, contract, profit, and the self-equilibrating exchange economy were being institutionalized in a number of Western countries, most notably Great Britain and the United States. In the United States, these ideas took the form of natural law: in politics as natural rights, and in economics as the theory of laissez faire.

The second phase of liberalism emerged in the latter part of the nineteenth century as the middle class overhauled the natural-law philosophy it had used against feudalism to equip itself better for the new problems and enemies that had appeared with industrialization. The doctrines of natural rights in politics and of laissez faire in economics were both gradually scrapped by advanced theorists as a host of liberal thinkers throughout Western society became increasingly concerned about the vitality, morality, and stability of industrial-urban corporate capitalism. Faced with the ravages and conflicts produced by hectic and undirected industrial expansion, liberal theorists came more and more to see social harmony, progress, and individualism not as emanations from a benevolent and rational natural order but as social products that had to be created through institutional management. Theorists such as John Stuart Mill (1806–1873), Thomas Hill Green (1836–1882), and Leonard Hobhouse (1864–1929) in England and John Dewey (1859–1952), James Harvey Robinson (1863–1936), Charles Beard (1874–1948), and Walter Lippmann (1889–1974) in the United States (along with many sociologists) demanded that people exhibit in politics the same creativity they had shown in science and business. In short, middle-class theorists recognized that a measure of intelligent state action was necessary to counteract the ills and cleavages of economic and social life.

The resort to state action by middle-class theorists was not so novel as one might think. Those in the middle class had supported royal centralization during the fifteenth and sixteenth centuries when their interests coincided with those of royal absolutism. When they turned against absolutism, they may have deposed of monarchs and even monarchy, but they kept the centralized legal and political institutions (the state, the crown) of absolutism as the necessary framework for individual freedom and private enterprise. The resort to state action (the so-called welfare state) during the nineteenth and twentieth centuries by the middle class marks merely another phase in the continuing rationalization of social life that began in the late Middle Ages.

Of course, in speaking of the late nineteenth century it is a misnomer to talk of a middle class, at least in Great Britain and the United States, if by that term one means a group standing between lord and serf. The "middle class" was supreme in Great Britain and the United States, while in France, its grip on society, though none too firm, was nonetheless strong enough to yield a liberal social system. Only in Germany, where the Prussian nobility remained supreme, could one still speak of a middle class—but it was a middle class confronted on the right by a powerful landed aristocracy and on the left by a working class committed to political *and* social democracy; as such it faced problems quite different from those it had faced in the past.

The problems and interests of the historic middle class differed, depending on its strength and national location. In France and Germany during the nineteenth and twentieth centuries (until World War II), the middle class was still engaged in a struggle over the system of society. In Great Britain and the United States a triumphant middle class was engaged primarily in managing a society of which it had full possession. The middle class had become an upper class of the very rich; an upper-middle class of successful business people, executives, and professionals; and a lower-middle class of small businessowners and farmers, lower-level professionals, and white-collar workers. Much of the political dynamics of mature liberal society comes from the competition among these three levels of the historic middle class to determine how society should be managed and how the goals of workers, socialists, and assorted radicals on both left and right can be contained.

Although rarely understood in this way, the role of sociology during the middle-class surge to power was to provide an anchor for liberal values and beliefs and to establish liberal society as the terminal of social development. After the triumph of the middle class, sociology also identified social problems and proposed solutions to them in ways that did not reflect badly on the liberal social system as such. Thus the empirical outlook, organized empirical research, and the social problems–social policy orientation emerged in the nineteenth century and combined after World War I to form the relatively coherent late-liberal perspective that has dominated sociology in the twentieth century.

The two phases of liberal social development are also related, therefore, to two distinct epistemological phases in liberal social theory—rationalism and empiricism—that also mark natural philosophy or natural science. The first phase of modern science (roughly 1500–1800) is the predominantly deductive, speculative science that runs from Copernicus to its high point in Descartes (1596–1650) and Newton. Throughout this phase, it was assumed that human reason and nature had identical structures, and that since experience is deceptive, one can more easily and truly investigate nature through rational discourse. This was an old assumption, to be sure, but post-Renaissance science was revolutionary in that mathematical logic supplanted formal logic or teleology as the medium of truth.

Beneath deductive science was a strong empirical current; it nourished and sustained the dominant deductive tradition and slowly gathered strength until it gained supremacy as the modal method of science in the nineteenth century. This revolutionary epistemology destroyed the static, mechanistic view of the world and resulted in two discoveries: first, that nature contained an intrinsic pattern of qualitative change and second, that nature was far more complex and mysterious than anyone had imagined. Nineteenth-century science, with its emphasis on an open-ended, evolving universe, had an affinity with the emphasis on intelligent adjustment that can be found in the general current of late liberal social thought. Indeed, all branches of science underwent change in the nineteenth century to meet the needs of a rapidly expanding industrial society confronted with a continuous flow of complex, novel problems.

THE CONCEPT OF POSITIVISM

Positivism Defined

For various reasons I have redefined the term *positivism.* There are a number of ways in which the term will be used. Broadly speaking, it will refer to the distinguishing characteristic of Western civilization: the belief that human beings can rationally understand and control phenomena. As Lovejoy has pointed out, the West's belief in the power of reason has never been an otherworldly idealism but always an attempt to connect reason with either the substratum or the structure of phenomena.[4] On the other hand, Western belief has never been content to accept the world as it is or as it presents itself to the senses. Even in its most empirical phase, Western thought has sought to abstract from nature its underlying laws. The main periods in Western intellectual history have been characterized by shifts from an emphasis on one type of reason to another and from reason (deduction) to an emphasis on fact (induction). In the period stretching from the origins of Greek philosophy through the Middle Ages to the Enlightenment, the modal emphasis of science was on logic—the logic of teleology and of mathematics. The Enlightenment reversed this emphasis on reason, or more properly on deduction, by establishing the revolutionary assumption that the validity of beliefs rests on their conformity with fact. In no case, however, was the shift from one modal methodology to the next an either/or proposition; it was always a blend of old and new ingredients. As Alfred North Whitehead was one of the first to point out, without the Greek faith in the rationality of the universe, Galileo and other modern scientists could not have probed for the basic laws underlying phenomena. Further, without the same faith in the orderliness of the universe, the Enlightenment could not have taken the revolutionary step of seeing reason in phenomena themselves. We are so used to taking for granted the Greek craving for metaphysics or the abstraction of laws from phenomena that we sometimes forget that the empiricism that has helped to make the post-Enlightenment world so dynamic is a special type of Greek rationalism. It is far removed from the more common empiricism, devoid of abstraction, that in Babylonia, Egypt, or China is associated more with traditionalism than with the active mastery of the world.

I shall also use the term *positivism* to refer to the continuing attempt by Western thinkers to bring human nature within the jurisdiction of reason (science), the view that refuses to see human beings as creatures of custom or as unpredictable creatures of passion, the gods, or other mysterious forces. Thus Socrates (470–399 B.C.) is the main figure in the Greek attempt to reason about human nature teleologically—that is, in the same way that

---

[4] Arthur O. Lovejoy, *The Great Chain of Being* (New York: Harper & Row paperback, 1960), originally published in 1936.

Greek natural philosophers had reasoned about nature. The next great figures are Hobbes (1588–1679) and Locke (1632–1704); each in his own way applied the new spirit of post-Renaissance rationalist (mathematical-mechanistic) science to the understanding of human nature. Shortly after Hobbes, the current method of thinking about human behavior–empiricism–slowly emerged. Sociological theory, one of its variants, is the subject of this study. Thus, while I shall refer to positivism in general as simply the most advanced stage of rationality, I shall use it mainly as a term to describe the broad modern emphasis on the need to derive knowledge and theory from empirical analysis.

It should be noted that the term *positivism* is not used this way in sociology although this use has some standing in the field of philosophy.[5] Sociologists tend to take stands for or against positivism (or neopositivism), a fact that obscures the fundamental acceptance of empiricism within sociology. That is, there is a general consensus that the methods of the natural sciences are applicable to human nature and human behavior.[6]

Types of Positivism

My broader definition of positivism, therefore, covers the empirical orientation common to all main branches of sociology. In addition, in order to identify the various methodologies and conclusions advanced during the general development of sociological positivism, I shall employ a number of subtypes. *Naturalistic positivism* deals with behavior in natural terms; that is, it deals in climatic, geographic, physical, biological, or psychological terms. *Sociocultural positivism,* on the other hand, deals with human behavior in terms of cultural factors and social interaction. Further, I shall use the terms *monistic positivism* and *pluralistic positivism*. Monistic positivism, usually naturalistic, is a theory that uses one method—usually logic, despite its verbal commitment to empiricism—and finds one principle or cause in human nature, usually biological or psychological. The term *pluralistic positivism,* usually sociocultural, refers to a theory that employs a plurality of methods to cope with the complex data of human behavior and that sees a multiplicity of causes in human affairs. Finally, I shall identify a minor tradition in sociology that rejects on *scientific grounds* [7]

[5] For a valuable survey and introduction to positivist philosophy, see Leszek Kolakowski, *The Alienation of Reason: A History of Positivist Thought,* trans. Norbert Guterman (Garden City, N.Y.: Doubleday, 1968), also in paperback, originally published in 1966.
[6] For variations in and departures from this consensus, see Part VI, Chapter 23 and especially Chapter 24.
[7] There is a sharp distinction throughout this study between those who reject the goal of a unified theory of human behavior on scientific grounds, and those who reject it on humanistic, philosophical, or religious grounds.

the idea of a unified theory of human behavior, whether natural or socio-cultural—a tradition I call *historical positivism.*

It is important to note that naturalistic and sociocultural positivism—and the deductive and inductive phases through which both have passed—share the same monistic (or metaphysical or nomothetic) goal: the reduction of all social phenomena to law, either separate from or merged with nature at large. I must state at the outset that I have serious reservations about the possibility of such a science. My own belief, derived from Weber and ulti-mately from Hume, is that empirical science precludes the idea of rational—or general or systematic—knowledge or theory. Science is fundamentally a tool to be used against the recurrent but also novel problems that human beings face. In Weber's terms, sociology has "eternal youth."

The above typology should help us to identify theorists and to see that some theorists who are against positivism are really against empiricism; it should be useful in establishing the similarities and differences that exist between theorists and in avoiding the often misleading "schools of thought" approach. These broadly conceived comparative categories will allow us to cite reasons for categorizing theorists and at the same time to note that many individual theorists are mixtures of these types and thus in some respects stubbornly idiomatic. Perhaps the chief merit of these theoretical types is that they provide the detachment needed for talking *about* sociological theory—something that must be clearly distinguished from sociologists talk-ing about society or about each other.

The Structure of the Study

Though my overall purpose is to view the development of sociological theory and social science in terms of its varying social base and its relation to other intellectual currents, I shall not follow a uniform pattern of exposi-tion. Part I analyzes liberal civilization as it emerged between the thirteenth and the eighteenth centuries. Chapter 2 briefly describes liberal society, while Chapters 3 and 4 present the basic transformation of the Western view of nature and human nature into the now-dominant liberal world view. My analysis includes a brief description of the emergence of capitalism and ends with an extended discussion of the rise of modern natural and social science (liberalism).

In providing this backdrop to the rise of sociology, I shall end my initial discussion of liberalism with the Enlightenment. This is no arbitrary deci-sion; the various forces that make up the many-sided historical phenomenon called liberalism reached their climax during the Enlightenment, when they merged to form a coherent world view. Indeed, the eighteenth century is best seen as a vast watershed period that at one and the same time climaxes earlier developments and inaugurates fresh advances. It saw an end to what

Lewis Mumford has called the water and wood stage of Western economic development and the revolutionary beginnings of the coal and iron stage. During this century English society secured the political gains it had made in the Settlement of 1688. Despite the widespread corruption of English political life during the eighteenth century and the constant threat of absolutism, the English political structure served as an inspiration to foreigners and its own colonists alike. This inspiration found expression first in the American Revolution and then in the cataclysm of the French Revolution. By the end of the century, political liberalism awaited only the further development of the coal and iron economy for full realization.

Riding the crest of centuries of economic expansion, the middle class during the Enlightenment took possession of the intellectual life of Europe, formulating as it did a relatively coherent and comprehensive metaphysical theory to justify its claim to social power. In natural science, the Enlightenment ended the deductive phase of modern science and set loose the revolutionary powers of empirical investigation. In social thought, it rounded out the growth of modern science by boldly proclaiming that human nature was also amenable to empirical study.

In attempting to combine empirical social science with the tradition of natural law, however, the middle class encountered a far-reaching philosophical dilemma arising from the deeply antirational nature of empiricism. Confronted with the need to develop a worldly, empirical social theory to justify the revolutionary society it was creating, the middle class looked for a new metaphysics. In so doing, it accepted the basic assumption of Western rationalism, namely that one can obtain both a total unification of data and a rational basis for morals. Though the middle class explicitly rejected the teleological world view, it ended by constructing a metaphysics that was not only a theory of natural law but was teleological as well. The teleological character of bourgeois metaphysics is especially apparent in the doctrine of progress that a growing number of liberal political and social philosophers in the eighteenth and nineteenth centuries used as the cornerstone of their moral or normative theory.

Sociological theory was the scientific wing of this metaphysical endeavor. Despite its antimetaphysical avowals, early sociology continued the Greek (metaphysical) quest for truth and virtue by claiming that empirical science could unify all knowledge and establish a valid morality. In Parts I and II, I shall examine the social and intellectual context in which sociology arose and compare the methods and ideas of sociology to those of natural science, showing the ways in which both disciplines fulfilled the scientific, the moral, and the ideological needs of an emerging capitalism.

In subsequent parts, I shall continue to analyze the relationship of sociological theory to natural science and to liberal society, examining these relationships concurrently with the theorists themselves. There will be no attempt to sketch out in a single place the general structure of liberal society or of natural science after 1800. The changing social and intellectual context in which sociology developed will be discussed in the chapters introducing each of the remaining parts and, because of the diverse national backgrounds in which sociologists worked, in the introduction and conclusion to each of the chapters devoted to their work.

PART I
The Civilization of Liberalism: 1200–1800

Chapter 2
The Origins and Nature of Liberal Society

The unique value and belief system called sociology could only arise from the unique value, belief, and institutional system called liberal society. It is not easy to construct the sociocultural context in which sociology emerged and flourished. Even maintaining a high level of abstraction and ignoring the differences among countries, the task of defining the origins and nature of liberalism is a heavy one. Fortunately, my purpose is not to present an exhaustive definition of middle-class civilization, but merely to provide a backdrop against which to understand the origins and nature of sociological theory.

THE FEUDAL BACKGROUND

In tracing the decline of the complex *Gemeinschaft* (feudal) society of medieval Europe and the rise of liberal civilization, one must avoid the lure of easy verbal contrasts that simplify causation and exaggerate both the rapidity and the evenness of social-system change. In point of fact, the old and the new social systems of Western Europe were intertwined for centuries, and many of the features of the old social and cultural structure actively promoted the rise of modern society; many, with slight changes, became important parts of the new system.[1] Social systems are exceedingly durable entities, and it is best to think of social-system change in terms of successive stages; conscious and unconscious actions, stemming from long-range causes, at last crystallize to form a qualitatively different social structure. If one is to understand the nature of the modern world, one must resist the notion of a unitary, creative, and progressive middle class. A number of "middle classes" emerged from the eleventh century onward with little continuity among them. After an initial burst of innovative economic activity, each of the various middle classes became conservative, and

---

[1] In this connection, see Gideon Sjoberg, "Folk and 'Feudal' Societies," *American Journal of Sociology* 58 (November 1952): 231–39, also a Bobbs Merrill reprint (S-270).

new groups of people would form to supply the energy and initiative for future capitalist expansion.[2] To complicate analysis further, one must not think in terms of single, autonomous social systems undergoing natural stages of development; rather, one must think in terms of the interaction of societies or—perhaps better—in terms of the relation between the division of labor within a society and the division of labor among societies (world system). The emergence of the uniquely capitalist division of social labor and world view cannot be explained without referring to complementary social systems—revitalized feudal systems, colonies, and dependent trading areas. The following discussion assumes, for example, that England's transformation into a liberal society was not simply an act of self-determination. England could not have specialized in wool so readily had Poland not specialized in grain and lumber, which helped to revitalize Polish feudalism. England's specialization in textiles was complemented by the plantation-slave economy and the cultivation of cotton in the American South. On a broader plane, one cannot explain the rise of parliamentary government in England without referring to England's economic expansion, and the latter cannot be explained without some reference to an international division of labor (or a redistributive world-economy) that supplied England with cheap raw materials and allowed the English economy to specialize in manufacturing and services. I shall not dwell on this aspect except to note that sociology has only begun to understand this process;[3] the failure of sociology in this regard is a conspicuous example of the ideological function it has served during its career.

The outstanding feature of a *Gemeinschaft* society is a passive attitude toward the problems of earthly existence. This was true even of the complex structure of Western feudalism. Medieval people assumed that their legacy of ideas, values, and practices was correct and good. The center of social gravity lay outside the individual, in a body of custom considered sacrosanct either because it was of divine origin or because it had successfully withstood the test of time. Custom not only regulated behavior, but, along with religion, it also gave individuals their basic identity. The core value in this body of custom stemmed from the idea of birth, though Western feudalism must not be thought of as a simple family-based society. The

---

[2] For a classic analysis, see Henri Pirenne, "The Stages in the Social History of Capitalism," *American Historical Review* 19, no. 3 (April 1914): 494–515, available as a Bobbs Merrill reprint (E-171).

[3] For the most notable start, see Immanuel Wallerstein, *The Modern World-System: Capitalist Agriculture and the Origins of the European World-Economy in the Sixteenth Century* (New York: Academic Press, 1974), the first of a projected four-volume study. Wallerstein's thesis that a new world system, the world economy, has replaced the cumbersome empire world system—and the implications that this holds for the social sciences—are succinctly stated in his essay, "A World-System Perspective on the Social Sciences," *British Journal of Sociology* 27 (September 1976): 343–352.

family, graded into noble and ignoble types, was used as a basis for assigning relatively complex religious, political, and economic statuses. The differentiation of statuses on this basis gave medieval Europe an estate type of social stratification in which the higher benefits and responsibilities of social existence, though distributed by birth, required a considerable amount of specialized training.

As an advanced civilization, therefore, medieval feudalism was an admixture of ascription and achievement, tradition and innovation; it included a relatively complex specialization of institutions, even though functional specialization coincided closely with position in the social hierarchy. In this complex agrarian society, the well-born performed functions that are accorded the highest priority in almost all traditionalistic cultures. Part of the nobility safeguarded, transmitted, and developed religious and philosophical values, while the rest concerned itself with maintaining family honor and performing political and military functions. In addition, as the controllers of land—the major source of wealth—the nobility supervised a primitive subsistence economy.

It is difficult for the modern mind to grasp the place of land in the feudal scheme of things. An individual's relationship to land was fixed by birth and derived from social custom. Land was not owned as private property to be bought, sold, and exploited for its best return. Land was primarily the physical setting for a complex set of social functions; economic behavior did not receive the importance we attach to it today.

The state as we know it today, a separate institutional order with special personnel and specific functions, did not exist. Political order was maintained mostly on a personal, customary basis. The population, considered either as individuals or as strata, was enmeshed in a web of personal loyalty stretching from serf to king. There was no impersonal, bureaucratic civil and military administration, and no state organized on a legal-territorial basis with attributes of sovereignty. There was no legal code, precisely worded in terms of logical categories to cover all possible contingencies, for settling disputes and protecting rights. In a feudal society disputes theoretically could not arise, since normative and behavioral structures supposedly coincided. Far from having a specialized legal code, feudal populations did not distinguish among law, custom, and morality, and they believed that the structure of intertwined norms in which they had their being had always existed as known at that time. Legislation in the modern sense was unheard of, and tampering with the time-hallowed canons of conduct was considered sacrilegious.

The responsibility for supplying society's material needs fell primarily to the lower stratum, the serfs, who made up the bulk of the population and provided food and personal services. In addition to the serfs, a small staff of skilled workers provided commercial and some manufacturing services and goods. The feudal attitude toward work was vastly different from our own; according to the dominant group, work was imposed by God as a punishment for sin. Economic work gave no prestige and was considered merely a means to the end of biological existence. Not surprisingly, the feudal attitude toward nature was one of passive conformity, a humble acceptance of both its bounty and its hardships. Economic activity was judged by need or use values, not by exchange or market values. Feudal society was a consumption economy in which work and production were for the immediate satisfaction of a static set of needs. There was no thought of production to meet the needs of tomorrow nor of the need to develop new technology, products, and services. Obviously, an economy based on human muscle power, rather than on machinery and brain power, is not likely to glorify and encourage economic motives.

No understanding of Western feudalism is possible without an insight into its unique religion. *Gemeinschaft* societies are heavily dependent on family and religion for their central values. In most such societies, religion is so intertwined and congruent with other social institutions that no institution, religion included, has a separate identity. If religion is based on a passive otherworldliness and the religious inequality of individuals, the resulting congruity between society and religion can lead to a rigidly articulated caste system. This is the case in Hinduism. Christianity, however, stands at the other extreme. Its doctrines contain the possibility of serious discord between the realm of Caesar and the realm of God. Its sharp separation of humanity from nature and God, its focused otherworldliness in which salvation is a reward for resisting nature's temptations, and its religious equality based on an explicit moral and ethical universalism—all are potential sources of tension with the claims of traditional particularism.[4]

Medieval feudalism was relatively indifferent to the benefits of intensive specialization. The division of social labor was based, of course, on the functional specialization of strata—nobility and serfs—and even these two main strata were somewhat specialized. One part of the nobility ruled and fought, and another prayed and thought; while members of the non-noble stratum performed an assortment of economic functions. Nowhere, however, was there a sharp functional specialization. The secular nobility indiscriminately combined family, political, legal, administrative, military, moral, religious, and economic functions into one all-embracing "political" function. For its part, the religious nobility combined religion, philosophy, logic, science, and aesthetics into one "spiritual" function. Indeed, involvement of the clergy in politics, law, administration, and warfare showed that it felt

[4] Particularistic norms emphasize not the abstract universal character of things or individuals, but their differences and uniquenesses. Thus, emphasis is placed not on humanity but on types of human beings (serfs, slaves, lords, wives, heroes); not on law, but on privileges; not on ethics, but on taboos; not on nature, but on types of nature (sacred grove, forbidden mountain).

no obligation to confine itself to purely spiritual tasks. If this was true of the upper stratum, it is not surprising that the lower stratum was also caught in a seamless social web in which no status could be separated from other statuses to insure either functional efficiency or a private identity. Thus, it is not surprising that the forces of custom, religion, and philosophy thought of social behavior as the embodiment of a seamless, static, hierarchic structure of objective and revealed truth whose only beginning and end were in the mighty drama of salvation.

LIBERAL SOCIETY:
ITS STRUCTURE AND MEANING

The period from 1200 to 1800 is a distinctive phase in the general history of liberalism, a turbulent period of social-system and world-system change. It is marked by a distinctive technology corresponding roughly to Lewis Mumford's eotechnic phase of development—the creative, preparatory technological complex based on water and wood, as distinguished from the post-1800 paleotechnic (coal and iron) and neotechnic (electricity and alloy) phases.[5] As both consequence and cause of eotechnic technology, new norms emerged to enforce the well-known bourgeois values of thrift, industry, pecuniary gain, and rational endeavor. Political and social thought reflected the basic individualism of economic practice, and leading liberal theorists soon came to picture society as a collection of self-propelled atoms. Out of the conflict and stalemate of contending factions, classes, sects, and churches in England came the norms of individual liberty and equality, toleration, and the supremacy of law. The period before the onrush of industrialization (say, before 1850), is sometimes called *early* or *classical liberalism*; it saw the development of the distinctive attributes of the modern state, be it liberal democratic (England) or authoritarian (Prussia). Though society was still predominantly agrarian, early liberalism witnessed the emergence of the focused authority of the national state, sovereign internally as well as in its relations with other states. With a centralized political structure, characterized by a superior legal order and a superior lawmaking structure—king or parliament—came centralized administration and the centralized emotions of patriotism. In short, the modern nation state emerged, its sovereignty matched in liberal democratic states by the sovereignty of the individual—each sovereignty making the other both possible and necessary.

The transformation and gradual replacement of feudal Christendom between the thirteenth and eighteenth centuries is the most profound social

[5] Lewis Mumford, *Technics and Civilization* (New York: Harcourt Brace Jovanovich, 1934), pp. 109–110. Mumford acknowledges his indebtedness to the British sociologist and urban planner Patrick Geddes (1854–1932) for the terms *paleotechnic* and *neotechnic,* and for teaching him to think of modern civilization in terms of contrasting technological phases.

event in recorded history. Out of the caldron of causation came the principle of achievement rather than birth as the constitutive (formal) principle of society. Out of the manifold and shifting forces that shaped modern society came a new value orientation, a new hierarchy of functions, and ultimately a radically new form of collective existence. The feudal value hierarchy gave top priority to an ill-defined mixture of family, religious, military, and political values and relegated the values associated with the control of nature to an inferior, if not despised, status. The new value hierarchy of liberalism sharply separated all social functions, placing them in a new scale of priority. The family as the source of social position and as the focus of multiple social functions was gradually undermined. The Roman Catholic church lost its position as the repository of otherworldly values and as the moral superintendent of society—a fate that eventually befell the various branches of Protestantism. Demands for rationality in politics, law, and administration—to match and make more effective the rationality of the capitalist economy—gradually eroded the cumbersome personal relations of political particularism. By the late eighteenth century, as a climax to centuries of political development, the emotional ties that bound individuals to their locality had shifted to the nation at large, and the passions of patriotism had replaced family and feudal fealty.

From the Middle Ages on, the personal qualities needed in the battle against nature were steadily established in social relationships and affirmed by the intellect. People were quick to notice that the talents associated with the control of nature were not distributed by birth, but seemed to flow from the rational and even hand of nature. Slowly people came to believe that such talents could be displayed by individuals from all stations in life, and that there might be a fairer, more natural system of inequality if individual rights were protected, opportunities enlarged, and competition encouraged.

With the growing power of the achievement ethic, the norms that had structured human behavior and given life meaning slowly lost their *Gemeinschaft* immediacy and diffuseness and became ever more functionally delimited, impersonal, and complex. Eighteenth-century theorists were fully familiar with machinery, with the rational techniques of commerce, and with the abstract formulations of science; it is no wonder that they began to think of society itself as a network of natural, as opposed to divine or customary, laws. With the growing sense of human achievement, it is also no wonder that by the end of the eighteenth century liberal theorists had announced a natural law of progressive world mastery, evoking the principle of the specialized yet versatile individual to replace the feudal principle of specialization by birth. The new society was characterized by the idea of rational world mastery through human effort—an idea that permeated social relationships and provided Western populations with a new criterion by which to judge the effectiveness of both themselves and their institutions. The history of this momentous development in Western thought is the subject of the next two chapters.

Chapter 3
Basic Transformations in the Western
View of Nature

In recent decades, theorists have come to think of natural science more in historical terms—that is, more as a social phenomenon and less as a result of genius or the immanent power of mind. When applied to intellectual activity, the historical approach is also called the *sociology of knowledge*. That beliefs and values can be traced to their origins in society is an old idea, and may be found, for example, in Plato's *Republic* and in Aristotle's *Politics*. Both theorists considered it axiomatic (however unfortunate this might be) that values and beliefs were rooted in experience. Though there were many anticipations of it, the first systematic effort to study the relation between thought and social structure appeared in the nineteenth century, pioneered by such thinkers as Karl Marx (1818–1883) and Emile Durkheim (1858–1917) and developed further by Max Scheler (1874–1928), Karl Mannheim (1893–1947), and R. G. Collingwood (1889–1943).

THE SOCIOLOGY OF SCIENCE:
SCIENCE AS HISTORY

One of the most important historical interpretations of science is R. G. Collingwood's *The Idea of Nature*.[1] Collingwood argued that the key to understanding science (as well as philosophy, which is essentially a reflection upon the findings of science) is history; stated differently, human beings' general presuppositions about nature and themselves depend on experience. Collingwood contended that Western thought has undergone three qualitatively different periods of natural philosophy, each producing a different idea of nature or cosmology, and each followed by an intensive reflection on the nature of mind. The first period began with the development of Greek science around 600 B.C. with Thales, and was climaxed by an intensive examination of mind by such figures as Socrates (470(?)–399 B.C.), Plato (c. 428–348/347 B.C.), and Aristotle (384–322 B.C.). The second

---

[1] New York: Oxford University Press paperback, 1960; first published in 1945.

period began with the development of modern science immediately following the Renaissance, as exemplified in the work of Copernicus, Galileo,
Descartes, and Newton, and was again followed by an intensive examination of mind by Locke (1632–1704), Berkeley (1685–1753), Hume (1711–
1776), and Kant (1724–1804). The third great cosmology emerged in the
nineteenth and twentieth centuries, stimulated by new discoveries in biology
and physics. The philosophical reflection inspired by these findings, putting
aside Hegel's (1770–1831) anticipation of this new cosmology, is found in
such thinkers as Bergson (1859–1941), Alexander (1859–1938), and
Whitehead (1861–1947).

In his analysis Collingwood did not mechanistically depict either the relation of natural science to philosophy or the relation of one cosmological
period to the next. Though he gave temporal priority to natural science, he
insisted that philosophy often accompanies science quite closely. His general theory of causation, however, has far-reaching significance: namely,
that the human view of nature is dependent not primarily on human reason,
but on historical experience. What precedes both science and philosophy is
society. In other words, society together with science and philosophy constitute the changing totality known as history, a totality that at any given
time provides the experience necessary for fresh advances of the intellect.
The key to understanding the relation between experience and science, said
Collingwood, is to be found in anthropocentrically inspired analogies.

> As Greek natural science was based on the analogy between the
> macrocosm nature and the microcosm man, as man is revealed to
> himself, in his own self-consciousness, as Renaissance natural
> science was based on the analogy between nature as God's handi-
> work and the machines that are the handiwork of man . . . ; so
> the modern view of nature, which first begins to find expression
> towards the end of the eighteenth century and ever since then
> has been gathering weight and establishing itself more securely
> down to the present day, is based on the analogy between the
> processes of the natural world as studied by natural scientists
> and the vicissitudes of human affairs as studied by historians.[2]

Collingwood's perspective on the historical nature of science can be augmented in several ways. Scientific developments can be explained by pointing to such variables as these: climate and geography; the uniqueness of
Western science as opposed to the traditional, nonabstract empirically
based lore and technology of other civilizations; the way in which science
is retarded or promoted by economic, political-military, or religious considerations (including the domination of one society by another, which helps
to explain its absence in geographical regions that are comparable in climate

[2] Collingwood, *The Idea of Nature,* p. 9.

and resources to the West); the sharp breaks, the sudden spurts, and the periods of quiescence that mark the history of science; the accidental or serendipitous nature of much of science; and, finally, its dependence on a cultural base from whence springs not only the cumulative nature of the growth of knowledge but also the well-known pattern of simultaneous discovery.[3]

SOCIETY AND VIEWS OF NATURE

Greek Natural Science

The belief that the structure of the world at large is accessible to the human mind has been a distinguishing characteristic of Western civilization since the time of the Greeks. Though we tend nowadays to separate philosophy and science, they should be thought of as interchangeable terms when discussing the origin of science among the Greeks. By engaging in disciplined thought about the universe around them, the Greeks invented philosophy and science simultaneously. The essence of their momentous invention was the process of rational abstraction, which freed the mind from the shackles of empirical knowledge. Though other civilizations had developed extensive empirical knowledge about nature and technology, and even about mathematics, the Greeks furthered the cause of knowledge by doing something that, ironically, is both the curse and the strength of Western science—they freed the mind from its dependence on fact. Their revolutionary view of things was their assumption that a structure of nature existed beyond the limited and ephemeral knowledge available through the senses. The Greeks felt that empirical knowledge or experience was superficial knowledge—only

---

[3] For a brief review of some of these aspects of science, see chaps. 1, 2, 9 of Bernard Barber's *Science and the Social Order* (New York: Free Press, 1952). For some pioneering essays in the sociology of science, see Robert K. Merton, *The Sociology of Science: Theoretical and Empirical Investigations* (Chicago: University of Chicago Press, 1973). Other valuable sources for understanding the sociocultural context of science are Philip P. Wiener and Aaron Noland, eds., *Roots of Scientific Thought: A Cultural Perspective* (New York: Basic Books, 1957); Marshall Clagett, ed., *Critical Problems in the History of Science* (Madison, Wis.: University of Wisconsin Press, 1959); A.C. Crombie, ed., *Scientific Change* (New York: Basic Books, 1963).

Other sources, focusing mostly on the institutional bases of science and the scientific career, are Norman W. Storer, *The Social System of Science* (New York: Holt, Rinehart, and Winston, 1966); Stephen Cotgrove and Steven Box, *Science, Industry, and Society: Studies in the Sociology of Science* (New York: Barnes & Noble, 1970); Joseph Ben-David, *The Scientist's Role in Society: A Comparative Study* (Englewood Cliffs, N.J.: Prentice-Hall, 1971); Roger G. Krohn, *The Social Shaping of Science: Institutions, Ideology, and Careers in Science* (Westport, Conn.: Greenwood, 1971); Diana Crane, *Invisible Colleges: Diffusion of Knowledge in Scientific Communities* (Chicago: University of Chicago Press, 1972); Leslie Sklair, *Organized Knowledge: A Sociological View of Science and Technology* (London: Hart-Davis, MacGibbon, 1973); and Jonathan R. Cole and Stephen Cole, *Social Stratification in Science* (Chicago: University of Chicago Press, 1973).

the mind was capable of penetrating to the core of nature. They developed structures of logic to achieve this penetration and to reduce the variegated vagrancy of nature to principle or reason. The basic contribution of the Greeks to science, in other words, was their belief that nature is orderly or rational and that its orderliness corresponds to the structure of the human mind when it engages in logical discourse.

In developing the assumption that reason can unlock the strongbox of nature, Greek science, especially from Socrates on, turned its attention to moral philosophy and made another revolutionary assumption—that human nature itself is amenable to reason. Thus, in less than two centuries— roughly between the time of Thales and the time of Socrates—Greek science accomplished the miracle of bringing all nature, physical and human, under the jurisdiction of reason. During this period Greek rationality firmly established itself against opposing views—views that pictured the universe as arbitrary and unpredictable or that saw life as a series of disconnected and discrete experiences that could be bound together only by force, piety, or the iron band of unconscious custom.

The scientific worth of Greek rationalism can be seen in its two greatest figures, Plato and Aristotle. In addition to systemizing the Greek faith in the rationality of the universe, Plato and Aristotle developed ways of thinking about the world that were destined to play an influential role in the rise of modern science. Plato's "otherworldly" idealism, which sought to expunge the particulars of existence, led him to champion radical abstractionism, especially the mathematical tradition stemming from Pythagoras (sixth century B.C.). The more worldly idealism of Aristotle made him anchor abstractions in the world of matter and predisposed him to think of nature as a structure of individuals. Thus, if scientific thought is defined as having two elements, a concern for abstraction and a concern for facts, the thought of each of the major figures in Greek philosophy had both elements; however, each emphasized one aspect of science and permanently imprinted it on the Western mind.

The peculiar blend of "otherworldly" and "this worldly" views in Greek rationalism eventually led to the idea of a *great chain of being*. As Lovejoy emphasized, Greek idealism was not a rejection of the world, but a thoroughgoing attempt to link the supersensible to the sensible. Lovejoy called Plato's belief that belief must find full embodiment in the world of actuality the principle of *plentitude*. Implied in this principle are two related ideas that stem mainly from the work of Aristotle: *continuity* and *gradation*, the principles that decree that there are no breaks or "leaps" between various beings, and that these things are arranged in a hierarchy of worth. These principles were eventually organized into an integrated world view by the

Neo-Platonists, said Lovejoy, and became the common coin of intellectual discourse down through the eighteenth century.[4]

Greek rationalism posed dangers for science, however, and the work of Plato and Aristotle was also a separation of philosophy from science. In effect, their thought represented a turning away from nature and a corresponding emphasis on mind. This is most obvious, of course, in Plato's radical rejection of experience as a source of knowledge, a view he modified somewhat in his later work. Even in Aristotle, one finds serious impediments to the successful pursuit of science. For all his empiricism, Aristotle preferred mind to fact, the contemplative to the active life, pure knowledge to practical knowledge. His preferences, like Plato's, were rooted in the same aristocratic disdain for the workaday world. It was a bias that was to have dire consequences for the subsequent history of science. Aristotle's syllogistic logic, for example, which yielded a rich universe of logical relations, had a way of remaining aloof from the universe of fact, while his logic of final causation or teleology undermined his more fruitful emphasis on efficient causation. Nowhere is the failure of Greek philosophy so ironically displayed as in Aristotle's teleological reasoning. In resorting to teleology to explain the nature of a thing, what he was saying was, in effect, that something is what it is because of what it is. Thus Greek rationalism, which began its career by escaping from bondage to the concrete, ended by succumbing to the empiricism of teleology—to a view, in short, that cannot go beyond the world as it is.

It is no denigration of Greek thought to point out that the Greek view of nature was anthropomorphic and Greek science was based on the Greeks' own historical experience—an experience that made them conscious of themselves as vital, purposive organisms and that they extended by analogy to nature.[5] Whatever the origin of Greek science, the fact remains that Greece invented the idea of reason, an idea without which modern science is inconceivable. However, the vast promise of Greek science had to wait for the work of others. Though it owed its existence to the stimulating

[4] *The Great Chain of Being* (New York: Harper Torchbook, 1960), originally published in 1936.
[5] This view of Greek cosmology may be found in the Introduction to R. G. Collingwood's *The Idea of Nature*. For a history that relates Greek science to technology and social structure in a sophisticated Marxian manner, see Benjamin Farrington, *Greek Science*, 2 vols. (Middlesex, England: Penguin Books, 1944); for a classic analysis of Greek religion in terms of its origin in social structure, which acknowledges its debt to Bergson and Durkheim, see Jane Ellen Harrison, *Themis* (Cambridge, England: Cambridge University Press, 1912); for an analysis that traces Greek philosophy to its origins in religion, and religion to its origin in society—and which acknowledges its debt to Jane Ellen Harrison and to Durkheim—see F. M. Cornford, *From Religion to Philosophy* (New York: Harper & Row paperback, 1957), originally published in 1912.

environment of the Ionian cities, Greek science could neither transcend nor prevent the failure of the Greek city-state. Reacting sharply to a social experience that seemed to offer only arbitrary and unpredictable about-faces, Greek thought sought refuge more and more in the certainties of philosophy (logical discourse) as against the perplexities and challenges of science (finding the logic of phenomena). Philosophy and science were separated to the detriment of both; philosophy became the domain of reason and science the domain of fact. By the end of the fourth century B.C., any hope of a continued interplay between reason and fact had ended. The genius of Greek speculation had been unwilling to grapple with the world of experience; after the rise of Macedonia, Hellenism's speculative side found fruition in religion, while its empirical side was congealed into the important but heavyfooted science of Hellenistic Alexandria.

Medieval Natural Science

The medieval view of nature, which was essentially the same as the Greek view, pictured nature as a teleological order. The emphasis on final cause meant that nature, as well as human beings and society, could best be known in terms of their ends or purposes. Everything and everyone had a purpose established in and through the mind of God, the first and final Cause. Each being, it was thought, had an essence it strove to realize, and its success was the measure of its participation in the mind of God. In finished form, the theology of the medieval Church did not so much alter the *Gemeinschaft* mentality of barbarian Europe as give it an Aristotelian preciseness and explicitness.

As formulated by Saint Thomas, the medieval view of human and physical nature was profoundly static. Nature was securely bound by the linkage of the great chain of being—a teleological orientation perfectly suited to an agrarian society whose whole experience militated against any prospect that things could be other than what they were. It should not be forgotten, of course, that by the thirteenth century, temporal conditions had undergone considerable improvement and that the Thomistic synthesis can also be regarded as a new emphasis on the this-worldly aspect of the great chain of being. The vastly enhanced importance that Thomas gave to natural and positive law—an enhancement that said, in effect, that the structure of morals and of society exists independent of revelation—can certainly be construed in this way. No matter how much Thomistic thought reflected the medieval Church's growing appreciation of the world, however, that world had burst the logical bonds with which Thomas had hoped to contain it—even before his work was finished. His union of the particular and the universal, the secular and the spiritual, the sensible and the rational (and both with revelation) was disputed by other scholastics long before the onset of secular science. This is a reference, of course, to the profound controversy between the realists and the nominalists. The realist position, which reached a modified form in Saint Thomas, rested on the assumption that real things are not only the particular things of the senses, but also universal essences. It is mind that gives form to matter by realizing its potential or essence and thereby makes it actual. The mind finds ascending levels of actuality until it reaches God, who is pure form and pure actuality. All this was challenged by the nominalists within the framework of Christianity.

The outstanding figure in the nominalist movement was William of Occam (c. 1290–1349), who systematized and enlarged upon the terminist or nominalist position that had emerged somewhat earlier. The aspect of Occam's thought that was decisively important for the success of modern science was his insistence that mind and nature be separated. For Occam, the operations of the mind dealt with relations among ideas, while nature contained only individual things and relations among them. The easy identification between mind and nature, which the Greeks had started and the medieval realists had continued, was ended by Occam, and each was given an independent existence. The mind no longer established universals, but only subjective abstractions based on the common properties or contrasts of things—abstractions that had no objective reality. The implications for science were enormous, for what Occam said was that knowledge comes not from logic, but from the direct perception of individual things and relations. The denial that reason can establish the reality of things also means, Occam insisted, that there is no logical proof of religious beliefs, including the belief that God exists. Thus, since religious beliefs cannot stem from sensory perception, they must rest on faith alone.

The upshot of Occam's work was not only to separate mind from nature, but also to separate religion from both. His definition of nature as a collection of individuals and relations among individuals contained neither the concepts of the mind nor the morals, purposes, or values of religion; this meant, in effect, that he was delimiting the special area and activity of science. Occam's razor, which saw in parsimonious precision the guarantee of knowledge, was also sharp enough to sever the unity of faith, reason, and nature and to leave each to stand on its own special feet.[6]

Post-Renaissance Natural Science

The emergence in philosophy of a nominalist outlook bears a strong relationship to the increased power that Westerners had acquired over nature. The nominalist separation of nature from its religious and teleological moorings

[6] For a concise account of four of the major figures in the controversy between the realists and the nominalists—Saint Augustine, Peter Abelard, Saint Thomas, and William of Occam—see Meyrick H. Carre, *Realists and Nominalists* (London: Oxford University Press, 1946). A technical discussion of Occam's logic, with a valuable chapter for the layman on the role of his logic in the development of science, may be found in Ernest A. Moody, *The Logic of William of Occam* (New York: Sheed and Ward, 1935), chap. 7, sec. II.

admirably suited it to serve the needs of an expanding economy. The old view of nature gradually gave way before the growth of technology, commerce, experimentation, and the new anti-Aristotelian metaphysics. By the time of Copernicus, but especially with Galileo and Newton, the Scholastic view of nature had undergone a momentous transformation. Nature now existed separate from God and human beings alike and no longer contained any purposes. It was simply a vast machinelike structure of dead, homogeneous matter in lawful motion. By the end of the seventeenth century, the mechanistic view of nature had largely displaced Aristotelian science and was firmly established in the intellectual community of Europe. Instead of searching for purpose in nature, science now tried to express nature's processes in abstract, quantitative terms.

With this revolutionary concept of nature appeared a number of dualisms with profound implications for the direction that modern philosophy and social theory would take. In the first place, God and nature were divorced, and God became, in E. A. Burtt's phrase, "the chief mechanic of the universe." Second, human nature and nature—or, more exactly, mind and matter—were divorced. All the qualities in nature that were so easily produced by medieval and Greek thought were banished: nature was pure extension—that is, pure geometry. The secondary qualities that human beings experience became mere appearances and were lodged in a different order of being, the mind. The distinction between the primary, objective world and the secondary, subjective world appeared first in Galileo and reached its final development in Descartes.[7] According to this view, only the objective, mathematical world constitutes scientific knowledge; the rest of the world, consisting of sights, sounds, and smells, belongs to a realm that cannot be known because it is not reducible to mathematics. This dualism between the world of human nature and the world of nature presented modern philosophy with its major problem. By defining the mind as the source of only insubstantial, secondary, or empirical knowledge, one is faced with the question of how is it possible for human beings to know nature itself, even through mathematics. One also faces the question of determining the nature of the type of knowledge produced by sensory experience, especially in view of the success of the experimental method.

The Enlightenment

The Enlightenment of the eighteenth century is a watershed in the development of modern science, and its thought is crucial for understanding the

---

[7] For a succinct analysis of this development, see E. A. Burtt, *The Metaphysical Foundations of Modern Physical Science* (Garden City, N.Y.: Doubleday paperback, 1954), originally published in 1924, pp. 83–90, 115–124. Burtt's characterization of God is on page 297.

origin and nature of sociological theory. On the one hand, the Enlightenment climaxed the Newtonian world view by battering it into the consciousness of Western populations, searching out its deepest implications, and giving it its widest application. On the other hand, the period initiated the post-Newtonian phase of science by making deep-reaching alterations in the West's concept of scientific method and in its view of nature. Few periods in the history of thought can rival the Enlightenment for its influence or for the profundity of its thought. To understand the Enlightenment properly, one must discard the view that the philosophes were naive rationalists—a view that stems in no small measure from Carl Becker's influential book, *The Heavenly City of the Eighteenth Century Philosophers*.[8]

Far from being naive rationalists, the philosophes fashioned a hard-bitten secular naturalism and realistically faced up to the prickly problems contained in this view. Their fundamental point of view was the revolutionary assumption that the world of reason and the world of phenomena formed a single, unitary structure.[9] In a sense, one can say that the philosophes were profoundly antirational—if *rational* means the tendency to prefer concepts to facts, logic to data, and speculation to observation. There is no doubt, of course, that the Enlightenment believed in reason and that it accepted the traditional touchstones of rationality, unity and permanence. However, the revolutionary significance of the Enlightenment lies in its transformation of the ideal of reason, an ideal that went far beyond the demand that reason be disciplined by facts; in a far-reaching reversal of the West's traditional distrust of the phenomenal world, the philosophes boldly declared that reason and facts were but opposite sides of the same coin. Reason could be seen as a "homogeneous formative power" that plunges into the multiplicity of data to reveal its unity; it is a force or agency that finds its own structure in the act of grappling with the world. Underlying this view is the faith that, while all statements and principles are provisional and relative, given the complexity of the world, the active intelligence will at last come to rest and be identical with the structure of facts. To be true to itself, reason must look beyond accepted explanations and seek out the organic

[8] New Haven: Yale University Press, 1932; now available in paperback (Yale, 1959). For a much-needed critique of the distorted view of the Enlightenment produced by Becker's famous book and in the writings of others, see the three articles by Peter Gay, "The Enlightenment in the History of Political Theory," *Political Science Quarterly* 69 (September 1954): 374–389; "Carl Becker's Heavenly City," *Political Science Quarterly* 72 (June 1957): 182–199; and "The Party of Humanity" in Peter Gay, *The Party of Humanity: Essays in the French Enlightenment* (New York: Alfred A. Knopf, 1964)—this collection of essays reprints Gay's article, "Carl Becker's Heavenly City." In a more positive vein, students of the Enlightenment are indebted to Gay's comprehensive reference work, *The Enlightenment: An Interpretation*, 2 vols. (New York: Alfred A. Knopf, 1966, 1969).
[9] The following account of the philosophical and scientific changes wrought by the philosophes is based on Ernst Cassirer's monumental work, *The Philosophy of the Enlightenment*, trans. Fritz C. A. Koelling and James P. Pettegrove (Boston: Beacon paperbound, 1955), originally published in 1932; first published in translation by Princeton University Press in 1951.

unity of existence or nature. Reason despairs of metaphysical solutions but rejoices in its power to make the world accessible to human reason and guidance.

The philosophy of the Enlightenment attacked "rational" as well as "biblical" physics. Throughout the century a concerted attack was mounted against system building, against science based on definition, logic, mathematics, or pure reason, and against any image of knowledge based on the distinction between essence and appearance. The philosophes did not create their ideal of science; rather they developed strands of thought that had appeared in the work of earlier thinkers. Somewhat uncharacteristically, they fully acknowledged their debt to these scientists—especially to Locke and more especially to Newton. Newton, they felt, had achieved a solid victory of the mind and had proved the power and validity of reason. However, it was Newton's method and not just his substantive conclusions that inspired the philosophes and profoundly influenced the direction of the philosophy of the Enlightenment. Significantly, Newton had presented his theory of gravity as a description of phenomena, not as a metaphysical principle; though he defined gravity as a universal phenomenon, he resisted the tendency in Cartesian science to seek the ultimate explanation of things.

In attacking Descartes's definition of knowledge, the philosophes had to find a methodology that could resolve the dualism between the realm of truth, on the one hand (which stemmed from the intuitively arrived-at and mathematically expressed structure of ideas that corresponds to pure, material extension), and the unintelligible realm of the senses, on the other. The philosophes seized upon the vast promise contained in Locke's sensationalist psychology, a promise that seemed to reduce knowledge to sensation without the loss of certainty. There was, however, in Locke's epistemology a dualism between sensation and reflection that the philosophes had to remove. Their task was to find the unitary mental substance that makes contact with the unitary substance of nature so that the relation between the two could be established and the dualism of mind and matter dissolved. Their search, which was conducted empirically, could locate only the causal efficacy of sensation. Though they were not unaware of the problems their findings contained, it soon became axiomatic among the philosophes that there existed some sort of energetic, sentient-thinking substance that made contact with and established knowledge about the outer world solely through sensory perception.

Acting under the pregnant presupposition that the phenomenal realm is inherently orderly—that is, rational—and assured of the fact that the sentient-thinking substance has an original power to apprehend that order, the eighteenth century went on to lay bare the many faces of nature. Stimulated by the mounting achievements against nature that emerged from the work of practical scientists, engineers, government officials, merchants, and manufacturers, the intellectual culture of the eighteenth century gradually became aware of the complexity of nature. New branches of knowledge slowly appeared and asserted their independence from physics. The heightened interest in physiology and psychology was followed by solid achievements in biology, botany, and chemistry. The biologist Buffon (1707–1788) expressed this new spirit when he flatly came out against any attempt to prescribe a monistic ideal for natural science. Above all, Cassirer points out, it was Diderot (1713–1784) who best captured the new spirit of science. It was he who espoused experiment and research, who decried not only a priori or mathematical methods, but reliance on any unitary method. Instead, he insisted that method must follow subject matter, and warned against compressing nature into artificial human molds. Against the absolute diversity and heterogeneity of nature, all knowledge, he asserted, must be considered relative.

Seen from the vantage point of centuries of social change, the Enlightenment climaxes the gradual separation of science from philosophy and theology and inaugurates science as a specialized, autonomous intellectual activity. But in calling for specialization within science proper, the Enlightenment, in effect, was superseding itself. The fulfillment of this new orientation toward nature had to await the nineteenth century, but one can already discern in the Age of Reason the institutionalized, flexible empiricism that was destined to make discoveries that would dwarf the accomplishments of the Age of Newton. As Lovejoy has shown, by temporalizing the great chain of being and by seeing nature as a creative advance,[10] the Enlightenment made substantive as well as methodological contributions to the future.

Despite the insight of the Enlightenment into the complexity and temporality of nature, its empiricism and relativity were still secondary emphases. The ideal of reason that the age set for itself was the same as it had been for the Greeks—only that which had unity and permanence could be considered rational. Not until the fuller development of romanticism and empirical science in the nineteenth century were changes effected in this hoary ideal. The modal thought of the Enlightenment found its center of gravity in a rationalistic monism based on a frankly stated naturalism. This monism drew into its orbit not only nature but also human nature and society, in effect climaxing in the realm of thought the long-term trend toward the secularization and rationalization of society. If there is any truth to the charge that the Enlightenment was naive, it lies, perhaps, in the attempt to provide liberalism/capitalism with a social metaphysics. Though the philosophes were following Hume somewhat when they reduced the role of reason in the study of nature, they had little concept of Hume's strict separation of the operation of reason, either as logic or as experience, and the realm of value. All this, however, is something to which I shall return later. I shall first trace the history of the Western view of human nature.

[10] Lovejoy, *Great Chain of Being*, chap. 8.

Chapter 4
Basic Transformations in the Western
View of Human Nature

The modern concept of human nature, like the modern view of nature, also followed the fortunes of liberal society and also reached its climax in the Age of Reason.

SOCIETY AND VIEWS OF HUMAN NATURE

The Greek View of Human Nature

The science of human nature, like the science of nature, begins with the Greeks, who first established and acted on the assumption that human nature is a suitable subject for rational investigation. Accordingly, the Greeks developed, along with moral philosophy, a social science—something similar but also quite different from what we understand by that term today. In referring to Greece, one usually means Athens, the greatest of the numerous Greek city-states; and when referring to Greek social thought, one usually has in mind Plato and Aristotle. In truth, however, a rich body of social theory developed throughout Greece, and while no other figures compare with Plato and Aristotle, there emerged over the centuries a number of theorists of considerable stature. Indeed, the social views expressed by Greek theorists were so rich and varied that—from the Sophists in the fifth century B.C. to Plato, Aristotle, the Epicureans, and the Stoics in the fourth and third centuries B.C.—almost every conceivable picture of human nature received formulation and currency. Even before Plato and Aristotle, the speculations of Greek thinkers, especially of the Sophists, had produced a sophisticated body of ideas about human nature.[1]

Greek social thought took place as a result of profound changes in Greek society, changes that for the first time in human history allowed reflection

[1] The major source of our knowledge about the Sophists, as well as of Greek philosophy in general, is the work of Plato and Aristotle. For an excellent brief summary of early Greek social thought, see Sir Ernest Barker, *Greek Political Thought: Plato and His Predecessors* (New York: Barnes & Noble paperbound, 1960), chaps. 3, 4; published originally in 1918 and reprinted many times. A fuller account may be found in the excellent study by Donald Kagan, *The Great Dialogue: History of Greek Political Thought from Homer to Polybius* (New York: Free Press, 1965).

to penetrate the sway of custom and superstition. The most important and best-known changes occurred in Attica (Athens). Highlighting a long process of detribalization and defeudalization, the reforms of Solon (638?–?559 B.C.) and Cleisthenes (570?–?508 B.C.) prepared the way for the golden age of Athenian democracy. After the Persian invasions, victorious Athens became the focus of the entire Mediterranean world but was unable to contain internal strife, overcome the challenge of war, or resist the temptations of imperial adventures and domination. Thus, Athenian society in the latter part of the fifth century was again threatened by social system change. The chronic instability of Greek city-state life was as much the cause as it was the consequence of the total and absolute manner in which various contending classes stated claims against each other. Each struggled to restructure society in the name of a comprehensive, uncompromising hierarchy of value based on birth, land, wealth, or numbers. With the struggle for power defined and practiced in such terms, and passion and interest not only magnified but also linked indissolubly, it is not surprising that the worst excesses of intrigue and strife were the commonplaces of Greek life. The one merit of this deeply-rooted conflict was that it stimulated reflection about the nature of human nature and of society; against this backdrop of chronic confusion and conflict, Greek speculation about human nature first developed among the Sophists. The Sophists were practical moralists and teachers and not given to broad theory. It was only when Plato and Aristotle tried to formulate the rational principles that governed human nature—principles that they felt, once acquired, would assure human beings a life of harmony and stability—that one can say that the science of human nature begins. With their thought, the belief that it is possible to obtain a cognitive grasp of human nature becomes a permanent part of Western intellectual life.

Characteristically, Plato and Aristotle sought to protect reason against convention, and consciousness against custom. From one point of view their thought was quite revolutionary, for in attempting to shore up the disintegrating city-state, they paid little heed to the claims of either birth or custom. Instead, they sought to place society on a natural, objective, rational basis. In place of the claims of blood and custom, they hoped to substitute the claims of reason, and they labored to develop a coherent consciousness about the nature and meaning of social life and to eliminate the immoral and unreliable stability of mindless custom. Although they went beyond the assumptions of customary society, Plato and Aristotle were also profoundly conservative, for they opposed the brilliant but chaotic spontaneity of Greek democracy. In particular, they rejected the stark opposition made by the later generation of Sophists between nature and convention; this opposition had been used to champion an assortment of claims such as individualism, equality, might, and hedonism against the conventions of society—and in the case of some to champion the relativity of convention against the supposed existence of right or nature. Plato and Aristotle could not accept such a distinction; for them, much of customary society had a rational or natural basis—especially its stability, its hierarchy, and much of its morality. What was lacking was a rational foundation for these values, one that could satisfy the ethical demand that submission to norms be conscious, and yet be persuasive enough to protect norms from the sway of passion and misguided interest.

In their effort to establish the objective structure of society, Plato and Aristotle used as an anchor the distinction between reason and experience. In adopting this distinction, their strategy was to block the attempt among early social theorists, especially among some of the Sophists, to base their ethical theories—most of which were of a hedonistic variety—on attributes that Greek (Ionian) natural science had found in nature. As idealistic rationalists, they also opposed the tendency on the part of some Sophists to rely only on the relativity of experience for their view of human nature and society. However, while Plato and Aristotle opposed the naturalism of much of sophistic thought, they too sought to base their social theory on the main assumptions and conclusions of Greek physical theory.

The method of Greek science was primarily speculative. As handed down by the Ionian scientists, a tradition developed that the task of science was to find the basic substance, the parent-stuff of which the fleeting multiplicities of experience were made. There are two main branches of this tradition, the materialist tradition descending from the Ionians and the idealist tradition started by Pythagoras. Underlying both traditions, however, was one general conclusion: that nature is basically a vital, purposive, orderly organism (in the first tradition expressing the nature of matter; in the second, expressing the nature of logic). As noted earlier, Greek cosmology was anthropocentric, derived ultimately from an analogy based on the experience of the Greeks as purposive, human organisms. This analogy, first extended to physical nature, eventually found its way into ethical thought with Socrates and social thought with Plato and Aristotle. Human nature, too, was thought to contain a substance that could stabilize the behavior of individuals and protect them from the deceptions and accidents of experience. Permeating the thought of both Plato and Aristotle was the conviction that the phenomena associated with human nature, no less than those associated with physical nature, are rational and thus accessible to human reason, and that people need not base their behavior on the waywardness of instinct, the shortsightedness of interest, or the ruts of an uncomprehended routine.

It is worth noting again that the social thought of Plato and Aristotle, no less than their cosmological thought, was not a flight from the world. As Lovejoy has pointed out, their belief in absolute being may have been otherworldly, but it was an otherworldly rationalism, not religion, and they were careful to maintain links with the world of experience. On both counts—their belief in a self-sufficient universe of rational discourse and their willingness to relate this mental universe to the world of experience— the social thought of Plato and Aristotle bears the genuine marks of a social science. The practical and empirical bent in Plato's social theory (if one defines the *Republic* as a utopia) is evident in the *Statesman* and the *Laws*, works that belong to the last of the four periods into which scholars have divided his thought. The empirical bent to Aristotle's thought is better known, of course, and was based on the insights developed by the later thinking of Plato. With a relative indifference to philosophy, his own included, Aristotle developed these insights in the *Politics*, a towering masterpiece of social analysis, which in its absorption with the lessons to be learned from the total experience of the Greek race still stands as a model of social science at its finest.[2]

Despite the fact that Plato and Aristotle transformed Greek science into philosophy and diverted human reason into a disproportionate concern for logic and morals, their social thought, even by modern standards, contains scientific insights of the first importance. They viewed society as fundamentally an exchange of services, a social division of labor in which all benefit from the performance of social functions; they had an acute sense of institutional or functional interdependence that made them think in terms of social systems; and they were almost as aware of the operation of the mundane, efficient causes of human behavior as they were of final causes. Above all, in trying to find the structure of society and the nature of human nature, they confined themselves to rational discourse and eschewed appeals to custom or religion.

Reference to the scientific elements in the thought of Plato and Aristotle should not be construed to mean, however, that the social thought of the past be viewed only in terms of its prefiguration of modern social science. On the whole, the social thought of Plato and Aristotle was markedly different from modern social science. It found its center of gravity in logic—and teleology, or the logic of final causes, at that. The thought of Plato and Aristotle differed sharply from modern assumptions about society in another respect—though it is not necessarily less scientific on this score. Neither theorist could conceive of an independent existence for the individual. For Plato and Aristotle, as for most Greeks, individuals were social animals; individuals became human beings only to the extent that they absorbed a social way of life. A being able to exist by itself, in Aristotle's famous phrase, was "either a beast or a God." In maintaining this view, Plato and Aristotle were not merely introducing into social theory their idealist bias against the contingent particular. In looking upon social life as

---

[2] Sir Ernest Barker's highly readable translation of the *Politics* (together with notes and a valuable introduction), first published by Oxford University Press in 1946, is now available as an Oxford paperback.

an agency for the cultivation and fulfillment of human powers—powers that would lie dormant without the stimulus of social interaction—they were also expressing the highest ideals of the Greek city-state. Their belief that reason could provide a valid moral and functional basis for human existence followed the traditional Greek view that society was a seamless, soul-nourishing unity of moral and functional imperatives. This view of society, together with the assumption that reason can provide a hierarchy of value, was destined to hold sway over the European mind for more than two thousand years, and despite the rise of modern scientific philosophy, it continues to hold a fascination even today.

The invigorating life of the Greek city-state could not fail to produce a variety of perspectives on society, including a biopsychological individualism that stood in sharp opposition to the "social individualism" of Plato and Aristotle. With the decline and destruction of the city-state, the biopsychological view was powerfully augmented by new philosophies that arose to register and relieve the growing feeling that social life was not a blessing but a burden. With Epicureanism and Stoicism a new ideal of behavior emerged, centered on individual self-sufficiency. Earlier Greek social philosophy, which had sought to absorb the individual into a comprehensive social life, slowly succumbed to the belief that the sources of well-being existed apart from society. Of these two new philosophical schools, the most important was Stoicism, for out of it came the clearly articulated doctrine of natural law that so profoundly influenced medieval and modern social thought.[3] The Stoics saw a correspondence between the rationality of the universe and the rationality of the individual: the individual qua individual, following the promptings of reason, possessed the capacity to acquire the virtues engrained in the nature of things and to bring them to bear on social life. The difference between this mode of thought and the thought of Plato and Aristotle could not be more complete. In Stoic thought individuals exist in their own right and are equal to each other in fundamental ways. Society is no longer thought of as prior to the individual and as the source of virtue—as a teleological magnet drawing humans to truth and goodness. Before society is the individual, while beyond it is the law of nature, the objective standard of justice and morality by which human beings can judge the shortcomings of their society. In short, the Stoics spoke of human beings and not of citizens. By proclaiming an individualistic universalism, in which the source of norms lay outside of society, they effectively bypassed the tight, hierarchic communalism that had been the main

---

[3] For background on Stoicism, see A. A. Long, ed., *Problems in Stoicism* (London: University of London, Athlone Press, 1971); and F.H. Sandbach, *The Stoics* (New York: W. W. Norton, 1975). For a general introduction to the varieties of natural-law thought from the Greeks to contemporary times, see Paul E. Sigmund, *Natural Law in Political Thought* (Cambridge, Mass.: Winthrop, 1971).

tradition in Greek thought. Despite the novelty of this view, however, it should not be thought that the contradiction that Stoicism introduced between the law of nature and the law of society necessarily created tension or inspired revolution; in Cicero (106–43 B.C.), for example, the contradiction was easily adjusted to the expediencies and inequalities of social life.

The Medieval View of Human Nature

The medieval view of human nature and of society was heavily indebted to Greek thought, especially to the idealism of Plato and Aristotle and the natural-law philosophy of Stoicism. Medieval social thought became a blend of these Greek elements with the social views contained in the Bible, the thought of the Church Fathers, and the customary codes of the barbarian tribes of northwestern Europe. The philosophy of Stoicism, for example, blended easily with Christianity,[4] while Aristotle's acceptance by and influence on the intellectual life of medieval Christendom are well known.

The most important intellectual figure of the medieval period is Saint Thomas Aquinas (1225–1274), who incorporated Aristotelian philosophy into the framework of Catholic Christendom. As applied to social theory, a subject with which Saint Thomas did not concern himself greatly, Aristotle's philosophy worked against and largely undermined the individualist and equalitarian flavor of Stoic thought. For Thomas, as for Aristotle, the world was governed by purpose. Everything in the vast, diverse, particular, contingent, finite world had a place, a function, a purpose. Acting under the internal urgings of its own nature, every being sought the good, the form of perfection natural to its kind. As for the nature of human nature, Thomas adapted Aristotle's logic of final cause to suit the needs of Christian social theory. Human beings, he claimed, had a twofold nature, and the higher, or spiritual, always ruled the lower, or material. Correspondingly, society might be viewed as a hierarchy of offices or functions based on the exchange of services. It was axiomatic for Thomas that those serving spiritual ends should rank highest, though in his overall view he was only a moderate papalist. He was content to affirm simply that all those who are in authority are from God; while they have different functions, they all exercise correlative jurisdiction over humanity's earthly and spiritual needs. In keeping with the teleological assumptions contained in the idea of a great chain of being, Thomas assumed that since nature had all its necessaries, the requisite social functions and the types of individuals needed to fulfill them were supplied as well. The primary purpose of society was to provide a

[4] E. Vernon Arnold, *Roman Stoicism* (New York: The Humanities Press, 1958), chap. 17; originally published in 1911.

setting for the acquisition and exercise of virtue, which in turn was a preparation for salvation.

Thomas's insistence that the institutions of society were natural to human beings, rather than a compromise made necessary by the Fall, is of considerable import. His rejection of social Augustinianism [5] represents not only the need by Christianity to put forth a positive doctrine and to anchor its own authority on rational grounds, but also the new appreciation in the West for worldly existence—a tribute to the vast improvement in the commodiousness of social life by the thirteenth century.

Though Thomas embedded "politics" in morals, he also carved out a large area for practical reason (or human-made positive law). Politics is also an art and not merely a theoretical science; prudence must take its rightful place alongside truth. Thomas's Aristotelianism is apparent in this respect. Aristotle, true to his view that different areas of inquiry require different methods, did not emphasize teleology in his moral or political theory, with the result that there exists in Thomas, as in Aristotle, a strong streak of pragmatism—that is, a strong suggestion that reason must accommodate itself to the exigencies of life.

The various questions about social organization that concern the modern mind (or, for that matter, that concerned Aristotle) did not trouble Thomas. He was not much interested, for example, in the relation between religion and society, in the problem of finding happiness or virtue through the perfection of social organization, or in the question of how individuals obtain their respective stations in life. He was content to accept the traditional medieval view that the rewards of this world are subordinate to those of the next. He saw a harmony between the spiritual and the temporal, believed in birth as a valid mechanism for assigning social status, and felt that since teleology guarantees that all authority is from God, the existing structure of norms is both valid and sacred. In short, in Thomas's thought, human beings aspired upward not forward.[6]

It was against this view that the modern view [7] of human nature had to fight. It is important to recognize that medieval intellectual culture—despite

---

[5] For Saint Augustine's (354–430) "central political insight—the idea of a politics of imperfection, a necessary consequence of human sinfulness—and his profound awareness of the inevitable limitations of a coercive political order," see Herbert A. Deane, *The Political and Social Ideas of St. Augustine* (New York: Columbia University Press, 1963), also in paperback. Not the least valuable aspect of this study is the careful attention given to recapturing Saint Augustine's thought in his own words and in relation to its historical context.

[6] A valuable collection of Thomas's views on society may be found in Dino Bigongiari, ed., *The Political Ideas of St. Thomas Aquinas* (New York: Hafner, 1953); a full-length exposition of Thomas's political thought, containing a valuable background on the legacy of ancient and medieval ideas with which Thomas worked, is Thomas Gilby's *The Political Thought of Thomas Aquinas* (Chicago: University of Chicago Press, 1958).

[7] Strictly speaking, there is more than one modern view of human nature—we are referring here to the modal viewpoint established by the Enlightenment.

its emphasis on order and harmony and despite the fact that its teleological orientation tended to erase tension between the "ought" and the "is"— contained elements that were far from congruous. For one thing, Christian mysticism and supernaturalism stood opposed to the naturalist rationalism of Greece; for another, Christian universalism opposed the provincialism of pre-Hellenistic Greek thought. Finally, Christianity and Greek philosophy contained elements that were deeply opposed to the customary, ascriptive particularism of feudalism. In short, despite deep pressures to unify it, medieval culture never congealed into a world view purged of incongruities and contradictions. Without the tension and friction of these incongruities, the modern view of human nature and society could never have arisen.

The Modern View of Human Nature: Phase One, Secular Rationalism

The political and social literature that appeared between Saint Thomas in the thirteenth century and the philosophes in the eighteenth is far too complex for useful generalization. It is safe to say, however, that the literature of this period, including even that which emerged from the religious controversies attending the Reformation, was profoundly this-worldly in orientation.

If the modern view of human nature was as much a revolt against Aristotelianism in social theory as in physical theory, it must also be noted that Aristotle was as instrumental in aiding that revolt in social theory as he had been in physical theory. On the whole, Greek rational naturalism helped to curb both excessive supernaturalism and excessive particularism, something we saw in the thought of Saint Thomas. Thomas was primarily interested in religion and philosophy, of course, and his social views never questioned the basic structure of feudalism. However, the tight linkages he forged between the layers of law bound heaven as securely to earth as they bound earth to heaven. The enlargement of the area of natural law (or the rational-moral proclivities of humankind that are independent of revelation) and the emphasis on positive law (or the adaptation of the dictates of natural law to the relativities of time and place) represent a genuine historical/secular bent in Thomas's thought.

Of greater significance, however, in understanding the modern view of human nature was the profoundly original thought of Marsilius of Padua (1290?–?1343). Writing in support of imperial claims during the struggle for supremacy between Ludwig of Bavaria and Pope John XXII, Marsilius wrenched Aristotelian naturalism free from the supernatural framework in which Thomas had hoped to contain it and used it to build a surprisingly modern theory of society. Marsilius also departed from Aristotelian thought, for in attacking the papal view that subordinated society to religious and theological ends, he also rejected Aristotle's attempt to cap social analysis with teleologically derived ultimate ethical ends. In effect, what Marsilius did was to merge the four causes of Aristotle and to think only of efficient causation. Along with this methodological change came a revolutionary change in the concept of human nature. For Marsilius, human beings had no propensities toward ethical or religious ends. They were not rational, but willful, appetitive creatures whose conduct was derived from a bundle of biological needs and not from teleological tendencies toward absolute moral and ethical values. Given the excesses of human biological desires and appetites, the problem of social peace and survival was almost exclusively the problem of channeling and controlling human biological nature. Social analysis, for Marsilius, could concern itself only with the means of establishing peaceful social concourse; it could not prescribe the goals of society, which came almost entirely from biological needs. Accordingly, society was primarily a structure for the satisfaction and augmentation of biological-economic needs, and its institutions had to be evaluated only in terms of how well they served these needs.

Marsilius's view of human nature and society was far more radical than one might suspect at first sight. What he effected was nothing less than a closely reasoned transformation of Aristotelian naturalism into a theory that allowed reason no capacity for establishing moral and ethical ends and that confined religion and the priesthood to a narrowly defined and socially irrelevant spiritual function. By turning reason into a means and religion into a purely spiritual exercise containing no consequences for the organization of social life, Marsilius revived the general presupposition of Aristotelian naturalism that society is a self-sufficient structure capable of providing all its moral and material needs. Further, he reduced social theory to a functional discussion of means and ends in which political and social requirements were determined independent of absolute moral and religious values. It was a secular, dynamic, and pragmatic view that was to be re-echoed ever more loudly in the following centuries.[8]

The path taken by the new view of human nature from Marsilius through the Renaissance and Reformation snaked its way through a tangled brush of controversy and invective. There is little need to follow it completely. The Renaissance, despite its continuity with medieval culture, was a distinctive period largely because of the new interest and delight that some individuals found in the exercise of their natural powers. Surprisingly, the religious revival known as the Reformation supported the same secular trend represented by the Renaissance. One of the great ironies of history is that the Protestant revolt, by smashing the strong elements of Christian

[8] The above account of Marsilius's thought is based on Alan Gewirth, *Marsilius of Padua, The Defender of Peace*, vol. 1: *Marsilius of Padua and Medieval Political Philosophy* (New York: Columbia University Press, 1951), especially chap. 2. Vol. 2 of this work contains Gewirth's translation of Marsilius's one great work, the *Defensor pacis*.

unity that had persisted in the face of nationalism and secularism, represented not so much the defeat of Rome as of Christianity itself. The religious individualism of Protestantism accorded well with the forces of secular individualism, providing a religious sanction to the worldly activity of individuals as well as the moral discipline that helped make secular individualism possible. This irony—that religious principles were instrumental in establishing the supremacy of economic values—was matched fully in the realm of political and social thought. Out of the renewed religious fervor that marked the Reformation, one overall ironic result stands out— the tendency of social theorists to separate the structure of society, and even the interests of people in general, from religion. This pattern emerged in a number of ways, but most ironically in the very theories that defended religion. In their efforts to protect religion from the Erastian tendencies of royal absolutism, both Protestant and Catholic monarchomachs and Jesuit thinkers used the tradition of natural law—as well as arguments based on the sanctity of custom—to contend that society was a natural structure and that the people were the source of all power.[9]

The religious strife that issued from the Reformation had a secularizing effect in a more direct fashion. In the century of the Reformation, religious war was so damaging to the peace and prosperity of France that people became more and more disposed to see a plague visited on all houses of worship. They began to think of social unity as something separate from religion, until at last the *politiques*, and especially the best known among them, Jean Bodin (1530–1596), arrived at the revolutionary conclusion that religious uniformity was not necessary for political unity.

By the sixteenth century the diversification of society (perhaps better stated, the coexistence of feudal and liberal values—values reflected in the antagonism of strata and the rivalry of secular and religious groups) had produced social systems racked by conflict and instability. In Italy, Machiavelli (1469–1527) sought to improve the efficacy of politics and to bring unification to the patchwork of principalities on the Italian peninsula. In France, Bodin sought relief from the bitterness of religious strife in the doctrine of absolutism and state sovereignty. Finally, in seventeenth-century England, Hobbes and Locke proposed the social contract as a solution to the plague of social and religious strife that had infected the body of English society. Despite the diversity of their aims and arguments, these theorists had one thing in common—all were intellectual contributors to the theory of liberal society and liberal politics. Machiavelli severed politics from morality by

[9] For a classic discussion of these theories see John Neville Figgis, *From Gerson to Grotius: 1414–1625* (Cambridge, England: Cambridge University Press, 1907), chaps. 5, 6. For the contribution of the Protestant monarchomachs to modern constitutionalism, see Julian H. Franklin, "Constitutionalism in the Sixteenth Century: The Protestant Monarchomachs," in David Spitz, ed., *Political Theory and Social Change* (New York: Atherton Press, 1967), pp. 117–132.

viewing the former as a means for dealing with mutable political problems, a means he felt should be unhampered by immutable moral principles. Bodin separated politics from religion by deciding that religious uniformity was not essential to political unity. However, the struggle to free politics from religion and feudalism received its most radical expression in the social contract theories of Hobbes and Locke.

The social contract, a much-misunderstood idea, was more than an attempt to set politics on a new basis. Its revolutionary significance lay as well in its new assumptions about the nature of society. Hitherto, the timeless, perfected hierarchical structure of society, reflecting the perfection of God and the wisdom of the past, had been thought of as prior to individuals and the only source of their identity. The social contract theory reversed the relationship with a sharp clean stroke, declaring that individuals had identities prior to society and that henceforth society would receive its identity from them. The idea that humankind is composed of individuals, all relatively equal and existing in their own right, and the accompanying idea that individuals create society instead of being its creatures, was a radical departure from the main current of Western social thought. It was an idea, however, that did not enter the world simply as an inspired solution to the problem of English society. For centuries, many Westerners had exhibited individualism in behavior, and had become accustomed to acting singly and from private motives. For centuries, they had been creating machines for every type of utility, and new legal and economic forms to exploit the opportunities presented by the machine. It is not surprising, then, that Westerners came to feel that society itself was not beyond their powers of creation.

In the work of Hobbes and Locke, therefore, we see the intellectual climax to the gradual emancipation of economic and political structures from the framework of feudal Christendom. The works of both thinkers bear the authentic marks of liberal society: individualism, private property, the primacy of economic motives and market relations, utilitarianism, and a separate and supreme realm of positive law. In the words of C. B. Macpherson, Hobbes and Locke and other seventeenth-century thinkers developed the central assumption of liberal social theory:

> . . . its conception of the individual as essentially the proprietor
> of his own person or capacities, owing nothing to society for
> them. The individual was seen neither as a moral whole, nor as
> part of a larger social whole, but as an owner of himself. The
> relation of ownership, having become for more and more men
> the critically important relation determining their actual freedom
> and actual prospect of realizing their full potentialities, was read
> back into the nature of the individual. The individual, it was
> thought, is free inasmuch as he is proprietor of his person and

capacities. The human essence is freedom from dependence on the wills of others, and freedom is a function of possession. Society becomes a lot of free equal individuals related to each other as proprietors of their own capacities and of what they have acquired by their exercise. Society consists of relations of exchange between proprietors. Political society becomes a calculated device for the protection of this property and for the maintenance of an orderly relation of exchange.[10]

Though Hobbes and Locke each made the distinction between private and public spheres in his own way, the effect was the same. Because the individual was intractably unruly, the only way to achieve society for Hobbes was through absolutism. However, because Hobbes provided no social content for his absolutism, it was in effect a demand for legal sovereignty, a sovereignty that could be wielded by any social interest(s). It was also an absolutism intrinsically connected to Hobbes's fundamental individualism. By failing to place it in the hands of any social group or stratum, by using it to destroy the validity of all intermediate claims on the individual—such as family, custom, and religion—and by justifying it only to the extent that individuals found it more useful to obey than to go their own way, Hobbes's absolutism stands as a milestone in liberal social thought.

For his part, Locke did not stress the need for sovereignty or state action to assure social peace. The individual was for him somehow sociable before society, and political authority was necessary only to settle the exceptional disputes that arise between social actors. Thus, individuals carried with them into society their natural rights to liberty, property, contract, and family—rights not derived from nor subject to the state. However, even Locke, in insisting on the legal monopoly of the legislature and on the prerogative power of the sovereign, admitted by the back door a sphere of public authority that somewhat balanced his almost anarchic emphasis on the naturally social individual.

Locke's work bears considerable interest for us because of its enormous influence during the eighteenth century, especially in France and the United States. Whereas Hobbes based his social thought on a scientific concept of natural law, reducing it to relations of cause and effect, Locke secularized and individualized the philosophical concept of natural law; his argument provided a moral justification for the emergent capitalist economy of England. Locke read into the state of nature the main features of the bustling market economy of his day: private property and market relations in credit, commodities, and labor. His core assumption—that an

[10] C. B. Macpherson, *The Political Theory of Possessive Individualism: Hobbes to Locke* (London: Oxford University Press, 1962), p. 3.

individual's labor belongs by nature to that individual—led to a full-blown moral justification for the appropriation of nature through capitalist institutions. As C. B. Macpherson has shown, however, the labor theory of value was not a simple, equal claim of right, but quite varied: it meant that individuals had the right to unequal and unlimited appropriation as well as the right to alienate (sell) their labor. What Locke was doing, of course, was putting his own society into metaphysical clothing. The economic individualism and exchange relations of his day were defined as natural to human beings, using traditional natural-law arguments. Locke also made the class relations of his day natural by arguing that unequal natural property made for socially unequal individuals and classes. Indeed, those in the propertyless laboring class were assumed not rational enough to be full members of society, a condition Locke considered permanent since laborers must of economic necessity live on subsistence wages. As for the able-bodied unemployed, not only did their moral depravity disqualify them for full social membership, but the state had a duty to enforce discipline and productive labor, even among children.[11] In any case, Locke's argument that acquisitive behavior was neither a social convention nor a matter for political sanctions and direction suited the interests and needs of the middle class. By the end of the eighteenth century the French and Scottish Enlightenments had taken these ideas, and those of Newton's mechanistic, self-balancing world view, and had constructed a comprehensive theory of society grounded not merely in the power of the middle class but in metaphysics as well.

Though overlooked and neglected, it was Hobbes who was more prophetic and profound in his depiction of the emergent capitalist society. His starkly stated pragmatism, his rejection of natural law and teleology, and his explicit image of society in terms of the exchange relations of the capitalist economy of his day rendered social existence totally problematic and prefigured the conflicts and moral uncertainties of the future. In his social philosophy as well, Hobbes was more prophetic and profound. Despite the bitter and costly strife unleashed by the Reformation, the expansion of commerce, industry, technology, and science continued unabated throughout the sixteenth century. By the seventeenth century the growing control and understanding of nature culminated in a scientific breakthrough, which rested on the master assumption that nature could be fruitfully understood as a collection of minute material particles in structured mathematical motion. In the development of social theory, a similar breakthrough is discernible. Out of the savage conflicts of the English Civil War, there came a vast debate about the nature of human nature and society, the upshot of which was the radical secularization and individualization of

[11] For Locke's theory and its relation to the needs of English capitalist society, see C. B. Macpherson, *The Political Theory of Possessive Individualism: Hobbes to Locke* (London: Oxford University Press, 1962), chap. 5.

natural law. Of even greater importance was the fact that beyond the noisy claims and counterclaims of normative social theory, there appeared for the first time a deliberate attempt to model social theory on the new natural science. The scientific assumption that physical nature could be thought of in terms of indivisible particles in motion bears a deep kinship to the social-contract theory, that revolutionary view which also dissolved society into individuals and also defined it as having a structure accessible to rational analysis. Given the deep metaphysical craving of Western society, it was no accident, of course, that during the seventeenth century the science of human behavior received an explicit and coherent formulation in terms very similar to those that had been successful in understanding the structure of physical nature.

The rise of modern social science did not result from empiricism any more than did the rise of natural science. Stemming from the new confidence in human capabilities that accompanied the growing mastery of nature, and especially from the new confidence in human reason, a social science arose that sought to apply to the study of human nature the successful methods and the revolutionary conclusions of natural science. Out of the ferment of the seventeenth century came the first of the many attempts during the modern era to model social thought on the methods and findings of modern natural science.

The modernization of social and philosophical thought took place on a wide scale during the seventeenth century. If social science is defined as the attempt to round out or unify human beings' concept of themselves to match their most rational concept of nature, then the works of Grotius, Francis Bacon, Hobbes, Pufendorf, and Spinoza must be thought of as pioneer statements in the development of modern social science. Perhaps the greatest of these attempts to bring the study of human nature and society up to date is the materialistic monism of Thomas Hobbes. Whereas the main current of physical theory through Galileo and Descartes explicitly confined science to nature, Hobbes's historic greatness lies in his systematic and conscious application of the method and content of mechanistic science to the study of human nature. The revolutionary question he posed can be stated simply: If deduction, especially geometrical deduction, can provide an understanding of a nature conceived as particles of matter in structured motion, is it not possible that human nature and society will lend themselves to the same treatment?

Even without this scientific bent to his thought, Hobbes would have been assured a high place in the annals of social thought. This he accomplished by posing the problem of social order as one of reconciling the sovereignty of competing egoisms, and by proposing a simple utilitarianism as a solution. In noting the significance of the social contract theory, we saw the revolutionary way in which Hobbes dismissed both feudalism and religion as the basis of society by declaring both incapable of producing peace and predictability, the prime staples of social existence. Only a focused structure of power, he argued, could bring unity out of the conflicting claims that mark the nature of society. By thus stating the problem of politics, Hobbes did more than gauge correctly, and give expression to, the trend toward centralized government that the current of economic and religious change had made inevitable; his originality went much further. In posing the sovereignty of the state as the only solution of the problem of social order, he did so without eliminating the sovereignty of the individual. By stating the problem of society as one of reconciling the basic egoism of individuals, by seeing unpredictable interaction among individuals as the main problem of social existence, by recognizing the rights of individuals to judge the power of the state in terms of its utility to their interests, and by condemning along the way the parasitical and contentious nature of feudal-military values, Hobbes was attempting to register in social thought the basic values and interests of the middle class.

Hobbes's stature as a social theorist, however, does not rest on this achievement alone. His theory of society was no expedient designed merely to bring social peace out of the bloody conflicts of the English Civil War, or to champion bourgeois values against feudalism. He deliberately set out to base his theory of society on unshakable scientific foundations—to complete, in short, the destruction of Aristotelian teleology in the realm of social theory that Galileo had accomplished in physical theory. It makes no difference that his attempt to equate human nature with physical nature failed, or that his theory lacked an empirical basis. He must receive the credit not only for envisioning the possibility of a science of human nature that would bring the spirit and substance of the new physical theory to bear on social theory, but also for providing modern intellectual culture with a brilliantly executed example of the problems inherent in such an approach. Viewed from a broader perspective, Hobbes's thought was the first systematic attempt by the newly emerging civilization of liberalism to pull together the scattered strands of its centuries-old revolution against theocratic feudalism, and to gain for itself a coherent identity based on an unshakable metaphysics. It was an attempt, as we shall see, that was to be repeated many times during the history of sociological theory, for in the long course of transforming Hobbes's deductive positivism into an empirical positivism, sociology in no way abandoned the search for a transhistorical definition of human nature and society.

The Modern View of Human Nature: Phase Two, Secular Empiricism

Despite the importance of the seventeenth century in the history of social science, it is to the eighteenth century that one must look for the emergence of an empirical science of behavior. During the multifarious flowering of the intellect known as the Enlightenment, the idea of a science of human behavior was firmly secured and its fortunes markedly advanced. We have already had occasion to look at the physical theory of the Enlightenment, and we must now show how closely social theory followed the main line of development in natural science. The Enlightenment, of course, is older than the eighteenth century and wider than the territory of France. Its essential spirit was already widespread in seventeenth-century French skepticism and science; and the same spirit of intellectual rebellion and reconstruction flowered all over Europe, though, of course, nowhere so brightly as in France.[12] It is also important to note that generalizations about the Enlightenment, while easy to make, are difficult to sustain, and that the term refers to the work of a large and rather disparate group of thinkers who are not easy to classify. One would be hard put, for example, to relate such thinkers as Hume, Ferguson, Montesquieu, Rousseau, and Herder to one another, or to the philosophes. Even among the philosophes there was such a diversity of opinion that it is necessary to qualify all generalizations about them carefully. The gap that existed—for example, between the political views of Voltaire and those of Helvetius; between the empiricism of D'Alembert and the rationalism of the Physiocrats; between Voltaire's deism and fear of materialism, and the atheistic materialism of Holbach; and between the static mechanism of La Mettrie and the evolutionary doctrine of Condorcet—makes it necessary to think of even the philosophes as individuals.

It is safe to say, however, that the Enlightenment, especially in France and Scotland, was a momentously important period for the development of social science, a period discussed much too hurriedly, if at all, by the historians of social science and sociology. The Enlightenment's revolutionary redefinition of human nature may be thought of on two different but related levels. First, the Enlightenment smashed the Cartesian restriction of science to nature, and loudly proclaimed and firmly established the applicability of science to the study of human behavior. On the second level, and of greater importance, the intellectual tendency of the age not only brought human nature and society within the jurisdiction of science, but also brought science to the school of fact. We have already noted the profound empirical bent of the Enlightenment's physical theory. By the eighteenth century the development of technology and industry had made it both possible and imperative that a systematic empirical science be established to allow

---

[12] For a review of the growth of the new spirit of enlightenment before the eighteenth century, see J. S. Spink, *French Free-Thought from Gassendi to Voltaire* (London: University of London, Athlone Press, 1960); Paul Hazard, *The European Mind, 1680–1715* (London: Hollis and Carter, 1953). For an account of an important concentration of enlightenment outside of France, see Gladys Bryson, *Man and Society: The Scottish Inquiry of the Eighteenth Century* (Princeton, N.J.: Princeton University Press, 1945). Peter Gay's *The Enlightenment: An Interpretation*, 2 vols. (New York: Alfred A. Knopf, 1966, 1969) remains the outstanding reference work on the overall period.

human beings to grapple at close quarters with a nature increasingly immune to long-range attack by logic. What was true of natural science was true elsewhere: a restless, pragmatic, earthbound bourgeoisie found that both Cartesian and Greek rationalism were no less of an obstacle in moral and social theory than they had been in physical theory. The method of Descartes left human nature unknowable, thus depriving the middle class of a metaphysical basis for their values; Greek rationalism placed most of the activities and things that the bourgeoisie most valued lowest in its teleologically derived hierarchy of values.

Thus, odd as it may seem, the Age of Reason opposed rationalism in morals just as it opposed it in physics. Or, put more positively, the profound achievement of the Enlightenment was to pioneer and to insist on the view that the phenomenal realm was in and of itself rational. The rationalism of eighteenth-century social science, therefore, was quite different from the rationalism of Hobbes. Hobbes's deductive, mathematical positivism was as uncongenial to the philosophes as was his absolutism. The inspiration for eighteenth-century social science came from another direction: from the earthy empiricism at the heart of Bacon's passion for induction and utility, from Bayle's zeal for accuracy, and from Locke's judicious attempt to relate the structure of the psyche to sensation. The nature of the Scottish Enlightenment, or of the so-called common or moral sense school—composed of Hutcheson, Hume, Adam Smith, Ferguson, Reid, Stewart, Monboddo, and Kames—was deeply empirical; it diligently applied this empiricism to the study of human nature and society.[13] Making allowances for the more advanced political development of Great Britain, the work of this group of thinkers bears a remarkable similarity to the main line of thought developed in France, from whence, incidentally, these thinkers drew much of their inspiration. Therefore, despite our emphasis on the philosophes as the main representatives of the Enlightenment, it should be understood that we are also speaking of Scottish developments.[14]

The trend toward empiricism expressed the middle-class need for specialized, flexible action and thought, a need that militated against the unwieldy interlocking structure of both feudal norms and scholastic reasoning. However, the empiricism of the Enlightenment had another side of equal significance. The humbling of reason implicit in the new orientation went far beyond the demand that logic be disciplined by facts. In a vast act of intellectual brilliance, the Enlightenment defined the intellect as a servant

---

[13] See Bryson, *Man and Society: The Scottish Inquiry of the Eighteenth Century*, chap. 1, for a valuable summary of the work of this remarkable group of thinkers.
[14] For a useful collection of selections from the work of the Scottish thinkers with a valuable introduction to their thought, which links it with present-day sociology, see Louis Schneider, ed., *The Scottish Moralists on Human Nature and Society* (Chicago: University of Chicago Press, 1967).

of the passions and of the interests of humanity, thereby asserting the claims of the appetites against the superiority and superintendence of reason.[15] Though only Hume, in one way, and Rousseau, in another, followed this line of thought to its fuller meaning, there was a broad consensus during the eighteenth century that the mind was a tool for the acquisition of knowledge, and that knowledge, in turn, was a means for satisfying human needs. Nothing illustrates the revolutionary discontinuity of the philosophy of the Enlightenment as much as this elevation of the passions to a position of superiority and respectability. Underlying this re-evaluation was the momentous assumption that the passions were not merely good, but also rational—that is, lawful. Indeed, it was their rationality that made the passions good. No longer were human passions automatically defined as evil, antisocial, and the source of intellectual confusion and deception. The explanation for this revolutionary about-face is undoubtedly complex, but any explanation of the Enlightenment's rejection of moral scarcity must take into account the accelerating expansion of European economic life. The inroads made by the West into material scarcity were not unrelated to an increasing intellectual impatience with doctrines that denied the human capacity for moral improvement. Perhaps nothing illustrates so well the deep gap separating the Enlightenment from the preliberal era of scarcity— an era, incidentally, in which one must place Hobbes—than this emphatic denial that human capacity for moral action was limited.

The Enlightenment's re-evaluation of the passions went hand in hand with its sensationalist epistemology. Under the general guidance of Lockean psychology, there was a diligent search for the natural individual—the psychic structure ordained by nature. Again following Locke, the philosophes reduced mind to its history—a static conception of history for the most part. In addition they emphasized the complex diversity of phenomena and the relativity between a particular sense and its subject matter—a tendency I noted earlier in my survey of the Enlightenment's physical theory—and went on to say that not reason but the will produced knowledge as well as values. Reason was defined in terms of its activity, a prelude to the more explicit and thoroughgoing transformation of mind into function that occurred during the nineteenth century.

Considerable light is shed on the hedonistic instrumentalism of the Enlightenment if it is interpreted as a moral and intellectual response to the needs of a burgeoning economy. This economy presented Westerners with an ever-new array of problems that only an instrumental reason could solve, and it required an upgrading of the appetites so that energies and talents

---

[15] Ernst Cassirer, *The Philosophy of the Enlightenment,* trans. Fritz C. A. Koelling and James P. Pettegrove (Boston: Beacon paperbound, 1955), pp. 102–108; originally published in 1932; first published in translation by Princeton University Press in 1951.

could be fused with the requirements of commerce and industry. In the simpler age of the eighteenth century, this new outlook could still be combined with a belief in the ultimate unity and permanence of physical and moral reality. Though Carl Becker's famous book, *The Heavenly City of the Eighteenth Century Philosophers*, has tended to distort our view of the Enlightenment, Becker is right in pointing to the large measure of continuity between the thought of the philosophes and the intellectual and moral tradition of Christianity.

For all its continuity with the past, however, the Enlightenment was a serious break with tradition in that it secularized and individualized the theory of natural law, and demanded that Christian values be realized *in this world*. In any case—and for all their insistence on empiricism and their awareness of the relativity of knowledge—the theorists of the Enlightenment were certain that norms of conduct existed that were absolute; just as they were certain that once the blinkers of custom and superstition were removed, human beings would obtain a knowledge of the natural order of things and would fashion their lives accordingly. Of course, the philosophes were not inclined to wait until humanity was ready to act for itself. They took it upon themselves to reveal in advance what would be found once the reign of reason had been established. They did not hesitate to announce that liberty, equality, fraternity, and happiness were the rational goods that nature had ordained for humankind's eventual enjoyment. Before the century ended, they added to this catalog of goods the idea that humanity would receive these benefits in accordance with a natural schedule of progress. Even before the publication of Voltaire's *Essay on Morals*, Fontenelle (1657–1757) and Saint-Pierre (1658–1743)—in rejecting the superiority of the ancients over the moderns—had discarded not only the doctrine of cyclical recurrence, but with it all ideas of a degeneration from a golden age, whether religious or secular, and had adumbrated for the first time the idea of progress. Formulated more explicitly by Turgot (1727–1781) in the middle of the century, the idea of progress passed into the literature of sociology with its subsequent acceptance by Condorcet, Saint-Simon, and Comte. Deeply needed as a metaphysical balm to soothe the wounds of rapid social change, the doctrine of progress, elaborated by a thousand other voices, soon became part of the core consciousness of Western populations, eventually becoming almost as much the cause of change as it was an effect.

The doctrine of progress stood at the heart of the intellectual and value orientation of the middle class, and it served as the epitome of the basic middle-class world view. Through it, the bourgeoisie affirmed its belief that the world was a worthy place in which to live and that mundane problems and hardships were not beyond the ken and stamina of human beings. While the philosophes were not agreed about the question of human natural goodness, they were completely agreed that there was no such thing as original sin.[16] In announcing their absolute faith in human beings' ability to achieve undreamed-of secular progress and to make their way in the world unaided, the philosophes knew that there could be no compromise with any view that sought to place absolute limits on human achievement.

The overall orientation of the Enlightenment thus contained a paradox: By directing attention to the values of this world and by advocating instrumentalism as the method by which these goods could be obtained, the Enlightenment was thoroughly historical; but in claiming that it was also possible to obtain the permanent principles underlying human nature and society, it was ahistorical. In a mighty act of intellectual synthesis, climaxing centuries of social change, the Enlightenment took both the Greek and the post-Renaissance concepts of science and brought them down to earth. In a momentous reversal of intellectual tradition, it declared that the empirical world was rational and constituted the only source of knowledge. At the same time, the Enlightenment broadened the blanket of science to include human nature, declaring that it too was amenable to empirical science. Thus, by deepening and broadening the West's view of science and by insisting that there was but one nature and one reason—with an essential relation between them that could be found by the sentient-thinking ego—it eliminated any distinction either between supernature and nature, or between history and nature. The Enlightenment thereby rounded out and gave coherent shape to the sociocultural universe of liberalism, a universe at once continuous with and in sharp opposition to the Western tradition.

In achieving this synthesis, however, the Enlightenment was as much a way station as a terminal, for it expressed forces that not only led to attacks on liberalism from the outside, but also drastically changed it internally. Politically, the period up to 1789 pointed the way toward universal suffrage and legal equality, institutional forms that eventually became the hallmarks of liberal democracy. Economically, the shift from wood, wind, and running water (and human muscle) as sources of power toward harnessing the power of steam marks the end of the "water and wood" stage of production and the start of the "coal and iron" stage—a technological transformation destined to visit cataclysmic changes on the life of Western populations. Scientifically speaking, the eighteenth century was also a turning point as well as a climax. Fortified by its past success, increasingly supported by industry and government, and endowed with its newly digested empirical method, science stood at the threshold of an undreamed-of expansion of knowledge. Of particular importance, of course, is that in consolidating the ideal of a science of human behavior, the eighteenth century set standards in methodology and substantive work that

[16] Cassirer, *Philosophy of the Enlightenment*, pp. 141, 159.

stimulated later generations to heights that would have astonished but pleased the philosophes.

Despite stupendous achievements across the entire breadth of intellectual life, the goal that stood closest to the heart of the Enlightenment—effecting a merger between history and metaphysics—presented a difficult and perplexing quandary. My analysis of sociology must wait, therefore, until I have considered the dilemma that stood at the heart of the fully formed civilization of liberalism, a dilemma that has plagued liberalism and sociology ever since.

THE DILEMMA OF LIBERAL RATIONALITY

By assuming an ultimate identity between reason and experience (or theory and fact) and between knowledge and utility (or reason and virtue), the Enlightenment helped to open the floodgates of knowledge and to usher in an era of intellectual plenty. By indicting other ages for their faith in logic, for their uncritical acceptance of miracles, and for philosophies that were irrelevant to humanity's needs, the Enlightenment effectively undermined the authority of logic, of revelation, of custom—and even of authority itself; it thereby helped to institute the self-conscious search for empirical knowledge that is so characteristic of the contemporary age. However, because it insisted that the goal of knowledge was unity and permanence—in effect accepting the traditional goal of metaphysics—while at the same time insisting that this goal be based on experience, it not only posed a threat to previous systems of philosophy, but to philosophy itself. My analysis of the history of sociological theory will be viewed as a continuing and (perhaps) futile attempt to solve the dilemma that this metaphysical urge posed for liberalism.

The Dilemma in Natural Science

Classical rationalism had based the unity of nature on the unity of God. By rejecting this proof, according to Cassirer, the Enlightenment was presented with a new problem:

> What is the use of freeing natural science from all theologico-metaphysical content and of limiting it to purely empirical statements, if we do not, on the other hand, succeed in eliminating metaphysical elements from its structure? And does not every statement which goes beyond the simple affirmation of an immediate object of sense perception contain just such an element? Is the systematic structure of nature, the absolute homogeneity of experience, itself a result of experience? Is it deductible from, demonstrable by, experience? Or does it not rather constitute a

premise of experience? And is not this premise, this logical *a priori*, just as questionable as any metaphysical or theological *a priori* could be? One should not only eliminate all individual concepts and judgments from the realm of empirical science: one should finally have the courage to pursue this tendency to its logical conclusion: one should even withdraw from the concept of nature the support of the concept of God. What will then become of the apparent necessity of nature, of its general, eternal, and inviolable laws? Is this necessity based upon an intuitive certainty, or upon any other rigorous deductive proof? Or must we forego all such proofs and make up our minds to take the last step, namely, to acknowledge that the world of facts can only support itself and that we seek in vain for any other firmer foundation, for a rational ground, for this world.[17]

The elimination of rational proof from science, continued Cassirer, which was inherent in Newton's inductive method, was powerfully augmented by the Dutch experimental scientists. In 1690, Huygens affirmed that physics did not admit of the same clarity that one found in mathematics and that it did not admit of intuitive certainty. A further implication of Newtonian theory was developed by S'Gravesande, who replaced the logical supports for universal causation with arguments based on human experience.

Cassirer also traced the problem of trying to base knowledge on experience in the fields of psychology and epistemology. Given the importance of sensory knowledge, a number of questions arose to plague the Enlightenment. Where, for one thing, do the "forms" that we perceive in the realm of reality come from? Does the psyche have an autonomous power of coordination, a process of consciousness that unites the data of each sensory organ and reveals the objective structure of reality? In answering these questions, the Enlightenment, in general, followed Berkeley.

All apriority of space is vigorously rejected; hence the question of its generality and necessity appears in a new light. If we owe our insight into the structural relations of space merely to experience, it is not inconceivable that a change of experience, as for instance in the event of an alteration of our psychophysical organization, would affect the whole nature of space. Henceforth the concept of space is indefatigably pursued through all its ramifications. What is the significance of that constancy and objectivity which we are accustomed to attribute to the forms of perception and of the understanding? Does this constancy predicate anything concerning the nature of things, or is not all that we understand by this term related and limited to

[17] Cassirer, *Philosophy of the Enlightenment,* p. 58f.

our own nature? Are the judgments which we base on this conception valid, as Bacon would say, by analogy with the universe or rather exclusively by analogy with man? With this question the problem of the origin of the idea of space develops far beyond its initial limits. We see now the circumstance which caused psychological and epistemological thought in the eighteenth century to recur again and again to this problem. For on it the fate of the concept of truth in general seemed to depend. If space, which is a fundamental element of all human perception, consists merely of the fusion and correlation of various sensory impressions, then it cannot lay claim to any other necessity and any higher logical dignity than the original elements of which it is composed. The subjectivity of sensory qualities, which is known to and generally acknowledged by modern science, accordingly, draws space too into its sphere. But the development cannot stop here, for what is true of space is true in the same sense and with the same justification of all the other factors on which the "form" of knowledge is based.[18]

All this, Cassirer continued, was given empirical confirmation in 1728 with the successful operation on a young boy who had been blind from birth. The fact that he had to learn to see confirmed the theory that there is no "inner affinity" between sense organs, but only a habitual connection. Thus there is no homogeneous space underlying the senses; experience contains neither unity nor permanence, but only the diversity and relativity of the senses. This is a view that extends itself to include all areas of thought: the intellectual, moral, aesthetic, and religious.[19]

The Dilemma in Social Science

The philosophes not only believed that the principles governing human nature could be found and that humankind could at last base ethics, morals, and social existence on rational foundations; they even ventured to outline the general structure of law and morals that nature had decreed for the governance and guidance of humanity. Through this act of intellectual legislation, however, the philosophes plunged headlong into the same dilemma in morals that lay at the heart of their physical theory. As Cassirer pointed out, Voltaire never faced up to the philosophical problem inherent in a doctrine of progress based on a belief in a constant human nature. Despite a genuine historical perspective—namely his view that the historian's function is to uncover the "hidden law" at work in historical phenomena, in the same way the natural scientist probes for law beneath natural phenomena—Voltaire failed to explain the relation between the

---

[18] Cassirer, *Philosophy of the Enlightenment*, p. 113f.
[19] Ibid., pp. 114–116.

empirical events of history or experience, and the constant spirit or reason of human beings. Ultimately, said Cassirer, Voltaire succumbed no less than Bossuet (1627–1704) to a teleological view of history.[20]

The same dilemma can be stated differently: For the philosophes, the idea of progress really meant progress in uncovering the original nature of human nature. The crucial problem for bourgeois social thought, from the seventeenth century on, was to construct a theory of natural law as free from religious and ecclesiastical control as it was from state absolutism. Such a version appears in Grotius who, in the fashion of the seventeenth century, argued deductively that there was an objective order of natural law that existed apart from human beings as well as from God. Though it could not accept the abstract rationalism of Grotius, preferring instead the more empirical rationalism of Locke, the Enlightenment accepted the general idea of natural law. Even Montesquieu, whose main line of thought lay outside the tradition of natural law, expressed his belief in natural justice. The Enlightenment accepted the whole idea of the a priority of law, and enthusiastically embraced the doctrine of inalienable human rights. Human beings, it felt, had the inherent good sense to see and act upon their duty toward others. The philosophes were certain that there existed a natural moral order, based squarely on the nature of human beings and not on the abstract declamations of reason or on the suprarationality of revelation. Out of the uniform appetites and inclinations of humanity, out of humankind's purely natural motives and interests, would come, they felt, a natural moral and social order. However, as Cassirer pointed out, referring especially to Voltaire and Diderot, such a belief, in combination with a sensationalist epistemology, led to a difficult dilemma. It was one thing for Grotius, for example, to affirm a doctrine of immutable law, since he based it on deduction. The philosophes, however, subscribed to a theory of knowledge that derived every idea from the senses—an epistemology that was at variance with the idea of natural law.[21]

Stated succinctly, the dilemma of liberal rationality was this: *How can the inherent power of reason or moral sense overcome experience, which is a chronicle of folly and fraud, when reason does not exist apart from experience?* The philosophes affirmed a set of standards by which individuals could judge society, while at the same time affirming, not only the power of society over human beings, but also its ethical monopoly to train human minds and personalities. Related to the Enlightenment's interest in empirical causation was the tendency to think of knowledge as a means or cause, and to judge it by its consequences. It was self-evident to the philosophes that inalienable rights existed in regard to such things as liberty, property, and happiness, and that rights not only would be realized through science but

[20] Ibid., pp. 218–222.
[21] Ibid., pp. 234–253.

were also based on science. However, the dilemma remains: *On what basis are these rights established when they have never been part of human experience?* How, in short, can one establish the institutional features of society on an argument based on natural law and self-evidence, while at the same time wielding the sword of empiricism?

The liberal dilemma, which was more acute in moral than in physical theory, evoked a rich variety of responses and solutions during the course of the eighteenth century. There is no better testimony to the realism and profundity of Enlightenment philosophy than the fact that it directly produced important lines of thought; while these lines of thought were able to transcend the assumptions of the Enlightenment, they could do so only by accepting and absorbing them. By being true to itself, especially by forcefully stating its assumptions and baring the problems inherent in them, the Enlightenment, in effect, superseded itself.

One of the most influential and important of the many attempts to solve the general dilemma plaguing the Enlightenment is found in the philosophy of Immanuel Kant. Another solution to the dilemma was sought in the categorical rejection of natural law, a view that tended to reduce norms to conventions. On the whole this was the direction taken by Hume and Montesquieu. As will be shown later, Montesquieu, in one phase of his thought, even went so far as to question the worth of any kind of society. However, this line of thought as a general solution to the liberal dilemma was developed only by Rousseau, who questioned the worth of all types of social existence, including one based on science, individualism, and progress.[22] Rousseau's rejection of both the past and the present and his simultaneous insistence that a genuine community is the destiny of humanity pitted him against the main thrust of the French Enlightenment. What separated Rousseau most from the philosophes was his suspicion that reason and science were no more related to humanity's true identity than were religion, warfare, or feudalism. Indeed, the emergence of reason as critical intelligence menaces rather than establishes society.

Rousseau's opposition to rationalism in all its guises and his refusal to equate humanity's true identity with the accepted institutions and consciousness of European society are clear. Though his attempt to specify the nature of the true world of humanity was vague, the thrust of his argument was unmistakable. Human beings have a moral nature that has been corrupted by all known institutions. The only way to realize the community intended for humanity is to allow this original moral force to manifest itself. While this

---

[22] *The Discourse on Inequality* (1754) and the *Social Contract* (1762) are Rousseau's most important works in social science. For a succinct description of Rousseau's radicalism and his relation to the philosophes, see Ernst Cassirer, *Philosophy of the Enlightenment*, pp. 153–158, 266–270.

force has been partially realized in the lives of plain people, only a radical reconstruction of society can make it manifest completely.

Rousseau's influence was wide-ranging. His stress on the moral will influenced Kant and the entire romantic reaction to the age of reason. His assertion that the moral sentiments of ordinary people are sound, his idealization of the communal will, and his vague but fervently expressed belief that humanity must make its own destiny found expression in conservative, liberal, and socialist movements, theories, and nationalisms.

Another attempt to solve the liberal dilemma, one which was of great importance for the origin of sociology, was the "evolutionary" doctrine that took shape during the second half of the eighteenth century. Finally, from all the foregoing responses, came many of the elements that were to make up the powerful intellectual currents that dominated nineteenth-century thought: romanticism, historicism, utilitarianism, and pragmatism. Though the thought of the philosophes contained aspects of all these responses, the philosophes never gave up the position that created the liberal dilemma in the first place, *the belief that a constant human nature, which manifests itself only through experience, is still capable of achieving at a certain time and place its ultimate perfection.*

Charles Frankel's carefully and concisely written *The Faith of Reason* [23] leads us to the liberal dilemma from another route. Like Cassirer, Frankel has developed the intellectual dilemma of the Enlightenment by tracing it back to the two opposing views of science that emerged in the seventeenth century. Cassirer contrasted Newtonian empiricism with Cartesian rationalism to lay bare the problem of knowledge that bedeviled the philosophes. Frankel made the same contrast, but did so more dramatically by using Pascal's empiricism rather than Newton's in contrast with the rationalism of Descartes. No lengthy review of Descartes's view of science is necessary; for him science was an exercise in speculative reason, a search for comprehensive certainty through mathematical deduction. The factual realm, for Descartes, was too deceptive and ephemeral to form a secure basis for knowledge. In contrast, Pascal argued that only that which was acquired through experiment and observation—that is, from within the realm of the factual—could properly be called scientific knowledge.

As Frankel has shown, these two views of science merged during the eighteenth century to form the philosophical problem we have referred to as the dilemma of liberal rationality. The philosophes accepted the Cartesian goal of unified and indubitable knowledge, but they wanted to base it on the empiricism characteristic of Pascal's thought. And, of course, the philosophes broadened and deepened the dilemma immeasureably by going

[23] New York: King's Crown Press, 1948.

beyond Descartes and Pascal, each of whom had excluded human behavior from the competence of science, and by declaring that a science of human nature and society was possible. Thus by formulating the science of human behavior in the above terms, the philosophes introduced the liberal dilemma into social science. As I shall show, evolutionary positivism was largely an attempt to get around this dilemma without going outside the framework of liberalism.[24]

If, as the Enlightenment believed, knowledge is assured because of a correspondence between human reason and the rationality of nature, and if the empirical method is the road to establishing this correspondence, then an empirical inquiry into the process by which the mind acquires knowledge is not only possible, but constitutes the first order of business. It is not surprising, therefore, that the Englightenment turned its attention to psychology, biology, and medicine, nor that mathematics and logic were reduced to positions of secondary interest. However, as the philosophes delved empirically into the foundations of belief, their perplexity mounted. On the one hand, science as an empirical method told them that knowledge came from experience. On the other hand, they felt that the realm of facts could be unified into a comprehensive set of scientific principles. However, if human beings learned from experience only, how could they be sure that their ideas were valid?[25] By reducing mind to a tabula rasa that recorded sensations, the philosophes were hard put to explain the validity of their own ideas, including the idea of the empirical method itself. If human beings had the rationality or reflective power to validate sensations, then why had they never done so before? If there was no such thing as revelation, and if chance could provide no basis for knowledge, why had the truth been revealed by natural processes to the theorists of the Age of Reason? Conversely, why, if human beings were rational, was their history

[24] For an analysis that relates other post-Enlightenment currents, especially Marxism and Utilitarianism, to the same philosophical dilemma, see R. V. Sampson, *Progress in the Age of Reason* (Cambridge, Mass.: Harvard University Press, 1956). Like Frankel, Sampson uses the contrast between Descartes and Pascal to point up the nature of science during the Age of Reason (chap. 2), and he too asks how is it possible for nature to produce evil or for enlightenment to take place so abruptly (pp. 53, 90, 118). But unlike Frankel, Sampson approaches this problem through Hume's analysis of natural law—an analysis, Sampson says, which led not only to the destruction of all rational foundations for values, but also to the construction of new schemes of thought, especially philosophies of history, each seeking a rational basis for morals. It is worth noting the Gladys Bryson's *Man and Society: The Scottish Inquiry of the Eighteenth Century* was also written primarily to search out the philosophical milieux that shaped the emergence of social science. However, though Bryson identifies a proclivity for value judgments, teleological reasoning, and metaphysics in the thought of the Scottish Enlightenment, she fails to point out or to emphasize the serious implications contained in the introduction of such intellectual habits into social science, merely raising the question for the reader to ponder. In this connection, see her Conclusion.

[25] Frankel, *The Faith of Reason*, p. 47.

a record of ignorance and error? By assuming that a stable and unchanging natural order could be revealed by a gradual growth of knowledge based on and manifested in experience, the theorists of the Enlightenment were trying to combine metaphysics with history, theory with practice, and abstract right with social actuality, thereby raising philosophical and social questions of the greatest complexity.

The problem of evil is closely related to the problem of error, since the philosophes tended to equate evil with ignorance. Despite many disagreements on other matters, the philosophes were agreed that there was no such thing as original sin; but if human beings were good, as some philosophes believed, then why, by their own admission, had the history of humankind been an uninterrupted chronicle of evil? One could not answer that it was due to ignorance and error, because these had not been accounted for either.

The intellectual dilemma of liberalism was matched by an institutional dilemma running through the newly emerging liberal social structure. Individuals, liberals said, were no longer to receive their identity from birth, custom, or religion. The individual was defined as a self whose reality lay in the unity and spontaneity of its psychological make-up. However, it was not reason that ruled the individual, but will, passions, and interests. Individual reason was no longer the avenue to truth and virtue, but a servant of the appetites and a tool of discovery and invention. Viewed sociologically, the Enlightenment effected a vast transformation in the intellectual tradition of Western society to serve the needs of a new social order. Its basic individualism meant that self-expression was socially valuable. The individual's need for self-expression required liberty of conscience and of speech at the very least, and insured individuals equal status before the law. It required a set of common legal norms that not only reflected the equality of individuals, but also insured them the predictability necessary to make their self-expression rational and meaningful. Law was no longer anchored in sacred usage, but was conventional and positive, the result of will—be it the will of the sovereign or of the people. However, law must also embody certain natural rights that lie beyond convention, especially the right of personal liberty and private property, and it must insure the sanctity of contractual agreements resulting from the conscious activity of the rational ego. Here again the intellectual problem of determining the relation between natural and positive law appeared as an institutional dilemma as liberalism put its ideas into practice.

This dilemma was not confined simply to law but pervaded all reaches of bourgeois institutional life. The family was removed from the central position it enjoyed under feudalism and Roman Catholicism and became a functionally limited structure serving the needs of individuals. However, in

Locke, at least, the family was thought to be a natural—not a social—institution, and there was a widespread desire to guarantee the natural status of the family, especially in regard to the inheritance of property. The natural right to property made it difficult to establish the public's right to restrict and regulate the uses of property, or to tax it. The presumed rationality of the economic order made it difficult to think about or take measures to cope with unemployment, exploitation, the steady alternation of boom and bust, or inflation. The nation as a moral community gave justification for military expenditures and territorial and economic expansion, but it enjoyed no such standing when it interfered with internal property rights or private economic power.

In political matters, there was a widespread feeling that the right to liberty meant more than mere equality before the law—it meant self-expression and participation in political decisions. Infused by the assumption that the combined result of rational political activity by all individuals would result in harmony and legislative rationality, bourgeois political institutions could discover nothing more dignified on which to base decision making than the irrational, historically bound expediences of compromise and majority rule. However, the harmony of the political process rested ultimately on the assumed harmony of economic life—an assumption that did not lose its vitality until well into the nineteenth century despite the deep economic conflicts that beset early industrialism and the large-scale political supports that were necessary to its stability and growth.

These institutional norms, which were hammered out slowly within a feudal context during the seventeenth and eighteenth centuries, were dynamic and disruptive. In effect, they declared that Western populations (especially those in England and France) were no longer content to obtain their identity from the static, ascriptive structure of feudal society. Henceforth, liberals proclaimed, society would derive its identity from the nature of the individual. There were limits to the dynamism, however, implicit in the attempt to find a natural basis for the new norms. The bourgeoisie wanted a centralized legal system to sweep away feudal and religious particularism, but also wanted protection against the new centralized state. To this end Locke placed most of society beyond the jurisdiction of positive law and insisted that constitutional procedures be followed before any legislative change. In the same vein, Grotius spoke of law as something that existed without religion or empirical evidence, while Montesquieu, despite his skepticism, was sure that a natural justice existed. Morality may be temporal and geographical, and human beings may be subject to the vargaries of experience, but the philosophes were certain that an immutable moral order existed.

As an intellectual and social structure based on the central value of world mastery through rational human effort, liberalism gained its dynamism by posing the "ought" against the "is," by separating the past and the future, by freeing economic activity from moral, religious, and social restraints, and by postulating the existence of a large area of knowable mystery, the key to which lay in the cumulative power of science. However, a variety of liberal thinkers braked this dynamism by carving out in detail an institutional structure enjoined, they claimed, by nature and therefore not amenable to human or historical change.

The attempt to establish a dynamic set of norms at once conventional and natural, to single out those norms that were merely historical conveniences from those immutably rooted in the nature of things, was jeopardized from the start by an inadequate philosophical formulation. The overall problem of liberalism stemmed from its revolutionary emancipation of the human ego. Subjected immemorially to the corruptions and deceptions of history, individuals were henceforth to be the arbiters of their own fate. They were not to live idiosyncratically, however, but rationally—that is, they would apprehend the social universe ordained by nature and live accordingly. However, the paradox remained. If individuals had hitherto been subject to historical determination, on what basis could it be assumed that they had finally escaped from their bondage? They might be told that ideas and institutions were relative to time and circumstance, but could they ever be sure that liberal ideas and institutions were valid? They might be told to regard all values and ideas as problematic and perhaps profane—they might be told that their egos must acquiesce before submitting to any value or idea structure—but what was to prevent the magnification of the errors and deceptions of history once differently conditioned individuals and classes began to assert their new-found authority? In short, a society that actively encourages individuals to think and act for themselves may be hard put to establish limits to thought and self-interest, or to contain the ensuing diversities and antagonisms if no natural order exists to arbitrate or integrate divergent egos or groups and social classes.

The philosophical and social thought of the eighteenth century became increasingly self-conscious about its philosphical dilemma. As the century progressed, the philosophes struggled to reshape their thought to overcome the metaphysical inadequacy of the world view that they had constructed to displace feudal Christendom. In the process they became increasingly historical in a new way. Their world view was already somewhat historical in that it directed attention away from the supernatural and toward the here and now. It was the static formulation of the here and now that had led to their dilemma in the first place, and as the century wore on they groped toward a more dynamic concept of history.

The first commitment to a genuine idea of progress emerged during the controversy between the ancients and the moderns when in 1688 Fontenelle

wrote his *Digression on the Ancients and the Moderns*. In this early formulation, however, the belief in progress was restricted to progress in knowledge. The first explicitly to equate progress in knowledge with social progress seems to have been Saint-Pierre, whose works appeared during the
early decades of the eighteenth century. Then quickly, and over a wide
geographical area, the new sense of progress, closely allied with a new
sense of history, began to permeate the intellectual climate of Europe.
Despite differences in outlook, a number of thinkers emerged who gave
expression to the new sense of history: Vico, Voltaire, Montesquieu, Turgot, Ferguson, Hume, Gibbon, Priestley, Lessing, Herder, and Kant.

As the century progressed, eighteenth-century thinkers came more and
more to think of the present as a stage in a lawful process of change. The
present was no longer sharply demarcated from the past, the particular no
longer separated from the general; both were seen as somehow involved in
and determined by what had occurred earlier. The overwhelming similarity
among most of these theories is their metaphysical cast, their attempt to
reduce the phenomena of history to a monistic principle. However, the
main speculative tradition of Europe during the eighteenth century was
centered in France, and it was there that the idea of lawful historical
change received its greatest development. In the development of sociology,
there is a direct line from Voltaire through Turgot to Condorcet, Saint-
Simon, and Comte. By the end of the century, the two meanings of the
word *historical*—the here and now as opposed to the hereafter, and the
temporally empirical as opposed to the statically rational—had crystallized
into a coherent social theory that is easily recognizable as sociological in
both method and content.

It is time, therefore, to end both this analysis of the liberal dilemma and
this description of the emerging civilization of liberalism, and to begin an
analysis of sociological theory proper. I shall begin by examining the work
of five theorists, Vico, Montesquieu, Condorcet, Saint-Simon, and Comte,
who bequeathed to sociology its major organizing ideas—paying close attention to their conscious and unconscious struggle to overcome the dilemma of liberalism. These five are not only the most important theorists
of the formative stage of sociology, but are also representative figures. In
pioneering the application of science to human behavior, they gave the
widest possible range of answers to the liberal dilemma without opposing
the fundamental interests of the middle class.

PART II
The Origins of Sociology

Chapter 5
The New Science of History: Vico (1668–1744)

After emphasizing that modern social science had its origins in the general current of rationalism, it is ironic that I must start my discussion of the formative period of sociology with an exception to this generalization— Giambattista Vico. Of course, if one judges theorists by their influence, the generalization holds, for Vico exercised almost no influence over the formative period of sociology. Indeed, his work went unrecognized until the nineteenth century, and even then gained recognition mostly on the continent of Europe. There are a number of reasons for the general neglect of Vico's work, which holds even to this day in the Anglo-American world: his geographical isolation, his failure to gain an academic forum from which to publicize his views, and his nonpolemical disposition.[1] Perhaps the major reason his work failed to gain either the recognition or the influence it deserved was that his thought, while congenial to the earthbound empiricism of the Enlightenment, was in radical opposition to its ahistorical rationalism. The opening of the eighteenth century was not an auspicious time to present, as Vico did, a philosophical view that saw meaning and truth in the historical past.

---

[1] Some small evidence of a growth of interest in Vico was the symposium held on the tercentenary of his birth: see Giorgio Tagliacozzo and Hayden V. White, eds., *Giambattista Vico: An International Symposium* (Baltimore: Johns Hopkins Press, 1969) and the more recent publication, *Giambattista Vico's Science of Humanity*, eds. Giorgio Tagliacozzo and Donald Phillip Verene (Baltimore: Johns Hopkins University Press, 1976). The latter volume contains a bibliography of all works on Vico printed in English since the nineteenth century. Though the essays in these volumes contain material relevant to understanding Vico's thought and its relation to currents of thought in philosophy, law, literature, and the like, they are written by specialists for specialists and none provides an overview of Vico's social theory and its relation to sociology and social thought. Two special issues of *Social Research* 43, nos. 3 and 4 (Autumn and Winter 1976), titled "Vico and Contemporary Thought, 1–2," with an updated bibliography, are also oriented toward specialists. Two recent, fuller treatments of Vico's thought, which unfortunately do not focus on his social theory and its relation to sociology and social thought, are Leon Pompa, *Vico: A Study of the 'New Science'* (Cambridge, England: Cambridge University Press, 1975) and Isaiah Berlin, *Vico and Herder: Two Studies in the History of Ideas* (London: Hogarth Press, 1976).

Giambattista Vico (1668–1744)

PHILOSOPHY AND METHOD

Vico's early philosophical essays clearly reveal his antirationalism and contain the seeds of his later work in social science.[2] Vico's core objection to Cartesianism was that it either neglected the moral sciences or else sought to absorb them into natural science; it assumed that only that which is absolutely certain can be called knowledge. This assumption, Vico argued, left out the vast and important area of probable or prudential knowledge.

In Descartes's case, knowledge about human nature was not possible—a position he was forced to take given his criteria of truth. Vico attacked

[2] The following account of Vico's philosophical position is based on Robert Flint, *Vico* (London: Blackwood and Sons, 1884), chaps. 5, 6, and on the excellent short summary of Vico's philosophy in R. G. Collingwood, *The Idea of History* (New York: Oxford University Press paperbound, 1956), pp. 63–71.

this position, dismissing Descartes's "clear and distinct" criterion with the simple declaration that there was a sharp difference between consciousness and knowledge, and that one could have a lively and sharp belief in something patently false. Vico's criticism went deeper, however; he deliberately brushed aside Descartes's attempt to equate knowledge only with that which can be expressed mathematically. With such a criterion of knowledge, one could be concerned only with the relation between ideas (or logic), and would have to consider the empirical world, including the realm of human behavior, as nonrational. The problem of empiricism, however, did not exist for Vico because of his revolutionary assumption that there was no order of ideas separate from an order of facts. A clue to this new perspective, said Vico, was the fact that the Latin terms *verum* and *factum* were convertible one to the other. Truth was merely facts, and facts were simply whatever had been made or done. Once accepted, these simple words undermined the foundations of rationalism, for their meaning was clear—no separate order of truth existed apart from facts or creation. Even mathematics, said Vico, anticipating developments in nineteenth-century mathematical thought, was a human creation, a set of fictions established by convention.

The Science of Human Nature

The core assumption of Vico's new science was that knowledge about human behavior requires an act of understanding, in which one empathizes with actors, not an act of perception, in which one attempts to link ideas with facts. As the title [3] of his masterwork (*Scienza nuova*) indicates, Vico was conscious that he had arrived at a new way of acquiring knowledge. In developing his new perspective, Vico rejected a number of representative theories of human nature. From the past, he rejected all systems of natural law based on teleology and all systems of thought that sought to interpret human behavior as physical behavior. Of particular interest is Vico's critique of the social theory based on the rationalism of his own age—a rationalism that, when it did not deny the possibility of rational knowledge about human behavior, sought to interpret it either through mathematically based systems of natural law or in terms that had been successfully applied to physical nature. Having refuted Descartes, the major philosopher of rationalism, Vico felt no qualms about setting aside the modern nonteleological systems of natural law that had been derived from that tradition. He specifically singled out for rejection the natural-law

[3] *Scienza nuova*, first published in 1725 and now available in English as *The New Science of Giambattista Vico*, revised translation by Thomas G. Bergin and Max H. Fisch (Ithaca, N.Y.: Cornell University Press, 1968) from the third edition (1744); henceforth cited as *New Science*. The abridged paperback edition (Harper Torchbook) is based on the first translation (1948).

systems of Grotius (1583–1645), Selden (1584–1654), and Pufendorf (1632–1694).

Human Nature and the Nature of Truth

The reader who peruses the first book of the *New Science* is soon aware that Vico's axioms tend to affirm a common theme, namely that human beings are above all creatures of action. Throughout Vico's writings, there is an unmistakable preoccupation with the interpretation of time and events. His references to human behavior emphasize the "indefiniteness" of the human mind; "will"; early humankind's childlike curiosity, imagination, and actions; the primacy of the passions, senses, and ego; and the tendency of individuals—especially during the infancy of the race—to engage in action without reflection, refinement, or moderation.

Perhaps the clearest expression of Vico's emphasis on action is his definition of truth. Human beings, he said, are naturally inventive; they fashion a mental and moral world by using the senses, the conceits of the mind, and bodily analogies; only gradually does reflection begin to play a part in human affairs. Under the guidance of Providence, human beings come to feel, act, and think in approximate accord with God's purposes. However, they are neither the puppets of Providence nor bound by necessity like the world of nature. Despite their fallen nature, human beings are autonomous actors who participate in the mind and heart of God. In a complex and mysterious interplay of human spontaneity and divine direction, individuals create the moral and social universes that God has ordained in His own mind. If they are to know God and themselves, Vico argued, they must avoid the conceit of the philosophers who seek God through the use of mathematics and related metaphysical approaches. Invariably, Vico referred to God as Providence, grace, or the "divine legislative mind." Rarely was it the God of love, law, or impersonal reason that Vico emphasized; it was the Old Testament God, the intervening God of the Hebrews who actively manifests Himself in history through His chosen instrument, the Hebrew people. God, in short, was more a demiurge for Vico than a principle or a spirit—like human beings, God was a dynamic entity.

God can be known, therefore, only by His acts; creation is truth. Similarly, individuals can be known only through their acts; no rational knowledge of human beings or of God is possible in abstraction from events and deeds. Enfeebled by sin, the human mind cannot ascend to divine truth, but it can obtain the truth implicit in its own creations. The mind can know the things of history not because they are material or physical things, but because they are human products and thus amenable to human understanding.

In the night of thick darkness enveloping the earliest antiquity, so remote from ourselves, there shines the eternal and never-failing light of a truth beyond all question: that the world of civil society has certainly been made by men, and that its principles are therefore to be found within the modifications of our own human mind. Whosoever reflects on this cannot but marvel that the philosophers should have bent all their energies to the study of the world of nature, which, since God made it, He alone knows; and that they should have neglected the study of the world of nations or civil world, which since men had made it, men could hope to know.[4]

Vico's revolutionary assumption that truth and creation are the same is also stated in these words:

The nature of institutions is nothing but their coming into being (nascimento) at certain times and in certain guises. Whenever the time and guise are thus and so, such and not otherwise are the institutions that come into being.

The inseparable properties of institutions must be due to the modification or guise with which they are born. By these properties we may therefore verify that the nature or birth (*natura o nascimento*) was thus and not otherwise.[5]

The search for knowledge proceeds both theoretically and empirically, or to use Vico's terms, through both philosophy and philology:

Philosophy contemplates reason, whence comes knowledge of the true; philology observes that of which human choice is author, whence comes consciousness of the certain.

This axiom by its second part includes among the philologians all the grammarians, historians, critics, who have occupied themselves with the study of the languages and deeds of peoples: both at home, as in their customs and laws, and abroad, as in their wars, peaces, alliances, travels and commerce.

This same axiom shows how the philosophers failed by half in not giving certainty to their reasonings by appeal to the authority of the philologians, and likewise how the latter failed by half in not taking care to give their authority the sanction of truth by appeal to the reasoning of the philosophers. If they had done this they would have been more useful to their

---

[4] *New Science*, 311; in accordance with Vico's custom, the numerical references to his work refer to paragraphs or axioms, not pages.
[5] Ibid., 147–148.

commonwealths and they would have anticipated us in conceiving this Science.[6]

The fundamental postulate that knowledge is possible only about things that are made or done not only gives access to the divine mind, but also is the way to knowledge about human nature. According to Vico, human beings think and act in rough accordance with the wishes of Providence even though they may not be aware of it. These thoughts and acts in one sense are divine products, and in another sense are human things. Individuals can know God and themselves only by framing their reasoning in terms of these two poles—the perfect but unknowable truth of God, and the realized portion of this truth that is human history.

Christianity and the New Science

Vico's advocacy of theory and fact (or philosophy and philology) was a keynote of eighteenth-century thought. Vico also shared the Enlightenment's revolutionary belief in an empirically based science of human nature. However, whereas the rationalism of the Enlightenment led the philosophes to adopt an ahistorical view of human nature, Vico's conception of science led him to a genuinely historical view of human nature and of society. The source of his unique historical orientation was undoubtedly his immersion in the Christian world view.[7] The defectiveness of human reason, which Vico used to undermine the pretensions of rationalism, was derived from the Christian doctrine of original sin. Further, by taking the dynamic elements in the Judaic-Christian conception of God, Vico used the doctrine of original sin to construct a dynamic Christian positivism.

The basis of Vico's theoretical edifice is the assumption that God *is* what He *does*. Though God is an eternal principle or reason, He is primarily an active shaper of events. From the dual nature of God, reason and will, Vico derived his dual methodology—the emphasis on philosophy, or reason, and on philology, or fact—and his assumption that theory and fact, reason and experience are separate but mutually supporting methods of knowledge.

Ultimately speaking, there is an identity between theory and fact. No truth could exist for Vico that is unknown, because truth cannot exist unless created, and if created, it must be known to someone and knowable to

---

[6] Ibid., 138–140.
[7] In discussing the relationship between Christianity and Vico's contribution to the science of history, both at this point and in the conclusion to this chapter, I have drawn heavily on Collingwood's general discussion of the way in which Christianity influenced the rise of historical thinking; see, in this respect, R. G. Collingwood, *The Idea of History* (New York: Oxford University Press paperback, 1956), part 1, secs. 1, 2.

others. The relation between theory and fact, in other words, is not an epistemological problem. At any given time, the true is that which is known, and, conversely, what is known is true. For human beings truth is historical, not absolute; indeed, human beings make truth as they go along. Truth is not a pre-existing realm of objective facts whose underlying uniformities thinkers can seize once and for all. However, said Vico, knowledge is still absolute in the sense that what human beings know exists in the absolute mind of God. Though human knowledge is relative to individuals and to their historical period, this knowledge is not relative if viewed in the overall context of God's purpose—which, whatever it is, renders human knowledge at once limited and absolute.

Human beings cannot know God or His purposes fully because of the Fall; but Vico's version of original sin is again in conformity with the assumptions of his new science. Original sin is not so much an absolute limitation of human powers as it is a historical limitation. Human knowledge of God, for example, can grow, though it ends at a certain point. This inability to know God completely is the same as the inability to know the future, for human beings cannot know what they have not yet done.

However, what human beings do know is of great value and validity. By defining the empirical realm as the manifestation of God's purposes, and by relating it to the truth that is God, Vico transformed what had previously been considered an irrational and unknowable realm into a fertile field of knowledge. Thus did Christianity promote the central assumption of social science—the belief that the diversity and contingency of the empirical realm is rational. The upshot of this momentous intellectual reorientation was that individuals could now obtain empirical knowledge about themselves. They did not obtain foresight, however, for they often did things that had consequences other than those they intended. However, even the intrinsic blindness of human action, which stemmed from original sin, was transformed by Vico into a beneficial process in which human beings became the unwitting agents of God. Though foresight was not possible, people could obtain hindsight—a true knowledge of what they had done in the past. This vast area of knowledge was opened because of Vico's basic postulate of knowledge: contemporary scientists could know what human beings had done and been in the past because their common humanity allowed them to participate in the emotions and thoughts of their forebears through acts of mental reconstruction. Thus Vico's method of knowledge was a process of understanding human nature, not a process for disclosing its permanent uniformities.[8]

---

[8] The use of subjectivity in scientific method (as well as its use as subject matter) in sociology did not come into its own until the end of the nineteenth century and will be treated more fully later. Some of the most important figures in this regard are Max Weber and Charles Horton Cooley.

SUBSTANTIVE WORK

The Concern with Origins

In keeping with his philosophical orientation that equates truth with creation, Vico devoted the greater part of the *New Science* to uncovering the
origins of society. Books Two and Three, entitled "Poetic Wisdom" and
"The Discovery of the True Homer," are attempts to discover the nature
of early human beings through an analysis of poetry, the characteristic
mental form of primitive times. The grand aim of Vico's research was stated
at the beginning of Book Two:

> We shall show clearly and distinctly how the founders of gentile
> humanity by means of their natural theology (or metaphysics)
> imagined the gods; how by means of their logic they invented
> languages; by morals, created heroes; by economics, founded
> families, and by politics, cities; by their physics, established the
> beginnings of things as all divine; by the particular physics of
> man, in a certain sense created themselves; by their cosmography,
> fashioned for themselves a universe entirely of gods; by astron-
> omy, carried the planets and constellations from earth to heaven;
> by chronology, gave a beginning to [measured] times; and how
> by geography the Greeks, for example, described the [whole]
> world within their own Greece.
>
> Thus our Science comes to be at once a history of the ideas, the
> customs, and the deeds of mankind. From these three we shall
> derive the principles of the history of human nature, which we
> shall show to be the principles of universal history, which prin-
> ciples it seems hitherto to have lacked.[9]

For Vico, the key to the growth of "human social institutions" was the
study of language, for language unlocked the meaning of poetry and rendered values and ideas of a period accessible to outsiders. Accordingly, Vico
devoted considerable attention to the task of constructing a science of
poetry and language. The first peoples were intellectually sensual; they
relied on metaphor to create their picture of the world, and on a robust
imagination undisciplined by criticism or reflection. Their morals were
sensual, too; "that is, they were virtues of the senses, with an admixture of
religion and cruelty. . . ." Out of the fear of Jove came piety and shame,
moral sentiments that eventually culminated in marriage—which Vico in
characteristic language refers to as "a chaste carnal union consumated
under the fear of some divinity." Out of religious fear, there emerged an
entire catalog of morals. Piety and religion made human beings prudent,
just, temperate, strong, industrious, and magnanimous, though these early
peoples were also fanatically superstitious as well as savage, proud, and

[9] *New Science,* 367–368.

cruel. The original state of society was neither a golden age of philosophy nor an age of innocence. It was an age of savagery softened by religion, in which human beings were humanized by their fear of a deity they themselves had created. It was really an Age of Gods, because the people soon created many deities, each of whom assuaged an anxiety or satisfied a social need.

The Discovery of Cultural Systems and Epochs

The first institution, the family, was also a miniature society, claimed Vico, a place "where the fathers teach only religion and where they are admired by their sons as their sages, revered as their priests, and feared as their kings." Out of the family came economic behavior, for the father's obligation to leave his sons a patrimony led to the development of the economic arts. The men who responded to religious discipline and became heads of families were called *heroes.* However, at a very early point the family included more than the offspring: The hero-fathers took under their protection the refugees who had wandered onto their lands in flight from the violence and misery of an existence as yet unsoftened by religious discipline. As economic and political asylum were added to religious and family institutions, the aristocratic Age of Heroes superseded the Age of Gods as the second type of society. The Heroic commonwealth reached its completion with the appearance of the first agrarian law regulating the status of the heroes or nobles in relation to their "clients" or serfs.

Vico believed that his findings were common to the origin and development of all humankind. All people, he stated, begin as people with the fear of Jove. Then, in the process of developing their own version of the Heroic Age, all people create a Hercules myth. This knowledge of the common origin and development of humankind confounds the conceit that makes each people think of itself as unique. However, Vico's search into the past also reveals cultural epochs in this history of nations; this confounds the conceit of philosophers who feel that things have always been the same. The philosopher's conceit, Vico explained, has misled modern thinkers about the nature of the Heroic Age. The meaning that the people of that period attached to the words *people, king,* and *liberty,* for example, is quite different from what is currently meant by these words. The *people* meant the patricians only, and did not include the plebs; *kingship* was aristocratic, not monarchic; *liberty* was not popular, but referred to the liberty of the lords. Only through his philological method, Vico insisted, could the past be truly understood, for only it could reconstruct the exact quality of life in bygone ages.

Vico's most brilliant use of his new method is in Book Three, "The Discovery of the True Homer." By analyzing the poems of Homer, Vico concluded "that the Greek peoples were themselves Homer." All the textual difficulties contained in those poems are resolved if one thinks of Homer not as an individual but as the entire tradition of heroic poetry spanning the centuries that lay between the beginning of the Heroic Age and its close.

> Thus Homer composed the *Iliad* in his youth, that is when Greece was young and consequently seething with sublime passions, such as pride, wrath and lust for vengeance, passions which do not tolerate dissimulation but which love magnanimity; and hence this Greece admired Achilles, the hero of violence. But he wrote the *Odyssey* in his old age, that is when the spirits of Greece had been somewhat cooled by reflection, which is the mother of prudence, so that it admired Ulysses, the hero of wisdom. Thus in the time of Homer's youth the peoples of Greece found pleasure in coarseness, villainy, ferocity, savagery and cruelty, while in the time of his old age they found delight in the luxury of Alcinous, the joys of Calypso, the pleasures of Circe, the songs of the Sirens, the pastimes of the suitors, and the attempts, nay the siege and the assaults on the chastity of Penelope: *two sets of customs which, conceived above as existing at the same time, seemed to us incompatible.*[10]

Regardless of whether or not Vico's analysis of Homer is valid, these closing lines attest to Vico's thorough grasp of the crucial factor in historical analysis—the knowledge that human beings who share a common biological and psychological make-up can lead qualitatively different kinds of life. It was this insight that prompted Vico to develop the assumptions and methods by which different sociocultural systems could be known. Though each way of life is ordained by God, the fact that makes them accessible to human understanding is that they are all human made. Human beings can know the epochs of the past by reconstructing them in their minds through philological analysis—that is, through the empirical analysis of actual behavior and belief—and through philosophy—that is, through logical analysis and a theological understanding of God's purposes. If one follows this new science, one will find that human behavior groups itself into logically compatible wholes, or cultural systems, and that these systems undergo qualitative transformations in accordance with the plan of God.

The Nature and Evolution of Cultural Systems

Arguing that nations or civil states pass through three ages—of Gods, of Heroes, and of Men—Vico carefully outlined the cultural structure of each of the first two ages, clearly specifying the type of personality, custom, natural law, government, language, jurisprudence, authority, and reason

---

[10] *New Science*, 879 (emphasis mine).

characteristic of each. Whether Vico's cultural types are acceptable is a separate question and should not be confused with the undoubted originality of his search for the inner logic of given complexes of historical phenomena. As we saw in his analysis of Homer, Vico had an acute insight into the qualitative differences that exist in human history—differences expressed in unique universes of ideas, values, and practices. Of special importance was his admonition that one must be careful to interpret a given fact in terms of its cultural context and not as a thing in itself. Unfortunately, Vico's last stage, the Age of Men, received little elaboration; however, its nature is clear. Under the sway of fully developed human reason, individuals in this stage are modest, dutiful, and benign, and enjoy an equality based on their common rationality.

Vico's search for unity within a given complex of facts was part of a larger attempt to find unity in all the facts of history. In addition to the unity within (and the sharp difference between) cultural periods, he also discerned a pattern or logic in the relationship among the periods themselves. The three ages form a cycle through which all humankind passes, but the cycle does not exhaust the phenomena of history in the sense that it occurs once and ends in a final golden age. After a cycle occurs, a recurrence takes place, similar but not identical in nature to the first. In the West, the three ages of the first cycle took place in the history of Greece and Rome and then the cycle resumed its course during the Dark Ages. Though all humanity is subject to this developmental pattern, Vico found that the nations of Asia, Africa, and the New World were not so advanced as European Christendom. In the West, however, by comparing the medieval to the ancient world, one could clearly discern a "first and a returned barbarism." By subjecting the medieval world to historical analysis, Vico found that it contained two of the earlier stages in the evolution of humankind: the Age of Gods, which corresponded to the Dark Ages, and the Age of Heroes, which corresponded to the Middle Ages. The recurrence of the third period might be found in the Renaissance, which inaugurated the second Age of Men—a period, Vico felt, that would eventually culminate in the perfect monarchy where alone human beings could be equal and free.

The last stage of the second cycle is of considerable interest because it represented to Vico a qualitative advance over its counterpart in the ancient world. Without undue emphasis, Vico argued that the main reason for this advance was that Christianity had entered the stream of historical development, thus making it possible for human beings to realize more fully their potentiality for rational behavior. Vico's references to the previous Age of Men, though sparse, usually emphasized its decadence. In referring to the new Age of Men emerging from the womb of the Heroic culture of medieval Europe, he was more favorably disposed toward it, and even allowed himself a moderate optimism about the future. In any case, there is no doubt that Vico believed that the recurrence of the cycle meant an upward spiraling of the fortunes of humanity.

Judged as a solution to liberal dilemma, Vico's theory of history is a brilliant attempt to find both permanence and change within the seeming chaos of human affairs without resorting to either religion or philosophy for his main explanation. On the contrary and despite his repeated references to Providence, religion plays a relatively minor part in his analysis. Although an orthodox Roman Catholic, Vico scarcely mentioned either the role of revelation or that of the Roman Church in the formation and development of society. His references to the new religious ingredient in the modern cycle are sparse and restrained. Though he often suggested in a vague way that individuals are prompted to action by Providence, his main assumption was that cultural and social structures emerge almost solely through the unaided efforts of human beings. However, if he was unwilling to say that God rules directly, neither was he willing to say that human beings are self-explanatory. It is not surprising, therefore, that Vico ended his study on a note that is apparent in a number of places in his work—with the attempt to secularize Providence, or, conversely, to rationalize the empirical. Simply expressed, Vico put forward a belief in the existence of a hidden logic lurking behind human actions, which orders and directs people to purposes that are often unknown to themselves.

The concept of a hidden agency in human affairs did not end with Vico. It appears again and again in sociological theory as a solution to the liberal dilemma. Faced with the same problem of reducing a manifold and ephemeral empirical realm to reason, sociological theorists—along with other types of social scientists—were to find the concept of a hidden agency an extremely attractive explanatory device. Vico's reliance on this concept, which he derived from the religious idea of Providence, is clearly seen in the following passage:

> It is true that men have themselves made this world of nations (and we took this as the first incontestable principle of our Science, since we despaired of finding it from the philosophers and philologists), but this world without doubt has issued from a mind often diverse, at times quite contrary, and always superior to the particular ends that men had proposed to themselves; which narrow ends, made means to serve wider ends, it was always employed to preserve the human race upon this earth. Men mean to gratify their bestial lust and abandon their offspring, and they inaugurate the chastity of marriage from which the families arise. The fathers mean to exercise without restraint their paternal power over their clients, and they subject them to the civil powers from which the cities arise. The reigning orders of nobles mean to abuse their lordly freedom over the plebeians,

and they are obliged to submit to the laws which establish popular liberty. The free peoples mean to shake off the yoke of their
laws, and they become subject to monarchs. The monarchs mean
to strengthen their own positions by debasing their subjects with
all the vices of dissoluteness, and they dispose them to endure
slavery at the hands of stronger nations. The nations mean to
dissolve themselves, and their remnants flee for safety to the
wilderness, whence, like the phoenix, they rise again. That which
did all this was mind, for men did it with intelligence; it was not
fate, for they did it by choice; not chance, for the results of their
always so acting are perpetually the same.[11]

The redefinition of reason as something to be found both in and beyond
experience, as something both overt and covert in the affairs of human
beings, as a hidden design revealed slowly to actors through their own
deeds, is one of the central features of historical social theories. This
orientation, which has played such a large part in modern thought, both
in sociology and beyond, received its first systematic statement in the work
of Giambattista Vico. A static version of the idea of a hidden logic had
emerged somewhat earlier in English and Scottish liberal thought and
reached its climax in the concept of an invisible hand in laissez faire economic theory. Perhaps the earliest figure to develop this idea is Bernard
Mandeville (1670–1733) whose *The Fable of the Bees or Private Vices,
Publick Benefits* appeared between 1705 and 1728.[12] The idea was widespread in the Scottish Enlightenment.[13]

CONCLUSION

While Vico's work emerged from presuppositions lying outside the rationalism of his age, his thought is not wholly dissimilar from the main intellectual current of the eighteenth century. The secular and empirical bent to
his thought brought him much closer to the Enlightenment than a superficial analysis might indicate. In addition, he shared the Enlightenment's
proclivity for deductive thought and its craving for metaphysics—that is, for
building a unitary, monistic view of things. Similarities aside, however,
there are deep differences between Vico and the Enlightenment.

To see these differences best, it is necessary to recall our classification of
the various types of sociological theory.[14] Methodologically speaking, the

[11] *New Science,* 1108.
[12] Available as a Capricorn Book, 1962, edited with an introduction by Irwin
Primer.
[13] See Louis Schneider, ed. and intro., *The Scottish Moralists on Human Nature
and Society* (Chicago: University of Chicago Press, 1967), xxix–xlvii, and part 4.
[14] See Chapter 1.

formative period of sociology was monistic (despite its avowals of empiricism), that is, it relied on one method, invariably deductive logic. It was not until the late nineteenth century that a pluralistic methodology arose, namely, a genuine commitment to the empirical method and to a variety of techniques for obtaining knowledge. In substantive matters, another important dividing line in sociology stems from differing views of subject matter. The main line of development in early sociology was the definition of behavior in biopsychological terms and the search for other natural causes of behavior such as geography, climate, and even physics (naturalistic positivism). A second line of development was to view human behavior as a function of sociocultural variables (sociocultural positivism).

What differentiated Vico from the main line of development in sociology was his pioneering sociocultural perspective. For Vico there existed a fundamental distinction between the realm of nature and the realm of society. Human beings do not exist as fixed entities, structures, or essences. They exist only in the sense and to the extent that there are specific institutional structures. In short, by making cultural structures, human beings make themselves. The basic distinction, therefore, between nature and society is that the latter is a human creation, something resulting from human powers and related to human "needs and utilities." The distinctively human capacity for creation not only separates people from nature, but also provides them with a method for obtaining knowledge about themselves. Humankind can know only what it has created, however; the mind cannot know more, for the rest is knowable only to God. God knows and then creates; human beings create and then know. Stated differently, people use their powers to realize the mind and heart of God. The purposes of God are contained within human beings, who as indeterminate beings can be thought of as a bundle of potentialities waiting for the divine spark to kindle the fire of history. Possessed with the "mental dictionary" that contains all things feasible, human beings grope their way under providential direction toward the earthly existence most pleasing to God. All nations, originating in religion, pass from the Age of Gods to the Age of Heroes and then to the Age of Men. As a distinct cultural entity, each age has an interdependent set of institutional structures that informs its entire life. Each represents the realization of a portion of human potentiality. Once finished, the cycle recurs, but as an upward spiral rather than as a repetition of the previous cycle. The second cycle is different because human existence, now under the sway of Christianity, has become more gentle and more rational than before.

It is evident that Vico was the first modern theorist to hold a thoroughly historical (sociocultural) point of view. The facts of social life, for him, could not be comprehended by the static logical or mathematical models that are useful in fathoming the structure of nature because social facts are different from the lifeless, repetitive processes characteristic of natural

phenomena. Social facts exhibit change, not mere change like the monoto-
nous changing of the seasons but qualitative change. Vico's emphasis on
the upward spiral in the second cycle clearly distinguishes his theory from
the cyclical theories of Greek and Roman historiography; and his emphasis
on the creative movement of sociocultural systems clearly separates him
from the idea of progress that appeared slightly later in French thought
(in Saint-Pierre and Voltaire), reaching full flower in Turgot, Condorcet,
Saint-Simon, and Comte. The idea of progress in the French Enlightenment was that of a process of intellectual and moral advance—science—
toward the full uncovering of a finished, objective world.

Modern because of his historical perspective, Vico is also modern because
of his sociological perspective. Despite his religious framework, there is no
doubt that he believed society could be studied apart from religion, provided it was studied empirically and socioculturally. To understand the
complexity of human affairs, one must be especially careful not to view the
past in terms of the present. Vico placed great emphasis on the need to
interpret facts within a meaningful historical or cultural context, a stricture
he followed brilliantly in his own work. His social theory was perhaps the
first systematic ordering of cultural and social facts since Aristotle's *Politics*,
an achievement not to be minimized because it was followed closely by the
similar and better known work of Montesquieu. Clearly informing his work
is the fundamental assumption behind cultural analysis—namely that a
social fact, whether it be in law, literature, politics, morality, or in the
economy, must be explained in terms of its relation to other parts of a
cultural universe. Indeed, Vico's focus on social structure as a viable historical entity with an identity of its own anticipates all the later social theories
that use a similar idea to justify a variety of causes, traditionalism, liberal,
or socialist.

Vico was also a harbinger of romanticism. He expressed a deep appreciation of the unique and the bizarre in human affairs, at the same time repudiating the rationalism of both mathematical and natural-rights theorists in
favor of a thoroughly historical and organic concept of society. In terms of
ideology, his thinking may be likened to French romanticism, in which the
organic concept of society was liberal in orientation, rather than to German
romanticism, in which the organic concept was conservative. In the Age of
Reason, when universalism and humanitarianism were the bywords of the
day, Vico's accent on the nation as a viable and unique structure was a prophetic anticipation of both the romanticism and the nationalism of the
following century.

Vico's evolutionary theory, it must also be noted, contained a dynamism
and a political ideology in keeping with the current of liberalism. There
was an unmistakable, if restrained, optimism in his view of history as a
movement toward liberty, equality, and rationality. Though he never lost

his emphasis on history as the movement of unitary cultural configurations, his definition of the last stage contained the unmistakable sign of liberal thought—a division between public and private spheres of life. Further signs of his liberalism were his belief that the Age of Men would be complete once the lag in political development was overcome, and his preference for an antifeudal, rational monarchy.

From another viewpoint, Vico was also the first figure in the development of liberal Catholicism. Though his political and social views were not so polemical nor so influential as those of Lamennais (1782–1854), they unquestionably represent an attempt to reconcile the divergent values and beliefs of Roman Catholicism and liberalism. His belief that Christianity is compatible with liberty and equality—that it even contributes to their development—and that authority, whether ecclesiastical or political, is similarly compatible with liberty and equality, are anticipations of beliefs that Lamennais was to popularize a century later.

One of the more interesting aspects of Vico's thought is the relationship between his religious orientation and his contribution to the emerging science of history. While many of the figures of the eighteenth century were influenced by ideas derived from the general outlook of Christianity, it was Vico's unique contribution to take the historical elements in Christianity and transform them into a genuine science of history. Vico's empiricism, for example, was derived from Christianity. By seeing the hand of God behind each event or deed, he transformed the despised empirical realm into a respectable field of study. Vico also derived from Christianity his awareness that human affairs can undergo qualitative change. We know, for example, that individuals in primitive cultures tend to think in terms of an "eternal yesterday"; but this static mode of thinking was also characteristic of the rational cultures of Greece and Rome. Reason was employed to search for the principle of human nature, the unyielding substance at the base of human existence. Christianity introduced a novel perspective on human nature, a perspective that provided one of the indispensable ingredients of eighteenth-century historical thought.

For the Christian, God is the only unchanging substance; human beings are merely created, contingent beings, though they do possess the capacity to rise above the animal nature that degrades them and the social nature that misguides them. Through the intervention of God in human affairs, human beings learn to use this capacity and thus to free themselves from the shackles of tribal or national custom. Once the word of God courses through their veins, their world can never be the same. The spiritual energy unleashed by the word of God transforms humanity's entire personal and even social existence. In the same way, the human mind is not left untouched. The birth of Christ is such a stupendous change in humankind's religious existence that change in other areas of life becomes a respectable intellectual possibility. It is quite possible, therefore, for a Christian to view the Bible as history, as a set of concrete empirical events, as a book of divine acts in which God manifests Himself in human affairs. Under this perspective the Pentateuch, the Books of the Prophets, and the Gospels represent the continuous revelation of God's will in human affairs, a revelation that continues through the operation of grace and the growth of human understanding.

It is not an unwarranted conclusion, therefore, to assume that Vico was inspired by this religious perspective when he made his contribution to the science of history. His image of God as Providence rather than as Law or Love provided him with the frame on which to weave the manifold events of history into a unified tapestry. It was Providence that explained why the tapestry of history had no loose ends, for in secularizing Providence, Vico did not eliminate the majesty and mystery of God. By stressing the importance of unintended consequences, a device he used to explain why fallible human beings act infallibly to achieve divine purposes, he made God historical and transcendental at the same time. The implications of this mode of thought for the science of history were enormous, for it also made human behavior historical and transcendental (or, in less theological language, historical and rational), thus providing the science of history with its fundamental assumption.

One must also acknowledge the religious source of much of Vico's liberalism. He was clearly aware that by denying the total inequality of the first Heroic Age, Christianity introduced a change that would someday, when matched by a growth of rationality, lead to a considerable growth in equality. So, too, his roots in Roman Catholicism prevented him from basing his liberalism and view of history on a philosophy of individualistic rationalism. Instead, he emphasized that individuals and the values by which they live emerge from the structural context in which they have their existence, and that the present is basically continuous with the past.

Nowhere is Vico's religious humanism, liberalism, and reliance on hidden logic expressed more pointedly than in the following axioms:

> Legislation considers man as he is in order to turn him to good uses in human society. Out of ferocity, avarice, and ambition, the three vices which run throughout the human race, it creates the military, merchant, and governing classes, and thus the strength, riches, and wisdom of commonwealths. Out of these three great vices, which could certainly destroy all mankind on the face of the earth, it makes civil happiness.
>
> This axiom proves that there is divine providence and further that it is a divine legislative mind. For out of the passions of men each bent on his private advantage, for the sake of which they

would live like beasts in the wilderness, it has made the civil institutions by which they may live in human society.[15]

As a solution to the liberal dilemma, Vico's general theory can be criticized on a number of grounds. Despite his empiricism, his theory is still heavily deductive. Though he displayed enormous erudition and employed a genuine historical approach, this did not prevent him from fitting his data into a prearranged scheme. Ultimately speaking, the facts of history for Vico were facts because they represented the manifestation of eternity in human affairs; they were contingencies that were ultimately absolute because of their significance in the divine plan. In the end, Vico's claim to have founded an Ideal Eternal History remained a contradiction in terms.

Despite the serious shortcomings of his general theory, however, Vico left a considerable legacy to social science. Though he had only a limited influence in the eighteenth century, he was the first to crystallize the new historical perspective of the age—and in a way that remained unsurpassed until the nineteenth century. The cornerstone of his original if neglected contribution was his insistence that human behavior was social in nature and that the facts of behavior had to be interpreted in terms of the cultural system in which they were found. However, his data, for all their richness in range and detail, were still meager in comparison with the full record of the human experience. Though his inclusion of Asia, Africa, and the New World into his subject matter represents a contribution to the development of a more universalistic outlook by Western scholarship (especially in comparison, say, with Bossuet's conception of history), his analysis of these expressions of the human potential was uninformed and highly deductive. A more serious criticism of Vico's work concerns the lack of an empirical theory of causation. The main emphasis of his empirical analysis was on understanding the *significance* of cultural data. His explanation of the qualitative change that he found in cultural structures, however, was extremely vague as to causal factors. Though he mentioned the influence of climate and geography, and casually referred to various natural instincts, passions, and faculties, he never concerned himself seriously with causation as an empirical problem. The main weight of explanation was borne by the concept of Providence. Thus, however much human beings may learn about the workings of history, God remains an inscrutable demiurge whose plans are ultimately veiled from the gaze of the human creatures whose destiny He guides. Sociology would have to wait for the *verstehen* sociology of Max Weber before Vico's methodology of understanding would be combined with a scientific theory of causation. That Vico's own contribution to historical science, derived from a religious source, would someday be influential in constructing a secular science of society is an irony that Vico would have deplored but probably understood.

[15] *New Science,* 132–133.

Chapter 6
The New Science of Society: Montesquieu (1689–1755)

While Vico remained in relative obscurity, it was quite different with his slightly younger French contemporary, Montesquieu. When Montesquieu's *The Spirit of the Laws* appeared in 1748, it enjoyed an enormous success and went on to exert a wide influence on political and intellectual leaders everywhere in the West. In Montesquieu's lifetime, France had begun to wrest the intellectual leadership of Europe away from England by opening a debate that was destined to excite the deepest reflections on the nature of humankind and of society. Written with this debate partly in mind, Montesquieu's long and scholarly work was interpreted as a tract for the times. In addition, his intellectual orientation was congenial to the rationalist temper of the age, even if his conclusions were bitterly denounced by thinkers who shared many of his philosophical assumptions. Indeed, much of the bitterness of the philosophes' attack stemmed from their frustration at seeing a secular-minded rationalist propound a theory of society so different from their own. In any case, Montesquieu did not oppose the philosophical current of his age in the way that Vico did, and his work entered the mainstream of European intellectual life at once.

This is not to suggest that the works of Vico and Montesquieu were diametrically opposed. Both men sought to comprehend social behavior in terms of culture patterns, and both were sharply opposed to the tradition of natural law. Montesquieu was acquainted with Vico's *New Science*, but it is unlikely that he was ever influenced by it.[1] His thought derived from a different intellectual tradition and was expressed in a manner quite different from Vico's. Further, Montesquieu's influence on intellectual thought and on the development of the social sciences was more immediate, extensive, and varied. Indeed, his thought is a landmark in the history of sociology and in social science in general.

[1] See, in this regard, C. E. Vaughan, *Studies in the History of Political Philosophy* (Manchester, England: University of Manchester, 1925), 1:253.

Montesquieu (1689–1755)

PHILOSOPHY AND METHOD

Montesquieu wrote no formal work on either method or philosophy, but
his general intellectual orientation is apparent in each of his three major
works.[2] These three works supplement each other, and though we will devote our major emphasis to Montesquieu's masterpiece, *The Spirit of the
Laws*,[3] a word must be said about his two earlier works, *The Persian Letters* and *Considerations on the Grandeur and Decadence of the Romans*.[4]

---

[2] *Lettres Persanes*, 1721, ed., trans., J. Robert Loy (New York: Meridian Books
paperback, 1961); *Considérations sur les causes de la grandeur des Romains et
de leur décadence*, 1734, trans. with notes and introduction by David Lowenthal
(New York: Free Press, 1965)—also in paperback; *L'Esprit des Lois*, 1748, trans.
Thomas Nugent (New York: Hafner Publishing Co. paperback, 1949) with a
valuable introduction to Montesquieu's thought by Franz Neumann.
[3] Henceforth cited as *Laws*.
[4] Henceforth cited as *Letters* and *Considerations*, respectively.

The literary genre known as Persian Letters holds great interest for the historian of the social sciences, for it reflects the impact on European intellectual life of contact with other cultures. Comparative studies (along with the contrasts provided by internal social change) had led to a growing detachment of European intellectuals from the legacy of received institutions, and to a growing critical sense about their validity. Montesquieu's The Persian Letters was the culmination and perfection of this literary tradition,[5] in which a "foreign observer" was allowed to express thoughts about the customs of the countries visited. In employing this device, Montesquieu brilliantly and audaciously satirized not just France, but European society in general. Nothing escaped his critical eye. Whether discussing politics, economics, religion, morality, the relation between the sexes, fashion, vanity, or urban, artistic, professional, and intellectual life, his mocking condemnation penetrated every aspect of French and European society and demolished whatever it saw. When he was through, he left the reader with no alternative; the institutions of the East seemed to be no better than those of the West. What remained was a genial if somewhat bitter skepticism about the validity of any set of institutions and about the capacity of human beings to establish even a moderately successful society.[6]

The Persian Letters is episodic, ambiguous, and contradictory, but it contains insights and arguments with far-reaching implications. In it, Montesquieu expressed the growing secular humanism of his age, though in a unique form. In keeping with the times (perhaps somewhat ahead of them), Montesquieu evaluated the passions, especially sexual passions, positively, and he championed the free intellect. However, his thought contained a matter-of-fact skepticism and relativism (reflecting, no doubt, the influence of Machiavelli and Montaigne) that separated him sharply from the main current of the Enlightenment.

Montesquieu's skepticism made him suspicious of beliefs supposedly based on the intrinsic worth of an object or practice, and led him to advocate toleration in matters of belief. It was a perspective that saw virtue and utility in the passions; it inclined him to judge beliefs and values by their consequences. In addition, it made him suspicious of the "universal decider" and of religious and philosphical zeal, and inclined him to accept

[5] G. L. Van Roosebroeck, Persian Letters before Montesquieu (New York: Institute of French Studies, 1932), chap. 1. For further examples of the growth of comparative studies, see Paul Hazard, The European Mind, 1680–1715 (London: Hollis and Carter, 1953), chap. 1, and European Thought in the Eighteenth Century (London: Hollis and Carter, 1954), chap. 1.
[6] Franz Neumann goes so far as to say that Montesquieu's Persian Letters is a protest against dehumanization by all institutions, and that his rejection of the human capacity to fashion a new and better society stems from a deeply felt pessimism (Laws, Intro., xiv–xix).

institutions that were working moderately well rather than to risk the dangers of novelty and hasty legislation.[7]

The innovations in social thought that Montesquieu expressed in *The Persian Letters* never left his thinking. His most important innovation was the rejection of the normative tradition of European social theory. Montesquieu not only raised the problem of human identity, but also strongly suggested that its solution was to be found in the actual expressions of human nature. Implicit in his general approach was a fairly conscious separation of questions of truth, value, and fact. Though he never formulated this separation as a philosophical maxim—that was left to his contemporary David Hume—it informed his thought throughout his life. The method that effected his release from normative social theory, and from ethnocentrism in general, was the comparative or historical method, a tool of analysis that was to have far-reaching implications for Western social theory. A warning is necessary, however, to counter any misconception over the use of the terms *factual* and *historical* in connection with Montesquieu's thought. Montesquieu was not an empiricist and he was historical only in a static sense. The factual and the historical aspects of his thought amounted to one thing: a shift to the here-and-now of behavior and away from a concern with abstract questions of right. He never said that empirical data are the only source of knowledge, and he never developed the other meaning in the term *history*—the recognition that dynamic social elements can produce deep, qualitative changes in the nature of human existence. Nevertheless, the intellectual innovation that he introduced in *The Persian Letters* and elaborated in his later works was an indispensable preliminary to the full development of both empiricism and historicism.

The novel historical method of *The Persian Letters* is also found in Montesquieu's work on Roman society, *Considerations on the Grandeur and Decadence of the Romans*. While the *Considerations* contained the factual, comparative approach of *The Persian Letters*, it had a new note. Montesquieu's skepticism was held somewhat in abeyance as he considered the institutions of Rome from a point of view more interested in understanding the operation of institutions than in satirizing them. Though the *Considerations* lacks Vico's genuine historical approach—the willingness to analyze and to accept the past in its own terms—the study reveals everywhere the curiosity about causation that Vico lacked; throughout, Montesquieu sought to understand why Rome achieved its success and why it

---

[7] Marshall Berman, *The Politics of Authenticity* (New York: Atheneum, 1970) rightly calls attention to Montesquieu's concern for personal identity and his positive view of the passions. Berman errs, however, in saying that *The Persian Letters* contains a "radical individualism" or an individualism that "legitimizes revolution."

decayed. Though his approach to causation is confused and static, it contains the unmistakable note of the Enlightenment, the belief that general laws govern the operation of social phenomena.

> It is not chance that rules the world. Ask the Romans, who had a continuous sequence of successes when they were guided by a certain plan, and an uninterrupted sequence of reverses when they followed another. There are general causes, moral and physical, which act in every monarchy, elevating it, maintaining it, or hurling it to the ground. All accidents are controlled by these causes. And if the chance of one battle—that is, a particular cause—has brought a state to ruin, some general cause made it necessary for that state to perish from a single battle. In a word, the main trend draws with it all particular accidents.[8]

Montesquieu's belief that mind and data, theory and fact are sufficient unto themselves and that the interplay of principle with the empirical realm will lead to a unified theory of behavior is clearly evident in the *Considerations*. This orientation blossomed into a more conscious and profound formulation in *The Spirit of the Laws*, a book that in many ways is the charter of sociology and modern social science. In it, the gap separating Montesquieu from the leading social theorists of the seventeenth century widened into a deep and permanent chasm. Whereas Locke had centered his thought on natural rights, effecting an individualization and secularization of the tradition of natural law, and Hobbes had hoped to construct a materialistic monism based on mathematics, Montesquieu looked for law in the raw stuff of social existence itself. Twenty years in the making, this new perspective eventually reached fruition as *The Spirit of the Laws*.

Montesquieu devoted his opening book (chapter) of the *Laws* to the laws of nature—a gesture that was partially a sop to the conventions of his day and partially a matter of conviction. There can be no doubt that he believed there were standards of justice, happiness, and morality beyond the conventions of society. Similarly, there is little doubt that he believed that these emanated not from revealed religion, but from nature or—what amounts to the same thing—from God. In addition to these absolutes, there are other laws of nature, "so called, because they derive their force entirely from our frame and existence." There are four of these, said Montesquieu, the laws of peace, of nourishment, of sexual attraction, and of the desire of living in society.

---

[8] *Considerations*, p. 169.

Having said this, Montesquieu disclosed his real interest. The laws of nature are physical needs and vague dispositions toward sociality. The real business of fulfilling them is done by society. As if his offhanded treatment of the laws of nature were not enough to dismiss the social-contract tradition, Montesquieu explicitly rejected the Hobbesian theory by declaring that hostility among individuals derives not from nature but from society. If we are to know what human beings are, we must analyze them not in the state of nature, but in society. Unlike physical nature, people do not lend themselves to abstract definition. Though Montesquieu never formally dismissed the tradition of natural law, allowing it to intrude here and there throughout his work, his real interest is unmistakably expressed in these last paragraphs of the opening book of the *Laws:*

> Law in general is human reason, inasmuch as it governs all the inhabitants of the earth: the political and civil laws of each nation ought to be only the particular cases in which human reason is applied.
>
> They should be adapted in such a manner to the people for whom they are framed that it should be a great chance if those of one nation suit another.
>
> They should be in relation to the nature and principle of each government: whether they form it, as may be said of politic laws; or whether they support it, as in the case of civil institutions.
>
> They should be in relation to the climate of each country, to the quality of its soil, to its situation and extent, to the principle occupation of the natives, whether husbandmen, huntsmen, or shepherds: they should have relation to the degree of liberty which the constitution will bear; to the religion of the inhabitants, to their inclinations, riches, numbers, commerce, manners, and customs. In fine, they have relations to each other, as also to their origin, to the intent of the legislator, and to the order of things on which they are established; in all of which different lights they ought to be considered.
>
> This is what I have undertaken to perform in the following work. These relations I shall examine, since all these constitute what I call the Spirit of the Laws.
>
> I have not separated the political from the civil institutions as I do not intend to treat of laws, but of their spirit; and as this spirit consists in the various relations which laws may bear to different objects, it is not so much my business to follow the natural order of laws as that of these relations and objects.
>
> I shall first examine the relations which laws bear to the nature and principle of each government; and as this principle has a strong influence on laws, I shall make it my study to understand

it thoroughly: and if I can but once establish it, the laws will soon appear to flow thence as from their source. I shall proceed afterwards to other and more particular relations.[9]

By focusing on human behavior in terms of time and place, Montesquieu consciously departed from the Western tradition of natural law; and by searching for the reason or principle underlying human behavior in behavior itself, he also denied the metaphysical tradition that claimed that no rational knowledge about the empirical world was possible. In this sense, Montesquieu brought theory to the school of fact not as an empiricist, but as a rationalist who assumed there was a fundamental identity between the structure of the mind and the structure of phenomena. As such, he everywhere assumed that relationships among the data of social experience could be expressed in terms of principle.

Montesquieu's revolutionary perspective did not stop here. The data of behavior would be interpreted not only in terms of principle, but also in terms of special functions and causes. A glance at his table of contents is enough to show this strikingly modern view—the heading of almost every book indicates a desire to know something in terms of its relation to something else. The very title of his study, which expresses *law* in the plural, indicates Montesquieu's empirical bent. Further, the idea that laws or norms of behavior are to be analyzed in relation to institutional functions, in relation to causes, and in terms of the interrelations of functions and causes, contains the concept of cultural structure, or as Montesquieu termed it, the *spirit* of the laws. Montesquieu's search for the spirit or the inner principle of a given structure of phenomena marked the introduction of the concept of *ideal type* in its modern form. Such types are not hypotheses or empirical generalizations, but the idealization of both the meaning and the order of facts.

If Montesquieu's search for the fundamental forms of social existence smacks of the Cartesian definition of science, it must be noted that he also tended toward the Pascalian view of science. In truth, his thought was influenced by a very diverse collection of thinkers, including, in addition to Descartes, Malebranche, Locke, Machiavelli, and Montaigne—many of whom exerted an antispeculative influence on his thought. Montesquieu's strong inclination for separating the realms of being and for assigning to each an appropriate subject and method constitutes the nominalist strand in his thought. God can be removed from the world by the thought of Descartes as well as by that of Pascal, and Montesquieu never altered his

[9] *Laws,* 1:6f.

belief that any attempt to unite the various realms of being is a debatable enterprise. Even within the human realm, one must separate the laws that govern each area of human existence, and distinguish among different types of causation.

On the one hand, therefore, Montesquieu hoped to achieve a unified theory of the sociocultural realm, suggesting that it was related in some way to the objective laws of nature. On the other, he expressed his belief, first, that such a unification was limited to the human realm, and second, that human life was too diverse to be unified. This dual approach to human behavior expressed Montesquieu's fundamental affinity with liberalism. It is true that he criticized and rejected the natural-law liberalism of Hobbes and Locke, but his fundamental position should be seen from a wider perspective. In effect, what he did was to reject the medieval attempt to link human nature, nature, and God into an all-embracing *Gemeinschaft*-type theory. He particularized the world and was concerned not with the intrinsic nature of being, but with the causes, operational relationships, and consequences that pertain to human beings.

To seek knowledge about something not as a thing in itself but in terms of something else—as relative to causes or functions—marks the scientific as opposed to the philosophical or theological mentality. Implicit in Montesquieu's approach was a semiconscious separation of questions of truth, of value, and of fact—a separation that allowed him to concentrate on the operation and consequences of social phenomena and to ignore the conundrums of conventional social thought. This perspective allowed him to see that social phenomena contained both moral and physical causes, an insight that he developed brilliantly and that made him an outstanding contributor to both sociocultural and naturalistic positivism.

SUBSTANTIVE WORK

At first reading, *The Spirit of the Laws* seems to belie the promise of the author's method; it is unsystematic in the extreme and often confused and irrelevant. The diverse influences that worked on Montesquieu's mind, however, combined to turn the absence of system and synthesis into the virtues of originality, openmindedness, and toleration, and made him sensitive to the complexities and nuances of human behavior. What *The Spirit of the Laws* lacks in unity and compression, it makes up for in its sprawling breadth and pervasive subtlety. To extract the scientific contributions of this extraordinary work, I shall focus first on Montesquieu's search for the fundamental forms of social structure, and second on his analysis of physical and moral causation.

The Principles of Government

Montesquieu began his analysis of the fundamental forms of social structure by distinguishing between the nature and the principle of government. The nature of a government is determined by the number of people who possess supreme power and by the way in which power is exercised. The laws that pertain to the nature of government, therefore, are concerned with the way in which numbers of people participate in political life. Of far more importance for sociology, however, was Montesquieu's search for the principle of government. "There is this difference between the nature and principle of government, that the former is that by which it is constituted, the latter that by which it is made to act. One is its particular structure, and the other the human passions which set it in motion." [10] Each of the three forms of government has a different principle: a republican government, which can be democratic or aristocratic, is motivated by civic virtue; a monarchy, by honor; a despotism, by fear. Each principle expresses the unity underlying a given constellation of laws and customs. Montesquieu was never very clear about the meaning of the word *principle*. Sometimes he appears to use it to denote the "ought," or the ethical precept behind behavior; and at other times he appears to be referring to empirical causation and uniformity. In short, he never clearly distinguished between "principle" as an ethical guide to action (or as a logical structure), and "principle" as a causal agency or empirical uniformity. In his clearest statement, he inclined toward the former:

> Such are the three principles of the three sorts of government: which does not imply that in a particular republic they actually are, but that they ought to be, virtuous; nor does it prove that in a particular monarchy they are actuated by honor, or in a particular despotic government by fear; but that they ought to be directed by these principles, otherwise the government is imperfect.[11]

The norms that govern education, the art of legislation, civil and criminal questions, manners, morals, the status of women, and military life correspond in logic and often in fact to the basic principle governing the life of a people. There is no better evidence of Montesquieu's revolutionary perspective than his view that the phenomena of social life, far from being in the realm of the nonrational, are interconnected parts of an organic whole whose constitutive principle can be identified. Through this perspective, Montesquieu not only affirmed the assumption that human nature can be brought within the jurisdiction of reason, but revolutionized this assumption

---

[10] *Laws*, 1:19.
[11] *Laws*, 1:28.

by declaring that reason can be found in the actual, empirical behavior of human beings.

Not all of this was original with Montesquieu, of course. Defining the nature of government in terms of the numbers who rule had been a staple of political thought from the time of the Greeks. The concept of a basic value or principle informing the entire structure of society was also a commonplace of works in social philosophy, most notably Aristotle's *Politics*, and Books XIII and IX of Plato's *Republic*. What is noteworthy in Montesquieu's work is the assumption, derived from the Newtonian world view, that general causes operate directly in social phenomena—an assumption, thanks to Montesquieu, that helped enormously in redirecting European social thought toward the study of actual human behavior. If the subsequent history of sociological thought concerned itself with finding a more adequate way to ascertain and to express the fundamental principles contained in social phenomena, it is only because later thinkers could take for granted Montesquieu's assumption that this was possible.

Physical Causation

One of the best known aspects of Montesquieu's innovative empirical approach is his interest in the effect on human behavior of climate, soil, geography, and population. The idea of interpreting behavior in physical terms was destined to exert a virtual monopoly on sociological thought for a century and a half after Montesquieu's death, and its success was in no small measure due to the impetus Montesquieu gave it. Not that the idea was original with him—as many commentators have pointed out. However, he analyzed physical factors in a more comprehensive and systematic manner, and placed more emphasis on this type of causation, than other thinkers had done.

Of the various physical causes, Montesquieu placed the most emphasis on climate. Cold or warm air acting upon the "external fibres" of the body either contracts or lengthens the fibers and thus influences a people's character. People in the North are more vigorous, bolder, and less deceptive, while those in the South are timorous, enervated, and passionate. These character traits, Montesquieu assumed, must be reflected in the laws—an assumption he explored at length, paying special attention to the relation between climate and the laws governing the various forms of slavery: civil, domestic (servitude of women), and political.

Montesquieu also devoted several books to the influence of soil and population on laws and customs, and attempted to correlate the laws of a country with its geography. Great plains produce despotism, we are told, while a geographical area containing natural divisions will produce liberty. A country's size also influences the character of its government: republicanism is appropriate to small territories, monarchy to a territory of moderate extent, and despotism to large countries.

It is apparent that Montesquieu took the idea of physical causation in human affairs seriously. However, his analysis of human behavior went far beyond physical factors, and it is extremely misleading to equate his contribution to social science with his emphasis on physical causation, as many commentators have done. Though his emphasis on what may be called moral or cultural causation is less systematic and less well known, it contains a rich and important—if somewhat confused—contribution to the development of sociological theory.

Moral (Cultural) Causation

That Montesquieu did not rely exclusively on physical factors to explain behavior can be seen on almost every page of the *Laws*. The most striking feature of the table of contents, for example, is its concern with understanding laws and customs in relation to a variety of causes, physical as well as moral. The human capacity to act morally (or, in more modern language, to act culturally) to offset the influence of climate is stated quite explicitly. Legislators can and should oppose the effects of climate; and manners and customs, however much they are influenced by climate, are also a reflection of laws. Montesquieu also developed a number of primitive but valuable insights into the correlations between beliefs and practices. Whereas in the early parts of the *Laws* he focused on the logical fitness of institutions conceived as ideal types, he later discussed institutions as causal agencies exerting a reciprocal influence on each other. This perspective is never systematically stated, but his references to the causal correlation of institutional structures are genuine sociological insights, however scattered and poorly expressed. For example, there is a relationship between type of economy and type of government: trade in luxuries is related to monarchy, while the enterprising commercial spirit is related to republican governments. There is also a relation between a commercial economy and the manners and morals of a nation: "... the spirit of commerce is naturally attended with that of frugality, economy, moderation, labor, prudence, tranquility, order, and rule." [12]

Political institutions can also exert an influence on society. In this regard, Montesquieu concerned himself mostly with the effects of liberty on the general character of a people. While his famous and widely influential doctrine of the separation of powers [13] is of only limited sociological interest because of its excessively legalistic nature, his attempt to correlate political liberty in England with the habits and values of the English people be-

[12] *Laws*, 1:46.
[13] *Laws*, Vol. 1, bk. XI.

speaks a genuine flair for sociological analysis. The attempted correlation is admittedly unsystematic and vague, but we are told that liberty provides an atmosphere that has causal efficacy in regard to trade, taxation, manners, and religion. In another place Montesquieu recognized the intrinsic connection among religion, commerce, and liberty in England.

In a fairly extended statement on the role of religion, Montesquieu equated Christianity with moderate government and Mohammedanism with despotic government. Within moderate governments, Catholicism is equated with monarchy and Protestantism with republicanism. Religion also influences economic behavior. A contemplative religion, according to Montesquieu, can prevent a people from engaging in economic activity; religious festivals can interfere with productive labor; and the suppression of religious festivals is more likely in Protestant countries, which have greater need of labor, than in Catholic countries.

The Science of Society

There is little doubt that much of Montesquieu's causal analysis is amateurish and unoriginal. What saves the *Laws* from being merely the random remarks of a well-read dilettante is the spirit of science that pervades every page. It is not only that his work has both breadth and specificity, though both of these qualities are necessary to the scientific spirit. Nor is his work scientific merely because he eschewed the natural-law tradition and directed his attention at understanding the concrete, historical manifestations of human nature in all its multiplicity and variety. The distinguishing mark of Montesquieu's scientific mentality is his struggle to understand cultural phenomena relationally in terms of efficient rather than final causes, and to see phenomena in terms of consequences rather than in terms of intrinsic attributes. His attempt to comprehend cultural phenomena in terms of both logical and causal relationships constitutes his pre-eminent contribution to the development of social science. Actually, it would not be stretching matters to say that Montesquieu's work represents a distinct anticipation of what is today known as functional analysis. It is true that he did not specify the various functions that must be served if a society is to survive. He was content to say that preservation is the end of all societies—a function, he felt, that could be satisfied by all three types of government (republican, monarchical, despotic) and by a variety of causes.

Montesquieu's tolerant outlook toward existing societies was at once the source of his scientific outlook and of the conservative bias that repelled the philosophes. This outlook allowed him to see a wide variety of mixtures in the values, beliefs, and practices of various people, and gave him an extraordinary insight into the fact that even the most diverse customs may be functional to a given society. In truly scientific fashion, he neither praised nor blamed the various cultural elements he found, but defined them in terms of their cultural context and their effects within that context. The confiscation of property, he explained, is functional under despotism but not moderate governments. Sale of public offices is functional to a monarchy but not to despotic government. The same is true of other cultural elements such as the power of the clergy, the dowry system, and bastardy: each is declared, not good or bad, but functional or dysfunctional depending on the context in which it has its being.

It cannot be said, however, that Montesquieu ever explicitly formulated a functional approach to cultural phenomena. He was more an explorer of new pathways than a map maker. His functionalism approached explicitness, however, in a number of places. He declared that false religions may serve useful social functions, and that ". . . the most true and holy doctrines may be attended with the very worst consequences when they are not connected with the principles of society; and on the contrary, doctrines the most false may be attended with excellent consequences when contrived so as to be connected with these principles." [14] In another explicit discussion that captures the full flavor of functionalism, he warned that the same laws have different effects in different settings, that laws that appear the same are not always made from the same motive, that contrary laws may come from the same motive, that laws must never be separated from the ends for which they were made nor from the circumstances in which they were made, and that uniformity of law is not always necessary since the same functions may be served by different laws.

Montesquieu's insight into the irony in social phenomena was developed quite differently from Vico's similar insight and, as we shall see, differently from the insights of Montesquieu's successors. It led him toward relativism, toleration, and conservatism rather than toward the idea of a hidden logic. The reason, undoubtedly, was Montesquieu's lack of metaphysical anxiety and his genuine acceptance of causal complexity and multiplicity. His unique version of empirical rationalism led him to a static conception of history and dampened his interest in social change. Able to resist the metaphysical urge to reduce phenomena to a single sovereign cause, Montesquieu also resisted the temptation to explain the irony in human behavior with the attractive idea that a hidden logic brings unity to social phenomena. Given his conservative tendency to look upon structures of behavior as functional to a given society, he was content, for the most part, to classify and correlate the many causes in human affairs, an approach that his successors in sociology neglected until the development of pluralistic positivism late in the nineteenth century.

[14] *Laws*, 2:38f.

CONCLUSION

It would not be extravagant to conclude that Montesquieu's *Spirit of the Laws* is the authentic beginning of sociological theory and, if one ignores the highly abstract social science of the seventeenth century, also the beginning of modern social science. The traditional search for a metaphysics of human nature through philosophy or theology is totally absent from this work; and the search for knowledge about humans is placed on a radically new footing. Henceforth rationalism was to search for its subject matter and laws in the existential world of human action, feeling, and thought. Alongside the rationalist bent in Montesquieu, however, is a contrary current that is skeptical about the power of reason to establish general truths and that is concerned more with operation and usefulness of institutions than with their validity. This is to say, of course, that Montesquieu combined in himself the two views of science that emerged in the seventeenth century—views that were destined to compete for the allegiance of social theorists throughout the modern period.

In adopting the Cartesian goal of generalized knowledge—that is, by searching for the principles of society—Montesquieu put aside Descartes's reliance on mathematics though not his deductive method. As a member of the Enlightenment, Montesquieu looked for rationality within phenomena, not beyond them. Fundamental to his point of view was the assumption that the mind can comprehend the structure of phenomena and reduce the seeming chaos of social existence to a few, constitutive principles.

While Montesquieu's social science employed deductive logic, his novel concern with phenomena resulted in a strong interest in empirical causation. Though he never became an empiricist, his causal analysis was a comprehensive attempt to establish the physical and cultural causes of behavior. This turn of mind—the search for the general structure of empirical causation—together with his deductive search for ideal types expressed in terms of their integrating principles, constitute the Cartesianism in Montesquieu's thought. It is true that Vico anticipated the sociocultural positivism in Montesquieu's thought; but, unencumbered by Vico's theological approach, Montesquieu was able to go far beyond him in the analysis of cultural causation. Further, by applying the models of thought in the natural science of his day to social phenomena, he also constructed a superior theory of physical causation. Unlike Vico's concept of social science, therefore, Montesquieu's embraced both naturalistic and sociocultural explanations of human behavior. Because of the breadth of his assumption that law can be found in social phenomena, because of the skill with which he applied this assumption, and because of the influence his work exerted over later thinkers, his thought became the fountainhead of all the variants of modern social science and of sociological positivism.

Montesquieu, however, lacked the temperament to commit himself to a monistic positivism of either the sociocultural or the naturalistic type. Ultimately speaking, his thought was a form of pluralistic, not monistic, positivism. He found, after all, three types of society, and he employed a theory of multiple causation. However, his pluralism went much further, exhibiting enough depth and self-consciousness to approximate the Pascalian definition of science. The fundamental skepticism and relativism that he acquired from Montaigne and expressed most bitingly in *The Persian Letters* never left his thought. His skeptical relativism enabled him to discuss a variety of institutional forms with a clinical detachment unique to social theory; and, while he condemned much of what he saw, he did so in the name of common decency and good sense, not of absolute standards.

Montesquieu's perspective, if anything, was more mellowed and more firmly held in the *Laws*, which on the whole contains a spirit of inquiry in close harmony with the Pascalian view of knowledge. His main thesis in the *Laws* is that knowledge about human beings in the abstract is not possible. It is only possible to have knowledge about particular individuals—what they have done and how they have fared under particular conditions. This attitude places Montesquieu outside the tradition of natural law because it interprets the multiple forms of culture as structures that take their shape from the necessities of social existence and physical nature, not as emanations of human nature. In those places where Montesquieu became somewhat explicit about his functional approach, he deliberately separated questions of truth and value from questions of functional success or failure. By so doing, he was not searching for the functional structure of society in general—as so many later functionalists were to do. His functionalism was based on a cultural relativity that interpreted cultural elements in terms of their own milieu. If Montesquieu did not fully realize that societies are not always unitary, but often contain contradictory and irrelevant beliefs and practices, and if he failed to see the implications of his own insight into the way in which a wide range of values could perform the functions of society, he avoided a facile reduction of human experience to an all-embracing formula. Whereas Plato took the idea of the ideal state seriously before he began to interest himself in the approximately best state, Montesquieu was interested in the second-best state from the start; in this respect his intellectual kinship lies with Aristotle. However, Montesquieu was not restricted by the ethnocentric distinctions—between Greek and barbarian; between freeman (or woman) and slave—that narrowed Aristotle's vision, and this enabled him to construct a global anthropology unique in the annals of social thought.

Montesquieu's aversion to monism opened a gulf between him and the Enlightenment. Actually, Montesquieu's deep insight into the nature of social phenomena and into the problems of constructing a social science prevented him from sharing the philosophes' faith in the power of reason. The philosophes might have accepted many of his insights, had these insights not been embedded in relativism and conservatism. What the philosophes found particularly distasteful was that Montesquieu focused his relativism and conservatism into a defense of the *thèse nobiliaire*—that is, of a monarchy tempered by intermediary bodies.

Despite his lack of enthusiasm for the possibilities of science and despite his conservatism, Montesquieu was no ordinary conservative. In the broader perspective of history, he must be counted a liberal—traditional minded and cautious to be sure, but a liberal none the less. The signs of the liberal mentality are unmistakable. Most notably, he showed no concern whatever for the rights of birth. Secondly, and more positively, the *Laws* contains many of the main features of the liberal state. There is a running distinction between the state and civil society, and between politics and morality. There is an extraordinary interest in economic issues—sources of wealth, efficiency, trade, utility, and the like—so much so that in the French edition of his *The General Theory of Employment, Interest and Money*, John Maynard Keynes is quoted as saying "Montesquieu was the real French equivalent of Adam Smith. The greatest of your economists, head and shoulders above the physiocrats. . . ." [15]

Another clue to Montesquieu's liberalism was his treatment of law. Law is separated from custom; it is made and not inherited; it is arranged in terms of social function and not in terms of a hierarchy of privilege; and law must give security and therefore must be precise and predictable. Even his distinction between the three types of government is basically a distinction between power that is exercised predictably according to law and power that is exercised capriciously according to will. His famous separation of powers was an attempt to secure liberty through a legalistic arrangement of political forms. All that is lacking for a complete bourgeois description of society is the concept of legal sovereignty, the definition of the state as a monopoly of legal power. Montesquieu was too concerned about the pretensions of absolutism for that, however, though the idea was no doubt familiar to him through his reading of Hobbes. Finally, his liberalism, however much disguised by his preference for feudal monarchy, is apparent in

[15] Quoted in Nicos E. Devletoglou's valuable examination of Montesquieu's economic thought, "Montesquieu and the Wealth of Nations," *Canadian Journal of Economics and Political Science* 29 (February 1963): 1–25.

his assumption that humanity and the individual exist apart from society, and that differences among individuals are due to the causes that control their lives. Though he seemed to resign himself to these causes, lacking as he did the philosophes' optimism about humanity's ability to master environmental causes, he always maintained an attitude toward society that tended to evaluate its compulsions in terms of their utility to human beings—an attitude not out of keeping with the bourgeois temperament.

Though Montesquieu was a practitioner of science and a liberal in many of his fundamental beliefs, he never suffered anxiety because of the liberal dilemma. His basic skepticism warded off the problem—indeed, kept it from arising. Unlike the philosophes, who faced up to the problem of finding truth within the context of a shifting and deceptive empirical realm, Montesquieu never concerned himself with the validity of beliefs, but only with their consequences, and he never concerned himself seriously with the problem of finding the basic identity of human beings. It is true that he touched on this latter problem in *The Persian Letters*, where he expressed a genuine puzzlement about the relationship between human happiness and freedom and the institutions of society. However, his answer flatly suggested that no answer is possible to the question of human identity, or to that of the set of institutions most suitable to its needs. It was a perspective that never left his thought.

The liberal dilemma never arose for Montesquieu because he never developed a sense of the sharp qualitative differences between cultures, nor did he ever develop Vico's sense of qualitative social change. His thought is curiously static; human nature is constant despite the influence of social and natural causes. His thought is historical only in the sense that he directed his attention to concrete historical existence and its causes. He never saw causes as dynamic agencies capable of producing qualitative changes in the life of society, and he never equated history and human nature as Vico tended to do. For Montesquieu, human nature was a given substance, and the only task of science was to portray the modifications made in that substance by the multiple causes to which it is subject.

Montesquieu's failure to recognize the drastic absorption of human nature by sociocultural forces constitutes the major indictment of his work. This failure is made all the more poignant by the fact that in directing his attention to the cultural context of human life, he himself gave ample evidence that while human beings create history, they are primarily its creature. It would be more appropriate, however, to emphasize Montesquieu's virtues instead of his faults and to acknowledge the healthy influence that he exerted on social thought. His doctrine of the separation of powers was widely influential on both the thinking and the practice of public figures; his grasp of factual detail was influential in the future growth of historical scholarship; and his many insights into the nature of law, religion, politics, family, and economics undoubtedly served to make theorists regard these institutions more sociologically.

Despite his deficiences, therefore, Montesquieu must be credited for raising the possibility of a general science of society and for publicizing the idea across the breadth of the Western world. His greatest influence on sociology was the impetus he gave to the development of monistic naturalism. It was the Cartesian spirit in his work—the spirit that defined knowledge as the derivation of general principles and that regarded only nature as a valid subject matter of science—that had an immediate influence on sociology. The side of his thought that approximated the Pascalian definition of science—the concern for accurate empirical information, the identification of a plurality of causes, physical and moral, and the pragmatic concern for the consequences of beliefs and practices—had less immediate influence.

The century and a half after Montesquieu brought vast changes to European society, but these did not allay the metaphysical hunger of European intellectuals. Both Vico and Montesquieu fed this appetite for metaphysics, the one by providing European intellectuals with the idea of history and progress, and the other by providing them with the idea of a general science of society. The major figures in sociology who followed them—Condorcet, Saint-Simon, and Comte—combined these two aspects into a single doctrine—though, of course, they obtained the idea of progress from French sources rather than from Vico. In any case, the effect was to minimize the anti-Cartesian elements that were so important in the thought of both Vico and Montesquieu. These anti-Cartesian elements did not reappear until late in the nineteenth century, when Max Weber effected a unification of Vico's dynamic sense of history and concern for understanding, and Montesquieu's sense of multiple causation, framed in terms of the irreducible plurality of social systems. However, before that time (and since), the science of society came into the hands of those who were inclined to think of social science in Cartesian terms. The three thinkers who did the most to shape sociological theory in that direction are the subject of the next chapter.

Chapter 7
The New Society of Science:
Condorcet, Saint-Simon, and Comte

In the half century after the death of Montesquieu, a momentously important transformation took place in the intellectual perspective of the Enlightenment. The faith in science, which had marked the Enlightenment from the beginning, had grown steadily. By the end of the eighteenth century, it had crystallized into a passionate belief that science was the key to understanding and mastering not only physical nature but the nature and destiny of humanity as well. This chapter treats the thought of the three theorists who more than any others linked the future of humanity (and sociology) with the progress of science, all within the boundaries of liberalism.

MARQUIS DE CONDORCET (1743–1794)

This new faith in science is in no place expressed in a more moving manner than in the piece of work written by the Marquis Marie Jean Caritat de Condorcet, *Sketch for an Historical Picture of the Progress of the Human Mind.*[1] Condorcet's fervent outpouring of faith in the redemptory power of science would not be enough to recommend his work, however, were it not for a new note that he added to the meaning of science. The novel element in his work was that he did not define science (or truth) in terms that suggest a sudden enlightenment, but rather saw it as an intelligible process of development. In effect, by combining science and the goal of truth with the idea of progress, Condorcet was offering a solution to the liberal dilemma.

---

[1] New York: Noonday Press, 1955; henceforth cited as *Progress of the Human Mind.* For an encyclopedic account of Condorcet's life and thought against the backdrop of the Enlightenment, see Keith Michael Baker, *Condorcet: From Natural Philosophy to Social Mathematics* (Chicago: University of Chicago Press, 1975).

Marquis de Condorcet (1743–1794)

PHILOSOPHY AND METHOD

The liberal dilemma stemmed from the need to explain the existence of error in a rational universe and the emergence of evil from a beneficent nature. How could a sentient being, subject to the vagaries of experience, secure permanent knowledge, and why was it that human beings had succumbed to error if the process of experience produced truth? The liberal dilemma had another feature illustrated in Condorcet's work itself. To Condorcet, the apprehension of truth was in some way connected with the development of natural "ties of interest and duty," a theme that appeared again and again during the Enlightenment, stemming from its assumption that truth and morality were connected and mutually supportive. However, if the Enlightenment's prospects for establishing truth were uncertain, its prospects for establishing the relation between truth and morality were even more uncertain.

Condorcet's attempt to place the problem of human behavior and human knowledge on a new basis was not made consciously or formally. His work was more the crystallization of the long, groping attempt by such thinkers as Fontenelle (1657–1757), Saint-Pierre (1658–1743), Turgot (1727–1781), and others to see progress in human affairs, than an original piece of work. Whatever its intellectual ancestry, however, the revolutionary import of Condorcet's perspective is apparent. His basic approach emerged from a distinction between the study of the development of human faculties common to all people (metaphysics) and the study of this development in a certain area and time (history).

> Such a picture is historical, since it is a record of change and is based on the observation of human societies throughout the different stages of their development. It ought to reveal the order of this change and the influence that each moment exerts upon the subsequent moment, and so ought to show, in the modifications that the human species has undergone, ceaselessly renewing itself through the immensity of the centuries, the path that it has followed, the steps that it has made towards truth or happiness.[2]

The contrast with Montesquieu could not be more complete. With these few sentences, Condorcet drastically altered the perspective of social science by placing human beings in a dynamic historical frame. His attempt to separate this approach from metaphysics is an important clue to his dissatisfaction with the static rationalism of the Enlightenment, but it should not be taken too seriously—there is no sharp demarcation between metaphysics and history in Condorcet's work. On the contrary, his work was a primitive attempt to transform metaphysics into history and history into metaphysics, something that was to have a rich future in social science. Rather than calling for a painstaking compilation of facts about human behavior, he assumed that the progress of the human mind contains "general laws" and that historical analysis will reveal its "order" of development. Indeed, so far was he from being scientifically detached that he revealed what his study would show before he began. Not only would it reveal progress, he claimed, but it would

> ... show by appeal to reason and fact that nature has set no term to the perfection of human faculties; that the perfectibility

[2] *Progress of the Human Mind,* p. 3f.

of man is truly indefinite; and that the progress of this perfecti-
bility, from now onwards independent of any power that might
wish to halt it, has no other limit than the duration of the globe
upon which nature has cast us.[3]

Condorcet did not set for himself the task of writing either a philosophical
or historical analysis in any formal meaning of those words. Furthermore,
it should not be thought that he seriously tackled the philosophical dilemma
contained in the position of the philosophes. His fundamental concern was
with supplementing their position and with finding added verification for
it. The purely meditative, speculative approach to truth, Condorcet argued,
should not exclude historical experience, nor should the concern for individual psychology exclude the attempt to know something about human
beings in general. Instead of relying on contemporary experience to substantiate truth, one must explore all avenues. Condorcet even suggested that
the explanation for error and evil somehow lies in the past. The bearing of
this approach on the liberal dilemma is obvious. It may be possible, Condorcet suggested, that error and truth, good and evil, can be placed in an
understandable and thus rational sequence of development. "If there is to
be a science for predicting the progress of the human race, for directing
and hastening it, the history of the progress already achieved must be its
foundation." [4]

It is clear that Condorcet's appeal to history is not a challenge to rationalism. For Condorcet, history was simply a neglected dimension of truth
rather than a separate approach or a separate kind of subject matter. His
view was that objective truth emerges through a developmental process
and that a knowledge of that process reveals the workings of nature. The
corollary of this belief is that, once apprehended, a truth or a natural law
has practical consequences for social organization and individual behavior.
In short, history is a supplement to, not a substitute for, rationalism. Its
study will help humanity find the hierarchy of morals and values hidden
in the bosom of nature.

It is clear that Condorcet stands squarely within the philosophical assumptions of the Enlightenment. He postulated that humans are sentient, rational
beings capable of finding the truth and morality in nature. To this he added
a belief that a determinate order of progress can be found in the experience of the race. Even if we suppose that there is no such order, he argued,
we can at least profit from the mistakes of others. His main goal, however,
was to show that the Age of Reason was not mistaken in its belief that
there is a natural order, the truths of which are accessible to human beings.

[3] Ibid., p. 4.
[4] Ibid., p. 11 (disputed passage). Since some of this work has not been au-
thenticated, it is necessary to indicate disputed passages.

He hoped to provide added proof of this belief by showing that it was sanctioned by the historical evolution of the mind.

By giving a historical dimension to truth, Condorcet summed up a current of thought that in one formulation or another was destined to dominate the thought of the future. Throughout his work, Cordorcet assumed that his analysis of the past would substantiate the major assumption of rationalism—that it is possible to find permanence and simplicity in the flux of a manifold experience. He never suspected that such a search might not reveal progress, nor that the historical approach was destined one day to challenge not only rationalism, but in some quarters the idea of reason itself.

SUBSTANTIVE WORK

Condorcet identified ten stages of human development, starting with a first stage in which human beings are "united in tribes." This is followed by a pastoral stage, and that in turn by an agricultural stage. Then, starting with the rise of philosophy in Greece during the fourth stage, Condorcet identified his remaining stages not in terms of the prevailing type of economy but in terms of intellectual activity. His main interest was obviously in the ninth stage, which begins with Descartes and ends with the founding of the French Republic, and in a future tenth stage, in which humanity's pace toward perfection will undergo enormous acceleration. The unifying thread that links each stage with its temporal neighbor, especially from the fourth stage onward, is the painful, hard-won progress of the human mind toward the truths and practices of science. It is the emergence of science, both as a metaphysics and as a method, that gives meaning and structure to each historical stage and that simultaneously makes each stage absolute and relative.

Causation and the Interdependence of Variables

Deficiencies in the Enlightenment's empirical approach should not blind us to the profound achievement implied in its quest for factual certainty. If Bayle (1647–1706) was the first practitioner of factual accuracy and the thinker who raised the problem of factuality itself,[5] then the work of Vico, Montesquieu, and Condorcet can be thought of as contributions to a more adequate handling of facts. Essentially their contribution was to identify the causal variables in human behavior and to think of them in terms of cultural configurations and contexts. Their empiricism had little concern,

---

[5] Ernst Cassirer, *The Philosophy of the Enlightenment,* trans. Fritz C. A. Koelling and James P. Pettegrove (Boston: Beacon paperback, 1955), pp. 201–209.

of course, for the accumulation of data as such or for the precise verification of hypotheses.

Many of the variables that have figured in modern sociology are found in Condorcet's work—for example, innate needs, sentiments, and genius. There are also casual references to the influence of forms of interaction, geography, political forms, and military events, and to the role of education and cultural accumulation. However, Condorcet reserved his greatest enthusiasm for economic, technological, and ideological causation. Though he made human beings more dependent on natural causes in the lower stages of development, and though he even attempted a rough correlation between economic-technological forms and social forms, it is clear that his primary interest was in the role played by ideological factors in retarding or stimulating a nation's economy, technology, and cultural forms. His greatest emphasis is on the influence of ignorance and superstition in holding back the development of the human race, and on the momentous importance of the rise of science—an occurrence that holds the promise of a permanent emancipation from the deceits of philosophy and theology. The rise of science promises nothing less than a final victory in humanity's battle to escape the darkness of ignorance and superstition; thus for Condorcet, it was history's major event. It has already become a causal agency of the greatest importance by extending the arts, industry, leisure, and education; but its greatest importance is that it provides a guarantee that humanity will henceforth be guided by the truth. Since all the operative causes in the physical and social realms are interdependent, the sciences are also interdependent. Despite his emphasis on ideology, Condorcet employed a multicausal approach to some extent, and he often referred to the reciprocal effect that causal factors have on each other.

Once this unity of all the sciences is recognized, the implications for social science and social improvement are enormous. It opens the possibility that precise mathematical knowledge can be obtained about the role of every conceivable factor in human behavior, including sex, climate, and population pressures; even more important, it gives humanity a scientific method for policy making in politics, finance, morals, education, and music and the arts. It holds, in short, not only the possibility of a science of society, but also of a society of science.

Condorcet's unitary conception of the various sciences and his belief that knowledge about human beings can be obtained in the same way that knowledge is gained about physical nature is in the authentic tradition of the French Enlightenment and of naturalistic positivism. His commitment to the idea of progress not only goes far beyond Montesquieu, who was much warier about identifying morals with knowledge, but also represents the profound difference that eventually developed between the French and the German sociological traditions. German intellectual culture offered a much greater resistance to the absorption of philosophy by science than was the case in other Western countries, and this made it possible for important segments of German social science to maintain a sharp separation between nature and human nature. It is not surprising, therefore, that much of German sociology developed more in line with Vico's sociocultural positivism than with French naturalistic positivism.

In Condorcet's approach, destined to become the dominant sociological tradition not only in France but also in England and the United States, social and moral achievement were closely identified with the development of science. Condorcet's belief that science leads to truth and that truth has normative social consequences represents the pioneer formulation in sociology of monistic naturalistic positivism. One need only say that human behavior is understandable in the same way as physical nature, and that it is subject to the same principles that govern the rest of the natural world, to have reached the fully developed stage of monistic naturalism of Saint-Simon.

The Hidden Logic of Events

The main contribution of the Enlightenment to sociological theory was to place human beings in a natural setting and to analyze them in terms of efficient causation. Its search for the laws that unify human sensory existence led straight to the liberal dilemma. One of the aspects of this dilemma that is of particular interest is that social theorists became aware that patterns of events often contained ironic consequences. They began to notice that human beings often engage in courses of action leading to consequences that defeat their purposes or work against their interests. The pre-Enlightenment metaphysical tradition had conducted its search for truth beyond experience largely because the empirical world that defeats individuals also defeats philosophers. However, the metaphysics of the Enlightenment was based on experience, and it could not take such a position; its task was to explain error, not to renounce it. It was imperative, in other words, that the Enlightenment find an explanatory structure for the irony that thwarts even the best-laid human plans. All error explained, so to speak, becomes truth.

Two types of historical explanation for the problem of error emerged during the eighteenth century. We met the first of these in the work of Vico, who in a novel application of the Christian world view saw history as not merely the record of error, but also as the record of truth; human beings cannot grasp the structure of truth once and for all, but they can know the past. The assumption behind Vico's theory is that a hidden logic operates within events to guide them, and that it remains hidden to human .

beings until after a given event has taken place. The hidden logic, of course, is the hand of God. Individuals can learn from experience and can understand the course they have taken, but they cannot learn enough to anticipate the workings of Providence and thereby act from perfect knowledge.

The other type of explanation is associated with Montesquieu. Like Vico, he too insisted that knowledge about human beings is of a different order from knowledge of nature because of human indeterminateness. However, Montesquieu's emphasis on the complexity of causation seemed to imply that the root of error lay strictly within discernible causes. He was too skeptical to participate fully in the Enlightenment's optimistic belief that once all causes had been comprehended, human beings could escape their bondage to ignorance and control their destiny. In any case, however, he not only directed attention to historical causation but also used it to explain both the successes and failures of human behavior.

Condorcet's achievement was to combine the type of explanation found in Vico (though derived from other sources) with Montesquieu's and to produce a theory of human nature and society that was destined to receive important elaboration from future thinkers. While Condorcet knew Montesquieu's work directly, it was Turgot rather than Vico who supplied him with the panorama of an unfolding history; or perhaps it would be truer to say that it was Christianity that supplied the Enlightenment with the idea that history had meaning. Condorcet rejected, of course, any recourse to religion; the realm of truth and the realm of fact were not to be united by the faith of religion, but by the faith of reason. The optimism of faith was also a Christian legacy, but it had been transmuted by the success of science into a purely secular belief that the forces of darkness could be defeated by the natural capacities of humanity. Condorcet's optimistic faith in reason allowed him to avoid the skepticism of Montesquieu and to face the chronicle of human folly with equanimity; and Condorcet's faith produced a novel perspective on the existence of error and evil—something that Frankel called the sociology of error.[6]

Like Montesquieu, Condorcet had a tendency to look at social data in terms of their function. However, by doing so within a more dynamic conception of history, Condorcet felt he could locate the causes of error and evil, and could thereby trace their history. If one can explain error and show that the causes that produce it are succumbing to those that produce truth, one has solved the liberal dilemma. In explaining error, Condorcet's main targets were the unscrupulous elites, especially religious elites, who

[6] Charles Frankel, *The Faith of Reason* (New York: King's Crown Press, 1949), pp. 136–140.

have deceived the masses. He even suggested sometimes that society itself separates the interests of an elite from those of the masses. Further, he was not unaware of the ironies in history, showing that the errors and deceits of an elite sometimes lead to its own destruction and to the promotion of truth and virtue.

However primitive Condorcet's causal analysis, it rests on the assumption that the explanation of history (and of error) can be analyzed in terms of empirically verifiable factors. However, his thought also contains an aspect lying outside the boundary of science—the belief that there is a hidden logic behind events, shaping and directing them in ways that are ultimately beneficial to human beings. The introduction of a deus ex machina, a belief in the demiurgical wisdom of history, cannot of course be verified by the science that Condorcet himself defended so stoutly. It is one thing to say that particular achievements in the history of science take place at certain times for concrete causes only to be smothered and stagnated by other causes; it is quite another to assert that behind these events lies a hidden logic that ordains the successive upswelling of truth and error into a pattern of progress. It is one thing to say that progressive forces arise, decay, and rise again; it is quite another to claim that there is a patterned and progressive process ordained by nature and therefore rationally comprehensible. As Frankel has pointed out, it never occurred to Condorcet that the new elite of the Enlightenment might itself succumb to stagnation, or that it might use its knowledge to serve its own class interests.[7]

There is little doubt that Condorcet brought a new note to the problem of linking the empirical realm with the realm of cognition. Ironically, he did this by sharply separating the two realms and by introducing a temporal sequence through which events and beliefs had to pass before the truth of the mind could emerge. Stated differently, Condorcet produced a secularized idealism that employed a new relationship between the actual and the potential. By interpreting the relativities of history as dynamic elements realizing their potential for truth and happiness, Condorcet gave the Enlightenment a dynamic bent and a faith by which to circumvent the liberal dilemma. It was a mode of thought that was to receive a more sophisticated presentation in the work of his successors. One need only take, for example, his idea of the emergence and decay of progressive forces and link it with the emergence of specific classes and specific cultural epochs to pass from Condorcet to Saint-Simon, and even to Marx.

---

[7] Ibid., p. 140. It should again be noted that the idea of a hidden logic had become a commonplace by the end of the eighteenth century in a more static form. The Physiocrats in France and British thinkers from Mandeville to Adam Smith had made wide use of this idea.

However, the basic idea informing the work of these later thinkers—that each stage of history is both false and true and that the ideas and actions of individuals, especially of elites, are both reactionary and progressive—is found in Condorcet. His thought, in short, prefigured the general concept of development (or evolution) that in one form or another was to dominate the physical and social sciences during the nineteenth century, and that exerts a pervasive influence to this day.

The purpose of this extended discussion of Condorcet's concept of hidden logic, therefore, is to alert us to its use in later sociological theory. The eighteenth century's great contribution to social science lay in its ringing declaration that the empirical data of human behavior are comprehensible and in its strenuous efforts to face up to the problems contained in comprehending them. It made notable contributions to the theory of causation, isolating causal variables, assigning priorities, and stressing causal interdependence. However, its thought contained a tendency—especially when confronted with the facts of error, evil, conflict, uniqueness, relativity, and irony—to rely on an unfounded faith in an inner logic of facts that somehow rendered these facts rational and progressive. The subsequent study of sociological theory will often come across this tendency to go beyond science and to impart cosmic significance and teleological causality to social phenomena.

CONCLUSION

Though Condorcet's ideas were more fully elaborated by nineteenth-century thinkers, his work represents the emergence of an important new phase in the momentous intellectual revolution introduced by the emergence of rationalism in the post-Renaissance period. First applied to the physical world in a deductive search for the principles of the universe, rationalism was applied to society in the eighteenth century in an effort to grasp the laws of human behavior. This approach was initially applied under the static assumptions of the mechanistic cosmology of the seventeenth century; however, those assumptions were discarded in favor of an evolutionary world view in which the facts of human behavior were seen as part of a general law of development.

It was Condorcet's rejection of the static perspective of early modern science that insured his place in intellectual history and that made him an important contributor to the post-Newtonian phase of science that was to dominate post-Enlightenment thought. Like early science, however, Condorcet's thought was still deductively metaphysical. Never stated in formal philosophical terms, his theory of history was essentially an act of faith. It expressed his unverified belief that scientific, moral, and social progress was neither accidental nor limited, but somehow rooted in the nature of things. As such, his theory did little to overcome the liberal dilemma.

However, the empirical-historical side of his thought contained many insights into the nature of social processes. The modern reader feels at home in reading Condorcet. The historiography of the *Progress of the Human Mind*, with its sense for the factual, its search for causation, its use of a chronological framework, and its oscillation between a dominant psychological approach and a weaker institutional approach, is the measure of Condorcet's contribution to the modern temper.

By accepting the idea that change is not only an inherent but a lawful feature of human life, Condorcet's work prefigured the nineteenth century's rejection of the finished world of medieval and post-Renaissance intellectual culture. In this sense, his thought is similar to Vico's; but Vico sharply separated nature and human nature, while Condorcet tended to unite them. In Vico's approach there was a deep awareness of the uniqueness of cultural epochs, conceived as value structures, and an awareness of the ponderous, slow-moving nature of social change. Though his work contained the idea of progress, the main weight of his emphasis was on the slow, almost glacial nature of historical movement. Condorcet was too deeply immersed in the dominant assumptions of the Enlightenment to be interested in either the validity or the importance of the past. His emphasis was on the present and the future, and he regarded the past as a necessary but not too important preliminary to the present. For him, the path of progress was a straight-line sequence of historical stages, a line of progress that had accelerated with science and would accelerate even more in the future. Condorcet's identification of the control of nature with human progress, together with his tendency to regard human beings as part of nature, was his bequest to evolutionary monism, the perspective that was to characterize much of naturalistic positivism during the nineteenth century.

Condorcet's emphasis on the importance of humankind's control of nature was more than a contribution to the development of naturalistic positivism. It also served to reveal the relationship between sociology and liberalism, a relationship that can be analyzed on several levels. Speaking generally, his work was a response to the intellectual needs of the new social system emerging unevenly across the face of Western Europe. By the eighteenth century the rise of liberal society, with its growing specialization of institutional life and its growing mastery over nature, had created a need for a thought structure that could resolve the inconsistencies between itself and feudalism, and one that could give expression to the growing confidence of the middle class. Earlier liberal thought had sought to resolve the contradictions between itself and feudalism by basing itself on the device of a social contract; but the social contract, while revolutionary when used as a weapon against feudalism, was essentially static. Even the philosophes, who abandoned the social contract and, on the whole, expressed themselves in more dynamic terms, tended to attack feudal institutions in the name of a natural order of society that was still relatively static. It was only in the work of Condorcet (whose work climaxed earlier doctrines of progress) that liberal society found a theory that adequately expressed its achievements and aspirations—a theory at once a rejection of feudalism and a dynamic vision of the new society that would replace it. His theory, in effect, supplied the middle class with a cosmic explanation and legitimacy both for their destruction of feudalism and for the new society they were busily creating.

Condorcet's liberalism is apparent on other levels as well. His thought contains all the central elements of capitalism: faith in the individual and in education, and a belief that technology and science can conquer ignorance and subdue nature, that science is automatically beneficial to society, and that the same techniques that are useful in industry are useful in social analysis and control. Condorcet was also a liberal in economics, reacting favorably to doctrines that saw harmony in the give-and-take of economic individualism.[8] His belief in laissez faire, of course, is a corollary to his belief in a hidden logic that harmonizes the forces of history and produces progress.

It is clear that the main ideas, values, and institutional practices of an emerging liberalism and the main features of sociological theory were brought to a focus in Condorcet's thought. Henceforth, sociological theory was to be conducted increasingly in terms of the assumptions of an industrial (capitalist) civilization. The practical, empirical mentality of the world of business found its corollary in the growing tendency in social thought to derive society from social practice. Banished were the deductively derived structures of society, whether Platonic, Thomistic, or Hobbesian. In the world of business only pragmatic individuals existed, not bloodlines or logic. If the individual seemed to be a separate entity in his empirical social and economic activities, then it would seem to follow that the separation of the individual and society was a valid presupposition of social thought. As such, the introduction of the individual as a category of social analysis in large part reflected the empirical individualism produced by the social and economic expansion of Europe. By the time of Condorcet, liberal society could formally assert its readiness to harness the energies of all individuals, the low born and the high born, and women as well as men. In Condorcet there is no trace of the deep suspicion of the individual that had characterized Western thought, a suspicion that was not absent even

[8] *Progress of the Human Mind*, pp. 130–132, 138f.

from the thought of some of the philosophes. On the contrary, Condorcet's work symbolizes the way in which individuals were redefined by the eighteenth century to make them respectable and responsible. The individual for Condorcet was no longer a fount of evil and folly, but a sentient-thinking being able to fathom the structure and purposes of nature. The individual as an analytical category had emerged in social thought as early as the social contract, but in Condorcet the idea was linked with a faith in the power of science to effect a piecemeal but ever-growing emancipation of human beings from the tyranny of ignorance and superstition. Furthermore, the extension of the idea of the individual to include women as well as men made the idea synonymous with the idea of humanity.

The concept of humanity had first emerged with the Stoics and was given a permanent place in Western life by the universalism of Christianity. Despite its reinforcement by Christianity, the idea succumbed to feudal particularism and lay dormant for over a thousand years. In the eighteenth century it re-emerged, but this time coupled with the revolutionary demand that its meaning be incorporated into the life of society. Gone from this new formulation was the suspicion of the unwashed and unlettered masses that had characterized the idea of humanity among the Stoics, the Christians, and even the early liberals. Instead there emerged a new, almost fatalistic faith in the ability of an individualized humanity to perfect the methods of science and, by so doing, to perfect itself.

Condorcet's thought was a unique mixture of hitherto disparate liberal ingredients. By taking the natural-law theory at the heart of the philosophical, political, and economic theory of the bourgeoisie, and combining it with the social dynamism characteristic of bourgeois science and economic behavior, he gave the hitherto static concept of liberal world mastery a historical perspective. If his emphasis on the individual explains much of the psychological bias of later sociological theory, and if his theory of history is superficial, his work is nonetheless important because it expressed the achievements and longings of a newly crystallizing civilization. Bourgeois civilization was given a richer and more definitive intellectual expression in the works of Saint-Simon and Comte, but its main ideas and values were first adumbrated by Condorcet. It was he who justified the cataclysmic changes in social structure that technology and science had introduced into European society, at the same time providing the intellectual and moral perspective by which theorists could think positively about the discontinuities of history. It was he who proclaimed the power of science to link the past with the present and both with the future, and to leap the gap between the known and the unknown in all fields. Finally, it was he who outlined more fully than ever before the values and disciplines by which Westerners would henceforth live. In place of the values of birth and religion, he substituted those of merit and science; for the tyranny of the past he substituted that of the future. In the dual discipline imposed

by science and by the postponement of gratification, he expressed the profound this-worldly orientation of the bourgeoisie. In large measure, he
expressed his faith that a society of science was the inevitable corollary of
a science of society. His thought, therefore, is of no little importance in the
history of sociology despite the fact that future sociologists had to struggle
to disentangle the legacy of faith, fervor, factuality, and final cause that
he bequeathed them.

COMTE DE SAINT-SIMON (1760–1825)

The hope that the study of human behavior could be brought within the
jurisdiction of science was given impetus and explicit shape by the erratic
genius of Comte Claude Henri de Saint-Simon, in many ways a watershed
figure in history of sociology.[9] Saint-Simon climaxed the formative stage in
which sociology committed itself to search out systematically and self-
consciously the implications contained in Newtonian science, and he also
inaugurated the post-Newtonian phase of sociology. Saint-Simon lived and
thought in two epochs—he grew to manhood in the eighteenth century, experiencing both the American and French revolutions firsthand, and he
experienced the postrevolutionary romantic flowering of the early nineteenth century.

This is not to suggest that Saint-Simon's work was a break with the past.
There is a direct line of continuity between his work and that of Condorcet,
though there are some important differences. Absent from Saint-Simon's
work, for example, is Condorcet's belief in natural rights and dislike of
religion and clerics. Above all, however, Saint-Simon accepted Condorcet's
view of the importance of science and his dynamic perspective. Saint-
Simon's historic function was to take Condorcet's ideas about progress and

---

[9] Except for the *Introduction aux travaux scientifiques du dix-neuvième siècle,*
found in vol. 1 of *Oeuvres choisies de Saint-Simon,* ed. Lemonnier, 3 vols. (Brus-
sels: Van Meenen, 1859), Saint-Simon's important works can be found in vols. 15,
18–23, and 37–40 of the *Oeuvres de Saint-Simon et d'Enfantin,* 47 vols. (Paris:
Dentu, 1865–1876; Paris: E. Leroux, 1877–1878). For a translation of selected
writings, see F. M. H. Markham, ed. and trans., *Henri Comte de Saint-Simon:
Selected Writings* (Oxford: Basil Blackwell, 1952), available in paperback (New
York: Harper & Row, 1964) under the title *Henri de Saint-Simon: Social Organi-
zation, the Science of Man and other Writings;* and Ghita Ionescu, ed., *The
Political Thought of Saint-Simon,* trans. Valence Ionescu (New York: Oxford
University Press, 1976), also in paperback. For a definitive intellectual biography,
to which I am greatly indebted, see Frank E. Manuel, *The New World of Henri
Saint-Simon* (Cambridge, Mass.: Harvard University Press, 1956), available in
paperback. Also valuable in assessing Saint-Simon's contribution to sociology is
Emile Durkheim's *Socialism and Saint-Simon,* ed. A. W. Gouldner and trans.
Charlotte Sattler (Yellow Springs, Ohio: Antioch Press, 1958), available in
paperback.

Comte de Saint-Simon (1760–1825)

the possibility of a science of human nature, and to give them a deeper and more explicit meaning.

PHILOSOPHY AND METHOD

Saint-Simon's conception of knowledge seems at first glance to be identical with that of the Enlightenment—knowledge comes from reason confirmed by experience, by theory in fruitful interplay with fact. Saint-Simon went considerably beyond the Enlightenment, however, by claiming that the two methods that correspond to theory and fact, the a priori and the a posteriori, have alternately contributed to the progress of knowledge. Thus some periods have been characterized by synthesis (constructive periods) and some by analysis (critical periods). The present era, he felt, was ripe for the flowering of a synthetic and constructive period.

The preference for the a priori approach that Saint-Simon displayed throughout his career indicates clearly that he was not an empirical positivist. He showed little interest in the careful examination of facts or in the need to increase the factual base from which to generalize; nor did he hesitate to claim that a total comprehension of the phenomenal world could be achieved. Without questioning the validity of this presupposition, he assumed throughout his career that a general law governed the universe, and that humanity, which had succeeded in establishing the unity of the world in ever-more progressive thought systems, was at last ready to formulate the real law of the universe in scientific terms. Despite his repeated claim that positive knowledge was different from metaphysical knowledge, it is apparent that Saint-Simon was not abandoning metaphysics, but attempting to place it on a new epistemological foundation.

Saint-Simon's thought structure rested on the assumption that a single scientific concept could fathom both nature and human nature.

> There are not two orders of things; there is only one, the physical realm.
>
> Phenomena are divided into two classes: solids and fluids.
>
> Man is a minature world; there exists in him, on a small scale, all the phenomena that take place on a large scale in the universe.[10]

There is no mistaking either the naturalistic positivism or the monism in this passage. Of special interest is Saint-Simon's belief that the human mind does not stand outside of nature. To believe otherwise would have made him a philosophe and embroiled him in the liberal dilemma. For Saint-Simon, the mind itself was part of nature and subject to nature's law of development. His central doctrine is that there is a natural process of development in which the mind, having made solid advances in its knowledge of physical nature, will now come to know itself. The conviction that intellectual progress is the law of the universe explains Saint-Simon's characteristic disposition to inaugurate every problem with a look to the past. He was firmly convinced that to know the past is to know the present and the future.

Saint-Simon used a number of related ideas to develop the idea of scientific progress, but he never synthesized them. His theory of the alternation of a priori and a posteriori methods has already been mentioned. He also argued that all phenomena can be explained by the struggle between fluids

---

[10] *Introduction, Oeuvres choisies,* 1:175.

and solids, thought of in terms of universal gravitation. Alternation and conflict are also present in the relation between social events and science, each of them acting alternately as cause and effect. The march of humanity is marked by profound and even bloody crises. A new discovery in science results in political turbulence, which in turn is a preliminary to further scientific discovery. Thus Copernicus is a preliminary to the political upsets accompanying the Protestant Reformation, and the rebellion of Luther leads to the work of Bacon, Galileo, and Descartes. The scientific revolution of the seventeenth century leads somehow to the English Civil War and the stage is set for the appearance of Locke and Newton—and there is no telling what enormous discoveries will stem from the French Revolution.

Saint-Simon also sought to understand the evolution of science by using a literal analogy between the growth of the individual and the growth of humanity. He also stated that all science begins by being conjectural and ends by being positive, and that it proceeds from the simple to the complex. These attempts to understand the development of science were based on the general notion that it is possible to make a rational periodization of intellectual history. But it must be scientific history, claimed Saint-Simon, by which he also meant that it must be the history of science.

The number of divisions that Saint-Simon saw in history varied slightly, though the theme of progress was common to all. In one place, he divided history into two parts, claiming that the idea of unity that Socrates introduced into philosophy was the most momentous act in all intellectual history. Later he distinguished four stages, two preceding Socrates and two following him: those of idolatry, polytheism, and theism, and a final period based on science. He finally settled on a three-stage division: the period of Preliminary Work (or Polytheism as it was called later), the Conjectural period (or Theism), and the Positive period (or Physicism).

Regardless of the numbers of stages, however, Saint-Simon's main theme was that humanity has progressed to an ever-higher comprehension of the unity of nature. Human beings begin by worshiping inanimate objects, proceed to polytheism and the belief in a plurality of causes, and finally arrive at a stage in which they see the world as a universe governed by a single cause. From the time of Socrates, who inaugurated this latter stage, a variety of metaphysical or conjectural systems, including the systems of Socrates himself, Christianity, Descartes, and Newton, have all searched for the one law of the universe. The final positive stage will complete this search by ceasing to think of the world as divided into distinct moral and physical spheres, and humanity will at last be in possession of the one law that governs all phenomena.

Saint-Simon developed the idea of a three-stage process of intellectual development by relating the structure and movement of this process to the interests and activities of specific social classes (something that will be analyzed as part of his substantive theory). His identification of human nature and nature, his resolve that human behavior must be studied by the same methods used in studying physical nature, and his belief that the substantive concepts of physical science can be applied to humans—all were destined to have a long career in sociological theory. However, Saint-Simon did more than merely point out the general direction that the science of human behavior would take. There are numerous passages in the *Mémoire* [11] where he tried his hand at knowing human nature by comparing it with the rest of the inorganic and organic worlds. In one place he indicated that knowledge about human beings will come only from physiology, stating flatly that the superiority of humankind over the rest of nature lies solely in its superior biological organization.

Saint-Simon's definition of reason was also highly suggestive and in keeping with his emphasis on biology. The main function of reason is to predict and to control the behavior of phenomena in order that individuals may benefit from useful phenomena and avoid those that are harmful. Reason is thus an instrument of adjustment to the external world—not a limited adjustment, however, but one based on a complete knowledge of the workings of the universe.

It is apparent that Saint-Simon's philosophical naturalism not only is anti-Christian, but also supersedes the more static rationalist and universalist tradition of the Enlightenment. The trend away from the Enlightenment was accentuated in his later works. In particular, he rejected the Enlightenment's equalitarianism in favor of an elitist theory, and became even more aware than he was earlier in his career of the emotional and religious basis of social life. He never ceased to think of religion, however, as anything more than the moral and emotional reflection of a given state of knowledge.

Saint-Simon's view of religion stemmed from his naturalistic monism, the fundamental turn of mind that saw all nature as a unity, and made him reject the compartmentalization of existence into distinct physical and spiritual spheres. When translated into social thought, this view led him to think of society as an organic, functionally specialized unity in which all sciences and institutions worked in concert to achieve a unity of knowledge and social existence. Saint-Simon's overall perspective insured him a place as the leading founder of monistic naturalistic positivism and as formulator of a philosophy of history based on the evolution of positivism.[12] Finally,

---

[11] *Mémoire, Oeuvres,* 40:73–110, 187–190.

[12] For a discussion in favor of the originality of Saint-Simon's ideas, see Emile Durkheim, *Socialism and Saint-Simon,* ed. A. W. Gouldner, tr. Charlotte Sattler (Yellow Springs, Ohio: Antioch Press, 1958), chap. 6, especially pp. 104–108 (available as a Collier paperback entitled *Socialism*); and Frank E. Manuel, *The New World of Henri Saint-Simon* (Cambridge, Mass.: Harvard University Press, 1956), chap. 29, also available in paperback.

his influence helped to make positivism in French sociology more organic and synthesizing in its orientation than the more atomistic positivism that developed in England and the United States.

SUBSTANTIVE WORK

Saint-Simon's fundamental assumption about social behavior was that it reflects given states of knowledge. If knowledge has gone through stages of development in a manner comprehensible to human beings, then it is logical to assume that social development has gone through corresponding stages and is also accessible to human thought.

The Stages and Movement of History

Saint-Simon's belief that a given stage of philosophical development has a corresponding form of social development was clearly stated early in his career. The first stage of knowledge is Polytheism, with its social form Slavery and Militarism; the second is Theism, with its social form Feudalism and Militarism; and the third is Positive Science, with its social form Industrialism.[13] In L'Organisateur,[14] Saint-Simon provided some details about the structure of the second and third stages, and gave an explanation of why change takes place. The Theological-Feudal stage, which began about the third or fourth century A.D. with the establishment of Christianity and the dissolution of the Roman Empire, reached its fullest development in the eleventh century A.D. No sooner did it reach its zenith, however, than "the germ of its destruction" was also born. In a two-pronged offensive, the free cities, which represent the industrial principle, began to undermine the "feudal power," and science, after its reintroduction into Europe by the Arabs, began to undermine the "theological power." Weak at first, but with constantly growing vigor, the new society grew alongside the old. Historians who depicted the violent events of the past seven or eight centuries as unexpected and unforeseeable were wrong, claimed Saint-Simon. These conflicts were part of the struggle between the old and the new systems of society, erupting after long preparations within the bowels of the old system, first in the sixteenth century with Luther's attack on the spiritual power, and then in seventeenth-century England with an attack on the temporal power.

According to Saint-Simon, historians were also wrong who depicted this period as the struggle between kings and popes, and who saw the free cities as merely their instruments. Quite the contrary, the communes had taken advantage of these quarrels to further their own interests. With a

[13] L'Industrie, Oeuvres, 19:22–27.
[14] Oeuvres, vol. 20.

"kind of admirable instinct" they supported whichever power was the most
liberal, sometimes siding with the nobles against the king, as in England,
and sometimes with the king against the nobles, as in France.

With the decline of the Theological-Feudal system came the gradual development of the new society. Fortunately, industrial and scientific "capacities" developed outside the old system (which was not the case in countries
like China and India) and were possessed by distinct and independent
classes. It should not be thought, Saint-Simon warned, that scientists, artists,
and artisans followed a preconceived plan. This error characterizes past
thinkers, who subjected the march of civilization to their views instead of
basing their views on the march of civilization. The law of progress is
beyond the control of human beings, and carries everything with it. Human
beings can only hope to know the course of events, and support it; the
only alternative is to be dragged along blindly. By acting solely against
nature, however, the scientists who provided the knowledge and the
artisans who applied it for the benefit of humanity might just as well have
been following a predesigned course. Ultimately, said Saint-Simon, the
primary urge of human beings is not to dominate their own kind but to
dominate nature. The growth of science and industry has promoted a
definite moral change in this direction. Thus, in confining themselves to
the task of subduing nature, the free cities were following a law predestined
to carry humanity from the Theological-Feudal stage to the Positive-Indus-
trial stage.

The Society of Science

The end of history will see the human urge to dominate other human beings
turn to focus instead on the domination of nature. This is a persistent theme
in Saint-Simon's writings and the key to an understanding of what he meant
by the Positive society. He expressed this theme in many different ways.
He once asserted flatly that the obligation to work should be substituted
for the golden rule—an assertion that illustrates his view that science and
industry are the bearers of a new morality. In *L'Industrie*, which is strewn
with admiration of industry, Saint-Simon identified liberty with the freedom to engage in economic activity and to enjoy its fruits. In regard to
social organization in general, he proclaimed that the one most favorable
to industry is the best, and he bluntly stated that politics is the science of
production.[15] So deep was his belief that the mastery of nature is the ultimate objective of the historical process that he unleashed a long diatribe
against what he called the antinational party of parasitic idlers.[16] In the same
vein was his famous attempt to assess the loss to France, if, on the one

---

[15] *L'Industrie, Oeuvres,* 18:81f, 128, 165f, 188.
[16] Ibid., 19:195–235.

hand, it should suddenly lose all its scientists, artists, and workers, or, on the other, if it should suddenly have to dispense with the services of the nobility and clergy. His answer was predictable—the first loss would make France a "lifeless corpse," while the second loss, however regrettable, would be of small consequence.[17]

In essence, Saint-Simon's new society would be an era without power, a period in which human beings would no longer dominate others. It would not be an era or period strictly speaking, for that implies time; in reality, it would be the end of time, the end of change. In the new society, all producers would be united by utility, morality, and friendship because of their common stake in economic values. Saint-Simon's belief that an essential harmony of interests would prevail in the new society never left his thought, though he lost his earlier interest in the theory of laissez faire. Whereas the old society was governed by individuals, the new society would be governed by principles. In this golden age, social direction would come not from a government, but from the entire society considered as a sovereign entity. It would not act arbitrarily, but according to principles derived from the nature of things. The proper course for society to take and the answer to every question would be clear and beyond dispute since all matters would be determined by science and not by human will. Once society was managed according to knowledge, the struggle for power would abate because social positions would be distributed according to capacity.

The problem of order would also cease to trouble the new society since the people would maintain order themselves. The coercive aspect of government would wither greatly since a large governmental apparatus for the maintenance of order is necessary only when the political system is not oriented toward the enhancement of social prosperity, and the government is obliged to consider the people as an enemy of the established order.

Regarding the institutional structure of the new society, Saint-Simon's writing is a little bit more concrete than usual, though his scattered remarks are still vague and unintegrated. However, his characteristic attitude toward the nature of society is apparent. From his earliest writings, Saint-Simon tended to think of society in terms of classes and leadership. In *L'Industrie* he compared society to a troop of soldiers led by an elite and posed the problem of contemporary France as the need to replace a decadent elite with a new one. In another place, he argued that the idea of equality popularized by the French Revolution was debased. True equality, he declared, comes when human beings receive benefits according to their capacity.

[17] *L'Organisateur, Oeuvres,* 20:17–26.

Saint-Simon's recourse to individual capacity as the criterion for distributing social position reveals a great deal about his image of society. He was
certain that once the old society disappeared, the task of judging capacity
would be a simple one. In this millennium of perfect knowledge, and thus
perfect justice, social functions would be distributed according to the
nature of human beings in general and of each individual in particular. In
developing this view, Saint-Simon abandoned, in effect, the belief among
some of the philosophes that people could be educated into equality.

A naturalistic positivist who equates the nature of human nature with
physical nature cannot easily accept a doctrine based on the assumption
that human nature is flexible and indeterminate. A monistic positivist is
more likely to accept a psychological, not a social or historical, definition
of human nature, and this is essentially what Saint-Simon did. He was
especially influenced by the French anatomist Bichat (1771–1802), who
had distinguished three human types: the brain, the sensory, and the motor
individual. These capacities, which all human beings possessed in some
measure, were mutually exclusive and distributed differently among individuals. Education could develop the dominant capacity in individuals
but could not change the classification into which birth—nature—had placed
them. In sketching the institutional structure of the new society, Saint-
Simon was undoubtedly influenced by Bichat's doctrine of psychological
types, though his reference to Bichat is brief and vague. The new society
is essentially a coordination of three classes, composed of scientists, artists,
and *industriels*, classes that correspond roughly to Bichat's three psychological types. Saint-Simon's definition of these classes varied. Sometimes
his references to scientists emphasized pure science and sometimes applied
science. The aesthetic realm, which covered the full range of aesthetic
expression, came in his later thought to include religion. His definition of
the *industriel* class, which at first included all workers from the lowest to
the highest levels of economic activity, referred only to large capitalists in
his later work.

Saint-Simon's failure to decide on the social equivalent of Bichat's types
prevented him from ever deciding clearly on the institutional order enjoined by human nature. The three functions of invention, review, and
execution, which were evidently supposed to be the political equivalents of
intrinsic human capacities and the categories of positive knowledge, were
assigned differently by Saint-Simon in his various writings. In *L'Organisateur* he spoke of a chamber of invention composed of practical scientists
and a minority of artists, a chamber of review composed of theoretical
scientists, and a chamber of execution composed of members of each branch
of industry in proportion to its importance. In the future the total material
and spiritual needs of society would be entrusted to these three chambers.

They would inaugurate vast public-works projects both useful and aesthetic; public holidays would celebrate the importance of all social statuses; luxury and refinement would become moral because they would be public and no longer the exclusive privilege of the few.[18] Later, in his "Catéchisme des industriels," [19] Saint-Simon outlined his new society differently. He still placed the management and education of society in the hands of those who can synthesize knowledge, adding a significant admonition that the rich should have no educational advantage over the poor. However, there is a new emphasis; a distinct role for artists is envisaged alongside the practical scientists, with the two somehow corresponding to the rhythm of of philosophical history—a rhythm that has seen Plato, the moralist, alternate with Aristotle, the materialist. Along with the new importance that he attached to the sentiments, especially to moral and religious sentiments, Saint-Simon declared that the most important class is the *industriels*, though he did not translate this importance into an institutional supremacy until one of his last works, *Opinions littéraires, philosophiques et industrielles*.[20] The artists and scientists are now seen as initiating projects for the educational and economic benefit of society, but it is the large industrialists who are charged with the tasks of reviewing and executing these projects.

It is significant that in Saint-Simon's final discussion of the political structure of the golden age toward which history is propelling humanity, he transformed the function of government almost completely into a task of administration. With adequate provision for keeping society abreast of moral and scientific knowledge, it is assumed that ignorance will disappear and human beings will no longer disagree. As such, there is no need for the political system to focus on the containment and reconciliation of warring groups, and government and politics dissolve into administration. Given this perspective Saint-Simon finally came to regard industrialists, who provide for the existence of all other classes and are the most experienced in administration, as the foremost class of the scientific society.

The superiority of industrialists should not be thought of in conventional political or social terms. Saint-Simon did not seek to substitute an aristocracy of wealth for one of birth, though this would no doubt emerge from his proposals. Social evils, such as injustice, greed, envy, and sloth, were for Saint-Simon merely historical manifestations that resulted from imperfect knowledge. Evil would disappear when all people, working in statuses enjoined by their natural capacities, were linked together in the common enterprise of subduing the forces of nature. Society would be unified by a

[18] *Oeuvres*, 20:50–61.
[19] *Oeuvres*, 39:25–44.
[20] *Oeuvres choisies*, 3:287–289.

belief in progress through science, a belief that progress can be achieved and enjoyed only through social specialization. Society for Saint-Simon was not a metaphysical abstraction, but a positive set of functions. Such a view obligates individuals to determine to which of the three main functional classes they belong, and to accept the identity given to them not by other human beings but by nature.

Saint-Simon's proclivity for thinking of society as a set of functions is yet another way of illustrating his inegalitarianism. The functional view of social phenomena, which is common to much of sociological positivism, can assume a number of forms. In Montesquieu, it was used mainly as a tool of observation, to measure the consequences and utilities produced by specified causes. In Saint-Simon, it was also flavored heavily with the idea of utility, but in addition there was a tendency to think of society as having a set of functions or needs much on the order of a biological system. Roughly speaking, there is the need for knowledge, for sentiments (artistic, moral, and religious feelings), and for material expression and satisfaction. The law of historical development decrees that three major structural systems—Polytheism, Theism, and Positivism—will emerge to satisfy these needs in ever more satisfactory ways. This functional view of society, which was only adumbrated in Saint-Simon's thought, was destined to exert a heavy hold over the field of sociology with the rise to prominence in the nineteenth century of the biological sciences.

Saint-Simon's organic picture of society had a number of sources. His favorable view of religion as a necessary stage in history made him receptive to the hierarchic conception of social unity that figured in the work of the French traditionalists.[21] He was especially impressed with the work of Bonald, whom he cited with some approval. Though Saint-Simon's version of society was uncompromisingly positivist and secular, there are important parallels between his view of society and the medieval conception of society as a hierarchy of cooperating "classes."

Saint-Simon was undoubtedly also influenced by Rousseau, whose works he knew, and by the romantic movement. He tended to define human beings as active creatures with emotional as well as intellectual needs, all of which had to be satisfied within the context of social existence. His last work, New Christianity, was in keeping with his belief that religion had

---

[21] The main figures in French traditionalism or counterrevolutionary conservatism were Joseph Maistre (1753–1821) and Louis Bonald (1754–1840), both of whom argued that society is not a voluntary, human creation composed of isolated individuals, but of divine origin (language is from God), hierarchic, and organic—a system held together by a network of traditional norms and functional groups that are logically and empirically prior to the individual. Their counterpart in England was Edmund Burke (1729–1797), who said less about religion, language, and reason and more about the wisdom of custom.

performed useful social functions in previous historical periods and that it was an indispensable part of social existence. Therefore, while he made a plea for Christianity to come abreast of science, his last book was also concerned with the need to translate science into religion—that is, into a set of emotional and moral imperatives useful to social existence.

Saint-Simon's leanings toward order and inequality were also influenced by his negative reaction to the excesses of the French Revolution. He thought of the Revolution as merely one phase of the long struggle by the positive spirit to extricate itself from its thralldom to theism. It was not the end of the old system, but merely a vast catharsis; the emerging new system was still heavily contaminated by the critical, destructive a posteriori spirit of the philosophes and overladen with metaphysical abstractions like liberty and equality. Though these abstractions were secular, they were not scientific and belonged more to the Theological than to the Positive stage of historical development.

As a champion of industrialization, Saint-Simon could not help but realize that the subjugation of nature would require an extensive division of labor—thus his constant tendency to think of society in terms of specialized functions serviced by specialized groups. His view that the "natural" human being would be the basis of social specialization in the new society, while presented as a way of satisfying the claims of truth and justice, was an argument that blended smoothly with the needs of an emerging industrial society. The concept of the natural person for Saint-Simon meant, after all, that human nature contained three qualitatively different types of human beings conveniently arranged in a hierarchy of worth. Saint-Simon wrote, it should be remembered, during a period of quickening industrial activity in which the long trend toward social inequality based on talent and wealth (class rather than estate stratification) was accelerating under the impetus of science, technology, republicanism, nationalism, and war. It was a social period vastly different from the one of Vico and Montesquieu, and different as well from the one that had engendered Condorcet's thought. In short, it was a period in which sociological theory, confronted by the fact of industrialization, took on its major ideological function: to explain and to justify inequality within the framework of liberal institutions. This was a function of which sociological theory rarely lost sight during its subsequent history—something that in no small measure is due to Saint-Simon.

CONCLUSION

Saint-Simon has an assured place in the history of sociological thought as the theorist who explicitly set forth the view that a unified scientific theory of natural and human behavior was possible. Because of his preference for the a priori method and his belief that the general law governing both human and physical phenomena had been found, he has been classified as a monistic naturalistic positivist. His definition of science was much closer to the spirit of Descartes than to that of Pascal, despite his emphasis on the need for positive knowledge and the fact that his thought was heavily tinged by utilitarianism. Though toward the close of his career he placed a somewhat greater emphasis on the importance of emotions and religion, he never abandoned his fundamental assumption that a unified scientific theory of all phenomena, material and moral, was the basic goal of human reason and history. His monism prompted him to develop a substantive theory that saw all phenomena conforming to the law of gravitation. Neither his preferences for the a priori method nor his appreciation of human emotional life ever undermined his belief that the world of physical and social phenomena had a lawfulness that could be grasped by the human mind. In short, he never ceased to be a child of the Enlightenment.

However, his view of the phenomenal world contained a dynamism that was absent in the work of most of the philosophes. Building on the work of Condorcet, he developed a dynamic monism based on the view that there was a law of progress in the realm of mind. For Saint-Simon, human beings can come to know the world they live in only gradually—a view with large implications for the liberal dilemma. In achieving its destiny, humankind must pass through three intellectual phases: Polytheism, Theism, and Positivism. Since society is merely the reflection of a given state of knowledge, it too passes through three stages. The last intellectual stage will end the conventional miseries that have plagued humanity; perfect knowledge means perfect control over both human and physical nature.

The doctrine that the control of nature is the answer to human ills is central, of course, to both liberalism and socialism. Though a case can be made that Saint-Simon presented a socialist doctrine—and many similarities to and influences on Marxian doctrine can be cited in particular—his essential affinity is with liberalism. It is true that he sharply separated himself from the liberals of his day, whom he criticized as a motley group united by vague sentiments, lacking a true doctrine based on interests. However, if one thinks of liberalism in wider terms, it coincides almost exactly with Saint-Simon's fundamental position that the objective of history is to achieve a rational mastery of nature through an institutional structure based on private property, the market, the neutral rational-legal state, and the allocation of social position in accordance with economic performance by naturally unequal individuals. Despite differences, there is a basic similarity between Saint-Simon's image of history and of the new society, and that of liberalism.

Fundamentally, Saint-Simon presented a doctrine conducive to the rise and success of liberal society. His exaltation of work and castigation of idleness, his appreciation of technology and pure science, his defense of private property and adulation of the large industrialists, and his equation of morality and personal worth with economic performance and belief in the distribution of social status according to that performance—all are derived from his fundamental view that the history of humanity is an evolutionary process that terminates in a society based on the mastery of nature. Even the technocratic aspect of the new institutional order that he outlined for the Positive society bears an intrinsic relationship to the nature of liberalism. His vision of a society without conflict coincides with the liberal doctrine of natural harmony—though it should be noted that Saint-Simon never adopted the theory of laissez faire.

His theory of history may also be seen as a solution to the liberal dilemma. According to Saint-Simon, human knowledge goes through stages, and the law of progress can be achieved only during the formative phase of the last stage. Therefore human beings are fated to have only incomplete knowledge until history has finished speaking. From this point of view, truth emerges from the fundamental teleological force at work in nature; it is not an entity that can be grasped all at once at any one time. It evolves from human nature, which undergoes no change in its essential nature but only in the knowledge made available to it by the historical process. Human beings are semiblind participants in this process, driven unwittingly by an instinct to know and to control the forces of nature, an instinct that makes them the agents of history's hidden logic. Only when the process has neared completion does the logic of history become apparent. Only then do the errors and evils of history assume their rightful place as the necessary concomitants of the progress of truth and goodness.

Without doubt, Saint-Simon occupies a high place in the history of sociology. His work gave a deeper and more dramatic formulation to the synthesis that Condorcet had begun to fashion between earlier scientific currents—the empirically based rationalism of Montesquieu and the historical perspective of Turgot and others. By eliminating Condorcet's belief in ahistorical natural rights, by linking intellectual and social progress to the values and interests of specific historical classes, and by reducing Condorcet's ten stages to three, Saint-Simon made the theory of progress more coherent and attractive to the needs of the nineteenth century. In short, his work updated sociology to meet the needs of the emerging industrial society. To Saint-Simon must go the credit, therefore, for giving explicit shape to the close relationship that exists between sociology and the institutional structure of capitalist society.

Saint-Simon's greatest influence was on the development of naturalistic positivism, but his assumption that the goal of sociological theory was to build a unified theory of human nature had influence on sociocultural positivism as well. Though sociologists today are much more wary about applying the concepts of the natural sciences to human behavior, and though many sociocultural theorists deny that this can be done, almost all sociologists still believe, as Saint-Simon did, that the natural and social sciences share, if not the same subject matter, at least the same aims and methods. One cannot doubt Saint-Simon's originality in conceiving this identity between empirical natural science and sociology. One can doubt, however, whether the inchoate state in which his theory was presented could have exerted the influence it did without the systematization it received at the hands of Auguste Comte. For this reason I shall postpone further criticism of Saint-Simon in order to examine the work of Comte. This examination will explain why the theories of both Saint-Simon and Comte were pseudoevolutionary and thus still well within the confines of the first or Newtonian phase of modern science—a phase that was an anachronism before either theorist laid pen to paper.

AUGUSTE COMTE (1798–1857)

Generally acknowledged as the founder of sociology, Auguste Comte contributed little to sociology that can be characterized as new. The strength of his work [22] lies in his undoubted ability to coordinate and systematize the material of others. Comte's historic achievement was to take a scattered intellectual trend and subject it to a rigorous process of theoretical agglutination. Using a framework he acquired from Saint-Simon, Comte pulled together the disparate strands of positivist thought and welded them into a vast systematic whole. It is somewhat of an injustice, of course, that Comte's diligence won him a greater reputation than did the originality of Saint-Simon. However, one must not minimize the importance of Comte's work. The ability to complete an idea, while exploring its every possibility

---

[22] Comte's thought is contained in two major works, the six-volume *Cours de philosophie positive,* which appeared between 1830 and 1842, and the four-volume *Système de politique positive,* which appeared between 1851 and 1854. *Cours de philosophie positive* has been condensed and translated by Harriet Martineau as *The Positive Philosophy of Auguste Comte,* (New York: Calvin Blanchard, 1855), henceforth cited as *Positive Philosophy.* Comte thought so highly of this condensation that he decided to substitute it for the six-volume French edition. Selections from Comte's work are available in: George Simpson, ed., *Auguste Comte: Sire of Sociology* (New York: Thomas Y. Crowell paperback, 1969); Stanislav Andreski, ed., and Margaret Clark, trans., *The Essential Comte* (New York: Barnes & Noble, 1974); Kenneth Thompson, ed., *Auguste Comte: The Foundation of Sociology* (New York: John Wiley, 1975); and Gertrud Lenzer, ed., *Auguste Comte and Positivism: The Essential Writings* (New York: Harper & Row paperbound, 1975).

Auguste Comte (1798–1857)

and extracting its every advantage, is just as important as the ability to conceive it in the first place.

PHILOSOPHY AND METHOD

The guiding concept in Comte's work was the law of progress:

> From the study of the development of human intelligence, in all directions, and through all times, the discovery arises of a great fundamental law, to which it is necessarily subject, and which has a solid foundation of proof, both in the facts of our organization and in our historical experience. The law is this:—that each of our leading conceptions—each branch of our knowledge—

passes successively through three different theoretical conditions: the Theological, or fictitious; the Metaphysical, or abstract; and the Scientific, or positive.[23]

Though Comte's stages of evolution were different from Saint-Simon's, their general concepts of historical evolution are almost identical. For both, the progress of human beings was bound up with the progress of the mind toward a unified scientific conception of the structure of the universe, a progress marked by critical (or destructive) and organic (or constructive) phases. Comte claimed that the mind of the race passes through stages that are akin to the stages of mind of a maturing individual. This theory is also found in Saint-Simon, and in Condorcet and others. Also familiar from Saint-Simon is Comte's assertion that knowledge develops differently depending on subject matter—the more general and simple sciences precede the more individual and complex sciences. The history of the mind confirms this logical proposition; the development of positivity in scientific areas was first in astronomy, then in physics and chemistry, and then in physiology. The one remaining area to be rescued from the domination of theological and metaphysical explanations was the most complex of all, the field of social phenomena.

The procedures for finding the laws of social phenomena are observation, experiment, comparison, and the historical method. Comte was careful to point out that mere empirical compilations are worthless and that theory precedes facts—or, more exactly, that "social science requires . . . the Subordination of Observation to the statical and dynamical laws of phenomena." [24] It is clear that Comte, like Saint-Simon, preferred the theoretical to the empirical approach and that he accepted the Enlightenment belief that human reason could fathom the phenomenal world.

The main weight of Comte's argument rests on the assumption that there is a natural order that human beings can comprehend. He assumed that this natural order contains a hierarchy of knowledge that discloses itself to human beings according to a natural law of mental progress; the culminating science is sociology, which itself gains theoretical and empirical unity and validity from the great law of progress. The law of progress decrees that social phenomena at any given time contain both structure and process. Though each of these is subject to invariable natural laws, they will merge into one concept as human knowledge increases. In short, a process of perception can reduce the unity, diversity, order, and movement of the physical and the moral universes to laws of factual uniformity. Moreover, as we saw in Saint-Simon, the process of perception is itself subject to the law of the three

[23] *Positive Philosophy*, p. 25.
[24] Ibid., p. 476.

stages—a law, Comte was sure, whose logical validity must have an empirical foundation.

SUBSTANTIVE WORK

Comte's attempt to verify his master concept of the law of three stages is a surprisingly sound piece of historical scholarship. Though his effort resulted in a philosophy of history that orders its materials to suit a pre-established scheme, his knowledge and handling of historical materials is impressive.

The Three Stages of Social Development

To develop his theory of history, Comte identified the social-system corollaries of his three-tiered structure of philosophical development. The Theological stage, according to Comte, went through three phases—fetishism, polytheism, and monotheism—and had as its social forms military conquest and slavery. In keeping with his principle of social statics, Comte argued that there is a fundamental agreement among all parts of the Theological society and its subdivisions. All in all, Comte's appreciation of the past, and his attempt to portray it accurately with the aid of an anthropological-cultural approach, constitute a notable contribution to historical scholarship.[25]

The Metaphysical stage, which started about 1300, went through two phases, Comte explained, a critical or destructive period and an organic or constructive period. It too is characterized by military values, but these have become defensive. The entire stage, however, merely marked a transition to the Positive stage. Characterized negatively, the Metaphysical stage went through a two-century period of spontaneous involuntary decline and then developed a systematic doctrine of revolution; it was the decline of the old system that produced the critical Metaphysical period, not the other way around. Characterized positively, the five centuries between 1300 and 1800 were a period of gestation for the Positive stage. New developments in industry, art, and science coincided with the decline of the theological and military spirit. From 1800 on, said Comte, the Metaphysical stage, which was now over-ripe, was destined to give way to the Positive stage at any time.[26]

The Nature of Society

Comte's early work did not dwell much on the Positive society, though it does contain his characteristic view of society. His fundamental disposition was to regard society as an organic whole. As for individuals,

[25] Ibid., bk. 6, chaps. 7–9.
[26] Ibid., bk. 6, chaps. 10–12.

they were an abstraction, not elements of society at all. Society's basic unit is the family, but it too is markedly inferior to the totality called society. The family, said Comte, developing a distinction between primary and secondary relations, is primarily an emotional and moral union, while society is more diverse and utilitarian, essentially an association based on the "division of employments." The division of employments means something far wider than economic specialization; it includes all intellectual and moral employments and extends within nations and without, linking the entire race in a structure of cooperation as yet only partly realized. Society is therefore a structure of specialization that in keeping with the law of progress, tends toward an ever-more exact estimate and employment of individual capacities.

Specialization is dangerous, said Comte, but fortunately society sets up a counterbalancing force that neutralizes the tendency toward dispersion. The true basis of a scientific theory of government is the spontaneous emergence of a specialized social organ to assert the spirit of the whole over the parts. Since the division of labor affects every aspect of social existence, the governing force must assert its sway over intellectual and moral pursuits as well as over material activities. Still relying on logic rather than observation, Comte argued that there is a principle of super-subordination in all sciences: a specialized function is always subordinated to a more general function, and the most generalized social function is governance. An increase in the material division of labor strengthens the governing organ because specialization provides the leisure to develop the intellectual and moral qualities on which political superiority rests. These qualities, Comte pointed out, are the possession of individuals and are much less affected by both the dispersive tendencies of the division of labor and the augmenting power of cooperation. Thus, concluded Comte, we have "the elementary tendency of all human society to a spontaneous government. This tendency accords with a corresponding system, inherent in us as individuals, of special dispositions toward command in some, and toward obedience in others." People are much more disposed to obedience than we suppose, and there can be no doubt that individual dispositions are in harmony with the course of social development.

Comte's analysis of "social statics" was based on the assumption that society, government, and the individual are natural structures containing inherent and spontaneous attributes and functions. When he turned to "social dynamics," it is not surprising that his analysis of social causation was thin and indifferent. In one place he casually cited three chief causes of social variation: race, climate, and political action. In another, he referred to ennui and to population expansion as causal factors—making it clear, however, that sociological analysis can reach only secondary causes. Causation is primarily the spontaneous action of phenomena taking place from one end of the scale of being to the other. On a whole, he relied on instincts for his explanation of human behavior and the movement of history. Some of these instincts are expressed constantly and some are developed over time, but all, with a kind of teleological foresight, are in accord with the progress of humanity. In short, Comte's causal theory was vitiated from the start by his belief that all causal analysis, the search for first as well as for final causes, is characteristic of prescientific metaphysics, and by his inability to separate psychology and sociology. The latter failure is endemic to sociological positivism, especially to its naturalistic variant.

The Positive Society and the Absence of Power

Comte's depiction of the terminal stage of history has features similar to Saint-Simon's vision of the Positive society. The final society, said Comte, will have a division between spiritual and temporal authority. The spiritual or speculative power will have little to do with theology. It will be composed of sociologists, and its main function will be to provide the sociological truths that alone can ensure the mental and moral health of the race. A totally new class will emerge spontaneously to fulfill this function. The emphasis of society will no longer be on force, political measures, or rights, but on morality and duties. The positive spirit, Comte insisted, is "the only one which duly systematized, can at once generate universal moral convictions and permit the rise of a spiritual authority independent enough to regulate its social application."

As for the temporal authority, all distinctions between public and private functions will be abandoned. Such division is appropriate only to the heterogeneous stages of development prior to positivism. The new economy and society will be composed of homogeneous elements, and therefore every function will be social. The law of hierarchy, which subordinates the simple and particular to the general, will ensure the coordination of social elements just as it insures the coordination of the elements in the rest of nature. The spiritual or speculative class will be foremost in the social scale, and within this class the philosopher-scientist is above the artist. Below them come the practical or active classes with bankers first, followed by merchants, manufacturers, agriculturalists, and finally laborers. The social nature of all statuses does not mean that private or individual methods will be eliminated. On the contrary, education will enable the individual to cultivate private economic activities and interests as free as possible from governmental direction. Though Comte warned against allowing private wealth and inheritance to become a means to social ascendancy, he was sure that education and moral training would curb the pretensions of wealth and at the same time would silence the clamorings of the poor. The spiritual authority, acting through the dispensation of speculative truth, would homogenize the morals of the population and insure all individuals the social position to which their capacities entitled them. Despite the existence of inequality, the result would be justice because it is based on a truth freely assented to.[27]

The Religion of Humanity

Comte's doctrine received a finished and slightly different form in the second of his two major works.[28] Satisfied that the intellectual supremacy of positivism had been successfully asserted in his earlier work, Comte spent his "second career" tracing the moral and religious aspects of his philosophy. His later writings, therefore, emphasized feeling instead of intellect, the subjective instead of the objective, and moral and religious considerations instead of scientific and sociological considerations. All in all, Comte's concern with establishing a "sociocracy" and a "sociolatry" indicates a deep desire to provide sociology and thus society with the moral unity and vitality he felt it needed. If this could be done, the three aspects of human nature, intellect, energy (or action), and feeling, would be synthesized, and the way prepared for the replacement of revealed religion by demonstrated religion.[29]

Comte wrote four prolix and highly abstract volumes in pursuit of the above goals, elaborating on much of the material from his *Positive Philosophy*. His most notable addition to the theory was to specify the emotional and religious correlates of the various stages of progress. The intellect, it will be remembered, goes through Theological, Metaphysical, and Positive stages, and activity goes through three corresponding stages, Military (Conquest), Military (Defense), and Industrial. To these, Comte now added the most fundamental principle of all—feeling, the source of order and thus of progress. Expressed as a social instinct, feeling is "merely civic in Antiquity, collective in the Middle Ages, and universal in the Final State," and represents the affective evolution that corresponds to evolution in the realms of intellect and action.

In bringing his theory to a close, Comte again relied on instinct as the main category of explanation. It is innate human altruism that makes a scientific theory of morality possible. Two things form the basis of complete positivity: sociological prevision and benevolent instincts; the former demonstrates the existence of the latter. The evolution of humanity is now seen in terms of the gradual elimination of egoism and the triumph of altruism. Indeed, in the true synthesis humankind itself emerges from

---

[27] Ibid., pp. 763–784.
[28] *System of Positive Polity*, trans. J. H. Bridges *et al.*, 4 vols. (London: Longmans, Green, 1875–1877), originally published in 1851–1854. Hereafter cited as *Positive Polity*.
[29] *Positive Polity*, 1: xi–xiii; 325–326. So important was this new orientation that Comte added a seventh science, morals, to the apex of his hierarchy of the sciences (2:352).

the womb of history. The overall process has seen first the family emerge, then the state, and now humanity. Comte focused his philosophical and religious interests on this latter stage. Humanity—or the great being as it is also called—is defined rather vaguely as "the whole constituted by the beings, past, future, and present, which cooperate willingly in perfecting the order of the world." All the subprocesses of evolution contribute to the eventual and inevitable emergence of humanity. Once the great being is fully realized as the basis of education, politics, and religion, future generations and individuals will be spared the earlier stages of evolution. Comte devoted the remainder of the fourth volume to an incredibly detailed picture of the new religion of humanity, expressing satisfaction that, having turned science into philosophy in the first half of his career, he had now succeeded in turning philosophy into religion.

Comte's new orientation, and indeed the whole range of his thought, may be obtained from the first half of Volume One of the easily available translation of the *Positive Polity*.[30] This selection contains the main features of Comte's new emphasis: the elevation of emotion over intellect, the adoration of women as moral agents, the appeal to the masses to seek regeneration in positivism, the attempt to develop an aesthetic theory based on positivism, and the climactic emphasis on the religion of humanity. Apparent throughout is Comte's belief that society is a lawfully changing reality, the nature of which will be fully understood only with the development of sociology; and his related belief that humanity will emerge from its period of historical—or, rather, natural—gestation only when sociology, embodied not in a speculative class but in a priesthood, is managing the affairs of society. As Pareto astutely pointed out, Comte's own intellectual evolution is exactly the opposite of the evolution he claimed for humanity.[31]

CONCLUSION

Although they assigned different names and dates to their three stages of progress, Saint-Simon and Comte presented philosophies of history that were almost identical. While Comte deserves little credit for originality—or, for that matter, for gratitude— [32] his achievement lies in having system-

[30] *A General View of Positivism*, trans. J. H. Bridges (New York: Robert Speller, 1957); other editions are available. This work was written and published separately in 1848 and then revised to become the general introduction to the *Positive Polity*.

[31] Vilfredo Pareto, *Mind and Society*, trans. A. Bongiorno and A. Livingston, 4 vols. (New York: Harcourt, Brace, 1935), 3: para. 1537.

[32] In naming his predecessors in the development of sociology, Comte makes no mention of Saint-Simon. Forced finally to face the question of his relationship to Saint-Simon, Comte (in the preface of Volume Three of the *Positive Polity*) denied that he had benefited from his association with Saint-Simon, dismissing him contemptuously as a "depraved charlatan."

atized the inchoate dream of a science of society, and in giving it a form
that insured its currency and standing in Western intellectual life.

Comte and Liberalism

Like Saint-Simon's, Comte's liberalism is difficult to discern at first because
he too seems to have violated the cardinal principle of liberal thought—
the spiritual autonomy of the individual. Also like Saint-Simon, Comte
could not bring himself to see individuals as basic social units; however, he
believed strongly that there were natural individuals with natural talents
and inequalities, and that the positive society would reveal who they
were. In addition, Comte had a fundamental belief that the destiny of
human beings was to effect a rational mastery of historical existence; this
stamps him as a liberal within the deepest and widest meaning of that
term. Despite Comte's fondness for the unity of medieval society, his
version of the organic society was not based on the dogmas of supernatural religion, the distinctions of birth, or the efficacy and wisdom of
tradition. Although he immersed the individual in the great being, humanity—and its social counterpart, the Positive society—his golden age was not
based on the socialization of either property or occupation. The Positive
society, on the contrary, allowed a wide scope for the expression of individual talent and action.

Like Saint-Simon, Comte constructed a theory of society that went beyond
the assumptions of feudalism and absolutism, and he worked to bring into
being a new civilization based on science and industry. In this sense, his
thought was radical and progressive. At the same time, however, it was
also deeply conservative. Comte's terminal stage of social evolution was
an organic, hierarchic society derived from the intrinsic inequality of
individuals. Thus for all its emphasis on science, industry, and evolution,
Comte's theory of society was simply another variant of the basic model
of Western social thought, the preindustrial model of hierarchy, authority,
and unity through homogeneity of belief and emotion.

Comte's theory was conservative on yet another level. The empirical methodology that he advocated (but did not practice) and the concept of
teleological causation (which he denounced but practiced extensively)
were both conservative—the former by framing the methods and subject
matter of science as a search for the invariable uniformities in social phenomena, the latter by conceiving phenomena in terms of the fulfillment of
pre-existing structures and functions. In an important and sophisticated
analysis from a Hegelian-Marxian perspective, Herbert Marcuse has argued
that positivism braked historical development by identifying reason with
the given and by defining society as a natural process—in effect denying
the existence of an autonomous reason capable of judging and criticizing

the empirically given.[33] Marcuse's analysis, however, tends to associate social dynamism with rationalism and conservatism with empiricism; this point of view causes him to overlook the fact that Comte is a teleological rationalist. In other words, belief in a transcendent reason does not always have dynamic consequences. Furthermore, the dynamic natural-law rationalism of the Enlightenment, which Marcuse cited approvingly, became the main source of liberal conservatism in the nineteenth century. In short, it is not always possible to associate "reason" with "revolution."

Marcuse's specific argument that sociological positivism—especially in its definition of society as a natural process—is associated with liberalism and social-system conservatism is well taken. However, sociological empiricism (positivism) is a variant of Western rationalism (idealism). Its ideological function has varied with time and place; it has had dynamic or conservative consequences depending on the historical and national context in which it has emerged and on whether it has become a naturalistic or a socio-cultural positivism. In this case, Marcuse tends to overemphasize Comte's interest in stability, dismissing the evolutionary emphasis in his work as mere propaganda for a middle class already solidly entrenched. There is some question, however, whether the French middle class was really entrenched during Comte's lifetime. The French middle class was under the pressures of right and left throughout the nineteenth century and indeed well into the twentieth century. Thus, while Comte's theory sought to neutralize the proletariat, it also sought to discredit the counterrevolutionary forces of monarchy and aristocracy by strongly emphasizing that science, industry, and merit were the emergents of a logically demonstrated, irrepressible process of social evolution.

Comte's thought, along with the rest of French naturalistic positivism, was part of the transformation of agrarian society that was placing science and industry uppermost in the West's scale of values. To this end, Comte constructed a society that had a stability based on homogeneity and a dynamism based on extensive functional specialization. Like his predecessors in naturalistic positivism, Comte performed two ideological services for a nascent capitalism: he justified the destruction of a feudal society based on birth and tradition, and he sought legitimacy for a new form of social inequality based on private performance and private property.

The affinity of Comte's thought with liberalism can be seen in still another way. To offset the divisive effects of individual specialization, he relied

---

[33] Herbert Marcuse, *Reason and Revolution* (New York: Humanities Press, 1954), pt. 2, chap. 2; available in paperback.

heavily on a social model that assumed the existence of a natural equilibrium—an intellectual device that is suspiciously similar to the belief in natural harmony that is so widespread in liberal economic and social thought. It is true that despite his belief in society's natural equilibrium, Comte still saw the need for positive social control. One can almost think of Comte as part of late liberalism. This tendency in late-nineteenth-century liberal thought sought to promote social integration through state action without rejecting private property, the market economy, and the idea of a natural harmony; it also tried to reconcile the idea of the autonomy and creativity of the individual with the growing realization that individualism is as much a derivative of a dynamic society as its source.

Comte and the Liberal Dilemma

In providing a solution to the liberal dilemma, Comte's thought is no more satisfactory than that of his two predecessors in naturalistic positivism, Condorcet and Saint-Simon. He was nonetheless aware of the problem; he recognized, for example, that Condorcet had failed to explain the emergence of novelty in human affairs. In Condorcet's theory, Comte argued,

> . . . the human race is represented as having attained a vast degree of perfection at the close of the eighteenth century, while the author attributes an entirely retrogressive influence to almost every doctrine, institution, and preponderant power throughout the whole past. Whereas, the total progress accomplished can be nothing else than the result of the various kinds of partial progress realized since the beginning of civilization, in virtue of the gradual onward course of human nature. Such a state of things as Condorcet describes would be nothing else than a perpetual miracle.[34]

Comte's solution to the problem of novelty was to assert that it is inherent in the nature of things. The principle that sums up the emergence of the new from the old, that gives unity to diversity and stability to change, is the grand law of three stages. However, neither Comte's idea of progress nor his explanation of progress marked any advance over the thought of his predecessors. The crux of Comte's theory is still that the mind has advanced through progressive stages of enlightenment and that the main epochs of advance form a rational law. In short, he never got beyond the point reached by Saint-Simon in the latter's attempt to improve on Condorcet's theory of historical progress. We are again confronted with an assertion, not an explanation. All the sciences, we are told, are united, but

[34] *Positive Philosophy*, p. 445.

not because they are essentially the same either in principle or in the elements out of which they are composed. They are united by a hierarchical relationship based on the complexity of subject matter, the simplest at the bottom and most complex at the top. There is no evolution in the subject matter of either physical or human nature, but somehow evolution does take place in the behavior of mind. Starting with the simplest science, the human mind conquers each field of knowledge, arriving at last at a Positive stage in all fields.

Comte's theory was still an attempt to read lawful significance into the achievements of modern science and into the impact of those achievements on European society. He approached this task not by using positive, empirical research into the past nor by constructing generalizations about the data collected, but by relying almost exclusively on logical discourse. It is true that Comte's knowledge of history was exceptionally good—much better than that of any of his predecessors in social science. In his day he probably had few peers as a historian. However, the center of gravity of his work was logic, not fact. One of the most striking qualities about his work is its abstractness. His reconciliation of order and progress and of consensus and dispersion (to use his terms for the problem of unity and diversity), was at bottom a logical integration. He was certain that the unity of logic was a guarantee of empirical unity. It is understandable that in Comte's day social change was seen as a threat to social order, casting up diversities that threatened stability and integration. Comte's characteristic answer to this problem was that society was intrinsically equipped to supply all its own needs. Questions concerning the dualism of order and progress and of unity and diversity are, of course, aspects of the liberal dilemma. The problem for social thought from the eighteenth century on was to explain the genesis of science and the implications for social existence of a widespread application of the new skills and values of science. In many ways, the problem of understanding the impact of industrialization on society is a connecting link between the work of the main body of sociological theorists from Saint-Simon on. The problem figures heavily in the work of such central figures as Spencer, Sumner, Durkheim, Simmel, Pareto, and Max Weber, and most of these theorists sought to provide a metaphysical answer to the problem within the framework of liberalism. Comte also advanced a metaphysical theory—a theory based on the logically induced faith that society is a self-sufficient reality, the features of which are discovered through science and are realized in practice in accordance with the lawful progress of the mind.

There are obvious dangers in Comte's predilection for deductive discourse. The shapeless elasticity of logic never left him at a loss for arguments. It allowed him to use instincts and teleology as explanations, to refer whenever necessary to a self-sufficient reality lurking behind the deceptions of empirical knowledge. Phenomena, in short, are subject to a hidden logic that insures the rationality of the world. Though Comte did not place as much emphasis on the rationality of conflict as did Saint-Simon, he too indulged in this sort of reasoning and tried to explain the progressive character of destruction and decay.[35] Finally, Comte's rationalistic approach permitted him to gloss over and digest any awkward fact or occurrence, as when he suddenly discovered that the Positive stage might have to go through a preliminary phase under the benevolent dictatorship of Louis Napoleon. An empirically minded theorist might have been more disposed to see the seemingly indelible cleavages wrought by the political and industrial revolutions as serious intellectual problems. A theorist committed to science could hardly place reliance on the spontaneous powers of history or on the imperatives derived from philosophical analysis, as Comte was wont to do.

Therefore, despite Comte's repeated emphasis on evolution, his explanation of change is extremely misleading. Far from being a new theory, his general position is a curious mixture of post-Renaissance, pre-Darwinian science with the thought of ancient Greece. Using Comte's own definitions, his thought more properly belongs to the metaphysical rather than the Positive stage of mind. Interestingly enough, his rationalism was not inadvertent; he consistently stated his preference for the theoretical, speculative approach to knowledge and invariably used the word *empirical* as a term of derogation. In short, the controlling disposition of his mind is identical with the major presupposition of Western thought derived from the Greeks—namely that the logical structure of mind must be the key to the structure of reality. Comte's tendency to see mind as a force whose purpose is to search out the structure of phenomena connects him with the Enlightenment, but his consistent recourse to teleological explanations is a throwback to Greek and scholastic thought. Indeed, his work amounts to a refutation of naturalistic positivism, for if the main assumption of this revolutionary perspective is that one can study the mind in the same way that one studies nature—either as a part of the rest of nature or as a unique biopsychic structure—then Comte's commitment to this position is largely verbal. On the contrary, his thought is actually retrogressive when compared with that of Saint-Simon—far from studying mind as part of nature, it is nature that is to be studied in terms of the operation of the mind. If positivism has a tendency to absorb the mind into nature, Comte's thought maintains a strict separation between them, a separation in accord with the Cartesian dualism of mind and matter and with the Enlightenment's separation of theory and fact. In short, for all Comte's brave talk about positivism, he stands squarely in the tradition of deductive, teleological idealism.

[35] Ibid., p. 637f.

The End of Pseudoevolutionary Positivism

Considered carefully, especially in the context of Lovejoy's discussion of the history of the concept of the great chain of being, Comte's theory of reality was fundamentally static, amounting in his day to a monumental anachronism. Before and during Comte's lifetime, a host of geologists and biologists had, in Lovejoy's words, "temporalized the great chain of being" and laid down the foundations for a genuine theory of evolution. All this, however, was beyond the purview of Comte. For him, there was no qualitative change in either physical or social nature, both of which he saw as connected parts of a finished external reality. Only the mind, by the unexplained substantive process of the law of three stages, undergoes change. This process, which unites humankind's multifarious experience into a rational unity, slowly reveals the unchanging reality of physical and human nature.

Not only was Comte's thought no advance over the eighteenth century, but his depiction of the nature of reality was actually retrogressive. Inspired by the findings of pre-evolutionary biology, Comte pictured nature as a stable, self-sufficient organism, a great chain of being whose main features accord with the logically derived principles of plenitude, continuity, and gradation.[36] Comte's view of nature as a moving but nonevolving organism, animated and directed by rational tendencies, is very similar to the Greek view of nature. Unable to escape from the liberal dilemma by using the mechanistic cosmology of the post-Renaissance world, and not yet familiar with the evolutionary cosmology of the nineteenth century, Comte in large part reverted to the cosmology of Greece in which nature is viewed as a vital, rational organism. As such, Comte is closer to Plato than he is to his chief rival in the field of evolutionary monism, Herbert Spencer— the thinker who brought a genuine evolutionary view into sociological theory.

Our characterization of Comte's thought as an attempt to construct a monistic naturalistic positivism is justified on two grounds: he used one method —logic—for the study of human behavior; and he tried to establish a unitary view of human behavior as a natural process—a view that in the final analysis rested on the assumption that human nature contains innate psychic propensities that gradually manifest themselves as scientific progress. He hedged his monism somewhat by saying that a single constitutive principle might never be found, but the major thrust of his theory was to reject multiplicity, contingency, and change—in short, to reject Pascal's argument that science can produce only limited knowledge.

Comte's claim that knowledge is based on the observation of the invariable laws of phenomena and his emphasis on functional relations are important

[36] See for example, his statements in *Positive Philosophy*, pp. 515f., 775. 827.

for understanding the development of sociology. Comte's thought contains, in other words, the two concepts that have figured so largely in the history of sociology and modern science, the concepts of structure and function. However, though he often viewed a phenomenon in functional terms— that is, not as a thing in itself but as it relates to something else and to the ends served—his emphasis was on structure—that is, on the intrinsic attributes and relations of things. Comte's dynamic approach, or functional approach as he also called it, was therefore always subordinate to statics. In the few places where this aspect of his thought surfaces, he argued that human nature must be studied by relating function to organ and by seeing functions solely in terms of acts and not as intrinsic objects; that the affections are stronger than the intellect and that human beings are prompted to action by a multitude of interior impulses; and that these impulses must be interpreted in terms of a mechanical equilibrium.[37] As we shall see later, it was Pareto who fully developed the inherently static nature of Comte's thought. Pareto, who knew Comte's work, also defined sociology as a functional search for the invariable laws of phenomena. However, in rejecting the idea of evolution, he revealed the intrinsically static nature of such an assumption.

An alternative to Comte's static methodology and substantive theory had to wait for the appearance of a genuine evolutionary view. The alternative took a number of variations, some within naturalistic positivism and some within sociocultural positivism. Speaking generally, however, the alternative to structural substantialism came from thinkers who tried to transform structure into function. In Collingwood's terms:

> If nature is a machine, the various motions of its parts will be motions of things which have structural properties of their own independent of these motions and serving as their indispensable prerequisites. To sum this up: in a machine, and therefore in nature if nature is mechanical, structure and function are distinct, and function presupposes structure.
>
> In the world of human affairs as known to the historian there is no such distinction and *a fortiori* no such priority. Structure is resolvable into function. There is no harm in historians talking about the structure of feudal society or of capitalist industry or of the Greek city state, but the reason why there is no harm in it is because they know that these so-called structures are really complexes of function, kinds of ways in which human beings behave; and that when we say that, for example, the British constitution exists, what we mean is that certain people are behaving in a certain kind of way.
>
> On an evolutionary view of nature a logically constructed

[37] Ibid., pp. 383–385, 819–821.

natural science will follow the example of history and resolve the structures with which it is concerned into function. Nature will be understood as consisting of processes, and the existence of any special kind of thing in nature will be understood as meaning that processes of a special kind are going on there.[38]

As we have seen, human beings' view of nature is heavily influenced by analogies from their own experience. The Greeks, the first to think of themselves as intelligent organisms, attributed to nature the characteristics that they found in themselves; the people of the post-Renaissance period, great builders of machines, came eventually to think of nature as a machine; and in the eighteenth and nineteenth centuries when Westerners began to experience qualitative social change, they began to think of nature in evolutionary terms.

The process is reciprocal, however; individuals attribute their own behavior to nature, but they also attribute nature's behavior to themselves. Comte's work may be thought of as culminating the first phase in the development of sociology. His thought marks not only the establishment of sociological positivism but also the consolidation of a two-hundred-year revolution in the West's image of itself. Roughly between the time of Hobbes and the emergence of French naturalistic positivism, European intellectuals reorganized their concept of human nature to bring it into line with Newton's synthesis in physics and with the prospect of a continuous extension of human knowledge and mastery over nature. Stimulated by this scientific progress and by the rapid qualitative social change of his time, Comte, like Condorcet and Saint-Simon, gave his thought an evolutionary flavor. Impressed by the progress of knowledge about nature, Comte, like his predecessors, sought to reduce that progress to a determinate pattern. Satisfied that this could be done, he tried to bring social phenomena within the jurisdiction of science and account for its structure in terms of the sequence of scientific progress. However, Comte's picture of nature as a static, hierarchic entity prevented him from actually immersing the world of human nature in nature. The evolving mind, which does not itself change but somehow makes sequential discoveries about the laws that govern a static world of physical and social phenomena, remained a miracle. In the end Comte was still pinned to the horns of the liberal dilemma.

The movement toward a genuine evolutionary view of society was accomplished by Herbert Spencer. By the nineteenth century the historical consciousness of Westerners was deep enough to see the emergence of a genuine evolutionary view in both the social and the natural sciences. In

---

[38] R. G. Collingwood, *The Idea of Nature* (New York: Oxford University Press paperback, 1960), p. 16f.

Spencer's thought human nature was deeply implicated in a cosmic process of lawful change; this view equated human nature and nature and
sought to explain them by a comprehensive theory of cosmic evolution
applicable to both. Spencer's theory, in other words, was a genuine theory
of evolution, as opposed to the static positivism of Condorcet, Saint-Simon,
and Comte. Working within the tradition of monistic naturalistic positivism,
Spencer pioneered in the transformation of structure into function—a transformation that was to have momentous implications when completed by
the sociocultural positivists. Indeed, the general climate of opinion called
functionalism was to blossom into a full-fledged cosmology absorbing the
attention of scientists in all fields. In social theory it not only came to
dominate all branches of sociological theory, but in its Hegelian-Marxian
form it also became a strong rival to liberalism.

The General Current of French Positivism

One of the most significant features in French sociology from Montesquieu
to Saint-Simon and Comte and on to Durkheim is its emphasis on the reality
of social structure. French sociologists and French social theorists in general, whether naturalistic or sociocultural, stressed the reality of society.
The main reason for their orientation was the chronically unsettled state of
French society from the Wars of Religion in the sixteenth century through
the post-1945 period.

The development of sociology in general was deeply influenced by the
national contexts in which it arose—as the case of France well illustrates.
Sociologists strongly reflected their national experiences in their theories,
and thus there arose a distinctive difference in theoretical orientation among
the various Western nations. One of the most useful categorizations in this
regard is the distinction between Anglo-American theorists, who were
much more individualistic and tended to take their respective societies for
granted, and Continental theorists, who generally stressed the reality of
society as a force, as a problem, or as an unrealized potential.

Of considerable interest in assessing the influence of social forces on French
positivism are the unique traditions of French romanticism and French
conservatism. While it is true that romanticism in general was a revolt
against rationalism and science, there is an interesting affinity between
empirical science (or positivism) and the romantic outlook. Considered in
general, positivism and romanticism shared a dislike of the abstract and a
concern for the concrete. Revolting against the teleological view of nature,
post-Renaissance science opened up the intellectual horizon of the West
by narrowing its outlook—by forcing Western thinking to disregard the
many faces of nature and to focus abstractly on a narrow slice of it called
physics. Thus, the astounding victory of the human mind that culminated

in Newton's synthesis was purchased at the expense of scientific breadth as well as depth. The rise of empirical science during the eighteenth century should be understood, therefore, as a revolt against the equation of science with physics as well as a revolt against the methodology of deduction. The equation of science with physics was considered not so much wrong as restrictive. By sharing the concern of empirical science for the uniqueness and diversity of nature, the romantic current, whether in art, literature, philosophy, or religion, helped to prepare the way for the triumphal march of nineteenth-century empirical science. Sociologically speaking, positivism and romanticism were both products of the revolutionary new social experience that Western peoples had undergone. This experience, composed of movement, novelty, conflict, and contradiction, made it increasingly difficult to think and feel in terms of the classical ideals of measure and balance, symmetry and form.

Some of the ideas in the general current of European romanticism were highly influential in molding the practice and theory of both politics and society. Lovejoy identified three basic ideas in late-eighteenth-century romanticism: holism or organicism, in which the individual is considered to be a meaningful entity only as part of a whole; voluntarism, in which a dynamic process of endless striving or struggle is considered to be natural and good in nature, art, and morals; and diversitarianism, in which diversity of taste, character, and even cultures is also considered natural and good.[39] These romantic ideas, which Lovejoy identified in order to suggest some of the historical roots of German totalitarianism, took on a unique flavor in France.[40] Of all the romanticisms,[41] French romanticism was the most progressive. After a brief association with reaction during the Empire and Restoration, it pledged itself to the ideals of the French Revolution and leveled a devastating critique against a social order that it considered unjust and degrading. Of special interest is the influence of the romantic outlook on the development of French sociological positivism. As we saw in the work of Saint-Simon and Comte, the idea of the whole, combined with the idea of growth and development, led to the view that the individual can be understood only within the context of society, and, in turn, that society

---

[39] Arthur O. Lovejoy, "The Meaning of Romanticism for the Historian of Ideas," *Journal of the History of Ideas* 2 (June 1941):257–278.

[40] For a valuable essay on romanticism in French literature and social theory during the second quarter of the nineteenth century, see David Owen Evans, *Social Romanticism in France, 1830–1848* (New York: Oxford University Press, 1951). Evans points up the reformist and even revolutionary character of French romanticism and describes the mutual influence that existed among such major figures as Saint-Simon, Fourier, Leroux, Proudhon, Hugo, Balzac, and Lamartine. His explicit distinction between German and French romanticism may be found on pages 97–99.

[41] For a valuable corrective to the error of thinking of romanticism as a unitary movement, see Arthur O. Lovejoy, "On the Discrimination of Romanticisms," *Essays in the History of Ideas* (Baltimore: Johns Hopkins Press, 1948), chap. 12.

can be understood only in terms of its location within the total process of history.

The romantic idea that something is to be known by its relationship to something else is similar to the method of science, and thus far from inimical to the positivist spirit. Romanticism is not so irrational as is sometimes supposed, or—stated better perhaps—science is more irrational than is often supposed. In any case, the romantic urge to think in terms of the relationships within a whole helped to shape French social science into an organic positivism.

As a product of the same forces that produced romanticism, Comte framed his science of society in ways that, at least to some extent, represented a revolt against the tradition of rationalism. His historical approach to social phenomena was akin to the romantic spirit in art and literature; he sought the significance of change and diversity for social science. Finally, of course, his attempt in his later years to give social existence an emotional and religious basis bears a fundamental kinship with the romantic outlook.

These features of Comte's (and Saint-Simon's) thought—the concern for finding unitary but hierarchic configurations within natural and social phenomena, the definition of society as consensus, and the concern for social integration (an integration that Comte in his later years hoped to achieve more through deliberate action than through the spontaneous action of organic forces)—had other sources besides romanticism. They were occasioned in no small way by Comte's awareness of the legacy of cleavage and conflict that the Revolution had bequeathed French society. His search for an alternative to the atomistic and universalistic rationalism of the seventeenth and eighteenth centuries, to which he attributed the loss of social unity, brought his thought in line not only with romanticism but also with conservatism (counterrevolutionary traditionalism). Like Saint-Simon, he looked with favor on the organic concept of society propounded by the traditionalists, although in his case he favored Maistre (1753–1821) rather than Bonald.

The influence of conservatism—and of the French Revolution—on Comte and sociology has been noted by Robert Nisbet.[42] Unfortunately, Nisbet's analysis is badly skewed and an unreliable interpretation of the formation of sociology. In his first article, his thesis is that sociology developed in "profound deviation" from most of the ideas of the Enlightenment, and that in response to the French Revolution it developed an acute concern with the group, with the role played by values (along with groups) in

[42] See his well-known articles, "The French Revolution and the Rise of Sociology." *American Journal of Sociology* 49 (September 1943):156–164; and "Conservatism and Sociology," *American Journal of Sociology* 58 (September 1952): 167–175.

maintaining social order, and with social and personal disorganization. Nisbet is more careful in his second article, where he points out that the role played by primary groups and values in establishing order was not recognized until later. Here he cites the conservative (counterrevolutionary) reaction to the French Revolution and modernity as a major reason for the later recognition and claims that its ideas of "status, cohesion, adjustment, function, norm, ritual, symbol" were given scientific standing first by Comte, then by Le Play, and finally by Durkheim. Three things must be said against Nisbet's general argument—aside from the fact that of the three men that Nisbet cites, Burke, Bonald and Hegel, the latter is a liberal and should not be categorized as a conservative or traditionalist. First, the psychological naturalism of Condorcet, Saint-Simon, and Comte has very little in common with the conservative idea of a network of social control made up of groups and customary norms. It is revealing that Nisbet bases the bulk of his argument on Comte's least scientific work, the *Positive Polity*, in which Comte simply creates the groups and norms he deems necessary to the Positive society and adds them to his theory. Second, most of the ideas of traditionalism are the staples of logical and social thought from the time of the Greeks on. Third, Nisbet fails to point out that while Comte and French sociologists shared conservatism's concern with social order—even to the extent of using conservative ideas—they nevertheless sought to establish society on radically new grounds. Unlike conservative thinkers, they wanted social order *plus* science, industry, and the allocation of social position according to economic and professional performance. And far from merely climaxing the absorption of conservatism's ideas into sociology, as Nisbet claims, Durkheim, whose thought is a high point of French positivism and will be analyzed in Chapter 14, showed that social integration could be achieved *either* by the homogeneous, hierarchic type admired by the conservatives *or* by the heterogeneous, industrial type admired by the middle class, and he clearly indicated his preference for the latter. Incidentally, Durkheim does not stand in the conservative tradition, as Nisbet claims, because he believed that behavior is social. So did Aristotle, Rousseau, and Marx, for example, all of whom have little in common with conservatism. Finally, Durkheim's view of history did not, as Nisbet claims, place "stress upon the disorganizational and alienative aspects of modern European development and upon the creation of the masses, lying inert before an increasingly omnipotent state." Durkheim was quite complacent about the viability of industrial (Organic) society, and *anomie* (or alienation) was a decidedly secondary theme in his work.[43]

---

[43] Nisbet has expanded the themes of these articles in his *The Sociological Tradition* (New York: Basic Books, 1966), a book badly marred by the author's curiously unsociological manner of wrenching thoughts from the context of a theorist's work and finding parallels with the similarly disembodied ideas of other theorists. Basically, Nisbet fails to understand that the ideas of conservatives, liberals, and radicals are anchored in different social systems and that while they share much, they are also distinctly—evenly violently—opposed.

In any event there is little doubt that the development of sociological positivism in France was influenced by the particularities of French historical
and social development. In searching for conceptual supports to counteract
the cleavages of the French Revolution, Comte, like Saint-Simon, accepted
ideas from conservatism/traditionalism, especially the idea of a homogeneous hierarchic society standing prior to the individual. Indeed, one of
the distinctive features of French sociological theory as a whole, from
Montesquieu through Durkheim, is its tendency to regard society as an
entity apart from individuals and groups; the main source of this tendency
is the preoccupation with the problem of social stability and integration.
To a large extent, this feature of French sociology—which separates it
sharply from the more atomistic positivism of Anglo-American sociology—
is explicable in terms of the unresolved conflicts that plagued the French
social system from the sixteenth century onward. These conflicts found
expression in French rationalism and romanticism as well as in French
naturalistic positivism. Ultimately, however, and despite similarities with
other social theories, whether conservative or socialist, French sociology
as a whole has been most closely identified with the ideological needs of
French capitalism.

Chapter 8
Science and the Problem of a Social Science

The dilemma of liberal rationality emerged when the middle class tried to derive a theory of natural law from its own experience. From Saint Thomas through Hooker (1553(?)–1600) to Locke, natural law was gradually secularized and individualized, finally becoming a belief in the spiritual independence and self-sufficiency of the individual mind. Applied at first mostly to political institutions, liberal natural law eventually became a full-blooded social theory; as such, it was centered on the belief that the individual, freed from the limitations of received opinion, could fathom the deepest reaches of nature and extract the normative standards by which to construct and enjoy a natural society. The climax of this development came in the late eighteenth century with the emergence of an economic theory based on natural law. In a momentous intellectual transformation, the Physiocrats in France and Adam Smith (1723–1790) in England placed economics outside the reach of traditional political, moral, and religious values by declaring it natural. The natural economic order was also said by some to contain a hidden logic that reconciled the self-interest of the individual with that of society—a proposal that can be seen as an attempt to solve the liberal dilemma.

THE METAPHYSICS OF LIBERALISM

The full development of early bourgeois social theory came with the idea of progress, an idea that allowed the middle class to reject the past and lay claim to the future. The emphasis on progress did not imply an open-ended attitude toward the future, however; it meant a sloughing off of the past in order to reach a period of naturalness—a period when social-system change would end and human beings could enjoy the fruits of their mastery over nature. It was futurism in the service of an emerging capitalist present. All in all, it was a strange mixture.

Liberalism wanted progress, but a progress sanctioned by nature; it wanted change, but not uncertainty; it wanted the past to be abolished, but the future to be familiar. It reveled in the new-found powers of human nature, but explained them in nonhuman terms. It accomplished a philosophical revolution by appealing to experience, only to reject experience as a self-sufficient basis for philosophical discourse. Finally, when liberalism took the form of sociology, it boldly proclaimed that human nature was amenable to scientific inquiry—only to read into human nature the needs of an expanding industrial society.

Either explicitly or implicitly the founders of sociology struggled to formulate a new way of looking at human nature and behavior that would be scientific and liberal and yet not succumb to the liberal dilemma. Save for Condorcet, they avoided natural rights—such a view was incompatible, for example, with Vico's deep-rooted historicism, with Montesquieu's skeptical relativism, and with the "evolutionary," organic positivism of Saint-Simon and Comte. All these theorists sought to find causation in human affairs, though only Vico and Montesquieu made lasting contributions in this respect. All expressed a sense of the relativity of behavior and belief, and tried to interpret social phenomena in terms of their social or historical functions; here also, Vico and Montesquieu were the most successful. Methodologically speaking, all of them saw difficulties in logic as a method, and all tried to come to grips with the concrete data of behavior. Of the five, Vico and Montesquieu were again the most successful. Finally, all sought to explain human behavior scientifically, although Vico clearly separated human from physical nature—followed in lesser degree by Montesquieu, Condorcet, and Comte. Only Saint-Simon made an explicit attempt to identify human nature and nature, though even he shrank from a full commitment to this position.

In any case, what had begun as a deductive social science in the seventeenth century emerged in the thought of Saint-Simon and Comte as an empirical social science—or, better still, as a plea for empiricism. Ultimately, their "evolutionary" monism was just as deductive and metaphysical as Hobbes's mechanistic monism. As an ideology, their new social science was admirably suited to the needs of liberalism, but as a solution to the liberal dilemma, it was a failure. It solved the dilemma only by making unverifiable assertions and a wide use of overt and hidden logic. Although Saint-Simon and Comte dismissed natural law as a prescientific relic, their theory smacks of the same rationalist conceit. Oddly enough, despite their emphasis on evolution, their theory of reality was basically static and closer to the view of the past than to that of their own century. In the end their theory was an unproved assertion that though human nature is constant, the human mind undergoes evolution and thereby gains an ever-greater knowledge about the static hierarchy of being.

In truth, no solution to the liberal dilemma emerged during the formative period of sociology. Condorcet shared many of the shortcomings of Saint-Simon and Comte; Vico relied on Providence to unify the phenomena of history; and even Montesquieu, despite his insight into the difficulty of unifying social phenomena and despite his functionalism and causal insight, was able to escape the rationalist assumptions of his age only by resorting to skepticism—that is, only by accepting the rationalist definition of truth. In short, the originators of sociology were metaphysicians who either could not go beyond the need for certainty or who substituted a new metaphysical theory for the metaphysics of natural law. While they developed some penetrating and permanent insights into the nature of society and social science, they did so within the confines of an obsolescing cosmology. Before I assess the work of their successors, it will be useful to develop more fully the problems implicit in a science of human behavior and to outline the various positions that can be taken in regard to the nature of such a science.

HUME AND THE DEFINITION OF SCIENCE

Hume's Theory of Knowledge

David Hume's philosophy rested on the fundamental assumption that all knowledge stems from experience.[1] His place in the history of philosophy stems from his thoroughgoing and consistent application of this assumption to the main branches of philosophy. Historically, his work climaxed the empiricism of Locke and is central to the definition of science. Indeed, Hume's definition of the two types of moral philosophy in Section I of the *Enquiry Concerning Human Understanding* corresponds roughly to the two definitions of science employed in this study. The first type of moral philosophy, said Hume, treats people as active beings and defines philosophy as a way to help them satisfy their feelings and values. The second type is concerned with finding the original principles that are the foundation of truth, goodness, and beauty. Hume did not hide his belief that the first type of moral philosophy most adequately defines the "proper province of human reason," and his supporting argument is simple and consistent. The perceptions of the mind are divided into "ideas" and "impressions." However, the former are merely copies of the latter; therefore, the traditional separation between reason and experience is without foundation. The objects of human reason fall under two headings: relations of ideas and matters of

---

[1] Hume's first work, *A Treatise on Human Nature: Being an Attempt to Introduce the Experimental Method into Moral Subjects,* Everyman Library, 2 vols. (New York: E. P. Dutton, 1911), appeared in 1739–1740. It failed to excite general attention, which prompted Hume to recast his ideas into more readable forms. Book I of the *Treatise* became the *Enquiry Concerning Human Understanding* (1748) and Book III became the *Enquiry Concerning the Principles of Morals* (1751)—both reprinted as Hume's *Enquiries,* ed. L. A. Selby-Bigge, 2nd ed. (Oxford, 1902). Selections from Hume's writings are available in Henry D. Aiken, ed., *Hume's Moral and Political Philosophy* (New York: Hafner Publishing Company paperback, 1948).

fact. The former is the domain of logic and consists of propositions that do not depend for their validity on the existential world. Matters of fact, however, are established in a different manner from logical propositions, because the contrary to every fact is conceivable and implies no logical contradiction. The evidence for a fact is always another fact, and this means that all reasonings about facts are based on cause-and-effect relationships.

Cause-and-effect relations are the "constant conjoining" of facts to give the impression that one causes the other. Therefore, custom or habit, not reason, is the source of human knowledge of cause-and-effect relations. The probability of an event taking place may vary from the uniform and constant to the irregular and uncertain, but knowledge of it is based on the necessity of probability, not on logic.

Hume's epistemology climaxed the nominalist tradition that dates from William of Occam. Hume completed this tradition by insisting that the traditional schools of philosophy had made excessive claims for the power of reason. Strictly speaking, he argued, the meaning of reason should be restricted to the logic of mathematics. It is a dangerous extravagance to claim that reason can penetrate the existential world and reveal its structural principles. The empirical realm exhibits no rational or logical necessity, and knowledge of it is limited to the rates of "customary conjunction" or probability—or, as one would say today, correlation. In other words, there is a strict and unbridgeable separation between knowledge based on reason or logic and knowledge based on fact.

Reason and Morality

Until Hume, it had been a basic assumption of Western thought that reason could establish rational measures of right and wrong and a moral scale of good and bad. Socrates's formula "knowledge is virtue" is the most famous example of this assumption. Over time this rational assumption became a hardened axiom of Western culture, though the various schools of rationalism disputed what could be derived from it. For the Stoics, for example, the unity of reason and morality emerged as a theory of natural law. They believed that reason, the common possession of all individuals, could provide humanity with a hierarchy of values and precise standards of conduct. The theory of natural law became an integral part of Christian (Roman Catholic) philosophy after the Thomistic synthesis of the thirteenth century. From Saint Thomas on, the theory lost none of its vigor, though it was gradually secularized and individualized. This transformation reached its climax in Locke's theory of natural rights, in which rights came to the individual by nature and existed, therefore, independent of ecclesiastical or social sanction. The full development of this concept of natural law came in the eighteenth century when the French Enlightenment developed it into a complete theory of human nature, morals, and society.

However, Hume's definition of reason demolished the entire structure of natural law and all moral philosophy based on it. His discussion of the relation between reason and morality and his denial of any intrinsic connection between them is most forcefully presented in the *Treatise on Human Nature*. Hume's argument is direct and to the point. Neither form of reasoning, the demonstrative (deductive) nor the probable (inductive), influences our actions. Strictly speaking, only a passion or impulse can affect another passion or impulse—and thus our will.

> Reason is the discovery of truth or falsehood. Truth or falsehood consists in an agreement or disagreement either to the *real* relations of ideas, or to *real* existence and matter of fact. Whatever, therefore, is not susceptible of this agreement or disagreement is incapable of being true or false, and can never be an object of our reason. Now, it is evident our passions, volitions, and actions, are not susceptible of any such agreement or disagreement; being original facts and realities, complete in themselves, and implying no reference to other passions, volitions, and actions. It is impossible, therefore, they can be pronounced either true or false, and can be either contrary or conformable to reason.[2]

Not only does morality lie outside the domain of demonstrative reasoning, but it is also separate from probable or empirical reasoning:

> Take any action allowed to be vicious—wilful murder, for instance. Examine it in all lights, and see if you can find that matter of fact or real existence which you call *vice*. In whichever way you take it, you find only certain passions, motives, volitions, and thoughts. There is no other matter of fact in the case. The vice entirely escapes you, as long as you consider the object. You never can find it till you turn your reflection into your own breast and find a sentiment of disapprobation which arises in you toward this action. Here is a matter of fact; but it is the object of feeling, not of reason. It lies in yourself, not in the object.[3]

The upshot of Hume's argument was that no form of knowledge, based on either logical or empirical grounds, can substantiate a given form of conduct. There can be no reasoning that proceeds from the "is" to the "ought"— that is, from either the rational or the factual to the moral. The new relation between reason and morality, in Hume's famous words, is that "Reason

[2] *Treatise*, 2:167f.
[3] Ibid., 2:177

is, and ought only to be, the slave of the passions, and can never pretend to any other office than to serve and obey them." In a less flamboyant passage, Hume wrote

> . . . that reason, in a strict and philosophical sense, can have an influence on our conduct only after two ways: either when it excites a passion by informing us of the existence of something which is a proper object of it; or when it discovers the connection of causes and effects so as to afford us means of exerting any passion.[4]

In Hume's philosophy, then, the operations of the mind are sharply separated into the unrelated procedures of logic and inference from probability—and both of these are separated from morality and values. The implications of this philosophy undermines the entire metaphysical tradition of the West, including the tradition of natural law and any social theory based upon it.[5]

The Implications for Social Science

Hume's epistemology undermined the Cartesian definition of science and all metaphysical attempts to know the world. Instead, it leaned toward the Pascalian view, which limits human knowledge to what can be learned from experience. Further, Hume's epistemology contained a solution to the liberal dilemma, or rather it prevented the dilemma from arising. The great puzzle that plagued the Enlightenment had no meaning for Hume since there could be no question of truth in regard to matters of fact. The very nature of the empirical world is that it cannot be logically lawful. The social realm of fact—history—can display novelty without violating logic since it has no intrinsic relation to logic.

In regard to the important question of the nature of human nature, Hume seems at first glance to be a radical skeptic. Human beings may seek to anchor their values and beliefs in nature, but values and beliefs are really human inventions that are obeyed through habit and utility, and all attempts to establish the existence of "modes and substances" must fail. Applied directly to human beings, Hume's theory also denies the existence of any mental substance, of any idea of self or personal identity: "The mind is a kind of theatre, where several perceptions successively make their

---

[4] Ibid., 2:168

[5] Not surprisingly, Hume's own social theory, the essentials of which can be found in Book III, Part II of the *Treatise*, was based on the general proposition that ideas and laws governing such questions as justice, property, and allegiance derive their authority not from nature but from convention and utility. For a comprehensive analysis of Hume's social theory, which was liberal though opposed to natural rights, see John B. Stewart, *The Moral and Political Philosophy of David Hume* (New York: Columbia University Press, 1963).

appearance; pass, repass, glide away, and mingle in an infinite variety of postures and situations. There is properly no *simplicity* in it at one time, nor *identity* in different; whatever natural propension we may have to imagine that simplicity and identity." [6]

Hume's skepticism was not so complete as it might seem. In the *Enquiry on Understanding*, for example, he expressed a belief that the laws of association are relatively uniform and that there is a harmony between the behavior of nature and the sequence of ideas. Later he argued that "action, and employment, and the occupations of common life" are too strong for radical skepticism or Pyrrhonism. He proposed instead a "mitigated" skepticism that recognizes the effectiveness of human understanding but only in the limited area of daily practice and experience. There is another and all-important limitation to Hume's skepticism—his belief that human nature is relatively constant and that it can be studied in much the same way that one studies physical nature.

There are two ways to interpret Hume's epistemology and its implications for social science. First, it can be assumed that social facts display a lawfulness or probability of occurrence that is inherent in their nature though not necessarily inherent in the nature of the mind. As such, knowledge of social facts is of the same order as knowledge of physical nature. By and large, this is the majority view in both main branches of sociology, naturalistic positivism and sociocultural positivism.

A second interpretation, however, is that the lawfulness or probability of social facts is temporal in nature and can be qualitatively changed either by new conditions or by deliberate action. As such, social facts are rooted neither in the constant promptings of emotions nor in the uniform relations of perception. On the contrary, they are unmoored, free-floating instances that can be known only in terms of the relationships and patterns they assume in the tides and tempests of history. Such a concept of knowledge is more in keeping, of course, with historical positivism and the general denial that a unified theory of human behavior is possible.

Hume's demolition of the tradition of natural law and of metaphysics in general was largely ignored by the enthusiasts of rationalism, especially in France. The belief in a basic identity between the worlds of mind and nature, between theory and fact, was too deeply implanted and too useful for the philosophes or their successors to give up. But the struggle to unite reason and fact in the service of French capitalism resulted in the liberal dilemma, a dilemma that French theorists were not disposed to solve by

---

[6] *Treatise*, 1:239f.; for a more extended discussion of Hume's denial of the existence of mental or external substances, see *Treatise*, 1:238–249 and 2:313–320.

trimming the wings of reason. Instead, the relationship between reason and fact was recast by Condorcet, Saint-Simon, and Comte so that fact became explicable in terms of a natural process of development in reason (or science) itself. In addition, the latter theorists ignored Hume's insistence that neither rational nor factual analysis could substantiate any value structure; these early sociologists assumed that there were normative imperatives attached to the cosmic pattern of development that they thought they had found.

During the Enlightenment the value of natural law as a critical weapon against feudal absolutism was too urgently needed by a French middle class out of power for the philosophes to take the Humian alternative seriously. The appeal to custom and experience was much more palatable— that is, suitable to the dominant oligarchy of which the middle class was now a part—in England, where the Settlement of 1688 had obviated the need for transcendent absolute principles either in philosophy or in politics. England had gone through its ordeal by ideology in the seventeenth century, and English thinkers tended to hew closely to the concrete actualities of precedent and tradition and to avoid appeals to a mercurial reason. In a sense, and despite his concern with abstract right, Locke was as anti-Cartesian as Vico, and it was this line of thought that Hume continued and completed. Even the traditionalism of Burke may be viewed as a development well within the basic tradition of British empiricism.

Just as the philosophes' theory of natural law was incompatible with Hume's theory of knowledge, so was their idea of progress. The attempts to merge these two ideas by Condorcet (who used the idea of natural rights) and by Saint-Simon and Comte (both of whom rejected natural rights) were errors of the first magnitude given the validity of Hume's analysis. The empirical world may well exhibit progress, but a doctrine of progress must be carefully stated in terms of fact, or better still in terms of cause-and-effect probabilities and explicitly stated value preferences. However, it can never be presented as a metaphysical doctrine. The mind has no jurisdiction over the existential world and can never pretend that its value preferences are derived from or substantiated by the factual uniformities it discovers. The early monistic sociologists ignored Hume's general injunction, though they insisted that their views were based on positive knowledge as opposed to the verbalisms of the metaphysicians, which tended to obscure the vast gulf between their own metaphysics and Hume's more modest estimate of the capabilities of empirical analysis.

Hume was ignored outside the field of sociology as well. By the nineteenth century, however, too much had happened for theorists to accept the old rationalism, and new ways of finding rational necessity in human affairs were developed. Through a process of intellectual alchemy, custom became reason—that is, custom was seen as embodying a deeper wisdom than was available to the unaided mind. In other formulations, the nation became the new Logos of the universe. When combined with a sense of development, custom and nation became the foundation of historical romanticism. Finally, in Kant and Hegel, attempts were made to reconstruct logical analysis so that a transcendental logic or a dialectical logic might be used to penetrate to the nature of things with an insight that Hume had denied ordinary logic.

THE "HISTORICAL" AND "METAPHYSICAL" APPROACHES TO HUMAN BEHAVIOR

The term *historical* approach has a variety of meanings and tends to be a source of confusion. Since there is no alternative to using it, the term must be defined carefully and used consistently. The much neglected masterpiece of R. G. Collingwood, *The Idea of History*,[7] is indispensable to my definition of history. Collingwood's objective in this work was to establish the field of history as something different from philosophy and from science (positivism). The main tendency in Greek thought, said Collingwood, was based on an antihistorical metaphysics. The idea of history, however, was clearly developed in the work of Herodotus, the first to use the word *history* to imply an inquiry into what human beings qua human beings had done. Though Collingwood ranked Herodotus and Socrates as the two innovating geniuses of the fifth century B.C., he pointed out that Herodotus had no successors (with the possible exception of Thucydides), whereas Socrates did. The failure of Herodotus to attract followers, said Collingwood, is crucially important for understanding the history of the idea of history. The Greeks became sensitive to history for the simple reason that they had experienced the violent fluctuations of social change. They came to feel that the world of flux could never be an object of cognition. No knowledge gained through the sensory perception of the inconstant world was reliable; only that based on the stationary could properly be called knowledge. Thus, the very uncertainty of temporal existence prompted the Greeks to search behind events for the unchanging substance. Ironically, it was history itself that engendered the mode of thought that outlawed the historical as knowledge and that led to the domination of history by philosophy.

In a survey of the historians of the Greco-Roman world, Collingwood showed how the propensity for metaphysics made the development of historical thought impossible.

> If its humanism, however weak, is the chief merit of Greco-Roman historiography, its chief defect is substantialism. By this

[7] New York: Oxford University Press paperback, 1956; first published in 1946. My indebtedness to this book is apparent on every page of this study.

I mean that it is constructed on the basis of a metaphysical system whose chief category is the category of substance. Substance
does not mean matter or physical substance; indeed many Greek
metaphysicians thought that no substance could be material. For
Plato, it would seem, substances are immaterial though not
mental; they are objective forms. For Aristotle, in the last resort,
the only ultimately real substance is mind. Now a substantialistic
metaphysics implies a theory of knowledge according to which
only what is unchanging is knowable. But what is unchanging
is not historical. What is historical is the transitory event. The
substance to which an event happens, or from whose nature it
proceeds, is nothing to the historian. Hence the attempt to think
historically and the attempt to think in terms of substance were
incompatible.[8]

The idea of history, Collingwood continued, received enormous encouragement from Christianity. For the Christian the only substance is God. However, God is an all-powerful and unknowable substance; this fact had
significance for the development of the historical perspective. That God
is a creator makes all things contingent—people, nations, and nature alike.
Because of this, human beings are prevented from thinking solely in terms
of substance, since the world emerged from nothing. God is unknowable
because of the defective nature of human beings, which emphasizes the
importance of the things human beings can know. The history of humankind illustrates God's purposes since God desires human well-being, and
therefore history is important. Since the purposes of God are beyond
human ken, events are ultimately explained by the idea of Providence, a
notion that in its many formulations is indispensable to the historical
mentality. Finally, Collingwood said, Christianity destroyed Greco-Roman
substantialism by making not only human beings creatures of God, but
nations as well. From a different vantage point, the substantialism of
Greco-Roman particularism was undermined by the universalism of Christianity. The injunction to regard all human beings as equally humbled and
equally glorified in God cuts across the notions of privilege, of a chosen
race or people, and of special classes and communities.

However, argued Collingwood, the Christian world view need not become
an historical view; it merely contains the possibility. Medieval historiography developed in a way that blocked the emergence of a genuine historical perspective. God was conceived more and more as a being outside
history, and thus the historical realm was rendered unimportant. The duty
of the scholar was to discover the objective plans of God for human beings

---

[8] Ibid., p. 42.

and not to be interested in what human beings were doing. The implications of this perspective for the development of a historical point of view are obvious.

The real development of the idea of history had to await the empiricism of the postmedieval period, from which Collingwood distinguished two main contributions, Vico's anti-Cartesian empiricism on the one hand, and that of Locke and Hume on the other. In effect, the empiricism of these thinkers, especially of Vico, gave empirical knowledge a validity that equaled or surpassed that of metaphysical knowledge.

Vico's empiricism, however, became a genuine historical point of view because he went beyond mere empiricism and transformed the nature of knowledge altogether. He rejected the rationalist tradition that presented the problem of knowledge as a relation between idea and facts, and he substituted the revolutionary view that the study of facts will lead not to the true as opposed to the false, but to an understanding of what human beings had done and been. The task of knowledge, in other words, is not to perceive the laws of the universe or the substance behind events and human behavior, but to understand human behavior. A human being can understand human behavior because the knower and the doer share a common nature. Since human beings have made (and unmade) themselves in so many different ways—personalities, societies, cultures—their behavior can only be known historically, through understanding not through perception.

The anti-Cartesianism of Locke and Hume was also a reorientation of philosophy toward history, said Collingwood, but in a negative way. They anchored knowledge in experience, denying the existence of innate ideas and any argument intended to bridge the gap between ideas and facts, and they judged knowledge by its usefulness and not its certainty. However, as I said in my analysis of Hume's theory of knowledge, British thought tended toward empirical positivism and failed to become truly historical.

In the following passage Collingwood describes the failure of the Enlightenment to develop a genuine historical perspective, at the same time raising the problem of the liberal dilemma.

> ... the historiography of the Enlightenment is apocalyptic to an extreme degree, as indeed the very word "enlightenment" suggests. The central point of history, for these writers, is the sunrise of the modern scientific spirit. Before that, everything was superstition and darkness, error and imposture. And of these things there can be no history, not only because they are unworthy of historical study, but because there is in them no rational or

necessary development: the story of them is a tale told by an idiot, full of sound and fury, signifying nothing.

Thus in the crucial case, namely the origin of the modern scientific spirit, these writers could have no conception of historical origins or processes. Pure reason cannot come into existence out of pure unreason. There can be no development leading from one to the other. The sunrise of the scientific spirit was, from the point of view of the Enlightenment, a sheer miracle, unprepared in the previous course of events and uncaused by any cause that could be adequate to such an effect. This inability to explain or expound historically what they regarded as the most important event in history was of course symptomatic; it meant that in a general way they had no satisfactory theory of historical causation and could not seriously believe in the origin or genesis of anything whatever.[9]

The philosophic revolution implicit in Locke's empiricism, and especially in Hume's demolition of the concept of spiritual substance, said Collingwood, opened up the possibility of historical thought by destroying the basis of substantialism. However, argues Collingwood, neither the Enlightenment nor Hume could overcome the tradition of substantialism. The following criticism of Hume contains the crucial difference that separates the "historical" perspective from the "positivistic":

> Hume's abolition of spiritual substance amounted to laying down the principle that we must never separate what a mind is from what it does, and that therefore a mind's nature is nothing but the ways in which it thinks and acts. The concept of mental substance was thus resolved into the concept of mental process. But this did not in itself necessitate an historical conception of mind, because all process is not historical process. A process is historical only when it created its own laws; and according to Hume's theory of mind the laws of mental process are ready-made and unchanging from their beginning. He did not think of mind as learning to think and act in new ways as the process of its activity developed. He certainly thought that his new science of human nature, if successfully achieved, would lead to further progress in the arts and sciences; but not by altering human nature itself— that, he never suggests to be possible—only by improving our understanding of it.
>
> Philosophically this conception was self-contradictory. If that which we come to understand better is something other than ourselves, for example the chemical properties of matter, our improved understanding of it in no way improves the thing itself.

9 Ibid., p. 80.

If, on the other hand, that which we understand better is our own understanding, an improvement in *that* science is an improvement not only in its subject but in its object also. By coming to think more truly about the human understanding we are coming to improve our own understanding. Hence the historical development in human nature itself.[10]

THE TYPES OF SOCIOLOGY

Collingwood's criticism of the Enlightenment and of Hume is also applicable to the founders of sociology. Montesquieu, despite his skepticism, approached the facts of behavior as a given set of data to be apprehended by a perceiving mind. He failed to see that human nature and the mind itself are drastically involved in the data of history. Condorcet, Saint-Simon, and Comte, despite their sense of time and their attempt to develop a theory of historical causation, did not really involve human nature itself in the process of history. Their fundamental assumption was that history is an encrustation on human nature and that beneath the historical process are human beings waiting to be freed from its corruptions. As thinkers Condorcet, Saint-Simon, and Comte were positivists in that they stood outside the historical process and analyzed it as an external spectacle of lawful facts. They did not assume that their analysis as an intellectual experience would transform their own nature. On the contrary, they assumed that their nature, which in reality was particularized by their experience as eighteenth- and early-nineteenth-century Frenchmen, was really human nature, and that their analysis would reveal the process by which humanity had emerged from the past. The fact that they employed a time dimension does not mean that they were historical, but only that they had developed a more dynamic ideological substantialism. They made a notable contribution to historical thought by their use of a time perspective, and in a lesser manner by their semiempirical analysis of social causation. However, they vitiated this contribution by interpreting human behavior not as a function of historical and social processes, but as a natural process.

The only genuine historical view of the eighteenth century was Vico's. In both his intellectual approach and his empirical research, he explicitly involved human nature itself in the historical process. There is no set of imperatives in human beings that remains unaltered by experience; human nature is what it has been, what it is, and what it will be. Clearly implicit in Vico's approach was the assumption that even though his new science had the power to reveal the past, it could not exhaust the possibilities of human nature. Indeed, an understanding of history will itself be further

[10] Ibid., p. 83f.

history and open up further development in human nature. What Vico's thought lacked in causal analysis was made up for by his emphasis on analysis through understanding. However, his emphasis on understanding, which effectively undermined the notion of a natural human nature, combined with a deficient causal theory, made him succumb to a different brand of substantialism. The same criticism that Collingwood made of medieval historiography can be applied to Vico. Ultimately Vico's theory of history rested on the Christian idea that only God is substance; though he saw God as the dynamic creator of history, his theory was still substantialistic in that it presupposed some agency outside the historical process itself.

The development of sociological theory from the ferment of the European Enlightenment and its crystallization in the theory of Comte was not therefore a move away from substantialism but rather the substitution of a new type of substantialism based on the idea that the mind can grasp the general law of mental development. None of the originators of sociological theory and, as I will show, none of their immediate successors developed a genuine historical view of human nature or of the knowledge that human beings can have of themselves.

In the following study of sociological theory, there is only one genuine historical approach, the sociology of Max Weber. Aside from Weber, there is only a variety of substantialisms, some naturalistic and some sociocultural, some dynamic and some static. In studying the various types of positivism, I shall not, therefore, merely compare naturalistic positivism with sociocultural positivism—that is, compare one type of substantialism with another. The interpretative categories that I shall use to structure and illuminate this analysis of the history of sociology will also include historical positivism.

Historical positivism defines social science as a method, as a tool for achieving social control through a knowledge of causal relationships and consequences. In short, it approximates the Pascalian definition of science. Metaphysical positivism, on the other hand, while it accepts much of this definition, attempts to go much further. For metaphysical positivism, science as a method leads to science as a metaphysics; this approach assumes that human behavior, whether defined in natural or in sociocultural terms, contains an objective reality the structure of which can ultimately be grasped through the application of scientific method. Whether it stresses logic (theory) or a multiplicity of methods; whether it focuses on biopsychic or sociocultural facts, on subjective intents and constructions or objective forces and institutions; whether it is monocausal or multicausal; whether it stresses statics or dynamics; or whether it uses a teleological or a functional approach, its objective is still a metaphysical quest for the timelessly true, a search for the properties or processes that are always and everywhere

true of human behavior. This craving for the total and permanent understanding of the constitutive principles of human nature distinguishes metaphysical from historical positivism. The latter view sees human beings as
actors not as entities, as both the creators and the creatures of their
own acts—acts that can be recurrent or unique, stable or transitory, rational
or nonrational, conscious or unconscious (always in keeping with sociocultural conditions and frames). Unlike nature, which is in bondage to a
registry of fixed structures and processes, human beings need not be what
they are.

SOCIOLOGY AS HISTORY

The metaphysical and historical perspectives contain a further implication
that can now be stated more fully. Though I shall continue my effort to
define both the details and the spirit of the major and representative theorists of sociology, I shall also assume that sociology is itself subject to the
historical perspective. Thus, while giving full credit and even sympathy to
the positivist substantialism at the heart of the sociological tradition, I shall
regard that tradition as I would any other intellectual system—as the symbolic defense of historically conditioned values and as the reflection of
historically conditioned intellectual and moral needs. That is, I shall continue to analyze sociology sociologically; far from being immune to historical conditioning or having escaped from it, sociological theory is itself subject to the sociology of knowledge. I shall continue to assume that its
methods, ideas, and values are the result of the confluence of previous
cultural elements and that it is therefore subject to cultural analysis in the
same way that the philosophy or art of the Golden Age of Greece, the religion of India, or the cosmology of a primitive tribe is subject.

In particular my analysis will continue to assume that sociology is a social
theory appropriate to the age of liberalism and that it is intimately connected with the intellectual and emotional needs of capitalism. The redefinition of human nature and society by the founders of sociology was a
brilliant but unsuccessful attempt to find a metaphysical basis for an emerging capitalist society. Its major scientific problem, the liberal dilemma, was
disguised by Condorcet, Saint-Simon, and Comte under the idea of progress—an idea that at bottom reflected liberalism's need to base its social
structure on a set of values and ideas that were at once natural and historical, stable and dynamic. As part of the scientific world view of liberal
civilization, sociology arose during the course of the Enlightenment to lay
claim to social science. In rejecting previous forms of social theory, sociology
had open to it two general scientific approaches, the metaphysical and the
historical. Although it drastically reorientated human thought toward secularism and empiricism, sociological theory became blatantly metaphysical.

While it accepted and continued the dynamic, instrumental norms of the liberal version of world mastery, it perpetuated philosophical substantialism under the guise of science and installed the philosophical tyranny of Greece into the intellectual and institutional structure of modern society. Finally, like all ideologies, sociological theory benefited some power groups more than others, not the least by disguising a middle-class structure of power—property owners and professionals in an exchange economy—as a natural, nonhistorical phenomenon.

PART III
The Maturing Tradition

Chapter 9
Evolution and the New Phase of Modern Science

The formative period in sociological theory took place during a transitional period in Western science. The pioneer sociologists went past the assumptions of the first phase of modern science without fully entering its second phase. Future sociologists were heterogeneous in many ways but had one thing in common that separated them from their predecessors—all were immersed in the genuine phase of empirical science. Since sociology did not embrace empirical science quickly or uniformly, it is necessary in analyzing the development of sociological theory after Comte to distinguish between an intermediate stage, composed of sociologists whose work was still under the spell of evolutionary monistic positivism, and a later stage that I have designated *pluralistic positivism*. Generally speaking, however, the main body of sociologists after Comte employed different assumptions about methodology and were inspired by the new developments of post-Newtonian science.

Though continuous with postmedieval science, nineteenth-century science inaugurated a new phase, the third great cosmology that has gripped the minds of Westerners. It is difficult to find a word that describes the new cosmology exactly. The view of nature that lasted from Thales to Saint Thomas and the view that lasted from Copernicus to Newton are readily described as organic-teleological and mechanistic-mathematical. It would be misleading, however, to describe the third great cosmology as evolutionary, though the idea of evolution is crucial to its meaning. Though I call it pluralistic positivism, the term *functionalism* would also be a useful epitome. In a sense, a capsule definition of post-Newtonian science is as misleading as it is presumptuous. For a number of reasons, however, there is a need for a working definition of the new, contemporary, scientific world view. For one thing, sociological theory cannot be discussed meaningfully without relating it to the other sciences. It is necessary, therefore, to outline the new perspective of post-Newtonian science in at least some detail. It seems best to interweave selected aspects of the new cosmology with a discussion of the specific types of sociological theory with which they were most closely related. The general structure of the new phase of science will emerge, therefore, partly in this chapter, introducing the work of Spencer, Sumner, and Ward; partly in Chapter 13, introducing the emergence of pluralistic positivism in continental Europe; partly in Chapter 18, introducing the development of pluralistic positivism in the United States; and finally, in summary form, in Chapters 23 and 24.

SOCIAL CHANGE AND THE THEORY OF EVOLUTION

Developments in post-Enlightenment science are best viewed as the ripening of Western experience with both social change and social-system change. Some theorists, for the first time in Western history, began to see change in a favorable light. The growing success in coping with the empirical world of day-to-day problems eventually produced a revolutionary attitude toward change as well as toward knowledge. In the centuries after the Middle Ages, the Greek derogation of experience as ephemeral and deceptive carried less and less weight for a middle class thriving on practical affairs. The world of facts and events made sense to the middle class—so much so that by the eighteenth century empiricism dislodged rationalism as the cutting edge of Western philosophy, forming, as it were, the intellectual counterpart to the economic and political dislodgement of the feudality.

In successfully coping with change, the middle class gradually discarded the Greek definition of change as nonrational and began to think of it more and more in terms of lawful, predictable development. The social experience of the middle class made change intellectually respectable and made the idea of evolution possible. The origins of the rapid social change, which did so much to alter human beings' view both of themselves and of nature, were in the increased capacity to master the physical environment—a capacity soon to be matched by an increased capacity to effect changes in social and personality structures. These changes, which went back to at least the twelfth century, reached their floodtide during the eighteenth and early nineteenth centuries, by which time there was a growing feeling that change and even conflict were endemic to nature and society and therefore had to be dealt with intellectually.

The historical bent of the Enlightenment, though pronounced, was still subordinate to its main concern with substance, with finding the permanent structure of nature and society. Throughout the eighteenth century, however, a genuine idea of evolution grew, as scientists and philosophers, to use Lovejoy's phrase, began to "temporalize the great chain of being." Though there were deep new insights into the processes that produce qualitatively new structures (as opposed to the static processes that can be found in Aristotelian teleology or in Newtonian physics), the philosophical crisis inherent in such a view was not felt until Charles Darwin's *Origins of the Species* in 1859.[1]

THE CRISIS OF EVOLUTION

It is difficult, if not impossible, to appreciate fully the deep impact of the idea of lawful change on the nineteenth century. Whatever name and shade of meaning it assumed, the idea that movement is characteristic of both nature and human nature permeated almost every aspect of nineteenth-century thought. The mechanistic universe of the post-Renaissance world that had replaced the static, purposive world of Medieval Christendom was itself replaced by the revolutionary idea that the world was no finished thing but a vital, growing process. The impact of the new cosmology on social thought was enormous. Superseding the pseudoevolutionary view of Saint-Simon and Comte, sociological theorists began to assume that qualitative changes were taking place in human nature and human history and that these could be rendered intelligible only in terms of natural evolutionary processes. This outlook created an intellectual crisis of the first magnitude.

The theory of evolution did not create a crisis because it placed human beings in nature—Western moralists had been only too aware of humankind's animal nature. Nor was it simply because the theory contradicted Genesis. The moral and intellectual crisis arose because Darwin seemed to have proved conclusively that nature was composed not of fixed but of evolving forms—a conclusion that rendered problematic the fixity of both morals and reason.[2] Greek as well as post-Renaissance science was based on the assumption that the structure of being was not only unitary but permanent. Moreover, both previous cosmologies had believed that the only permanent and unitary structure was mind, or reason, or perhaps better still, logic. The view of nature in these two periods had differed because the definition of logic had differed: the earlier cosmology had employed the logic of final cause and the latter the logic of mathematics to construct their versions of reality. In both cases, however, the structure of ideas produced by logical discourse was assumed to be the source not only of what was true but also of what was real. Conversely, the empirical realm was considered unreal because it was ephemeral and multiple. Even the Enlightenment's revolutionary declaration that the empirical realm was

---

[1] For a fascinating and comprehensive account of the evolution of the idea of evolution in all fields of natural science from the time of Newton until the synthesis of Darwin, see John C. Greene, *The Death of Adam* (New York: Mentor paperback, 1961).

[2] In this regard, see John Dewey, "The Influence of Darwinism on Philosophy," *Popular Science Monthly* (July 1909); reprinted in B. J. Loewenberg, ed., *Darwinism* (New York: Holt, Rinehart, and Winston, 1960), chap. 13.

rational really meant that natural phenomena contained both structure and unity and were therefore not merely accessible to but identical with the structure and unity of reason. Because of the liberal dilemma, the Enlightenment had been unable to achieve a cognitive apprehension of phenomena as long as it held a static definition of truth; slowly, it recast its definition to make truth more dynamic. Alongside the revolutionary commitment to empiricism, therefore, there grew the revolutionary assumption that change is cognitively graspable. By the nineteenth century, for the first time in Western intellectual history, the world of change and novelty was removed from the realm of the irrational and given the traditional hallmarks of reason, structure and unity.

Within the genuine evolutionary perspective, there are two opposing views, the Hegelian view, confined mostly to Germany and later to Russia, and the Darwinian view, influential mostly in France, England, and the United States. However different the two schools, both agreed that evolutionary change in nature is the same as it is in culture, thus illustrating again the strong penchant of Western rationalism for a unified theory of the universe.[3]

The evolutionary approach had enormous impact on early Anglo-American sociology. I have selected three theorists, Spencer, Sumner, and Ward, to represent the initial involvement of sociology in the new phase of science. Though all three worked to bring social thought into line with new developments in natural science, they were not genuinely empirical in their outlook. They are best seen as part of a developing or maturing empirical tradition in sociological theory. Their work is important for two reasons. First, in working within the main tradition of Western rationalism, they sought a unification of phenomena in terms of the new, up-to-date substantive principle of evolution. Second, despite the failure of the principle of evolution to provide a satisfactory unification of knowledge, they explored and established in sociology some of the important methodological implications that the idea contained. Because of the twentieth-century reaction against the literal application of evolution to social phenomena the reputation of these theorists has faded. This is an injustice, particularly in the case of Spencer and Sumner, for it overlooks their important methodological contributions. The main claim to unity in sociological theory after Comte is not so much the establishment of substantive laws of human behavior as

[3] For a masterly and succinct discussion that identifies and contrasts these two views of change and compares them with the Aristotelian attempt to understand change through teleology, see F. S. C. Northrop, "Evolution in Its Relation to the Philosophy of Nature and the Philosophy of Culture," *Evolutionary Thought in America*, ed. Stow Persons (New York: George Braziller, Inc., 1956), chap. 2. Not the least valuable part of Northrop's analysis is his depiction of the way in which these two schools sought to combine the philosophy of nature and the philosophy of culture, and his affirmation of the validity of such a quest in spite of the fact that it cannot be done in terms of evolution.

the development of a scientific methodology. Spencer, Sumner, and Ward belong to the post-Comtean tradition of sociology primarily because of the methodology that they culled from the genuine doctrine of evolution. Their achievement in this regard links them to the more fully developed empirical methodology that also emerged in the latter part of the nineteenth century in the work of the pluralistic positivists.

THE AGE OF METHODOLOGY

The fortunes of empiricism are not associated solely with biology and the theory of evolution. A number of European and American symbolic movements, each in its own way, helped to alter the static, rationalist picture of nature and human nature that had prevailed up to the time of the Enlightenment. Given the growing power of the middle class and its exhilarating experience of deep and largely beneficial social change, it is not surprising that all reaches of Western intellectual life sought escape from the stultifying effects of formal logic. Above all, the new experience with change meant that truth, and therefore virtue, could no longer be defined in terms of either formal or mathematical logic, but had to take on a "historical" dimension. If there is one abstraction that unifies the intellectual culture of the post-Enlightenment period, it is antirationalism. It is this abstraction that brings a certain measure of unity, for example, to such figures as Wordsworth, Shelley, Austin, Bagehot, Pusey, Pearson, and Graham Wallas in England; Chateaubriand, Bonald, Lamennais, Gobineau, Manet, Henri Poincaré, Bergson, and Maurras in France; Schelling, Wagner, Nietzsche, Windelband, and Scheler in Germany; Lobatchevsky, Bolyai, Kierkegaard, Mach, Pavlov, Freud, and Mosca elsewhere in Europe; and James, Dewey, Holmes, Veblen, Watson, Beard, James Harvey Robinson, and Robinson Jeffers in the United States.

Of course, such high-level abstractions are only moderately illuminating. Any adequate depiction of Western intellectual culture since the Enlightenment would have to pinpoint the diverse formulations of antirationalism, as well as trace the diverse consequences that flowed from similar theories and the similar consequences that resulted from different formulations. My purpose in resorting to the broad abstraction of antirationalism is to note that serious criticisms of rationalism emerged from a wide group of theorists. Insofar as my interest is in the new climate of science, it is important to note that one of the most fertile forms of antirationalism took place in the field of logic. Of the thinkers cited above, many made rich contributions to logic. Thus developments in mathematics, physics, and ultimately in philosophy, along with biological and evolutionary theory, and romanticism in art, music, and literature all contributed to the new climate of opinion in which pluralistic positivism in sociology appeared. Ironically, much of the modern attack on rationalism was made in the name of science.

Following earlier trends, post-Enlightenment science humbled the claims of reason while at the same time affirming its faith in the power of a reason rightly understood. The genuine empirical phase of science, therefore, was not against logic or even against the older forms of logic. Rather, it fostered a new consciousness and discipline about the employment of logic. The post-Enlightenment period, therefore, can be seen as the age of methodology or even as the age of new logics. Aside from the so-called logic of the heart— of dubious scientific worth—there appeared Hegel's dialectical logic, probability and non-Euclidean logics, and a rich collection of thought forms that despite their names were similar: inductive, analytic, symbolic, predictive, pragmatic, instrumental, and functional logics.

There is an important distinction among the new logics. Among them, only Hegelian logic was avowedly ontological; despite its novelty, it adhered to the main philosophical tradition of the West by claiming a real existence for logic (reason, mind). The other logics, which were more directly related to ongoing scientific work, contained implications of wide-reaching significance. Climaxing the empirical bent of the Enlightenment was a new and drastic re-evaluation of the nature of reason, especially of the traditional claim that reason had an ontological status. Far from being a fixed feature of the universe, reason came to be thought of as a human, historical creation, as a many-pronged instrument of knowledge and adjustment. This emphatically did not mean the abandonment of the traditional Western dream of establishing a unified theory of phenomena. That dream was too deeply fixed to be given up so easily. It was assumed, however, that one must guard against premature world views and that the goal of unified knowledge must wait until science developed new logical structures to uncover and record the many faces of nature. The empirical method, unhampered by outmoded concepts of logic, would one day be in a position to establish a comprehensive theory of phenomena.

In subsequent chapters introducing the advent of pluralistic positivism and twentieth-century American sociology, I shall say more about the development of positivism in science and philosophy, especially about the continuing commitment of positivism to substantialism and even idealism. For now, it is enough to indicate that while nineteenth-century science radically altered the West's intellectual and moral outlook by transforming reason into method, the main body of theorists, both in and out of sociology, continued to believe in the possibility of a monistic metaphysics. As noted earlier, the philosophy of Hume, which prefigures the main line of scientific development in the nineteenth and twentieth centuries, contained implications that were profoundly antimetaphysical in all traditional senses of the word. However, few theorists interpreted Hume in this fashion; few developed positions devoid of the traditional substantialism of Western thought. While reason was rapidly reduced to method, the rationalist tradition of the West remained intact. The idea that human experience is inescapably diverse and contradictory, that it undergoes change and decay and therefore is not suitable to cognitive appropriation—and perhaps not even subject to control through cognition—was as uncongenial to the nineteenth century as it had been to the Greeks. All this lies ahead, however. My first task is to show how the antirationalism of biological and evolutionary theory bore rich scientific fruit in sociology, and how sociological theory began not only to reflect but to contribute to the new knowledge and modes of thought that emerged during the nineteenth century.

Chapter 10
Herbert Spencer (1820–1903)

It takes great effort today to appreciate Herbert Spencer's enormous sway over the English-speaking world during the nineteenth century. His work, a remarkable attempt to synthesize all knowledge, has suffered from neglect and stands in general disrepute. Nonetheless, it was an incredible feat of intellectual systematization with few parallels in the history of Western philosophy.[1]

Spencer's first book, appropriately entitled *First Principles*, was followed by explorations into the special sciences of biology, psychology, sociology, and ethics. This series, entitled *Synthetic Philosophy*, attempted to break down the divisions among the sciences and to comprehend them according to laws applicable to all.

Spencer's work represented a significant departure from the positive tradition. For two hundred years, roughly from Hobbes to Comte, the positive current had attempted to interpret human behavior using the latest developments in science. There was a variety of expression within this period, but it was dominated by one fundamental concept. Whether viewed deductively or empirically, or in terms of mechanics or of biology, nature was conceived as being essentially static. Even when thinkers employed the concept of evolution, they were referring to the evolution of human knowledge about nature, not to processes taking place in nature. It was this latter idea, that nature itself is undergoing change, that is the revolutionary basis of Spencer's thought. Whereas Condorcet, Saint-Simon, and even Comte had greatly concerned themselves with vindicating the right of science to

---

[1] Modern readers are indebted to J. D. Y. Peel's brilliant analysis of Spencer's work seen from the standpoint of the sociology of knowledge, *Herbert Spencer, the Evolution of a Sociologist* (New York: Basic Books, 1971). Also useful is *Herbert Spencer on Social Evolution: Selected Writings*, ed. J. D. Y. Peel (Chicago: University of Chicago Press, 1972). Philip Abrams's excellent *The Origins of British Sociology 1834–1914: An Essay with Selected Papers* (Chicago: University of Chicago Press, 1968) provides a detailed analysis of the social and intellectual context in which Spencer worked.

deal with social phenomena, Spencer for the most part took this for granted and devoted himself to applying both the methods and the substantive concepts of science to the study of human behavior. The locus of his social thought, therefore, was squarely within the confines of science. This allowed him a more extensive use of social data than had been the case with French sociology, and he had no hesitation in applying the genuine idea of evolution to human behavior.

PHILOSOPHY AND METHOD

Long before Darwin, theorists such as Buffon, Lamarck, and Lyell had speculated about the possibility that both the inorganic and the organic realms were undergoing qualitative change. Not only the pseudoevolutionary currents in French sociology but the general current of romanticism and the development of Hegelian philosophy as well had discarded the static universalism of the Enlightenment in favor of the idea of movement and development. However, it was Darwin's empirical verification of evolution that placed the idea on an unshakable scientific basis. Spencer's immersion in this new cosmology is what makes him of such interest to the historian of sociological theory. Of all the sociologists I have analyzed, he was the first to assume the nonfixity of the structures of nature, and his work was the first thoroughgoing attempt to apply the laws of nature at large to human nature. In evaluating Spencer's work, it should be noted that his genuine evolutionary theory preceded Darwin's by a number of years, and that, without using the term "natural selection," he also anticipated Darwin's explanation of the causal mechanism by which evolution takes place.[2]

The Metaphysics of Evolution

Spencer's philosophical study, the *First Principles*, begins with a discussion of the relationship between the unknowable, the domain of religion, and the knowable, the domain of science. His discussion illustrates one of the most persistent themes in the history of sociology, the attempt to extricate thought from the philosophical tradition and from the search for essences or substances. Science, Spencer contended, can establish only relationships, not the intrinsic nature of things. Spencer did not reject philosophy's belief that knowledge consists in obtaining the highest degree of generality; however, philosophy must do its generalizing in a new way. Henceforth, it will consolidate and unify the generalizations that emerge in each of the sciences. The simplest formula is thus: "Knowledge of the lowest kind is *un-unified* knowledge; Science is *partially-unified* knowledge; Philosophy

[2] Spencer's ideas appeared in a number of articles and were applied to social phenomena in a book entitled *Social Statics*, which appeared in 1850.

Herbert Spencer (1820–1903)

is *completely-unified* knowledge." [3] What Spencer has done is apparent—
he has yoked philosophy to science. A more precise and succinct definition
of positivism would be impossible.

Spencer also hoped to reconcile religion and science. He argued that the
inability of science to form a cognizable picture of the unknown—or, as he
also called it, the unconditioned—does not mean that there is no reality.
Though knowledge is limited to the phenomenal world, it is based on the
presupposition that there is an unknowable absolute. This effects a reconciliation between science and religion, for beyond the disputes of the day

---

[3] *First Principles,* 6th ed. (New York: Appleton, 1904), p. 119.

both depend and agree on the existence of the unknowable. Conflicts between science and religion are due to the differences in their historical
"spheres and functions." As knowledge progresses and as more of what
theorists have regarded as supernatural is brought within the sphere of
natural explanation, conflicts develop. But eventually, said Spencer, science
and religion will be content to remain within their respective jurisdictions,
and there will be a harmony between them.

The scientific name for the unknowable is *force,* which is the ultimate of
ultimates. The world is neither matter nor any of the entities proposed by
religion; similarly, space, time, and motion are not real entities. The real
subject matter of science consists of the relationships produced in our consciousness by the manifestations of force in the phenomenal world. More
precisely, the persistence of force is the ultimately unverifiable principle
on which science depends. Any reduction of the various attributes of force
to a formula must also account for the deep-rooted dynamics in the phenomenal world.

> The law we seek, therefore, must be the law of *the continuous
> redistribution of matter and motion.* Absolute rest and permanence
> do not exist. Every object, no less than the aggregate of all ob-
> jects, undergoes from instant to instant some alteration of state.
> Gradually or quickly it is receiving motion or losing motion, while
> some or all of its parts are simultaneously changing their relations
> to one another. And the question is—what dynamic principle, true
> of the metamorphosis as a whole and in its details, expresses these
> ever-changing relations? [4]

Spencer's answer, of course, is the principle of evolution, which he defined
as

> . . . an integration of matter and concomitant dissipation of mo-
> tion; during which the matter passes from a relatively indefinite,
> incoherent homogeneity to a relatively definite, coherent heterog-
> eneity; and during which the retained motion undergoes a parallel
> transformation. [5]

Unlike French sociologists, who applied evolution to intellectual development only, Spencer applied it to all orders of existence, including all social
products, such as language, art, music, dress, and architecture, which obey
all the laws to which physical nature is subject. Though the *First Principles*
is filled with naturalistic interpretations of mental and social phenomena,
one example will suffice to show Spencer's radical naturalism:

[4] Ibid., p. 252.
[5] Ibid., p. 367.

> The phenomena subjectively known as changes in consciousness, are objectively known as nervous excitations and discharges, which science now interprets into modes of motion. Hence, in following up organic evolution, advance of the retained motion alike in integration, in heterogeneity, and in definiteness, may be expected to show itself both in the visible nervo-muscular actions and in the correlative mental changes.[6]

Though Spencer explicitly rejected metaphysics and its concern with "essences," "potentialities," or "pre-established harmonies," he was no less a metaphysician for all his emphasis on science and all his talk of an unknowable absolute. His approach to science is unmistakably Cartesian in spirit, not Pascalian. Despite Spencer's immersion in the tradition of British empiricism and the fact that much of his thought is Humian in character, his thought is explicitly modeled on the grand speculative tradition of Western metaphysics. Working within an up-to-date scientific tradition, Spencer altered the content of Western rationalism but not its longing for a unified theory of phenomena. The great chain of being is no longer static, of course, but has a dynamism summed up as the law of evolution. Significantly, Spencer's metaphysics does not separate the age-old dream of cognitive unity from its age-old concomitant, stability. Almost offhandedly Spencer declared that the process of evolution has a terminal point. All nature will eventually reach a state of "equilibrium" and "quiescence," and human beings will one day achieve a harmony between their mental nature and the conditions of existence. No further proof is needed of the metaphysical nature of Spencer's thought or of the enduring tyranny of Greek philosophy.

The Logic of Life and the Functional-Organic Method

Beneath the morass of deductive reasoning to which Spencer, like Comte, was addicted is a mode of thought that appears persistently in the literature of sociology. Spencer consistently sought to understand the evolutionary process as a change in the structure and function of a given subject matter. The grand law of evolution could be analyzed and explained, he felt, only in terms of the lawful emergence and interplay of new structures and new functions.

The notion of function is crucial to the scientific temperament. Science assumes that cognition is possible only in terms of cause-and-effect relationships and that given objects, beliefs, or practices can be understood only in terms of their performance within given contexts. The first deliberate and systematic effort to study social phenomena in terms of function was

[6] Ibid., p. 362.

by Vico, who used a cultural approach, and by Montesquieu, whose approach was both cultural and natural. After Vico and Montesquieu, the
functional approach came more and more under the sway of the natural
sciences. Biology was especially influential in developing the functional
approach; human and social behavior were increasingly interpreted as
analogous, if not identical, to the behavior of biological organisms. This
trend, which emerged somewhat in Saint-Simon and Comte, was most fully
developed in the work of Spencer.

Spencer's organic approach is clearly evident in his earliest full-length
work, *Social Statics*, where he stated his fundamental belief that all of
nature is subject to the same lawful forces, and that, in consequence, ethical and social phenomena are just as amenable to scientific analysis as is
any other part of nature. Applied to social development, the law of evolution can be defined as a progressive rise in the human capacity to adjust
to conditions. What human beings think of as evil, said Spencer, is non-
adaptation to conditions. The process of evolution is progressive in that
evil gradually disappears as nature produces more adaptable forms.[7] Later,
Spencer made the pregnant comment that in its progress toward more
effective adaptation, social organization takes on forms that are essentially
similar to the various forms found in animal organization.[8]

The full implications of the biological analogy for social thought were developed in Spencer's *The Study of Sociology*.[9] This work is popular in style
and much the most readable of Spencer's works. Conscious of himself as a
pioneer in social science, Spencer devoted considerable space to analyzing
and demolishing the obstacles confronting social science. Despite his self-
righteous compulsion to catalog the intellectual sins of others—a self-
righteousness exceeded only by the later work of Sumner and Pareto—
Spencer's analysis is clear and to the point. Humankind, he said, is subject
to an enormous range of biases that block scientific social analysis. The chief
source of all bias is the widespread and stubborn belief that human nature
is constant and forms an order of phenomena separate from the rest of
nature. There can be no social science so long as this belief continues to
influence social thought. However, even after this belief is dispelled, the
problem remains of defining the subject matter and method of a social
science. In attempting this definition, said Spencer, one must not hesitate
to use the mental disciplines and skills that characterize the physical
sciences. From the abstract sciences, logic and mathematics, one can acquire a sense of the "necessity of relation," and from the abstract-concrete

---

[7] Herbert Spencer, *Social Statics* (London: Williams and Norgate, 1868), pp.
45–80.
[8] Ibid., pp. 493–498.
[9] Published in 1873; available as a University of Michigan paperback (Ann
Arbor: 1961) with an introduction by Talcott Parsons.

sciences, physics and chemistry, one can acquire a sense of "simple causa-tion." But, Spencer cautioned, these types of science tend to be static and overly simplified. They must be supplemented by the concrete sciences, astronomy, geology, and biology, from which one can acquire concepts of "continuity, complexity, and contingency." These concepts are supplied chiefly by biology, since it alone has the concept of "fructifying causation." Actually, biology supplies the most important concepts for the study of society. It alone provides the idea of the individual and society as organic wholes whose differentiated parts are functionally interdependent. This idea, originally borrowed by biology from political economy, is now ready to return to social science, greatly enriched by its use among biologists. It has developed into an "all-embracing truth" that allows human beings to see that not merely industrial but all social relations are characterized by a division of labor.[10]

The idea that society is fundamentally a division of labor and can be con-ceptualized in terms of the functioning of an organism is hardly original with Spencer. It is a staple of ancient and medieval social thought, which is not surprising given the organic-teleological cosmology of those periods. What the theorists of the premodern period had done was to impart to nature the same attributes they had experienced in themselves as self-conscious animals. Not surprisingly, during the early modern period, which was dominated by the idea that nature was a machine, the use of biological models to interpret social phenomena played a relatively minor role in social science. It was only as the mechanistic-mathematical world view waned in the eighteenth and nineteenth centuries that the organic analogy was revived.

Spencer's organic theory, however, was novel enough to be an innovation in social thought. Unlike most previous thinkers, Spencer deliberately pro-ceeded from nature to human nature, not the other way around. There is a full-fledged commitment to the view that the methods and findings of biological science can be used to study human beings. In reality, the ancient and medieval uses of the organic model were based on logic, not on biology. Spencer, on the contrary, disavowed "logic" in favor of "life."

One of the consequences of Spencer's new outlook is that he developed a far more dynamic perspective on the nature of human beings and society than any previous sociologist. Gone from his thought is the logically de-rived image of society as an organic unity composed of static, hierarchic strata. Far from being static and hierarchic, society is a structure evolving toward individualism and equality. Whether or not Spencer successfully

[10] *The Study of Sociology*, chaps. 13, 14.

reconciled individualism with the organic view in a separate matter, but there can be no doubt that individualism was a novel feature in his organic approach.

The radical naturalism of Spencer's methodological and substantive theory went beyond the traditional antirationalist trend; in some ways it constituted a threat to the validity of science itself. Like Comte, Spencer emphasized the emotional basis of human conduct and deplored the fact that legislatures assume that individuals are guided in action by cognition.[11] However, Spencer went further; unlike Comte, he was not an ideological determinist. His work does not emphasize the growth of science as the chief emergent and causal variable in social evolution, a view characteristic of French sociology before Durkheim. He was quite conscious of this difference and specifically criticized Comte for being too ideological.[12] For Spencer, it was not that rationality is an emergent of history, but rather that *emergence is rational*. It was this point of view that permitted him to say in the *Social Statics*, in *The Study of Sociology*,[13] and in a more extended way in the *Principles of Sociology* that each stage of social evolution, with all its modes of thought and values, is valid in its own right. The adaptability of functional thought to a variety of viewpoints, radical and conservative—and even to both at the same time as in Spencer—is something that occurs again and again in sociological thought.

Spencer's theory of evolution is also a deeply sophisticated solution to the liberal dilemma. The distinctions between truth and falsehood, new and old, good and evil have been largely superseded by his evolutionary naturalism. The following statement is the most fitting indication of Spencer's tendency to go beyond the mere critique of traditional rationalism and assume the lawfulness of the hitherto irrational, a tendency that connects his thought with the vitalism of Bergsonian philosophy in which the Cartesian dualism of mind and matter is reconciled by a new substantive principle, the principle of life:

> There can be no understanding of social actions without some knowledge of human nature; there can be no deep knowledge of human nature without some knowledge of the laws of Mind; there can be no adequate knowledge of the laws of Mind without knowledge of the laws of Life. And that knowledge of the Laws of Life, as exhibited in Man, may be properly grasped, attention must be given to the laws of Life in general.[14]

---

[11] Ibid., pp. 324–340.
[12] Ibid., p. 299f.
[13] See, e.g., *Social Statics*, pp. 447–455 and *The Study of Sociology*, p. 356.
[14] *The Study of Sociology*, p. 355.

SUBSTANTIVE WORK

Spencer based his formal treatise on sociology on three assumptions: that evolution is as true of the human realm as it is of every other kind of existence, that the data of human behavior can be treated as natural data, and that the purpose of science is to find the generalizations embracing the largest possible collection of facts. In pursuing these assumptions, Spencer made an enormously important contribution to the development of sociology in that his starkly stated naturalism removed all equivocation from the positive tradition and thereby helped to reveal its strengths and weaknesses in terms of its own assumptions.

The Data of Sociology

Spencer's concern for establishing his principles on a factual basis prompted him to devote more than four hundred pages of Volume I of the *Principles of Sociology* to what he called "The Data of Sociology." All in all, his classification of data is surprisingly good. Sociology, he claimed, deals with two types of primary factors, extrinsic and intrinsic. The extrinsic factors, influencing human behavior, include such things as climate and geography and their attendant flora and fauna. The intrinsic factors, influencing the growth and structure of society, are based on the physical, emotional, and intellectual characteristics of the individual. The possibility of social evolution rests primarily on these two sets of factors. Once the primary factors have exercised their force, however, evolution itself produces a number of secondary or derived factors. Listed briefly, these are:

1. the modification by society of its extrinsic environment

2. population growth

3. the reciprocal influence of society and its parts—the series of actions and reactions between the community and each member and the consequent change in their nature

4. relations between societies

5. the accumulation of superorganic products such as material appliances, language, mathematics and science, law, and the arts

Once these secondary factors come into play, they each become potent causal forces and are often more important than the primary factors.

The Interpretation of the Data

Spencer's classification of data contains, at least implicitly, two broadly different assumptions about the nature of social phenomena. First, he suggested that social facts are similar to physical facts—thus the emphasis on the physical, physiological, and psychological character of social pheonmena in his list of primary factors. This tendency is carried over in the first two secondary factors, the transformation of the physical habitat and population growth. However, the last three secondary factors imply that a different mode of interpretation is possible. Here Spencer was referring to social relationships and cultural facts, and there is a suggestion that at least part of social behavior is different from the behavior of natural objects. In short, he suggested that social interaction, which takes place according to historically created technologies, values, and norms, may constitute an important and different type of sociological data. However, while he sometimes interpreted data in this way, his commitment was to the first mode of interpretation.

In a long introduction Spencer focused on the two types of primary factors, especially on the psychological nature of primitive human beings. He surveyed a vast store of anthropological knowledge, and he canvassed and cited with methodical exactitude strange and nonrational customs and ideas. However, he showed little evidence of what today is called cultural analysis. On the contrary, he attributed the origin and the development of the primitive mentality to the psychological nature of human beings and to the play of natural forces. He stated that although the superstitious belief structure of primitive human beings is psychologically based, it is still subject to the law of evolution. In addition, there are certain underlying similarities in the wide variety of superstitions that characterize primitive mentalities. Beneath all the varieties of religion and political authority lie two fears, the fear of the dead and the fear of the living. Through these two fears primitive people, whose raw psychology renders them unfit for social existence, are conditioned for cooperation.

Only after Spencer finished an extensive analysis of the psychological basis of social customs and beliefs did he shift his attention to secondary factors. Social science is now in a position, he asserted confidently, to analyze the growth and performance of the functional structures of society: the family, which replenishes the race; the governmental, ecclesiastical, and ceremonial structures, which regulate and protect society; and the producing structures, which insure the material support of society. Associated developments in language, knowledge, morals, and aesthetics must also be analyzed. However, he cautioned, the overall analysis will not be complete until developments in all areas are correlated with one another and the interdependence of all structures, functions, and social products considered in their totality.

The Organic Nature of Society

Spencer's definition of society was at once a methodology, or a way of thinking about society, and a substantive statement about its nature.

Society is not merely a collection of individuals with no existence of its own: it exists in the regular relations of its component members. Spencer's focus on society as a system of relationships is the mark of his scientific orientation. The same orientation is found in his famous organic analogy. Society can be likened to an organism, he argued, because it too grows and develops a more complex structure and its various unlike parts engage in unlike activities.

Spencer made it clear, however, that he was making an analogy, not an identification, between society and organic life. For one thing, cooperation between the parts of society is effected by the language of the emotions and the intellect. The most important difference, however, stems from the fact that society, unlike other organisms, is composed of discrete units that are wholes in their own right.

> In the one, consciousness is concentrated in a small part of the aggregate. In the other, it is diffused throughout the aggregate: all the units possess the capacities for happiness and misery, if not in equal degrees, still in degrees that approximate. As, then, there is no social sensorium, the welfare of the aggregate, considered apart from that of the units, is not an end to be sought. The society exists for the benefit of its members; not its members for the benefit of society. It has ever to be remembered that great as may be the efforts made for the prosperity of the body politic; yet the claims of the body politic are nothing in themselves, and become something only in so far as they embody the claims of its component individuals.[15]

Here Spencer was again suggesting that social phenomena are different from physical phenomena, a difference that stems from the fact that human behavior entails consciousness. However, Spencer's naturalistic positivism was too strong for him to pursue this line of thought very far.

The Evolution of Social Types

The organic analogy held Spencer in good stead in analyzing the evolution of both social relations and social types. It was axiomatic for him that a phenomenon could be understood only in terms of its genesis and development. He shared this assumption with many other thinkers, but he gave it a distinctive flavor when he assumed that the relations between the structures and functions of a living organism could also be applied to social relations. Accordingly, he spent considerable effort in defining social activities and beliefs in terms of the structures and functions found in animal organisms. There was no doubt in his mind that there would be a

[15] *Principles of Sociology*, 3rd ed., 3 vols. (New York: Appleton, 1910), 1:461f.

significant gain in scientific understanding if economic institutions, for example, were defined as sustaining and distributing systems, and if political institutions were thought of as regulative systems. Each subsystem, Spencer insisted, is subject to evolution in the same way as the rest of nature. Similarly, on a more complex level, the totality of systems that make up society is also subject to evolution. The master trend is toward the increased differentiation of society into specialized functional subsystems and a significant advance into a qualitatively more adaptive social system. Social types may be distinguished according to which of the two main structural-functional organs is dominant, the regulative (political) or the sustaining (economic). When the regulative function is paramount, there exists a Military type of society, "in which the army is the nation mobilized while the nation is the quiescent army." Social activities and values in Military society are subordinated to the requirements of government and war.[16]

Whereas the Military social system is characterized by "compulsory co-operation," the second type of society, the Industrial, is characterized by "voluntary cooperation." All its social activities, ranging from worker-employer combinations to philanthropic bodies and from political to aesthetic organizations, are permeated by the principle of voluntary cooperation. The main reason for this structural change is the emergence of industry and its characteristic relation, free exchange for mutual benefit.

These two social types may not exhaust the fertility of evolution. A new social type may evolve in which the "products of industry" will be used for "higher activities" and "the belief that life is for work" will be inverted into "the belief that work is for life." [17] In this [Ethical] society:

> The ultimate man will be one whose private requirements coincide with public ones. He will be that manner of man who, in spontaneously fulfilling his own nature, incidentally performs the functions of a social unit; and yet is only enabled so to fulfill his own nature by all others doing the like.[18]

Despite this strain of utopianism and his general belief in progress, one should not hastily infer that Spencer was a naively optimistic nineteenth-century liberal. He was too aware of the complexities of social phenomena to adopt simple solutions or doctrines. He was certain, of course, that social data exhibit all the features of cosmic evolution, and he never faltered in his conviction that the data overwhelmingly supported his theory of evolution. However, he expressed definite reservations about a straight-line development in social evolution. He was aware that industrialization is compatible with militarism and cited Germany and France as illustrations.

[16] Ibid., 1:556–564.
[17] Ibid., 1:575.
[18] Ibid., 3:611.

Even England, the most advanced example of Industrial society, showed signs of retrogression toward the military type because of an increase in international war and because of the increasing tempo of social legislation. All in all, he could summon up only a "relative optimism."

Causation

Spencer's consistent adherence to a structural-functional approach held great promise for the movement of sociological theory toward a concern for causal factors. In his original classification of factors, Spencer outlined the physical and psychological phenomena that influence social structure and showed that he was aware of the causal power of social interaction and culture. In his general discussion of the organic nature of society and its evolutionary development, he referred again and again to the emergence and influence of new forms of interaction stemming from changes in international relations or from advances in such fields as transportation and communication facilities. His causal formula was based on the pregnant assumption that social structures adjust to fit new activities. Unfortunately, he never developed this idea, though he constantly verged on an image of society as a structure of relationships different from those of natural phenomena. His naturalism was too strong to permit him to shift to a more historical-cultural viewpoint.

Spencer's institutional analysis, which has a modern, textbooklike flavor, cannot receive extended treatment even though it contains an often fascinating survey of "domestic, ceremonial, political, ecclesiastical, professional, and industrial institutions." The range of Spencer's scholarship is almost incredible, even allowing for the fact that he had research assistants. Each volume contains an extensive bibliography of references to the cultures of almost every known portion of the globe. However, the most important aspect of his analysis, aside from the fact that the material is compressed into an evolutionary scheme, is that he treated specific practices and beliefs in terms of their functional purpose in a given stage of social development or a given type of social system. To take just one example, a section on ceremonial institutions shows a grasp of the importance of the lesser structures of society in producing social control, and it contains fascinating insights into the way specific beliefs and practices perform social functions quite apart from the intrinsic value or purpose of the ceremony. Spencer's work in this regard anticipated Simmel's insight into the sociological importance of the lower reaches of society—an anticipation that also included Simmel's acute sense of the importance of seemingly obvious and trivial relations. Further, Spencer's wide-ranging functional approach anticipated Durkheim's insight into how beliefs and practices, especially those connected with religion, serve the wider ends of social life. Spencer's strict adherence to a relational approach also allowed him to see universes of data. He had an acute sense of the unity underlying the various institutional structures of society and was able to show the correlations (or, as he called them, the *coexistences*) that obtain within a given social system at a given stage of development.

Ultimately, however, Spencer's theory of causation is faulty and represents a subsidiary interest in his work. Though he listed the operative factors in human behavior and consistently viewed them in relational terms, he never focused on the problem of deriving an adequate causal theory. Even his keen ability to see patterns within social phenomena never led to an adequate causal theory; correlation is not the same as causation, just as description is not explanation.

The major reason for Spencer's deficiency in causal analysis is his initial definition of social phenomena. It is not merely that he equated human behavior with physical and biological behavior—a naturalistic positivism need not be deficient in causal explanation. It was his metaphysical positivism, his decision to commit his data to the all-embracing principle of evolution, that negated the need for an adequate theory of causation. Though Spencer had an acute sense of the complexity of data and made constant reference to sociocultural factors and to the special factors that influence events, he never allowed data to control his ideas. On the contrary, he assumed that the data of behavior would fit the evolutionary mold, a mold that he always assumed to be a natural, biological-like process. As for so many other naturalistic positivists before and after him, events for Spencer happened because they happened. His failure to define social phenomena as cultural and to attach primary causal importance to interaction and culture led him straight into a teleological explanation in which final cause supplants first cause. However, if he had acknowledged the importance of sociocultural factors, he would have been forced to modify drastically his reliance on psychological and racial factors—though he could have continued to use such factors as climate, geography, and population growth as causal variables. In short, Spencer would have had to shift his explanation of social change from evolution to history, something manifestly impossible given the presuppositions behind his thought.

CONCLUSION

The Contribution to Method

Though Spencer's rigid naturalistic-evolutionary scheme was a dead end in the history of sociology, his methodology was a rich contribution to the science of society. Though Spencer failed to make an adequate distinction between the method of science and its substantive concepts, his work is nevertheless characterized by the crucial methodology of science. In particular, he employed the scientific idea of _system_ with a deliberateness and consistency unusual in the previous annals of sociology. The concept of system was not new with Spencer, of course. Conceiving something as a whole with interrelated parts had been a commonplace of Western intellectual life since the time of the Greeks. In social thought Plato and Aristotle and such thinkers as John of Salisbury (d. 1180), Saint Thomas (1225–1274), Bonald (1754–1840), and Maistre (1753–1821) had all conceived of society as an organic unity based on a division of function. For the most part, however, these thinkers had conceived of society as a logical system, as an organized whole that they derived from logic. At best it was mind organizing experience; at worst, it was mind ignoring or going beyond experience.

Though Spencer was highly addicted to the use of deduction and abstractions, the measure of his stature as a social scientist lies in his deep, if implicit, rejection of logic as a scientific method. For Spencer, it is not that which is rational that exists; it is that which exists that is rational. He was also addicted to metaphysics, though in his quest for a monistic principle he made a significant scientific contribution when he insisted that science can concern itself only with relations and functions and that it must give up the search for the essence or inherent structure of things. Thus Spencer did more than merely climax trends that had appeared in earlier sociology; he also stands as the first figure in the development of the empirical phase of sociology, a phase in which sociology sought a more adequate definition of its subject matter and method from the new developments that were taking place in the natural sciences. Spencer's lasting contribution to empirical sociology was mostly methodological, consisting of an attempt to think in terms of functional relationships. In his substantive theory, however, he never realized that the substantive concepts of natural science might be inappropriate when applied to human beings, and his work has been called transitional, an anticipation of the full-bodied empirical tradition that flowered later in the century.

Spencer's strictures on the need to come to grips with phenomena and to search for relational rather than substantive knowledge, unlike similar exhortations by earlier sociological theorists, were practiced as well as preached. Like others before him, Spencer conceived society as an organic unity, but he did so in thoroughgoing naturalistic terms. For him, society was a moving equilibrium of natural, existential forces, and its parts as well as its unity could be known not through a logical analysis of the nature of being, but only in terms of functional relationships. Though he vitiated his theory by hinging it on an almost straightforward identification between social and biological processes, Spencer was clearly aware of the interactional and cultural basis of behavior. Finally, though he obscured causal analysis by committing himself to an evolutionary monism, he was still relatively aware of the complexity of the causes in human affairs and the complexities and even perplexities of social development.

Though Spencer's work contained both the natural and the sociocultural models of interpreting social data, his emphasis on the first model vitiated his overall theory. For all his evolutionary dynamism, his open-ended view of social development, and his open-armed welcome to novelty, Spencer was ultimately expounding a static substantialism. By failing to separate the method of science from its substantive content, he severely limited his perception of social data and of human capabilities. It is in this light that Spencer's commitment to, indeed, unconscious absorption into, a specific historical social system is most readily seen.

Spencer and English Liberalism

Of all the sociologists, Spencer is most easily identified as an ideological champion of liberal society. His work blatantly equates the specific institutions of English liberalism with a necessary, beneficent, and thus rational cosmic process. It is important to note that Spencer's liberalism is English, since it has a distinctly different flavor from the liberalism of the Frenchmen Saint-Simon and Comte. The difference stems primarily from Spencer's individualism and his greater belief in the intrinsic harmony of social processes. The radical laissez faire theory that he propounded never left his thought, though it took on a more mellow and sophisticated flavor in his later years. While Spencer used natural selection and even conflict to explain change, he was only a moderate social Darwinist. Given the advanced state of English economic and social development, it is not surprising that he was more disposed to trust individuals and to think of them as consciously rational participants in social processes. Nowhere in the previous literature of liberal social thought, except in Hobbes and Condorcet, is there such a heavy disposition to separate the individual from society and to shift the center of gravity from society to the individual.

Spencer's theory, however, is not a crude psychological vitalism, nor is it a typical liberal overestimation of the rationality of the individual. If that were so, he would have been mired in the liberal dilemma of earlier rationalism. By thinking of society as a natural process in which conflict and superstition are rational for given stages of development, he was offering a more advanced version of the developmental theory of French pseudo-evolutionary sociology. As I emphasized earlier, Spencer's radical naturalism lacked the ideological causation of Comte's evolutionary thought. For Comte, the emergence of rationality made possible the development and eventual rationality of society. For Spencer, the development of new modes of adjustment to conditions was in itself rational at each stage of social

development—that is, the development of functional structures was in and
of itself the development of rationality. It was in this sense that Spencer
used his famous phrase, "the wise severity of nature's discipline."

For Spencer, the process of human development originates in an individual's
psychology and racial attributes,[19] but the individual is soon caught up in
the organic social relationships that slowly equip him or her for an even
better adjustment to conditions. Finally, industrial relationships place individuals on their own, and free competitive markets, the contract, private
property, and limited government become the best institutional arrangements for adjusting to conditions. The future holds promise that eventually
"man may be fully adjusted to the social state," by which Spencer meant
that there will be a perfect identity between the compelling needs of society
and those of the individual, and that it will no longer be necessary to rely
on suffering, sacrifice, and superstition to preserve and advance the interests of society.

Spencer placed great emphasis, of course, on the transition from Military
to Industrial society, and his description of this transition is a perfect
model of liberal thought. The contrast between these two societies is one
of the major strands running through the whole of sociological theory. It
is found in one form or another in almost every major theorist. In Spencer's
version, the transition is from a relatively homogeneous society, in which
the individual is controlled by society and government for purposes of
war, to a relatively heterogeneous society based on a more rational division
of labor in which the individual is trained for peaceful pursuits.

In making this contrast almost every sociological theorist states the major
difference between the stages of evolution, or between types of society,
in terms of economic institutions—invariably the specific institutions of
bourgeois civilization. It is not industrialism itself that marks a qualitative
change in evolution, Spencer warned, pointing to the case of Bismarckian
Germany, but the accompanying institutions whose essential characteristic
was "voluntary cooperation." Like so many of his fellow sociologists, Spencer argued specifically against the dangerous allurements of socialism.
Despite his acceptance of novelty, uniqueness, and dynamism, Spencer was
content to limit progress to the specific institutions of English liberalism.
His overall theory reflected features that have exercised wide influence
in the Anglo-American world down to the present day: the notion that the
individual is more real than society; that voluntarism is a real force and

---

[19] The tendency to use psychology as the substantive explanation for social
behavior easily slides off into a racial theory. Spencer constantly did this, though
he never emphasized race as a major variable.

requires institutions in which it can express itself—essentially private property and free contractual relations; that cooperation and harmony are somehow inherent in a free, voluntary society; and that the future will take care of itself.

Spencer's general contrast of past and present was a moderately accurate description of the emergence of modern English society. Despite his advanced scientific outlook, however, Spencer hypostatized the social process he uncovered. Like others before him, he turned his analysis into a metaphysics by framing the specific historical forms of English liberalism in substantialistic terms. Spencer's grand theory of evolution was obsolete even before his death—it was an early industrial image applied to a relatively advanced industrial society. By the end of the nineteenth century the internal differentiation of English society was too complex and its imperial entanglements and rivalries too vast for the simplistic scheme that Spencer proposed. This was something Spencer himself sensed. In some respects he deeply misunderstood the developments around him. He overlooked, for example, one of the most significant developments of nineteenth-century English life, the creation of a powerful, efficient, centralized civil service. In a sense, Spencer misread the entire development of English political life—the English state was enfeebled neither by the Settlement of 1688 nor by the rise of Parliament. On the contrary, it grew consistently from the Civil Wars on, becoming fully centralized and bureaucratic during the nineteenth century. In short, Hobbes was as much the prophet of English social development as Locke.

The theory of an automatic and beneficent social evolution and the concept of a magical market were understandable outcomes in a "lead" society. England was the first to experience industrialization and the first to experience social-system change with its many tangible benefits. The theory of evolution and the doctrines of individualism and voluntarism were understandable developments in a stable society that had settled most of the main questions of social existence and could take its values and institutions for granted. A dynamic society creates a continuous stream of psychological problems—the concept of automatic progress through individual competition in free markets helped the English and the American middle class overcome its anxiety about an uncertain future. Unlike Continental liberalism, English and American liberalism had no coherent social enemy by the nineteenth century. Saint-Simon and Comte had conducted an ideological debate with the forces of monarchy in what was still predominantly an agrarian society. The "enemy" faced by the English middle class was a vague and open-ended future, a future for which it had no coherent model on which to base its actions. The theory of evolution, along with the ideas of automatic equilibration and progress through natural selection, were admirably suited to overcome such anxieties and to help ward off the new enemies that appeared with industrialization, the urban working class and socialism.

If Spencer had been content with an accurate description of the development of society, his theory of evolution would have been transformed into a theory of history; ultimately he may even have raised the possibility that history itself has no one pattern and no one meaning. Nonetheless, Spencer's thought is a landmark in social theory, for it is the first statement in sociology that goes beyond the Newtonian phase of science. In Spencer, the experience with social-system change, by and large a beneficial experience for the English middle class, led to a new cosmology in which nature, human behavior, and mind were turned into functional processes, ultimately into the same dynamic, evolutionary, natural process. Spencer's evolutionary-functional cosmology reflected powerful and complex social currents, and it is not surprising that contemporary populations and theorists are still struggling to clarify its meaning. However, even as Spencer wrote, the complexities and conflicts of urban-industrial development were leading Anglo-American theorists into a later stage of liberalism—basically to the recognition that explicit human control had to be exercised over social evolution and that society and government were forces that could and must be made amenable to human purposes and volitions. In England, late liberal sociology is represented in the work of Leonard Hobhouse (1864–1929), Morris Ginsberg (1889–1970), and Karl Mannheim (1893–1947). In the United States, the debate within liberalism as to whether it should adopt a more positive, instrumental, and interventionist stance toward government and society appeared in the work of Sumner and Ward. Nothing illustrates the monopoly of American liberalism so well as the fact that this debate continues to constitute what most Americans in private and public life, as well as those in sociology, mean by social theory. It is to this debate that I now turn.

Chapter 11
William Graham Sumner (1840–1910)

The establishment of sociology as an independent discipline in the United States is due in no small measure to the work of William Graham Sumner. A good part of Sumner's success is explained by the fact that his work took place within the setting of a university—Yale—something that was to become increasingly characteristic of sociologists. Sociology did not find immediate acceptance, however, either inside or outside the academic world. Of course, Sumner's attitude toward the conventional disciplines, expressed in barbs and taunts about the unscientific and useless character of much of what passed for intellectual activity, was not calculated to endear him to the academic community.

Unlike his predecessors in sociology, Sumner saw no need to construct a philosophy of positivism. He once made a serious proposal that the teaching of philosophy be abolished at Yale. His objection to philosophy stemmed from a deep-rooted nominalism that made him suspicious of all formal intellectual activity. Sumner's deep distrust of abstract thought, which he shared with American pragmatism, did not mean that he made any significant alteration in the tradition of monistic naturalistic positivism. Despite his avowed nominalism and well-known contribution to cultural analysis, Sumner's work never veered from the basic goal of early sociology, the search for the truth about human nature and society in terms of natural, physical-psychological causation.

PHILOSOPHY AND METHOD

Characteristically, Sumner wrote no formal treatise on the logic of social science. Nevertheless, his work provides significant insights into the nature and development of positivism and the logic of scientific method.[1] Much

[1] Sumner devoted his early career mostly to economics and topical political issues, and with the exception of a few articles, his early work contains little of interest to the historian of sociology. As sociology came to dominate Sumner's

William Graham Sumner (1840–1910)

of the world's mischief, Sumner argued, can be laid at the door of those who explain things by reference to ideas or ethics. In one of his few philosophical essays, "Purposes and Consequences," he distinguished between those who rely on ideas and ethics, or purposes, and those who

---

intellectual interests, he undertook a large-scale treatise on the science of society that was never finished. Sumner's reputation rests mostly on a portion of this work, *Folkways* (1906; reprint ed., Boston: Ginn and Company, 1940), available as a New American Library paperback. The larger treatise was completed by Sumner's disciple Albert G. Keller, under joint authorship, as *The Science of Society*, 4 vols. (New Haven, Conn.: Yale University Press, 1927). Since its spirit and content do not differ from the main bent of Sumner's mind, it will be considered an organic part of his work. A running commentary with a liberal sprinkling of quotations from Sumner's writings, especially from *Folkways*, is provided by Maurice R. Davie, *William Graham Sumner* (New York: Thomas Y. Crowell, 1963).

rely on science and facts, or consequences. Any attempt to impose ethical considerations on the world of fact, he argued, is unacceptable to the scientific spirit. "In fact, the judgment of probable consequences is the only real and sound ground of action." [2] The world is in an age of transition, he concluded, between a period when purposes and consequences have been united and a period when they will be divorced and metaphysics left behind.

Sumner's bias against metaphysics was not directed only against medieval survivals. He was if anything even more intent on assailing the metaphysics of the Enlightenment and what he felt was its grossly unscientific concept of natural rights. Eschewing any recourse to formal philosophical analysis, he peremptorily dismissed the idea of natural rights as unworthy of scientific belief. In such essays as "Rights," "Equality," and "Liberty" he rejected all efforts to establish absolute standards prior to social life. It is clear that Sumner was protesting not so much against the idea of individual rights as against the natural-law basis on which theorists had sought to establish them.

The rejection of natural rights is not new to sociological theory; Saint-Simon, Comte, and Spencer, for example, also saw them as relics of a prescientific age. Saint-Simon and Comte had ignored individual rights altogether. Sumner, like Spencer, accepted them but on different grounds; both theorists were inclined to think of individual rights in utilitarian terms, as both the product of human adjustment to nature in the past, and the means for waging a more successful struggle for existence in the future. Sumner, however, was too unphilosophical to attempt, as Spencer had done, a cosmic philosophy of evolution in which human beings are simply one aspect of an evolving nature. He was content to say simply that individual rights come from experience.

Underlying the entire range of Sumner's thinking is the crucial assumption of the struggle for existence, an assumption that the source of knowledge about human beings was their relations with nature. As philosophical nominalism, this assumption expressed Sumner's belief that these relations are unalterably empirical rather than rational since there is "no disposition at all in nature to conform her operations to man's standards." It was a philosophical position, in short, that had abandoned the Enlightenment's belief in the corresponding structures of the human mind and of nature. For Sumner, population-land ratios and capital formation were the primary determinants of intellectual life and of all social relations. His economic determinism is most clearly expressed in such essays as "Power and Progress," "Consequences of Increased Social Power," "The Absurd Effort to

---

[2] William Graham Sumner, *Selected Essays* (New Haven, Conn.: Yale University Press, 1924), p. 5.

Make the World Over," and "Earth Hunger or the Philosophy of Land
Grabbing." In the second of these essays he stated flatly that individualism
developed in the United States not because of metaphysical discourse but
because of economic conditions.

> Is not this the correct interpretation of what has happened in
> America? If it is, then the dogmatic or philosophical theorems, in-
> stead of being the cause of our social arrangements, are only the
> metaphysical dress which we have amused ourselves by imagining
> upon them. We are not free and equal because Jefferson put it
> into the Declaration of Independence that we were born so; but
> Jefferson could put it into the Declaration of Independence that
> all men are born free and equal because the economic relations
> existing in America made the members of society to all intents
> and purposes free and equal. It makes some difference to him
> who desires to attain to a correct social philosophy which of these
> ways of looking at the matter is true to the facts.[3]

The facts of human behavior are not too various and unstable to admit
of generalization. On the contrary, Sumner was convinced "that social phenomena are subject to law, and that the natural laws of the social order
are in their entire character like the laws of physics".[4] Even though he
sharply denied that the mind can find moral law in nature—a position that
in its Humian rigor is unprecedented in sociological theory—he did feel that
science can provide a guide for action:

> The moral deductions as to what one ought to do are to be drawn
> by the reason and conscience of the individual man who is in-
> structed by science. Let him take note of the force of gravity,
> and see to it that he does not walk off a precipice or get in the
> way of a falling body.[5]

Sumner's identification of morality with the factual world amounted to
an almost fatalistic acceptance of social and historical structures, a conscious equation of might with right. Sumner's concern for facts led him,
like Spencer, into a massive exploration of ethnography. Sumner's conviction that the data of behavior and belief can be traced to the conditions
of existence is central to his best-known work, the loosely structured *Folkways*, and his fundamental nominalism is clearly evident in the structure
of *The Science of Society*. The latter contains no methodological analysis;
it simply states some starting points, or self-evident propositions about the
relationship of human beings to nature. Significantly, Sumner relegated the

---

[3] Ibid., p. 149.
[4] *War and Other Essays*, p. 191.
[5] William Graham Sumner, *What Social Classes Owe to Each Other* (Caldwell,
Idaho: The Caxton Printers, 1952), p. 137f.

discussion of scientific social thought to the end of the last volume of text. Basically, science consists of "trained and organized common sense," and its mode of procedure is to plunge into the realm of facts in order to obtain the generalizations necessary to intelligent adjustment. Once obtained, these generalizations will effectively separate sociology from metaphysics as well as from history.

Sumner shared many philosophical assumptions with his predecessors in sociology. Like them, he articulated a positivism that was avowedly anti-metaphysical. Distinctive in his philosophy and method was his rejection of what he felt were the exaggerated claims that had been made on behalf of reason. He was unique in his definition of reason as an instrument of adjustment. In this respect his antimetaphysical bias allowed him to go even further than Spencer in transforming mind into function. However, Sumner also believed that the mind as science was somehow capable of unearthing the underlying pattern that controls the destiny of human beings, a pattern that he identified as the law of evolutionary adjustment.

SUBSTANTIVE WORK

Population-Land Ratios

The relationship between human beings and nature, which for Sumner constituted the starting point of all social science, was stated more precisely as the relation between population and land.

> How much land there is to how many men is the fundamental consideration in the life of any society. The ratio between these two factors means the ratio of numbers to sustenance, or of mouths to food; for the fact that all food comes in the last analysis from the earth should not be let slip because it is obvious. This relation of numbers to sustenance affords a firm, unspeculative, unselected footing for a science of society. It is a matter of observation and of recorded experience. It is also determinative for organic life in general. Where Mother Earth has more children than she can nourish, they die or exist in misery; where beasts or men are fewer, they get more nourishment and may live on in comfort. This simple and objective relation furnishes, we say, a firm footing for a science of society; we start with an incontrovertible and, indeed, implacable fact of life, and not with any speculative considerations.[6]

In addition to his "economic" determinism, Sumner believed that there were elemental motives or interests behind the struggle for adjustment.

[6] *Science of Society*, 1:4.

> There are four great motives of human action which come into play when some number of human beings are in juxtaposition under the same life conditions. These are hunger, sex passion, vanity, and fear (of ghosts and spirits). Under each of these motives are interests. Life consists in satisfying interests, for "life," in a society, is a career of action and effort expended on both the material and social environment. However great the errors and misconceptions may be which are included in the efforts, the purpose always is advantage and expedience.[7]

Sumner never formulated an explicit biopsychological theory of society; that is, he never said that elemental human needs are directly translatable into human behavior. In the passage just quoted, for example, the fact that human beings must be in "juxtaposition" suggests that interaction is necessary before the four motives become operative. Furthermore, his "economic" determinism, together with his cultural approach, by illustrating the variegated forms that these elemental urges could take, contained the broad suggestion that social existence makes possible a wide transcendence of biology and psychology. Though Sumner never satisfactorily defined the role of biopsychological forces in human behavior, he tended to limit them as explanatory factors, suggesting that human nature is a set of indefinite promptings upon which society builds.

Folkways and Mores

Perhaps the best known aspect of Sumner's work is his contribution to the understanding of social values and norms—in his own terms, *folkways* and *mores*. The belief that the values and norms by which human beings live can be understood scientifically, and not in terms of revelation, authority, reason, or specially endowed human beings, is implicit in the entire tradition of sociological theory. All the sociological theorists whose work has been examined attempted, at least in some way, to explain the origin and nature of social norms. Sumner's careful choice of the terms *folkways* and *mores* indicates his desire to make a fresh start in this area. He signaled this approach by insisting that the most important thing about social norms is that they arise "without rational reflection or purpose" from the struggle of the human animal to cope with the pitiless forces of nature.

The folkways arise from pleasure-pain responses. The mechanism of pleasure-pain produces, first, a "strain of improvement toward better adaptation of means to ends"; next, there develops "a strain of consistency" to bring norms into line with each other. Groups characteristically elaborate sentiments of solidarity, ethnocentric emotions that differentiate in-group

---

[7] *Folkways*, p. 18f.

from out-group and serve to strengthen the rest of the folkways. Relative to time and place, the folkways prescribe the good and the true. When they involve the welfare of society itself—that is, when they involve such things as property, sex, and power—they become mores—that is, they become deeply lodged in the personality.

Two themes emerged in Sumner's analysis of folkways and mores. The first received the most attention and constitutes Sumner's contribution to the concept of culture. Like Spencer, Sumner was greatly influenced by the ripening discipline of cultural anthropology. However, Sumner went beyond Spencer and revived the cultural emphasis that figured so heavily in the work of Vico and Montesquieu. The second theme, which Sumner never developed adequately, grew from his insight into the cultural sources of behavior. If social existence takes place through the medium of culture and is not directly derived from natural forces, then it follows that folkways and mores can be discussed in terms of the relations of human beings to each other, that is, in terms of interaction or social process.

Types of Social Process

Sumner's main concern was to show that norms originate in the relationship between human beings and nature. However, he was aware that relationships among human beings also affected the nature of norms and the functioning of society. In his discussion of the four motives, Sumner was careful to add that these motives come into play only when individuals are in juxtaposition. His awareness of social interaction as a sociologically important variable is apparent in such phrases as "near each other," "mutual reactions," "methods of interaction," and "adjustment of adjacent interests." Sumner also developed, at least embryonically, the related idea of social status or "fixed positions," and the idea that the totality of relations and positions connected to social functions can be conceived as a structure. Sumner's interest in interaction also led him to accept the idea of "suggestion" as the origin of norms. In the same connection, he made fleeting references to the importance of subgroup membership, references that suggest a crude awareness of what has come to be known as reference-group theory.

Though Sumner's insight into the importance of interaction was deeper than that of Spencer, his contribution in this area was minimal. His ideas about interaction were incidental to other concerns, and he never focused on social relationships as the core of sociological analysis as did, say, Durkheim and Simmel. He was far more disposed to regard norms as arising from human beings' relation to nature than as a product of interaction. His failure to identify interaction as an important sociological variable is one of emphasis rather than of omission, and he managed to say a number of interesting things about the causes and types of social process. He was aware that population density influences the quality of social relationships, as does the growth of what he called the "industrial organization." This development, which stems from human efforts to cope more efficiently with the forces of nature, affects social relationships by disciplining individuals and by restricting both liberty and equality—a price, Sumner said, not too high for the benefits organization brings.

Sumner's awareness of the increasing complexity of society, especially in the economic sphere, links him with Saint-Simon, Comte, Spencer, and the entire sociological tradition. Though some sociologists, such as Comte, Durkheim, and Max Weber, were concerned about the stability of a complex society, almost all felt that the increased division of labor was ultimately functional. Basically, Sumner was disposed not to worry about this question; indeed, he developed a number of ideas to show that the grand idea of automatic evolutionary adjustment through specialization posed no problem for social unity and stability. *Antagonistic cooperation,* for example, which is unconscious and basically akin to the processes of the natural world, reconciles antagonistic interests so that common purposes can be achieved. Though Sumner failed to develop the idea in his later work, he nevertheless maintained that antagonistic cooperation was the primary mechanism by which society benefits by the division of labor and competition and by which society insures its own integration.[8]

Also relevant to the explanation of social stability and integrity is Sumner's concept of *conventionalization.* This is the process whereby certain standards and practices are placed in a special category by convention, thus preventing a clash with the general body of mores. These socially acceptable inconsistencies contribute to the richness and diversity of social unity, often acting to reconcile nonrational remnants with the growth of new mores and rationality.

Society as an Evolutionary Functional Structure

Underlying Sumner's discussion of folkways and mores is the idea of functional adjustment to life conditions, an idea that bound together the whole range of Sumner's thought. Again and again he affirmed his belief that norms do not emerge from the ruminations of philosophers, but as solutions to the problems of existence. They are relative to life conditions and survive only to the extent that they satisfy human needs. The only criterion for judging mores, therefore, is by their utility for social existence; mores are "bad" only when they outlive their historical usefulness. Despite their deep "inertia and rigidity," the mores nonetheless exhibit "changeableness and variation." As new conditions arise, the mores either assume new forms or are discarded. The entire process is natural, though great societal crises

[8] *Science of Society,* 1:28f; 3:2231–2237.

or revolutions are often necessary to cleanse society of its backlog of outmoded mores. Finally, Sumner concluded, little can be done to modify
this process through artificial human effort. "There is logic in the folkways,
but never rationality." The logic presumably emerges from the workings
of the automatic strains toward improvement and consistency that are
natural to society.

Sumner also had faith in the inherent rationality of interaction. When
human beings come together in the struggle for existence, their interaction
seems to have an inherent capacity for producing both functional mores
and functional patterns of behavior. If the *Folkways* has any theme apart
from the emphasis on the cultural sources of behavior, it is that social norms
are explicable only insofar as they can be related to environmental conditions and to social purposes. Despite the fact that, on the whole, the
Folkways is heavily deficient in causal theory, Sumner insisted that norms
and practices be viewed in terms of time, place, and need. For example,
such practices as slavery, cannibalism, abortion, infanticide, killing the
old, polygamy, and polyandry are products of economic necessity. Such
practices, Sumner argued, may be quite functional to one society and
should not be judged by the standards of another.

Sumner's realistic appraisal of culture and social life held forth the possibility that his sociology would fulfill the promise of Spencer's work, but
neither the *Folkways* nor *The Science of Society* went beyond Spencer in
any significant way. It is true that the overall framework of *The Science
of Society* is stated in functional terms. The institutions of society are described in terms of how well they fulfill the four human motives, and
society is repeatedly defined as an interdependent survival unit that gradually builds institutions around these motives or interests. Unfortunately
the promise in this vague but genuinely scientific approach never bore
fruit. In regard to how human beings cope with nature, Sumner made
little theoretical advance beyond the *Folkways*. He made a small effort
to identify evolutionary stages and to correlate them with economic systems. There are also some scattered references to the economic basis of
such phenomena as slavery and family forms, but these merely repeat insights in the *Folkways*. In truth, Sumner made no serious effort to tackle
empirically the problem of causation. He was content to reiterate his
vague assertion that adjustments to natural conditions determine the structure of both culture and society. Similarly he made no theoretical advance
in regard to a second type of environment, relations among human beings.
All in all, Sumner's faith in the automatic nature of evolution made it unnecessary for him to take the question of causation seriously.

However, Sumner's treatment of a third type of environment, the world of
ghosts and spirits, holds considerable interest for the historian of sociology.

Sumner regarded religion as part of the human attempt to adjust to a hostile world, in this case the world of the unknown. Religion, along with the rest of the mores, is therefore subject to the law of evolution and the "strain toward consistency." Arising as a naive anthropomorphism and evolving through definite stages, religion gradually developed an awareness of First Cause. Historically, said Sumner, religion has often retarded social evolution. It adjusts less slowly to new situations and in many cases blocks required adjustments by insisting on beliefs and practices that are detrimental to economic progress. Sumner's interesting and rather unexpected conclusion to all this is that while religion often obstructs rational solutions to human problems, on the whole it plays a positive role in the "strain toward improvement." Indeed, Sumner went on to argue that religion is indispensable not only to the formation of social order, but to economic and scientific progress as well. It contributes to evolutionary adjustment in many ways; it disciplines individuals, provides the sanctions for nonreligious mores, causes labor to be performed, and settles disputes between contending factions. Finally, its intuitive statements about the forces of the universe are the crude but necessary beginnings of the long, self-correcting intellectual process known as science.

Sumner's evaluation of the nature and function of religion was not an isolated feature of his sociology. On the contrary, his proclivity for finding utility in beliefs and practices that violate the canons of science, already pronounced in the *Folkways,* became an important unifying thread in *The Science of Society.* His emphasis on the social value of error was matched by an emphasis on the social value of evil. One practice after another—coercion, inequality, injustice, slavery, war, infanticide, killing the old, human sacrifice, polygamy, monarchical absolutism, monasticism, feudalism—is cited and justified in terms of historic utility. Behind this approach is a genuinely functional spirit, which Sumner stated in more theoretical terms: a given cause may have different consequences depending on time and place, while different causes may have the same consequence. The motives of any actor may have no relation to consequences—that is, a given purpose may have consequences quite at variance with a person's intentions. Sumner even recognized that the distinction between intentions and consequences implied a rejection of psychology as the basis for social science.

Sumner's functionalism stemmed from his assumption that science can never establish the intrinsic worth of any objective or subjective fact. Like Montesquieu and Spencer, the two most consciously functional thinkers before him, Sumner sought knowledge about human behavior by relating given practices to given contexts. However, Sumner had a deeper intellectual kinship with Spencer than with Montesquieu. Like Spencer, he employed a relational approach to knowledge without becoming a relativist. For Sumner, science is not defeated by the multiplicity and contradictoriness of human affairs; the phenomena of the social realm are ultimately lawful. He admitted that Spencer's biological analogy had been misused and that organic and societal evolution cannot be equated, but he said that this does not mean cultural and social structures are not natural. The science of society must still model itself after the natural sciences and conduct an unremitting search for law. Thanks largely to the work of Herbert Spencer, the science of society

> ... has worked out a conception of society as a unified whole—
> as a great entity, self-maintaining and self-perpetuating, some-
> thing more and greater than the sum of its parts, whose evolu-
> tion and life are susceptible of investigation, whose forms pass
> from phase to phase, from the most primitive up to the most
> sophisticated, remaining yet constantly interdependent in the
> most intimate and intricate of relations.[9]

Sumner felt that the ability of social science to find law in facts—to generalize—separates it from the art of history and gives it its supreme generalization, the law of evolution. Society does not dissolve into a series of unrelated and disparate historical complexes. Society is a natural structure having a natural sequence and thus is as immune to political control as it is to ethical criticism. Whatever exists at any given time is necessary, expedient, true, and good; the only standards by which to judge the workings of society are its own needs and its responses to these needs.

Despite Sumner's nominalism and emphasis on culture, therefore, his thought is more in keeping with the tradition of monistic naturalistic positivism stemming from the work of Condorcet, Saint-Simon, Comte, and Spencer than it is with the sociocultural positivism of Vico and Montesquieu. Though his profound nominalism disposed him toward an acceptance of the given, and was therefore conservative, it was not traditionalistic. While his work lacks the glowing optimism and commitment to science that informs the work of his predecessors in naturalistic positivism, Sumner firmly believed that the evolutionary development of society stemmed from the rise of science, especially as it translated itself into economic efficacy. Though never stated in systematic terms, there is throughout Sumner an undercurrent of tension between the mores and science. While the mores

---

[9] *Science of Society*, 3:2194; for a further depiction of society as a functional system, see 3:2220.

are always functional for their time, they are also always under attack by new and better ways of coping with the problems of existence. Sumner expressed this contrast between the "rational" and the "more rational" in a number of ways, most frequently by posing the mores against science. However, he also made the contrast by posing folkways and mores against such things as interests, rational reflection, legislative action, and positive law.

The tension between mores and science also emerged in Sumner's efforts to understand the phenomenon of social stratification. His theory of stratification was based largely on Galton's (1822–1911) psychology. Society, Sumner argued, tends to select those who are best equipped to serve social interests. Fundamental to all societies is a division between the masses and the classes; the former embody the mores and resist change, and the latter introduce variation and change. As the conditions of life change, a new elite arises to realize the new possibilities for satisfying interests. In a manner reminiscent of Saint-Simon, Sumner argued that very often there are unexpected consequences, good and bad, that flow from the selfish actions of classes. The historical trend has been to place the direction of the masses in the hands of the sober and responsible middle class. Any action by the working masses on their own would be disastrous to society. At the apex of society are the few individuals of genius and talent; at its base are the defective and delinquent.

Sumner's theory of social stratification in *Folkways* differed little from the ideas in his famous essay, "What Social Classes Owe to Each Other," published more than twenty years earlier, though the Darwinian emphasis is perhaps more strongly and callously expressed in the earlier work. Modern society, Sumner argued, has evolved from a system based on customary status to one based on rational contract, and it now provides individuals with the opportunity to prove themselves. Merit is inherent in the individual; society merely brings it out through the processes of education and competition. The muddle-headed talk of the reformers notwithstanding, liberty and equality are intrinsically opposed to each other. All schemes to help the weak are wrong-headed interferences with nature's stern commandment that survival depends on "labor and self-denial." Such schemes are doubly injurious because they also penalize the diligent and resourceful individual, an allusion to the middle-class individual, or "forgotten man," that Sumner defended throughout his career. Just as nature owes an individual nothing, so classes owe each other nothing except for the mutual recognition that individuals are obligated to help only themselves.

Sumner's wide acquaintance with ethnographic data allowed him to see the multiple bases on which inequality can rest. Though he failed to use the term *class* with any precision, he distinguished between inequality based on birth, whose extreme form is caste, and inequality based on wealth, whose extreme form is plutocracy. The crucial insight is that "among primitive peoples wealth is perhaps more likely to be a result of power than power of wealth."

All history, Sumner went on, is primarily a struggle between classes, especially in regard to living standards. In this struggle, classes use both ideas and political power to bend society to their own interests. The historical trend is toward inequality based on economic performance. Citing two of his favorite authors, Lippert (1839–1909) and Gumplowicz (1838–1909), and again referring to Galton, Sumner concluded that inequality and struggle are intrinsic to human nature and social evolution. The process of evolution creates new and unequal rights by giving power to those best equipped to carry on the struggle for survival. The corollary of this process is the weeding out of the unfit. Any attempt to protect the weak through ethical doctrines or through state action can lead only to social stagnation and destruction.

Though this is never stated systematically, Sumner's theory of social stratification is organically connected with his belief in a pattern of emerging rationality in history. Social strata are the embodiment of the differences and tensions that exist between the mores and science, between "rational" and "more rational" beliefs and values. Sumner's equation of social adjustment with inequality again connects his thought with that of Saint-Simon and Comte and, for that matter, with much of later sociological theory. His beliefs that conflicting views of social welfare and adjustment are embodied in specific social classes and that these classes, often unwittingly, serve as the agents of social change are similar to ideas in Saint-Simon and, of course, in Marx. However, whereas Saint-Simon saw the climax of history in the triumph of a scientific and industrial elite and Marx saw it in the victory of the proletariat, Sumner, who was almost as critical of the plutocracy as he was of the proletariat, felt that history had ordained the dominance of the individualistic middle class.

Though Sumner never openly embraced a doctrine of progress, it is clearly implicit in his work and therefore raises the liberal dilemma. His efforts to overcome the liberal dilemma are characteristically his own, despite the fact that like some of his predecessors he eventually resorted to the idea of a hidden logic to pull together the loose ends of his thought. He avoided first of all an explicit contrast between evil and good and between error and science. Evil, for Sumner, often contributes to the adjustment of society and can therefore be a source of good. As for error, it also contributes to rational adjustment and can therefore be "scientific." For from envisioning a sudden and miraculous enlightenment that enables human beings to transcend experience, Sumner saw human progress as a piecemeal, fitful process completely confined to historical experience. In one place he even went so far as to say that human beings have "stumbled upon" science.

The rise of science and the evolution of society, however, are not haphazard, accidental occurrences. Individuals may be caught in the grip of an irrational culture with no metaphysical standards to which to appeal, error and evil may tenaciously obstruct adjustment, the interests of individuals may be deeply antagonistic to each other; but underneath humanity's blind strivings a hidden logic meshes these feeble efforts into a unified structure of evolution. The antipathies among the interests of individuals are harmonized by the automatic process of antagonistic cooperation. Even when the interests of a group seem in fundamental conflict with the interests of humankind, evolution insures rational adjustment.

CONCLUSION

Sumner's Radical Nominalism

Sumner is the most consistently antimetaphysical of the theorists whose work I have examined. Taking his cue from Spencer but eschewing Spencer's belief that the science of society should be based on a formally constructed cosmic philosophy, Sumner based his thought on a frankly stated naturalistic nominalism. Like Spencer he was greatly interested in ethnographic and ecological data, but whereas Spencer was avowedly metaphysical, so great was Sumner's nominalism that one even hesitates to classify him as a monistic positivist. However, Sumner's monistic temperament is unmistakable. The distinction between the monists and pluralists rests not so much upon the amount of data contained in their work as upon their basic orientation toward and appraisal of social facts. The monists are interested of course, in facts, but the pluralists tend to be far more concerned with the adequacy of their methodology and far more cautious and tentative in their conclusions. Sumner never particularly concerned himself with the methodology of social science for the simple reason that he considered all such discussion to be philosophy and thus futile. It was self-evident that one had to be "tough-minded," that facts are facts, and that a few patent assumptions were all one needed to uncover the empirical realm. Sumner's genuine awareness of the historical and cultural sources of behavior did not extend far enough to force him to re-evaluate the methods and assumptions of earlier positivism. Like his predecessors, he remained a naturalist in that he defined the data of social behavior in terms of experience and in that he believed human behavior contains the same unalterable kind of law as physical nature. His reliance on psychology illustrates the fact that he was ultimately a naturalistic, not a sociocultural positivist.

Sumner never sensed the dangers of assuming that generalizations about physical nature can be stretched to cover human behavior. His awareness of cultural causation did not alert him to the inescapable role of ideas in empirical research—not ideas in the sense of logic but ideas as derivatives of the social scientist's own experience. One need only compare Sumner's nominalism with the equally radical nominalism of his contemporary Pareto (see Chapter 16) to see that similar methodologies can lead to appreciably different overall theories. Sumner's and Pareto's conclusions contained a host of assumptions and values derived from different cultural experiences —in Sumner, the social perspectives of an Anglo-Saxon Protestant culture aware of its progress; in Pareto, the frustrations of Italian and French society. Neither thinker ever developed an acute historical-cultural perspective and neither realized the complications of assuming that since physical and human nature are both lawful, the same laws must obtain in each.

The shortcomings of Sumner's nominalism can also be seen as a deficiency in causal analysis. Though he sometimes suggested a multicausal analysis— at one point making a rather interesting, almost Marxian distinction between economy and superstructure, even indicating that the superstructure of society can affect the maintenance structure [10]—he was content to reiterate his belief in the causal efficacy and logic of population-land ratios. He seemed completely unaware that his treatment of religion amounted to a contribution to causal theory and gave his work a strong flavor of ideological determinism.

In effect, Sumner's deficiency in causal analysis was enough to vitiate his nominalism and transform it into metaphysics. By assuming that social facts, no matter how unscientific, are self-explanatory and always rational and functional to social existence, he was propounding an ill-disguised substantialism. Despite the elaborate structure and carefully delineated subdivisions of *The Science of Society*, it remains a strangely shapeless book displaying little theoretical advance over the *Folkways*. Like the *Folkways*, it is a vast catalog of customs that substitutes description for explanation and fact for theory. Its only unifying thread is Sumner's faith that ideas and practices emerge automatically to further the evolutionary adjustment of the race. His deep antipathy to abstraction prevented him from unifying his data in terms of causation or social-system types. Like the mores themselves, Sumner's thought contains a logic that is not always rational—nor for that matter is it always logical. Judged by his own criterion of rationality, his thought is not rational because he failed to judge modern mores by

[10] Ibid., 3:2239.

their efficacy, and he is not logical because he used efficacy to judge only primitive mores. Though he hinted that contemporary institutions might someday be superseded, the day he had in mind is very vague and distant. Underlying and ordering his material is the assumption that the institutions of liberal society are products of an automatic, natural evolutionary process and that they thereby possess an efficacy for human welfare that renders them inviolate from criticism or reform.

The Commitment to Liberalism

Sumner's deep commitment to liberalism is apparent on almost every page of his writings. With the possible exceptions of the works of Condorcet and Saint-Simon, and perhaps of Ward, there is no greater attempt in the annals of bourgeois social thought to define human nature and society strictly in terms of the mastery of nature. It is axiomatic for Sumner that since the relationship of human beings to nature not only defines their moral nature but determines the structure of society as well, this relationship will be the subject matter of sociology. His view that the human struggle to achieve a more rational control of nature has led to an ever-more complex division of labor is a standard feature of sociological thought in particular and of liberalism in general. Though his thought lacked an explicit doctrine of progress, he suggested this idea when he said that the trend of history was toward an ever-more satisfactory adjustment to nature. Since satisfactory adjustment in Sumner's thought meant science, the destiny of society was ultimately dependent on the success of science.

Sumner's eagerness to subordinate philosophical, political, moral, and ethical values to economic need identifies his thought in a more general way with the main trend of bourgeois civilization. In some ways his thought is part of the late-liberal current in that it recognized the social and historical roots of individual rights. However, the current of late liberalism used this perspective to justify reform proposals to achieve a more adequate social adjustment and to insure the spread of social benefits; Sumner used it to reject reform proposals and to insist on the historic necessity of inequality. His deep suspicion of government and his belief that governmental acts are always less rational than economic acts is also characteristic of early liberal thought. Human beings, he felt, had to fight for rights because they lived in a world of scarcity. Accordingly, Sumner chose the free competitive economy as the best mechanism for distributing rights and integrating and directing society. Thus did Sumner wed the sociological insights of late-liberal thought to the laissez faire metaphysics of early liberalism.

Sumner's liberalism can be seen most simply in his belief that society is fundamentally composed of autonomous beings. Although he hedged on psychological explanations, there is no mistaking the affinity between his idea of the four motives and the social-contract theory of early liberalism. Sumner's individualism, which he made no attempt to disguise, is the social counterpart to his philosophical nominalism. His nominalism is related to liberalism in yet another way. His definition of reason as a means-ends relationship and his denunciation of those who seek to define reason in terms of purposes rather than consequences coincided perfectly with the pragmatism inherent in the needs of an advanced business civilization.

However, Sumner's liberalism was not so utilitarian and historically pragmatic as the foregoing might suggest. For one thing, he never abandoned the belief that the data of social behavior are reducible to general laws analogous to those in physics. Despite his cultural approach, he never discarded psychology as a permanent variable in the drama of evolution. Like some of his predecessors in sociology, Sumner explained social inequality as a derivative of the innate inequality of individuals. He based his theory of class largely on Galton's psychology, just as Saint-Simon and Comte had used the similar theory of Bichat. The thought of Sumner, like much of sociology, sought to base the historical need of an expanding, industrial capitalism for social specialization in human nature itself.

Sumner's belief that the multifariousness of human history can be reduced to a determinate pattern of evolution is unabashed liberal substantialism. If this belief was inconsistent with his deeply held nominalism, so was his attempt to specify the institutional structure that he regarded as the climax to the pattern of evolution. Though his sarcastic critique of metaphysics did not spare the liberal metaphysics of the Enlightenment, Sumner was not averse to accepting the ironclad economic laws of Thomas Malthus (1766–1834) and David Ricardo (1772–1823); nor did he hesitate to adapt the older idea of natural harmony and adjustment through laissez faire to the newer idea of harmony and adjustment through natural selection and antagonistic cooperation. His theory, in short, was based on the monistic conclusion that the empirically given always contains the necessary elements of social adjustment, that the process of adjustment is comprehensible as a law of rational evolution even though its elements are often nonrational and exceedingly complex, and that the given is always moral because it stems from the iron necessities of the struggle for survival.

All this suggests that the empirical functionalism of Sumner's thought, which foreshadowed the dominant intellectual mood of twentieth-century sociology, was historically determined, and that the scientific method itself must always be judged by the context in which it is used. Montesquieu's functionalism, for example, was innovational in that it was directed against natural law, but at the same time it was heavily conservative—something that did not escape the notice of the philosophes who shared many of Montesquieu's assumptions. So, too, Spencer's functionalism was innovational and dynamic in that it showed the superiority of the Industrial to the Military society, but it was also conservative in that it was identified with laissez faire economics during a period when laissez faire was itself the chief obstacle to social adjustment.

In much the same way, Sumner's functionalism and the overall theory in which it was embedded served a number of different and contradictory functions. It is generally overlooked, for example, that his ideas were quite dynamic and progressive, especially if contrasted with the Populist reform proposals inspired by the agrarian-humanitarian ideals of the eighteenth and early nineteenth centuries. From the standpoint of the sociology of knowledge, one can identify Hamilton as the progressive figure in American life and Jefferson as the conservative. Sumner's position, in effect, was in direct harmony with the dynamic world-mastery orientation of the middle-class civilization that had shattered and replaced the static world-accommodation orientation of the medieval world. This cultural and social revolution raised economic ideas and values from their traditional subordination to moral and social values. Thus, Sumner in effect upheld the authentic liberal perspective during the post-Civil War period of American industrial expansion and defended it against reform proposals that threatened to blunt the capacity of the American people to achieve a new plateau of mastery over nature. By combining the classical economics of Malthus and Ricardo with the nominalism and morality of science and Protestantism, within a framework inspired by the Darwinian theory of natural selection, Sumner led the struggle of American capitalism to update an earlier liberalism based on the agrarian-commercial economy of the pre-Civil War period. Earlier liberalism had not only an outmoded economic theory, but dangerously high and rigid moral and political standards. Sumner had an instinctive distrust of attempts to subordinate the workings of a free, individualistic market economy to ethical and moral judgments. This distrust stemmed from a belief that stagnation and disaster await those who deviate from the real world of competition, "labor," and "self-denial." No other sociologist, with the exception of Max Weber, saw so clearly the sharp antagonism between the demands of a "rational" economy and ethical and moral values.

In another sense Sumner was a conservative, a right-wing liberal. Much of the reform movement he opposed was perfectly compatible with the needs of an expanding industrial society and posed little threat to the core norms of liberalism. Indeed, even in his own day his ideas had become outmoded; their very success had transformed the United States from a nation of scarcity to one of relative plenty, from a nation of small economic units to one of large-scale, even monopolistic structures, and from a nation with a clear sense of direction to one beset by a growing sense of anxiety about the cosmic processes that were supposed to harmonize disputes and reward sacrifice and effort. Of course, Sumner's rejection of natural rights separated him from the main stream of late-nineteenth-century American conservatism (or right-wing liberalism). Regardless of differences, however, right-wing liberals aggravated the problems of advanced industrialization by defining social advance and adjustment as a natural process. It is ironic that in derogating rational adjustment through human effort and foresight, right-wing liberals were sharply limiting the sovereign goal of bourgeois civilization, the mastery of human destiny. To some extent, Sumner could not envisage this goal more broadly because his thought was an ideological reflection of a given stage of economic development. This is again ironic, for the intellectual tools with which this indictment can be made were forged by his own strenuous efforts to show that ideas, including those of early liberalism, are valid only insofar as they reflect economic conditions.

Chapter 12
Lester F. Ward (1841–1913)

===

The discipline of sociology in the United States is no less indebted to Lester Ward for its inception and furtherance than it is to Sumner. Like most of the theorists' work I have discussed, Ward's was heavily influenced by the natural sciences. Though Ward was not unique in this respect, he also had personal experience in the natural sciences as a practicing botanist and geologist. Unlike Sumner, who had no such experience, Ward explicitly modeled his thought on natural science. Again unlike Sumner, his thought was deliberately speculative after the manner of Comte and Spencer. Indeed, Ward's work bears a deeper relationship to Comte and Spencer than is apparent, being in effect an attempt to combine the distinctive insights of these earlier theorists.

PHILOSOPHY AND METHOD

Ward's commitment to monistic positivism was deep and explicit. At the base of his thought [1] is the assumption that human nature and nature are one and that both are subject to the universal principle of evolution, a principle that produces not only knowledge but virtue (or "utility") as well.

The Evolutionary Levels of Nature

Ward gave credit to Spencer for having laid down the fundamental ideas in the theory of evolution, although he said he preferred the term *aggregation* to evolution. He distinguished three levels of evolutionary phenomena:

[1] Ward's first major work (1883) was *Dynamic Sociology*, 2 vols. (New York: Appleton, 1902). Later major works include *Pure Sociology* (New York: Macmillan, 1925), originally published in 1903; and *Applied Sociology* (Boston: Ginn, 1906). In addition, Ward wrote two other works: *The Psychic Factors of Civilization* (Boston: Ginn, 1906), originally published in 1892; and *Outlines of Sociology* (New York: Macmillan, 1897). A selection from Ward's works is available in Israel Gerver, ed., *Lester Frank Ward* (New York: Thomas Y. Crowell paperback, 1963). For a collection of Ward's writings that focus on his promotion of the late liberal interventionist state, see Henry Steele Commager, ed., *Lester Ward and the Welfare State* (Indianapolis: Bobbs-Merrill, 1967).

matter, life, and society. Basic to all levels is the law of material aggregation, which is guided in its choice of products by the principle of adaptation. It is apparent that Ward's thought lies within the genuine tradition of
evolution (qualitative changes occur in phenomena), that it is a monistic
theory (all phenomena are subject to its workings), and that it belongs to
the tradition of naturalistic positivism. In all these respects his theory is
much closer to Spencer's view of evolution than to Comte's. However, Ward
did not discard the distinctive aspect of Comte's view of evolution, the
belief that the fundamental result of nature's itinerary through time is the
acquisition by humanity of full knowledge about the laws of nature.

Methodology

Though Ward repeatedly referred to the philosophical assumptions behind
science, he wrote little about methodology, engaged in no social research
of his own, and made little use of the research of others.[2] Actually, his approach to knowledge was highly deductive, reminding one more of Comte
than of Spencer—though even Comte had more to say about methodology
than Ward. Ward's lack of interest in the data of human behavior is also
more like Comte than like Spencer, though Comte was far more inclined
to use historical data than Ward. Ward was content to make extensive
analyses in the field he knew best, natural science, and then to apply his
findings to social behavior. As such, his basic methodological tool was logic
with a heavy emphasis on homological and teleological reasoning. In the
single chapter in the whole of his work devoted to methodology, Ward's
approach was stated in philosophical rather than scientific language. "The
basis of method," he said, "is logic, and the basis of logic is the sufficient
reason or law of causation." [3]

Though Ward paid special attention to efficient causation, criticizing Comte
severely for failing to distinguish between efficient and final causation, his
emphasis on the need for a viable theory of causation should not be mis-
interpreted. He never questioned the assumption that the logical structure
of the mind is identical with the structure of phenomena. His fundamental
philosophical and methodological orientation, therefore, was continuous
with the basic orientation of the Enlightenment, which itself was continuous
with the basic orientation of Western idealism or rationalism. Like his predecessors in monistic positivism, Ward continued the prescientific acceptance of a great chain of being, assuming like them that humanity's place
in the hierarchy of being can be established only through the rigorous
pursuit of science. Since human beings form part of an ultimately unitary

[2] The one exception is Ward's last work, *Applied Sociology,* where he made
extensive use of the research data of other social scientists to support his contention that human beings could be educated into equality.
[3] *Pure Sociology,* p. 45.

Lester F. Ward (1841–1913)

structure of being, what holds for some parts of nature must hold for other parts, and logic is therefore a reliable tool in establishing the unity that obtains among nature's various parts. In other words, Ward began his work with the conclusion that a monistic principle governs the universe.

In defending his view that sociology is a science, Ward was answering two sets of critics, those who claimed that sociology can arrive only at "probability or moral certainty" and those who would deny it the status of a science because human phenomena cannot be known with mathematical precision. It is a mistake, Ward said, to think that even natural science is based only on mathematics. Its basic task, like that of social science, is to establish the uniformities in phenomena, something that has been done successfully in many areas without the aid of mathematics. The basic method of science, Ward insisted, is generalization, and exactness in the complex sciences is possible only at the upper levels of abstraction. As the most complex of sciences, Ward went on, sociology searches for the generalizations in phenomena, using details only as aids in finding law. It does not even establish its own data, which are supplied by the special social and natural sciences. Its basic task is to coordinate data until unity has been found.

Given this orientation, it is not surprising that Ward had little to say about methodology and that his thought succumbed to homological and teleological reasoning. Such an orientation also prevented him from suspecting that there might be a deep and unbridgeable gap between human and physical nature and from ever wondering whether or not a great chain of being really existed.

SUBSTANTIVE WORK

Creative Synthesis

In his later work, *Pure Sociology*, Ward tightened his theory of evolution under the general concept of *creative synthesis* and tried to specify the concrete mechanism of evolutionary development and the causal links between natural and social evolution. Nature, he claimed, is everywhere characterized by struggle and striving, an "eternal pelting of atoms," a restless surging. In short, the main cause at work in the universe is not matter but "collision." Though there is a monistic principle unifying all existence, there is also a dualism or polarity in nature that produces conflict. The process that mediates this conflict and produces new evolutionary products is *synergy*. Essentially a process of equilibration, synergy explains the existence of structure at every level of nature. However, the overall process of creative synthesis is not yet explained. Ward, who had a penchant for establishing and then qualifying universal principles, introduced a distinction between social statics and social dynamics, a distinction that required a further set of principles: *difference of potential, innovation,* and *conation,* all unconscious agencies of social progress.

Such is the general scheme of evolution. Nature in its struggle to achieve ever-higher forms of organization finally produces human beings and thus society. The general process is unconscious and wasteful, marked by conflict and crisis, yet somehow functional and progressive. At the highest level of organic development stand human beings, who emerge out of the lower levels as sentient beings capable of ever-more-complex behavior. Within the

general history and constitution of humanity are two fundamentally different agencies or causal processes. The first, *genesis*, is an unconscious process
and its history is the history of all nature. The second process, *telesis*, is
marked by consciousness, and while it has existed from the beginning of
time, its real history lies in the future.

The Social Forces

The distinction between conative (or efficient) cause and intellectual (or
final) cause is central to Ward's thought. These two causes form what he
called the *social forces*, the special class of variables that make up the
domain of social science. The social forces fall into two general categories:
the physical forces, hunger and sex, and the spiritual or moral, aesthetic,
and intellectual forces. Out of these forces come the institutional structures
of society.

The division of the social forces into physical and spiritual—or biological
and psychic—also contains, implicitly at least, Ward's distinction between
conative cause and intellectual cause, or, more simply, genesis and telesis.
The truly dynamic or efficient cause in human affairs is the conative, or what
Ward also called feeling or desire or the subjective aspect of mind. The
basic desires, hunger and sex, are the source of a host of derivative desires.
All desires express themselves in obedience to pleasure and pain, and "all
social progress, in the proper sense of the phrase, is a movement from a pain
economy toward a pleasure economy, or at least a movement in the direction of the satisfaction of a greater and greater proportion of the desires of
men." At work in human affairs, in other words, is the law of parsimony, or
marginal utility, which is conative and therefore unconscious.

At the beginning, said Ward, the ends of nature and of humanity were identical, and human feelings were merely means to secure the functional needs
of nature, basically the need to perpetuate and increase life. Since evolution had special plans for humanity, the feelings developed and awareness
or *interest* began. The individual became an actor in the drama of evolution. Henceforth, a conflict of interests developed between the creature and
nature and between the individual and the race. This development, said
Ward,

> . . . was nothing less than the dawn of mind in the world. Before
> its appearance all nature had been mindless and soulless. Hence-
> forth there was to be *animated nature* with all that the phrase
> carries with it. In it were contained the psychic world and the
> moral world. With it came pleasure and pain with all their
> momentous import, and out of it ultimately grew thought and
> intelligence. Nature cared nothing for any of these. They were

unnecessary to her general scheme, and not at all ends of being. Mind was therefore an accident, an incidental consequence of other necessities—an *epiphenomenon*.[4]

Though the self has emerged and individuals have become conscious of themselves, they are not yet aware of the direction of nature or of the fact that it is under rational, efficient direction. Evolution throughout its history has been under the control of genesis—impelled by blind, natural, subjective forces. Evolution has achieved its purposes unconsciously through trial and error, evolving products at "enormous expense and involving infinite sacrifice of life and energy." It has produced egoism to satisfy desire, and it has constructed vast systems of religion to counteract selfishness, often leading to "extravagant follies and shocking practices."

Full consciousness and economy of effort, said Ward, will come only when evolution is placed under the direction of telesis. Under telesis, evolution will operate according to the dictates of humanity's objective faculties, which will bring "knowledge" about the workings of nature and will enable human beings to make "artificial" and economical adjustments of means to ends with the grand object of reducing nature to human service.

However, the human telic capacity, which has existed from the beginning of time and is itself an accidental and unintended product of genesis, has so far been unable to impose its husbandry on nature. On the contrary, it has been subservient to feeling and thus has helped to perpetrate "dark deeds and sinister practices." This is because the telic faculty always proceeds through indirection. When one human being uses it against another, it takes the form of "deception" and is fundamentally immoral. Deception and its various forms, ruse, cunning, shrewdness, strategy, and diplomacy, are the basis throughout history of the fundamentally exploitative character of religion, the economy, politics, and law. However, when the telic agent is directed against nature, it results not in deception but in "ingenuity." [5]

Ironically, the chief beneficiary of deception is telesis itself. Deception produces inequality, inequality produces leisure, and the surplus intellectual energy that leisure makes available is used by the telic faculty in a "nonadvantageous" manner—that is, in a manner that is not concerned with satisfying immediate and direct needs. The Greeks, Ward continued, developed marvels of telic speculation, though their use of mind alone resulted in a fruitless anthropomorphism in which human beings projected their own intelligence into nature. However, the Greek philosophers who

---

[4] Ibid., p. 128.
[5] An almost identical emphasis, it will be remembered, is found in Saint-Simon's work.

speculated about matter made a great contribution to knowledge even though they were seriously handicapped by an insufficiency of facts. With the slow accumulation of facts in the postmedieval world, the same speculative genius that the Greeks had displayed produced a vast expansion of knowledge. Telesis has begun at last to free itself from its bondage to genesis. Beginning with astronomy in the fifteenth century and climaxed by the greatest generalization of all, the law of evolution, telesis has achieved nothing less than the conquest of nature, a conquest that includes knowledge about human as well as physical nature.

The Origin and Nature of Social Structures

Ward's theory of society was based explicitly on biology and psychology, and therefore his explanation of the origin of society requires only a brief treatment. His explanation of how biopsychic traits are translated into social institutions is the weakest and least credible part of his work. Indeed, his explanation of the origin and nature of society is everywhere vitiated by vagueness and excessive reliance on logic. In Ward, the general process of evolution emerges out of material relationships and ascends from the inorganic to the organic levels of nature. From organic nature there emerges mind or reason, which is a combination of feeling and intellect—two aspects of mind that can also be described as psychic factors, social energy, or social forces. At first, feeling dominates intellect and is in perfect harmony with the general aim of nature that the race should multiply and survive; or, as Ward also stated it, the structure of human instinctual nature is in harmony with its function. All this changes as time passes, for with the growth of feeling there also grows an antagonism between the psychic structure of the individual and the function of individual and racial survival.

The idea of conflict became quite important in Ward's later work. In *Pure Sociology* he elevated the idea into an evolutionary principle of considerable importance, especially in explaining the origin and nature of society. He was prepared, for example, to accept Gumplowicz's and Ratzenhofer's (1842–1904) theory that the origin of society arises from racial struggle. In Ward's own language, the social forces (physiological-psychological desires) are mutually antagonistic and threaten the survival of the race. Thanks to the process of social synergy, however, these destructive forces are transformed into social structures that perform social functions. The struggle for greater efficiency is the struggle for structure. Human institutions emerge to control and use social energy. The essence of social energy, "the primordial, homogeneous, undifferentiated social plasma" out of which institutions develop, can also be called the "group sentiment of safety." Out of this social energy (or psychic energy) develops religion and then morals, law, politics, and all other institutions. In short, the social forces, which by themselves are destructive and constitute a menace to

human existence, are transmuted by social synergy, or conflict, into beneficial, functional institutions.

Each of the social forces leads to the formation of a social structure. The
physical or essential forces, hunger and sex, lead to economic and family
institutions; the spiritual or nonessential forces lead to moral, aesthetic, and
intellectual structures. Ward's account of how the biopsychological forces
become social institutions is unconvincing, not clearly saying where political and religious institutions come from. While social institutions must certainly be lodged in biotic and psychic structures, it is quite another thing
to say that society is unilaterally derived from these structures.

The Network of Causation

If one of the measures of a theorist's contribution to sociology and to social
science is his insight into causation, Ward's work did little to advance
humanity's knowledge of itself. Actually, his causal theory was retrogressive.
Despite his wide familiarity with the work of other sociologists, Ward
failed to advance or even to absorb their insights into social causation,
largely because he had made up his mind from the beginning that social
phenomena could be explained exclusively in terms of biology and psychology. Like many naturalistic positivists, Ward assumed that the social
realm is part of a unitary natural structure accessible to scientific method.
Like his predecessors in monistic positivism, he also assumed that all effects
have antecedent causes and that these causes are reducible to the one
cause that informs all phenomena. However, Ward's predecessors, while
searching for a unified theory of causation, managed to identify a variety
of causes such as climate, soil, population, interaction, invention, and
norms. Ward was content from the beginning to stake his entire system on
a single cause, the effects of biotic and psychic evolution. Committing himself to this idea confronted Ward with an insurmountable difficulty. It is
one thing to trace the development of the human organism as it makes its
way from primordial slime into biopsychic time, but in attempting to equate
this process of biopsychic time with social time, one encounters the fact
that human beings had fully evolved long before the start of significant
social evolution. In other words, one cannot use a constant (human nature,
biology, psychology) to explain change.

To circumvent this difficulty Ward was forced to rely on the very type of
thinking that science had struggled so mightily to supplant—philosophical
discourse. He constantly fell back on the assumption of a great chain of
being that is self-sufficient and continuous. While Ward defined being in
naturalistic terms, he also carried forward the prescientific faith that being
is replete with all its necessaries and contains no radical breaks or gaps.
Under this assumption the avenue to knowledge is logic, and since being or

nature is a unity, it is quite permissible to use homologous reasoning. In point of fact, Ward made extensive use of this type of logical explanation, especially when trying to explain the translation of psychic factors into social effects.

Ward's use of homologous arguments, however, is only one aspect of his overall acceptance of logic as a legitimate avenue to truth. He also indulged in an extensive use of teleological explanation. Just as logic presupposes a unitary structure of being connected by a single cause, which once identified in one area can be used homologously to explain behavior in another, so too it presupposes that any given effect, however far removed from an important cause in another area, must somehow be related to that cause. In other words, because of his underlying conviction that nature is a unitary structure, Ward simply assumed that social phenomena are part of the process of evolution. He simply assumed that the tremendously important process of evolution that had been identified in geology and biology must somehow be related to sociology. Further, since the same assumption cannot permit irrationality in nature, the process of evolution must be purposeful. Thus does teleological reasoning short-circuit science to produce two corollaries: the belief that all effects or historical manifestations have been for the best, and the belief that it is scientifically respectable to use the device of a hidden logic to explain the intermediate steps between ultimate principle and remote effect.

Ward's work is no exception to this pattern of quasi-scientific reasoning. Logic superseded science at every vital juncture in his thought, as, for example, when he attempted to justify the ultimate worth of all historical events and practices and when he used explanations based on hidden logic. From the flux of matter come inorganic and organic forms. With the development of life emerge feeling and intellect to form mind. Even within the purely biological-psychological sequence of development, Ward abandoned causation when he attributed the development of feeling and intellect to accident. His explanation of the origin and development of society is no less unscientific. The flux of human passions, he argued, is transmuted into social structures by the static or constructive principle of synergy and by the dynamic principles of difference of potential, innovation, and conation. In explaining the transition of mind to society, he again abandoned causation in favor of homologues and attributed social effects to a blind, wasteful, but ultimately functional set of processes called synergy and dynamic principles. The entire process called genesis everywhere simulates telesis despite its basically unconscious, accidental, and wasteful mode of operation.

Framed in terms of the liberal dilemma, the breakdown of Ward's causal theory becomes even more evident. Why is it that a rational universe has produced waste and pain or error and evil, and that human beings, who possess the telic capacity to see the lawfulness of nature, have failed to do so, except in a sporadic and error-filled way? The liberal dilemma posed no problem for Ward to the extent that he adopted a Spencerian naturalism in which there is no separate order of truth and error or good and evil but only an empirical "is" that absorbs both the true and the good. However, Ward also accepted the distinctive feature of Comte's view of evolution, that the main purpose of evolution is to supply human beings with a hierarchy of truth and goodness that is ultimately realized in the social life of humanity. Fundamentally, Comte's theory of evolution was based on the view that the universe, including humankind, is static but that somehow human beings obtain progressively more knowledge about first physical and then human nature. By accepting Comte's belief that truth and goodness are the terminuses of evolution, Ward's theory floundered on the liberal dilemma. Though evolution manifests itself in ways that seem to be erroneous and evil, Ward was convinced that it is basically orderly and progressive. Appearances to the contrary, he asserted, those things that philosophers have characterized as error and evil are in reality rational and moral.

The philosophical assumption underlying Ward's attempt to explain away error and evil is that conflict between particulars is not a barrier to law, but its essence—conflict is how nature works to produce law. The mixture of unlikes is a principle at work within sexual forces as well as within society. When conflict manifests itself as war and imperialism, it is really leading to progress because these social manifestations increase social activity. When the forces of nature take social shape as inequality, caste, slavery, exploitation, elitism, or deception, they are progressive because they discipline human beings and release the "surplus social energy" that is eventually used to direct the telic power of individuals away from themselves and toward nature.

Religion also participates in this process. Religion is unscientific, but because it stems from nature it can be thought of scientifically as the "instinct of group safety." Religion could not have come into existence, Ward argued, if it were not basically advantageous to the human race. The clergy has been among the elites who have benefited humanity through their possession of "surplus social energy."

As an evolutionary monist, therefore, Ward was ultimately forced to argue that everything is for the best and that error and evil disappear when placed in an evolutionary frame. Thus, in a way that we have encountered from Condorcet on, Ward was saying that everything in society works for the conservation of the group; that the proper attitude toward any institution is not to condemn it out of hand but to examine it to see what stage of evolution it is in; and that the majority of customs around the world are conducive to race safety.

Ward's fatalistic optimism was matched by a faith in hidden logic. Even the crowning glory of evolution, the modification of nature by human beings, is an accident. Science, knowledge, and invention, like the mind, are the results of haphazard processes. Egoistic telic action by the individual is the cause of that wasteful and pernicious but ultimately functional and progressive process known as social genesis. Even though humanity's "whole career has been marked by belligerency, internecine strife, and universal rapacity," the ultimate evolutionary effect of nature's forces is to produce social telesis, the stage of evolution in which human beings will have knowledge of themselves and can thus consciously control their own destiny. The beginnings of this terminal stage in the history of humankind can already be seen in the growth of collectivism, which is an outgrowth of natural evolution. However, knowledge about human nature is merely a higher stage of knowledge about physical nature, and it too must presumably emerge from accident. Thus social telesis, the apex of social evolution, the period in which human beings will run their affairs with full knowledge and full consciousness, is a social state that emerges from a magically efficacious process beyond human ken.

Social Evolution

Though Ward's sociological thought was permeated by the idea of evolution, he said surprisingly little about the various stages of social evolution. While constantly referring to the genetic and telic stages of social development, he rarely described them in terms of their characteristic institutions. His few references to concrete stages of social evolution were not developed systematically, nor did he place any great emphasis on them. In *Dynamic Sociology* he briefly referred to a fourfold pattern of social aggregation: the solitary or autarchic, the constrained aggregate or anarchic, the national or politarchic, and the cosmopolitan or pantarchic stages. However, having mentioned them, he never referred to them again. In another place he referred casually to the hunting, agricultural, and pastoral stages of development, and after a crude attempt to identify the psychic traits appropriate to each stage, he dropped the matter.[6] In his last work, there is a brief but unexplored allusion to "national freedom, political freedom, and social freedom" as stages within the process of evolutionary development.[7]

Ward's only real effort to identify stages of social development is found in *Pure Sociology*, but even here he showed no great interest in the problem. He expressed his general agreement with Gumplowicz and Ratzenhofer that

[6] *The Psychic Factors of Civilization*, 2nd ed. (Boston: Ginn, 1906), p. 186.
[7] *Applied Sociology* (Boston: Ginn, 1906), p. 26.

the origin of society is to be found in racial struggle. Again displaying his penchant for analogues, he likened social development to the biological process called *karyokinesis*. Both here and elsewhere, however, he never explicitly defined in terms of concrete stages the struggle between genesis and telesis, the essence of cosmic evolution. Ward's work contains neither a definite philosophical nor a social series, nor does it make any attempt to correlate the development of thought with the development of society. The process of evolution, it would seem, grinds out its qualitative changes so gradually that no discernible divisions can be found.

In marking the divisions in intellectual history, Ward used a simple distinction between theological, dualistic and scientific, monistic explanations of phenomena, or, as he also called them, *theo-teleological* and *anthro-teleological* explanations. The primary distinction in intellectual history is between those who view the antecedents of phenomena as "arbitrary and independent" of phenomena and those who view them as "constant and connected necessarily" with phenomena. The theological stage, said Ward, is anthropomorphic in origin. In it, individuals impute to nature or to deities characteristics derived from an awareness of their own willful, purposeful behavior. When individuals direct their attention to theology, spiritual things, or pure thought, stagnation results; only when they direct their attention to matter does their thought become dynamic.

Ward was slightly more informative about social evolution. The displacement of theo-teleological explanations by anthro-teleological explanations in the natural sciences will eventually find its counterpart in social science, and human beings will be in a position to install a true system of society, one based on knowledge of human nature and devoted to human betterment. Ward's depiction of the terminal stage of social evolution, however, is no more carefully delineated than the previous stage. Of all the monistic naturalistic positivists that I have discussed, only Comte was willing to give a detailed picture of the scientific society. Ward's picture of the final society, however, is unmistakable in its general outlines. It rests on the assumption that science is inherently serviceable to human beings. On the assumption that all individuals are educable, he predicted that scientific legislation would translate social knowledge into social practice. The essential equality of human beings, a belief Ward held throughout his life, rests on a distinction between intellect, the untrustworthy source of the theo-teleological world view, and intelligence, the intellect infused and disciplined by knowledge. Ward argued that intellect is equal in all human beings but that intelligence differs because of faulty social organization. Therefore, society has always been divided into two classes, the informed exploiters and the uninformed exploited. However, history shows that the informed class has been infused steadily by new blood; it now remains only for the masses to be uplifted. If this is true, Ward concluded, the Helvetian doctrine of intellectual equalitarianism, which assumes an equal capacity for achievement, means that no individual can be excluded from eventual membership in society's highest class.

After a careful scrutiny of existing research, Ward became convinced that his intuitive belief in the essential equality of human beings was supported by facts. The new society, therefore, must and will eliminate the causes of unequal intelligence. The main fault in the organization of society is the system for distributing knowledge. The avenue to economic equality, and to the achievement of happiness in general, lies in the systematic and intensive education of all individuals. No other problem can be solved until inequality in education has been eliminated.

Ward concluded his final book by spelling out the principle of attraction that underlies applied sociology. It is fundamental to social science, he insisted, that the laws of mind and thus of human behavior obey the same Newtonian laws that govern nature. Once the law of parsimony is united with the principle of attraction, the prospects for scientific legislation will be almost boundless.[8] Scientific legislation may also be called *attractive legislation* as opposed to prescientific *compulsory legislation*. The forces of human nature can be steered in directions that are beneficial to both the individual and society, and the traditional repression of these forces can be discarded. Though Ward stated that his discussion of the Telic society in *Applied Sociology* superseded previous discussions, he was still vague about the institutional structure of the new society.

The fundamental condition for scientific legislation is an educated people guided by sociologists. In the Telic society all aspects of social life will awaken to the touch of enlightened legislation. In particular, economic production will be facilitated, not through public control or ownership of industry but by making labor attractive. Giving credit to Charles Fourier (1772–1837) for first propounding the principle of attractive labor, and agreeing with Veblen (1857–1929) and Ratzenhofer that the distaste for work is due to caste traditions, Ward gave a high priority to the problem of making labor satisfying in his schedule of reform. According to Ward, once labor is attractive, there will be a vast increase in social efficiency and improvement.

The Telic society is also characterized by the absence of social opposition to the individual; it is a social state in which one can "conceive of the final disappearance of all restrictive laws and of government as a controlling agency." This view, of course, is similar to Saint-Simon's image of the Positive society, to Marx's picture of the classless society, and to Spencer's

[8] Ibid., pp. 331–334.

Ethical society. Though Ward used organic analogies more sparingly and less rigorously than Spencer, he did use one to envisage the future society. In animals and human beings, he noted, the brain as it has grown has steadily taken over the body's unconsciously performed functions, and social development can be seen in analogous terms. As the homologue to the brain, the state will see to it that an ever-more-perfect coordination of parts and functions takes place socially. However, Ward cautioned, Spencer was correct in not carrying the analogy too far. Unlike in the organic world, the perfection of the social whole will be for the benefit of its parts. The superior achievement of the Anglo-Saxon race up to now has been because it has been able "to see and act upon the principle that while individual initiative can alone accomplish great results, *it must be free*, and that, under the influence of the normal and natural forces of society, and taking the whole of human nature into account, it cannot be free unless the avenues for its activity be kept open by the power of society at large." [9]

In short, society, guided by the knowledge that there can be a full congruity between its own self-consciousness and that of the individual, will set itself to realizing a full measure of liberty, equality, and happiness for all—a goal that is possible only through the accumulation and distribution of knowledge.

CONCLUSION

Ward and the Positive Tradition

Ward's general theory of society is an amalgam of the distinctive features in the evolutionary theories of Comte and Spencer. To the extent that he framed his theory of evolution in terms of material relationships and insisted that all aspects of nature undergo qualitative changes, his thought was in line with Spencer's and with the authentic scientific view of evolution. As a consequence, Ward placed human beings themselves in a natural setting and then sought to explain their psychic attributes as products of a process of natural evolution. However, in making an explicit identification between the growth of biopsychic traits and the structure and development of society, Ward parted company with Spencer. Whereas Spencer had sensed the difficulty in equating biology and psychology with social behavior, Ward felt no such qualm and adopted a thoroughgoing doctrine of biopsychological evolutionism. Furthermore, Spencer was somewhat aware that an evolutionary point of view precluded a terminal point, especially one in which conflict, the very stuff of evolution, was eliminated simply because science

[9] *Pure Sociology*, p. 567f.

emerged in full possession of the uniformities of nature; Ward, however, believed that the conflict-ridden process of evolution would end when human beings obtained total knowledge about their universe. To the extent that he adopted this view, his thought is similar to the pseudoevolutionary theory of Auguste Comte.

The similarity between Ward's work and Comte's can be seen in a number of other ways. Both believed that evolution must eventually produce a society that would embrace humanity; that the growth of human knowledge and consciousness comes from teleological causation; and that the terminal social system would be superintended by sociologists. Even Ward's notion of scientific legislation based on the principle of attraction is a curious throwback to the static cosmology of Newtonian physics and thus also Comtean in outlook. Ward, who wrote long summaries of the theories of both Comte and Spencer in *Dynamic Sociology*, never noticed Comte's failure to develop a genuine evolutionary view and never recognized the contradiction entailed in his own acceptance of Comte's ideological evolutionism. Of course, Ward's equalitarianism separated him from Comte, and from his contemporary Sumner. Finally, Ward's emphasis on an interventionist state separated him from both Spencer and Sumner, though Spencer, like Ward, was more disposed to think of the future society as a realization of individual equality.

Ward and Late Liberalism

Like his predecessors in both naturalistic and sociocultural positivism, Ward is easily identified with liberal civilization. His thought represents the equalitarian strand of the Enlightenment far more than the thought of any of his predecessors in sociology with the exception of Condorcet. Whereas Comte had found in evolution the justification for hierarchical industrial society, and Spencer and Sumner had found a justification for atomistic individualism (or early Anglo-American liberalism), Ward found a justification for the late-liberal belief that society should liberate the individual by perfecting its institutional structures.

Ward's liberalism is apparent throughout his work. Informing his entire point of view was the belief that egoism is the fundamental feature of human nature. Throughout his writings egoism appeared again and again in various guises. Egoism is lawful in that it proceeds according to pleasure and pain as measured by the principle of parsimony or marginal utility. Ward's use of a term from liberal economic theory was not coincidental. His entire attitude toward human nature, especially toward the passions, was authentically liberal. Gone are the theological and the rationalist distrust and fear of human passions. In a straightforward, hedonistic fashion, the conventional terms of moral philosophy are given a naturalistic basis. Happiness and the good are the same as pleasure, while evil comes from pain. Virtue is merely the performance of the necessary functions that make for individual and racial adjustment and survival.

Gone too is the traditional definition of human passions as too empirical to be known. It was axiomatic for Ward that human passions are structured and therefore knowable. Furthermore, the passions are good: they serve useful purposes as means toward other ends as well as being ends in themselves. It is not surprising that with such an orientation, Ward, an authentic son of the Enlightenment, looked upon history as a process that produces secular happiness; nor is it surprising that he thought of the conquest of nature, or more exactly of the intellectual conquest of nature, as the key to happiness. Intellectual progress, which human beings translate into the economic conquest of nature, stems from the organism's struggle to adjust itself to its environment. The more successfully individuals adjust themselves to the forces of nature, the more they will have conquered ignorance and evil. The struggle to conquer nature, however, is not a conventional or haphazard process; it emerges from within nature itself—that is, from human nature defined in terms of egoism or self-interest. It is individual rationality (individual telesis), spurred on by hunger and sex, that is the driving force behind the patterned process of scientific and economic achievement. Ward assumed throughout his work that while the use of human reason against other human beings is immoral, its use against nature is inherently beneficial. The net effect of these views was to provide a metaphysical basis for the ideas and values of an expanding industrial capitalism.

Ward is a late liberal in that the forces of egoism do not lead directly or automatically to social harmony and welfare. A tension emerges early in the evolutionary process between the individual and the group. Individuals are creative actors, but their creativity poses a danger to society and it is necessary to curb them. Social control, however, is not a product of random conventionalization or the outcome of political struggle and compromise; it is a natural outgrowth of natural processes. The structures of control, at first centered mainly in religion and then the state, are natural evolutionary products. The nation-state is the highest product of the process of social *karyokinesis*.

Ward's definitions of property and the state are further clues to his late-liberal orientation. Property, he insisted, is private and individual, not because of an abstract doctrine of natural rights but because of law and the state. Indeed, there are no rights at all except in and through the state. The state is the prime mechanism for controlling unbridled egoism, and without the state there can be neither unity nor individualism. However, the individual and the state are not in permanent opposition. Once the Telic society has emerged, social control will achieve its ends through the release of the socially beneficial capacities of individuals. Since the exercise of these capacities is beneficial to the individual as well, the individual and society are reconciled. They are in opposition only because of the faulty organization of society. However, in pointing out the defects in society, Ward did not question liberalism's basic institution, the market economy. For him, the main institutional defect in liberal society was its failure to distribute knowledge properly. Once this defect is corrected, social efficiency and social improvement will be powerfully augmented, since an educated population is more productive and supportive of scientific legislation.

Ward's immersion in the thought structure of liberalism is evident in yet another way. He thought of evolution as a process in which the continuous manifestation of egoism and its continuous reconciliation with society resulted in progressively better adaptation to nature. The defective nature of Ward's theory was pointed out in the discussion of his causal theory. His explanation can now be seen as a naive attempt to place the natural-law theory of liberal society on a scientific basis. Ward merely restated the Anglo-American commitment to laissez faire, in which self and society are in a continuous process of equilibration, in naturalistic, evolutionary terms, with the novel addition that the reconciliation must be made more consciously by public agencies. Nature was still basically orderly in Ward's theory, except that it now decreed a greater role for human beings in establishing social order than could be found in earlier liberal thought.

Ward, who criticized anthropomorphism in prescientific thought, is himself subject to analysis in terms of the sociology of knowledge. As a naturalist who believed in the automatic emergence of a mind destined to have full knowledge of the universe at large, he was ultimately a substantialistic idealist. Had Ward maintained that the growth of truth was a consequence of the biological growth of mind, he would have been wrong but consistent, and he would have avoided the liberal dilemma. However, to maintain that the telic capacity of human beings emerged before the dawn of science and that it was once used to produce false and immoral doctrines is to espouse a theory that pins him to the horns of the liberal dilemma.

Ward's theory can be thought of as a reflection of American society in the late nineteenth century. Industrial conflict and economic concentration required a rethinking of traditional American assumptions about society. Sumner used science to explain and justify the conflicts and hardships of industrialization in terms of the Darwinian struggle for existence. Ward, however, used science to show that the struggle for existence in nature and society, while purposeful, is extremely wasteful, and that just as individuals can bring nature under control through knowledge, they can also control society. Human beings who are natural creatures, are somehow miraculously able to separate themselves from nature and to rise above its dictates. Nowhere is Ward's commitment to Western idealism more apparent than his belief that mind, though subject to the compulsions of nature, is able ultimately to transcend nature's deceptive and destructive ways.

Ward, experiencing the growing conflicts of post-Civil War American society, read this experience into all human history. His experience with economic conflict and economic concentration, combined with his deep commitment to equality (and his origins in the American Midwest), gave him a fresh perspective on society. However, in formulating his concern for American society and his reform proposals, Ward went far beyond what was warranted by either his experience or his scholarship. He read his ideas into the cosmos at large. The ideological nature of his analysis and main reform proposal should not go unnoticed. Ward was aware that human history up to his own day was a vast catalog of misery and blindness, and he could not have been unaware that a rampant capitalism was increasingly identified as a major cause of instability and exploitative inequality. However, despite his awareness of waste, conflict, and injustice and his deep sensitivity to human suffering, Ward placed the main cause of social insufficiency in education.

Looking back, one is struck by the unreality of much of what Ward had to say about social behavior. Admirably equipped as a natural scientist, Ward was out of touch with the complexities of human behavior. The root trouble lay not only in his belief in a unified theory of human nature based on biopsychic forces, but also in his lack of historical and social knowledge. Of all the monists whose work I have covered, Ward was the most lacking in any real insight or knowledge about human behavior. He had no qualms or inhibitions about indiscriminately applying the substantive concepts of natural science to human behavior. His predecessors in monistic positivism all had in their thought secondary strands based on a wider knowledge of the empirical data of human behavior. They were thus able to discern social and cultural processes and causes and to avoid a total interpretation of human behavior in terms of physics, psychology, or biology.

Little schooled in history, Ward perceived all social data in natural-science terms. No insight into the cultural and social sources of behavior could penetrate the fine mesh of his positivism, which assumed that human behavior was reducible to naturalistic, biopsychological processes. In this sense, Ward's early career in natural science and his late entry into sociology explain and somewhat excuse his inability to question the literal identification of human beings with nature. Even his wide acquaintance with the literature of sociology never freed him from his single-minded emphasis on biopsychological evolutionism.

Ward deserves a place within the maturing tradition of sociology for a number of reasons. Like Spencer and Sumner, he frankly accepted a naturalistic approach to human behavior and thus helped to establish the respectability of a scientific study of society. Like Spencer, Ward made a literal identification of human nature and nature and thereby made the negative contribution of showing the limits of a biopsychologically based social science. Ward's naturalism included an open acceptance of the passions as the avenue to human welfare and a rejection of transcendental moral and rational approaches to human behavior. However, though his thought is everywhere marked by a suspicion of reason and a commitment to empirical investigation, Ward, like so many of his predecessors, succumbed to the temptations of both overt and hidden logic, and in this way he smuggled prescientific thought forms into the structure of sociology.

PART IV
The Emergence of Pluralistic Positivism

Chapter 13

The New Phase of Modern Society and Science

Western society in the early nineteenth century was unique in a number of ways that have a bearing on sociological theory. Above all, the advent of significant economic changes, which ran the gamut from intensified capitalist agriculture to the factory system, unleashed forces that tipped the scales irrevocably against feudal Europe. One of the most immediate consequences of this qualitative change in Europe's economy was a novel concern, expressed differently from country to country, for what historians have come to call the *social question*.

INDUSTRIALIZATION AND THE "SOCIAL QUESTION"

The social question was primarily a concern for the condition of the people, especially those subject to physical deprivations.[1] From the mid-eighteenth century on, due in no small measure to the significant increase in food supply that stemmed from the cultivation of the lowly potato, the population of Europe increased rapidly. With this population explosion, and with the displacement of small farm holdings by large landlords, cities experienced a large surplus of people. Millions lived in destitution and there seemed little hope that their energies could be harnessed by employment or their suffering alleviated by welfare programs.

Interest in the social question was a novel occurrence in Western thought. Obviously, thinkers and officials throughout history had concerned themselves with the general condition of the masses and had devised public policies to deal with it. What happened in the nineteenth century was

---

[1] For an excellent portrait of this period, see William L. Langer, ed., *The Rise of Modern Europe* (New York: Harper & Row, 1969), vol. 14, William L. Langer, *Politics and Social Upheaval, 1832–1852*, especially chaps. 1 and 6.

unique because both the holders and the near-holders of power saw their own fate bound up with the condition of the people. Previously, those in power had simply assumed a natural and fixed hierarchic order of things and human beings. The dominant groups took the people and their suffering for granted; whatever their condition, it was ordained by nature and was normal and familiar.

By the early nineteenth century all this had changed. The French Revolution and its aftermath had convulsed European society. Above all, the quickened tempo of economic life had wrought abrupt and unsettling changes in domestic and external power relations, and the future seemed pregnant with even more fearful changes. What was novel about all this was that powerful groups could no longer take their societies for granted. The widespread changes in social life had the effect of preventing the upper classes of Europe from directly experiencing their own society—a situation that seemed to be politically dangerous to many and a situation that must have been unsettling to almost all. An immediate result of this situation was a widespread desire to gain more knowledge about the social question, or condition of the ordinary people. As I shall discuss shortly, this new interest led to a vast growth of intelligence gathering, from domestic police spying to the establishment of census bureaus.

The Main Forms of Modern Social Theory

Another result of the ferment generated by an industrializing Europe is of particular interest to the historian of sociological theory: it helped to crystallize the main forms of modern social theory, conservatism-traditionalism, liberalism, and socialism, each with its variations and subtypes.[2] Out of the ferment of economic dislocation and political instability came a rich flower-

---

[2] The changes in the social theory and politics of Christianity that emerged with industrialization cannot be fully analyzed here. By and large Protestant churches continued to be differentiated in theology, ritual, organizational structure, and political and social orientation by class. However, a significant number of reform and even radical movements emerged from nineteenth-century Protestantism, such as the Social Gospel in the United States and Christian Socialism in England. The attempt by the Roman Catholic priest Hugues-Félicité Lamennais (1782–1854) to persuade his church to promote and support liberal democracy failed despite the phenomenal success of his writings throughout Europe. The most powerful branches of the Roman Catholic Church, those in France, Italy, Spain, Central Europe, and even Germany, were too deeply tied to feudal-monarchical reaction to allow the papacy—had it been so disposed—to embrace the current of liberalism. In England, Ireland, and the United States, Roman Catholicism was a minority and was far more disposed toward change and liberalism. The papacy began the process of disentangling itself from feudal-monarchical traditions in the encyclical *Rerum novarum* (1891), whose treatment of the condition of the working class signaled a clear start toward its present position, that the church can accept any political and social system that acknowledges certain elementary clerical and human rights.

ing of social theory as theorists searched for the absolute principles that would set society right again. Social redemption was found in the past in traditionalism; in the present in utopian theory, anarchism, and Blanquism; and in the near and distant future in evolutionary liberalism and Marxism. A wide variety of economic and political action accompanied the new phase of modern society. The landed aristocracy, still powerful everywhere in Europe, mounted a policy of opposition to liberalism and on the Continent adopted a systematic policy of repressing all forms of modernism. The landed aristocracy squeezed out small landholders to make their own holdings more efficient and productive. In turn, there were peasant and worker uprisings that fed the fear of the "dark masses." For its part, the middle class, as new property owners, asked for a share of power but did so in a low voice as it looked uneasily at the stirrings of the unpropertied masses.

In social theory the middle class faced a novel and troublesome situation, though one that varied from country to country. Until the nineteenth century it had lived in a relatively stable society, a circumstance that had found expression in the characteristic social theory of liberalism—social Newtonianism, or the tendency to think of society as a great machine. For centuries, the middle class had faced only a relatively backward landed aristocracy, which it considered not so much an enemy as a group to be emulated and even joined. After the cataclysm of the French and Industrial revolutions, the middle class was confronted by a more self-conscious, stiff-backed landed aristocracy *and* by a working mass beginning to stir and make demands on society.

Of considerable importance, therefore, in understanding contemporary sociology is that it matured during a period of vast social-system change, choice, and consolidation, and that it had coherent social and ideological enemies, perceived as such, on both right and left.

Sociology and the Challenges of Right and Left

The challenges faced by liberalism and sociological theory varied from country to country, depending above all on the strength of the middle class. In the United States liberalism faced relatively no challenge (save for the Southern plantation aristocracy) from either right or left. The American middle class for all intents and purposes is and has always been coextensive with society. In Great Britain, the landed aristocracy of the right and liberal commercial and manufacturing classes engaged in a long struggle for power relatively unhampered by the working classes of the left. The defeat of Chartism in the 1840s dramatically illustrated the power of the British upper classes and gave them ample time to resolve their differences and to develop a relatively full set of compatible and protective institutions (parliamentary government, rule of law, centralized civil service) before the rise of the Labor party toward the end of the nineteenth century. Essentially, British conservatism-traditionalism and liberalism joined to form a common front against socialism.

In France things were quite different. The social question became and remained a question of what form society should take. The 1830s and 1840s were a period of social-system turbulence throughout Europe, but nowhere did society quake as in France. Powerful monarchical-aristocratic forces, liberals of various stripes, most of whom wanted a property-based system of representative government, and radicals, ranging from utopian theorists to militant anarchists, and from reformist to revolutionary socialists, contended among themselves for control of the French social system. No understanding of French sociology or its creativity is possible without understanding the weakness of French republican institutions and the constant threat from both right and left from 1789 down to the post-1945 period.[3]

In Germany the situation was still different. Crucial to understanding both German history and German sociological theory is the Prussian aristocracy's defeat of liberalism in 1848 and the general tendency of the German middle class thereafter to ally itself with the forces of authoritarianism against socialism. One consequence of this historic compromise was that German sociologists, and liberal German thinkers in general, suffered from a deep-rooted ambivalence—it was not easy for them to see liberal values and beliefs, including love of country, become embedded in and subservient to an efficient, paternalistic, militaristic state dominated by landed aristocrats.[4] However, in Germany as in France, the sharp and explicit social conflicts spurred sociologists to new heights of theoretical creativity.

CONSERVATIVE SOCIAL THEORY

A conservative social theory can be broadly defined as any defense of the present or the past. Its specific content varies, of course, depending on historical circumstances—and it need not even call itself conservative. The conservative cause—conservatism-traditionalism—in the early nineteenth century was pitted primarily against liberalism. The two leading conservative theoreticians were Bonald and Maistre, who mounted an attack on the French

---

[3] For an illustration of the challenge from right and left against the liberal middle, see Michael Curtis, *Three Against the Republic: Sorel, Barrès and Maurras* (Princeton, N.J.: Princeton University Press, 1959).
[4] For background, and for how three sociologists (Toennies, Sombart, and Michels) fared in Imperial Germany, see Arthur Mitzman, *Sociology and Estrangement* (New York: Alfred A. Knopf., 1973).

Revolution and its individualistic image of society.[5] In contrast to liberalism's atomistic image of society, conservatives argued that the true society was static, hierarchical, organic, and based on hereditary relations to land. Given the rapid industrialization of Europe, this brand of conservative social thought had little future and by the end of the nineteenth century had taken other directions.

Irrational Conservative Social Theory

By the end of the nineteenth century the defenders of landed property, status, and hereditary privilege were faced by a heterogeneous urban-industrial society in which political power was acquired through broad-based electoral processes. Another characteristic of this urban-industrial society was that it generated insecurity and anxiety and had no established procedures for allaying them. One of the directions taken by the conservative-traditionalist current was an appeal to mass emotions in an effort to develop a popular power base. Elements of the old traditionalism, especially in France, Germany, and Italy, were transformed into an explicit irrationalism that glorified the nation, animal energy, heroism, the will, and the passions in general over reason. In the name of country, cooperation, "socialism," justice, property, opportunity for the average individual, heroism, racism or anti-Semitism, it called for the submergence of particular wills in the common will. Despite its use of radical terms and its critical tone, it was a conservative or even reactionary theory because it asked that the existing order of things and people be the basis of cooperation and sacrifice.

Irrational conservative social theory could draw on the rich history of irrationalism that had emerged earlier in nineteenth-century thought, for example Arthur Schopenhauer (1788–1860), Thomas Carlyle (1795–1881), Friedrick Nietzsche (1844–1900), and sundry aesthetic philosophies. The negative reaction to modernism, to such conditions as industrialization, urbanization, and popular government, appeared most pointedly in social thought and politics in Maurice Barrès's (1862–1923) concept of *integral nationalism* (also called *national socialism*) in the decades before World War I [6] and in Charles Maurras's (1868–1952) similar views to which was added an element of anachronistic monarchism.[7]

Nourished by the dislocations and hatreds of the First World War, the irrational elements that had congealed in Barrès and Maurras found ex-

[5] See the section "The General Current of French Positivism" in Chapter 7 of this text for a discussion of these two thinkers and their influence on Saint-Simon and Comte.
[6] For Barrès's thought and its basic similarities and differences with later fascist thought, see Robert Soucy, *Fascism in France: The Case of Maurice Barrès* (Berkeley: University of California Press, 1972).
[7] For Maurras's thought, see William C. Bushman, *The Rise of Integral Nationalism in France* (New York: Columbia University Press, 1939).

pression in the postwar period in a wide number of radical right-wing groups, most notably in Hitler's National Socialists and Mussolini's Fascists. No significant current of irrational conservative social theory appeared in either Great Britain or the United States,[8] and for good reason—the defense of society was in the hands of a far more sophisticated theory.

Rational-Liberal Conservative Social Theory

The traditionalist's emphasis on birth, custom, and land and the irrationalist's emphasis on will, animal energy, and action without thought are fundamentally incompatible with the effective long-term management of an industrial society. There is, however, another, more rational theory that defends the existing order of things and people. At the heart of rational conservative theory is an idea that has been characteristic of dominant groups throughout history, the idea of a constant human nature. Invariably, conservative (and, of course, other) theorists argue that society must be based on the permanent characteristics of human nature, the most important of which is the inequality in basic human endowments. The agrarian version of this idea argued essentially that *families* are unequal. Under industrial conditions, this idea was transformed by conservative-liberal theorists into the idea of a fixed human nature in which *individuals* are unequal. For liberals, society was still conceived in terms of an elite, but an elite composed of whatever individuals had risen to the top by dint of work and ability. From the time of Hobbes and Locke down through the French and Scottish enlightenments and on to the French and American revolutions, this liberal image of society was revolutionary in that it opposed the feudal concept of a hierarchy of hereditary families. However, with the advent of industrial society, there emerged another theory of industrialism—socialism—and liberalism ipso facto became the main form of conservative social theory.

The key idea behind the conservative nature of contemporary liberalism is well expressed in Ossowski's concept of *nonegalitarian classlessness*. Liberal theorists assume that society is already organized (or without radical change can be organized) to reveal the natural elite in any given population. (As I shall discuss shortly, this assumption is characteristic of both capitalist and Soviet-style communist societies.) Actually, the idea that society is or should be based on a natural elite is characteristic of many theorists and dominant groups and those who speak for them: Plato, Adam Smith, James Madison, fascist groups, Joseph Stalin, and some sociologists,

---

[8] An approximation of this type of theory in the United States is the disguised protection given to the status quo by a brand of populism practiced in the American South, most notably by Huey Long and George Wallace.

most notably biopsychological theorists such as Saint-Simon, Sumner, and Pareto.[9]

One of the most important transformations in modern social theory, therefore, is the decline of the concept of hereditary inequality and hierarchy and the emergence of democratic elitism. Accordingly, society must organize itself to allow the merit residing in each generation of individuals to assert itself. With equality of opportunity, especially in education, and with competition in all spheres, a natural inequality should emerge to provide society with the leadership it needs. The net effect of the liberal doctrine of "meritocracy," of course, is to transfer dominance from landed individuals as such to those who own or control economic assets in general. It is little wonder that agrarian conservatism often blended with and allied itself with liberalism during the nineteenth century, especially when both were threatened by democratizing forces.[10]

Today conservative social theory is synonomous with liberalism in the capitalist countries and with Stalinism in the Soviet-style communist countries: both systems of thought believe that their own system of society is based (or with reform can be based) on nonegalitarian classlessness. Of greater relevance for sociological theory is the fact that liberal thought has a right and left wing. On the right are the early liberals, who stress the natural individual and the self-equilibrating society; on the left are the late liberals, who stress the need for government and voluntary groups to help individuals realize and differentiate themselves and to make society, especially its private economy, work better. Reformist and radical liberals in the United States are conservative because they do not envision a different order of things and people but assume that liberal ideals can be achieved within a liberal social system.

SOCIALIST SOCIAL THEORY

For those living in a capitalist society, the study of socialist social theory provides a relatively systematic way of envisioning a social system different from capitalism. It allows social theorists to think about the ideals of the industrial West and contemporary social trends and problems in a more

[9] For an analysis showing this similarity in thought among apologists for a wide variety of social systems, see Stanislaw Ossowski, *Class Structure in the Social Consciousness,* trans. Sheila Patterson (New York: Free Press, 1963), pp. 172–180.
[10] For a fascinating depiction of this process in German history from the eighteenth century through Hitler and National Socialism and into the post-1945 period, see Walter Struve, *Elites Against Democracy: Leadership Ideals in Bourgeois Political Thought in Germany, 1890–1933* (Princeton, N.J.: Princeton University Press, 1973).

comprehensive and sophisticated manner than if they had to rely only on the thoughtways of their own society. It allows theorists to raise questions about the conscious and unconscious presuppositions underlying social theorizing within fully established liberal societies.

Sociology also provides comparative insight into the fundamentals of society, but only within limits. Throughout its history, sociology characteristically identified and contrasted communal and associational societies, and in some cases it distinguished between the associational society perfected by science and all prescientific societies.[11] Rarely, however, did sociology take seriously the socialist argument that economic variables are the key cause in human affairs and that the main theoretical difference between societies is whether or not productive facilities are privately or publicly owned.

For this reason and because of the political significance of the various socialist movements, socialist social theory is important to social theory in general, as well as for understanding the development of one form of social theory, sociology, from the middle of the nineteenth century on. Emerging industrial capitalism was challenged on the left by a variety of socialist thinkers and movements: in England by the Labor party and the Fabian movement; in France by syndicalism and socialism and after World War I by communism; in Germany by the Social Democratic party; and in the United States by the Socialist party, which peaked in 1912. Of considerable significance for understanding the political and intellectual climate in which twentieth-century sociologists have worked is the collapse of the czarist regime in Russia in 1917 and the ascension to power of the Communist party under the leadership of Lenin. Between the two great wars, the USSR was the lone representative of a determined and radical effort to build a socialist society; however, it was joined by many others after 1945. The rivalry between capitalist societies, led by the United States, and socialist societies, led at first by the USSR and now composed of various camps and nationally oriented parties, is especially important for understanding sociological theory since 1945. The rise to prominence in post-World War II American sociology of holistic, functional theory (most notably in Talcott Parsons) is undoubtedly related to the challenge to liberalism by a militantly chiliastic USSR. In a still wider setting the reformist, evolutionary, developmental themes in American sociology and social science after World War II reflected the need of the United States to project a positive image against the socialist camp and to develop a foreign policy in keeping with its position of leadership of the reconstituted capitalist world economy.

[11] Important additions to social-system comparison were made by Durkheim and Weber, whose work will be discussed shortly.

Early Socialism

In the early nineteenth century it was not possible to say in any precise way what socialism meant. The term *socialism* referred mostly to an effort to direct thought to social as opposed to political questions, especially to problems of poverty, exploitation, ignorance, and injustice—the social question. There was a general tendency to denigrate and oppose unproductive elements, competitiveness, and politicians and governments who did not reflect the values and interests of the productive segments of society.

Today many of the most important of the early "socialists" would be characterized as liberals: Robert Owen (1771–1858), Saint-Simon, and Charles Fourier (1772–1837).[12] The main feature that distinguishes liberalism from socialism is liberalism's assumption that a society based on the private ownership of productive forces is compatible with individualism, freedom, and harmony. Of the many social theorists who questioned this compatibility, the most important is Karl Marx.

Marx's Social Theory

Though there are many other contributors to socialism, its essential elements are largely the work of Marx. Though this section will stress the differences that separate Marxism and liberalism, there is much overlap between these two images of society, and there are many people who still confuse liberal reform, such as government programs to help the needy or to regulate industry, with socialism. It should be quite clear, though, that liberal reform is perhaps the most effective way to prevent socialism and that it is thus a conserving force. There is also much overlap between liberal "social science" and the "scientific" socialism of Marx. Marx's contribution to empirical investigation, for example, and his interest in the "condition of the people" are well known. Likewise, Marx accepted the secular historicism of the Enlightenment, the functionalism of classical economics, and along with

[12] For a good sample of the thought of the most interesting of the utopian sociologists, see *Design for Utopia: Selected Writings of Charles Fourier,* trans. Julia Franklin, intro. Charles Gide, foreword by Frank E. Manuel (New York: Schocken paperback, 1971). Fourier stressed the need for small-scale society to provide outlets and stimulation for all the senses, especially those involved in work and sex, for all ages and sexes. Fourier pioneered many ideas that were to gain greater currency later. He argued that civilized society harmed people by repressing passions; that individuals could develop their unique capacities only through sensual variety; and that the life cycle produced different problems for individuals. Though Fourier was highly critical of the world around him and paid special attention to the needs of labor, he remains a utopian sociologist and liberal because he accepted private property and assumed that individuals had biopsychic structures that society should reflect.

many liberal theorists sought knowledge in the relation among variables, especially in an evolutionary frame.

Despite this overlap between Marx and liberalism and despite Marx's contribution to sociology, the truth remains that Marxism and liberalism are quite different.[13]

Most fundamental to Marx is that he was a materialist, which among other things means that he rejected ideological causation, the belief in an immanent movement of ideas that carries society and humanity with it. According to Marx, ideological causation, whether found in liberals such as Condorcet, Saint-Simon, Comte, or Hegel, masks history's mainspring, the economy, and therefore helps to distort understanding of human behavior, problems, and destiny.

Another fundamental perspective in Marx is his rejection of any notion of a fixed human nature with fixed differences, especially in its liberal formulation that claims an individual's place in society rests on his or her innate talents. He also rejected any notion that the division of labor as found in any known historical society is compatible with social harmony and justice.

The key cause of human behavior and human consciousness, for Marx, stems from the human relationship to nature. Marx termed this cause the *forces of production,* or the material conditions of life—land, resources, technology, and technical skills. A given level of productive forces leads to a distinctive set of social relations or *mode of production:* economic relations especially; but also the legal order, especially property forms; forms of the state; and the ideological order, including religion, philosophy, and

[13] The substance of Marx's social theory may be found in the Communist Manifesto and on a more sophisticated level in *The German Ideology,* especially Part I. Three good readers on various aspects of Marx's thought are: T. B. Bottomore and Maximillien Rubel, eds., trans. T. B. Bottomore *Karl Marx: Selected Writings in Sociology and Social Philosophy* (New York: McGraw-Hill paperback, 1964), originally published 1956; Lewis S. Feuer, ed., *Basic Writings on Politics and Philosophy: Karl Marx and Friedrich Engels* (Garden City, N.Y.: Doubleday paperback, 1959); and Robert C. Tucker, ed., *The Marx-Engels Reader* (New York: W.W. Norton paperback, 1972).

Three useful commentaries on Marx's thought are Henri Lefebvre, *The Sociology of Marx,* trans. Norbert Guterman (New York: Random House paperback, 1969), originally published 1966; Robert C. Tucker, *The Marxian Revolutionary Idea* (New York: W.W. Norton paperback, 1969); and Alan Swingewood, *Marx and Modern Social Theory* (New York: John Wiley, 1975). One of the merits of the Swingewood work is that it presents Marx by systematically (and somewhat dogmatically) contrasting most of his major ideas with what the author believes are the similar but essentially different and inadequate ideas—not always presented accurately or empathetically—of bourgeois thinkers, sociological positivists, phenomenological-reflexive-radical-critical sociologists, and assorted stray Marxists such as Trotsky, Lukacs, and Marcuse.

art. In Marx's shorthand illustration, "the hand mill will give you a society with the feudal lord, the steam mill a society with the industrial capitalist."

History is essentially the story of the changing human relation to nature. As the forces of production change, they contradict the mode of production (or superstructure). This leads to a conflict between classes, which have emerged from the division of economic labor, and to eventual revolution, or social-system change. As the new forces of production crystallize into a new modal form, they develop a new set of social relations to correspond to their new needs. Two aspects of these new social relations are a new, corresponding type of human being and a new concept of human nature. For Marx, therefore, society takes its essential structure from the prevailing level of technology, and it is the individual's relation to the means of production that determines his or her class level, personality, and consciousness. Rather than seeing economic and social structures as the result of human talents, drives, or needs, Marx always focused on social variables, especially technology and the economic system in which it was embedded. Strictly speaking, the crucial factor in the creation of society's basic form is not technology as such but the *ownership* of technology—the means of production. The simple dichotomy of owner and nonowner is the key to understanding both the structure and the processes of society. All other factors, income, occupation, education, or political power, are for Marx derivative and secondary.

Marx was greatly influenced by liberal social theory. Like other socialists he accepted and transformed the Lockean labor theory of value. He also absorbed the various liberal ideas of conflict. For example, he substituted a dialectical materialism, in which conflict, social movement, ideas, and creativity emerge from economic variables, for Hegel's dialectical idealism, in which reason and society emerge from the clash of ideas.[14] Marx also accepted Adam Smith's and David Ricardo's ideas that the interests of landowners, capitalists, and workers—or those who live off rent, profit, and wages, respectively, were different and antagonistic, and he seized on Saint-Simon's idea that the dynamics of historical advance is embodied and expressed in conflicting classes. However, Marx transmuted these ideas into a distinctive conflict theory of society. Liberal theorists who stress conflict to this day tend to interpret it as contributing to the health of capitalist society; this is true, for example, of Adam Smith, Saint-Simon, Spencer, Sumner, Ward, Dahrendorf, and Coser. For Marx, conflict leads not to a healthy capitalism but to revolution, social-system change, and ultimately

---

[14] For Hegel's philosophy and its relation to other currents of thought, including Marx's, see Herbert Marcuse, *Reason and Revolution: Hegel and the Rise of Social Theory* (New York: Oxford University Press, 1941), also in paperback. The radical incompatibility between Hegel's thought and Italian and German fascism is a particularly valuable feature of Marcuse's conclusion.

socialism. Fundamental to Marx's conflict social theory was the fact that all material value is the result of labor. However, because of the power inherent in property, the owners of the means of production receive more than they produce by their own labor. Therefore, there is a basic antagonism between their interests and the interests of all non-property-owning workers. Once Marx identified economic classes on the basis of the ownership and nonownership of land, tools, factories, he identified social classes as well because beliefs and values and overt behavior outside of work correspond to economic behavior, beliefs, and values. Also decisive for Marx's explanation of class formation, as well as for his theory of the dynamics of class struggle and social change, was his assumption that one can distinguish between progressive and reactionary technological forces. The basic criterion that Marx used for making this distinction is the concept of *human fulfillment*. Some technological forces, and the social system embodying them, retard human progress, and others advance it toward emancipation from historical necessity. A class is progressive when it represents the emergence of new forms and levels of liberating technology, as for example, the middle class between the sixteenth and nineteenth centuries. Inevitably, however, a particular class becomes conservative and reactionary, a "ruling class," because it can make larger and larger profits without distributing the fruits of the machine to the general populace, as, for example, the upper-middle class or *grande bourgeoisie* in the nineteenth century.

Capitalism's very success in mastering nature dooms it to failure. (Like other metaphysical theories in modern social science Marx relied heavily on irony and the efficacy of a hidden logic.) Try as it may, capitalism cannot overcome the primary contradiction between the social nature of production and private control and gain. The law of accumulation locates this contradiction at the very heart of capitalist society, the process of capital formation itself. If one thinks of total capital as having two parts—technology, or constant capital, and labor, or variable capital—the inevitable process of capital formation leads to a growing proportion of constant capital and a decline of variable capital. Since exploited labor is the only source of profit, total profit declines, which intensifies the rationalization of industry (i.e., the use of more efficient technology) and leads to a lower proportion of labor, growing unemployment, lower profits, more rationalization, and so on. At a certain point the state of technological development will result in a revolutionary situation: a huge working class living at or below subsistence level and conscious of the contradiction between the essentially social nature of production and the private ownership of the means of production.

Marx was not clear about the actual process of revolution, suggesting in places that in a country like England the proletariat, which forms the vast majority of the people, will simply take over through established parliamentary machinery. Marx was also reticent about the nature of the future socialist society. However, his general vision of history was explicit enough:

individuals will be alienated from themselves, from each other, and from nature as long as there is material scarcity. Alienation is especially acute in capitalist society, with its propensity for turning human beings into commodities. The key to the reduction and elimination of material, and thus moral, scarcity is technology. Once material abundance has been reached, historical systems of economic inequality, with their corresponding structures of moral scarcity (original sin, noble vs. ignoble birth, master-slave, lord-serf, owner-worker, government-citizen, police officer-criminal) will disappear and a classless society of human fulfillment will emerge. It is clear that the classless society represents the end of the control of human beings by blind economic forces and also represents the end of human beings' alienation from themselves, from each other, and from nature. In short, humankind will leave the "kingdom of necessity" and enter the "kingdom of freedom." Under communism there will be a full unleashing of productive forces and a full development of all human faculties. All people will contribute to society according to their abilities, and all will receive according to their needs.

Perhaps the most important aspect of the classless society, and not the least of its appeal, is that it will be a community, thus ending the alienation inherent in all historical societies. Nowhere are the distinctions among the main streams of nineteenth-century thought so easily seen as in the placement of the idea and reality of community: conservatives-traditionalists put community in the past, socialists put it in the future, and liberals sought it in the present or near-present. Not only did socialism absorb many of liberalism's key ideas and values, but in giving fraternity an equal footing with liberty and equality, socialism acquired a potent ideal in an age of industrial atomization and dehumanization.

Marxism: Kautsky, Bernstein, Luxemburg, Lenin, Mao

Marx made predictions about capitalism that have not come true. Even in his own lifetime, there were developments that seemed to contradict his theory. The basic trends that created difficulty for Marx and those who carried on in his name can be listed briefly:

1. Instead of increasing misery, industrialization saw a rise in living standards.

2. Instead of a polarization between big property owners and a uniform working class, there was a broadening of the middle class, including a new white-collar middle class.

3. The growth of representative government seemed to be ushering in a period of cooperation, negotiation, and compromise among conflicting interest groups and classes.

4. Far from being an instrument of narrow class rule, the capitalist state seemed able to intervene in economic and social matters to soften economic hardship, direct economic life, and curb economic excesses.

By the end of the nineteenth century, Marxism contained two modal theoretical emphases: orthodox Marxism (itself somewhat diverse) and revisionist Marxism. The leading theoretician of orthodox Marxism was Karl Kautsky (1854–1938),[15] who stressed the main tenets of Marx: (1) the belief in the breakdown of capitalism because of its inherent contradictions; (2) the belief in the growing wretchedness and revolutionary consciousness of the proletariat; and (3) the belief that the state is an instrument of class rule and oppression.

Kautsky was opposed by the Marxian revisionists led by Eduard Bernstein (1850–1932), who challenged some of Marx's basic tenets, especially his predictions of the inevitable breakdown of capitalism and of the growth of revolutionary consciousness among the working class, and his belief that the state can only be an instrument of class rule and oppression.[16] Instead, the revisionists argued that socialism could be achieved through evolution, especially through social action and political reform.

Opposed to both revisionism and to Kautsky (who must now be called a centrist Marxist) were the radical or militant Marxists, who stressed the need for inciting social revolution. The two main theorists of this position were Rosa Luxemburg (1870–1919)[17] and Vladimir Lenin (1870–1924).[18] Both emphasized the voluntaristic aspects of Marx's thought by stressing the masses' need for leadership (though Luxemburg also stressed Party accountability to the masses)[19] and both explained the apparent health of

[15] Kautsky's basic views were developed in *The Economic Doctrines of Karl Marx* (1887); *Erfurt Programme* (1892); *The Agrarian Problem* (1898); and *The Social Revolution* (1902).
[16] For Bernstein's main statement see *Evolutionary Socialism: A Criticism and Affirmation*, trans. Edith C. Harvey (New York: B.W. Huebsch, 1909), originally published 1899. For a fuller discussion of Marxian revisionism, see Peter Gay, *The Dilemma of Democratic Socialism: Eduard Bernstein's Challenge to Marx* (New York: Collier paperback, 1962), originally published 1952.
[17] The most important of Luxemburg's writings is *The Accumulation of Capital*, trans. Agnes Schwarzschild (London: Routledge and Kegan Paul, 1951); also see her response to criticisms of this work in *The Accumulation of Capital–An Anticritique*, ed. Kenneth J. Tarbuck, trans. Rudolph Wichmann (New York: Monthly Review Press, 1972). This work also includes Nikolai I. Bukharin's *Imperialism and the Accumulation of Capital*.
[18] Selections from Lenin's works may be found in James E. Connor, ed., *Lenin on Politics and Revolution* (New York: Pegasus, 1968), and Robert C. Tucker, ed., *The Lenin Anthology* (New York: W.W. Norton paperback, 1975).
[19] For an argument that Marxism in the industrial heartland of Europe developed into "a largely evolutionary and positivistic doctrine whereas the activistic and voluntaristic interpretation of Marxism was mainly developed by intellectuals in the industrially undeveloped rimland of Europe," see Lewis A. Coser, "Marxist

capitalism by pointing to imperialism. Capitalist countries, they argued, could continue to make profits, raise wages, and develop domestic welfare programs because they had turned to exploiting the resources and labor of colonies.[20]

With the collapse of the European and Japanese colonial systems after World War II, a number of new Communist countries have emerged, along with a new international power system, and the meaning of Marxism and socialism has become more diverse accordingly. Socialist governments have come into power in capitalist countries, and the Communist parties of France and Italy and in the Communist societies of Eastern Europe have tended to stress their independence from Moscow. Perhaps the most significant development in Marxist thought and practice was the attempt by the Chinese Communist party under the leadership of Mao Tse-tung (1893–1976) to adapt Marxism to a deeply backward, peasant, colonial society and to profit from the Soviet experience. Essentially Mao upheld a voluntaristic image of the power of the masses while stressing the need of the Party and masses to unite with the Chinese middle class against foreign domination in the acquisition of power and in the construction of socialism. Of special significance was Mao's emphasis on guerrilla warfare as a means of coming to power. Also significant was Mao's emphasis, after coming to power in 1949, on developing antielitist institutions to prevent the separation of Party, managers, and professionals, on the one hand, and the masses on the other—a separation that is pronounced in the Soviet Union and most other Eastern European Communist countries. In striking ways, Mao's thought is a creative amalgam of Lenin and Luxemburg.[21]

Socialist Social Theory

It would go beyond my purposes to even outline the rich flowering of socialist and radical-left thought, either within or outside of Marxism, during

---

Thought in the First Quarter of the Twentieth Century," *American Journal of Sociology* 78 (July 1972): 173–201. Coser adds that "the only two Marxist theorists of marked originality who emerged after the First World War," the Italian, Antonio Gramsci, and the Hungarian, Georg Lukacs, were similar to Luxemburg and Lenin in both their antideterminism and voluntarism, and in their location on the agrarian rim of industrial Europe.

[20] For revisions in the Marxian theory of imperialism, see pages 539–540.

[21] For selections from Mao's writings, see Stuart R. Schram, ed., with a lengthy introduction, *The Political Thought of Mao Tse-tung* (New York: Praeger, 1963), and Mostafa Rejai, ed., *Mao Tse-tung on Revolution and War* (Garden City, N.Y.: Doubleday, 1969). Mao's success in raising China's living standards and simultaneously promoting egalitarianism is confirmed by Stuart R. Schram, ed., *Authority, Participation, and Cultural Change in China* (London: Cambridge University Press, 1973) and by the United States Information Agency's publication, *Problems of Communism*—its symposium on twenty-five years of Communist rule in China is in volume 23, September–October, 1974.

the twentieth century.[22] However, some sense of the overall alternative provided by socialist thought is a useful counterweight to liberalism and sociology. Methodologically, socialists stress a morally imbued rational-empirical approach, tending to see the alleged value-free empirical approach as a reflection of the status quo. Substantively, the basic elements of social as opposed to liberal democracy are:

1. Socialist theory tends to be sociocultural in a way that goes beyond the theories of most Anglo-American late liberals.

2. It rejects the idea of a biopsychological entity that behaves and therefore shapes the contour of society.

3. It also rejects the idea of a separation between the individual and society—the estrangement between or among human beings and their society is purely historical.

4. It places the reconciliation of human beings and society in a future social system.

5. It believes that all historical societies are sundered by contradictions and contain conflicts that are irreconcilable within extant social systems. Liberal democracy, in other words, cannot reform itself beyond certain limits or fully achieve any of its basic values.

6. It believes that the essential contradiction of capitalism springs from a privately owned economy that permits some to live at the expense of others and that makes a permanent mockery of equal justice and equal opportunity for self-development.

7. It believes that all behavior and all issues in history must be conceived in terms of an interlocking institutional structure (society and an interlocking system of societies) whose center of gravity is the domestic and international economy.

THE ADVENT OF ORGANIZED EMPIRICAL
SOCIAL RESEARCH

One of the more significant developments in the nineteenth century was the advent of organized empirical research in both the natural and the social sciences. Along with the empirical *outlook* (which I shall trace in the remainder of this study), systematic, organized empirical research arose to

---

[22] For a brief discussion of how socialist and radical-left thought has impinged on contemporary sociology, see the sections "Phenomenological-Ethnomethodological Sociologies" and "Radical Humanism" in Chapter 24.

become the modal *practice* of Western intellectual-moral culture. Of course, empiricism is multifaceted, and much of it precedes the nineteenth century. As nominalism in William of Occam and others, it helped to sever the medieval world's logical merger of God, nature, and human nature, and freed each for conquest by different means. The empirical outlook appears as a delight in and curiosity about the natural world during the Renaissance, as skepticism in Montaigne, and as pragmatic statecraft in Machiavelli. The Protestants' rejection of reason or theology as the avenue to God and their belief that nature was God's handiwork engendered a Protestant positivism that furthered the rise of experimental science in the seventeenth century. The empirical outlook emerged in literature in the picaresque novel, with its sense of chronic human chaos, and again in the bourgeois novel, with its concern for material things and individual human beings—for example Defoe's *Moll Flanders* and *Robinson Crusoe* and Fielding's *Tom Jones*. The empirical value orientation is evident in the realistic portrayals of individuals by Rembrandt and other Dutch painters, some of whom meticulously depicted the household possessions of their burgher patrons.

The empirical outlook and practice was furthered, above all, by the accelerated pace of technological development from the Middle Ages onward and by the rise of central government and absolutism—especially by the creation of bureaucratic administration with its interest in fact gathering. (Significantly, the words *state* and *statistics* have the same root.) Also not to be overlooked is the empirical bent of military life, in which the life and death of nations rested on up-to-date military technology, skill, and organization. Perhaps the key event symbolizing the empirical trend in military life was the victory of the English fleet, using naval technology tested in piracy, over the Spanish Armada, which put its faith in God.

However, a unique occurrence in the nineteenth century was that empirical research became routine, a modal activity in natural science and a widespread activity of government, business, and voluntary groups. The enormous import of this development is captured in Whitehead's remark that the most important discovery of the nineteenth century was "the invention of invention." The same attitude is suggested by the fact that Thomas Edison went into the occupation—nay, the business—of invention. It was an assumption in the nineteenth century that anything could be invented, that all goals could be turned into problems and solved.

Invention was not limited to science and technology—it was equally pronounced and noteworthy in social life. Legislatures began routinely to manage the multiple and tangled affairs of nations. The standardized interchangeable machine part found its counterpart and fulfillment in disposable labor and the factory system. The gold standard was established; utopian communities were organized by the thousands; voluntary groups for every conceivable purpose, from fighting fires to electing government officials, were created. Perhaps the most important social creation of the nineteenth century, however, was the corporation, that great engine of collective capital formation. Legally declared a person by the American government and accorded its full measure of rights under the Constitution by the Supreme Court, the corporation became the center of power in American society.

The abstract coordination of the myriad empirical activities of vast aggregates of individuals, implicit in all these organizational creations, intrigued people and made them curious about causation. The theory of laissez faire was humankind's grandest scheme for understanding empirical behavior, and its grandest mistake. In any case, there seemed to be some near-magical process that made possible such things as insurance, banking, political machines, and capital formation, and the search was on to uncover it. (Probability mathematics would eventually make sense out of much of the above.)

The emergence of organized empirical social research was a highly significant development. However, it must not be seen as a process intelligible unto itself or as merely part of the triumphal march of science and democracy against ignorance, superstition, exploitation, and misgovernment. Two things especially must be borne in mind: creative empirical thought and creative empirical practice developed separately, and both were outcomes and servants of a new system of social power.

The Separate Growth of Empirical Theory and Empirical Research

The institutionalization of empirical social research that began early in the nineteenth century was nowhere combined with sociological theory as such. The major figures who pioneered the empirical outlook (pluralistic positivism) in sociology did so quite independently of, and sometimes in opposition to, the burgeoning research activities that were taking place around them. Max Weber, who was far from opposed to empirical research, helped create the German Sociological Society in 1910 in opposition to Germany's leading research organization, the Association for Social Policy Legislation, which under the leadership of Gustav Schmoller viewed empirical research largely as an adjunct to legislation and government.[23] Sociology in Britain also had to struggle against a theory-less statistical empiricism.[24] Organized

[23] See Susanne Petra Schad, *Empirical Social Research in Weimar-Germany* (Paris: Mouton, 1972), chap. 1.
[24] See Philip Abrams, *The Origins of British Sociology: 1834–1914* (Chicago: University of Chicago Press, 1968), pt. 1.

empirical social research and sociology also grew independent of each other in France [25] and the United States.[26] This affirms again that all knowledge is acquired with theory. Without words (ideas, concepts, logic, theory) with which to see, arrange, and interpret facts, no knowledge is possible. Of course words do not emanate from a self-sufficient mind or an immanent scientific process, but flow from experience. If experience creates a certain line of words, then knowledge can be acquired, or, depending on the line words take, knowledge can be blocked in favor of custom or magic. Alternately, if one's experience is pleasant and contains few surprises, then the thoughts one develops and keeps are likely to depict a static, benign reality and express satisfaction with the world. If one's experience is unpleasant and filled with unexpected shocks, one will more than likely come to think of the world as malevolent and unpredictable. It is important to remember, therefore, that the creative advances in nineteenth- and early-twentieth-century sociology were made by empirically oriented theorists, not by research-oriented theorists. One of the more ominous implications of all this should be clear—the linking of theory and research in twentieth-century sociology (accomplished first in the United States by the Chicago School during the 1920s and then spreading, especially after World War II, to all parts of the West and even to many parts of the non-West) may represent the absorption of thought by the given. Or, to put the matter in its most insidious form, if the given social world becomes a successful, hierarchical, class-based welfare state (whether organized under capitalist or communist auspices may make little difference), then sociologists and social scientists in general could well become traditionalistic, especially if their occupations are secure, well paid, and research oriented.

Symbolic Activity and the Needs of Power

Like all symbolic activity, empirical research is related to the structure of social power. Those who accept the conventional view of the development of empirical science and of liberal political institutions as a growing emancipation from error and evil have themselves succumbed to the blandishments of power. Knowledge helps to make human beings free, but not all of them. Indeed, the knowledge that sets some people free results in the nonfreedom of others. Knowledge about how a legislature works, for example, can result in laws that free some from tax burdens while placing

[25] Sociology in France is different from sociology in other countries, having emerged quite early. It cannot be said that sociology and empirical research were linked even by Durkheim and his disciples who clustered around the leading sociological journal of the time, the *Année Sociologique*.
[26] For background, see Anthony Oberschall, "The Institutionalization of American Sociology," in Anthony Oberschall, ed., *The Establishment of Empirical Sociology: Studies in Continuity, Discontinuity, and Institutionalization* (New York: Harper & Row, 1972).

heavier burdens on others. Empirical research can certainly contribute knowledge and help in the clarification and realization of values, but like sociological theory in general, its known historic forms cannot automatically be equated with knowledge, morality, and the common good.

The use of the intelligence quotient (IQ) is a well-known example of how theory enters into empirical research and how both must be related to social power. Early research into intelligence quotients was conducted under the assumption or theory that human beings are innately unequal. As a consequence, the science of IQs became a potent instrument for creating and maintaining a capitalist division of labor—especially when educational systems adopted the IQ as the measure of ability and worth with the enthusiastic endorsement of the middle classes. The facts about unequal IQs can also be interpreted as a function of social power: people are made unequal in IQ, as well as in occupational skills, tastes, goals, and so on by the hierarchy of social class. This gives the researcher a very different view of the same facts.

Historically, empirical social research undoubtedly originated with the absolute monarchy, especially its mercantilist phase. The dynamics of internal and external power relations made it imperative that the state rationalize (bureaucratize) its operations.[27] Hand in hand with routine administration, the keeping of accounts, the codification of laws, and the minting and printing of money went the development of intelligence-gathering agencies: domestic and foreign spies, informers, police reports, inquiries and commissions concerning population, the state of the fishing or textile industry, surveys of public lands, and so on. Significantly, all these activities of the absolute state hastened the demise of feudal society in the advanced countries of the West and helped create liberal society.

The case of England is especially instructive in understanding the power functions served by the widespread institutionalization of empirical research. The symbolic development of England can be thought of not merely as the emergence of science and democracy, but as the record of acquiring, consolidating, and employing power in an economically dynamic society. In the seventeenth century Hobbes and Locke shattered and displaced the feudal symbolic world in the name of an emergent middle class. In the eighteenth century Adam Smith found rationality *in* capitalist society, not beyond it; Hume clipped the wings of reason, in effect saying that thought cannot be used to transcend or critically evaluate society; and Burke extolled the wisdom and efficacy of custom. The nineteenth century saw the growth

---

[27] For an informative account of a crucial period in the formation of the modern state and the European system of states, see Walter L. Dorn, *Competition for Empire, 1740–1763* (New York: Harper & Row, 1940), especially chaps. 1–3; vol. 9 of *The Rise of Modern Europe,* ed. William L. Langer.

of a series of deductive disciplines such as economics, political science, and sociology, all within the capitalist assumptions of laissez faire economics, utilitarianism, progress, and social Darwinism. These disciplines eventually flowered as the liberal arts—liberalism's higher education. Alongside this symbolic development, but not linked to it until much later, there grew a tradition of empirical social research, a nontheoretical grappling with the problems of an established capitalist society rapidly becoming industrialized and urbanized.

In the early nineteenth century, Britain had a well-established though adaptable and somewhat open set of ruling elites. There was an obvious need for intelligence, and it was assumed from the first that facts were to be used for purposes of formulating public policy. As Abrams has shown so well,[28] the basic form of research in Britain's centralized society was the massive government inquiry, and the basic roles that were encouraged were those of statistician, administrator, and reform politician. Further, as Abrams also points out, Britain's dominant classes held some distinctive views about society that deeply influenced the nature of empirical social research: a deeply rationalist concept of society, a focus on individuals as the basic unit of analysis, and the idea of automatic social integration and consensus through the invisible hand. Essentially, the purposes of fact gathering were to uncover the natural laws that constituted society, to expose artificial obstacles that impeded their operation, and to promote the consensual natural society through social legislation and government administration. Characteristically, researchers felt that there was no need for theory since one was searching for pure facts. Of course there was a theory behind this fact gathering; as Abrams points out, its characteristic units of analysis were

> the state, the individual (moral or immoral) and occasionally, the classes. What is missing is any developed concept of the social system, any extended or general analysis of structured interactions between individuals or classes, any theory of the social basis of the state. Where there *is* a model of society it is typically an administrative one suffused with moral judgment.... time and again the terms of analysis are the custodial state standing face to face with individuals in need of help, correction, or regeneration.[29]

So narrow was the definition of empirical social research and so dependent was it on the needs of government that sociology had first to fight the prevalent

[28] Philip Abrams, *The Origins of British Sociology: 1834–1914* (Chicago: University of Chicago Press, 1968), pt. 1.
[29] Abrams, p. 48f. For further evidence of the partisan uses of pure empirical research, see M. J. Cullen, *The Statistical Movement in Early Victorian Britain: The Foundations of Empirical Social Research* (New York: Barnes and Noble, 1975), especially his conclusion.

empirical tradition in order to establish its identity and then struggle to incorporate empirical research into its theoretical outlook.

Sociology grew, indeed prospered, at the end of the nineteenth century largely because many of the basic principles of early liberalism had been discredited. Of special importance in Anglo-American countries, where laissez faire theory had taken hold, was the gradual abandonment of a belief in natural harmony and social integration through an invisible hand. Far from being even-handed and integrative, the invisible hand of the market was stroking some and punching others, subjecting society to unhealthy ups and downs, and failing to incorporate many into society. It became clear that integrative processes other than the free market had to be found or created. Everywhere in the industrial West, a late-liberal movement surfaced to spearhead a more positive and comprehensive program of social reform within the assumptions of capitalism. The development of pluralistic positivism in sociology, along with its sociocultural emphasis and its involvement in social reform, is one aspect of late liberalism, its scientific left wing so to speak. In the United States, Sumner was overshadowed both by Ward and by the politics of reform. (In England Hobhouse played Ward to Spencer's Sumner.) With no laissez faire tradition to overcome, French and German sociologists developed a pronounced sociocultural orientation and became involved in the political issues of the day. In all countries alike, there was a clear recognition that empirical social research and social reform were positive forces to prevent socialism.

In any case, to return to the new interest in fact gathering, it is clear that its main sources were government, business, and voluntary groups, and that its motives were political, economic, humanitarian—and the fear of the masses and of socialism. In an informative essay,[30] Nathan Glazer has argued that the upper classes' new interest in facts stemmed from a feeling that they were surrounded by a society they neither knew nor could know using conventional methods such as reading or personal experience. However, Glazer does not complete his insight. One of the main functions of the new urge for empirical research was to provide the dominant classes with the intelligence they needed to possess their society fully. The primary significance of data gathering is that it helps consolidate, update, and legitimate a particular system of domination. The important reason that England was able to pioneer and develop the empirical arts more fully than other nations is not merely as Glazer points out, that it was the world's most advanced industrial country. All European countries were troubled by the social question during the early nineteenth century; all saw the growth of large numbers of destitute people both in the countryside and in the burgeoning

[30] "The Rise of Social Research in Europe," in *The Human Meaning of the Social Sciences*, ed. Daniel Lerner (New York: Meridian paperback, 1959), chap. 2.

industrial cities and towns. However, among the major countries of Europe, it was only in England that the social question was successfully separated from revolution. Certainly the threat to civil order and to the order of society itself, represented mostly acutely by the Chartist movement, stimulated social research as well as political rivalry and creativity among the dominant landed and commercial-industrial classes. However, the defeat of Chartism made England safe for liberalism, and the task of the dominant classes henceforth was to run, not to think about, their society. From then to now, the great flowering of empirical social research went hand in hand with the major achievement of British society, the successful incorporation of the working and destitute classes into a capitalist society. Empirical research supplied the intelligence for the reforms that forestalled revolution and even helped to turn socialism into reformism.

Organized empirical research was part of the monumental formation of the centralized state that was essentially completed, though not in any uniform manner, everywhere in Europe and the United States during the nineteenth century. From the establishment of the Prussian bureaucracy under Fredrick the Great in the mid-eighteenth century to Napoleon Bonaparte's creation of the modern French civil service to the Pendleton Act of 1883 in the United States, the process of bureaucratization (rational administration) manifested itself everywhere. Britain was no exception. Britain's construction of a highly centralized state machine during the nineteenth century is perhaps a better index to the realities of social power, both there and elsewhere, than the extension of the franchise or the emergence of cabinet government.[31]

The sanctities of government and politics; the moral cloak of voluntary organizations, including churches; the iron necessities allegedly governing economic life; and the prestige of science—all served to mask the essentially partisan nature of empirical research. However, if one views the activities of these institutions as ways of developing private solutions to public problems, then empirical research falls into place as another way in which the dominant classes solved their problems, invariably through solutions that created problems for the lower classes.

The eventual unification of organized empirical social research and sociological theory completed the social revolution called modern society and should be thought of as the intellectual corollary of the economic, political, and social revolution called liberal (or capitalist) society. With the triumph of liberalism, philosophy and social theory no longer serviced a landed-clerical elite; symbolic culture no longer emphasized the next world and denigrated

---

[31] For the development of Britain's centralized administration, see K. B. Smellie, *A Hundred Years of English Government* (New York: Macmillan, 1937).

this one; and contemplation and transcendence were no longer feasible social ideals. Philosophy, social theory, and organized empirical social research became ways of dealing with the here and now—that is, by camouflaging the here and now in evolutionary garbs, organized empirical research effectively pre-empted the future while safeguarding the present. In any case, given the class uses and advantages of empirical social research, one must resist equating it with science or social theory—though it has a clear affinity with sociology, and indeed with any system of domination from absolute monarchy, liberal constitutionalism and the welfare state, or the dictatorship of the proletariat.

Empirical Variation in the Rise of Empiricism

In the remainder of this history of sociological theory I shall be dealing with the world of empirical sociology or pluralistic positivism. To understand this world one must be wary of all notions suggesting a uniform symbolic development or the growth of objectivity. Each country developed the empirical orientation differently to suit its own conditions, traditions, and needs. Some of the implications of this empirical variation in the rise of empiricism are worth repeating. The social theorist must be wary of those who assert the existence of a pure process of fact gathering. By necessity facts are gathered in keeping with ideas and values, and like any social activity fact gathering must be related to and explained by the imperatives of social power. Furthermore, the basic advances in empirical sociology from the late nineteenth century on were made by theorists quite independent of organized social research, though of course theorists did engage in research and made use of the research of others.

Another important existential condition behind the development of sociological theory has already been suggested: the very different social experience available to Anglo-American as opposed to Continental thinkers. Given their settled system of society, settled even beyond the consciousness of most of their intellectuals, Britain and the United States produced no sociological theorists of the stature of Durkheim or Weber (or of the stature of Marx). Theory in both countries was primarily a legitimation of existing society, and both countries developed a full-bodied research infrastructure to supply data to cope not so much with the problems of theory as with social problems.

In contrast, France and Germany did not solve the social question for almost a century and a half and were racked by social-system challenges from roughly the French Revolution until after World War II. It was not until the post-1945 period that France and Germany emerged as functioning liberal democracies. Thus early French and German theorists had to think about the nature of society in a far deeper sense than did Anglo-American theorists. As a consequence liberal, conservative, and socialist social theorists were far more creative on the Continent than were their counterparts in the English-speaking world.

THE NEW PHASE OF MODERN SCIENCE

Before examining the thought of some representative pioneers of pluralistic positivism in sociology, it would be helpful to provide an overview of the new empirical phase of modern science in terms of the new analytical tools that scientists forged to help them see and collect facts more systematically. Though biology was the outstanding field of science during the nineteenth century, certainly from the standpoint of tracing the influence of natural science on social science, there were enormously important advances in almost every branch of science. Indeed, the nineteenth century has become known as the century of science. Its reputation, however, does not rest merely on gains in scientific knowledge and technology. With the emergence of a full-blown capitalist social system, science was no longer a contradictory and alien element in society. Not only did it become deeply institutionalized, but as an integral part of the new social system, it found support and reinforcement from other institutions, most notably from industry. For the first time in human history, common people in the West began to feel the effects of applied technology and to interpret their lives more and more in terms of a secular, scientifically based ethos.

So extensive were the gains made by science during the nineteenth century that there also occurred a qualitative change in its general outlook. As noted in a previous chapter,[32] the new phase of modern science, which can be dated conventionally from 1800, was intrinsically related to the radically new character of social life that emerged as a consequence of increasing human mastery over nature. The new outlook in science meant that individuals, especially males in the dominant classes, began to think of reason more and more in functional terms in order to keep abreast of the fast-moving and ever-changing array of economic and political problems. It was the increased tempo and complexity of practical life that ultimately led to a radically new view of nature and to the full development of an empirical methodology.

The Contemporary View of Nature

The mechanistic view of nature that had held sway as the organizing cosmology of European and American life since the seventeenth century was gradually supplanted during the nineteenth century by an evolutionary or functional view. The new cosmology abandoned the idea that nature was a structure with fixed properties. Climaxing generations of scientific work,

[32] See Part III, Chapter 9.

Western intellectual culture slowly reached the assumption that it would be more fruitful, as well as more consonant with established facts, to think of nature in dynamic terms. The Newtonian view saw nature as a fixed structure with fixed effects. In restricting science to physics, and physics to mechanics, the Newtonian world view had given the West a static and narrow view of nature. However, despite Newton's dominion over European intellectual life for more than a century after his death, countercurrents of scientific thought slowly gathered force. By the middle of the nineteenth century Western science was ready to transcend the Newtonian view in the same way it had transcended the Aristotelian view—by formulating a more satisfactory and productive image of nature.

Perhaps the most significant aspect of the new cosmology was that it rejected any distinction between structure and function. According to the mechanistic view, nature contained autonomous structural properties having fixed effects or functions. Under the new view, "structure is resolvable into function," that is, any regularity or seemingly autonomous natural property or structure is really a kind of activity, process, or behavior.[33] This change in the perception of nature had two important consequences: it opened scientists' eyes to processes that produce qualitatively new forms or structures or functions, and it made them aware of the plurality and complexity of the structures that constituted nature.

The Triumph of Empiricism

Empiricism, then, had become the modal methodology of science, and scientists were becoming wary of imposing on nature selected and thus arbitrary features of the human mind. It was painstaking observation or experiment that had found biological evolution, that had unified such seemingly diverse phenomena as light and electricity, that had uncovered new insights into the structure of gas, and that had established the laws of thermodynamics. It is not surprising that the empirical method rose to dominance.

Above all, the empirical method is a search for the relationships between precisely identified variables, not for the nature of the variables themselves. To an important extent, this general approach had characterized the main tradition in early modern science, the deductive or Mathematical approach. For example, Galileo's famous formula for falling bodies, $d = 16t^2$, was a precise mathematical description of a relationship between precisely identified variables. However, much of early modern science had assumed that mathematical deduction or causation was identical with the structure of

[33] R. G. Collingwood, *The Idea of Nature* (New York: Oxford University paperback, 1960), p. 16f. For a more extended picture by Collingwood of the new view of nature and the attempts to derive a new cosmology from it by philosophers such as Bergson, Alexander, and Whitehead, see pp. 9–27 and all of pt. 2.

phenomena and was therefore the primary, if not the only, method; late modern science found it increasingly necessary to separate the mind from nature and to subordinate it to the logic of phenomena. The crucial difference between the first and second phases of modern science, therefore, is that the latter emphasized efficient or empirical causation and downgraded logical causation. However, the rejection of logic as the embodiment of truth and as a method did not mean that logic became less important to the scientific enterprise. On the contrary, a whole series of new logics emerged during the nineteenth century, enormously enhancing the ability of Westerners to understand both physical and human nature.

THE NEW LOGIC OF PROBABILITY

The most important of the new logics was probability mathematics. However, the core idea of probability, namely that chance occurrences are lawful and that uncertainty can be calculated precisely, is older than the nineteenth century. Major beginnings in probability mathematics were made during the seventeenth century by Pascal and Fermat and there were numerous advances during the eighteenth century, but it was only in the nineteenth century that both the logic of probability and its application came into their own. An enhanced stature for probability mathematics was predicted in a major treatise by Pierre Laplace (1749–1827), an individual conscious of his place in the historical development of the subject and of his role as a synthesizer.[34] By the end of the century the theory of probability had been greatly advanced and had become an integral part of scientific methodology.[35]

Throughout the nineteenth century probability mathematics was applied to one field after another, reaping a rich harvest of knowledge.[36] Perhaps more

[34] In 1819 Laplace wrote a popular introduction to his technical treatise on probability that is now available in English: A Philosophical Essay on Probabilities, trans. Frederick W. Truscott and Frederick L. Emory (New York: Dover, 1951). Laplace provides a historical perspective on the development of probability theory in the concluding chapter. One of the major themes of Laplace's essay is his confident assertion that moral and social phenomena, no less than natural phenomena, can be rendered scientific through the application of probability mathematics. To this end, Laplace wrote a number of chapters marking a crude but pioneer attempt to apply probability theory to insurance, morals, and political and legal decision making.
[35] An outstanding exponent of the theory of probability in the late nineteenth century was Karl Pearson. See The Grammar of Science, rev. ed. (New York: Meridian, 1957); originally published in 1892, revised in 1900, issued in final form in 1911. Pearson's summary of the meaning that probability had acquired for the practicing scientist, including emphasis on the new idea of correlation, are in chaps. 4 and 5. The theory of probability meant more to Pearson than a method of investigation; it was for him, as well as for a growing number of other scientists, part of a full-blown, thoroughgoing Humian nominalism.
[36] John Theodore Merz's A History of European Thought in the Nineteenth Century (London: William Blackwood and Sons, 1903), 2:chap. 12, is a valuable

than anyone else, it was Darwin who stimulated interest in the scientific potential of the logic of possibilities. His discovery of the lawfulness of random mutations in biological evolution was a dramatic confirmation that one of the most complex portions of the empirical realm was rational. Of special significance for the logic of science, however, was the fact that this rationality was statistical in nature. This discovery was matched by similar discoveries in other fields. Mendel (1822–1884) and Galton (1822–1911) made important applications of statistical laws to biological and psychological phenomena; Maxwell (1831–1879) and Boltzmann (1844–1906) formulated the behavior of gas molecules in statistical terms; and such later scientists as Max Planck (1858–1947) and Werner Heisenberg (1901–1976) established that the atom was statistical in nature.

As illlustrated by the rise of probability mathematics, the development of empiricism during the nineteenth century did not mean that Western science dispensed with reason; rather, reason became subordinated to fact and had to justify itself by performance. The habit of abstract thought was too deeply planted and too fruitful to be discarded easily by Western scientists. As long as raw experience, and even experimentation, was contradictory, misleading, or inefficient, just so long would scientists be disposed to summon logic to their aid.

PROBABILITY AND SOCIOLOGY: QUETELET (1796–1874)

During the nineteenth century the logic of probability was also applied successfully to the study of social phenomena. Its record in this regard is not unimpressive, even in comparison with its accomplishments in natural science. The origins of statistical reasoning about social phenomena (not mentioning works with evidence of statistical rationality such as the *Domes-*

---

survey of the historical development of probability theory and of the extensive uses to which it was put during the nineteenth century. Another valuable source of information about the theory of probability itself, also containing numerous references to its application in various fields, is Morris Kline, *Mathematics in Western Culture* (New York: Oxford University Press, 1953), chaps. 22–24; available in paperback. A beginning of a history of quantification in sociology is Paul Lazarsfeld's informative essay, "Notes on the History of Quantification in Sociology—Trends, Sources and Problems," in Harry Woolf, ed., *Quantification: A History of the Meaning of Measurement in the Natural and Social Sciences* (Indianapolis: Bobbs-Merrill, 1961), pp. 147–203. Additional examples of the growing use of quantitative methods during the nineteenth century may be found in Nathan Glazer, "The Rise of Social Research in Europe," *The Human Meaning of the Social Sciences*, ed. Daniel Lerner (New York: Meridian paperback, 1959), chap. 2. As noted earlier, Glazer's essay directly relates the increased use of statistics to the rise of empiricism in social research and also relates the rise of empiricism to the need of governments, reformers, business leaders, and intellectuals to know a society whose foundations were being drastically altered by rapid social change.

day Book and the social bookkeeping of ecclesiastical records) are traditionally dated from the work of two seventeenth-century Englishmen, John Graunt (1620–1674) and William Petty (1623–1687), the founders of "political arithmetic."[37]

Whereas Laplace had merely stated that probability was applicable to social phenomena, the credit for actually demonstrating its usefulness belongs to Laplace's student and friend, the Belgian scientist and mathematician Adolphe Quetelet. Previous developments in the application of statistics to social phenomena converged and found their focus in this remarkable individual. It was Quetelet, says Hankins, who by his development of the statistical method, research, and activities in various European scientific societies did more than anyone else to promote the use of statistics in all branches of science.[38] Quetelet used statistical analysis to study social phenomena in a new way and with new scope. In many ways, he occupies a unique place in the history of social science, and his work deserves to be discussed more extensively than can be done here. However, since he was probably the first practicing empirical positivist [39] in the history of modern social science, his work deserves more than passing mention.

Like other positivists, Quetelet believed that there were scientifically ascertainable social laws. What distinguishes his positivism, however, is his belief that these laws obey the normal curve of error or, as he called it, the "law of accidental causes." [40] In following this law, argued Quetelet, social phenomena obey the same law as the rest of nature. They are not only similar in this regard to physics, but Quetelet even suggested vaguely that they follow the laws of Newtonian mechanics.[41]

Quetelet's positivism was also distinctive in that he actually conducted empirical research. The work embodying most of this research appeared in

[37] For background, see G. N. Clark, "Social Science in the Age of Newton," in Anthony Oberschall, ed., *The Establishment of Empirical Sociology* (New York: Harper & Row, 1972), pp. 15–30; and M. J. Cullen, *The Statistical Movement in Early Victorian Britain: The Foundations of Empirical Social Research* (New York: Barnes and Noble, 1975), "Prelude: Social Statistics in Britain, 1660–1830," pp. 1–16. For a contrast between English and German developments with an emphasis on the seventeenth-century German Hermann Conring, see Paul Lazarsfeld, "Notes on the History of Quantification in Sociology—Trends, Sources, and Problems," in Harry Woolf, ed., *Quantification: A History of the Meaning of Measurement in the Natural and Social Sciences* (Indianapolis: Bobbs-Merrill, 1961), pp. 149–164.

[38] Frank H. Hankins, *Adolphe Quetelet as Statistician* (New York: Columbia University Press, 1908), chap. 2. For additional material on Quetelet, see Lazarsfeld, *op. cit.*, pp. 164–179.

[39] Not only because he dealt directly with precisely recorded quantitative data about human behavior but because he also formulated a general theory of behavior.

[40] The clearest statements of this oft-repeated belief may be found in the second of Quetelet's two major works in social science, *Du Système social et des lois qui le régissent* (Paris: Guillaumin et Cie, 1848), Preface; bk. 1, sec. 2, chap. 5.

[41] *Ibid.*, pp. 16–17; bk. 3, chaps. 9–10.

1835 and constitutes a landmark in empirical social science.[42] Quetelet's goal was to demonstrate that all effects must have proportionate causes and that these causes can be determined through the application of probability. Fundamental to his approach was the belief that there are general underlying causes as opposed to secondary, trivial, or apparent causes, and that these general causes appear as effects in properly collected and analyzed social data. However, said Quetelet, one cannot ascertain these causes by studying the individual; rather, one studies the "average man," the "fictitious being" who truly represents the operation of general causes. Once identified, Quetelet claimed, the "average man" will reveal not only the truth about human beings, but also what is good and beautiful about them.

Quetelet's classic work is divided into two parts: an analysis of data pertaining to human physical characteristics, including such things as births, deaths, stature, and weight, and an analysis of human intellectual and moral qualities. The second part, in which Quetelet analyzed statistically such things as mental alienation, suicide, temperance, and crime, is of special interest for the historian of sociology. Here can be seen both the strength and weakness of his approach, especially in his treatment of crime, to which he devoted most of his attention. Quetelet's strength lay in his statistical empiricism, his careful compilation of data with a view toward establishing the causal variables in criminal behavior. However, his weakness is also apparent. In listing the major causes of crime, he cited age as by far the most important, followed by sex, season, climate, "frequent mixture of people," profession, "inequality of fortune," and passing "rapidly from a state of comfort to one of misery"—not poverty, but abrupt poverty.[43]

As his list reveals, Quetelet had only a limited appreciation of the sociocultural basis of behavior. The major presupposition of his work was that social behavior stems from constant physical and innate physiological-psychological causes. The weakness of Quetelet's approach is, in fact, a variant of monism in naturalistic positivism. He frequently remarked on the constancy of his data, a constancy that confirmed his belief that there are static regularities in social phenomena in much the same way as in Newtonian physics. In other words, Quetelet lacked data that expressed variations in the behavior of variables over time, and he lacked the comparative method in which the effects of variables are studied in different cultural contexts.

To be understood properly, therefore, Quetelet's thought must be placed in the context of the deductive mathematical tradition of early modern

[42] Adolphe Quetelet, *Sur L'Homme et le développment de ses facultés, ou Essai de physique sociale*, 2 vols. (Paris: Bachelier, 1835); translated as *A Treatise on Man and the Development of his Faculties* (Edinburgh: W. and R. Chambers, 1842); reproduced in 1969 in facsimile with an introduction by Solomon Diamond by Scholars' Facsimiles and Reprints, Gainesville, Florida.
[43] *A Treatise on Man*, p. 95f.

science. Such theorists as Galileo, Spinoza, Descartes, and Hobbes assumed that since the structure of mathematical logic corresponds to the basic structure of phenomena, it can be employed as the primary method of science. Quetelet's thought is part of this rationalist tradition, for though he looked for the logic in phenomena directly and used the theory of probability rather than geometry, his thought was nonetheless deductive and static. In the final analysis, what he did was to impose the logic of probability on his data by carelessly assuming that correlations always express causation. Given his assumption that social behavior can be explained in terms of a set of constant physical and biopsychological causes, this was especially harmful. Partly because of Quetelet's influence and partly because of the general climate of naturalistic positivism, these shortcomings entered the main stream of social science to plague the entire application of mathematics to the study of human nature, the most conspicuous example of which has been the search for innate intelligence quotients.

These deficiencies aside, Quetelet's use of probability theory to analyze social phenomena was a notable achievement, one that was to receive ever-wider currency and refinement in the decades ahead. Interestingly, the greatest fruits of his approach were reaped by Emile Durkheim, who extracted its full theoretical benefits by placing it in the context of a sociocultural form of positivism (see Chapter 14). Durkheim not only reversed the priority that Quetelet had given his causal factors, but he also had the theoretical acumen to transform Quetelet's casual reference to "frequent mixture of people" into the concept of "moral density" or social interaction. Durkheim also explored the enormous implications for social structure contained in Quetelet's reference to professional statuses, and transformed Quetelet's insight into the significance of abrupt poverty into the enormously fruitful sociological concept of *anomie*.[44]

No survey of the flowering of the statistical method would be complete without mentioning the work of such thinkers as Mayhew (1812–1887),[45] LePlay (1806–1882),[46] and Booth (1840–1916).[47] Though none of these

---

[44] There is no direct proof that Durkheim picked up these ideas from Quetelet. However, Durkheim did know Quetelet's two major works. Both are cited in Durkheim's rejection of Quetelet's explanation of suicide in his own book, *Suicide*, trans. J.A. Spaulding and G. Simpson; ed., G. Simpson (New York: Free Press, 1951) pp. 330–304, 317f.

[45] Henry Mayhew's investigation of the lower classes of London appeared in newspaper accounts as early as 1849. His overall work, *London Labor and the London Poor*, appeared in three volumes in 1851, was reprinted with changes in 1861, was supplemented by a fourth volume in 1862, and is now available as a reprint (New York: Augustus M. Kelley, 1967, 4 vols.). For background on Mayhew's career and his accomplishment as a social investigator, see Eileen Yeo and E. P. Thompson, *The Unknown Mayhew* (New York: Pantheon, 1971).

[46] Frédéric LePlay, *Les Ouvriers européens* (Paris: Imprimerie imperiale, 1855). This was a one-volume abridgment by LePlay of his case studies of the family; a second, revised, and expanded six-volume edition appeared in 1877–1879

thinkers employed the logic of probability, using instead the more inefficient approach of statistical description or enumeration, their works
are landmarks in the growth of the quantitative-empirical method that was
to play such a prominent part in twentieth-century sociology.

Though LePlay's work, with its emphasis on the case-study method and
direct observation, is a notable contribution to empirical social science both
for its general method and its influence, its importance has been greatly
exaggerated.[48] LePlay's social theory was a mixture of piety, paternalism,
and platitude, and his investigations were largely designed to substantiate
his belief in revelation, universal moral law, and original sin. While his
diligent study and classification of the family in terms of expenditures,
geographical habitat, and source of income and work bespeaks a genuine
empirical approach, to a large extent his findings remained an unstructured
miscellany of data. Deficient even as a theory of the family, his work was
also deficient as social theory, for he invariably equated society with family. Such an equation is not true even of complex agrarian societies, and
LePlay's distaste for modern society made him incapable of appreciating
the decreased importance and the qualitatively different status of the family in industrial society. Far from meriting a place among "the most prominent masters of social science," as Sorokin claims, LePlay is a decidedly
secondary figure in the history of sociology and social science.

THE NEW LOGIC OF NON-EUCLIDEAN GEOMETRY

While the development of probability produced no crisis for mathematics in
general, this was not true of nineteenth-century developments in geometry.
To understand this crisis, one must appreciate the reverence with which
geometry had been held from the Greeks on. Because geometry seemed
to possess unity and permanence amidst an irrational world of diversity
and change, Greek philosophy thought of it as the core of mathematics

---

published at Tours by A. Mame *et fils*. A translation of Volume I of this second
edition, which contains the whole of LePlay's general method and theory, may be
found in Carle C. Zimmerman and Merle E. Frampton, *Family and Society* (New
York: D. Van Nostrand, 1935), pt. 4.

[47] Charles Booth, ed., *Labor and Life of the People*, 2 vols. (London: Williams
and Norgate, 1889–1891), a book that eventually expanded and acquired a new
title: Charles Booth *et al.*, *Life and Labor of the People in London*, 3rd ed., 17
vols. (London: Macmillan, 1902–1903). For a discussion of Booth's life and his
place in sociology, see the introduction in Charles Booth, *On the City: Physical
Pattern and Social Structure*, selected writings, ed. Harold W. Pfautz (Chicago:
University of Chicago Press, 1967), pp. 3–170.

[48] For example, see Pitirim Sorokin, *Contemporary Sociological Theories* (New
York: Harper & Row, 1928), chap. 2.

and the bastion of human rationality. Of special importance in the Greek view of geometry was the fact that in the development of mathematics from Pythagoras to Euclid, mathematical reasoning was defined not only as being internally logical but as resting on axioms that were consonant with the external world. It is not surprising, therefore, that mathematics was given ontological status and that thinkers believed that the human mind (as it expresses itself in mathematics) and the world of nature at large were not only orderly but identically orderly.

Overshadowed by Aristotelian logic until the late Middle Ages, mathematics emerged during the early period of modern science to spark an incredible expansion of knowledge. Indeed, so startling was the success of the mathematical method in uncovering nature's laws that each day seemed to bring added confirmation that nature was constructed along mathematical lines. Even during the height of its success, however, the dominant role of mathematics in scientific research was being challenged by new modes of thought. By the end of the eighteenth century, a many-pronged empirical assault against nature had gone a long way in removing mathematics from its dominant position in scientific methodology.

The position of mathematics changed even more drastically during the nineteenth century. Out of the work of Lobatchevsky, Bolyai, Gauss, and Riemann came a number of non-Euclidean geometries, all of which rested on axioms that contradicted those of Euclid. This development eventually afforded new insights into nature, the most important of which was Einstein's theory of relativity. Of great significance to modern intellectual life was the fact that out of non-Euclidean geometry came a sense of the relativity of mathematics itself. The axioms of Euclid were no longer considered axiomatic except in a logical sense; that is, they were not indubitable truths about physical nature lodged in the human mind, but only subjective estimates about the structure of nature. Far from being ontological in nature, mathematical axioms, to use words made famous by Henri Poincaré, were "conventions, disguised definitions"—mental forms that, far from constituting the foundations of being, were simply "advantageous" assumptions. Mathematical reasoning, in other words, was not a feature of the human mind that corresponded to the features of nature but, like the rest of human ideas, a product of experience. The nature of mathematics, in short, was to be found not only in philosophical or logical analysis, but in history, or again to quote Poincaré, in "ancestral experience."

Significantly, mathematics was exalted as well as humbled by these developments. By freeing itself from its dubious links with nature—that is, by emptying itself of content and remaining true to its primary function, the development of abstractions—mathematics could construct a whole series of logical structures and provide a continuous flow of new and hitherto unsuspected insights into nature. Mathematics, in short, had become a *method*, a fate that the nineteenth century had in store for mind in general.[49]

As the nineteenth century progressed, therefore, there developed a heightened awareness of the dangers lurking in the unsophisticated use of human reason. Whatever reason lost in metaphysical stature, however, it more than gained in its enhanced power to grapple with facts imaginatively and efficiently. Whereas many nineteenth-century currents of antirationalism rejected the entire rational tradition, antirationalism in science led to a renewed optimism about human reason, provided only that one was willing to recast the methodological principles of science and to accept the fact that the substantive principles of science stand in need of continuous revision. Chastened by a growing awareness that human knowledge rests on historically conditioned assumptions and problems, and that essentially it is a cumulative process rather than a one-shot, ahistorical stab at synthesis, science changed its tenor and tempo and settled down to the tedious and complex task of unraveling the ever-less and ever-more mysterious processes of nature. In short, nineteenth-century science began to take on the characteristics that had been advocated by the Enlightenment and especially by Diderot: methodological diversity within a common empirical approach. However, in adopting a deep-seated nominalism, nineteenth-century science repudiated the rationalism of the Enlightenment and, in effect, made David Hume the prophetic figure of the eighteenth century. Its nominalism, however, did not produce skepticism or pessimism about human rationality. Despite the fact that nature was becoming at once more shapeless and more structured, more remote and more accessible, and despite the fact that methodology was itself becoming problematic, there was no denying one sovereign fact—incredible expansion was taking place in human knowledge about and control over nature.

THE SPECIALIZATION OF SCIENCE

The intensified division of labor in industrial and social life, a marked feature of nineteenth-century society in the West, was matched by a grow-

---

[49] Henri Poincaré's discussion of the implications of non-Euclidian geometry for the mathematics of space may be found in his *Science and Hypothesis*, especially chaps. 3 and 5. This work, originally published in 1902, together with his *The Value of Science* (1905) and *Science and Method* (1909), were translated by George Bruce Halsted and published as *The Foundations of Science* (New York: Science Press, 1913). *Science and Hypothesis* by a different translator, identified only as W. J. G., is available as a Dover paperback. The Halsted translation of *The Value of Science* is available separately as a Dover paperback.

An even more radical reduction of geometry to experience and an even sharper separation of the "*several* sufficing geometries" from physical reality may be found in Ernst Mach, *Space and Geometry in the Light of Physiological, Psychological and Physical Inquiry*, trans. Thomas M. McCormack (Chicago: Open Court Publishing Co., 1906). A similar concept of geometry may be found in Karl Pearson, *The Grammar of Science*, chap. 6.

ing division of labor within science itself. Forced by the success of empiricism, and by the empiricism of social life in general, into a fruitful and healthy specialization, Western science began to carve out special subject matters and develop special methods of study. During the nineteenth century a host of specialized fields in natural science, each with its subdisciplines, emerged to challenge the dominance of physics, while a parallel development in social science gave rise to a number of specialized sciences such as history, political science, jurisprudence, economics, anthropology, and sociology.

In the general trend toward specialization, there were two interesting developments in sociological positivism. First, the traditional reliance on the substantive principles of natural science for interpreting social phenomena came into increasing disrepute. This is not to say that natural-science principles did not continue to exercise an enormous, even predominant, influence on sociological theorists during the nineteenth century. Darwin's theory of evolution was widely influential in almost every phase of Western culture and held effective sway over Western intellectual life, especially in Great Britain and the United States, up to World War I. However, despite the virtual monopoly of evolutionary thought, there was an important countertrend even within evolutionary theory. There slowly appeared a more critical attitude toward the literal application of the principle of biological evolution to social change. Increasingly social evolution was explained in terms of empirically verified variables relevant to the special nature of social phenomena.

The second notable development in sociological positivism was a heightened contrast between naturalistic positivism and sociocultural positivism. Both main branches of sociology and social science were enormously affected by the new climate of nineteenth-century science. For one thing, both tended to avoid monistic theories based on the established principles of the natural sciences. For another, both types of sociological positivism became part of what has been called *pluralistic positivism*—that is, both became more empirical, problematic, diversified, and flexible in their methodology. Though many single-factor and essentially deductive monistic theories remained in sociology, the important new trend was toward genuinely multicausal, empirical explanations. Finally, both forms of positivism continued to be part of the general current of philosophical naturalism, the current that in its various guises has dominated the intellectual climate of the West from the Enlightenment to the present.

Because of these similarities, the differences between the main branches of sociological positivism are modal and relative, not absolute. Naturalistic positivism refers to any theory that seeks to explain social behavior in terms of such natural forces or agencies as geography, climate, physics, biology, or psychology. Of these, the most important approach, of course, has been some variant of the biopsychic explanation. Sociocultural positivism, on the other hand, tends to see human behavior as primarily a function of social and cultural structures. Its main achievement has been to call attention to the causal power of types and levels of interaction and to the symbolic as well as the material elements encompassed by the concept of culture.

However, the changes in sociological positivism did not entail a change in one important goal—the development of a unified theory of social phenomena. Sociologists continued to believe in the ultimate unity of social phenomena, and many continued to cherish the idea that social and natural phenomena could be unified. While this latter dream is especially true of naturalistic positivism, which has always hewed close to natural science in defining its methods, subject matter, and objectives, it is not absent in sociocultural positivism.

PLURALISTIC POSITIVISM: THE MENTALITY OF FUNCTIONALISM

The growing nominalism of the nineteenth century had important implications for sociology. In philosophy proper, nominalism found diverse expression as pragmatism, phenomenalism, phenomenology, existentialism, and logical positivism. In natural science proper, it took an extreme form in the work of Karl Pearson and Ernst Mach, a less extreme form in the work of Henri Poincaré, and an even less extreme form in the work of Albert Einstein, who could not bring himself to believe that "god played dice with the universe." The authentic note of the new empirical phase of natural science was struck by Poincaré when he referred to scientific methodology as "unconscious opportunism." While this phrase was not characteristic of his thought in general, it suggests the general ad hoc character of the new phase of science.

Whether or not "ad hoc empiricism" is an accurate description of the spirit informing contemporary science, there is no denying that the main result of late-nineteenth-century thought was the transformation of mind into function. In the remainder of this study I shall analyze this transformation. Almost all the remaining sociologists whose work I shall examine made important contributions to scientific method, contributions that had a marked similarity both to each other and to developments in other fields of thought. I shall refer to this general development as *pluralistic positivism*, though the term *functionalism* could easily be substituted.

The deeper significance of this new world view lay in the notion that perhaps no objective or substantive world exists at all, and that far from being able to comprehend natural and moral phenomena, reason was nothing but a tool, inescapably circumscribed by historical conditions. However, this implication was not developed by the main traditions in sociology or social science. Whereas experience strongly suggested that reason could never be more than a means for solving problems and realizing nonrational ends, most Western intellectuals looked upon the new intellectual perspective as a guarantee of truth—as a way, in short, of unifying theory and fact and thus solving the liberal dilemma. Of all the post-Enlightenment sociologists, only one, Max Weber, was content to accept Hume's conclusion that the shoulders of reason were too narrow and feeble to support the heavy metaphysical load that the Greeks had placed on them.

The work of the pluralistic positivists will be analyzed against this background, starting with some major representatives of this tradition on the continent of Europe (Chapters 14–17) and concluding with some of the major figures in the United States (Chapters 18–22). The sociologists whose work will be discussed all fall within the period between the last decades of the nineteenth century and the present. The work of these theorists will be regarded as the current or contemporary mode of thought in sociology because of the unity in their general methodology and in many of their substantive findings. For one thing, they all (with one exception) continued the substantialist (or metaphysical) tradition that entered sociology during the Enlightenment, though they did so less proudly and knowingly than their forebears in sociology. In their substantive theories, they all expressed a deep commitment to liberal society, and most tried to avoid the tradition, so prevalent in monistic positivism, of interpreting social phenomena in terms of the substantive principles of natural science.

To point out the similarities among the pluralistic positivists, however, is not to forget that broad abstractions often hide and distort the particularities of phenomena. It is important, therefore, not to obscure the individuality of these theorists nor exaggerate the extent to which their thought converged. Of crucial importance in interpreting their individuality will be the varied economic and political backgrounds from which their theories emerged. Economic development was markedly different in the various Continental countries: industrialization was slow, gradual, and often stagnant in France, late but explosive in Germany, and chronically backward in Italy. The path of political liberalism also differed among these countries, especially when contrasted with its development in Great Britain and the United States. In France, the path of liberal democracy was rocky and precarious but at least passable compared with the dead ends it encountered in Germany and Italy. The doctrines of individualism, equality, progress, and laissez faire failed to establish themselves on the continent of Europe. Forced to work against a background of political and social instability, Continental theorists not surprisingly rejected either or both of the two main threads in Anglo-American sociology: the biopsychic approach born of a successful individualism and the evolutionary approach born of a successful pattern of social-system change and subsequent development. The result, especially in the work of Durkheim and Weber, was a revolutionary shift in the nature of sociological theory. In forging the intellectual weapons to overcome the biopsychological evolutionism that had come to dominate Anglo-American sociology, these two thinkers went outside the framework of naturalistic positivism to lay down the foundations and much of the superstructure of contemporary sociocultural positivism.

Chapter 14
Emile Durkheim (1858–1917)

The career of Emile Durkheim is an excellent illustration of the fertilizing power a discipline acquires once it accumulates a heritage of ideas, data, and felt problems. Of considerable importance in understanding Durkheim's unusually creative contribution to sociology [1] is the fact that he inherited Europe's richest legacy of social science, the brilliant tradition of French sociological positivism. Possessing a genuine capacity for empirical research and a unique flair for conceptualization, Durkheim more than extended that legacy. Out of his penetrating inquiry into the methods by which human beings acquire knowledge about their own nature and behavior, he effected a far-reaching reorganization of the methodology and substantive theory of sociological positivism. In his quest for a science of behavior, he did not hesitate to criticize and reject the work of the two most influential figures in nineteenth-century sociology, Auguste Comte and Herbert Spencer. That Durkheim wrote his doctoral dissertation on Montesquieu and lectured on Rousseau will suggest the direction his criticism took.[2]

---

[1] Of Durkheim's many writings, the most important are *The Division of Labor in Society* (1893); *The Rules of Sociological Method* (1895); *Suicide* (1897); and *The Elementary Forms of the Religious Life* (1912). Probably the best collection of selections from his work is Anthony Giddens, trans. and ed. *Emile Durkheim: Selected Writings* (New York: Cambridge University Press, 1972), also in paperback. Durkheim's stature as a creative sociologist has prompted essay and chapter-length examinations of his work by a large number of theorists and the following, more recent full-length treatments: Dominick LaCapra, *Emile Durkheim: Sociologist and Philosopher* (Ithaca, N.Y.: Cornell University Press, 1972); Steven Lukes, *Emile Durkheim: His Life and Work* (New York: Harper & Row, 1972); Ernest Wallwork, *Durkheim: Morality and Milieu* (Cambridge, Mass.: Harvard University Press, 1972); and Robert A. Nisbet, *The Sociology of Emile Durkheim* (New York: Oxford University Press paperback, 1974).

[2] Both Durkheim's dissertation and his lectures on Rousseau have been published as *Montesquieu and Rousseau: Forerunners of Sociology*, trans. Ralph Manheim (Ann Arbor: University of Michigan Press, 1960); also in paperback.

Emile Durkheim (1858–1917)

PHILOSOPHY AND METHOD

Durkheim's treatise, *The Rules of Sociological Method* [3] is a landmark in the history of sociology. The sociocultural outlook in Vico and Montesquieu had not become a major force in social science. Instead, the main tradition in sociology had emerged as an attempt to model social science on natural science. Concrete advances in empirical methodology within this tradition

---

[3] Trans. S. Solovay and J. Meuller, ed. G. Catlin (New York: Free Press, 1950), also in paperback. Henceforth cited as *Rules*. Durkheim's *Suicide* is also one of the classic studies in the history of methodology, especially in the sense that it represents an actual application of his method to empirical materials. However, since the *Rules* contains a comprehensive statement of his methodology, I have chosen to treat *Suicide* as part of his substantive work.

were inspired by developments in biology—for example, in the work of Spencer and Sumner. Other advances had been made by applying mathematics to human behavior—for example, in the work of Condorcet, LePlay, and Quetelet. It was Durkheim's historic role to disentangle the methodological advance that had emerged from the application of biological science and probability mathematics to social phenomena and graft it to the unrealized potentialities of the sociocultural outlook. Aside from a few technical terms that have failed to gain currency, Durkheim's *Rules* breathes the air of modernity. Indeed, its main orientation is likely to strike the contemporary reader as platitudinous since many of its perspectives have become the truisms of contemporary sociology. It is important, however, to examine how Durkheim developed his orientation in order to see that the commonplaces of science are really the hard-won victories of the human mind over less scientific but tenaciously held commonplaces.

The Definition and Study of Social Facts

A factually oriented sociology had been proposed many times before Durkheim. It is not this that distinguishes his work, but rather his redefinition of the nature of facts.

> Here is a category of facts with very distinctive characteristics: it consists of ways of acting, thinking, and feeling, external to the individual, and endowed with a power of coercion, by reason of which they control him. These ways of thinking should not be confused with biological phenomena, since they consist of representations and of actions; nor with psychological phenomena, which exist only in the individual consciousness and through it. They constitute, thus, a new variety of phenomena; and it is to them exclusively that the term "social" ought to be applied. And this term fits them quite well, for it is clear that, since their source is not in the individual, their substratum can be no other than society, either the political society as a whole or some one of the partial groups it includes, such as religious denominations, political, literary, and occupational associations, etc. On the other hand, this term "social" applies to them exclusively, for it has a distinct meaning only if it designates exclusively the phenomena which are not included in any of the categories of facts that have already been established and classified. These ways of thinking and acting therefore constitute the proper domain of sociology.[4]

Elsewhere we are told that

> . . . a social fact is to be recognized by the power of external coercion which it exercises or is capable of exercising over individuals, and the presence of this power may be recognized in its

---

[4] *Rules,* p. 3f.

turn either by the existence of some specific sanction or by the resistance offered against every individual effort that tends to violate it.[5]

In yet another place, a pithier statement is found:

> A *social fact is every way of acting, fixed or not, capable of exercising on the individual an external constraint;* or again, *every way of acting which is general throughout a given society, while at the same time existing in its own right independent of its individual manifestations.*[6]

Normal and Pathological Social Facts

The most pervasive aspects of Durkheim's sociology are his denial of a distinction between science and ethics and his belief that science, while remaining true to itself, has the power to illuminate and solve ethical problems. Durkheim claimed that science can distinguish between "normal" and "pathological or morbid" types of social facts. By viewing society as a survival unit and by evaluating individual and group behavior in this light, thought can service action and knowledge can service ethics. However, in broaching the idea that a scientific study of society must distinguish between beneficial and harmful social facts, Durkheim avoided associating the idea of social pathology too closely with individual pathology. A general or normal fact is presumed functional in the sense that it has survived the test of time and circumstance, though all traits are not useful, nor are all useful traits normal. One must be careful to explain a general social fact and not merely to observe that it exists.

In order to decide what is normal, one must relate social facts to causal conditions. If a general fact was produced by certain conditions in the past and those conditions have changed, then the fact is abnormal. By using such a method, said Durkheim, sociology acquires a reference point for judging the normal for any society or any given state of social development.

The aim of sociology is to determine the causes and functions of a social fact. This is no easy task, and one should not too easily identify the normal with the possible or with the most useful. To show the necessity of following his method carefully, Durkheim developed his famous functional view of crime. Far from being pathological, he said, crime is normal to society: "It is a factor in public health, an integral part of all healthy societies".[7] If one does not view crime morally or from the standpoint of some absolute standard, one will see that crime is necessary for the existence of society.

---

[5] Ibid., p. 10.
[6] Ibid., p. 13 (the emphasis is Durkheim's).
[7] Ibid., p. 67.

The absence of crime is possible only when the collective conscience is absolute, something that is patently impossible. Even if the collective conscience becomes stronger, it will become more sensitive and demanding and define new things as criminal. There can be no society "in which the individual does not differ more or less from the collective type," and therefore "it is inevitable that among these divergences, there are some with a criminal character." [8]

Thus, crime is the necessary cost of progress since creativity and change are possible only if the collective conscience is not rigid and all-encompassing. Crime may even lead to progress, as in the case of Socrates.[9] Durkheim's view of crime was central to his method of viewing all social facts in terms of their function in a given social system and in terms of their consequences for the health of a given society. Social facts must not be viewed as intrinsic or substantive things or according to substantive criteria. However, while Durkheim warned that a given fact if viewed differently becomes different, he did not set up the mind as the criterion of knowledge. Many of the pluralistic positivists, such as Simmel, Weber, and Cooley, were deeply influenced by Kant and German idealism in general and gave subjectivity an important role in scientific method. Durkheim, however, remained true to the modal Anglo-French tradition of naturalistic positivism that denies subjectivity a role in science. For Durkheim, the mind, using correct methods, does not bring order to the world, but reveals it.

The Classification of Social Types

Durkheim said that the classification of social types is a necessary branch of sociology "since a social fact can be construed as normal or abnormal only relatively to a given social species." [10] Such an approach avoids the "nominalism" of historians and the "extreme realism" of philosophers. It is not necessary, however, to study each society intensively and to compile a complete catalogue of social types before beginning to compare and classify. This would pose an impossible task for science. The scientific method, however, looks for "*decisive* or crucial facts, which by themselves and independently of their number, have scientific value and interest." [11] In other words, theory and fact work together to reveal each other—on the basis of some knowledge, a type is constructed and becomes the basis of a new perspective and new knowledge. The classification of social types is facilitated because social elements can form only a limited number of compounds and because a social system must maintain a certain functional logic

[8] Ibid., p. 70.
[9] Ibid., p. 71; see also p. 96, where Durkheim points out that another function of crime is to reinforce collective sentiments, which would diminish if no one violated them.
[10] Ibid., p. 76.
[11] Ibid., p. 79.

in its various values and institutions. It is therefore possible to develop the logical alternatives that exhaust the possibilities of human behavior and social organization.

The Causal-Functional Method

Durkheim's revolutionary methodology appeared most clearly in his criticism of Comte and Spencer. These theorists, argued Durkheim, were mistaken when they said that phenomena exist because they are useful. "To show how a social fact is useful is not to explain how it originated or why it is what it is." [12] Comte and Spencer erred in assuming that human nature wills the things that are useful to it.

> Unless we postulate a truly providential and pre-established harmony, we cannot admit that man has carried with him from the beginning—potentially ready to be awakened at the call of circumstances—all the intentions which conditions were destined to demand in the course of human evolution. It must further be recognized that a deliberate intention is itself something objectively real; it can, then, neither be created nor modified by the mere fact that we judge it useful. It is a force having a nature of its own; for that nature to be given existence or altered, it is not enough that we should find this advantageous. In order to bring about such changes, there must be sufficient cause. [13]

Therefore, concluded Durkheim, "*When the explanation of a social phenomenon is undertaken, we must seek separately the efficient cause which produces it and the function it fulfils*". [14]

By separating cause and function, Durkheim argued that the traditional idea of utility has no scientific value since it relies on teleology and short-circuits genuine explanation. He shrewdly noted that there is a fundamental connection between teleological and psychological theories and that Comte and Spencer were as guilty of the one as of the other. It is a fundamental mistake, he argued, to think that society emerges from the needs or consciousness of the individual, or that it is simply a sum total of the bio-psychic natures of its individual members.

Durkheim developed his revolutionary contribution to sociocultural positivism as a counter to the psycho-teleological view. Focusing on association as "the source of all the innovations which have been produced successively in the course of the general evolution of things," Durkheim argued that

[12] Ibid., p. 90.
[13] Ibid., p. 92.
[14] Ibid., p. 95 (the emphasis is Durkheim's).

. . . by reason of this principle, society is not a mere sum of individuals. Rather the system formed by their association represents a specific reality which has its own characteristics. Of course nothing collective can be produced if individual consciousnesses are not assumed, but this necessary condition is by itself insufficient. These consciousnesses must be combined in a certain way; social life results from this combination and is, consequently, explained by it. Individual minds, forming groups by mingling and fusing, give birth to a being, psychological if you will but constituting a psychic individuality of a new sort.[15]

Durkheim warned, however, that one would be mistaken

. . . if, from the foregoing, he drew the conclusion that sociology, according to us, must, or even can make an abstraction of man and his faculties. It is clear, on the contrary, that the general characteristics of human nature participate in the work of elaboration from which social life results. But they are not the cause of it, nor do they give it its special forms; *they only make it possible*.[16]

Far from using innate psychological states, instincts, or sentiments to explain society, the sociologist proceeds in the opposite direction because "sentiments *result* from the collective organization and are not its *basis*." [17] This leads to the following methodological principles: "*The determining cause of a social fact should be sought among the social facts preceding it and not among the states of individual consciousness*" and "*the function of a social fact ought always to be sought in its relation to some social end*." [18]

Further, said Durkheim,

. . . if the determining condition of social phenomena is as we have shown, the very fact of association, the phenomena ought to vary with the forms of that association, i.e., according to the ways in which the constituent parts of society are grouped. . . . *The first origins of all social processes of any importance should be sought in the internal constitution of the social group*.[19]

Thus, he concluded,

The principal task of the sociologist ought to be to discover the different aspects of [the human] milieu which can exert some influence on the course of social phenomena. Until the present we have found two series of facts which have eminently fulfilled this

[15] Ibid., p. 103.
[16] Ibid., p. 105f (the emphasis is mine).
[17] Ibid., p. 107 (the emphasis is Durkheim's).
[18] Ibid., p. 110f (the emphasis is Durkheim's).
[19] Ibid., p. 112f (the emphasis is Durkheim's).

condition; these are: (1) the number of social units or, as we have also called it, the "size of a society"; and (2) the degree of concentration of the group, or what we have termed the "dynamic density." By this last expression must not be understood the purely physical concentration of the aggregate, which can have no effect if the individuals, or rather the groups of individuals, remain separated by social distance. By it is understood the social concentration, of which the size is only the auxiliary and, generally speaking, the consequence. The dynamic density may be defined, the volume being equal, as the function of the number of individuals who are actually having not only commercial but also social relations, i.e., who not only exchange services or compete with one another but also live a common life.[20]

Durkheim's emphasis on interaction, which formed a main theme in all his works, should help to clear him of the charge by Sorokin and Parsons that he explained social activity and social change in terms of a biological increase in population.[21] The same causal influence, Durkheim went on, should be expected from relationships in the partial groups of society. Family or professional groups, for example, will develop a different life for their members depending on their numbers and the types of relationships in which they engage. However, these groups are always subject to the influence of the general social milieu. "This conception of the social milieu as the determining factor of collective evolution is of the highest importance. For, if we reject it, sociology cannot establish any relations of causality." [22] Without this assumption, Durkheim insisted, there can be no explanation of social phenomena, since neither the psychological nor the teleological explanation is satisfactory. A belief in historical evolution is not adequate since it is a fallacy to argue from effect to cause; one can establish causation only between facts.

It is in relation to this milieu that the utility or, as we have called it, the function of social phenomena must be measured. Among the changes caused by the social milieu, only those serve a purpose which are compatible with the current state of society, since the milieu is the essential condition of collective existence. . . . the conception we have just expounded is, we believe, fundamental; for it alone enables us to explain how the useful character of social phenomena can vary, without, however, depending on a volitional social order. If we represent historic evolution as impelled by a

[20] Ibid., p. 113f.
[21] For a more detailed clarification of this point, see Leoe F. Schnore, "Social Morphology and Human Ecology," *American Journal of Sociology* 63 (May 1958): 622–626.
[22] *Rules*, p. 116f.

sort of vital urge which pushes men forward, since a propelling tendency can have but one goal, there can be only one point of reference with relation to which the usefulness or harmfulness of social phenomena is calculated. Consequently, there can, and does, exist only one type of social organization that fits humanity perfectly; and the different historical societies are only successive approximations to this single model. It is unnecessary to show that, today, such a simple view is irreconcilable with the recognized variety and complexity of social forms. If, on the contrary, the fitness or unfitness of institutions can only be established in connection with a given milieu, since these milieus are diverse, there is a diversity of points of reference and hence of types which, while being qualitatively distinct from one another, are all equally grounded in the nature of the social milieus.[23]

Sociological Proof

Durkheim's discussion of methodology was climaxed by an analysis of the nature of sociological proof. Since experiment is impossible, the sociologist must employ the comparative method. Of all the procedures that facilitate comparison, the most valid is "the method of concomitant variations or correlation." [24] This one method offers a wealth of available data; historical periods of every variety have left their imprint, and contemporary society has a rich store of phenomena, such as crime and birth rates, that vary according to profession, religion, and so on. However, the sociologist must be careful:

> One cannot explain a social fact of any complexity except by following its complete development through all social species. Comparative sociology is not a particular branch of sociology; it is sociology itself, in so far as it ceases to be purely descriptive and aspires to account for facts.[25]

SUBSTANTIVE WORK

In the preface of his first major work, *The Division of Labor in Society*,[26] Durkheim affirmed two major themes that never left his thought: first, that a science of the moral life or of ethics is possible using the methods of the

---

[23] Ibid., p. 119f.
[24] Ibid., p. 130.
[25] Ibid., p. 139 (the emphasis is Durkheim's).
[26] Trans. George Simpson (New York: Free Press, 1949), also in paperback. Henceforth cited as *Div. of Labor.*

positive sciences, and second, that such a science cannot be based on principles borrowed from any of the positive sciences. Affirming his belief that social science is no different, methodologically speaking, from natural science, Durkheim asked

> . . . why does the individual, while becoming more autonomous, depend more on society? How can he be at once more individual and more solidary? Certainly these two movements, contradictory as they appear, develop in parallel fashion. This is the problem we are raising. It appeared to us that what resolves this apparent antinomy is a transformation of social solidarity due to the steadily growing development of the division of labor. This is how we have been led to make this the object of our study.[27]

The Social Division of Labor

The division of labor, said Durkheim, which received its first theoretical emphasis in Adam Smith, has come to dominate all of modern life; economy, science, politics, administration, law, art, and education have all become progressively more specialized. The evaluation of this phenomenon according to abstract moral principles has led nowhere; some commentators praise it and others condemn it. For his part, said Durkheim, he would put abstract principles aside and study the division of labor itself, paying special attention to its function or the social need that it satisfies, its causes and conditions, and the classification of its abnormal forms.

To say that the division of labor produces civilization (industry, art, and science) does not settle the question of its moral effects, Durkheim argued, since on the whole civilization is morally neutral. However, a clue to the moral effect of the division of labor may be found in friendship patterns and the development of the family. In friendship, an individual often likes those who do not resemble him or her as well as those who do. When people complement each other, become friends, and exchange services, a moral effect, a feeling of solidarity, develops. The division of labor also produced the conjugal family and has rendered it more solidary. The implication is inescapable—might not the division of labor have the same moral effect on more extensive groupings?

To find the answer, said Durkheim, one must begin by classifying types of social solidarity. However, solidarity is a subjective phenomenon and does not lend itself readily to the scientist's methods. How can it, then, be analyzed? The answer lies in examining law, the visible symbol of solidarity. Classified according to the sanctions employed, two legal systems can be

[27] *Div. of Labor,* p. 37f.

distinguished, one emphasizing repression and the other restitution. When the solidarity of a society is based on sameness—that is, when the collective or common conscience absorbs almost the entire personality—then law is repressive. Its unity may be called *mechanical solidarity* and any violation of its "social similitudes" is considered criminal. However, said Durkheim, "we must not say that an action shocks the common conscience because it is criminal, but rather than it is criminal because it shocks the common conscience." In the event of such an act, everyone reacts strenuously and immediately to punish the infraction of the communal ethic. The function served by punishment, however, is not merely to expiate the crime:

> Its true function is to maintain social cohesion intact, while main-taining all its vitality in the common conscience. Denied so cate-gorically, it would necessarily lose its energy, if an emotional reaction of the community did not come to compensate its loss, and it would result in a breakdown of social solidarity. It is neces-sary, then, that it be affirmed forcibly at the very moment when it is contradicted, and the only means of affirming it is to express the unanimous aversion which the crime continues to inspire, by an authentic act which can consist only in suffering inflicted upon the agent. . . . We can thus say without paradox that punishment is above all designed to act upon upright people, for, since it serves to heal the wounds made upon collective sentiments, it can fill this role only where these sentiments exist, and commensurately with their vivacity.[28]

Therefore, concluded Durkheim, "in determining what fraction of the juri-dical system penal [repressive] law represents, we, at the same time, mea-sure the relative importance of [the mechanical form of] solidarity."

The second great system of law, the restitutive or cooperative type, is characterized by a different type of solidarity, the *organic*. Unlike repressive law, cooperative law is itself specialized and must be applied by special organs and specially trained personnel. It is removed from the common conscience since its task is to provide specialized social areas and spe-cialized consciences with guideposts to correct behavior.

Durkheim's argument is clear and simple. Societies can be studied as func-tional systems and divided into two types on the basis of kind of integration and the method for achieving and maintaining it. A society with mechanical solidarity is homogeneous and has a simple division of labor; its "social sim-ilitudes" dominate the personality and "consciences vibrate in unison." Its repressive system of law maintains solidarity in two ways, one manifest and

[28] Ibid., p. 108f

one latent: it punishes and represses deviant behavior and, by doing so, re-vitalizes beliefs by reminding community members what their sentiments are.

A society with organic solidarity is heterogeneous and has an advanced division of labor. Its specialized areas dominate the personality of specialized individuals. The organic society is no less a society for all its diversity and lack of a concretely articulated collective conscience. Its ultimate unity is provided by restitutive law, which reflects the needs of its specialized behavior structures. The function of restitutive law is to restore disturbed relations to normal in all areas of specialized activity. The "normal" in organic society is not the sanctity of the collective conscience, but the sanctity of the division of labor, which has created a vast structure of interlocking, specialized sentiments and norms. In short, an advanced division of labor puts millions of individuals into specialized orbits, each with its appropriate values and norms, evolving at the same time a legal system that at once reflects and upholds this new form of unity.

Here is the answer to Durkheim's original query as to why individuals, while becoming more autonomous, depend more on society, and as to how they can be at once more individual and more solidary. People become individuated through the intense training necessary for performing society's specialized tasks, but at the same time they are ever-more subject to the rules of a delicately balanced interdependent sequence of specialties. Thus the division of labor not only is related to morality, but is at once its source and guardian—an answer that is a profound contribution not only to social-structure analysis but to the sociology of law.

Sociocultural Causation

Durkheim searched historical records in an effort to show, by comparing modern with premodern legal codes and by noting the decline of religion and of the use of proverbs, a trend toward the progressive development of organic solidarity. There are, he said, two ideal social types in history, and there is a trend away from the homogeneous and toward the heterogeneous. However, the nature of this trend, said Durkheim, is quite different from Spencer's depiction of it. The development from Military to Industrial society (Spencer's two types of society) does not represent the emancipation of the individual from a coercive society and the emergence of an individualistic, voluntary society. On the contrary, the difference is merely that society, always the formative agent, is producing a different type of social agent to correspond to its new needs. The contractual relations of modern society are not free, spontaneous exchanges among autonomous individuals but are themselves socially derived and enforced. Far from there being a decrease in social regulation, the evidence points to the growing regulation of life by society, a fact that has enhanced both the self and social unity.

Utilitarian theories, which argue that human need or desire for happiness or pleasure inevitably leads to specialization and progress, do not explain the division of labor. The real causes, argued Durkheim, must be sought in the emergence of new structures of interaction. The dissolution of mechanical solidarity takes place when

> . . . social life, instead of being concentrated in a multitude of little centres, distinctive and alike, is generalized. Social relations—more exactly, intrasocial—consequently become more numerous, since they extend, on all sides, beyond their original limits. The division of labor develops, therefore, as there are more individuals sufficiently in contact to be able to act and react upon one another. If we agree to call this relation and the active commerce resulting from it dynamic or moral density, we can say that the progress of the division of labor is in direct ratio to the moral or dynamic density of society.[29]

Durkheim's discussion of the causes of an increase in social density was brief. It stems, he said, from population concentration, especially in urban areas, and from an increase of communication, transportation, and population. Social change is produced by a change in the quantity and quality of interaction, changes that in turn are necessary to given historical conditions.

In his analysis of the development of modern society, Durkheim seemed less interested in establishing a specific priority and sequence of causal factors than in establishing the fact that regardless of the phenomena being studied, the causal agent is society and not the individual. The entire section on causation is mostly a restatement of his general anti-Spencerian position. Again and again Durkheim reiterated his master contention that society determines social change, all values, institutions, needs, and individual consciences, and that there is no discernible teleological or psychological process at work shaping the structure or direction of society. All that the scientist can affirm, he said, is that society is an independent entity in its own right and that it is suitable to the circumstances in which it finds itself.

The Division of Labor and Abnormality

Although Durkheim introduced his famous concept of *anomie* in his analysis of the abnormal forms of the division of labor, it was not fully elaborated until his study on suicide. His main concern in the earlier work was

[29] Ibid., p. 257.

to show that the division of labor is not, as had been claimed, a source of social dissension and instability.

There are three types of the *anomic* division of labor, all of which are exceptional developments. The first takes the form of industrial strife, and its cause is the social separation of management and labor. The second is the class war, caused by injustice or the forceful imposition of social status on individuals in violation of their natural talents. The third form is anomie proper, which occurs during economic recession or depression, or, in Durkheim's terms, when the functional activities of individuals are not properly coordinated. Throughout, Durkheim referred to these abnormal forms as artificial and transitional. The normal division of labor, if it suits the needs of the times, can lead only to solidarity. In short, unity comes from diversity, not in spite of it. The argument, of course, was directed squarely at Comte, and implicitly at Saint-Simon and Marx.[30] *The Division of Labor* is therefore more than a tract against Spencer. It also refutes the Saint-Simonian and Marxian concern with the alleged antagonisms in social development and the corresponding need for an elite to maintain consensus and give society direction—an emphasis continued by Comte in the liberal tradition and by Lenin in the Marxian tradition. Durkheim argued, against Spencer, that society is the source of heterogeneity and individualism and, against Saint-Simon and Comte, as well as socialist theorists, that unity and justice do not have to come from an elite-imposed homogeneity.[31]

One of the implications of the division of labor, said Durkheim, is that individuals can specialize and avoid the mediocrity of the well-rounded individual. Specialization is good for individuals since it develops capacities intensely, and it is also good for society, for whoever "gives himself over to a definite task is, at every moment, struck by the sentiment of common solidarity in the thousand duties of occupational morality." In addition, "the ideal of human fraternity can be realized only in proportion to the progress of the division of labor." The hope for solving the crisis through which society is passing, said Durkheim, lies in removing the aberrations that interfere with its functioning.

The unifying theme in the *Division of Labor* is that society is a reality sui generis, which can be studied scientifically according to society's own

[30] Durkheim was interested in socialism from the beginning of his career. In 1895–96, he gave a lecture series on socialism that has been published as Emile Durkheim, *Socialism and Saint-Simon*, ed. A. W. Gouldner, trans. Charlotte Sattler (Yellow Springs, Ohio: Antioch Press, 1958); available as a Collier paperback entitled *Socialism*.
[31] This latter point is also an attack on the quite different tradition of French monarchical conservatism and its longing for the unity of medieval society. It will become apparent that Durkheim's thought was essentially different from conservatism (traditionalism). For an opposite view, see Robert A. Nisbet, *The Sociology of Emile Durkheim* (New York: Oxford University Press paperbound, 1974), Introduction.

method of operation—that is, as a functional system whose parts contribute to its development and maintenance. Throughout the work, Durkheim made constant use of analogies between the functioning of the biological system and that of the social system. However he was careful to establish analogies, not identities, between society and biology, extracting from biology its mode of thinking while discarding its substantive principles. His main objective was to establish the reality of society through a discussion of the division of labor. He established that social solidarity can be achieved in two different ways, through either mechanical or organic solidarity. Neither form of solidarity, however, reflects the psychology, the instincts, or the racial character of the individual. Solidarity stems from society itself, from resemblances in the one type and from differences in the other. Durkheim categorically denied the Spencerian position that society is a voluntaristic, rational exchange of services among individuals. He also denied the Saint-Simonian and Comtean position, and implicitly the socialist position, that complex society tends to degenerate and needs explicit public regulation. In short, Durkheim advanced a brilliant defense of industrial capitalism and liberal democracy, a theory that was to influence profoundly the science of sociology.

Social Structure and Deviance: Suicide as Social Behavior

Durkheim's classic work, *Suicide*,[32] is not only a penetrating analysis of the phenomenon of suicide but also a brilliant example of how the sociological categories in his earlier works could be combined with a straightforward empirical method. One cannot understand the significance of the book, however, if one thinks of it merely as a study of suicide. Here, as always, Durkheim's main interest was to establish his functional-sociologistic method and extend his understanding of social structure.

Durkheim tried to explain suicide by looking for "concomitant variations," that is, for correlations between suicide and other phenomena. After eliminating extrasocial factors such as the organic-psychic disposition of individuals and the physical environment, Durkheim focused on social variables. Using the crude statistical data and methods of his day, he tried to account for *rates* of suicide rather than for individual suicides. He found three patterns in the diverse phenomena of suicide, which he called *egoistic, altruistic,* and *anomic.*

After surveying data pertaining to religious, family, and political statuses, Durkheim reached the general conclusion that "suicide varies inversely

---

[32] Trans. J. A. Spaulding and George Simpson, ed. George Simpson (New York: Free Press, 1951); also in paperback.

with the degree of integration of the social groups of which the individual forms a part." He noted carefully that suicide cannot be explained by the intrinsic nature of the sentiments or beliefs of the institutional areas involved, but rather by the degree to which the individual is integrated into the group, or, in his own terms, *the degree of moral density*. When integration is low, when "the individual ego asserts itself to excess in the face of the social ego and at its expense, we may call egoistic the special type of suicide springing from excessive individualism." Altruistic suicide stems from an opposite cause. Whereas "excessive individuation leads to suicide, insufficient individuation has the same effects." Altruistic suicide is a social duty and is found in the cultures of Japan and India. There is one area in Western society in which altruistic suicide takes place—the army.

Society, said Durkheim, can be seen as a regulative force—that is, as having strong or weak attachments between itself and the individual. When regulation breaks down, the characteristic form of suicide is the anomic. An economic breakdown is a potent generator of suicide, not because it induces poverty but because it breaks down established expectations. Sudden prosperity can also cause anomic suicide because it too represents a break in an individual's normal routine and leaves him or her unprepared for elevated status. Anomic suicide also results from disrupted family relations, such as widowhood or divorce, because the individual's normal, predictable relationships are upset.

To understand the phenomena of anomie certain other things must be understood. Unlike animals, said Durkheim, human beings are not severely restricted by their bodily equipment or environment. In regard to wants and aspirations, individuals can expand their appetites almost endlessly and

> . . . nothing appears in man's organic nor in his psychological constitution which sets a limit to such tendencies. . . . It is not human nature which can assign the variable limits necessary to our needs. They are thus unlimited so far as they depend on the individual alone. Irrespective of any external regulatory force, our capacity for feeling is in itself an insatiable and bottomless abyss.[33]

Fortunately, just such a regulatory force exists:

> As a matter of fact, at every moment of history there is a dim perception, in the moral consciousness of societies, of the respective value of different social services, the relative reward

---

[33] Ibid., p. 247.

due to each, and the consequent degree of comfort appropriate on the average to workers in each occupation. The different functions are graded in public opinion and a certain coefficient of well-being assigned to each, according to its place in the hierarchy. . . . A genuine regimen exists, therefore, although not always legally formulated, which fixes with relative precision the maximum degree of ease of living to which each social class may legitimately aspire.[34]

A sudden break in this regulative structure produces anomie: "When society is disturbed by some painful crisis or by beneficent but abrupt transitions, it is momentarily incapable of exercising this influence; thence come the sudden rises in the curve of suicides which we have pointed out above.[35] It is the same whether the crisis stems from an economic downswing, or from an upswing. In either case there is a temporary derangement of social values and thus a loss of social cohesion.

The significance of the concept of anomie in Durkheim's thought must not be exaggerated. On the whole, it played a subsidiary role in his work. In the *Division of Labor,* Durkheim took the view that the various disturbances in the Cooperative (or Organic) society were temporary and superficial rather than chronic and deep seated. Parsons has suggested, however, that the concept of anomie became much more important to Durkheim after the *Division of Labor* and that Durkheim became much more pessimistic about the prospects of European society.[36] It is true that Durkheim became more concerned with the troubles of modern industrial society, that he became more aware of the growing disjointedness of society, and that he came to depict society more in terms of a growing absence of regulation. He was also aware that different types of rates of suicide are intimately related to social types, and that "our very egoism is in large part a production of society." He admitted that there is a relationship between the central values of a society and its form of suicide, thus identifying the irrationality of suicide with even the basic ends of Organic society. "The entire morality of progress and perfection is thus inseparable from a certain amount of *anomie.*" Finally, Durkheim was well aware that the suicide rate had grown enormously during the nineteenth century. Nonetheless, he never changed the fundamental position that he outlined in the *Division of Labor.* Despite his insights into the relation between deviance and social structure, he was far from concluding that modern society is stricken mortally or that suicide is even a major problem. Suicide, like crime, is normal to society

---

[34] Ibid., p. 249.
[35] Ibid., p. 252.
[36] Talcott Parsons, *The Structure of Social Action* (New York: McGraw-Hill, 1937; reprinted, New York: Free Press, 1949), p. 338; also in paperback.

because both stem from social norms, though Durkeim did concede that there is currently an excessive suicide rate that is pathological. However, the sickness is due to the rapidity with which modern society has appeared and not to its intrinsic nature.[37]

Despite Durkheim's insights into social deviation, therefore, he never changed his belief that industrial society was a structural-functional whole containing value and behavior imperatives that insured its functional vitality. He continued to believe that the division of labor (a term that to him was synonomous with progress, perfection, individualism—in short, with liberalism) was compatible, indeed synonomous, with social health. His ultimate judgment on suicide was that it is a transitional phenomenon associated with the rapid emergence of Organic society. He felt that suicide and other social ills could be curtailed without changing the basic structure or values of Organic society if one applied the scientific method and the knowledge it yields about the nature and operation of society. Science had already suggested one such reform, the creation of occupational groups or corporations to generate the interaction or moral density necessary for individual discipline. Such groups would form intermediary bodies between the individual and the remote state. The moral reintegration of the individual with society cannot be performed by the family, education, the state, religion, the province, or political department.[38] Durkheim gave this reform a prominent place in a new preface for the second edition (1902) of the *Division of Labor*. He even went so far as to say that occupational corporations . . . will become the foundation or one of the essential bases of our political organization.[39]

Durkheim's monograph on suicide was a brilliant contribution to empirical sociology. Through a skillful handling of statistical data, he revealed a number of complex causal patterns that related suicide rates to social structure. Yet he never lost his basic belief in the soundness of Organic society nor his faith that the historical trend was toward a functional social system based on an advanced division of labor. Had Durkheim taken seriously his insight into the social nature of suicide, he would have had to reevaluate the basic institutional and value complex of liberal society. He would have become more interested in the whole range of social deviation, the instability of industrial society, and the possible antagonisms lurking in the

[37] Robert A. Nisbet, *The Sociology of Emile Durkheim* (New York: Oxford University Press paperbound, 1974), chap. 9, also exaggerates the importance of Durkheim's concept of anomie; indeed, by saying that Durkheim was rather pessimistic about modern society, that he stressed "alienation, estrangement, moral isolation, social disorganization, and social disintegration," Nisbet has given a deeply erroneous view of Durkheim's basic stance toward modern society.
[38] *Suicide*, pp. 370–392.
[39] *Div. of Labor*, p. 27.

class form of social stratification.[40] Instead of pursuing such questions, however, Durkheim became sidetracked. In his last major work, *The Elementary
Forms of the Religious Life,* he chose to search for the underlying functional
processes that insure the stability and vitality of social systems. He focused on
the fundamental insight that informed the *Division of Labor, Suicide,* and the
Rules—that social systems have inherent functional processes—and ignored
his earlier interest in classifying social types and in understanding social
variation and deviation. If all behavior, values, and beliefs are social, he
seems to have asked, could it be that the classification of societies according
to the extent of the collective rather than the individual conscience was
fundamentally misleading? Might not the fact that every collective conscience imposes a functional unity and vitality on human behavior be more
important than the fact that sometimes it does so by enforcing a homogeneous existence and at other times by enforcing diverse behaviors and
personalities? Might not the possibility that there is a universal tendency
toward functional social health be far more important than the fact that
both individualism and deviation are social products—and might not this
possibility be the strategic path for sociology to follow? In short, might not
the empiricism of social phenomena, that is, their variety and temporality,
be epiphenomenal, and should not sociology therefore search for the underlying processes that give unity to the variety of social types and social
deviation? Actually, Durkheim's train of reasoning did not, of course, take
this form. Perhaps it would be truer to say that he had always been interested in such things as the division of labor, law, social types, crime, and
suicide for the light that they could shed on the general nature of social
structure. As such, the single-minded focus on social structure in his last
major work is continuous with the basic orientation of his earlier career.

Religion and the Elementary Forms of Social Life

Durkheim's interest in religion in *The Elementary Forms of the Religious
Life* [41] was not new. As early as the *Division of Labor,* he had related
religion to the type of solidarity characteristic of Mechanical society, broadly
suggesting that religion is a social product. In his work on suicide, he declared authoritatively that religion was "the system of symbols by means
of which society becomes conscious of itself; it is the characteristic way of

---

[40] Modern sociology has built heavily on Durkheim's concept of anomie. In particular, Robert K. Merton's "Social Structure and *Anomie," American Sociological
Review* 3 (October 1938):672–682 was a notable contribution to the theory of
anomie precisely because Merton used a class analysis to relate "antisocial behavior" to the core values of society. More generally speaking, Durkheim's concept of anomie is usually evident when sociologists, especially in the field of
criminology, explain behavior in terms of the inadequacy of normative and interaction structures.
[41] Trans. J. W. Swain (New York: Free Press, 1954), available as a Collier paperback; hereafter cited as *Elem. Forms.*

thinking of collective existence." [42] In the *Elementary Forms*, however, Durkheim tackled the study of religion directly, though as always his main interest was to enhance his knowledge of society. His basic assumption was that there is an elemental reality behind all religion that can be analyzed sociologically.

> At the foundation of all systems of beliefs and all cults there ought necessarily to be a certain number of fundamental representations or conceptions and of ritual attitudes which, in spite of the diversity of forms which they have taken, have the same objective significance and fulfill the same functions everywhere. These are the permanent elements which constitute that which is permanent and human in religion; they form all the objective contents of the idea which is expressed when one speaks of *religion* in general.[43]

To find the fundamental elements of religion, Durkheim chose to study the totemic tribes of Australia because their simple structures had not yet been complicated by historical development. Thus, hoping to see the nature of the universe in a grain of sand, Durkheim went to the origins of history to arrive at an unhistorical explanation of all social behavior. The fundamental thesis that emerges from the *Elementary Forms* is that religious ideas, practices, and objects are human inventions that result from social interaction and serve collective needs. Out of the intensity and "effervescence" of collective life or interaction, the individual begins to feel and believe in a life different from his personal life, to recognize a distinction between the sacred and the profane, between the ideal and the real. Once these distinctions crystallize into a system of religious beliefs and rites, human beings acquire a social identity. Henceforth, the function of religion is to transmit and reinforce the sentiments that insure the continuity, unity, and survival of society. Though the fundamental purpose of religion is to bring people together to interact in ways that insure the general sameness, it also promotes art and recreation and helps individuals escape the debilitating drudgery of workaday existence. The contents of religious rites and beliefs are not important since they are not true or false in any religious or philosophical sense. The truth or validity of a practice, sentiment, or belief lies in its success in performing social functions, especially the function of integration. Content is not important, for the same content can serve different functions and different contents can serve the same function.

Durkheim's *Elementary Forms* is a major contribution to the sociology of knowledge. The study of religion is really the study of philosophy and science as well, since the basic categories of the intellect are founded on

[42] *Suicide*, p. 312.
[43] *Elem. Forms*, p. 5 (the emphasis is Durkheim's).

and derived from religious beliefs. Since religion stems from society, the basic categories of cognition are social products serving social functions whether they stem indirectly from religion or more directly from the peculiarities of social organization. The categories of understanding, said Durkheim, are not innate and could never have suggested themselves to the isolated individual. In developing his sociology of knowledge, Durkheim devoted much of the *Elementary Forms* to tracing relationships between social organization and ideas of space, the rhythm of social life and ideas of time, and religious rites and beliefs and such ideas as class, force, personality, causality, and totality. Indeed, totemism itself, which is the only authentically elementary religion, has an intimate relationship to the clan or family and is thus social in origin as well as' in function. Durkheim's sociology of knowledge is related, of course, to his functionalism, which assumes that the only way to understand a phenomenon is to see it in context or in terms of a system. "For the sociologist as for the historian, social facts vary with the social system of which they form a part; they cannot be understood when detached from it." Further, ideas are functional to a society because they express that society's collective might and personality and provide a common, unifying vocabulary of discourse.

Durkheim's perspective on religion and ideas could easily have led to philosophical nominalism and relativism and could even have inclined him toward historical positivism. However, he remained true to his substantialistic beginnings. That religion and ideas originate in society, he argued, does not make them any less valid. This mistake is made by those who forget that society is part of nature and who do not recognize the value in natural science of socially derived ideas.

> From the fact that the ideas of time, space, class, cause or personality are constructed out of social elements, it is not necessary to conclude that they are devoid of all objective value. On the contrary their social origin rather leads to the belief that they are not without foundation in the nature of things.[44]

CONCLUSION

The last decades of the nineteenth century witnessed a momentous alteration in sociological theory, one that paralleled similar changes in the moral-intellectual culture of the West. Out of a sweeping re-examination of the methodology and subject matter of sociology, there emerged the point of view that was to dominate twentieth-century sociology, *pluralistic sociocultural positivism.* This term is extremely abstract, referring in a loose way to the highly variegated output of a number of theorists. Yet the term is

[44] *Elem. Forms*, p. 18f.

exact enough if one thinks of it as containing the reflections and conclusions of those sociologists who challenged the general tradition of monistic naturalistic positivism. In general, the sociologists who made up this
movement stopped trying to explain human behavior in substantive concepts borrowed from the natural sciences. Instead, they recognized the
complexity, variety, and instability of human behavior, which led to a
growing awareness that social phenomena are qualitatively different from
natural phenomena. Out of the ferment of the nineteenth century, there
emerged a revolutionary distinction between human behavior and human
nature. Theorist after theorist abandoned the idea of a structured biopsychic human nature and adopted as explanatory principles the concepts
of society and culture.

Durkheim as a Pluralistic Sociocultural Positivist

As a brilliant pioneer in all these respects, Durkheim deserves a pre-
eminent place in the history of sociological theory. By repudiating the
teleological and psychological evolutionism of Comte and Spencer and by
developing the empirical method that they had espoused but had practiced
so poorly, he helped to recast the entire tradition of sociological positivism.
Despite Durkheim's devastating critique of the main sociological tradition,
he gave to sociology the functional method, which extended the range and
depth of empirical investigation far beyond anything that social science
had hitherto attained. Furthermore, he identified a realm of subject matter
that was, while natural, distinct from the rest of nature. His functionalism,
which broadly speaking was synonomous with his concept of "comparison"
or the identification of variables in a cause-effect framework, employed
both qualitative and quantitative concepts and techniques. His concept of
the subject matter of sociology, though focused on the topics he analyzed
in his major works, included an interest in developing a scientific basis
for ethics, education, and the family and brought him into contact with the
disciplines of history, philosophy, and anthropology. The genius of Durkheim's empirical method lay in the fact that, unlike British or American
empiricists, he refused to dissolve his subject matter into individuals or
particulars. He insisted that the totality of social phenomena formed a
structural entity that must be studied in its own right. If he dissected
society for purposes of study, he did so in terms of nonpsychological variables or "social facts"—beliefs, sentiments, symbols, and interaction. In
this process of analytical dissection he always insisted that these social facts
had meaning and reality only as part of a general system of collective
existence.

Durkheim's theory and his efforts to delimit a field of study for sociology
have been interpreted as a belief in an occult, collective mind;[45] as agelic

[45] George Catlin in the Introduction to *Rules*, xxii-xxviii.

transcendentalism;[46] and as a belief in the reality of a social mind, as psycho-organicism and/or medieval realism.[47] However, none of these views stand as an ultimate interpretation of his work. For one thing, Durkheim explicitly argued against transcendental concepts of society.[48] More important, his writings are best interpreted as a pioneer identification of the two pillars of contemporary sociology, the concepts of *interaction* and *culture*. Without being completely clear about these concepts or the relation between them, he identified in a groping but unmistakable way a range of facts clearly cultural in nature (technology or material density, legal codes, proverbs, suicide statistics, cognitive forms, and religious dogmas and symbols) and a range of facts that clearly refer to social interaction (association, moral density, "effervescence," group, ritual).

Durkheim's work has also been interpreted as containing stages of qualitative development.[49] Though true in some respects, this interpretation obscures the fundamental unity and continuity in his work as a whole. Durkheim's unity and continuity are evidenced by his life-long insistence on and interest in social facts and in functional analysis, an orientation based on the assumption that social phenomena cannot be understood as essences or substances (psychological or teleological) but only as general systems of causal-functional relationships.

Parsons failed to recognize the importance of both functionalism and interaction in Durkheim's work. He noted Durkheim's functionalism, of course, but did not see it as the kingpin of his theoretical system; and he overlooked Durkheim's focus on interaction as the explanation of social change in the *Division of Labor* and as the process that originates and maintains both religion and society in the *Elementary Forms*. Though Parsons recognized that the function of ritual for Durkheim is to maintain social solidarity, he failed to see the full implications of the idea of effervescence. Instead, he maintained that Durkheim's stress on the functional significance of religious ritual was pointing toward a voluntaristic theory of action—that he was abandoning his earlier positivism and objectivist bias and closely approaching Weber's concept of *verstehen*.[50] It is true that Durkheim's last work emphasized the subjectivity of individuals and that it left off dealing

---

[46] Emile Benoit-Smullyan, "The Sociologism of Emile Durkheim and His School," *An Introduction to the History of Sociology*, ed. H. E. Barnes (Chicago: University of Chicago Press, 1948), pp. 499, 510–514. Agelicism holds that society totally determines the ideas, feelings, and actions of individuals.
[47] Pitirim Sorokin, *Contemporary Sociological Theories* (New York: Harper & Row, 1928), pp. 464–467.
[48] Emile Durkheim, *Sociology and Philosophy*, trans. D. F. Pocock, intro. J. G. Peristiany (New York: Free Press, 1953), pp. 23–26, 28, 62, 86–90, 94.
[49] See Talcott Parsons, *The Structure of Social Action* (New York: McGraw-Hill, 1937; reprinted, New York: Free Press, 1949), p. 304; and E. Benoit-Smullyan, *op. cit.*, p. 510.
[50] Parsons, *op. cit.*, pp. 435–442.

with categories signifying objective data such as legal codes and suicide statistics and concerned itself more with the subjective category of religious ritual and dogma. This represented a shift from his earlier position, in which he tended to make a sharp separation between individuals and their motives, and social facts (which he defined by the two criteria of exteriority and constraint). However, in changing his earlier focus, Durkheim was extending the fundamental achievement of his early work, not abandoning it. He still rejected the utilitarian position that located rationality in the individual. Far from recognizing the role of human effort and willfulness in behavior, Durkheim continued to assert the primacy of society over individuals; he emphasized in a new way the almost total dependence of individuals on society, and he placed rationality (functional adjustment) squarely within sociocultural objects and processes. In his earlier career, Durkheim had felt he could use objective data, implying that society was a concrete, empirical thing separate from the individual. In his last writings Durkheim sought to avoid such mysticism. In *Sociology and Philosophy* and especially in the *Elementary Forms*, he found a solution to this problem. He had never sought to understand the intrinsic worth of the objective data of legal codes or suicide statistics, but only their social functions; therefore he easily arrived at a position where he placed the individual, on the one hand, and objective and subjective social facts, on the other, in a theoretical system of mutual identity, dependency, and functional interrelation. Durkheim's stress on action and subjectivity was not, therefore, a preparation for voluntarism, as Parsons claims. Rather, it was an attempt to unite action and thought, emotions and beliefs, into a comprehensive structure of explanation. Far from leading to voluntarism, Durkheim's later thought worked individuals into an ever-tighter web of social and cultural relationships outside of which they had no existence. It was the logical climax to a scientfic orientation that saw the meaning and existence of human actions, not as isolated acts, but only as parts of a sociocultural system that creates and sustains them.

By tracing empirically the causal and functional networks that constitute society and link the individual to the collective conscience, Durkheim's *Elementrary Forms* concluded an effort begun seventeen years earlier in the *Rules.* Far from developing a theory of voluntarism, Durkheim elaborated a theory that questioned not only the validity of individually inspired activity and belief, but their very existence.[51] In Parsons's judgment, Durkheim never escaped the empiricist-idealist dilemma, coming finally to an idealistic position in which he focused on systems of "value ideas" in and of themselves instead of in relation to action.[52] Further, Parsons claimed that Durkheim's whole career reflected a concern for substance and not

---

[51] It should be noted that in Parsons's later works he has come to identify Durkheim as one of the founders of the key concept of *internalization* and that he has abandoned the stress on voluntarism in his own theory.

[52] Parsons, *op. cit.*, p. 446.

process, for order and not change, and that he came finally to concern himself with values in terms of their "intrinsic properties as eternal ebjects." The result, he said, was that Durkheim relegated the functional interrelations of normative elements to a secondary position. Finally, concluded Parsons, only the voluntaristic concept of action focuses on these interrelationships and is thereby in a position to reveal dynamic processes.[53]

Durkheim's considerable success in escaping from the empiricist-idealist dilemma is the heart of his contribution to sociology.[54] His precise achievement was to explain "value ideas" (culture) as natural products of social interaction. In turn he related culture to action by thinking of both as parts of a general system of causal-functional relationships that the individual internalizes to become an actor. Although Durkheim's thought is on the whole static, it does contain a vague evolutionary flavor. If he is to be criticized, it is on the grounds that his search for the lawful, timeless reality underlying society led him to minimize the dysfunctional consequences in interaction and cultural patterns and their relation to each other. Though Durkheim helped through his concept of anomie to bring the nineteenth-century experience with conflict and disorder into greater conceptual clarity, his work in this regard was peripheral to his main interests and not nearly so significant to sociology as the liberal theory of conflict of Simmel and Weber and the socialist theory of conflict that crystallized in Marx.

Durkheim as Metaphysician and Liberal Ideologist

Despite Durkheim's keen historical-empirical approach and his dismissal of the monistic naturalistic tradition, he never veered toward historical positivism. His contribution to pluralistic sociocultural sociology, in other words, was never a rejection of unified theory. Throughout his career, he maintained his belief that science had the power both to unify phenomena and to establish a moral order. In this respect, his thought stands squarely within the substantialist tradition of the West, a tradition with diverse formulations but with the common belief that the unaided human mind can provide human beings with both truth and a rational system of values.

Related to this metaphysical strand in Durkheim's thought is a deep ideological element. His work takes on added meaning if one examines the way in which he adjusted the ideals of the Enlightenment to suit the needs of late-nineteenth-century French liberal society. The nature and development of French society can be understood only in the light of the unreconciled cleavages that emerged from the political and economic revolutions

[53] Ibid., pp. 448–450.
[54] Durkheim himself felt that he had escaped from the empiricist-idealist dilemma. See, for example, *Sociology and Philosophy,* pp. 62, 67, and *Elem. Forms,* pp. 13ff., 445–447.

of the eighteenth and nineteenth centuries. The Revolution had split France into two societies, one longing for the feudal monarchy based on birth and privilege and one determined to preserve the new social hierarchy founded on property and talent. Long before the bitterness engendered by this conflict was reconciled, there emerged a third value-belief system, socialism. Without a viable political system to adjudicate economic conflicts, the new-found consciousness of French workers developed in opposition to both the nobility and the bourgeoisie.

The slow development of French industry during the nineteenth century allowed France ample time to debate the political questions of the eighteenth century. With poor coal and iron resources, a deeply entrenched small-business and artisan tradition strongly committed to family life, a Roman Catholic value-belief tradition, and a rich soil that kept her tied to agriculture, France lagged badly in economic development in comparison with England, Germany, and the United States. Thus, it is not surprising that France never developed a wholehearted commitment to economic individualism, laissez faire, and unending progress, nor that the fruits of economic plenty never appeared to numb the memory of the past and to create a spirit of compromise and optimism. The constant juggling to contain the antagonistic multiplicities in its population and the chronic lag in problem solving, which resulted only in their aggravation and accumulation, characterizes the history of modern France into the post–World War II period.

France's problems did not abate during Durkheim's life. If anything, his generation experienced the tensions and frustrations of French society in some of their most acute forms. Durkheim's generation experienced the French military defeat at the hands of Prussia, and the savage butchery of the Paris Commune; they witnessed the continued hostility of monarchical elements to republican institutions, marked by incidents such as the Boulanger Affair; and they saw the Roman Catholic Church stage a remarkable counteroffensive against the modern world, capping the Syllabus of Errors and the Vatican Council with the condemnation of Modernism and the encouragement of the religious fervor that swept France at the end of the century. Finally, Durkheim's main creative years coincided almost exactly with the soul-searing hostilities of the Dreyfus Affair, in which the right-wing forces of aristocracy, civil service, army, and clergy came together to turn the trial of Captain Dreyfus into a struggle for supremacy between authoritarian and republican systems of society.

Over and above these political and religious legacies from the Great Revolution, new and more complicated problems began to emerge from the quickening tempo of industrial life, problems that could not be contained by Louis Napoleon's paternalism and police. Durkheim witnessed the growing problem of the French proletariat, who were transforming their disinheritance from the benefits of French society into a tradition of violence and revolution based on syndicalism and socialism.

Viewed against this background, it is not difficult to identify Durkheim's thought as part of the French tradition of rational social theory, a tradition that concerned itself primarily with the problem of social integration and stability. Nor is it difficult to identify the origins of Durkheim's interest in society as such, nor his pervasive tendency to interpret social phenomena in terms of their contribution to the unity and stability of society.[55]

The ideological elements in Durkheim's work are also easy to identify. In his first major work, *The Division of Labor,* he argued that social specialization was producing a new type of social unity; this represented a healthy historical insight into the multiple bases of social organization and presented a much-needed corrective to the monism of both right and left in French politics, as well as to the monism of the earlier sociologists. However, the way in which Durkheim accounted for the new unity represents a major ideological transformation of the ideals of the Enlightenment. In a revealing argument, Durkheim denied that the division of social labor is promoting moral progress because it forms the indispensable condition for the rise of civilization. If this were its function, it would be remote to moral life because civilization, whether considered as economics, art, or science, is morally neutral. The division of labor, he said, produces morality in and of itself by subjecting individuals to the duties of their specialized existence.

Durkheim's argument, simple as it may seem, has far-reaching implications. In effect, he discarded the ideals of early liberalism, which sought to found a new society on a new moral consensus based on liberty, equality, and reason. The growth of civilization, stemming from the free exercise of individual reason and creativity, does not lead to moral progress and cannot be thought of as the basis of liberal society. Instead—and the brilliance of Durkheim's argument should not blind one to its ideological quality— the new moral unity is based on *moral particularism.* The rationalism of the Enlightenment, which declared the universe and the individual mind to be in fundamental harmony, is refuted as dangerous to moral unity. This was Durkheim's ideological corollary to his denial of individual psychology as the source of society. The integration of society comes, he declared, from the way in which a given population is incorporated into the existing social structure. It is almost as if he were enunciating a fear that the ideals of the Enlightenment can only make human beings impatient with the necessary inequalities of historical society. When inequality exists that is unjust or

---

[55] Durkheim would be the first to appreciate an analysis that related his sociology to its social origins. He would also be the first to point out that the validity and objectivity of a conceptual or logical scheme is not undermined if one shows its social origin.

disruptive, said Durkheim, the social scientist tries to achieve reforms based on the need to perfect the division of labor (as opposed to the social philosopher, who would base reforms on philosophic doctrines). Ruptures in unity such as class conflict, economic depression, and anomie do not stem from the fundamental defects of liberal society, but rather from the malfunctioning of the division of labor. The only reform that Durkheim could propose, aside from the conventional liberal doctrine of equal opportunity, was his well-known idea that new moral energies would be unleashed and old ones more effectively transmitted if individuals were incorporated into the discipline of occupational organizations.[56]

The early liberal emphasis on the individual, equality, and moral and legal universalism had already been modified by the sociology of Saint-Simon, Comte, and even Spencer and Sumner. Despite their differences, these early sociologists tried to explain the existence of inequality and, in the case of Saint-Simon and Comte, the need for social hierarchy, by referring to innate differences among individuals. Durkheim, however, tried to explain and justify inequality and social hierarchy as inherent not in human beings but in the nature of society. Though he significantly modified the liberal tradition, he did not cease to be a liberal. Most revealing is Durkheim's acceptance of the general liberal commitment to specialization and to the primacy of a private economic realm. Liberal thought, especially outside of England and the United States, found it difficult to conceive of an economic order based on private property as a realm of harmony and unity. Even in the work of Adam Smith and certainly in the early-nineteenth-century English classical economists, there is no facile acceptance of the harmony of economic life. It was not until laissez faire was fused with Darwin's theory of natural selection that Anglo-American theorists accepted the idea that specialization, competition, and economic life in general were ultimately orderly and beneficent. It was Durkheim's historic role to disgorge from liberal theory the indigestible elements from evolutionary theory and to spell out the ways in which a specialized economy and society created specialized norms and relationships to insure integration and stability. Durkheim's liberalism is apparent, therefore, in his acceptance of specialization; in his assertion of the primacy and viability of a private market economy, which included a mild advocacy of the corporate state; and, of course, in his sociology of law, which emphasized the specialized, restitutive functions of law, which on the legal level paralleled his redefinition of the moral universalism of early liberalism.

Durkheim's emphasis on society as a functional system was a valuable contribution to social science—especially when combined with his caution

---

[56] See *Div. of Labor*, Conclusion, for many explicit statements identifying individual personality, liberty, morality, progress, and human fraternity with the division of labor.

that functions can be separated from concrete value and behavior structures and, of course, from human nature. In his analysis of the problems of industrial society, however, Durkheim not only underestimated their seriousness, but identified the crucial social function of unity with a specific institutional content. It is one thing to argue against the utilitarian individualists that society is a regulative system prior to the individual, and quite another to propose how that regulation should take place. In other words, by accepting the existing liberal division of economic and social labor as an adequate and sufficient regulatory system, Durkheim introduced a major ideological element into his thought and into sociology.

Durkheim is open to criticism on a different level. It never occurred to him that the division of labor could be chronically disruptive, let alone an insidious, corrosive force eating away at moral, economic, and political consensus. Since the economy presented no problem for Durkheim, he never developed an interest in or appreciation of the potentials of liberal political institutions for supplying a rational and moral direction to the conflicts of the market. He never realized that giving political and social recognition to occupations (even if a formula of political representation could be worked out) would freeze social change or else obstruct peaceful solutions to social conflicts. Although he denied it, Durkheim tended to regard the economic division of labor as equivalent to social structure; as a consequence, reforms within the division of labor are tantamount to social reform and thus beyond the ability of conscious human effort. Thus, there is little need to discuss tax, welfare, property, contract, or labor reforms. In the case of French labor, for example, Durkheim was hopelessly utopian in thinking that French workers would accept the discipline of trade-union or factory organization while the political, legal, and economic structures of France saw to it that they were excluded from the benefits of French society—benefits the workers insisted on measuring, at the least, by the yardsticks of the French Revolution. Durkheim, in short, not only rejected as unscientific the equalitarianism of the Enlightenment and the evolutionary monism of early sociology; he did so in a way that implied that the inequality and shortcomings of industrial society were phenomena rooted in the nature of society. While remaining in the liberal camp, his scientific critique of individualism, equality, and progress unduly narrowed the possible catalog of value and behavior structures that could perform the functional prerequisites of social life.

The ideological element in Durkheim's other works does not require extended discussion, for these works reveal the same pattern. A certain amount of crime and suicide, he said, is normal to society because they either serve functions or are related to the basic values of society and are thus necessary costs; excessive rates of crime and suicide are abnormal, and thus transitional. In other words, the excesses do not challenge the validity of the existing social system, which is in the process of transition to a new functional unity where excessive rates of deviant behavior will disappear.

After his book on suicide, Durkheim's thought could have gone in two directions. He might have become a historical positivist. There is a bent in his thought that is strongly historical: he saw a diversity of social types, each unique and explicable only in its own terms; and he believed that knowledge accrues only in developmental processes on a comparative basis. If Durkheim had seen and interpreted social facts as conventional and not as natural forces, having both functional and dysfunctional consequences for social existence and having no necessary relevance for the health of society, he might have moved toward historical positivism. He might have come to see friction and disorder as integral features of complex society, sometimes contributing more to social disease than to social health. Perhaps, in becoming as interested in change and disorder as he was in structure and unity, he might have specified more clearly the dynamics of change and might have moved toward a classification of types of disorder and diversity. Then, in seeing no natural process of equilibration in society, he might have cited a need for the more explicit management of social affairs.

There was, however, a substantialist element in Durkheim's thought. This bent sought to abstract the element of time, to reduce behavior to principles about humankind rather than to principles about social types, to find laws that transcend historical determination, and to objectify or unify the collective conscience. This is the direction that Durkheim's thought took after *Suicide,* a course in which he remained true to his original orientation, which may be called a *metaphysical functional-positivism.* Though Durkheim rejected the philosophical monism of Comte and Spencer, he could never come to accept philosophical pluralism. Society, he felt, everywhere tended toward a functional equilibrium rooted in the nature of things— though he was sometimes careful to account for historical diversity by pointing out that social functions could be fulfilled in a plurality of ways. After his study of suicide, Durkheim put the study of contemporary society aside and devoted a major research project to the primitive totemic tribes of Australia to search for the functional reality that he felt must underlie all social existence.

The book that resulted, the *Elementary Forms,* completed Durkheim's transformation of early liberalism. Progress is no longer measured in terms of advance toward liberty and equality nor in terms of human ability to subdue nature. Progress no longer emerges from the work of the critical intelligence, which sloughs off outmoded institutions as it gains power through the acquisition of knowledge. For Durkheim, progress was now something less than concrete, a mysterious commodity that emerges from the bowels of society from whence come all the virtues and few vices.

Though the collective conscience varies in content, it always exhibits a natural tendency toward unity and harmony; when one finds disharmony, it is only the world of appearance. Beneath appearance, the collective conscience of humanity is groping unerringly for a new structure of objective moral and social unity. Durkheim's substantialism and ideology are nowhere better revealed than in his attitude toward the individual. By radically submerging the individual in society, Durkheim smothered early liberalism's belief in the critical intelligence of the individual, which, at least in part, is able to pass valid judgments on the deficiencies of society. In a curious exchange, the power and responsibility for effecting good and evil, once attributed to the individual, have now been transferred selectively to the collective conscience—selectively because society now achieves good only; whatever evil is produced is attributed to the heavy-handedness of history.

Durkheim's claim that his sociology has revealed the functional reality underlying every society, and his belief that an emerging humanity is marching toward an ever-richer cultural life free from functional defects, identifies him as a substantialist late liberal. Also in his thought are the faint overtones of later authoritarianism and fascism—especially his denial of individual rationality, his mild advocacy of the corporate state, his emphasis on the vitality and unity of the collective will, and his concern with the coordination of social functions more as an end in itself than as a means for realizing stated values.

The failure to employ rigorous and essential distinctions among various types of societies and social theories can obscure much of one's understanding of the history and nature of social and sociological theory. This is more than evident in the case of Durkheim—for example, the claim that Durkheim was a conservative (not a liberal seeking to consolidate and conserve liberal society, but a conservative along the lines of traditionalist, agrarian thinkers like Maistre and Bonald who stressed the need to resist individualism and curb human passion by supporting the hierarchic, static social order ordained by nature) is clearly wrong. Durkheim himself further obscured his position on the spectrum of social thought by mistakenly equating the regulation of property and a more equitable distribution of economic benefits—policies he favored—with socialism. All in all, there is little doubt that Durkheim worked consciously to support republican institutions, that he accepted a private market economy and "free" or private professions, and that his emphasis on the authority and power of the divison of labor and education included a carefully worked out claim that liberal society would produce individualism, a true morality, and social stability, and that it would achieve all these ends without explicit human effort.

Durkheim's sociological theory, therefore, must be considerably discounted as an ideological defense of a problem-laden French capitalism. However, his functional methodology supplied sociological theory with a sharp analytical instrument, and he provided brilliant examples of empirical research, especially in his study of suicide. Unfortunately he blunted the cutting edge of the instrument he honed so carefully when he wielded it in support of an almost fatalistic belief in the infallibility of a vaguely defined collective conscience. In Durkheim's mind, the inherent propensity of the collective conscience to seek a functional equilibrium, in much the same way that the laissez faire economy tended toward harmony and rational adjustment, was sufficient justification to assert its supremacy over the individual and to absolve it of any responsibility for the shortcomings of liberal society. If he had become a thoroughgoing historical positivist, he would have seen sociology as a method of shaping social existence. As a substantialist, however, he identified the values and institutions of liberal society with reality, which meant that social existence would continue to shape sociology.

Chapter 15
Georg Simmel (1858–1918)

One of the more notable contributions to the development of the contemporary empirical age of sociology was made by Georg Simmel, whose life span coincided almost exactly with Durkheim's. Though Simmel's work contains many similarities with Durkheim's, his contribution to the new empirical sociology was quite different from that of his great French contemporary. To be understood, Simmel's contribution must be set in the German intellectual tradition. Unlike the French, English, and American traditions, which tended to identify human beings and nature, German intellectual culture insisted that knowledge about human beings and about nature were two different things. Despite Durkheim's revolutionary insistence that human behavior must not be absorbed into either biology or psychology, he argued that society, though distinct from nature, was still natural and could therefore be studied in the same way one studies the rest of nature. In Germany, however, it was a commonplace by the end of the nineteenth century that nature was the realm of necessity and human behavior the realm of freedom. Individuals, unlike nature, imposed law on themselves, and since they freely legislated their behavior they were free to follow, modify, or even annul that legislation. Throughout the nineteenth century German intellectual culture struggled to preserve this perspective against the rising prestige and success of natural science.

As one would expect, those who defended human uniqueness against the claims of naturalistic positivism found the source of that uniqueness in human volition and reason. The implications that German intellectuals drew from this defense were profoundly important for social science. Not only must human consciousness be included in the subject matter of social science, but also social scientists must recognize the necessary role of subjectivity in the formation of knowledge itself. Unlike the physical scientist, who works with data already systematized into recurrent natural processes, the investigator of human behavior must bring order into the chaos of experience. This orientation, so reminiscent of Vico, was inspired mostly by the philosophy of Kant. The fundamental assumption of Kantian philosophy is that knowledge about experience is impossible without mental

Georg Simmel (1858–1918)

categories with which to shape the world of experience. Without the a priori categories of human understanding to give form to the shapeless world of experience, no knowledge is possible. Simmel attempted to incorporate this tradition into the methodological and substantive theory of sociology.

PHILOSOPHY AND METHOD

Simmel's writings in sociology, which appeared mostly as essays and articles from the 1890s on, were finally collected and published in 1908.[1]

---

[1] Georg Simmel, *Soziologie, Untersuchungen über die Formen der Vergesellschaftung* (Leipzig: Duncker and Humblot, 1908).

The final statement of his philosophical and methodological orientation appeared in 1917, a year before his death.[2] Simmel's concern in his last work was to vindicate a method and a subject matter for sociology and to refute the criticisms that had been made against it. His commitment to Kantian philosophy is apparent throughout. The possibility of a science of society, he said, has been denied because society "does not exist outside and in addition to the individuals and the processes among them." On the other hand "it is said all that men are and do occurs within society, is determined by society, and is part of its life; there is no science of man that is not [sic] science of society."[3]

As a neo-Kantian concerned with defending the study of human behavior from absorption by the natural sciences, Simmel not surprisingly directed most of his criticism at the concept of society that seeks to reduce it to individuals. Simmel declared that without the "synthesizing subject" and without a method of knowing that does not reduce knowledge to particulars, all knowledge is destroyed.

> The alleged realism that performs this sort of critique of the con-
> cept of society, and thus of sociology, actually eliminates all
> knowable reality. It relegates it into the infinite and looks for it
> in the realm of the inscrutable. As a matter of fact, cognition must
> be conceived on the basis of an entirely different structural prin-
> ciple. This principle is the abstraction, from a given complex of
> phenomena, of a number of heterogeneous objects of cognition
> that are nevertheless recognized as equally definitive and con-
> sistent. The principle may be expressed by the symbol of the

[2] Georg Simmel, *Grundfragen der Soziologie* (*Individuum und Gesellschaft*), (Berlin and Leipzig: de Gruyter and Co., 1917); available in English as Part One of *The Sociology of Georg Simmel*, trans. and ed. Kurt H. Wolff (New York: Free Press, 1950), also in paperback—henceforth cited as *Soc. of Simmel.* Parts Two through Five, of Wolff's work are translations of much of Simmel's *Soziologie* (1908), and the last chapter of Part 5, "The Metropolis and Mental Life," is a translation of an essay originally published in 1903. In addition, two more chapters of *Soziologie*, "Conflict" and "The Web of Group-Affiliations," have been translated by Kurt H. Wolff and Reinhard Bendix as *Conflict and the Web of Group-Affiliations* (New York: Free Press, 1955), also in paperback—henceforth cited as *Conflict.* Other translations of Simmel's work are in: Georg Simmel, *Sociology of Religion*, trans. Curt Rosenthal (New York: Philosophical Library, 1959); and *On Individuality and Social Forms: Selected Writings* (including selections from Simmel's *The Philosophy of Money*), ed. Donald Levine (Chicago: Chicago University Press, 1971), also in paperback. Essays about various aspects of Simmel's work as well as some further translations of short pieces may be found in Kurt H. Wolff, ed., *Georg Simmel, 1858–1918: A Collection of Essays with Translations and a Bibliography* (Columbus: Ohio State University Press, 1959), also a Harper paperback. A useful collection of essays on Simmel has been compiled by Lewis A. Coser, ed., *Georg Simmel* (Englewood Cliffs, N.J.: Prentice-Hall paperback, 1965).

[3] *Soc. of Simmel*, p. 4

different *distances* between such a complex of phenomena and
the human mind. We obtain different pictures of an object when
we see it at a distance of two, or of five, or of ten yards. At each
distance, however, the picture is "correct" in its particular way
and only in this way. . . . All we can say is that a view gained at
any distance whatever has its own justification. It cannot be replaced or corrected by any other view emerging at another
distance.[4]

In these pithy sentences, Simmel has rejected the positive tradition of
France, England, and the United States and its assumption that the mind's
sole duty is to grasp the pre-existing order in particulars. In place of the
objective empiricism of positivism, in which the mind plays a relatively
passive role in the acquisition of knowledge, he asserted a subjective
empiricism in which the mind plays a creative and independent role.

In the history of European philosophy up to the Enlightenment, a persistent assumption gave unity to its diverse expressions. From the Greeks
on, it was always assumed that rational knowledge of particulars, of experience, of temporalities is impossible. Rational or metaphysical knowledge is
a stable unity; it cannot be based on transistory particulars. The positivism
of the Enlightenment sought to reshape this tradition by assuming that the
world of particulars, if properly investigated, exhibits the unity and order
that are the signs of rational knowledge. Thus the orientation of early
empiricism or positivism was fundamentally within the tradition of Western
idealism. The philosophy of Kant must be viewed in this context. For
Kant, it is the mind that brings order into experience and therefore achieves
knowledge. Not the sharp separation of mind and particulars, but their
interplay, is what distinguishes Kantian idealism and establishes Kant as a
true member of the Enlightenment.

Simmel's methodological objective was to "idealize" sociological theory
using this Kantian framework. However, a theory claiming that the mind
is nourished by the data of history cannot be an ordinary idealism. The
subject must consciously inject itself into the maze of data using the "one-
sided abstraction that no science can get rid of." Simmel pictured mind
as far more instrumental and pragmatic than any old-fashioned idealism
could allow. Knowledge is relative to the viewpoint or category adopted,
and categories are chosen not because they are part of a seamless logic
but because they produce useful results. The mind, however, though
disciplined by facts, still charts an autonomously creative course; the relativities that are unearthed because they are products of valid cognition are
also objective. In short, Simmel is in the tradition started by Vico, which

[4] Ibid., p. 7f.

assumes that knowledge about human beings, history, and society is possible without using "naturalistic" or rationalistic methods.

For Simmel, sociology did not embrace the various disciplines but provided for the "mutual fertilization of problem areas that is suggested by the common involvement of human sociation in all of them." [5] In his fuller definition of sociology, he distinguished three problem areas and defined the type of sociological approach applicable to each. The first was the sociological study of historical life, or general sociology. The contents (or culture) of human life can be studied in their own right as individual creations and as objective forces. However, they can also be studied as the products of society. Using this approach, one can undertake studies of such things as "the fall of the Roman Empire or of the relation between religion and economics in the great civilizations or of the origin of the idea of the German national state or of the predominance of the Baroque style." [6] One looks for determinate rhythms or patterns in historical change; for the factors that give the group its strength and vitality, and for the value relations between collective and individual behavior.

The second type of approach was in the study of the epistemological and metaphysical aspects of society, or philosophical sociology. On this level, but based on superempirical sources, "factual details are investigated concerning their significance for the totality of mind, life, and being in general, and concerning their justification in terms of such a totality." [7] All sciences presuppose an epistemology and a metaphysics. In one sense, by providing the various disciplines with a method, sociology "emerges as the epistemology of the special social sciences, as the analysis and systematization of the bases of their forms and norms." [8] In another sense, when it supplies the fragmentary empirical realm with significance, sociology becomes social philosophy.

The last type of approach was in the study of societal forms, or pure or formal sociology. Simmel felt that this area represented the real focus of sociology. "If society is conceived as interaction among individuals, the description of the forms of this interaction is the task of the science of society in its strictest and most essential sense." [9] Proceeding like geometry or grammar, sociology abstracts from the heterogeneity of human behavior the element of "interaction" or "sociation." [10] Diverse social groups and

[5] Ibid., p. 15.
[6] Ibid., p. 19.
[7] Ibid., p. 23.
[8] Ibid., p. 24.
[9] Ibid., pp. 21f; for further comments on the meaning of the distinction between form and content, see pp. 40–44, 200, 214, 270fn, 384–387; and in *Conflict*, p. 172.
[10] The term Simmel uses is *Vergesellschaftung*, which Wolff translates as "sociation" (*Soc. of Simmel*, p. lxiii), adopting a term coined by the Christian social philosopher and sociologist J. H. W. Stuckenberg (1835–1903).

interests may exhibit identical forms of sociation, and sometimes the same content or interest complex can assume different forms. The subject matter of sociology, strangely enough, resembles its methodology. Its method is to inject mental shape into the world of unordered phenomena; however, those shapes are not static and stable but vary with the perspective of the synthesizing subject. The stress on relations in Simmel's methodology had a counterpart in his image of society. Society consists of relationships not substances, events not essences, and can be studied in terms of effects or consequences and in abstraction from the subjective content of those relationships.

Simmel's methodological contribution consisted mostly of ideas with which to see and study social structures. He formulated no method in the stricter sense of the word. He did not develop an experimental, empirical, historical, or comparative method, and made no mention of statistics, case notes, or historical or personal documents. However, Simmel was not opposed to these forms of empirical research; in 1910 he joined Max Weber and others in organizing the German Sociological Society and through it participated in organizing research into German newspapers and clubs.[11] His main contribution to the development of a genuine empirical climate in sociology, however, came from his conviction that the mind plays a creative role in the formation of knowledge—not the mind as the possessor of truth but mind as an instrument that sharpens itself and finds its function and structure in the process of investigation. Like other late-nineteenth-century liberal intellectuals, Simmel reduced reason to method, and, though he did not emphasize this as much as Durkheim, he saw reason as the product of interaction. As in liberal intellectual culture in general, Simmel's redefinition of reason was intended not to enfeeble reason but to enhance it by better defining its powers and jurisdiction.

SUBSTANTIVE WORK

Simmel's substantive ideas about human behavior were so diverse and idiomatic that they are exceedingly difficult to categorize. His agile mind saw angularities, uniquenesses, and paradoxes as well as symmetries and universalities in human behavior. Unfortunately, his insights were never incorporated into a unified theory. His attempt to identify, classify, and explain the forms of social interaction, however, gave his work at least a semblance of unity.

[11] For details, see Theodore Abel, "The Contribution of Georg Simmel: A Reappraisal," *American Sociological Review* 24 (August 1959), p. 476f.

The Extent of Interaction

One of Simmel's basic contributions to sociology was his warning against an exclusive concern with the larger structures of society and his insistence that interaction is a far more pervasive phenomenon than sociologists had hitherto recognized. It is appropriate to introduce his work with his attempt to orient sociology toward the uncharted lower reaches of society.

> Without the interspersed effects of countless minor syntheses, society would break up into a multitude of discontinuous systems. Sociation continuously emerges and ceases and emerges again. Even where its eternal flux and pulsation are not sufficiently strong to form organizations proper, they link individuals together. That people look at one another and are jealous of each other; that they exchange letters or dine together; that irrespective of all tangible interests they strike one another as pleasant or unpleasant; that gratitude for altruistic acts makes for inseparable union; that one asks another man after a certain street, and that people dress and adorn themselves for one another—the whole gamut of relations that play from one person to another and that may be momentary or permanent, conscious or unconscious, ephemeral or of grave consequence (all from which these illustrations are quite casually chosen), all these incessantly tie men together. Here are the interactions among the atoms of society. They account for all the toughness and elasticity, all the color and consistency of social life, that is so striking and yet so mysterious.[12]

Thus parties, social games, coquetry, and conversation are standardized forms of interactions that exercise authority over individuals. Though Simmel was never sociologistic in the manner of Durkheim, the effect of his argument was to reduce the area of spontaneous, nonsocial behavior. In a similar vein, he showed the sociological derivation, autonomy, and function of faithfulness, which he called "the inertia of the soul," and of gratitude, which he called "the moral memory of mankind." [13] Regardless of the motives that lead to a given relationship, there emerges from interaction a sense of obligation without which society cannot function. Aside from their social function, faithfulness and gratitude serve the individual as well, since they stabilize and pattern the deep emotional flux of the personality.

It is not possible to itemize Simmel's many insights into the social nature of a vast range of human activities and sentiments. He never failed to preface his discussion of any topic by calling attention to its interactional

---

[12] *Soc. of Simmel*, p. 9f.
[13] For Simmel's discussion of faithfulness and gratitude, see *Soc. of Simmel*, pt. 5, chap. 1.

nature. The stranger, the renegade, the liar, the secret society and its members, and the slave, along with adornment and fashion and a wide range of virtues and emotions, are derivatives of interaction, expressing or serving individual and social functions.[14] Even ignorance and irrationality are essential elements in social life. All relationships must be based on some reciprocal knowledge, on some degree of predictable expectations. However, "in view of our accidental and defective adaptations to our life conditions, there is no doubt that we preserve and acquire not only so much truth, but also so much ignorance and error, as is appropriate for our practical activities." [15] Even the lie performs functions for the individual and society. In a tacit acceptance of moral relativism, Simmel argued that the lie has a different meaning in different societies, and that it may even have positive social functions:

> In addition to this relative sociological *permissibility* of the lie under primitive circumstances, there is also its positive expedience. Where a first organization, arrangement, centralization of the group is at stake, this organization will take place through the subordination of the weak under the physically and intellectually superior. The lie which maintains itself, which is not seen through, is undoubtedly a means of asserting intellectual superiority and of using it to control and suppress the less intelligent. It is an intellectual club law as brutal, but on occasion as appropriate, as physical club law. It may operate as a selecting factor to breed intelligence or create leisure for the few for whom others must work; for the few who need leisure for producing higher cultural goods or for giving a leader to the group forces.[16]

The Numerical Determination of Interaction

"The quantitative determination of the group" is perhaps the best known aspect of Simmel's work. Certain group purposes and values, he argued, can be realized only in small groups. The numerical factor is an important determinant for socialist groups, certain religious sects, and aristocracies, none of which can retain their distinctive character if they grow beyond a certain size.[17] Simmel also noted that emotional radicalism is characteristic of the small group since it can command the full allegiance of its members. He was careful to mention, however, that radicalism is also possible among large groups under the sway of the demogogue. A change in the size of the group also changes the relationship between the minority and the majority

---

[14] For references, see the index to *Soc. of Simmel;* Simmel's treatment of fashion as distinguished from adornment is available in *The American Journal of Sociology* 62 (May 1957): 541–558.
[15] *Soc. of Simmel,* p. 310.
[16] Ibid., p. 314.
[17] Ibid., pp. 87–93.

within the group, even if the ratio between them is held constant. For example, the effectiveness of a rebel group of four in a parliamentary party of twenty is quite different from that of a rebel group of ten in a party of fifty, even though the ratio between the groups has not changed.

Amplifying his theme, Simmel pointed out that the form of social unity changes when the size of the group changes and that there is a relation between group size and group norms. The small group relies, he said, on custom, on the "undifferentiated 'normative as such.' The more special regulations, religious, moral, conventional, legal, are still enfolded in it, are not yet ramified and separated out." [18] With the group's enlargement, the normative structure is differentiated into law, custom, and morality. Knowledge, admitted Simmel, cannot yet characterize precisely the relation between the form of a group and its quantitative aspects, though there are some small groups where this can be done. With penetrating insight, he cited the reforms of Cleisthenes as an example of the profound significance of numerical designation for group life. "Numerical characterization as a form of organization marks an important step in the development of society. Historically, numerical division replaces the principle of the sib." [19] When numbers are used to designate either equals or unequals, depersonalization can take place. A similar defacement or absorption of individuality occurs when organization is reduced to "arithmetic relations."

Small Group Theory: The Monad, Dyad, and Triad

Though Simmel applied his analysis of the influence of number on behavior to groups of all sizes, he devoted the bulk of his attention to smaller groups. His analysis is a rich contribution to small-group theory. Paradoxically, argued Simmel, the isolated individual or monad [20] is not a nonsocial being. The individual's condition "is determined by sociation, even though negatively. The whole joy and the whole bitterness of isolation are only different reactions to socially experienced influences." [21] The monad, therefore, has a specific relationship to society. Isolation is a characteristic of the group and should not be thought of as "mere negation of association." So too, the idea of freedom is mistakenly construed as the absence of sociation. In reality, freedom is a specific relationship of an individual toward others. In fact, it is a twofold relationship, a process of liberation from the monopolistic claims of given relationships and a process of making personal

[18] Ibid., p. 99.
[19] Ibid., p. 109.
[20] The terms *dyad* and *triad* are not Simmel's but have been supplied by his translator Kurt Wolff. The term *monad* seems to be a useful synonym for the isolated individual.
[21] *Soc. of Simmel,* p. 119; for a similar relationship, see Simmel's discussion of "The Stranger," pt. 5, chap. 3.

claims against others. In any case, freedom is a relationship and not a substance or static state of rights.

The dyad, or relationship between two individuals, is characterized by triviality and intimacy and is the most fragile of group formations. It gains its force from the immediacy of interaction in relative isolation from extraneous influences. Thus monogamous marriage has a dyadic form but is too heavily controlled from the outside to be a true dyad. The basic meaning of the dyad lies in the fact that there is no delegation of duties and responsibilities to an impersonal group structure, and thus no lowered sense of personal responsibility. The individual in a dyadic relationship is never faced by a superindividual collectivity and tends to remain an individual. Simmel distinguished between two types of individuality, the *decided* and the *strong*. The decided individual must find sustenance in dyadic relationships, where he or she cannot be overruled by a majority, while the strong individual thrives on opposition.

The addition of a third element to a dyadic relation forms a triad and can change the relationship in three directions. First, when the third element is nonpartisan, there can be a reduction of affective intensity and an introduction of a mediating impartiality.[22] The addition of a third element can also take the form of the *tertius gaudens*, "the third who enjoys." Here the third party serves its own egoistic interests by exploiting a pre-existing dispute between the other two or benefits inadvertently from a quarrel between them. A third change, similar to the second, can take the form of *divide et impera* if the third party actively and intentionally produces discord to serve its own interest.

Numbers and the Group Structure of Society

Perhaps more important than Simmel's contribution to small-group theory was his analysis of the relationships between groups on the basis of number. Curiously, Simmel failed to give any prominence to his insights into group relationships. While he devoted a chapter to "The Importance of Specific Numbers for Relations Between Groups," he concerned himself mostly with the outside control of group performance through the use of legal regulations prescribing either maximum or minimum size. Society is sometimes cognizant of the way numbers affect the inner life and functioning of groups, and it sometimes uses this knowledge to insure the adequate performance of given groups. Sometimes society sets a minimum number of group members as, for example, in some laws of incorporation or in judicial proceedings. Sometimes it prescribes a maximum number to stymie political opposition or to prevent immorality or rioting through mass contagion. However,

---

[22] It may lead, however, to an increase of emotional ties between parents in the case of the birth of a child. (Ibid., p. 146.) It will be noticed that the family is a special type of small group.

Simmel's most penetrating remarks on the interaction of groups as groups are interspersed almost incidentally in his discussion of the dyad and triad. Explaining Voltaire's statement about the political usefulness of religious anarchy, Simmel said that "within a state, two rivaling sects inevitably produce unrests and difficulties which can never result from two hundred." [23] Periods of general excitement and mass movements tend to polarize commitments and divide the total group into two parties. Arranged on a continuum, the group structure of a society may range from one pole based on "the radical exclusion of all mediation and impartiality; at the other, tolerance of the opponent's standpoint as legitimate as one's own." [24]

Simmel enriched his discussion of triadic relations among groups with historical illustrations. The logic of numbers in the external relations of groups is fairly similar to that which develops *within* the group. When a third group is nonpartisan, group relations tend to become objective in nature. In the case of a labor-management dispute, for example, the third party may be a board of conciliation; the function of group order and survival is thus provided by intellect instead of will and by objectivity and mediation instead of subjectivity and conflict.[25] The unity and equilibrium of the total group may be served if the third element provides a new sense of the whole and if it allows for a fresh employment of stalemated energies. Such was the case in England when the impasse between estates and Crown forced them to bring in a third element, the common people.[26]

The relationship of the *tertius gaudens* can come into play among groups in a number of ways. Two antagonists can benefit a third, as was the case when English labor benefited from factory legislation sponsored by the Tories to curtail the power of liberal manufacturers. The consumer as third party can benefit by the competition of manufacturers. Sometimes in the fight between two antagonists, even a very small third party can be very influential, as in the case of parliamentary parties, or small countries in international relations. The ability to exert a balance of power can accrue in the favor of a third party—for example, England against the divided continent of Europe or the Roman bishop against other bishops. A reconciliation between disparate elements removes the power of the third party, as in the case of hostile craft unions who reconcile their differences and can no longer be exploited by employers. Sometimes the mere stability of a group allows it to benefit from a large variety of disputes between other parties (here Simmel cited the example of the Catholic church).

When the relationship takes the form of *divide et impera*, the third group actively promotes or aggravates discord for its own benefit. The general

---

[23] *Soc. of Simmel*, p. 139.
[24] Ibid., p. 142.
[25] Ibid., pp. 147–150.
[26] Ibid., p. 153.

process entails the systematic isolation of the other parties or their reduction into individual units. The Anglo-Saxon kings scattered the holdings of their feudal lords; George III prohibited the "party principle" and recognized only individual contributions to the Crown; employers may refuse to deal with negotiators drawn from outside the union movement; and a ruler may promote jealousy by creating ranks with differential privileges and prestige, foment suspicion and distrust by using spies and informers, or support the cause of one against another and then turn on the victor. The objective in every case, Simmel concluded, is to atomize one's opponents and render them helpless against one's superior power.

Stratification: Superordination and Subordination

Simmel's theory of domination and social stratification is one of the few great statements about social inequality in the history of sociological theory. One of the sharp differences between Simmel and theorists such as Comte, Spencer, and Durkheim is that he singled out the vast and complicated subject of social stratification for serious analysis. One must go back to Saint-Simon for a comparable appreciation of class structure. However, Simmel's Kantian heritage, which enjoined the mind to shape the data of experience rather than transcend it, freed him of any temptation to rely on a master scheme as Saint-Simon and many others had done. Indeed his Kantian background gave his analysis of social domination a pluralistic-historical cast that is absent from the work of all his predecessors in sociology and again points up the empirical bent of his mind.

Characteristically, Simmel pointed out that even domination is a two-way relationship regardless of how one-sided the relative strengths of the parties. The reciprocity of effects makes domination, even in its harshest form, a societal relationship. Those who are acted upon are never wholly passive. In the relationship between a teacher and a class, a speaker and an audience, or a journalist and the mute multitude, there is an important counterinfluence exerted by those who are acted upon. In the case of domination through law, even the most unilateral legal expressions never lose the character of interaction if only because the ruler is also bound by the law. "The elimination of all independent significance of one of the two interacting parties annuls the very notion of society." [27]

Simmel distinguished two varieties of domination, objective and subjective. Objective domination becomes authority. It can be acquired by an individual who has displayed a personal superiority for objective behavior, or it can be given to an individual in his capacity as an official. Subjective domination, or prestige, is based on subjective factors and can be acquired

[27] Ibid., p. 181f.

only by the magnetic individual. Though Simmel never used this distinction to unify his overall analytical scheme, he was fairly consistent in applying it to his material. He referred to impersonal, rational, and normative
forms of domination, which, of course, are similar to his definition of authority, and to emotional and personal forms of domination, which correspond to his definition of prestige.[28] Strictly speaking, Simmel did not discuss social stratification as such; for the most part, his analysis of domination
was a continuation of his major preoccupation with the forms of interaction,
especially as they were affected by the nature of the group, in terms of both
its internal and external relations. Though Simmel made important conceptual distinctions between such phenomena as group behavior, mass
behavior, and the behavior of associations, he did not systematically employ
these distinctions. This failure gives a sometimes confusing shapelessness to
his work and makes it necessary to order his material in a way that is not
present in his own exposition. Of special importance was his failure to
establish and insist on a distinction between group and stratum. The other
great theorists of social stratification, such as Karl Marx and Max Weber,
focused on the material and value contents of social life and their causal relation to inequality; Simmel, however, sought to discuss the general question
of domination merely as interaction. Though this gives his analysis an air of
unreality, it also allowed him to explore the nuances of domination from a
fresh angle. However, Simmel indiscriminately discussed groups (religious
sects and churches, cities, families, clubs) and strata with no distinction
between caste, estate, and class types. He also discussed the domination of
the group over the individual and vice versa, the group over another group
or groups, and societies over each other without making any careful attempt
to distinguish these forms of domination.

In Simmel, the two types of domination can appear in three different forms:
domination exerted by an individual, by a plurality, or by an objective
force, social or ideal. These forms of domination can be either rational or
emotional, or both—that is, certain types of domination can be based on
both authority and prestige—and each can lead to different results. Superordination under an individual can lead to the unity of a group or groups
either through or against the leader, but on occasion, if an attempt is made
to unify groups that are too disparate, it can also lead to enmity between the
groups. The unification of a society through common subordination can
take two forms: leveling and gradation. The strong ruler can enhance his
position by leveling all subjects beneath him, a process that results in equality for the masses vis-à-vis the former intermediate bodies. The ruler usually
accomplishes this leveling through law, that is, by elaborating the objective
criteria that establish the relation between the ruler and the rest of the

---

[28] Simmel's forms of domination correspond quite closely to Max Weber's distinction between class and status types of social stratification and rational-legal and
charismatic forms of domination.

population. Since other aspects of the personality are not engaged in the political relationship, despotism or absolutism can lead to a large measure of equality and individual liberty. Domination under an individual can also take place through gradation, through either downward gradation or upward gradation, or a mixture of both. As opposed to domination through leveling, gradation tends to order a population into hierarchical relations. The major distinction implied between leveling and gradation is that between absolute and feudal monarchy.

The second form of domination is based on the superordination of a plurality over individuals or groups. The results for the subordinate vary considerably. An impersonal plurality may be more just and objective than an individual ruler, as in the case of slaves of the state or employees of a large corporation, or it may be irresponsible and callous, since it reduces individual responsibility and tends to neglect personal considerations. Large pluralities may be more just than small ones, as in the case of British rule in India as opposed to rule by the East India Company, or they may be more vindictive or exploitative.

Individuals facing domination by a divided plurality may suffer severe conflict, especially if the claims made upon them are absolute and cannot be compartmentalized. The claims of God and Caesar, for example, can both engage the personality and cause severe psychic damage. However, subordination under a divided plurality may have beneficial results for the individual, sometimes removing subordination altogether. This is true when the idea of the *tertius gaudens* enters the domination relationship. The individual under a plurality of opposed masters can play one against the other. The same applies to group relations, as in the case of the English commons vis-à-vis the Crown and nobility. The growth of diversity or pluralism may lead to the growth of freedom just as the growth of monistic despotism may lead to equality. When there is contact between the top and bottom of a stratification structure, said Simmel, the individual faces an opposed but graded plurality and becomes the object of attention of the ruler who is in opposition to the aristocracy; here Simmel was referring to the frequent historical phenomenon of Caesarism. When the graded plurality is rigidly articulated and there is no contact between top and bottom, or the top must reach the bottom through the middle, there is a downward pressure that results in the exploitation of the masses. Simmel's analysis, it will be noticed, is very similar to his previous discussion of domination through leveling and gradation.

Simmel included a semihistorical treatment of the emergence of objectivity in family, economy, justice, morality, and ethics, which, while tantalizing in its suggestiveness, never went so far as to construct stages of social development or even social types. First, Simmel said, society produces a set of norms to fulfill its own needs (and he referred to a well-known theory about the social origin of norms—in all probability a reference to Durkheim). These norms eventually become a set of superindividual and supersocial norms that exercise absolute authority. In the same way, the relations between superordinates and subordinates undergo a historical development in which personal domination is replaced by impersonal domination. For example, the power of the father is transformed when his will is replaced by the norms of the idealized family. In the economic realm a similar process occurs when personal economic relations are replaced by an impersonal economy, which bends everything to its technical requirements. This analysis is Simmel's closest approach to a theory of social development or of social types.

Role Theory and Degrees of Domination and Freedom

There are degrees of domination, especially in relation to freedom, and freedom, like a coin, has two sides. One side is a process of liberation from subordination, but on the other side there is a gain in domination over some other group or individual. As such, freedom is relative to given conditions and group structures, and in the struggle for freedom the most interesting variety of combinations is possible. A struggle for freedom may see enemies combine for a purpose, only to struggle for dominance once their common purpose is accomplished, as for example, the alliance between the middle class and the masses against the kings and the feudality in England, France, and Germany. The demand for freedom by a church, guild, or city or state government may be a screen behind which the leaders of the group seek to dominate and exploit its members. Sometimes freedom may be granted to individuals in order to dominate the masses more effectively by depriving them of leadership, as when exceptional individuals from subjugated races are deemed equals or when individuals from the working class are promoted.[29]

Simmel briefly noted the sociological error of socialism and anarchism, both of which want the general social organization to be based on the coordination and not the supersubordination of individuals.

> The reasons *usually* advanced against this possibility are not at issue here.... No measure, it is argued, can eliminate natural differences among men, nor can any measure eliminate the expression of these differences through some upward-downward arrangement of commanding and obeying elements. The technique of civilized labor requires for its perfection a hierarchical

[29] On the whole, Simmel does not discuss domination in terms of its social functions except to say generally that forms of domination lead to unity. In this example of social mobility, however, he shows how the rebel against authority, by succeeding as an individual, serves to maintain authority; see especially *Soc. of Simmel*, p. 281f.

structure of society, "one mind for a thousand hands," a system of leaders and executors.[30]

In addition, there is inevitably a surplus of qualified individuals beyond the number of available superordinate positions.[31] In short, freedom and the recognition of individual merit are intrinsically related to domination and inequality. This issue led Simmel to perhaps his most valuable insight about the nature of domination and stratification, an insight he developed as part of his argument against socialism. The accommodation between the antinomy presented by liberty and equality is based on the capacity of the personality to "decompose" itself, that is to compartmentalize its activities. It is possible, he argued, to develop types of subordination that do not involve degradation. This is especially true of subordination to an objective force, as in the modern impersonal economy or army. Individuals may submit to the discipline of both structures with only part of their egos. Another interaction involving domination without degradation occurs when an individual is superior in one capacity but inferior in another, as in groups with an elected leader. Here Simmel expanded his insight into the operation and stability of stratified democracies. Citizens may be rigidly subordinate to law, and yet they elect the lawmakers. Simmel cited other examples of the unity that is possible through the "interlacing of alternating superordinations and subordinations," such as the relation between the Anglican church and Parliament, husband and wife, and the Puritan who is an obedient soldier in Cromwell's army but delivers the sermon to officers and men on Sunday. He concluded that this societal form has favorable results because "the sphere within which one social element is superordinate is very precisely and clearly separated from those spheres in which the other element is superordinate." [32]

Simmel's insight into the flexibility of the human personality, combined with his discussion of "outvoting," [33] or the problem of evoking a common will through voting procedures, produced a valuable insight into the functional operation of complex societies. Simmel saw the phenomenon of voting as essentially a mechanism to accommodate the individual to society and to bring unity out of diversity. The forms it takes are varied: if voting requires unanimity, the minority victimizes the majority; if majority rule prevails, the majority may dominate the minority. The difficulty with both positions, said Simmel, stems from the basic dilemma of human existence that requires the individual to coexist with others, thereby running the risk of having his or her individuality controlled from the outside.

[30] Ibid., p. 282.
[31] Ibid., pp. 300–303.
[32] Ibid., p. 289.
[33] Ibid., pp. 239–249.

Conflict as Interaction

One of the more important of Simmel's many legacies to modern sociology was his view of conflict as a form of interaction. He said that conflict in some form is an intrinsic and functionally necessary part of social life, and not necessarily antisocial. Further, diversity and change, which usually accompany conflict, are not opposed to unity and stability. These are ideas that grate against the substantialistic presuppositions of Western intellectual and moral culture. Simmel, of course, did not pioneer the reinterpretation of conflict. The problem of change and conflict had received considerable attention from modern social theorists, especially from the eighteenth century on. Many of the major battle lines of nineteenth-century intellectual life were drawn in terms of differences between rival interpretations of conflict. On the one hand stand Hegel and Marx, with their view that history results from the dialectical development of opposites; on the other hand stand Maistre and Bonald, with their search for unity and harmony and their hatred of conflict and change. Standing in the middle is sociology, with its various views of conflict. Saint-Simon gave class conflict a positive historical function, while Comte found it a threat to unity. Spencer saw in the competitive clash of individuals a great force for progress, as did most of the social Darwinists, but social Darwinism as well as Marxism saw stability as the goal of history. Conflict through diversity was merely a means of reaching a stage of repose.

Durkheim altered this tradition by declaring quite flatly that social unity is served by both the homogeneity and the heterogeneity of its constituent elements. For Durkheim, social diversity led to unity; the conflicts that attend diversity were for him transitional phenomena. However, while Durkheim saw positive social functions served by such deviant behavior as crime and suicide, his overriding concern was with stability as an absence of conflict. He nevertheless served to divorce the idea of diversity from conflict and to increase its respectability.

Simmel's great contribution was to go beyond Durkheim and the general tradition of Western social theory by examining conflict in its plural manifestations as positively contributing to social functions. If conflict is seen as a positive phenomenon, Simmel argued, then all social phenomena change their character. The assumption that relationships contain either a positive or a negative contribution to unity must be avoided:

> Concord, harmony, co-efficacy, which are unquestionably held to be socializing forces, must nevertheless be interspersed with distance, competition, repulsion, in order to yield the actual configuration of society. The solid, organizational forms which seem to constitute or create society, must constantly be disturbed, disbalanced, gnawed-at by individualistic, irregular forces, in order to gain

their vital reaction and development through submission and resistance. Intimate relations, whose formal medium is physical and
psychological nearness, lose the attractiveness, even the content
of their intimacy, as soon as the close relationship does not also
contain, simultaneously and alternatingly, distances and inter-
missions.[34]

Simmel developed the concept of conflict partly because of his belief that
the individual exists apart from society. The dualism of individual and
society, according to Simmel, is irreconcilable and a chronic source of tension and conflict. The main problem is that society attempts to impose its
claims on individuals, who in turn are trying to round out their own existence
according to their own needs. Simmel also talked about the individual's
inborn need for love, hating and fighting, and accentuation, all of which
have a relation to conflict.

Simmel also used the idea of conflict to refer to the type of interaction that
helps to shape both the individual and society. If conflict is not necessarily
an antisocial phenomenon, in what specific ways does it serve social functions? For individuals, conflict may help to stabilize, concentrate, and purify
their personalities. For the internal relations of a group or even of a total
society, conflict may lead to greater unity and centralization and to the
formation of new unities or groups. When it takes the form of competition,
conflict may socialize and civilize individuals by making them aware of
others and of the rules that make coexistence and conflict possible. Thus
competition or conflict may simultaneously serve social and personal functions.[35]

So far the functions served by conflict are more or less conventional. Of
more importance is Simmel's insight into how conflict promotes social adaptation. The existence of conflict may reveal the need to adjust to new conditions and create new power relations. Simmel's views about conflict in this
connection, though fleeting, reveal a deep insight into the nature of social
change and liberal democracy. Latent hostilities may lie undetected within
an imposed unity until new conditions bring them to the fore to wreak their
destruction. Furthermore, there are different ways of institutionalizing
hostility to preserve the group. These are all just hints, but they do suggest
that institutionalized conflict helps a social structure adjust to new conditions and forge new power relations, and thereby move to new levels of
unity. Change, then, may be thought of as intrinsically related to stability

---

[34] Ibid., p. 315; for further references to Simmel's new view of conflict, see pp.
15f., 16f., 20–25, 29, 107f.
[35] *Conflict*, pp. 60–107.   The fact that conflict presupposes a consensus on rules is
stated by Simmel on pp. 25–28, 34–38 in a way that suggests Durkheim's emphasis
on the noncontractual elements in society.

and not necessarily opposed to it. Simmel suggested that perhaps vast reservoirs of grievances and resentments lie beneath the fragile surface of society, ready to erupt destructively for want of sufficient outlets via institutionalized channels.[36]

These insights, combined with Simmel's role theory and belief in the flexibility of the human personality, offer a deep insight into the overall dynamics of social structure. Simmel's basic idea is that the interaction that produces change involves only parts of the personality. Thus, serious lags and splits can occur within the personality, and different sections of a population, each with its own special interaction, may change at different rates. Consequently, there may be blind or unintended social change because one hand does not know what the other is doing.

Role Theory and Multiple Statuses

In "The Web of Group Affiliations," [37] Simmel extended his contribution to role theory by drawing attention to the importance of multiple statuses. This contribution is continuous with his general orientation and needs no great elaboration. Despite a real but perhaps intended disorderliness and disregard for system, Simmel's work, if not unified, does reveal unities. It is informed everywhere by an acute empirical sense that should be seen as a sensitivity for nuance, paradox, and complexity rather than as a search for lawful behavior among particulars. Simmel's sense of the infinitely complex nature of human behavior made him aware that the individual personality does not exist in isolation but in large part reflects the interaction patterns in which individuals find themselves. The empirical-historical bent of Simmel's mind allowed him to see the variety of these patterns and led him to focus on multiple statuses. His most complete statement on the implications of multiple statuses is in "The Web of Group Affiliations," where he developed the idea of status; multiple statuses and the different possible criteria of status; the logic of status combinations; the relation between personality enrichment, individualization, and the statuses offered to an individual; and the possible confusions and conflicts that multiple-group participation may entail. The remainder of his essay is largely devoted to a discussion of how modern society, unlike all previous societies, provides the individual with many possible group memberships, most of which engage only parts of his personality. Through this process, according to Simmel, not only is the personality enriched but a new type of unity develops based on rationality and diversity. Thus Simmel provided yet another insight into the functional viability of diversity, a viability that benefits the individual as well as society.

---

[36] For all these hints, see *Conflict*, pp. 37ff., 49, 64–67, 84f., 91f., 98–103, 193f.
[37] *Conflict*, pp. 125–195.

CONCLUSION

Simmel and the Development of Pluralistic Positivism

Simmel's sociological theory was an important and influential contribution to the revolutionary redefinition of sociology that occurred in the late nineteenth century. On the methodological level, his work helped to revive aspects of the Enlightenment that had been neglected by French, English, and American naturalistic positivism. Though the Enlightenment inaugurated the Age of Empiricism with its revolutionary assumption that the human mind was capable of deciphering the phenomenal world directly, it still insisted on the need to obtain rational knowledge. Thus, it asserted the autonomy and creativity of reason, stressing the need for an interplay between concept and fact. This emphasis on the active nature of the mind was slowly forgotten by naturalistic positivism. Simmel's primary methodological contribution to sociology was to reassert the autonomously creative function of the mind as against the more passive definition that had gained dominance in Anglo-American and French sociology. By adapting Kant to the study of society, Simmel was declaring that the social scientist is no mere spectator of human behavior. Since there is no underlying substantive principle upon which behavior is founded, the mind can see, and does see, only in terms of the categories it introduces into experience. To do this consciously, argued Simmel, is central to sociology.

Simmel was not substituting philosophical discourse for empirical investigation. On the contrary, he made a profound contribution to the development of a genuine empirical methodology in sociology by developing a special brand of empiricism. The deep empirical bent of his mind enjoined him to ferret out the significance of the commonplace, to delve into the empirically obvious in order to reveal its complexities, paradoxes, and singularities, and above all to search for relationships and consequences and not for substances. Just as the mind is defined by its relationship to its subject matter, so individuals are defined by their relationship to others. Social relationships, the myriad forms of association, are the structure of society and thus the subject matter of sociology. Through this focus, Simmel unveiled aspects of society that had been hidden by the deductive impatience of early sociology. Far more than Comte or Spencer and even more than Durkheim, Simmel shunned the search for the one principle that could explain human destiny. As such his work stood as a corrective to the deeply deductive and abstract nature of much of naturalistic positivism.

In many ways, however, Durkheim and Simmel were similar. They both agreed that one knows a phenomenon, including human behavior, only in terms of functional relationships between determinate things. Both saw society in most of human behavior including seemingly nonsocial behavior, Durkheim seeing it in such occurences as crime and suicide and Simmel in loneliness, conflict, and trivial conversation. Finally, both saw the positive social functions served by these phenomena. However, Durkheim looked for the relationship between behavior and the collective conscience (culture), as well as the relationship between behavior and interaction, all within a total sociocultural conceptual framework; Simmel on the other hand, focused on interaction among individuals and groups independent of content (or culture) and without placing his analysis in the context of clearly conceptualized social-system types.

Simmel's single-minded focus on interaction was a major contribution to the development of modern sociology's analytical distinction among society, culture, and personality. More than anyone else Simmel helped to establish the view that society is a structure of reciprocal relations that exist and function independent of psychology and culture. By shifting attention from the larger social structures of state, church, and economy to the almost infinite number of lesser social structures that support the larger ones and are so important to personality development, Simmel significantly extended the range and accuracy of sociological analysis. In so doing, he provided sociology with a host of analytical leads and insights that had considerable influence on the development of sociology. Simmel's thought was effectively established, for example, at the University of Chicago, which had the foremost American sociology department during the first third of the twentieth century, because of the interest in his work by Albion Small (1854–1926) and Robert E. Park (1864–1944). His thought undoubtedly influenced the development of a number of important American perspectives and interests such as symbolic interactionism, exchange theory, small-group analysis, and role theory.[38]

This is not to say that Simmel neglected the larger structures of society. Less well known than his other work but perhaps of greater importance was the sociology of power that emerged from his study of the relations between groups and the relations of domination. It was here that Simmel directed attention to large-scale trends and factors in social causation, the ironies of the historical drama that make a unified theory of either society or power so difficult, and the way in which a variety of structures and processes can serve similar personal and social functions.

Despite these substantial contributions to the development of pluralistic sociocultural positivism, Simmel's sociology contains serious shortcomings. Though he had a dramatic sense of the paradoxes and ironies in social interaction, his sociology is curiously bloodless. Simmel was in his personal life

[38] For a discussion of Simmel's influence on sociology, see the introduction to Donald N. Levine, ed. *Georg Simmel: On Individuality and Social Forms: Selected Writings* (Chicago: University of Chicago Press, 1971), pp. xliii–lxi. For a fuller discussion of Simmel's impact on American sociology, see Donald N. Levine, Ellwood B. Carter, and Eleanor Miller Gorwan, "Simmel's Influence on American Sociology: I–II," *American Journal of Sociology* 81 (January, March 1976):813–845, 1112–1132.

a sensitive and refined gentleman in the best European tradition, yet his writings, despite their subdued zest for life and colorful illustrations, are oddly detached—unengaged, as the French would say. While scientifically valuable, Simmel's detachment also led to his greatest defect, the abstractness that characterizes so much of his work. Though in practice he always dealt with the norms and values that spark and direct interaction, his indifference to content was perhaps his chief shortcoming. His backhanded way of analyzing values means that there could be no systematic treatment of the functional consequences for behavior of specific ideas, values, and idea-value complexes. Simmel's isolation of interaction as the focus of sociology was an important contribution to sociology, but the fact remains that he tried to treat interaction in a vacuum; Durkheim was on sounder ground here. Simmel was also defective in causal analysis except insofar as he pointed out the determination of behavior by the factor of number and the autonomous interaction form. By neglecting the normative and material structures that animate human behavior and by not emphasizing the origin of norms in interaction, Simmel was again outmatched by Durkheim. Even Simmel's profound contribution to the sociology of power suffered by his failure to go beyond the factor of number. Though he was forced to include some nonquantitative factors, his analysis badly needed a sociology of interests and ideas to supplement the focus on number. Even his grasp of the conflicts and congruences that emerge from the interplay of interests and ideas in no way matched the analytical rigor or historical sense of Aristotle, Montesquieu, Marx, or Max Weber, though his insight into the art of acquiring and maintaining political power ranks with that found in Machiavelli's *The Prince* (1513) and in Aristotle's *Politics*.[39]

Without a cultural orientation, no theorist is likely to conceive of social interaction as a system of behavior structures that derives its impetus from a determinant value system; one is much more likely to view interaction as personal in origin and personal in purpose. It is not surprising, therefore, that the orientation of much of Simmel's sociology was heavily psychological, psychological in the sense that social interaction is thought to arise from the inborn needs of the psyche. Again and again, Simmel reduced society to the forms produced by the innate promptings of the individual, even asserting that inequality comes as much from individual differences as from social need. Here again Durkheim, who sharply separated sociology from psychology, had the surer vision.

Simmel as a Liberal Ideologist

The authentic mark of seventeenth-century liberal social thought was the belief in the existence of a nonsocial individual, and it is this belief that

[39] See Book V: "Causes of Revolution and Constitutional Change," *The Politics of Aristotle,* trans. Ernest Barker (London: Oxford University Press, 1946).

constitutes one aspect of Simmel's liberalism. However, Simmel was a liberal in another sense—his interest in showing the social and historical determination of individual behavior. In this sense he is also in the tradition of nineteenth-century late liberalism, a tradition that combined the idea that individuals have substantive identities of their own with the idea that the individual's identity is expressible only in terms of social situations or interaction with others. Viewed from this perspective, Simmel's distinctive insights into the nature of society may also be interpreted as a defense of the complex industrial society of the nineteenth century. A basic feature of liberal thought is that there is a never-ending tension between the rights and claims of the individual and those of society. In the seventeenth century this tension existed between the individual and the state; in the nineteenth century it included civil society as well. Awareness of tension is found throughout Simmel's work, signifying his acceptance of as well as his contribution to the analytical framework of late liberalism. However, lest such a tension be interpreted as a need for social reconstruction, liberal theorists, Simmel among them, also pointed out that the claims of society can be beneficial to the individual. For Simmel, the various forms of interaction gave the individual emotional and intellectual statisfactions and at the same time shaped and stabilized the personality. Indeed, like Durkheim, Simmel pointed out that the individual finds increased opportunities for individualism in a society with a rich multiplicity of interaction patterns. Again reminiscent of Durkheim, Simmel pointed out that the heterogeneous society finds stability and adjustment in its very diversity. Even social phenomena such as conflict and domination, which to the naive mind suggest social deficiency, were extremely functional for Simmel because of the capacity of the personality to decompose itself. It is almost as if Simmel were arguing that the integration of society is based on the nonintegration of its members. Like Durkheim, Simmel left behind the early-liberal ideal of the integrated individual in his effort to see social functions in diversity and conflict. Finally, like Durkheim, he gave a fresh impetus to the tradition that runs throughout sociological theory, the sociology of error and evil. This outlook, which prompted Simmel to see positive functions for ignorance, deceit, and the emotions, is a measure of the advance made by empiricism over rationalism and is heavily emphasized in sociology from the late nineteenth century on. It is very curious that living in Imperial Germany, with its severe social cleavages and its authoritarian structure posed precariously over deep religious and class antagonisms, Simmel could find so little to say about the dysfunctional aspects of social interaction.

Simmel's work, while a brilliant analysis of the associational society that had emerged in the nineteenth century, was also a subtle identification of that society with the substantive needs of all individuals and all societies. Because it was a social structure that had achieved the fullest development of sociational forms, Simmel mistook it for the structure that best expressed the needs of human existence. He took the interaction and the values of liberal society as the elemental urgings of an innate personality instead of seeing them as the source and molder of personality. Despite his insight into the diverse content manifested by identical forms and the diverse forms taken by identical content,[40] Simmel made no systematic effort to divorce the functions served by forms of interaction from the content they embodied. The result was an identification of the needs of the individual and society with the content or values of liberal society. Almost without qualification he accepted the presuppositions of liberal society as the organizing categories with which to analyze human behavior. His preference for the rational, impersonal, *Gesellschaft* social structure is evident throughout his work. His acceptance of the fundamental liberal dichotomy between freedom and equality is also evident and finds expression in his derogation of the mass and of socialism. However, his contrasts never became a systematic search for social types, for the logic, principles, or value complexes that differentiate social systems, though he related in an isolated passage that "every historical group is an individual." [41] To have done so might have reduced the associational social structure itself to a "historical individual," thus necessitating a re-examination of its fundamental assumptions. To have done so would have meant the introduction into sociology of a truly historical point of view in which the thinker subjects society to a searching examination in the light of the full range of human experience. Simmel disregarded his own insight that human experience could be enormously enriched and augmented through the manipulation of interactional patterns, and its implied emancipation of human beings from naturalistic and perhaps historical determination; he disregarded his own Kantian imperative that experience takes shape only through the activity of mind. He allowed the categories of liberal society to control his thought. His excursion into historicism and utilitarian and relational philosophy succumbed to a substantialist positivism in the end because he allowed himself to become a passive describer of a society whose individuals and social processes he conceived as a substantive spectacle.

Simmel's contribution to pluralistic positivism lay in his reorientation of empiricism away from a search for the whole to a search for the particular. He also helped to readjust the philosophy of the Enlightenment to the needs of industrial capitalism. He continued the Enlightenment's concept of mind as an active instrument in the acquisition of knowledge. In emphasizing and developing the role of subjectivity in scientific method, he made the perspective of the Enlightenment more historical but not less substantialist. He was unable to reduce all cognition to a process whereby the mind engages in an instrumental grappling and shaping of experience. He could never bring himself to see that the forms of interaction that make up the structure

[40] *Soc. of Simmel,* p. 22.
[41] Ibid., p. 257.

of behavior might simply be the temporal patterning of behavior in terms
of historical values. The Enlightenment assumed an order of nature; therefore, if the mind is shaped by nature, the result is truth. However if there
is no natural, objective order, then the mind is subject to the historical
categories it inherits. If this happens without its awareness, then the mind
is adrift, and all this because of (not despite) its efforts to live up to the
criteria of science. If society and the individual are functions of situations
and conditions, then the mind too is a function of experience and the only
escape from historical determination is through the adoption of an open-
ended historical positivism or historical-functional point of view. Instead of
exploring this tack, Simmel reified his concepts about the behavior structures of liberal society and thus constructed his own brand of liberal substantialism. Both Simmel and Durkheim argued against naive empiricism
and idealism and both enlarged the horizon of sociology through their
identification of the sociocultural realm, in each case helping to make the
interplay between mind and data more fruitful and creative. Eventually,
however, they both succumbed to experience, Durkheim by identifying
liberal society with nature and Simmel by identifying it with the human
nature.

Chapter 16
Vilfredo Pareto (1848–1923)

The rejection of a priori thought structures, which is a common feature of pluralistic positivism, is nowhere more evident than in the work of the Italian sociologist and economist Vilfredo Pareto. Durkheim and Simmel each developed a distinctive brand of empiricism as against the a priori monisms of early sociological theory; in Pareto, there is still another variation in the developing empirical outlook. Philosophically, Pareto is an heir of David Hume, though Hume's name is nowhere to be found in Pareto's major sociological work.[1] Nevertheless, the structure of Pareto's sociology rests on the Humian distinction between fact, reason, and value as separate and nonconnectable aspects of reality and on the belief that the mind can establish no causal relationships between facts but only relationships of probability. Pareto's contribution to pluralistic positivism lies in his radical application of this philosophical position to the study of human behavior. At the heart of his approach is the assumption that there is an unbridgeable gap between theories based exclusively on facts or experience and theories based on metaphysical principles, logic, ethics, religion, and the like. In his emphasis on the sovereignty of fact, a sovereignty unqualified even by the existence of causal laws, Pareto is a pioneer contributor to the twentieth-century school of logical positivism. Pareto's special contribution to pluralistic positivism is his emphasis on the sovereignty and complexity of facts, on the worthlessness of all superexperiential or monocausal explanations, and on the need to build theory carefully from fact in a series of "successive approximations." In his investigation of human behavior, Pareto came to

---

[1] *Trattato di Sociologia Generale*, 1st ed., 2 vols. (Florence, 1916); English title, *The Mind and Society*, ed. A. Livingston, trans. A. Bongiorno and A. Livingston, 4 vols. (New York: Harcourt Brace Jovanovich, 1935); also a Dover paperback, 2 vols. A selection of readings from *Mind and Society* with an introductory essay has been prepared by Joseph Lopreato, *Vilfredo Pareto* (New York: Thomas Y. Crowell paperback, 1965). Another collection of various writings by Pareto, together with an introductory essay, has been prepared by S. E. Finer, *Vilfredo Pareto: Sociological Writings* (New York: Frederick A. Praeger paperback, 1966), trans. Derick Mirfin. A collection of essays on Pareto's life and work has been edited by James H. Meisel, *Pareto and Mosca* (Englewood Cliffs, N.J.: Prentice-Hall paperback, 1965).

the conclusion that an overwhelming proportion of human action is non-rational. By examining human beliefs, values, and actions according to what he called the *logico-experimental method*, in which reason is defined in terms of means-ends relationships, Pareto helped enormously to open up the scientific study of nonrational human behavior. His assumption that non-logical behavior is not only lawful and thus subject to scientific scrutiny, but also socially functional constitutes his unique contribution to socio-cultural positivism.

PHILOSOPHY AND METHOD

The student who undertakes to read the *Mind and Society* faces an exciting but exasperating experience. It is undoubtedly the work of an original and creative mind that, by sheer piledriving persistence, detached itself from some of the familiar paths of Western social thought. Pareto was a debunker of the first rank, a twentieth-century Bayle who delighted in cataloguing the errors of others, and he achieved a detachment and perspective unique to sociological literature. However, he has other traits that make him difficult to read or appreciate; he is long-winded, pedantic, desultory, and often arrogant.

The Logico-Experimental Method

The heart of Pareto's approach is his logico-experimental method. The out-pourings of the human mind can be divided into two types, each with its own criterion for truth.

> The standard of truth for propositions of the first class lies in ex-perience and observation only. The standard of truth for the second class lies outside objective experience—in some divine revelation; in concepts that the human mind finds in itself, as some say, without the aid of objective experience; in the universal con-sensus of mankind, and so on.[2]

By distinguishing between the logico-experimental and the nonlogical-experimental, Pareto struck a line between positive and metaphysical knowl-edge in a manner reminiscent of early sociology. The line he drew, however, was far more radically nominalistic. His search was not for essences or principles, but for factual uniformities. His position is quite different from the Kantian orientation found in Simmel, which assumed that the mind

---

[2] *Mind and Society,* 16 (in accord with Pareto's custom, references to *Mind and Society* are by paragraph number).

Vilfredo Pareto (1848–1923)

plays an active, creative role in the formation of knowledge. The role of the mind is radically depreciated by Pareto's fundamental assumption that it is totally dependent on pre-existing factual uniformities.

Though Pareto occasionally suggested that the mind plays at least an instrumental or operational role in the formation of knowledge, he conducted his investigations under the assumption that knowledge is not created but exists for the mind to find. Basically, science is a cumulative body of knowledge that develops through a process of "successive approximations." Starting with vague concepts, it becomes increasingly more precise about the factual realm. Inquiry into social behavior, therefore, is contingent and relative, and results are more or less probable. Though Pareto claimed, somewhat offhandedly, that sociology is the synthesis of all the social sciences, he did not consider his own work as a synthesis or as a unified, general theory, but rather as a scientific first approximation, a theory about society in general.

Given his respect for facts, it is not surprising that Pareto had a passion for precision. In words that any semanticist would approve, he mounted a strong warning against the distortion implicit in the use of language. He regarded the quantitative expression of reality as the goal of all the sciences, and he clearly separated analysis from synthesis, identifying the former with the logico-experimental method and the latter with metaphysics.

Pareto believed that scrupulous attention to his procedures would uncover the uniformities underlying behavior. However, these uniformities imply no necessity, no cause and effect, no "must" or "ought," no certainty; they are strictly probabilities. It follows, of course, that if the mind can discover no certainty, no necessary sequence of events, then it cannot enjoin necessary behavior. The realm of moral necessity, the "ought" as opposed to the "is," disappears. There is no necessary connection between the true and the good, or, in Pareto's words, there is no necessary connection between the truth, or the logico-experimental validity of a belief or action, and its utility for social life.

The Concepts of Interdependence, System, and Equilibrium

Of course no scientist can dispense with the idea of causation altogether— in one way or another, one must assume that causation takes place. Pareto's rejection of cause-effect relationships was intended mainly as an attack against philosophical absolutism. In its place he introduced the concept of multiple causation and the related ideas of *interdependence, system,* and *equilibrium.*

In mechanics—and Pareto was careful to point out that he was developing an analogy not an identity—one speaks of forces acting on a point in terms of time. In sociology, one should also specify the forces influencing a social or economic situation and describe their effect in terms of the concept of *equilibrium,* the state they reach when they have spent themselves or are at rest through counterbalancing. The equilibrium is composed of *ties* (bond, condition, correlation, and so forth) as distinguished from active influences or *forces.* A social group, said Pareto, can be compared to a mechanical *system;* it results from all the forces and ties (dynamics and statics). Taken together, ties and forces can be called *conditions,* and at any given time the state of the system is determined by its conditions. It undergoes a change to a new state only through a change in conditions. Determinism, however, cannot be assumed a priori but must be demonstrated within the limits of the space and time being investigated.

There are two different types of movements, *real* and *virtual*. Real movement is the empirical movement that really takes place; virtual movement takes place when for theoretical purposes a condition is assumed to be different from what it is. Virtual movement should be used with extreme caution, Pareto warned, since social phenomena are extremely complex and are never independent. Not only are conditions in a state of mutual influence, but even the effects of conditions act back and influence the conditions. Therefore, one must think of all the facts of society, both conditions and their effects, as being in a state of *interdependence*, with changes in one affecting one or more of the others with varying degrees of intensity. The use of virtual movements in scientific work is dangerous because one cannot trace all the causal ramifications of a hypothesis, especially when dealing with the past; one cannot ask what would have happened if such and such had occurred because no knowledge is possible on that basis. Knowledge is possible only after the fact. Experience, in short, precedes knowledge. Even further, by divorcing knowledge from utility or practicality, Pareto eliminated the capacity of reason to transcend experience as well as to shape and control experience. The sole function of reason and sociology is to investigate and describe the "is." As such, Pareto's methodology is in the tradition of naturalistic positivism, being quite similar to that of his contemporary, William Graham Sumner.

SUBSTANTIVE WORK

Despite the verbose and chaotic way in which Pareto developed his substantive theory, his master work contains a definite structure. Central to his analysis is a classification of theories into two types, those in accord and not in accord with experience. In addition, theories can be classified in terms of their subjective origin in individuals and their subjective appeal to individuals. Finally, theories can be considered with reference to their utility, a matter quite separate from their validity.[3]

Pareto's reference to subjectivity did not denote an interest in meaning as a causal factor. Such an approach would imply that beliefs and values have major causal significance and would require special methodological attention. Pareto in no way employed the method of understanding (the *verstehen* tradition in German social science) started by his countryman Vico, whose work he castigated. When Pareto focused on subjectivity,

[3] *Mind and Society*, 13, 14.

it was not to show the power of culture in shaping society, but to argue that individuals respond to a variety of fictitious beliefs and values in accordance with their intrinsic dispositions. It is not culture that shapes society, but the differing propensities and capacities of individuals. Pareto's intention, therefore, was to analyze the theories by which human beings live in order to reveal the fundamental dispositions in human nature.

Residues and Derivations

Pareto's investigation of theories and behavior was guided by one standard, the conformity of a belief or action to experimental truth. Though individuals invariably believe all their actions are logical or efficacious, "from the standpoint of other persons who have a more extensive knowledge," most actions are nonlogical.

Though Pareto's analysis is ostensibly inductive, it varies considerably from contemporary empirical standards. He never investigated facts first-hand, nor did he use the firsthand investigations of others. He relied mostly on his library and contemporary newspapers for his facts. Moreover, his disavowal of a priori concepts was not honored in his own work. At the outset he introduced all the major ideas and results of his theory, all of which bore only the most tenuous relationship to the facts he recited. The prevalence of nonlogical elements in human actions; the distinction between the two major tendencies in human action, innovation and persistence; the existence of constant and variable elements in human behavior; and elites as a permanent feature of human society—were all introduced in the second chapter.

Starting with a survey of proverbs, maxims, magical beliefs and practices, and witchcraft, Pareto quickly established that nonlogical forms of behavior are far more prevalent than logical forms. Since the nonlogical usually has a logical exterior, one must be careful to probe beneath the surface of statements. Accordingly, he conducted a long and critical examination of almost every major intellectual position in Western culture. These pages defy summary. He unleashed a devastating assault on the metaphysical masks that hide nonlogical actions. Here every form of substantialism, from ancient Greece to the present, is analyzed and demolished. Included in the onslaught are Plato, Aristotle, Cicero, Saint Augustine, Saint Thomas, Descartes, Spinoza, the philosophes, and many others. No one escaped his fury. Natural law was a particularly choice target for his wrath. "A glance at history," he related, " . . . is enough to show that natural law is just a rubber band: the powerful can stretch it to whatever length they choose." [4] The same applies to all intellectual positions—they

---

[4] Ibid., 1689.

are merely ideologies, rationalizations, "pleasing fictions," or, more technically, *derivations*. Referring to accord with metaphysical entities, he said:

> This derivation figures in all reasonings that appeal to "Reason," "Right Reason," "Nature," "the goal of mankind," (or other such goals), "Welfare," "the Highest Good," "Justice," "Truth," "Goodness," and, in our day more particularly, "Science," Democracy," "Solidarity," "Humanity," and the like. Those are all names that designate nothing more than indistinct and incoherent sentiments.[5]

Having completed his "inductive" survey, Pareto announced his major findings. All theories or derivatives have two elements, *residues* and *derivations*, both of which have their source in sentiments and instincts. The residues are the overt manifestations of basic human sentiments, and the derivations are the verbal manifestations of the same sentiments. It is important, however, not to attribute objective existence to residues, derivations, or even sentiments; implicit in this warning is Pareto's general assumption that science deals with concrete events, with manifestations not substances.[6]

Pareto outlined six general classes of residues: [7]

I. Instinct For Combinations.

II. Group-Persistences (Persistence Of Aggregates).

III. Need Of Expressing Sentiments By External Acts (Activity, Self-Expression).

IV. Residues Connected With Sociality.

V. Integrity Of The Individual And His Appurtenances.

VI. The Sex Residue.

In an earlier passage, Pareto had cautioned that to complete the list of forces that shape society, one must include "simple appetites, tastes, inclinations, and in social relationships that very important class called 'interests.'" To the extent that appetites and interests emerge as nonlogical theories or actions, they fall into the above list of residues. The sexual appetite, for example, becomes a separate category altogether. Interests, by

---

[5] Ibid., 1513.
[6] Pareto does not define residues and derivations very clearly nor their relation to sentiments and instincts. One must extract what he means from a number of different paragraphs, the most relevant of which are 850, 868, 870, 875, 1689, 1690.
[7] *Mind and Society*, 888.

which Pareto meant economic activity, fall into Class V, the integrity of the individual and his appurtenances. Pareto said, however, that "they are of such great intrinsic importance in the social equilibrium that they are best considered apart from residues." The reason for this is that, while interests can become nonlogical, they represent the one area in social science that, with minor exceptions, has achieved a logico-experimental status.

The various types of residues are self-explanatory. Class I refers to the human instinct to combine things. As the translator points out, the original Italian term might also be translated as "inventive faculty," "ingeniousness," "originality," and "imagination." Class II, group-persistences, refers to the sentiment that conserves or consolidates. It is analogous to "mechanical inertia: it tends to resist the movement imparted by other instincts." These first two classes of instincts or sentiments represent the innovational and customary in human affairs and are by far the most important in establishing the social equilibrium. Though Pareto discussed classes III, IV, V, and VI, he eventually discarded them when he constructed his general theory of society.

Pareto devoted less attention to derivations. He reiterated, though, that derivations receive their force from sentiments; that they are sophistical arguments that purport to validate the sentiments; that they are surface indications of the main forces that determine the structure of society; and that the same residue may have many different derivations attached to it.

The Elite and Class Circulation

Pareto next examined residues with reference to their intensity, distribution among individuals, and variation in time. He warned one must be careful to study residues of constant and increasing intensity not as straight-line phenomena, but in keeping with their rhythmical nature as undulating curves. Citing cases from a wide range of historical materials, Pareto concluded that residues vary little in substance, though forms may vary widely, and that variations increase as one goes from residues to subclasses or from residues to derivations. Though they change slowly if at all, residues may differ widely in different societies because of the differences in intensities of Class I and Class II residues. Further, residues are not evenly distributed in social strata, and while they can and should be correlated with occupation, one must avoid single-factor explanations and think in terms of multiple causes in a process of interdependence.

Heterogeneity, Pareto insisted, is fundamental to society. "Whether certain theorists like it or not, the fact is that human society is not a homogeneous thing, that individuals are physically, morally, and intellectually different." If one examines the facts irrespective of value judgments and assigns individuals a rank according to their actual and not their potential ability in the various branches of endeavor, one finds two strata, the *nonelite* and the *elite*. The upper, elite stratum can be divided into two parts, a *governing elite* and a *nongoverning elite*. Further, an important phenomenon within this hierarchy is *class circulation*. Though there are always aristocracies, said Pareto, particular "aristocracies do not last. Whatever the causes, it is an incontestable fact that after a certain length of time they pass away. History is a graveyard of aristocracies." [8] The key to continuous class circulation are the changes that take place in the proportion of Class I and Class II residues in each stratum.

> Revolutions come about through accumulations in the higher strata of society—either because of a slowing-down in class-circulation, or from other causes—of decadent elements no longer possessing the residues suitable for keeping them in power, and shrinking from the use of force; while meantime in the lower strata of society elements of superior quality are coming to the fore, possessing residues suitable for exercising the functions of government and willing enough to use force.[9]

The Social Equilibrium and the Concept of Utility

Having established that residues and derivations are the key elements in human nature and that their distribution forms social classes, Pareto discussed the general form of society.

> The form of a society is determined by all the elements acting upon it and it, in turn, reacts upon them. We may therefore say that a reciprocal determination arises. Among such elements the following groups may be distinguished: 1. soil, climate, flora, fauna, geological, mineralogical, and other like conditions; 2. elements external to a given society at a given time, such as the influences of other societies upon it—external, therefore, in space; and the effects of the previous situation within it—external, therefore, in time; then 3: internal elements, chief among which, race, residues (or better, the sentiments manifested by them), proclivities, interests, aptitudes for thought and observation, state of knowledge, and so on. Derivations also are to be counted among these latter.[10]

In examining a "social system," Pareto warned, one must be careful to think in terms of interdependence or reciprocal determination. The complicated series of forces that make up the social equilibrium must not be thought of as cause and effect but as forces that influence and are influenced. The various forces, sentiments, economic conditions, customs, laws, intellectual

8 Ibid., 2053.
9 Ibid., 2057.
10 Ibid., 2060.

conditions, scientific knowledge, and so on may be combined into groups of facts and considered independently of each other. An important way to group them is according to whether they are variable or constant. The long-range goal of sociology is to construct mathematical indices that express the lawful behavior and the amount of influence of every force in human affairs.

Pareto shared much of the functional orientation that is such a striking feature of sociological theory. However, unlike the functional view of Durkheim, which was inspired by biology, or that of Simmel, which was historical, Pareto's was derived from mechanics. His fundamental view that facts are to be studied in terms of identifiable consequences places Pareto in the functional camp. His residues are essentially a list of social functions, while his recognition that residues can vary widely in form implies the existence of functional equivalents. Finally, his stress on the need to interpret facts in terms of the concepts of interdependence and system is in line with the general functional emphasis on a multicausal organic context.

Also central to functional theory is the concept of utility, which Pareto first introduced when he distinguished between the truth of a theory and its utility. In developing this distinction Pareto warned that one must not assume that human beings live at variance with facts just because nonlogical theories predominate in human behavior. Residues are more or less related to reality—if one of them goes astray, it is corrected by other residues that inspire sophistical derivations to get human beings back to reality. Thus, for Pareto, there is a cunning in the nonscientific empiricism of the residues and in the bad logic of the derivations that somehow keeps humanity more or less in accord with the facts. Thus a false theory has the latent function of directing people toward at least a partial recognition of the facts. All this, of course, is in line with Pareto's general tendency to distinguish between what today are called manifest and latent functions: not only can a nonlogical theory be useful, but a logical theory (truth) can lead to dysfunctional results.

Still in search of the ultimate structure of society, Pareto elaborated his idea of utility. Unlike the functional theorists who were inspired by biology, Pareto did not stress survival or functional prerequisites. This is understandable, given his static mechanistic orientation; for Pareto, social survival and functional prerequisites were not problematic, but were taken for granted. Thus he identified the state of utility most beneficial to individuals and society with X, the state of equilibrium.

The concept of utility is helpful, said Pareto, only if one specifies the units involved (the individual, the family, a community, a nation, the human race) and remembers that there is no necessary harmony of benefits or identity of interests among the units. The total of all utilities, direct and indirect, that an individual receives is an index of benefits under given circumstances and enables us to determine the state at which an individual or community receives the maximum utility. However, Pareto warned, utilities are not the same for everyone since individuals are different.

Pareto's discussion of utility is somewhat ambiguous and confusing. He suggested that it is merely a way of conceptualizing the best adjustment that a given society can make under given circumstances. He offered a valuable analytical tool when he proposed that every system has a point of equilibrium that is best for it. However, he created confusion in saying that every state of equilibrium has utilities that are different for different individuals and that there are conflicts between the utility of individuals and that of society. How is it possible, then, for the objective observer to state the point of maximum utility? Finally, of course, his tendency to accept the given state of equilibrium as normal identifies the state of maximum utility with the state of actual utility.

Pareto interpreted the social equilibrium in terms of what he called *cycles of interdependence*. The elements that make up a society can be grouped into four categories: residues, interests, derivations, and social heterogeneity and circulation. Among the economic elite, there are two different types of "capitalists," the *speculators* or entrepreneurs and the *rentiers* or savers. In the speculator group, Class I residues predominate, while in the rentier group, Class II residues predominate. There is a deep cleavage between the interests of these two groups, sometimes as deep or deeper than between "capitalist" and "proletariat." The type of civilization will be determined by the proportions of each type in combination, while the general utility is derived from the proportion of Class I and Class II residues in the ruling class and the population at large.

Elaborating on his idea of the elite (which has assumed a central position in his theory of social equilibrium), Pareto asserted that every governmental system is run by an elite despite the variety of forms under which it is masked:

> One may say, in general and speaking very roughly, that the governing class has a clearer view of its own interests because its vision is less obscured by sentiments, whereas the subject class is less aware of its interests because its vision is more clouded by sentiments; and that, as a result, the governing class is in a position to mislead the subject class into serving the interests of the governing class; but that those interests are not necessarily opposite to the interests of the subject class, often in fact coincide with them, so that in the end the deception may prove beneficial to the subject class.[11]

---

[11] Ibid., 2250.

That deception can be beneficial to the deceived is related to Pareto's insistence on separating truth and utility. Oftentimes individuals in the ruling class are carried along by a "system" and unwittingly perform acts that have negative consequences for themselves and for others. The idea that individuals act in partial blindness to thwart their own intentions is a legacy to sociological theory from Christianity and Greek tragedy, a legacy probated by the work of Vico and appearing in many forms in the history of sociological theory. It is not surprising to find the idea in Pareto's work since it is consistent with his overall emphasis. However, it is a little startling to hear him speak of a "system" controlling individuals when his whole emphasis up to this point has been that the individual's nature determines the nature of society.

Pareto thought of elites as the individuals who best embody the qualities most valuable and functional to a society at any given time. Class circulation takes place as social values and needs change. However, when an individual becomes part of the ruling class, his or her behavior changes. In an industrial society, an individual endowed with Class I residues will behave logically performing economic duties, but that individual's behavior becomes nonlogical once he or she becomes part of the ruling class. The nonlogicality of all political action is fundamental to Pareto's thought. The ruling class often enacts policies that have unforeseen and even disastrous consequences for themselves as well as for others. Pareto's rejection of the concept of social "needs" also illustrates his belief that political behavior is nonlogical. There is no way to determine the public's needs; almost anything, declared Pareto, can be cited as a need. Even if needs can be defined, they cannot necessarily be achieved by logical political and social action. Again emphasizing the nonlogicality of political action, Pareto insisted that a ruling class is successful only if it is capable of using force and cunning. Even the concept of "public needs" is a device of a ruling class to justify its own power. If a ruling class cannot use force and cunning, it will fail. These are the facts of political life as shown by the nature of human beings and society. A ruling class that hopes to govern logically is a historical impossibility. In an extended analysis of Roman society, Pareto attributed the stagnation of the Roman economy to the stultifying effects of political planning and the deadening influence of bureaucracy, factors Pareto saw again on the upswing to the detriment of modern society.

The Social Equilibrium and Its Movements

Pareto took considerable pains to determine the "mutual correlation between an undulatory movement in residues and an undulatory movement in derivations, and between both those movements and other social phenomena, among which, very especially, the economic." He asserted that although the rhythmical or oscillatory movements in social phenomena are well

known, theories purporting to explain these undulations have been derivations. Plato and Vico were the worst offenders of the logico-experimental
method, and Polybius (205?–?125 B.C.) and Machiavelli were closest to
experimental reality. Attempts to explain these undulations have led to a
number of errors, ranging from a failure to take account of their existence
to errors of interpretation. The main source of interpretive errors has been
the tendency to impose on data some nonexperimental cause or direction
and to assume that what is need not have been.

Since the sentiments are basically constant but may appear in various
intensities and mixtures, Class I residues may be emphasized in one period
and Class II in another, resulting in periods of skepticism followed by
periods of faith. The crucial point, however, is that neither residue can be
eliminated; the human mind oscillates between the extravagances of each.
Both residues, when they inspire derivations, are equally false in relation
to logico-experimental knowledge.

The central concern of the social scientist is the operation of the residues,
which give society its structure and movement and control intellectual
activity. There are three factors at work here, residues, logical residues or
interests, and the fact of individual heterogeneity, expressing itself as class
circulation. Using these three elements, Pareto briefly analyzed Western
civilization in a wide-ranging quest for the social equilibrium. He focused
first on Athens and Rome, then skipped to the medieval world, the Renaissance, the Reformation, and finally the modern world. As expected, the
data of history fall into place and the movement of history corresponds
to the relative influence of residues, interests, and class circulation. Pareto's
historical survey ends with a warning against the belief that the modern
period represents a trend toward progress and reason. This belief mistakes
segments of the wave for the total wave and forgets that "reason" in political
and social activities is different from "reason" in the sciences and economics.
Judging the total society, one cannot observe any qualitative difference between the modern and former periods of history. It is not difficult to understand the reasoning behind this conclusion, given Pareto's crucial assumption—that social phenomena emanate from residues, which are relatively
constant though they form different mixtures under different circumstances.
If the basic forces behind behavior are constant, if they simply check and
counterbalance each other, and if all other causes have only a secondary
influence, then the flow of behavior from the residual substances of human
nature can exhibit only cyclical or undulatory movements, and no historical,
qualitative change can take place.

CONCLUSION

The best way to assess Pareto's contribution to the pluralistic sociocultural
climate of opinion is to think of him as a theorist who revised rather than

rejected the tradition of naturalistic positivism. On the level of methodology, he continued the English utilitarian tradition, the stronghold of naturalistic positivism, by accepting its definition of reason as a means for obtaining ends—ends that reason cannot supply. However, he refined the methodology of earlier utilitarian positivism by making it, at least in aim, more rigorously empirical and less remote from human experience. Pareto made another revision in the early positive tradition. By identifying the world of belief and values as lawful and functional to human beings and society, Pareto included this world in the subject matter of science. Though beliefs and values are overwhelmingly nonrational, they are nevertheless the constituent forces of human behavior and cannot be dismissed as epiphenomena.

Pareto shared many of the perspectives and conclusions of the other pluralistic positivists. Like Durkheim and Simmel, he rejected approaches that saw the sociologist's task as a search for essences, all-explanatory monistic principles, or principles that would unite human beings and nature. Like them, he took an empirical approach to social phenomena, emphasizing the complexity, uniqueness, and multicausal nature of human behavior; like them, he saw society as a structure of functional relationships rather than as a substance. As a thinker, especially in methodology, he was closer, of course, to Durkheim than to Simmel. While all three thinkers separated human beings from nature, Pareto, like his great French contemporary, insisted that the beliefs and behaviors of human beings be regarded as an objective order of facts amenable to the same scientific methods that pertain in natural science. Both Pareto and Durkheim were concerned with the problem of getting at the complexity of social facts, and both devoted considerable attention to methodology. Pareto, however, went much further than Durkheim in his emulation of the natural sciences. Placing himself squarely in the tradition of philosophical and scientific nominalism, he explicitly rejected cause-effect relationships in favor of multifactor causation conceived in terms of probability analysis. (Durkheim, of course, did something quite similar when he equated scientific proof with "concomitant variations.") In the same spirit, Pareto demanded precision in dealing with empirical data, emphasizing that the ambiguity of language made it all the more desirable that the social sciences reduce social phenomena to mathematical terms. Durkheim identified science and ethics; Pareto separated them sharply and with great relish catalogued the distortions produced by explicit or implicit value judgments. Durkheim's belief in the promotion and realization of values as the ultimate justification of science stamped him as an offspring of the Enlightenment. Pareto severed the historic connection between sociological positivism and the social ideals of the Enlightenment by insisting that science and values, or truth and utility, could not be identified, and that in truth they are often opposed.

Pareto's attempt to conceptualize society as a structure of interdependent forces in equilibrium was an even more explicit use of scientific methodology than Durkheim's functional method. Durkheim's functionalism, however, was superior in that he explicitly sought to interpret a social fact in terms of the social function it performed, whereas Pareto made no explicit effort to relate residues and derivations to social functions. Notwithstanding Durkheim's superiority in this respect, however, Pareto was more conscious of the scientific need to develop a value-free and unambiguous terminology with which to realize the dream of science, an economical description of data in terms of conditions and consequences.

Pareto had one foot planted firmly in the authentic tradition of the Pascalian definition of science. His assertion that the science of sociology could establish neither a metaphysics nor an ethics and his insistence that his *General Treatise of Sociology* was not a unified general theory of society but a theory in general are in this tradition. Also characteristic of the nonmetaphysical definition of science is his definition of rationality as an efficacious relation between means and ends based on knowledge derived from observation. The Pascalian strand in Pareto's thought enabled him to make a devastating and on the whole valuable assault on the natural-law philosophies of the scholastics and the philosophes as well as on the deductive tradition in monistic sociology.

Pareto's single-minded attention to the logico-experimental validity of beliefs led him to his fundamental substantive finding, the fact that nonlogical behavior is the outstanding characteristic of human society. It was not that Pareto discovered this fact by himself. Many of the earlier sociologists, including Vico, Montesquieu, Saint-Simon, Sumner, Durkheim, and Simmel, emphasized the role of religion and other nonlogical elements in human behavior and were concerned with finding the functionality behind these elements. Pareto denied, however, that society was evolving from nonlogical to logical forms, and he insisted that human nature was essentially and unalterably nonlogical; this clearly distinguished him from the main current of Western social theory and the evolutionary optimism of earlier sociology. Pareto's new emphasis on the extent and permanence of nonlogicality in human behavior made him a prime contributor to the antirationalist current of the last decades of the nineteenth and first decades of the twentieth century. Along with his methodology, this emphasis constitutes his distinctive contribution to the emerging current of sociocultural sociology.

Pareto as a Naturalistic Positivist

Pareto's recognition of human nonlogicality is one thing—his explanation of it another. In explaining nonlogicality he smuggled into his work the second view of science, the Cartesian assumption that science deals with ultimate explanations. At the base of human behavior, Pareto claimed, is

an indefinable bundle of sentiments that can be known only as they manifest themselves in behavior. Science cannot define the sentiments directly
but can classify their manifestations as they appear in beliefs and other
behavior. These manifestations, which are the facts of sociology, can be
ordered into two main groups, residues and derivations. The six classes
of residues are the constant, nonlogical elements in human nature, and the
derivations are the variable, nonlogical intellectual masks that seek to
justify the residues. The entire range of human behavior falls within the
six classes of residues; all emotions, drives, and impulses, and their manifestation as social behavior, stem from them. Similarly, all intellectual
formulations are related to some residue, with radically different ideas
sometimes belonging to the same residue. Of all the residues only the sub-
class called interests, which is economic behavior, has attained the status
of a logical derivation—as economic theory. The structure of society is formed
by the operation of the residues, derivations, and interests. Since these
forces are distributed unequally among human beings, society everywhere
exhibits a sharp split between an elite and a nonelite. Changes in society
are not really changes, but fluctuations due to class circulation. The circulation of classes, which dooms all aristocracies, takes place partly because
of changing social needs but mostly because individuals with elite residues
appear among the nonelite and individuals in the elite fail to manifest the
appropriate ruling traits. In any case, the sharp separation of elite and nonelite always reappears and the social equilibrium re-establishes itself. The
fluctuation of society, however, produces nothing new; the same combination of residues still makes up the two strata of society, the elite having
primarily Class I residues (instinct of combinations) and the nonelite, Class
II residues (group-persistences), though the verbal expression of these
residues may be radically different.

The fluctuation of society is essentially an oscillation between Class I and
Class II residues and exhibits no linear or qualitative movements. Since the
elite, in addition to having the greater capacity for fabricating derivations
(fraud), must also use force to rule successfully, there is always a qualitative
difference between political behavior and the logical type of economic behavior that Pareto called *the manifestation of interests*. This behavior is
logical because individuals pursuing their economic interests base their
behavior on knowledge obtained through observation, thereby supplying
subjective desires with the necessary objective means. Attempts by a government to interfere in economic affairs are bound to fail because government can never perform rationally. Even if it could, rational behavior has
no necessary social utility.

The validity of Pareto's theory hinges on his concept of sentiments. Despite
his explicit disclaimer, it is apparent that he regarded the sentiments as
a set of objective forces in control of human behavior. Pareto discussed

the sentiments at one step removed by calling them "residues" and "derivations"; nevertheless, he could not disguise the fact that he assumed the
sentiments were a set of empirical uniformities that can be uncovered by
science. By unconsciously assuming that the ultimate forces that constitute
individual behavior, and thus the structure of society, can be found, Pareto
transformed his sociology into a positivistic substantialism. Despite his radical commitment to science, Pareto's position has many similarities with
traditional philosophical discourse. His concept of the sentiments, which
manifest themselves as residues and derivations, is similar to the concept
of potential in philosophical idealism. For example, the sentiments contain
one of the fundamental attributes of the idea of potentiality: at one and
the same time, they are both variable and constant. Pareto's recourse to
numbers, letters of the alphabet, and neologisms to overcome the limitations of language could not disguise his use of the old metaphysical dualism,
the eternal (the residues) and the contingent (the derivations). Of course,
this dualism results in the old idealist distinction between appearance and
reality. Despite the enormous apparent diversity of human customs and
beliefs, they all fall into the six classes of residues that express the underlying reality of human nature.

These six eternal types, which receive profane realization at the hands
of fallible human beings, eliminate the problem of novelty. Pareto solved
the liberal dilemma by acting as if the Pascalian and Cartesian views of
science were really one, and by disguising old philosophical concepts in
the garments of scientific terminology. He solved it by merging his method
and results so that the analytical concepts of system, interdependence, and
equilibrium also became substantive structures representing factual uniformities. Perceived differently, the same facts might well reveal conflict,
qualitative change and diversity, progress, decline, and so on, but in Pareto's
eyes the facts of society always tended toward functional equilibrium.
Society itself is ultimately an eternal type because it is composed of the
complex, interdependent, equilibrated forces that correspond to the unchanging biopsychological forces that constitute the eternal individual.

Pareto also solved the liberal dilemma by resorting to the idea of the
cunning of empiricism and false theory and to the concept of unintended
consequences. Somehow the sentiments manage to provide all social functions, even when human beings fail to act logically in the pursuit of goals.
However, the sentiments also insure that human beings fail even when they
act logically since truth has no necessary relation to utility. Thus, Pareto
solved the liberal dilemma by eliminating the capacity of human beings,
individually, collectively, or as rational-scientific agents, to produce anything new. The Enlightenment viewed science and reason as instruments
with which humanity would uncover a natural order rooted in the rational
structure of the universe; movement in that direction was progress toward
something qualitatively new in human affairs—a movement, of course, that

also raised the liberal dilemma. Pareto eliminated the dilemma by saying that science has not discovered a rational, natural order, but a nonrational order that has always existed; therefore, there is nothing new to explain.

Pareto's attempt to uncover the uniformities of human behavior was hopelessly compromised from the start by his basic supposition that these uniformities are the manifestation of a set of unchanging sentiments. The idea that all human conduct can be reduced to six classes of residues not only is metaphysics, but yields few results of scientific value. The same residue, it seems, could manifest itself in a variety of diametrically opposed practices: for example, those who revered a Roman Catholic saint and those who revered Rousseau were giving expression to the same residue.[12] However, the concept of residue lost all meaning when Pareto began to elaborate the subclasses of each residue. He almost completely abandoned his own canon of terminological precision. Every type of behavior seems to have a specific residue: there is a residue of veneration, one to prevent the discarding of old beliefs, one of uniformity, one for the endurance of pain and sacrifice, and so on.[13]

Pareto's characterization of the residues was contradictory in the extreme. Residues are constants but they also change, though slowly; they are unchanging substances but assume different forms depending on time and place or the influence of other residues; they are present in every society but differ widely in appearance and intensity from one society to another; they sometimes die out but can be revived; and they are in qualitative competition with each other but have the capacity to blend into an almost infinite number of mixtures to produce all the personality types known.[14] Pareto's master concept begins to resemble a bottomless portmanteau capable of carrying any load. In a way, it resembles the systems of natural law that Pareto likened to rubber bands that stretch to suit the interests of power groups. In short, Pareto's concept of residues has an elasticity that covers every intellectual problem and solves none.

Similarly, Pareto's attempt to correlate the relationship between the residues and derivations was laudable in intent but poor in execution and adds little to the sociology of knowledge. No relationship can be established, since residues and derivations can be combined in almost any manner, with the added complication that the same residue can have two or more derivations.[15] Here again, Pareto's failure stemmed from his general failure to construct an adequate causal analysis. The linchpin of his entire structure

---

[12] Ibid., 1712; for other illustrations see 863, 865–866, 1854.
[13] For these specific residues, see Ibid., 799, 1129, 1195; for further evidence of this elaboration, see vol. 2, *passim*.
[14] Ibid., 850, 877, 928, 968, 1114, 1165, 1695, 1720, 1755, 1845, 1847, 1854–1856, 1932, 2044–2045, 2410.
[15] For examples, see Ibid., 1416, 2086.

of thought was the presupposition that an irreducible, unchanging, ultimately inexplicable set of sentiments controls human behavior. A radical
nominalism, which assumes its data as given and complete, renders it inexplicable and therefore eliminates the need for causal analysis.

Despite occasional references, therefore, to the influence exerted on human
behavior by geography, social needs, intellectual currents, the political and
social system, or values,[16] Pareto's theory is overwhelmingly biopsychological, not cultural, social, or historical. The impulse to behavior comes
not from given sociocultural structures, but from residues in the individual.
The differences among human beings are not based on social power or the
operation of historical circumstances, but are innate. Despite Pareto's contribution to pluralistic sociocultural positivism, his elaborate theoretical
edifice is simply an updated version of naturalistic positivism. Like the
theories of Comte and Spencer, it collapses once one accepts Durkheim's
simple conclusion that there is no way to link directly concrete human behavior to biopsychological drives, traits, mechanisms, or energies.

The above characterization of Pareto's work is almost at total variance with
Talcott Parsons's interpretation in his widely influential book, *The Structure
of Social Action*.[17] The heart of Parsons's argument is that Pareto did not
have a psychological theory because his theory of the nonlogical includes
nonscientific value attitudes as well as unscientific theories. Pareto's emphasis on values, together with his critique of social Darwinism, claimed
Parsons, led him to define society as a system of common ends. From this,
Parsons developed a number of other propositions. Pareto, he claimed, employed the sociologistic theorem and was concerned with the tension between nonscientific values and science, and with the sociological framework
necessary to the operation of science and pure economics. While it is true
that a few such references can be found in Pareto's work, Parsons has taken
a few casual remarks made by a very unsubtle thinker and magnified them
all out of proportion. Such a procedure is acceptable as long as Parsons
is concerned with building his own theory out of clues provided by Pareto;
it is not acceptable, however, for Parsons to interpret these insights as
central to Pareto's analysis. Pareto was far from employing the sociologistic
theorem, which emphasizes the social roots of behavior, and far from appreciating the role of value ideas in determining behavior; indeed, he devoted
chapter after chapter to demolishing value ideas and declaring them inferior
to scientific reasoning. Nowhere did he seriously examine the nonlogical
sources of logical behavior, though he did refer rather offhandedly to the
cunning of unreason, nor probe into the instability and tension that ensued

---

[16] For his casual reference to these factors, see Ibid., 928, 1695, 1845, 1847, 2044–
2045, 2254, 2262, 2268.
[17] New York: McGraw-Hill, 1937; reprinted, New York: Free Press, 1949; also in
paperback, 2 vols.

from the emergence of science. To have raised these problems seriously would have caused Pareto some uneasiness about the validity of science. It would ultimately have led him into the liberal dilemma, which, in terms of his theory, would have questioned how new knowledge can emerge from the unchanging sentiments. Instead, Pareto solved these problems with the catchall concept of the residues and derivations, the belief in the heterogeneity of individuals, and the belief in the inherent tendency toward the equilibrium of all three emanations of the sentiments: the unscientific, nonscientific, and scientific forms of beliefs and behavior.

In regard to the sociologistic theorem, nowhere did Pareto conceive society as a sociocultural structure having no direct basis in biopsychological imperatives. Nowhere did he conceive of it as a sociocultural system that draws individuals into behavior and value complexes both satisfying and frustrating, unifying and disintegrating, nonlogical and logical. This orientation is certainly possible starting from Pareto's radical nominalism, but it took place not in his thought but in that of Max Weber. A cyclical theorist who denies the possibility of qualitative change and relates all social phenomena to a set of unchanging sentiments cannot possibly be concerned seriously with values or interactions as variables. Once Pareto introduced the all-explanatory sentiments, he took a turn that in the end left him without anything to say about society or culture as such.[18]

Pareto and Liberal Ideology

Is it unfair to characterize Pareto as a liberal in light of what has been said? Did he solve the liberal dilemma by ceasing to be a liberal? The answer is no. It is true that his theory eliminated the political strand of the liberal tradition. Nowhere was Pareto more content than when heaping derision on the ideals of representative government, equalitarianism, and humanitarianism. Indeed, he eliminated the entire liberal theory of social progress when he outlawed the possibility of genuine historical change. However, Pareto transformed rather than rejected liberal theory; the telltale marks of the liberal are everywhere in his work. For example, he assumed throughout that the individual and society have separate identities, that the interests of the individual and of society both overlap and conflict, that diversity is as normal as unity, and that a changing configuration of utilities is normal over time. The emphasis on unity within diversity is evident in Pareto's references to the abstract polar types of society: on the one extreme, he conceived of a theoretical social type based exclusively on sentiment and instinct and, on the other, of a type whose behavior is governed only by logico-experimental reasonings. Human society, said Pareto,

---

[18] Sorokin, who appreciates Pareto's work almost as Parsons, criticizes Pareto for being in the end a psychological theorist; see his *Contemporary Sociological Theories* (New York: Harper & Row, 1928), pp. 60–62.

is neither of these; it has diversity rather than homogeneity and change rather than stagnation. In addition, Pareto not only retained the liberal faith in science, something that in itself separated him from the current of conservatism-traditionalism, but he labored to deepen its meaning and widen its application.

Pareto's liberalism is most clearly revealed in his definition of economics and in his theory of the relationship between economic behavior and politics. Of all human theories, he said, only economic theory has attained a logico-experimental status. This is because human beings act logically only when they are serving their economic interests unhampered by outside interference.[19] Pareto's account of the relation between economic and political behavior was in keeping with the entire liberal tradition and its deep ambivalence toward political institutions. In liberal social theory, including its sociological variant, there is a widespread denial that society can be managed democratically or rationally through direct political action. Liberal thought almost universally restricted the right of the masses to function politically by making the right dependent on a status derived from non-political sources, basically property or, what amounts to the same thing, education. The sociological tradition upheld the characteristic middle-class fear of allowing the unlettered masses to acquire political power. Condorcet was an exception—his acceptance of natural rights implied a right to public participation, but even in Condorcet there was an implied need for science and education to validate political participation. Saint-Simon restricted political participation to the call for leadership; ultimately politics would be eliminated by the full flowering of industry and replaced by administration. In Comte, a manufactured religion based on science glued society together and gave it direction. Spencer and Sumner explicitly rejected an important role for government, while Ward emphasized public action to make human beings free and equal, which really amounted to a call to perfect existing economic institutions and to improve education. Even in late liberalism and late sociological theory, the acceptance of the need for greater political management was curiously qualified by the liberal aversion to the idea of a rational politics—thus politics often obtained its rationality from civil society, as in Durkheim; through inadvertence, that is, the sociology of error and evil; or through improvisation, for example the welfare state, the New Deal, and so on.

Pareto's view of politics was squarely within this tradition, though he went one step further than even William Graham Sumner in his derogation of

[19] Of the numerous references to economics as a science and to economic behavior as logical, see Mind and Society, 824, 2011ff., 2079, 2091, 2106–2107, 2146, 2585–2612.

politics. For Pareto, political behavior was inherently and inescapably non-logical, though in his characteristic way he added that nonlogical politics can be functional nonetheless. It is especially nonlogical and nonfunctional when it interferes with economic behavior.

Pareto's separation of the economy and politics into distinct realms of behavior is a sure sign of the liberal mentality. However, in Pareto this separation took a new twist. In politics, he proposed an elite that rules through a mixture of fraud and force, and in economics, a structure of laissez faire. In the eighteenth century, a similar combination of "absolutism" in politics and individualism in economics appeared in the work of the Physiocrats. However, the political theory of the Physiocrats was based on enlightened despotism; Pareto's denial of political enlightenment, together with his deep belief in the innate inequality of individuals, exhibit the fundamental affinity of his work with fascism.

One of the fascinating aspects of intellectual analysis is to see how similar ideas become utterly different and serve different ideological functions depending on the intellectual and moral framework in which they become embedded. For example, Pareto's view that human beings have been and always will be inherently unequal is very similar to a basic strand in liberal sociological thought represented by such figures as Saint-Simon, Comte, Spencer, and Sumner. However, these latter figures, with varying degrees of emphasis and optimism, placed inequality in an evolutionary, progressive framework, claiming that true inequality would be a feature of the terminal stage of social development.

Pareto's reputation as the "Marx of the bourgeoisie" points to other examples of how similar ideas vary in terms of context. Pareto and Marx shared two key ideas: that antagonism between ruler and ruled is basic to social existence, and that the theories and values by which human beings live are nonlogical or ideological masks to cover up power interests. Seen in context, however, these views have totally different meanings. For Marx, power was a sociocultural phenomenon taking qualitatively different shapes in different technological periods and was destined to disappear. For Marx, human beings lived in a moral universe of decision and volition, and the function of a scientific study of power was to help humanity bring society under conscious control. Pareto viewed power as a static, nonmoral, naturalistic phenomenon, distributed unevenly. All power relations are the same; the theorist can never denote the social and personal functions of power, only assert its existence and analyze the eternal nonlogical techniques by which it manifests itself. Lacking even a rudimentary sociocultural outlook, Pareto was unable to correlate power with social structure or observe historical differences in its structure and consequences. In this sense he stands on the periphery of the main Western tradition in social thought, which from Plato and Aristotle on has always sought to define the nature of power in terms of social and moral functions.

Pareto's belief that theories are nonlogical masks or ideologies for covering up the power impulse is again quite different from Marx's theory of ideology. Marx accepted the ideological nature of social theory, but believed that all theories serve a rational and progressive function in the historical process before becoming outmoded—that is, ideological. Thus Marx stands in the main Western tradition of social theory in that he attributed some degree of choice and rationality to both the holders and the aspirants of social power, something Pareto denied flatly.

Pareto's rejection of this tradition prevented him from completing his major contribution to functional analysis in sociology. Durkheim's and Simmel's view of power was on much sounder ground; based on a sociocultural orientation, their view developed into a functionalism that was able to distinguish different structures of power and relate them to nonpsychological causes and to the performance of personal and social functions. In Durkheim's case, this was most obvious in his sociology of law. Simmel's contribution to a functional analysis of power was even more impressive. His sociology of domination revealed strikingly different types of power structures and correspondingly different types of consequences. Simmel cited illustrations of power holders who quite consciously used rational means to obtain ends, and he also called attention to power coalitions and relationships—all of which escaped Pareto's narrow classifications. Given his definition of human beings as fixed entities, Pareto was unable to round out his functional theory. Like all theorists and dissident groups who hold fixed, biopsychological world views, he was forced in the end to adopt a conspiratorial theory of power.

What Pareto did was to accept the Enlightenment's view of a fixed human nature, but to discard its view that human nature will be revealed when humanity has stripped itself of the past. The net effect was to erase the small historical perspective in the early liberal tradition. Pareto's static, nominalistic view of power and human behavior can be related to his own experiences. Pareto was a practicing engineer, and his experience in mechanical science, in which one searches for the regularities and constants in natural phenomena, undoubtedly inspired him to apply the logic and principles of engineering to social science. Furthermore, given his experience in the political and social environment of Italy and France, it is not surprising that he was unimpressed with the theory of progress. It is no accident that the most progressive sociological theories, those combining progress with individualism, emerged in England and the United States, where progress amidst order was an everyday fact of life. As an Italian, Pareto inherited a social legacy in which the Reformation, the Enlightenment, and liberal democracy were absent, a social legacy in which intrigue, corruption, and disorder occurred with dreary repetition. It is significant that antirationalism, which formed such an important part of late-nineteenth-century Western intellectual culture, was reconciled with liberty and equality in some countries, notably England and the United States, whereas in continental countries it was often used to refute liberal values and to support authoritarianism. Not unexpectedly, therefore, Pareto's theory of power is in line with the nonhistorical, elitist tradition that is such a vital feature in Italian social theory from Machiavelli to Mosca (1858–1941). Given his background it is not surprising that Pareto adopted a radically static nominalism that saw social phenomena as data—that is, as entities and processes that are fixed and given. Such an assumption prevented Pareto from focusing on the novelties and innovations in social behavior. Thus for Pareto the structure and function of power were never really explained; elites were merely data and while data can be described in terms of uniformities, they can never be explained. It is true that Pareto sometimes referred to power and class structure in terms of economic factors. On the whole, however, he was content to say vaguely that these structures take shape depending on the supply of social elements—and often merely with a casual "whatever the causes." At this point Pareto's radical nominalism coincided with radical rationalism in a common substantialism.

Try as he might, however, Pareto could not banish the spirit of the Enlightenment from his work. In the tradition of the Enlightenment, he accepted the revolutionary idea that human passions are lawful and useful to both human beings and society. Though he denied humanity a past and a future and explicitly rejected any theory of progress, Pareto brought in by the back door what he ejected from the front. In the end he smuggled in the idea of progress and thereby raised the liberal dilemma in much the same form it had taken in the eighteenth century. If human beings are governed by sentiments, which are always the same, there is no way to explain the growth in knowledge that stems from the use of the logico-experimental method—a growth of knowledge that has produced a qualitative change in the human ability to control nature and to understand economic behavior. Pareto's belief in a realm of factual uniformities is comparable to the philosophes' belief in a natural order. So too, his logico-experimental method has a close affinity to the Enlightenment's emphasis on the need to bring reason and phenomena into fruitful interplay. In both theories the same problem arises: if a realm of truth exists and if human beings have the capacity to discover it, why do they do so at a particular time and place?

The philosophical dilemma of liberal ideology emerged in the work of Pareto as a moral dilemma as well. In a characteristically liberal way, though in accentuated form, he insisted on a separation between law or political power and morality. However, while insisting that power is what it does (and what it must do), he also condemned it for violating morality

and for interfering with the logicality of the marketplace. It is rather contradictory for him to insist that the facts of social behavior are lawful in the
manner of physical facts, then to criticize them when they fail to conform to
moral standards, especially when he labored so heavily to show that moral
standards are inescapably nonlogical and can have no basis in fact. It is
illogical, in short, to insist that logical action cannot be found in political
affairs and then to become indignant when politicians intervene in the
logical realm of economic behavior. Pareto's difficulty, of course, was an
outgrowth of his claim that human beings are always the same while also
claiming that a change has taken place that has brought with it a new truth
and a new morality. The dilemma of liberalism is nowhere better illustrated
than in Pareto's claim to have transcended the nonlogical world through
the use of a superior method for obtaining the truth, while insisting that
human affairs are substantively, permanently, nonlogical.

Chapter 17
Max Weber (1864–1920)

The high point of pluralistic sociocultural positivism is the work of Max Weber, perhaps the greatest of all sociologists. The intellectual dilemmas and value paradoxes of not only German life but the entire Western and Eastern worlds came to a focus in the thought of this remarkable thinker. His unique intellectual and moral perspectives constitute a brilliant and perhaps unparalleled contribution to social science.[1]

Weber's philosophical orientation is a unique blend of the subjective idealism and the sociocultural historicism of the Enlightenment, in effect a blend of Hume, Kant, Montesquieu, and Vico. Though he was profoundly original in many ways, Weber's most novel contribution to sociology was an attempt to incorporate the skepticism of Hume and Montesquieu into sociological theory. Thus, it is not surprising that Weber expressly repudiated the possibility of a general, unified theory of society. Although he was working on a more systematic statement of his position when he died, there is no indication that he intended any fundamental revisions in his basic orientation,

---

[1] Weber's attempt to systematize his sociology was interrupted by his untimely death. Major portions of this unfinished book, first published in 1922 as *Wirtschaft und Gesellschaft*, 2 vols. (Tübingen, Germany: J. C. B. Mohr) and in an extensively revised 4th ed. in 1956, have been translated under the following titles: *From Max Weber: Essays in Sociology*, ed. and trans. H. H. Gerth and C. Wright Mills (New York: Oxford University Press, 1946), also in paperback; henceforth cited as *From Max Weber;* and *Max Weber: The Theory of Social and Economic Organization*, trans. A. M. Henderson and Talcott Parsons and intro. Talcott Parsons (New York: Oxford University Press, 1947), also in paperback; henceforth cited as *S.E.O.* Translations of other portions of this work are cited below. A full translation incorporating most of these earlier translations may be found in *Economy and Society: An Outline of Interpretive Sociology*, ed., rev., and partially trans. Guenther Roth and Claus Wittich, intro. Guenther Roth, 3 vols. (New York: Bedminster Press, 1968). Weber's other major work, *Gesammelte Aüfsatze zur Religions-soziologie*, 3 vols. (Tübingen, Germany: J. C. B. Mohr, 1920–1921), contains his special studies and essays in religion. The various translations of Weber's work in this area are cited below.

Max Weber (1864–1920)

and on the whole his philosophical and methodological position is clearly stated.[2]

Weber's contribution to pluralistic sociocultural positivism came from yet another brand of empiricism, one that sought to separate the cultural sciences both from philosophy and from the natural sciences. Though

[2] Weber's general philosophical and methodological position (epistemology) is in the three essays in Max Weber, *The Methodology of the Social Sciences*, trans. and ed. E. A. Shils and H. A. Finch (New York: Free Press, 1949), henceforth cited as *Methodology*, and in *From Max Weber*, chaps. 4 and 5. His more systematically expressed methodology for social inquiry is in *S.E.O.* chap. 1. The essays in *Methodology* also have frequent references to the specific procedures and logic of social inquiry.

similar in some respects to the methodological orientation of Pareto and Simmel, Weber's orientation was profoundly different from any that I have yet discussed.[3]

PHILOSOPHY AND METHOD

The Rejection of General Theory

For Weber, as for Hume, there was an unbridgeable dichotomy between the realms of reason (concepts), science (facts), and values (faith).[4] Science can deal only with facts and means-ends relationships: the solution of problems, the selection of means, the clarification of alternatives, the delineation of the possible consequences of different courses of action. It can never prescribe an end and can never validate or justify any course of action or any value as either true or good.

Weber in his radical nominalist orientation bears a close affinity to Pareto: both separated reason, fact, and value; both were instrumental in their use of ideas; both tended to think of factual uniformities in terms of probability; both defined rationality in terms of the efficacy of means-ends relationships; both used the distinction between the rational or the scientific and the nonscientific to classify and analyze the range of human behavior; and both accorded a predominant role in human affairs to nonrationality.[5]

However, the Humian empiricism from which both started can be developed in two radically different directions. On the one hand, there is the position taken by Hume and Pareto: that facts are unchanging structures that reveal themselves to a fixed process of perception. On the other hand, one can assume along with Weber that facts are changeable, both in themselves and

[3] Many fine studies of Weber's work exist though none has caught the full meaning of his skepticism. For general accounts, see Theodore Abel, *Systematic Sociology in Germany* (New York: Columbia University Press, 1929); Raymond Aron, *German Sociology* (New York: Free Press, 1957); H. Stuart Hughes, *Consciousness and Society: The Reorientation of European Social Thought, 1890–1930* (New York: Alfred Knopf, 1958); also in paperback. For a fuller treatment of Weber's work, see Reinhard Bendix, *Max Weber, an Intellectual Portrait* (New York: Doubleday Anchor paperback, 1962). For perhaps the finest short account, see Julien Freund, *The Sociology of Max Weber,* trans. Mary Ilford (New York: Vintage paperback, 1969). For essays on various aspects of Weber's work, see Dennis Wrong, ed., *Max Weber* (Englewood Cliffs, N.J.: Prentice-Hall, 1970); *Max Weber and Sociology Today,* ed. Otto Stammer, trans. Kathleen Morris (New York: Harper & Row, 1971); Reinhard Bendix and Guenther Roth, *Scholarship and Partisanship: Essays on Max Weber* (Berkeley: University of California Press, 1971). For an analysis of the political aspects of Weber's thought, see David Beetham, *Max Weber and the Theory of Modern Politics* (London: George Allen and Unwin, 1974).
[4] This is the main theme of *Methodology,* chap. 1; also see pp. 49–63 of chap. 2. In *From Max Weber,* see pp. 77, 120–128, 142–156.
[5] The kinship in these respects with Sumner should also be noted.

in terms of differences in the perceptual stance taken by observers. Despite a common starting point, therefore, Weber's sociology was quite different from Pareto's. Pareto hewed closely to natural science and developed a naturalistic or biopsychological theory, while Weber developed a sociology that bears a strong affinity with the sociocultural "historicism" of Montesquieu and Vico.

If one thinks of the historical function of empiricism from William of Occam on as the attempt to free the Western perception of the phenomenal world from its bondage to logic and thus allow it to see new things and relationships, then Weber's orientation was the high point of this tradition in social science. By transforming ideas into methodological fictions, or acts of imagination, whose main purpose was to illuminate an unstructured empirical social world, Weber was able to see not only what was, but what had been and what could be. The rise of the empirical method was a necessary counterpart to the development of capitalism. A dynamic, expansive economy must overcome the resistance of a fixed logic and a fixed morality. Just as Weber's subjective eclecticism was the culmination of this tradition in social science, the high point of emancipation in natural science also came in the late nineteenth century with the emergence of what Poincaré called "unconscious opportunism."

Accompanying the sharp separation of philosophy and science in Weber's thought was a sharp separation between social science and natural science. Weber developed the difference between social and natural science through an analysis of the role of ideas in the social sciences. For Weber, reason cannot underpin values, nor can it stand by itself as a complete system of logical categories. Rationalism in the sense of Platonic or Scholastic realism is dead; the empirical is the only reality. The task of the social sciences, however, is not to grasp conceptually this empirical reality once and for all. There is a profound difference between knowledge about nature and knowledge about human beings. Knowledge about nature is a question of causal behavior and no more; knowledge about human beings is concerned with meaning as well as with causation. Since people behave in terms of values, the task of the social sciences is to understand these values and their origin and operation. Weber studied values not because he believed that one value system was truer than another; the scientist must always operate with "meaningful action" in a "meaningless universe." He was interested in values simply because human beings, including scientists, cannot act except in terms of a hierarchy of values. Values are always arranged in unique, historical configurations; no set can claim a universal validity. Therefore, universal, abstract, general laws are worthless for understanding human existence. The theorist cannot proceed "presuppositionlessly" in search of absolute truth, but must investigate in terms of value and in terms of some need or problem connected with that value. The empirical reality that is investigated can never substantiate the evaluative idea that prompted the investigation.

Since one cannot avoid approaching reality with evaluative ideas, one should employ them deliberately and with as much precision as possible. One can exercise "ethical-neutrality," however—that is, the nonevaluation of behavior. Evaluative ideas are not ethical imperatives to be realized, nor are they hypotheses to be proved—they are merely expository aids to help bring interest areas into relief.

> The *elementary duty of scientific self-control* and the only way to avoid serious and foolish blunders requires a sharp, precise distinction between the logically *comparative* analysis of reality by ideal-*types* in the logical sense and the *value-judgment* of reality on the basis of ideals. An "ideal type" in our sense, to repeat once more, has no connection at all with *value-judgments,* and it has nothing to do with any type of perfection other than a purely *logical* one. There are ideal types of brothels as well as of religions.[6]

Ideal types, it should be emphasized, are not hypotheses to be proved or disproved in an attempt to reduce the empirical world to law.

> It is not the "actual" interconnections of "things" but the *conceptual* interconnections of *problems* which define the scope of the various sciences. A new "science" emerges where new problems are pursued by new methods and truths are thereby discovered which open up significant new points of view.[7]

Thus, said Weber, ideal types do not exhaust empirical structures, most of which are a combination of types or in a state of transition between types.

> By the terminology suggested here [pure types of domination], we do not wish to force schematically the infinite and multifarious historical life, but simply to create concepts useful for special purposes and for orientation.[8]

Much of the flavor of Weber's utilitarian approach to ideas is implicit in his approving reference to an old saying that "an ingenious error is more fruitful for science than stupid accuracy." [9] However, he cautioned against introducing ideas from the natural sciences into the social sciences. Weber's

---

[6] *Methodology,* p. 98f.
[7] *Methodology,* p. 68.
[8] *From Max Weber,* p. 300.
[9] Max Weber, *General Economic History* (New York: Collier paperback 1961), p. 40.

criticism of the German historical school is applicable to the entire range of naturalistic positivism and to sociocultural positivism as well. Theorists of the historical school, said Weber,

> . . . still hold in many ways, expressly or tacitly, to the opinion that it is the end and the goal of every science to order its data into a system of concepts, the content of which is to be acquired and slowly perfected through the observation of empirical regularities, the construction of hypotheses, and their verification, until finally a "completed" and *hence* deductive science emerges. . . .
>
> This conception was, in principle, impregnable within the framework of the classical-scholastic epistemology which was still fundamentally assumed by the majority of the research-workers identified with the Historical School. The function of concepts was assumed to be the reproduction of "objective" reality in the analysts' imagination. Hence the recurrent references to the *unreality* of all clear-cut concepts. If one perceives the implications of the fundamental ideas of modern epistemology which ultimately derives from Kant, namely, that concepts are primarily analytical instruments for the intellectual mastery of empirical data and can be only that, the fact that precise genetic concepts are necessarily ideal types will not cause him to desist from constructing them. The relationship between concept and historical research is reversed for those who appreciate this; the goal of the Historical School then appears as logically impossible, the concepts are not ends but are means to the end of understanding phenomena which are significant from concrete individual viewpoints.[10]

Those who claim that the use of primitive ideal-type constructs reflects the adolescence of a science are right, said Weber, but for the wrong reason:

> There are sciences to which eternal youth is granted, and the historical disciplines are among them—all those to which the eternally onward flowing stream of culture perpetually brings new problems. At the very heart of their task lies not only the transiency of *all* ideal types *but* also at the same time the inevitability of *new* ones. . . .[11]

Weber summarized his philosophical orientation thus:

> In the empirical social sciences, the possibility of meaningful knowledge of what is essential for us in the infinite richness of events is bound up with the unremitting application of viewpoints of a specifically particularized character, which, in the last analysis,

---

[10] *Methodology*, p. 106.
[11] *Methodology*, p. 104.

are oriented on the basis of evaluative ideas. These evaluative ideas are for their part empirically discoverable and analyzable as elements of meaningful human conduct, but their validity can *not* be deduced from empirical data as such. The "objectivity" of the social sciences depends rather on the fact that the empirical data are always related to those evaluative ideas which alone make them worth knowing and the significance of the empirical data is derived from these evaluative ideas. But these data can never become the foundation for the empirically impossible proof of the validity of the evaluative ideas. The belief which we all have in some form or other, in the meta-empirical validity of ultimate and final values, in which the meaning of our existence is rooted, is not incompatible with the incessant changefulness of the concrete viewpoints, from which empirical reality gets its significance. Both these views are, on the contrary, in harmony with each other. Life with its irrational reality and its store of possible meanings is inexhaustible. The *concrete* form in which value-relevance occurs remains perpetually in flux, ever subject to change in the dimly seen future of human culture. The light which emanates from those highest evaluative ideas always falls on an ever changing finite segment of the vast chaotic stream of events, which flows away through time.[12]

The Method of Understanding

"Sociology," argued Weber, "is a science which attempts the interpretive understanding of social action in order thereby to arrive at a causal explanation of its course and effects."[13] Underlying this formal definition is Weber's belief that social action refers to human behavior that has meaning for individuals and that interpretive understanding refers to the interpretation of individuals' subjective states. The word *meaning*

> . . . may refer first to the actual existing meaning in the given concrete case of a particular actor, or to the average or approximate meaning attributable to a given plurality of actors; or secondly to the theoretically conceived pure type of subjective meaning attributed to the hypothetical actor or actors in a given type of action. In no case does it refer to an objectively "correct" meaning or one which is "true" in some metaphysical sense. It is this which distinguishes the empirical sciences of action, such as sociology and history, from the dogmatic disciplines in that area, such as jurisprudence, logic, ethics, and aesthetics, which seek to

[12] *Methodology*, p. 111.
[13] *S.E.O.*, p. 88.

> ascertain the "true" and "valid" meanings associated with the objects of their investigation.[14]

And, Weber continued,

> All interpretation of meaning, like all scientific observation, strives for clarity and verifiable accuracy of insight and comprehension. The basis for certainty in understanding can be either rational, which can be further subdivided into logical and mathematical, or it can be of an emotionally empathic or artistically appreciative quality.[15]

It is sometimes difficult to rethink or refeel the particular subject under investigation, especially when the values of the subject are remote or alien to the investigator. Imaginative participation is easiest with logical or mathematical propositions or when dealing with rational behavior—that is, when someone employs adequate means to secure an end. It is most difficult when dealing with emotions and the irrational behavior that emerges from them—the kind of situation that the ideal type is designed to overcome. "For purposes of a typological scientific analysis it is convenient to treat all irrational, affectually determined elements of behavior as factors of deviations from a conceptually pure type of rational action." [16]

By constructing a hypothetically rational scheme of action, a scheme of action in which adequate means are employed to achieve objectives, the investigator can attribute deviations from this course to emotionality, error, and the like.

> Whatever the content of the ideal-type, be it an ethical, a legal, an aesthetic, or a religious norm, or a technical, an economic, or a cultural maxim or any other type of valuation in the most rational form possible, it has only one function in an empirical investigation. Its function is the comparison with empirical reality in order to establish its divergences or similarities, to describe them with the *most unambiguously intelligible concepts,* and to understand and explain them causally.[17]

The ideal type, Weber cautioned, is a " . . . methodological device. It certainly does not involve a belief in the actual predominance of rational elements in human life. . . . "

If the main task of the sciences of human behavior is understanding, then what is the specific procedure of understanding, or *verstehen?* The first level is "observational understanding," but the more important level is what

[14] *S.E.O.,* p. 89f.
[15] *S.E.O.,* p. 90.
[16] *S.E.O.,* p. 92.
[17] *Methodology,* p. 43; also see pp. 89–112 for a more extended discussion of ideal types.

Weber called "explanatory understanding," which gives the motive or intention of the actor, an operation "which consists in placing the act in an intelligible and more inclusive context of meaning." Establishing the motive of an actor must be distinguished from causation because it is often difficult to find situations where the motive is clear or conscious to either the actor or the observer.

> A correct causal interpretation of a concrete course of action is arrived at when the overt action and the motives have both been correctly apprehended and at the same time their relation has become meaningfully comprehensible. A correct causal interpretation of typical action means that the process which is claimed to be typical is shown to be both adequately grasped on the level of meaning and at the same time the interpretation is to some degree causally adequate. If adequacy in respect to meaning is lacking, then no matter how high the degree of uniformity and how precisely its probability can be numerically determined, it is still an incomprehensible statistical probability, whether dealing with overt or subjective processes. On the other hand, even the most perfect adequacy on the level of meaning has causal significance from a sociological point of view only in so far as there is some kind of proof for the existence of a probability that action in fact normally takes the course which has been held to be meaningful. For this there must be some degree of determinable frequency of approximation to an average or a pure type.[18]

Weber insisted that, in establishing causation, heavy reliance be placed on the comparative method, and that the subject matter of sociology always be the behavior of individual human beings. Collectivities such as states, nations, or families must be thought of as the actions of individuals. Collectivities may be approached as functional systems, said Weber, but caution must be used.

> It is the method of the so-called "organic" school of sociology to attempt to understand social interaction by using as a point of departure the "whole" within which the individual acts. His action and behavior are then interpreted somewhat in the way that a physiologist would treat the role of an organ of the body in the "economy" of the organism, that is from the point of view of the survival of the latter. How far in other disciplines this type of functional analysis of the relation of "parts" to a "whole" can be regarded as definitive, cannot be discussed here; but it is well-known that the bio-chemical and bio-physical modes of analysis of the organism are on principle opposed to stopping there. For purposes of sociological analysis two things can be said. First this

[18] *S.E.O.*, p. 99f.

functional frame of reference is convenient for purposes of practical illustration and for provisional orientation. In these respects it is not only useful but indispensable. But at the same time if its cognitive value is overestimated and its concepts illegitimately "reified" it can be highly dangerous. Secondly, in certain circumstances this is the only available way of determining just what processes of social action it is important to understand in order to explain a given phenomenon. But this is only the beginning of sociological analysis as here understood. In the case of social collectivities, precisely as distinguished from organisms, we are in a position to go beyond merely demonstrating functional relationships and uniformities. We can accomplish something which is never attainable in the natural sciences; namely the subjective understanding of the actions of component individuals. The natural sciences on the other hand cannot do this, being limited to the formulation of causal uniformities in objects and events and the explanation of individual facts by applying them. We do not "understand" the behavior of cells, but can only observe the relevant functional relationships and generalize on the basis of these observations. This additional achievement of explanation by interpretive understanding, as distinguished from external observation, is of course attained only at a price—the more hypothetical and fragmentary character of its results. Nevertheless, subjective understanding is the specific characteristic of sociological knowledge.[19]

Weber was careful to deny that his focus on the individual implied an "individualistic system of values." He also warned against attributing human action to psychology, a view consistent with his sharp separation of the natural from the social sciences. In his discussion of the specific procedures of sociology, Weber also separated sociology from history, and by implication, from philosophy and philosophy of history. Sociology offers "limited generalizations," that is, it can go beyond history's bondage to the unique, though it cannot supply universal generalizations. It uses the methods of science, but to achieve a type of knowledge suitable to its subject matter, human behavior. It must resist turning human existence into natural existence as historians and sociologists of the old (naturalistic) positivist orientation have tried to do. However, sociology must not succumb to the temptation to look for a philosophical or metaempirical meaning to human existence.

Rational and Nonrational Types of Action

Separating the methodological aspects of a theorist's work from the substantive aspects is always difficult. This is especially true of Weber, who

[19] S.E.O., p. 102ff.

insisted on the intimate relation of each to the other. His use of the concept of *rationality* to order the subject matter of sociology is an important example. Difficult to define, the concept of rationality assumed different shades of meaning in various contexts, which is not as inconsistent as it sounds given Weber's thoroughly instrumental attitude toward ideas. Weber's definition of rationality is best approached by showing how it was used in a number of key contexts, which will also introduce his famous methodological tool, the ideal type.

In his methodology, Weber insisted on a steady interplay between theory and fact, a cardinal principle of Enlightenment philosophy. He differed from the Enlightenment and its heirs in his belief that the purpose of that interplay is not to uncover social reality, but to render portions of it amenable to human understanding and control. In the interaction between value-relevant ideas and data, each illuminates the other. The epistemological problem of the validity of knowledge about human beings and society was irrelevant for Weber; neither the subject matter (human action, biology, psychology, history, society, state) nor the method (science, empiricism, logic, mathematics) is the source of knowledge; and yet together they are. Knowledge results from a morally imbued process of perception, not from the fixed attributes of mind, method, or subject matter. Knowledge is the process of perception itself, and it emanates from felt value needs that rely on arbitrary images to clarify the empirical world in terms of those needs. In turn, the empirical world helps to form those images and thus shapes the scientist's ability to satisfy or select values.

Weber's orientation explains his interest in the concept of rationality and in the exploratory image called an ideal type. Without a fixed point in either fact or logic, analysts must develop their own guidelines. By deliberately developing an image of how a practice or institution would work if it were ideally rational, the analyst can then see how the empirical world deviates from the ideal type. An example of an ideal type is Weber's classification of forms of social action.

> Social action, like other forms of action, may be classified in the following four types according to its mode of orientation:
> 1. in terms of rational orientation to a system of discrete individual ends, that is, through expectations as to the behavior of objects in the external situation and of other human individuals, making use of these expectations as "conditions" or "means" for the successful attainment of the actor's own rationally chosen ends;
> 2. in terms of rational orientation to an absolute value; involving a conscious belief in the absolute value of some ethical, aesthetic, religious, or other form of behavior, entirely for its own sake and independently of any prospects of external success;
> 3. in terms of affectual orientation, especially emotional, determined by the specific affects and states of feeling of the actor;

4. traditionally oriented, through the habituation of long practice.[20]

Running through Weber's classification is a distinction between instrumental, means-ends, "formal" rationality and absolutist, "substantive" rationality, a distinction that occupied a central position in his thought. It is similar to the distinction employed in this study between historical and substantialist types of knowledge about human behavior. This perspective stemmed from Weber's distinction between reason, fact, and value, and he developed it in a number of ways. For example, he characterized value-idea orientations as based on an ethic of responsibility or on an ethic of absolute ends—that is, individuals must accept responsibility for the consequences of their action or they must follow certain ethical imperatives regardless of consequences.

Weber's distinction between types of rationality is full of ambiguities, especially when as he himself noted, the definition of absolute rationality includes every and any variety of philosophical orientation. Weber reshaped the distinction between formal and substantive rationality to suit the problem he was working on. He employed his distinction between types of rationality to analyze economic, political, administrative, and religious institutions. However, his classification of human actions according to the criterion of rationality was a methodological device—he was not interested in verifying hypotheses, in attributing rationality to the world of behavior, or in formulating metaphysical entities. The terms are shaded to render them useful in whatever context they are employed, the main purpose being to uncover modes of empirical behavior so that causation and problems can be more effectively understood in keeping with a researcher's felt values.

SUBSTANTIVE WORK

The Problematic Nature of Society

Weber's overriding interest was not merely the problem of modern Western society, but society itself. A concern for society is, of course, not rare in intellectual history; what distinguishes Weber's work is his unique formulation of this concern. Like Durkheim, Simmel, and Pareto, Weber could not accept the easy optimism and logic of the evolutionary school, liberal or Marxian, or of any doctrine that sought to explain human existence in terms of a single principle. Much more explicitly than any other sociologist except Montesquieu, Weber regarded social existence as problematical in and of itself.[21] However, given the more pragmatic atmosphere of the late nineteenth century, Weber also thought of society in terms of particular prob-

---

[20] S.E.O. p. 115.
[21] Hobbes, who also raised the problem of order, never questioned the existence of order somewhere.

lems and solutions.[22] Since no universal standard exists by which to judge society or its problems, the only appeal is to history—that is, to an analysis of the historical causes of society and a comparison of variables on a cross-cultural basis.

Weber was not problem oriented, however, in the ordinary meaning of the term. His interest in the empirical study of specific problems was genuine enough, though he did not seem to view such studies primarily as pathways to an understanding of social structure, as Durkheim had done. His interest seemed more political and ameliorative than theoretical. Weber's problematic mentality expressed itself most creatively in his study of perennial academic or social philosophical issues, hoping only to attack those problems in a more scientific way. The questions that concerned him were the origin of society, its decay and rebirth, sources of social stability and tension, the role of ideas in history, and the question of causation in general. Out of his concern came a series of analyses with revolutionary import for sociological theory.

Weber was not content to view these issues solely from within his own society or even as a Westerner. If, as he believed, the scientist's perception illuminates the world, then it is important to enrich perception by exploring a subject from every possible viewpoint. Weber's restless quest for Olympian detachment may be explained perhaps by his personal life,[23] or by his experiences in a social structure that generated a strong intellectual culture by its failure to develop normal political outlets for the talented members of German society. Whatever the reason—and one should remember Weber's own admonition that "men are not open books"—Weber found himself exploring the innermost nature of liberal society through comparisions constructed on a vast historical and global scale. Throughout his studies, he followed his own caution against mixing science and personal preferences. Despite a passionate nature with deep moral and political commitments, he rarely revealed his own preferences. One can infer, of course, from his research interests and the themes he emphasizd and returned to, what his values were; after all, he followed his own method, which laid heavy stress on the need to select research in terms of felt problems and values.

[22] Weber not only engaged in empirical studies of agricultural and industrial labor, but he used, and seemed greatly interested in, quantitative methods; in this regard see Paul F. Lazarsfeld and Anthony R. Oberschall, "Max Weber and Empirical Social Research," *American Sociological Review* 30 (April 1965):185–199.

[23] For a biography by Weber's wife, see Marianne Weber, *Max Weber: A Biography,* trans. Harry Zohn (New York: John Wiley, 1975), original German edition 1926. For a brief but excellent biographical sketch, see the Introduction to *From Max Weber,* by H. H. Gerth and C. W. Mills, pp. 3–31. For a brilliant Freudian analysis of Weber, which is also a superb examination of his intellectual development, see Arthur Mitzman, *The Iron Cage: An Historical Interpretation of Max Weber* (New York: Alfred Knopf, 1970).

Types of Economic Action

Weber's deep interest in economics, even when it led him into seemingly technical or remote research topics, was always focused to shed light on the origins, nature, and destiny of capitalism. It is not surprising, therefore, that when he constructed categories for understanding economic action he did so on the basis of the distinction between formally rational (capitalist, exchange, or market) and substantively rational (socialist, household agrarian, and natural) economic systems. The result is a series of fascinating contrasts in such specialized economic topics as credit, money, occupations, division of labor, accounting, and motivation. The contrast between these two rival economic systems was developed in many ways: by discussing the conditions necessary for a capitalist economy; by referring to the inevitable tension between the two systems; by arguing that centralized economic planning and socialism are incapable of formal rationality and must inevitably succumb to traditionalism. Weber's detailed description of the conditions that produce formal economic rationality is central to his argument:

> The following are the principal conditions necessary for obtaining a maximum of formal rationality of capital accounting in productive enterprises:
>
> 1. The complete appropriation of all the nonhuman means of production by owners and the complete absence of all formal appropriation of opportunities for profit in the market; that is, market freedom;
>
> 2. Complete autonomy in the selection of management by the owners, thus complete absence of formal appropriation of rights to managerial functions;
>
> 3. The complete absence of appropriation of jobs and of opportunities for earning by workers, and conversely, the absence of appropriation of workers by owners. This involves free labor, freedom of the labor market, and freedom in the selection of workers;
>
> 4. Complete absence of substantive regulation of consumption, production, and prices, or of other forms of regulation which limit freedom of contract or specify conditions of exchange. This may be called substantive freedom of contract;
>
> 5. The maximum of calculability of the technical conditions of the productive process; that is, a mechanically rational technology;
>
> 6. Complete calculability of the functioning of the public administration and the legal order and a reliable formal guarantee of all contracts by the political authority. This is formally rational administration and law;
>
> 7. The most complete possible separation of the enterprise and its conditions of success and failure, from the household or private budgetary unit and its property interests. It is particularly important that the capital at the disposal of the enterprise should be clearly distinguished from the private wealth of the owners, and

should not be subject to division or dispersion through inheritance. For large-scale enterprises, this condition tends to approach an optimum from a formal point of view in the fields of transport, manufacture, and mining, when they are organized in corporate form with freely transferrable shares and limited liability. In the field of agriculture, relatively long-term leases on a large-scale constitute formally the most favorable situation.

8. A monetary system with the highest possible degree of formal rationality.[24]

The foregoing is more than a sketch of economic conditions. It depicts an entire institutional system, including specific structural requirements for family, political, administrative, and legal relationships.

Types of Domination: Politics, Law, and Administration

The same Balzacean urge to bring order into the rich variety of human behavior is found in Weber's political analyses. Not surprisingly, his political orientation is in the tradition begun by Machiavelli; he insisted that politics and morality are separate and often at variance.[25] Yet he also recognized that human beings do not reveal their interests nakedly but clothe them in garments of legitimacy. Individuals submit themselves or dominate others in terms of what they believe are valid principles of authority. As a result, power structures can become qualitatively different from each other and produce qualitatively different consequences.

Though there are numerous admixtures of the "structures of domination," there are three pure types of legitimate authority: *rational-legal, traditional,* and *charismatic.*[26] No attention can be given to the subvarieties of political types or to the combinations of types that Weber outlined except to warn again against thinking of Weber as a formal theorist. The basic spirit of his work is directed against any form of conceptual realism, and he took great pains to keep his ideal types in constant touch with the rich abundance and diversity of human experience. Within his three main types of authority he found distinctive political forms that he also characterized in ideal-typical fashion. These include types of administration under such headings as bureaucracy, gerontocracy, patriarchalism, and patrimonialism; the forms and problems peculiar to charismatic authority; types of social and political structures that limit authority through such devices as collegiality (rule by

---

[24] *S.E.O.*, p. 275f.
[25] *From Max Weber*, "Politics as a Vocation," esp. pp. 117–128.
[26] *S.E.O.*, pt. 3. Note the similarity of these types with Simmel's classification of superordination and subordination in terms of subjection to an objective principle, the group, or one person.

equal and independent colleagues), separation of powers, and representation; types of political-party organization; and types of legal structure.[27] However, perhaps the best way to understand domination, for Weber, was through an analysis of types of administrative structures, again classified by type of rationality.

Weber distinguished two basic forms of administration, the patrimonial and the bureaucratic.[28] Bureaucratic behavior emerges from the application of science to administrative problems and exists in a stable modal form only in modern society. Such behavior ensues, said Weber, when the canons of formal rationality begin to pervade the relationships of human beings with each other as well as with nature. Once established, this rationality begins to rule out all nonrational factors such as family, birth, race, emotions, and religion as the basis of administrative performance. A strict hierarchy of relationships based on impersonal rules is established, and the recruitment of personnel is based on professionalism. The business of the bureaucracy is sharply separated from the individual's other interests, especially the family, as to both location and equipment. The bureaucratic mechanism is far more efficient and responsible than patrimonial administration. In the latter form of administration, responsibilities are embedded in a diffused, undifferentiated complex of political, family, and religious obligations, and the administrator's status and equipment are both obtained through ascriptive right and thought of as personal property.

Types of Domination: Social Stratification

Weber's brief essay, "Class, Status, Party," [29] is a far-reaching contribution to social-stratification theory. The essay's definition of law and power are similar to those found in the positivist branches of modern legal and political theory.

> Law exists when there is a probability that an order will be upheld by a specific staff of men who will use physical or psychical compulsion with the intention of obtaining conformity with the order, or of inflicting sanction for infringement of it. The structure of every legal order directly influences the distribution of power, economic or otherwise, within its respective community. This is true of all legal orders and not only that of the state. In general, we understand by "power" the chance of a man or of a number of

---

[27] *Max Weber on Law in Economy and Society,* ed. with introduction and annotations by Max Rheinstein, trans. Edward Shils and Max Rheinstein (Cambridge, Mass.: Harvard University Press, 1954), also in paperback.
[28] *From Max Weber,* chap. 8.
[29] *From Max Weber,* chap. 7.

men to realize their own will in a communal action even against the resistance of others who are participating in the action.[30]

Power for Weber could come from law, economic status, or considerations of "honor." With these simple distinctions, Weber opened the door to a wide-ranging critique of Marx's theory of social stratification and of all monocausal theories of inequality, economic or otherwise. For Weber "class" stratification—that is, the distribution of life chances in terms of economic status—was merely one factor among many in the creation of social inequality. He agreed with Marx that the economic factor is extremely important and that the distinction between propertied and propertyless is crucial. However, Weber insisted, even within a purely economic focus there are types of class structure and of class struggle, given the variations in types of property and in those who are propertyless. Thus, he distinguished different types of market situation: credit, commodity, and labor.

Running through Weber's analysis is the distinction between communal action (feelings of solidarity) and societal action (the rationally motivated pursuit or adjustment of interests). A class situation may or may not engender communal action, or in Marx's terms, class consciousness and struggle. The extent of class action is dependent on the "transparency" of the class situation, that is, on the extent to which actors can attribute class stratification to the economic system rather than to unalterable natural or divine causes. In opposition to Marx, Weber insisted that a class situation emerges not from the interaction of members of a class but from the interaction of *different* classes. All in all, concluded Weber, not much can be said of a general nature about the specific kinds of class except to point out that a struggle over the price of credit, over commodities, and over labor has been characteristic, respectively, of the ancient, the medieval, and the modern world.

Stratification analysis, Weber continued, must clearly distinguish between class or economic causation and "status" causation, or causation that stems from principles of "honor." Stratification by status may be based on breeding, birth, ethnicity, religion, democratic equalitarianism, or even property. It is linked in innumerable ways to class, but it always fights the sheer principle of property and the class-related spirit of formal rationality that knows no personal distinctions; it is often decisive in its struggle with the economic order. Stratification by status can proceed in all directions to control both material and psychic goods and often has a strong and even controlling impact on an economy. Its characteristic interests are expressed in such phenomena as endogamous marriage provisions; entailed estates; honorific

[30] *From Max Weber,* p. 180.

costumes, foods, and skills; and the monopolization of preferred occupations. Most of these phenomena impose nonrational restrictions on the free play of market interests, especially the withholding of land from the jurisdiction of the market through entail. Where the logic of status stratification is carried out fully, status groups develop into *castes*. In caste stratification, "rituals" are added to convention and law to stereotype all interaction and thus insure total and rigid inequality. Caste is especially possible with a radically inequalitarian religion such as Hinduism.[31]

A stable economy supports status stratification whereas dynamic economic conditions retard its influence. Weber's discussion of social stratification trailed off into a fragmentary statement about "parties," or groups that struggle to obtain political power. The structure of the political party varies with the prevalent form of domination; it may represent class and/or status interests; it may use the most varied means of obtaining or influencing communal power; and its existence presupposes an advanced societalization —that is, a substantial degree of formal rationality, often leading to separate political and legal institutions.

The implications of Weber's theory of social stratification go far beyond his criticism of Marx. Weber dismissed, for example, through complete indifference, the entire naturalistic psychological tradition in which theorists such as Saint-Simon, Comte, Spencer, and Sumner had sought to explain inequality (and Ward had sought to explain equality) by direct reference to human qualities. In keeping with the general spirit of his work, Weber went beyond the mere refutation of Marx's monocausal class theory—he also denied that a unified theory of social stratification, monocausal or multicausal, is possible.

Types of Religion

Weber's profoundly original and influential essay, *The Protestant Ethic and the Spirit of Capitalism,"* [32] is more than an attempt to show the causal power of religion. It also illustrates Weber's fundamental methodological perspective that social phenomena can be understood only in terms of the widest possible grasp of comparative materials. This perspective is reflected in his decision at the end of the essay to continue his study of the reciprocal effects between religion and society, especially on a comparative basis. Thus,

---

[31] For Weber's substantive work on Hindu caste stratification, see his *The Religion of India*, trans. and ed. H. H. Gerth and Don Martindale (New York: Free Press, 1958), chaps. 1–3, also in paperback; excerpts from these chapters may be found in *From Max Weber*, chap. 16.

[32] Trans. and intro. Talcott Parsons, 1930 (New York: Charles Scribner paperback, 1958).

in tackling the problem of the origin and nature of capitalism, Weber turned from an internal historical examination of capitalism to a study of capitalism from the outside. Though Weber went on from *The Protestant Ethic* to studies and essays on comparative religion, he did so in a value-neutral sense—that is, he was interested in the social, and especially the economic, impact of religion, and not the truth of religion. Furthermore, he did not regard religion as the only or even as the most important cause of capitalism, only as a necessary cause.

Though Weber's unfinished synthesis of sociology, *Wirtschaft und Gesellechaft*, contains a long section entitled "The Sociology of Religion," [33] neither here nor elsewhere does his work contain a precisely stated religious typology. The general logic of his analysis is relatively clear, however, and with the help of the above work can be extracted almost completely from his two essays, "The Social Psychology of the World Religions" and "Religious Rejections of the World and Their Directions." [34]

In constructing religious types Weber used two sets of polar opposites: first, the analytically and causally relevant distinction between "material" existence (geography, technology, stratification, mundane exigencies) and "ideal" existence (the realm of meaning and conceptions of the supermundane); and second, the analytically and causally relevant distinction *within* the sphere of meaning between nonrational and rational conceptions of the ideal. In the latter distinction, Weber again arranged his material in terms of his master problem, the identification of the variables associated with the rise of capitalism.[35]

Weber's first distinction in his dissection of the incredibly complex realm of ideal existence was between magic and religion proper, or irrational and rational religion. Magical religions are thoroughly and completely conservative; in Weber's words, they "safeguard the traditional" because they employ ad hoc solutions. The norm type of magical religion is the taboo—that is, the nonabstract rule relevant only for concrete persons, objects, and situations. Magical religion tends to develop a polytheistic or pantheistic image of the world, that is, a nonabstract image of the world's causal process. As

---

[33] Now available as *The Sociology of Religion,* trans. Ephraim Fischoff and intro. Talcott Parsons (Boston: Beacon Press, 1963), also in paperback.

[34] *From Max Weber,* chaps. 11, 13. In addition to these works, Weber wrote detailed studies on Confucianism, Judaism, and Hinduism, available in translation as *The Religion of China: Confucianism and Taoism,* trans. and ed. H. H. Gerth (New York: Free Press, 1951), also in paperback; *Ancient Judaism,* trans. and ed. H. H. Gerth and Don Martindale (New York: Free Press, 1952), also in paperback; *The Religion of India,* trans. and ed. H. H. Gerth and Don Martindale (New York: Free Press, 1958), also in paperback.

[35] *From Max Weber,* pp. 293–294.

such, it is neither substantively nor formally rational, but an irrational "empiricism." Its effect on practical conduct is to mire a people in the immediately given by blocking a cognitive grasp of the empirical realm.

When the magician is replaced by the priest and the prophet, the bearers of rational religion, a sharply opposite impact on society develops. For Weber, religion was not rational in the sense of being true or scientifically valid, but rational to the degree that it departed from magic. The primary norm type of rational religion is ethics—that is, an abstract body of rules governing all conduct under all conditions. Rational religion develops a fixed goal of salvation, it establishes its theology and ethics apart from nature and the empirically given, and it prescribes methodical, pragmatic means of attaining religious goals. Its image of God is monotheistic and the power of God or prime cause is universal. Rational religion emerges when human beings develop a systematic and rationalized redemptory stand against the world. Though there are many types of redemptory religion, "behind them always lies a stand toward something in the actual world which is experienced as specifically 'senseless.' Thus, the demand has been implied: that the world order in its totality is, could, and should be a meaningful 'cosmos.' " [36]

Weber then identified five rational or world religions, Confucian, Hinduist, Buddhist, Christian, and Islamist. This identification was a preliminary toward his real objective, which was to identify *substantively* rational as opposed to *formally* rational religions. The key to Weber's argument is the religious phenomenon known as prophecy. Rational religions may be classified into two main groups, *exemplary* and *emissary* prophecy. Each orientation has a different concept of God and a different way of realizing religious values.

> Exemplary prophecy points out the path to salvation by exemplary living, usually by a contemplative and apathetic-ecstatic life. The emissary type of prophecy addresses its *demands* to the world in the name of a god. Naturally these demands are ethical; and they are often of an active ascetic character. . . .
>
> In the missionary prophecy the devout have not experienced themselves as vessels of the divine but rather as instruments of a god. This emissary prophecy has had a profound elective affinity to a special conception of God: the conception of a supramundane, personal, wrathful, forgiving, loving, demanding, punishing Lord of Creation. Such a conception stands in contrast to the supreme being of exemplary prophecy. As a rule, though by no means without exception, the supreme being of an exemplary prophecy is an impersonal being because, as a static state, he is accessible

[36] *From Max Weber,* p. 281; further material on the above may be found in *The Sociology of Religion,* chaps. 1–5.

only by means of contemplation. The conception of an active God, held by emissary prophecy, has dominated the Iranian and Mid-Eastern religions and those Occidental religions which are derived from them. The conception of a supreme and static being, held by exemplary prophecy, has come to dominate Indian and Chinese religiosity.[37]

Though different social strata have always had specific affinities for different types of religion, Weber contended that the type of religion has also been influential in shaping social strata. One of the important empirical facts of religious history is that human beings have been stratified in the eyes of religion. The most obvious case is Hinduism, but differential religious quali-fications also exist in the Calvinistic doctrine of predestination, where the grace of God falls only upon the Elect. The idea that only a few, whether shamans, sorcerers, ascetics, or intellectuals, can achieve religious values is what Weber called *virtuoso religiosity* as opposed to mass religiosity. Virtuosity has always been in conflict with the hierocratic church, which seeks to institutionalize grace for the masses. Whether the form of virtuosity is exemplary or emissary will have profound consequences for economic and social life, a fact that looms large in Weber's analysis of the rise of capitalism.

The Origins of Capitalism: Multiple and Nonunitary Causation

The nature and origin of capitalism was a problem for German intellectuals in a way that was not true in other Western countries, especially England and the United States. Given the gradual development of capitalism in England, its beginnings in small-scale enterprise and its association with economic individualism and political-legal liberty and equality, English social theorists largely agreed on one fundamental point: the mainsprings of economic and social development were in the individual. In Germany, however, capitalism emerged abruptly and was associated with large-scale economic units and authoritarian political and military policy. For German intellectuals, therefore, the origins and even the very nature and survival of capitalism were problematic.[38]

Weber directed most of his writings on capitalism against two of his country-men, Karl Marx and Werner Sombart (1863–1941). In his arguments,

---

[37] *From Max Weber,* p. 285f; for more details, see *The Sociology of Religion,* chap. 4, where these two types of prophecy are called *exemplary* and *ethical prophecy.*
[38] For a comparison of Marx and Weber along these lines, see Norman Birnbaum, "Conflicting Interpretations of the Rise of Capitalism: Marx and Weber," *British Journal of Sociology* 4 (June 1953):125–141; also available as Bobbs-Merrill reprint S-26.

Weber enjoyed a supreme advantage. His incredible scholarship had familiarized him with almost every civilized area of the globe: Mediterranean antiquity, the Middle East, India, China, medieval and modern Europe, and even the United States. He had a comprehensive grasp of four major areas of human behavior—economics, law, politics, and religion—and related interests and skills in the analysis of administration, warfare, technology, and urban existence.

Weber summarized his views on the rise of capitalism shortly before his death.[39] He rejected the idea that capitalism was caused by an increase in population, as he rejected Sombart's view that it came from the influx of precious metals. He cited geography, military requirements, and the luxury trade as favorable factors, but "in the last resort the factor which produced capitalism is the rational permanent enterprise, rational accounting, rational technology and rational law, but again not these alone. Necessary complementary factors were the rational spirit, the rationalization of the conduct of life in general, and a rationalistic economic ethic." [40]

According to Weber, the main enemy of the "spirit of capitalism" is traditionalism, especially the stereotyping of economic behavior by magic. The Jews did not develop capitalism because their dualistic ethics forbade impersonal economic relations with one's tribal brother. In addition, they were an outcast guest people, and, above all, were strongly traditionalistic. However, Judaism transmitted to Christianity the strong hostility to magic that had emerged in its prophetic tradition. A prophecy strong enough to deliver human beings from their bondage to the magical was absent in China but was present in India. However, Indian religion was exemplary and aristocratic, developing an otherworldly asceticism for only a thin stratum of intellectuals and monks. Only Judaism and Christianity developed as plebian religions, religions that defeated magic and held up obligatory commands for all. However, the traditionalism of Judaism was matched by that of medieval Catholicism. Medieval Catholicism also developed an otherworldly form of asceticism (monasteries), and its magical sacraments, which delivered salvation in an ad hoc, piecemeal fashion, were a great barrier to the development of a methodical, rational way of life.

The Reformation eliminated the dualistic ethics of both Judaism and the Roman church as well as tendencies toward virtuoso religion by otherworldly adepts. Protestant Christians were called one and all to do God's work in this world and to accept the problems of the world as a challenge to their character. As Protestants they could neither withdraw from the

---

[39] These have been reprinted as *General Economic History,* trans. F. H. Knight, 1927 (New York: Collier paperback, 1961), pt. 4.
[40] Weber, *General Economic History,* p. 260.

world nor accommodate themselves to it under the auspices of an ecclesiastical hierarchy. Given the need to avoid creatural temptations, Calvinism soon came to see work as a calling in which one administers what God has given. As a result there emerged a methodical, impersonal, individualist type of conduct, especially in economic affairs, that combined with a religious brake on consumption to stimulate both capital formation and the spirit of capitalism. Out of the Reformation came a merger of religious and economic behavior in which economic success signified religious worth and religious status provided economic motives and credentials.

Weber did not think of religion either as the only or even as the major cause of capitalism. If anything, his major emphasis was on economic factors, followed by political and religious factors. However, while he was multicausal, he put no emphasis on establishing priorities; he was more interested in citing the many and complex causes of behavior. Thus he emphasized economic factors such as the emergence of technology, especially in the textile industry; the pre-eminent importance of coal and iron, which freed industry from inorganic and organic limitations; and the rise of new forms of economic organization such as the joint-stock company. He also emphasized political factors such as law, administration, warfare, and types of urban existence. Weber had a strong interest in urbanization, which led him to argue that a special type of city emerged in the West, especially during the medieval period.[41] Only in the medieval city, Weber asserted, did a community develop—that is, a general sense of sameness expressed in a common political and legal identity. This development went hand in hand with differences in military requirements. In the West, the city was set against the countryside, whereas "in the East the army of the prince is older than the city." As a community of merchants and artisans, the Western city developed an elaborate legal and administrative structure to further its economic and political interests.

All of the above factors, said Weber, together with a relatively congenial religious climate, were the cause of capitalism. While religion invariably stagnates, even suffocates, rational economic and social action, Christianity did not. Though medieval Christianity sought to block capitalism, it could not do so; indeed, Christianity contained religious elements that, once separated out as Protestantism, actively aided the rise of capitalism.

Weber's multicausal theory was distinctive in two ways. First, while other theorists such as Durkheim, Simmel, and Pareto had stressed multiple causation, Weber's causal theory was based on a more comprehensive grasp of materials. Second, one must go back to Montesquieu to find a

---

[41] Max Weber, *The City*, trans. and ed. Don Martindale and Gertrude Neuwirth (New York: Free Press, 1958), also in paperback.

parallel to Weber's insistence that there is no unitary thread to human causation. It is this feature of his thought that separates Weber from the other pluralistic positivists and makes his theory the least substantialistic in the history of sociology.

Weber's sense of the fortuitous nature of causation is best expressed, of course, in his explanation of the origins of capitalism. His insistence that religion, ethics, ideas, and values be incorporated into causal theory in no way implied that any version of normative culture was true or inherent in human nature. What Weber meant was that human beings live by values and ideas, and that when values and ideas are taken seriously, they affect behavior. However, while normative culture affects material culture and society, these in turn affect normative culture.

Weber's denial that human nature had inherent propensities, together with his wide grasp of historical materials, led him away from general or systematic theory. His nominalism led him only to limited or historical generalizations. Wherever he found a sequence or uniformity, he was careful to qualify his observation by pointing out that a different development emerged from a similar situation. His antipathy to systematic sociology also marks his characterization of capitalism; in Weber's overall theory capitalism emerges only because of a fortuitous confluence of factors, some new, some old or dormant, and some ironic and unintentional.

There are two poles of emphasis in Weber's work, and the stuff of history is hung between them. One pole is rooted in the idea of social integration and interdependence. Social institutions tend to form coherent systems with an underlying logic or spirit. Structures of behavior and values tend to be congruent and to reinforce each other. Vast crystallized structures can take hold of a population and hold it in sway for long periods of time. The unity of these structures may derive from religion, tradition, or bureaucracy.

The other pole of human behavior is buried in the soil of conflict and tension. Again and again Weber pointed to the incompatibilities between institutional areas and their values, attributing conflict and disjointedness sometimes to chance and other times to charisma or unintended consequences. The awareness of social conflict and contradiction was a widespread feature of nineteenth-century intellectual culture, but Weber's orientation was by far the most sophisticated. He saw social life as an unending series of choices between alternatives in which one value or idea had to be paid for in terms of others. His view was stark and uncompromising and amounted to a skeptical utilitarianism that saw no ultimate harmony or terminal point to the incessant moral nature of human life. It was this outlook that gave him a unique perspective on capitalism. Far from being the terminal of humanity's rational development, capitalism was history's greatest irony. In the very act of rationally conquering the world, capitalism had put its moral and emotional bases in jeopardy; yet there was no turning back and no going ahead.[42]

There is another way to express this polarity in Weber's thought. On the one hand, Weber believed that the material and normative forces of history produced a regularity in human behavior that made it amenable to scientific analysis. On the other, he insisted on the multiplicity and historical nature of causation, and on the inability of any one force or combination of forces to explain history. Not only does causal pluralism account for the diversities and incongruities in human affairs, but it produces the irreducible plurality of sociocultural systems that Weber called the traditional, the charismatic, and the rational-legal.

CONCLUSION

Weber's Unique Nonmetaphysical Sociology

Weber's unique definition of science enabled him to make a far-reaching and unusual contribution to sociological theory. In line with a major trend in nineteenth-century intellectual culture, Weber defined reason as a tool or method for solving problems. However, he went much further when he denied that reason could solve metaphysical problems. Reason, for Weber, was strictly a historical tool capable of solving only historical problems.

Up to a point Weber's unique position ran parallel to the German philosophical tradition with its sharp separation between the study of human beings and that of nature. Weber's position, however, was based on science not philosophy. His ultimate perspective was that while the moral sciences could not achieve rational conclusions, they could achieve scientific knowledge, provided two conditions were met: first, the investigator must apply the ordinary canons of scientific logic and empirical verification to human behavior, and second, because of the rich, complex subjective nature of human behavior, the investigator must give shape to empirical reality by empathically constructing a typological inventory of all data relevant to any given problem. The results yielded by this twofold procedure cannot be considered truth in either a physical or metaphysical sense, but only as an understanding of the causes and the meaning of the many, ever-changing, and unconnected empirical regularities in human behavior. For Weber, *verstehen* sociology was not a search for the underlying principle of existence, but a conscious search for insights and solutions to the unique and

---

[42] For Weber's most formal statement of sociocultural incompatibilities, see *From Max Weber*, chap. 13, "Religious Rejections of the World and Their Directions," sections 4–9.

changing problems that human beings face, an orientation that Weber stated epigrammatically when he said that social science has "eternal youth."

Thus, while repudiating the Anglo-French-American tradition of monistic naturalistic positivism, Weber also repudiated the German tradition that sought knowledge about human existence in metaphysical analysis. The unique amalgam he created out of these rival traditions may be called *historical positivism*. His contribution to sociological theory may be put into broader perspective by saying that he combined the instrumental concept of the human mind that emerged from the Enlightenment with Vico's maxim that humanity can know the truth about itself because human behavior is a human creation and therefore amenable to human understanding. Basically, Weber's position was that science cannot lead to unified or metaphysical or substantialist knowledge, and that it cannot validate any system of values. His position made him unique and separated him from the essentially metaphysical tradition of modern social science, liberal and Marxian, as well as from all forms of religious and philosophical opposition to science and modernity in general.

The diffusion of Weber's thought to the United States (and to Canada and probably elsewhere) has been highly selective. It would make a fascinating exercise in the sociology of knowledge to see which parts of Weber's work were congenial to American social science and therefore accepted and which were not, and why. In any case, many of Weber's ideas (bureaucracy; class-status-power; rational-legal, charismatic, and traditional types of authority; the separation of values and science; multiple causation; religion and the rise of capitalism) are the stock in trade of almost every practicing sociologist. Yet, most of these sociologists would probably be very much surprised to learn that by and large Weber did not believe in truth. Rather, he was a reluctant "relativist"—or, perhaps better stated, a "stoic" and "existentialist," not in opposition to but because of science. Ultimately Weber was a moralist who did not believe in the validity of any set of morals.[43]

---

[43] Even Reinhard Bendix, one of the most authoritative interpreters of Weber, has not grasped the full meaning of Weber's skepticism. In "Two Sociological Traditions," in Reinhard Bendix and Guenther Roth, *Scholarship and Partisanship* (Berkeley: University of California Press, 1972), chap. 14, Bendix identifies two traditions in modern sociology. The first, the Baconian or Saint-Simonian tradition, takes its cue from natural science; this is the tradition upon which Durkheim built. The second tradition of Burckhardt and Tocqueville has a developmental orientation and takes its cue from disciplines concerned with the genesis of historical configurations and the cultivation of human judgment; it is upon this tradition that Weber built. This characterization tends to associate Weber with the German philosophical rejection of science and fails to emphasize that his rejection of a science of human behavior (general theory) was based on science itself. In reviewing this book [*American Sociologist* 1 (May 1972):200–203], Talcott Parsons quite rightly pointed out that the spirit behind Durkheim is Cartesian rather than Baconian, but mistakenly insisted that Weber was converging with Durkheim and others toward a science of human behavior and a view that presupposed the essential unity of all intellectual disciplines.

It was not that Weber did not have strong convictions, or that he lacked principles—actually he had passionate views about many things. However, this is the point—his views were passions, not metaphysical abstractions or longings, and more importantly he knew it. To be metaphysical is to accept the assumption begun by the Greeks that the structure of the human mind corresponds to the structure of the natural and moral realms. To be metaphysical is to assume either that this correspondence allows the mind to fathom reality by itself (the deductive approach preferred by the Greeks and medieval philosophers) or that the mind must grapple with phenomena directly to find itself (the inductive temper of the post-Enlightenment world). To be metaphysical is to assume that the main characteristics of the human mind are unity and permanence and that because the natural and moral realms are rational or lawful, they too are unified and permanent.

That Weber rejected the metaphysical tradition of the West is sometimes obscured by the fact that he insisted on the role of ideal or normative elements in human behavior. Weber's view in this regard was far removed, however, from the metaphysical idealism that makes up the bulk of Western philosophy. Simply, his view was that human beings live lives of meaning —in today's language, one would say that behavior is cultural, energized by values and norms—and therefore social scientists must study social relationships as patterns of meaning. However, none of these meanings has any intrinsic validity.

Weber's antimetaphysical position is probably also obscured by his wide use of ideal types and his fertile creation of concepts in general. He was not, however, trying to impart to reality the nature of reason, nor to find reality through reason—for Weber, there was no ultimate reality.

> The fate of an epoch which has eaten of the tree of knowledge is that it must know that we cannot learn the *meaning* of the world from the results of its analysis, be it ever so perfect; it must rather be in a position to create this meaning itself. It must recognize that general views of life and the universe can never be the products of increasing empirical knowledge, and that the highest ideals, which move us most forcefully, are always formed only in the struggle with other ideals which are just as sacred to others as ours are to us.[44]

Standing directly on the skeptic side of Hume, as filtered down through Kant, Windelband, Simmel, and Rickert, Weber sharply separated the realms of value, logic, and fact, declaring them not only separate but unconnectable. Contemporary social scientists, of course, say something superficially similar: a scientist must use concepts carefully, avoid bias and value

[44] *Methodology*, p. 57.

judgments, and relate his concepts to the facts accurately. (Sometimes it is even said that the facts identify and speak for themselves and that the social scientist is better prepared for their message if he avoids excessive conceptualization.) However, Weber's insistence that these three realms are not connectable, not now and not in the future, immediately separates him from the main tradition in social science. It is a wide separation, much wider than we are aware, and the divergent paths that emerge from this difference lead further away from each other.[45] Alone among modern social scientists (always excepting Montesquieu), Weber accepted the idea of a world without truth. Social science as usually understood is something that science (and Weber) says is impossible. Or, again to use Weber's well-known words, far from being a stripling that will ripen into a wise old age, social science has "eternal youth."

Weber's separation of values and science has also been badly misunderstood. Simply put, what Weber meant was that theorists cannot be "presuppositionless," cannot avoid attaching meaning to whatever they do, even in science. Their choice lies not in whether to make value judgments or not, but in whether to make them consciously or unconsciously. Values are what prompt science. (Even science, said Weber, is a value peculiar to our culture.) Values are focused and clarified by logical analysis, and the means for attaining them are found by determining the causal sequences in the empirical world. Of course, values cannot be based on either reasoning or factual determination for the simple reason that reason and facts have no necessary relation either to each other or to values.

Weber derived his definition of *fact* from the historicist opposition to natural science. The facts of human behavior are not "givens" or data, but the nonnecessary creations of history. As phenomena that need not be, facts are not sovereign in relation to either ideas or values. The nonmetaphysical social scientist need never accept facts in the way that a natural scientist must. Indeed, he or she can decide to accept or reject a given range of facts, something that can be done only in terms of values. To say that values should not be employed in social science is to say that the values implanted and sustained in the present factual social order are valid—a value judgment by inadvertence, a disguised, a priori perpetuation and legitimation of a social reality created by a historical structure of power. Not to see all this,

---

[45] One reason Weber's divergence from mainstream, substantialist social science is not more widely known in the United States is that his work was introduced by Americans who were—quite legitimately—trying to extract the meaning of his writings for general theory (e.g., Talcott Parsons, *The Structure of Social Action,* 1937). Another reason is that a great many theorists acknowledge their debt to him, and then proceed to write works quite contrary to the spirit and substance of his thought (e.g., Seymour M. Lipset and Talcott Parsons). The American social scientist closest to the spirit of Weber's work is probably C. Wright Mills.

said Weber, is to engage in ideology, the partisan defense of a particular historical structure of fact (power) in the name of objectivity and neutrality.

Weber accepted aspects of Greek philosophy, of course. He accepted logic, but only as an analytical tool—in fact so much so that to some extent his systematic sociology was at odds with his historicism. He also accepted the Socratic value idea that consciousness is desirable and useful—human beings may not be able to apprehend the world rationally or to derive a hierarchy of good from cognitive processes, but they can and should be conscious of the forces that act on them even if consciousness is a burden—which for Weber it was.

The substantive side of Weber's work is so rich and comprehensive that it defies summation. His global comparisons gave in-depth insights that make the work of Simmel, Pareto, and even Durkheim look superficial and parochial. His insistence on both the angularity and the symmetry of sociocultural structures and his skillful oscillation between these two points of emphasis produced sparks of insight that lit up vast reaches of human behavior hitherto shrouded in darkness. By ranging in and out and around Western society, Weber brought into relief a singularly dynamic sociocultural structure. By showing the inherently static quality of Oriental religion and philosophy, including the secular ethics and pragmatic philosophy of China, he raised questions much broader than the relation of religion to economic behavior.

Implicit in Weber's work were the following questions: To what extent has the nonscientific substantive rationalism of Greek idealism and Christian theology and religion provided the indispensable mental-moral climate for the West's scientific mastery over nature and Westerners' belief that they could achieve a similar mastery over themselves? What substitute is there for the dynamism inherent in the various Western substantialisms, which despite their differences, have always insisted that there is more to the world than the profanity and deceptions ordained by experience and power? To what extent has modern positivistic substantialism become an idea-less empiricism nurtured by neither a spiritual nor a historical awareness of the infinity of possibilities for ordering human life? Is it possible that the formal rationality of modern society, including its intellectual culture, will come more and more to resemble the unimaginative and static pragmatism of Imperial China? Will sociology itself, to the extent that it tries to depict every nuance of the empirical world, develop the pictographic mentality of traditional China? Can it be said that a one-sided emphasis on either substantive or formal rationality incapacitates human beings for affirmation and adventure? What combination of substantive and formal rationality is necessary to prevent the Indian "flight from the world" or the Chinese "ossification of the mind"? Weber's global sociology gives insight into questions like these. The methodological base of Weber's thought was a belief in the necessity of an imaginative interplay between value-relevant ideas and historical data. Conducted consciously, this interplay yielded not metaphysical truth but scientific social truth, a penetrating understanding of empirical processes as a preliminary to the rational control of a human-made and therefore human-controllable sociocultural environment. Through his development and use of this method, Weber made an incredibly rich contribution to the understanding of human behavior.

Weber's Liberalism

An evaluation of a theorist's work that does not place it historically would be incomplete. Viewed in terms of the sociology of knowledge, Weber's work reveals ideological features, some explicit and some implicit.[46] Though he explicitly denied any connection between his *verstehen* sociology and the values of individualism, and though he rigorously maintained a sharp separation in his work between science and values, his work can still be interpreted as a defense of the institutions and values of liberal society. The sociology of knowledge assumes that ideas are always related to the problems and values of a given time. The fact that Weber explicitly agreed with this does not exempt his own work from scrutiny. The first maxim of the sociological analysis of knowledge is to construct the sociohistorical context in which ideas and values originate and flourish. In other words, the social scientist seeks to detect the beneficiary of an idea or value.

In what ways, then, is there a beneficiary in Weber's thought, and in what ways can it be said that his sociology represents the apogee of liberal social theory? One may always label Weber through the logic of elimination: he is neither a conservative (agrarian traditionalist) nor a socialist, and therefore must be a liberal. One may point to the general tenor of his presuppositions— his insistence, for example, that the individual is the only knowable unit of society, or his constant use of the dualism between individual and society, a hallmark of liberal thought, or his emphasis on unity as well as diversity. Such views, of course, are antithetical to the conservative belief in the

[46] Weber himself would be the first to insist on such an analysis, provided it were done to understand and not merely to debunk. Weber made a large contribution to the sociology of knowledge: his insistence on multiple causation; his search for the causes and effects of subjectivity; and his analysis of the role of social strata in receiving or blocking religious ideas under the concept of "elective affinities"; together with his analysis of the relationship between bureaucracy, education, and values. For the concept of *elective affinity*, see *From Max Weber*, p. 284, and for the relation between bureaucracy, education, and values, see *From Max Weber*, chap. 8, "Bureaucracy," and chap. 17, "The Chinese Literati." It must be emphasized, however, that Weber's sociology of knowledge, unlike the important contributions to this field by such figures as Marx and Durkheim, was part of an orientation that denied the possibility of truth.

organic, monarchical nature of society and the Marxian view of society as an objective process of class struggle.

The identification of Weber as a liberal, however, need not rely on this kind of logic alone. Central to Weber's work was the distinction between formal rationality or science and substantive rationality or philosophy, a distinction with rich methodological possibilities for the social sciences. In Weber's hands, however, science was associated only with liberal institutions. What Weber did was to locate formal rationality in the capitalist West and to deny it could serve other forms of society. Thus, he clearly identified liberal society with scientific rationality and he clearly implied that the civilization of capitalism was based on the bedrock of scientific behavior, and other civilizations on the quicksands of substantive rationality. Weber did not say merely that the intellectual culture of modern society had become increasingly scientific. For Weber, the entire institutional network of liberal society was based on scientific or formal rationality: the market economy, its political-legal institutions and bureaucratic mode of administration, its emissary-individualistic religion and ethic of responsibility, and even its music.[47] The institutions of liberal society form a unique functional unity, each part tooled to form a dynamic, pluralistic social structure. This uniquely moral world, Weber felt, was threatened by the traditionalism inherent in any form of substantive rationality, including socialism. In the case of traditional authority, where the value of family, age, or war takes precedence over formal rationality, only a consumption economy can ensue.[48] Where substantive rationality is based on the values of those who advocate planning or socialism, the only outcome can be traditionalistic stagnation.[49] Nor can religion hope to reconcile itself with formal rationality. Even ascetic Protestantism is eventually transformed into a secondary value and a means by triumphant capitalism. It is clear, in other words, that Weber identified rationality or science with the specific institutions of capitalism.

It is true that Weber expressly repudiated the liberal doctrine of laissez faire with its rational individual who promotes the general interest by promoting his own. However, he did so as part of a general movement within liberalism in the second half of the nineteenth century, a movement that despite its diverse expression, had a unity based on the common recognition that free and rational individuals can exist only in a free and rational society. Though mainly associated with political and social philosophers such as John Stuart Mill, Thomas Hill Green, Leonard T. Hobhouse, John Dewey and others,

[47] Max Weber, *The Rational and Social Foundations of Music*, trans. Don Martindale, Johannes Reidel, and Gertrude Neuwirth (Carbondale, Ill.: Southern Illinois University Press, 1958), also in paperback.
[48] S.E.O., pp. 325–329.
[49] S.E.O., pp. 189–191; 197–199; 203f; 228.

late liberalism received wide support in sociology. The essential temper of
the overall movement was a belief that liberal society could be reformed
from within through the application of science. The early liberal beliefs in a
presocial rational individual and economic order were the first casualties
of an updated liberalism.

Weber remained true to the Age of Reason, though he could no longer accept
its belief in the rational individual or in the ultimate congruence of the
human mind with an objective order of nature. Accepting in general the
definition of mind as function, he sought a meaning of rationality that
would support liberal institutions and at the same time identify those that
threatened rationality and individualism. Believing that only society could
create and sustain the individual, but without embracing either conservatism
or socialism, Weber must be classified along with the other liberal revisionists. In point of fact, Weber consciously accepted liberalism. Obviously, his
liberalism was quite different from much American liberal thought—for one
thing, he was aware he was a liberal in the social sense of the term. For
Weber, there was no scientific validity to liberalism, and he was quite prepared to admit that its chances of success were limited. His ironic turn of
mind, derived from his encyclopedic historical-comparative studies, also saw
the menace for social existence posed by formal rationality. Liberalism enjoyed no superhistorical status in Weber's thought, and he did not think
of capitalism in the usual evolutionary terms as the terminal stage of human
development, busily perfecting itself through gradual progress. Liberalism
for Weber was simply a historical individual, a meaningful segment of a
meaningless world process. In all likelihood he would have seen evolutionary
thought as the main way in which bourgeois social theory had sought escape
from the epistemological dilemma posed by the rise of empirical science. In
any case, science, unlike religion, does not require the "sacrifice of the intellect"—the evolutionary-progressive view, based on the inherent validity of
science, private property, the market economy, and political-legal equality
(or its Marxian counterpart), was just such a sacrifice, the laying of all eggs
in one metaphysical basket, and this Weber refused to do.

The End of Rationality: Weber's Tragic Vision

Like most social thinkers in the nineteenth century, Weber was emotionally
and intellectually involved in the problem of deciphering the meaning of the
cataclysmic change that had taken place in the structure of Western society.
The early sociologists had discerned a cosmic meaning in social-system
change. Liberal society was more than the unique result of unique causes; it
was written in the nature of things. This merger of the historical with the
normative through the concept of evolution was drastically revised and
eventually abandoned by late-nineteenth-century sociology. Methodologi-

cally speaking, I have called this revision a shift from monistic to pluralistic positivism, and substantively speaking, a shift from a naturalistic to a socio-cultural orientation. The upshot of this shift in sociological theory was a thoroughgoing redefinition of human rationality.

The questions raised by this change had more than academic meaning for Weber. They signified more than a dispute between philosophical systems; they concerned the validity of philosophy itself. To others, the problem of reason had a solution: one could revert or cling to religious optimism or despair; assert the supremacy of will or physics; point to a higher, more flexible reason that spun itself out in time; or point to the unconscious or the subjective as the spring of existence. None of these was acceptable to Weber, and yet he was denied the Enlightenment's simple faith in reason too. Reason was not enough, and it was all he had. It could not establish a hierarchy of value, and its nature was ambiguous and paradoxical. It could deal only with means and ends, in causes and consequences; but so often its operation in human affairs ended in ways that thwarted the actor. What Christianity called Providence, Hegel the *cunning of reason,* and Marxists *false consciousness,* Weber referred to prosaically as *unintended consequences.* Again and again, he cited instances of success that amount to failure, and movements and ideas that result in something quite opposed to the values of the individuals involved.[50]

The introduction of rationality into the institutional structure of Western society was itself the best example of the paradox of reason. Human beings freed themselves from magical bondage to reach new heights of technical mastery over nature and ethical mastery over themselves, only to find that reason, science, industry, progress, and the other shibboleths of the Enlightenment had consequences undreamed of by the philosophes. Reason establishes certainty, but it also serves as the spur to change. It necessitates the acceptance of a certain range of values, but also threatens to bring all values into question and eventual disregard. Even the Weberian version of reason, which was shorn of all ethical substance, has paradoxical social consequences. On the one hand, it gives human beings technical control of their environment and enhances the possibilities for ethical dignity and responsibility by clarifying choices and consequences. On the other hand, however, it leads to impersonalization, if not to depersonalization, as it slowly builds the vast bureaucratic structures that "parcel the soul" and threaten the

---

[50] "The final result of political action often, no, even regularly, stands in completely inadequate and often even paradoxical relation to its original meaning. This is fundamental to all history. . . ." *From Max Weber,* p. 117. The best known example of historical irony, of course, is Protestantism's furtherance of capitalism only to be relegated to a secondary position by an established and triumphant capitalism.

liberty and spontaneity of whole populations by engulfing them in a mind-less efficiency.

The process of "disenchantment" was depicted by Marx as the alienation of human beings from others and from themselves. For both Marx and Weber the source of alienation was historical in nature. Weber, however, could not accept Marx's metaphysical solution to the problem of history. In focusing on the separation of human beings from the means of administration and violence as well as from the means of production, he sketched out a structure of society so complex and impersonal that the web of causes and conse-quences could never be fully unraveled. As such, he was more pessimistic than Marx, for no millennium awaited the sturdy sufferers of history. Though the problems raised by the nature of history and reason seemed intransigent, Weber refused to solve them through either religion or dialectical material-ism. Western society was unique and its problems were relative to itself; human beings could not extricate themselves from their problems through the use of a deus ex machina. Weber sought rather to get around the para-dox of reason by redefining it to mean science, that is, by restricting it to the analysis of means-ends relationships. He constructed a methodological instru-ment that probed the depths of social existence and provided vast insights into the operation of social systems. In the end, however, his paradox reap-peared in the knowledge that science and the rational society would have been stillborn without the aid of nonrational metaphysical and religious support.

Weber's thought had a tragic element, a somewhat pessimistic view of political and social life as uncongenial to the modern temperament as his nonmetaphysical social science. One of the reasons for Weber's pervasive sense of unease was his polytheistic value system. Unlike most people, and most sociologists, Weber was not anchored to one culture and his values did not have the easy consistency that comes from living in the well-worn grooves of a single way of life. His empathetic or *verstehen* method, in which one puts oneself in the place of the thing to be studied, is not without its psychic dangers. Again and again Weber showed a deep respect, if not outright liking, for many of the values of preindustrial society—charismatic heroism, the grace and dignity of aristocratic life styles, eroticism, the sense of immediacy and "naive unambiguity" with which life was lived, and so on.

Of course, Weber also placed great value on industrial culture. He valued ascetic Calvinism for promoting responsible individualism (and hated Lutheranism for promoting servility to the state). Actually, there was much in Weber's complex and contradictory nature that was rooted in the petty-bourgeois Anglo-American stage of capitalist development. He believed in the liberal separation of institutional spheres because it promoted and re-flected formal rationality. He believed strongly in the value of a free sector of voluntary groups. For Weber, the free, individually scaled arena of voluntary life promoted versatility and choice, a counter to his fear of bureaucratization and its remorseless "parceling-out of the soul." Here individuals could compete freely and accurate judgments could be made about their capabilities.

Weber was also a German nationalist and realistic about the compromises and expedients intrinsic to political life; and yet he espoused a personal ethic of brotherhood, denounced the Kaiser during wartime, and supported parliamentary government as a counterweight to Prussian bureaucratic bungling. As a liberal, it is not surprising that he valued the formal rationality of liberal law. Unlike traditional society with its diffused and personalized legal obligations, capitalism separates law from morality and attempts to govern itself through clearly defined legal norms, something that helps make government predictable and responsible as well as promoting choice in general. Of course Weber was also committed to science, to the intellectually honest kind of science that makes no claims unwarranted by its capabilities. All in all, Weber's liberalism rested on the belief that only a rich, complex, nonintegrated culture based on formal rationality could provide choice and therefore genuine moral action (ethic of responsibility). Above all else, Weber's values centered on the supreme value of moral action itself, on the rendering of all values as problematic and thus subject to choice.

Given his comparative-*verstehen* method and his personal experiences in a society torn by rival world views, it is not surprising that Weber found little inner peace. But for whatever reason, he was denied the comfort of conviction. Modern society was a rich congeries of choices and thus preferable to the immoral peace of agrarian and socialist existence, but it was also a congeries of conflict and contradiction with no roots in the universe that ensured its survival. While Weber valued liberal society above all others, he could not "sacrifice his intellect" to its illusions or withdraw to the psychic security of a romanticized past or a utopian future.

Ultimately, Weber's tragic vision came from a view of science that destroyed all "illusions," including the belief that science is the gateway to truth and virtue. Unlike sociology and liberal social theory in general, which attacked the metaphysics of feudal-absolutism in the eighteeneth and early nineteenth century and then turned its fire on its new metaphysical enemy, socialism, Weber attacked all "convictions," liberalism's included.

No one can say what Weber would have thought about mature industrial society. He might well have seen much of what passes for progress as the standardization of life, the blotting out of opportunities for heroic encounters, the end of a manageable moral universe of diversity and tension. He might well have considered the growing interpenetration of economy and state as the end of the limited pluralism that early capitalism had managed to develop and tolerate, and the beginning of that "iron cage" of meaningless efficiency he feared so much. Even in his own time he sensed the menace represented by capitalism's growing grip over all spheres of life. The growing inner unity of liberal society might have worried Weber on a number of levels. He might well have asked whether industrial society was not a permanent halfway house, providing some freedom for the few and the illusion of freedom for the rest. So, too, he might have asked how it was possible to narrow effective choice or moral action through (not despite) the universalistic values of liberty, equality, progress, and so on. Of course, Weber realistically faced up to the possibility that none of capitalism's values could be achieved by anybody for any length of time. He was aware that formal rationality might well be destined to erode the sentiments that energize liberal society and usher in "a polar night of icy darkness and hardness."

The supreme irony for Weber was that human beings had escaped bondage to magic, ignorance, naivety, hunger, and disease by basing their life on science and methodical effort, only to risk the destruction of all meaningful social existence. His tragic presentiment, however, was not merely a belief that liberal society was unworkable, but that science had destroyed the possibility of any kind of society. Once eaten, the apple of knowledge cannot be disgorged. For Weber, the values of the past were lost forever; the values of the future, where they were not state capitalism in disguise, were utopian; and a meaningful present was becoming less and less possible as the relentless march of bureaucratization turned means into ends and placed life in a never-to-be-achieved set of abstractions—progress, perfectability, equality, happiness, and the like. Weber knew that his own work would contribute to this process of disenchantment and yet he wrote, and not without a streak of Promethean defiance.

Weber felt in himself the deep-rooted incongruities of a liberalism that sought to base a historical society on a nonhistorical basis. As such he experienced the liberal dilemma in its most acute form. His passionate commitment to the liberal doctrine of the free and responsible individual was more than a creed based on science. It was a value position he knew could not be proved by reason; ultimately it was a nonrational, substantive belief in the efficacy and value of reason. Although Weber used reason to probe relentlessly into the meaning of existence, he knew it was not a touchstone. Able as he was to escape many of the assumptions of his own culture, he was unable to make a complete break with the substantialist tradition of the West. Whatever the reasons—and they may be looked for in his mother's religious background, or in his class, educational, and national background—they prevented him from becoming a pragmatic historicist within the full meaning of the term.

Despite his unmatched awareness of the variability of institutions and the "inexhaustible diversity of historical existence," Weber allowed his thought to be circumscribed by the alternatives he constructed with his ideal types. Though he claimed no empirical validity for these types and warned against the dangers of reification, he unwittingly came to hypostatize his own creations. Though he constantly emphasized that mixed types of almost every conceivable variety existed, his thought was based on a few rather rigid pattern alternatives. He forgot that he was viewing the data of history through mental eyes that he himself had created. Ultimately his passion for precision made him view the social structures created by his ideal types as discrete entities. For all his historicism, Weber could not escape the need for certainty. His insecurity stemmed from the threat that science seemed to pose for values. He never fully realized the implications of his own insight— that while science could not validate values, it could create them, and that with its ability to judge the relevance of social institutions to values, science attained a uniquely nonmetaphysical yet nonhistorical status. Weber never came to appreciate fully the fact that by preventing the institutional and value closure of society, science could help create a pluralistic society in which conflict and value erosion placed a premium on intelligence and conscious choice. He failed to see that the very paradox of science, its reliance on nonscientific ideas and values for its existence, was also its strength and nourishment. Instead of leading to pessimism or metaphysical anxiety, the paradox of science can as easily lead to optimism. Implicit in Weber's general position is the view that research into the past and the present is really a step into the future, since its main goal is to enhance human life by cataloguing the possibilities of behavior and by suggesting new levels and types of cooperation between the ethic of absolute ends and the ethic of responsibility.

PART V
Pluralistic Positivism in the United States

Chapter 18
Pragmatism: The New Phase of Science in the New World

The new approach to human behavior found in the pluralistic positivists was not confined to continental Europe. It also appeared in the United States, though in somewhat different versions. By the end of the nineteenth century, American philosophers and social scientists, like their counterparts in Europe, had become increasingly reluctant to derive knowledge from logic or to apply unthinkingly natural-science principles to human behavior. Thus, the relevance of biological evolution for social science had to be re-evaluated. Just as the Continental pluralistic positivists discarded evolution as a synthesizing principle, it was also rejected, by and large, by American sociology after Sumner and Ward.[1] Sociology's rejection of evolution, however, was no isolated event. It was part of a general shift toward a more empirical and functional definition of nature, human nature, and society that began to permeate American moral and intellectual life. Ironically, it was Darwin's empirical confirmation of the evolution of biological forms that sparked the growth of empiricism in the United States and led to the revolt against monistic evolutionary theories. Less surprising, the theory of biological evolution also helped to bring about the same transformation of reason into method that I traced in the development of European intellectual life.

PRAGMATISM AND EVOLUTION

Even as the vogue of Spencerian sociology swept the United States, developments were afoot destined to undermine not only the traditional metaphysics of philosophical idealism but the evolutionary social metaphysics

---

[1] An explicit evolutionary emphasis remained in the thought of Cooley and has reappeared in the thought of Talcott Parsons and Gerhard Lenski. As I shall note in subsequent chapters, thinking of social change in terms of biological evolution, a necessary process of adaptive upgrading that progressively realizes liberal ideals, is an anachronism, reflecting more the needs of the liberal power structure than the dictates of science.

that had appeared in Sumner and Ward. From the work of Chauncey Wright (1830–1875), Charles S. Peirce (1839–1914), and William James (1842–1910) came the relatively new and distinctive American philosophical orientation known as pragmatism. Directly inspired by the Darwinian theory of evolution,[2] pragmatism attempted to update philosophy in the light of scientific advances.

The new phase of modern science that appeared in the nineteenth century, especially after the 1840s, was nowhere so distinctive or uniform as in the United States. Explicitly based on science and congenial to the needs of a dynamic, nontraditional society, pragmatism absorbed almost all of America's intellectual energy. Thanks to the favorable conditions of the New World, pragmatism emerged as a clean-cut, militant positivism, seeking to define philosophy in terms of natural science. Unlike in Europe, the new phase of science in the United States was not obscured or obstructed by entrenched antiscientific philosophies. Despite rival schools, most notably Hegelianism, pragmatism exercised a near monopoly in American philosophy, and despite differences, pragmatists were in broad agreement on an important core of basic ideas. Under the influence of evolutionary science, said Weiner, pragmatism has

> . . . fostered, first, an *empirical* respect for the complexity of existence requiring a *plurality* of concepts to do justice to the diverse problems of mankind in its evolutionary struggles. Secondly, it has abandoned the eternal as an absolute frame of reference for thought, and emphasized the ineluctable pervasiveness of *temporal* change in the natures of things. Thirdly, it has regarded the natures of things, as known and appraised by men, to be *relative* to the categories and standards of the minds that have evolved modes of knowing and evaluating objects. Fourthly, it has insisted on the *contingency* and precariousness of the mind's interactions with the physical and social environment, so that even in the most successful results of hard gained experimental knowledge, what we attain is *fallible*. Finally, American pragmatism upholds the *democratic freedom of the individual* inquirer and appraiser as an indispensable condition for progress in the future evolution of science and society.[3]

Darwin's painstaking research not only confirmed that development was a central feature of certain reaches of phenomena, but it strongly reinforced

---

[2] For the effect of the theory of evolution on the founders of pragmatism, as well as for a valuable introduction to the nature of pragmatism, see Philip P. Weiner, *Evolution and the Founders of Pragmatism* (Cambridge, Mass.: Harvard University Press, 1949).

[3] Philip P. Weiner, *Evolution and the Founders of Pragmatism*, p. 191.

the linchpin assumption of empirical science that facts are structured. By finding a pattern or structure in the seemingly multiple, temporal, fortuitous occurrences of biology, Darwin gave tremendous impetus to empirical science by showing that far from being the enemy of law, contingency contained law. Aware of the importance of evolutionary theory, the pragmatists were content for the most part to extract from evolutionary theory its methodological principles, and to resist monistic identifications of human behavior and nature. In pragmatism the antirational trend of post-seventeenth-century philosophy and science finally congealed into a thoroughgoing theory of empiricism. Instead of viewing the mind as an autonomous substance capable of finding truth in itself or of penetrating to the structure of the universe, the pragmatists viewed the mind in functional terms, as a tool for analyzing and controlling phenomena. For the pragmatists, the mind was not a passive process of cognition, but an instrument for knowledge and adjustment. Pragmatism, however, did not abandon the search for a metaphysical synthesis. Under its lead, science donned the garb of humility and came to think of itself as a method, not because it had accepted a historical definition of philosophy but because it was pausing to regroup for a fresh assault on truth or substantialism.

PRAGMATISM AND SOCIAL THOUGHT

The rise of pragmatism was part of a larger transformation in American intellectual culture.[4] From the end of the nineteenth century to the 1930s, the leading figures in American social theory exhibited a remarkable uniformity in approach.[5] Pragmatism in philosophy entered directly into social theory in the person of John Dewey. However, as Morton White has shown, the underlying assumptions of pragmatism also pervaded the thought of Oliver Wendell Holmes (1809–1894) in law, Thorstein Veblen (1857–1929) in economics, and James Harvey Robinson (1863–1936) and Charles A. Beard (1874–1948) in history and politics. The "revolt against formalism" was an attempt to go beyond the deductive rationalism of the traditional social-science disciplines and place them on solid scientific ground. All five thinkers, said White, shared a common historicism and cultural organicism.

> By *historicism* I mean the attempt to explain facts by reference to earlier facts; by *cultural organicism* I mean the attempt to find explanations and relevant material in social sciences other than

[4] For a comprehensive description, see Henry Steele Commager, *The American Mind* (New Haven: Yale University Press, 1950), also in paperback.
[5] The following account draws heavily on Morton White's brilliant analysis, *Social Thought in America: The Revolt Against Formalism* (Boston: Beacon Press paperback, 1957).

the one which is primarily under investigation. The historicist reaches back in time in order to account for certain phenomena; the cultural organicist reaches into the entire social space around him.[6]

The influence of evolutionary theory on social thought was selective, however—its methodological clues were avidly seized upon even as its substantive principle, evolution through genetic mutations, was discarded. In short, the pragmatists adopted the empiricism that had yielded such dramatic results in biology and natural science in general but abandoned the direct application of natural-science laws to social phenomena. The biological principle of organic adaptation was transformed into a methodological principle as social theorists began to see the possibilities of viewing social phenomena as functional, adaptive systems.

The revolt against formalism was not simply a revolt against the cruder formalism of deductive sociology, history, economics, political science, or jurisprudence. As Morton White has shown, pragmatism was also faced with the problem of criticizing and re-evaluating the tradition of British empiricism from Hume through Jeremy Bentham (1748–1832), John Austin (1790–1859), and John Stuart Mill (1806–1873). British empiricism presented a problem because it was static and nonhistorical; while it sought to base knowledge on experience, it emphasized *fixed* modes of experience. As such, British empiricism had become mired in the mechanistic world of Newtonian rationalism. Dewey, who was especially concerned with this question, eventually concluded that British empiricism was simply "a disguised *a priorism.*"

The goal of the pragmatic social theorists was the control and creation of experience, not the passive acquisition of and adjustment to either deductive truths or fixed modes of existence. However, as White has pointed out, these theorists were still concerned with finding truth, or more exactly with using science to fathom the structure of fact and obtain both objective knowledge and a scientific morality.

The revolt against formalism also signals the emergence of late-liberal social theory in America. The autonomous, self-propelled, rational individual of early liberal social theory was replaced by a more historical individual whose nature could be neither understood nor fully unfolded without the aid of a congenial social context. Confronted with mounting evidence that the individual is as much the product of society as its creator, late liberals

---

[6] Morton White, *Social Thought in America,* p. 12.

increasingly abandoned the deductivism and atomism of earlier liberal thought, adopting instead a more dynamic, organic empiricism.

Despite flirtations with socialism and Marxism, the revolt against formalism was also a deeply conservative movement whose basic thrust was to preserve the traditional liberal structure of American society. As many commentators have noted, liberalism's core values of individualism, private property, market economy, political-legal equality, and faith in progress have seeped into the marrow of American life to become a traditionalism that brooks no competition. America's deeply ingrained liberalism is evident in the various political movements from the 1890s through the New Deal, the period that Richard Hofstadter has characterized as the Age of Reform.[7] The reforms and ideas of this period attempt to realize the original definition of America as a society of free and equal individuals. Though the ideas of natural law and natural rights were gradually discarded, the individual as a given category of social theory and organization remained. Instead of being rational biopsychic actors, however, individuals were increasingly thought of as emotional, highly socialized egos who needed a rational social environment to realize their true nature.

Like the main movements in philosophy and social science at the turn of the century, sociology also became increasingly concerned with the problem of methodology and became heavily committed to social reform. The similarities between sociology and other intellectual currents do not end there. Despite the increasingly problematic nature of the individual and the growing sociocultural flavor of sociological theory, few questioned the central liberal assumption that the individual was a significant causal entity.[8] The continuance of this assumption led to a vast identification and confusion among biology, psychology, social psychology, and sociology in American social science. Sharing the same assumptions as the rest of American intellectual life, sociology after Sumner and Ward became suspicious of monistic, formal theories and settled down to rethink its approach

[7] *The Age of Reform* (New York: Knopf, 1955), also in paperback. A supplement to White's analysis, this book is expressly concerned with the middlebrow figures that helped to spark America's three great reform movements, Populism, Progressivism, and New Dealism. Though Hofstadter distinguished between the moralistic and absolutist character of Populism and Progressivism and the more realistic and opportunistic character of the New Deal, it should be noted that no serious challenge to the core beliefs and values of liberalism emerged from any of these movements.
[8] In their survey of American sociology, *The Development of Modern Sociology* (New York: Random House paperback, 1954), Roscoe and Gisela Hinkle emphasized the pervasive American consensus on "voluntaristic nominalism," the "assumption that the structure of all social groups is the consequence of the aggregate of its separate, component individuals and that social phenomena ultimately derive from the motivations of these knowing, feeling, and willing individuals" (Preface, p. v).

to social knowledge. Like its counterparts in other disciplines, it accepted the methodological implications contained in biology, constructing from them an empirical-functional orientation that was to inform the thought of almost all major theorists. But sociology also continued the metaphysical or Cartesian branch of science, seeing in the new empirical methodology a gateway to truth or general or systematic theory.

Stemming from the dynamic new conditions of American society, the empiricism at the heart of pragmatic philosophy and sociology brought both disciplines in closer touch with American life. However, the attempt to derive a metaphysics from empiricism was to keep American sociology mired in the liberal dilemma. Ironically, it also promoted lines of thought that were irrelevant and perhaps even dysfunctional to a society sorely beset by the problems of advanced industrialization. In satisfying its craving for metaphysics, twentieth-century sociology never fully realized that it was a product of new social conditions and that its methods and aims bore the marks of unique historical forces. As Rytina and Loomis have noted, pragmatism's attempt to derive truth from experience subjected pragmatism to social power, or the forces behind the organization and maintenance of experience.[9] Under such conditions, pragmatism did not confront the fact of social power—indeed, by stressing organic adaptation, empirical information, piecemeal reform, and education, pragmatism became the ideological agent of social power. It is of some importance, therefore, to trace the general relationship between the new phase of empirical science in sociology and the new social or power structure of twentieth-century America.

PRAGMATISM AND SOCIAL CHANGE

Under the powerful pressures of industrial expansion, both the tenor and tempo of American life were drastically transformed during the post–Civil War decades. Climaxing a process of economic expansion that had begun even before the Civil War, the 1890s mark a watershed between agrarian and industrial America and the end of a distinctive period in American life. Early America's self-image had been derived from a number of pre-industrial sources: Calvin's theology and religious individualism, Locke's doctrines of natural rights and limited government, Montesquieu's mechanistic theory of politics, and, to some extent, Adam Smith's economic theory based on natural law and individualism. America's self-image was relatively congruent internally: the forces of religion, science, politics, and economy meshed to promote the idea of the free individual as the basis

[9] Joan Huber Rytina and Charles P. Loomis, "Marxist Dialectic and Pragmatism: Power as Knowledge," *American Sociological Review* 35 (April 1970): 308–319.

of social organization. Further, its self-image was relatively congruent with the realities of social life. Spread out in a fertile land with a congenial climate, unburdened by the weight of feudal custom, and animated by selected elements from the gamut of Western culture, Americans were in fact as well as in theory an individualistic people.

The United States had inherited a purified, streamlined version of the liberal dream of world mastery, a dream that found expression in the static, absolute terms of political and economic natural law. Deeply colored by the general climate of Newtonian science and the French Enlightenment, these norms easily defeated the claims of theocracy and aristocracy and established themselves in American life in a relatively pure and unchallenged state. The monopoly of liberalism is of the utmost importance for interpreting American history.[10] Save for the southern plantation society, the United States, alone of all emerging industrial nations, had no significant social group opposed to the main ideas and values of liberalism. As such, American norms were not only congruent with the experience of Americans, but because these revolutionary norms were so widely accepted they became thoroughly traditional. There was no continuing debate in the United States, as there was in seventeenth-century England and in eighteenth- and nineteenth-century France, about the nature of human nature and society. Given their unanimity on fundamental questions, Americans could devote themselves to the problems of everyday life. There emerged a pattern of behavior unified by the individualistic logic that informed all institutional spheres. Along with this behavior structure emerged a normative structure closely allied to the logic of experience, a static structure of explanation in which the harmonious processes of Newtonian physics and Lockean natural law provided a metaphysical basis for the American experience.

The curious part of American traditionalism is that much of what Americans accepted as true and good, and therefore unalterable, was dynamic and creative. The combined effect of Protestant and bourgeois beliefs and values could not help but create a social type at once self-sufficient, adaptive, and enterprising. Further, the fact that the standards of the Protestant-bourgeois ethic were universalistic made it obligatory that all should strive to better themselves. The surge of commercial and industrial expansion had the ironic effect of making the original definition of America more and more remote to Americans' experience. To bring this definition abreast of new

---

[10] For a pioneering contribution to the understanding of American history as a liberal monopoly, see Louis Hartz, *The Liberal Tradition in America* (New York: Harcourt Brace, 1955). For a sophisticated Marxian analysis with the same theme, see Herbert Marcuse, *One-Dimensional Man* (Boston: Beacon Press, 1964), also in paperback.

conditions, two major alterations occurred in preindustrial America's normative structure. The first was evolutionary monism, which I have already traced in the work of Sumner and Ward, and the second was pragmatism.

As the specialized demands of a complex economy began to affect American behavior, it is not surprising that the prosaic pragmatism of the workaday world received philosophical expression. The conflicts and tensions produced by hectic industrialization could be neither explained nor justified by the old faith that nature provided a cosmic guarantee of liberty, equality, justice, and harmony. Nor did the evolutionary scheme quiet the moral conscience or suit the activistic optimism of America. By the late nineteenth century a determined critique was mounted not only against the natural-law theory of the founders of the American republic, but against the monistic theories of evolution as well. This critique found partial expression in the querulous person of William Graham Sumner. However, despite Sumner's rejection of natural law and his reluctance to accept a cosmic scheme of evolution, his thought was deeply fatalistic. Thus, while Sumner upheld the principle of world mastery, he denied human beings the capacity to interfere with the workings of society, thus denying them the ability to achieve that mastery through deliberate effort. As such, Sumner's theory was incompatible with both America's optimism and its activism. It became increasingly obvious to a new breed of observers and reformers that evil—or social problems—was located not in human beings, nature, or evolution, but in the concrete, willful, and alterable policies of individuals and groups, and that these, in turn, could often be traced to outmoded institutions. Out of the pragmatic individualism of the American socioeconomic system, therefore, came a mounting critique of the intellectual and moral basis of traditional institutions and a growing feeling that America's basic institutions bred injustice and were dangerous to social survival.[11]

The developments that swept over American life were similar to developments in European science and philosophy. In many ways, however, Americans embraced the new phase of science more deliberately and easily than the Europeans. The load of received ideas and values was lighter on their backs. America had no deeply entrenched intellectual or aristrocratic stratum dedicated to the preservation of preliberal codes of conduct or belief. Except for the Civil War, the struggle between power groups in the United States had always been a struggle between different types of liberalism. Though liberalism exercised a near monopoly over American life, it contained an intrinsic dynamism that put it in perpetual tension with the deficiencies and contradictions of social practice. The Protestant-bourgeois

[11] For an early depiction of the correspondence between pragmatism in philosophy and social science and middle-class experience from the Civil War to World War II, see Thelma Herman, "Pragmatism: A Study in Middle Class Ideology," *Social Forces* 22 (May 1944): 404–410.

ethic was conservative in many ways to be sure, but it also had elements that could not be contained by limited success or blunted by the easy compromises of history. Even before the Civil War, it had reflected and helped to further the forces that were to undermine the agrarian foundations of early American liberalism. However, if the dynamism of the Protestant-bourgeois ethic helped to destroy the structure of agrarian America, its flexibility and futurism helped Americans forge the awareness and determination they needed to transcend their age of innocence. The nominalism of Protestantism, its individualistic and equalitarian outlook, and its moral transcendentalism and antagonism to the world supplied many of the elements that made the new outlook possible. Combining these elements with secular liberalism, Americans built a new structure of awareness about themselves and their society in a relatively short time.

By the first decades of the new century the intellectual transformation wrought by pragmatism had had far-reaching effects on American thought. The closed society, the finished morality, the fixed hierarchy of virtues, and the rationality of the individual slowly gave way to views proclaiming the open society, the developing morality, the problematic hierarchy of virtues, and the need to supplement the rationality of the individual with the rationality of social institutions. The new optimism and faith in science was based, paradoxically enough, on new insights into the passion-driven, habit-inhibited nature of individuals, who were now judged incapable of transcending the forces within or outside themselves without the aid of a humane and rational social system.

PRAGMATISM, LIBERALISM, AND SOCIOLOGY

American pragmatism is another phase in the growth and refinement of the empirical epistemology the origins of which go back to William of Occam. The social basis of empiricism was the need of an expanding social system to rethink continuously its world orientation and to discard outmoded and irrelevant ideas and modes of thought. The nineteenth century climaxed the growth of empiricism in that a dynamic intellectual culture emerged to complement the dynamism of industrial capitalism. However, the dynamism of empirical science should not be misunderstood. All symbolic activity including empiricism is subject to social power. The growth of organized empirical research and the philosophy of empiricism/pragmatism should both be seen as serving the needs of power.[12] Pragmatism therefore represents the American response to the moral and intellectual needs of a dynamic industrial system, a system whose dynamism was confined to perfecting existing society. It provided the empiricism, the open-minded futurism, the moral voluntarism, and the fresh faith in mind that

[12] See the section, "Symbolic Activity and the Needs of Power," in Chapter 13.

American capitalism needed. The inconclusiveness, diversity, and even the ambiguity of industrial life, experiences that had never before enjoyed philosophical standing, were no longer defined as departures from reason, but as features essential to a truly rational society. The main weight of eighteenth-century liberal political and social theory was based on the assumptions and conclusions of Newtonian physics, acquiring thereby a deep ahistorical cast. The United States acquired and developed a selected version of the liberal tradition, one that emphasized the rational, self-reliant individual and the decentralized, intrinsically harmonious society whose institutions were static in their structure but progressive in their effects. When this ahistorical concept of human nature and society was infused by the dynamism of evolutionary theory, it did not change the assumption that the individual was the primary datum of social science. Individualism was so strongly established in the Anglo-American way of thinking that evolution never led to radical social organicism.[13] The leading Anglo-American sociologists, Spencer, Sumner, and Ward, were all biopsychological theorists who instinctively dissolved society into its last divisible particle, the individual human being.

Even after the evolutionary sociologies faded from the forefront of social science, the individualistic approach remained. In keeping with the American tradition of liberalism, American social science developed a naturalistic, essentially psychological, approach to human behavior; that is, it did not seriously question the ahistorical definition of human nature it had inherited.

Another way of pointing to the ahistorical bias in American culture is to note that the United States has had little political theory but a great deal of political science, and little social theory and a great deal of social science. The explanation for this bias lies in the unique circumstances under which the American nation was founded. The United States is a nation without history. It did not develop out of a previous social system but was founded *de novo*. It bears none of the scars of social struggle or social-system change. It had no great debate about the nature of human nature and no defeated power groups to reconcile or accommodate. It was founded on two miraculously derived set of norms: Christian revelation and the natural law of secular rationalism. The United States did not emerge as a historical society painfully created out of half-understood historical pressures and circumstances. It emerged as a revealed society erected on religious and rational truth, a society that thought itself free of the corruptions and compromises of historical existence. The Revolutionary period in American life was an attempt to scrape away the layers of European custom so that a homogeneous humanity could emerge. The battle cries of the moment may

---

[13] Radical social organicism is the belief that society is actually an organism that functions the way human biology functions.

have been "no taxation without representation" and "liberty or death," but the deepest significance of the American Revolution is probably best contained in the words "a virgin human nature on a virgin continent." It is no wonder, therefore, that social science flourished in a nation that considered itself free of the observation-distorting corruptions of history—that believed, in short, that it had achieved a perfect correspondence between human nature and social institutions.[14]

American history had done little to disturb America's ahistorical definition of itself. In Hofstadter's words: "The United States was the only country in the world that began with perfection and aspired to progress." In economics, perfection and progress were reconciled by thinking of economic institutions as perfect mechanisms for producing progressive material enrichment. Morally and socially, perfection and progress were reconciled by thinking of reform as a way to realize the perfect values of the republic's founders. Even the great reform movements of the Populist, Progressive, and New Deal eras did not upset America's basically ahistorical world view. As Hofstadter has pointed out, the first two movements fought either to realize the absolute standards that were embodied in America's original definition of itself or to forestall conspiracies against the imagined innocence of America's origin and early history. Even the New Deal, for all its experimentation and innovation, its fetish for organization and technique, and its attack on laissez faire economics, failed to go beyond the basic presuppositions of liberal social theory or social organization. Society was still conceived as basically a question of reconciling the egoism or self-interest of human nature with the public good. The New Deal's basic innovation was to repudiate the idea of a natural reconciliation of self-interest in favor of a managed reconciliation—to turn, in effect, from the liberalism of Locke to that of Hobbes.

If the reform movements of American political life continued to express the individualism of American life, it is not surprising that the individualistic approach remained strong in American sociology. Both American reform movements and American social science (which were closely related) emerged out of a cultural matrix in which the idea of the potent individual had long since become an unconscious presupposition of political, social, and intellectual life. It is not surprising, therefore, that both should accept this definition of human nature or that both should continue to think of society as either a natural or a created equilibrium of individuals in motion. Nothing illustrates better the indelible conservatism of American reform politics and social science than this twentieth-century reversion to the thoughtways and values of seventeenth- and eighteenth-century rationalism.

[14] For a valuable analysis of political science along these lines, see Bernard Crick, *The American Science of Politics: Its Origins and Conditions* (Berkeley: University of California Press, 1959).

Chapter 19
Charles Horton Cooley (1864–1929)

Empirical sociology in the United States is greatly indebted to Charles Horton Cooley, who taught sociology at the University of Michigan between 1894 and 1929. Deeply steeped in the evolutionary outlook of the nineteenth century, Cooley nevertheless developed a sociological perspective with many of the emphases of pluralistic positivism. His work is still another example of the amazingly diverse and fruitful impact of the theory of evolution on modern intellectual culture. Out of the matrix of evolutionary thought, Cooley developed many of the elements of the functional empiricism and the social behaviorism that have come to play such important roles in twentieth-century American sociology. Most social behaviorists in American sociology, including the major figures whose works I shall cover in Part V (Cooley, Thomas, Sorokin, and Parsons), have taken the position that a scientific understanding of subjective human behavior is possible. In this sense, the main line of American sociology has accepted one of the important premises of sociocultural positivism. This behavioristic approach should be carefully distinguished from Watsonian behaviorism and from the neonaturalistic positivism of such figures as George A. Lundberg and Stuart C. Dodd, in which subjectivity is defined as scientifically unknowable.

PHILOSOPHY AND METHOD

Like many of his predecessors in sociology, Cooley was convinced that social life was governed by an evolutionary process that made it ever-more rational—that is, he saw a growth in the human ability to adjust to and even to control life.[1] Unlike much of the previous sociological tradition,

---

[1] Cooley's first major works, *Human Nature and the Social Order* (1902, rev. ed. 1922) and *Social Organization* (1909) are now available in a one-volume edition, Free Press, New York, 1956. All references to these works are from this edition; each is also available as a Schocken paperback. His last major work, *Social Process* (New York: Charles Scribner's Sons, 1918), is available in paperback from Southern Illinois University Press. Cooley's most explicit and extended treatment of

Cooley placed no great emphasis on the growth of science, on the struggle of modern society to escape from its thralldom to a less rational social system, or on the achievement of social perfection through total knowledge. What Cooley meant by the growth of rationality was not the growth of scientific knowledge, but the growth of conscious mental, moral, and aesthetic activity—a growth in the quality and quantity of symbolic interaction.

Subjectivity and the Method of Dramatic Perception

In step with a major trend in pluralistic positivism, Cooley stressed the emotional basis of human nature. The growth of human consciousness, far from being a result of human reason and hard-won scientific knowledge, emerges from an evolutionary process that is essentially unconscious. In criticizing rationalist explanations of social development, Cooley developed arguments that were similar to Durkheim's. Like Durkheim, he argued that the development of society could not be explained in psychological or biological terms, and again like Durkheim, he directed his main argument against Herbert Spencer. Cooley acknowledged Spencer's great service to the cause of social science. He concluded, however, that Spencer was fundamentally ill-equipped for social observation because he lacked both the quality of sympathy and the literary-historical education that constitute the major sources of knowledge about human beings. Given this deficiency, Cooley argued, Spencer was forced to rely on analogies from other orders of phenomena and on a faulty utilitarian-individualistic psychology. Unlike Spencer, Cooley said,

> We now believe that the individual is born with decisive but quite rudimentary capacities and tendencies, owing little or nothing to direct inheritance of the effects of use. For the development of these into a human personality he is wholly dependent on a social environment which comes down from the past through an organic social process. This social process cannot be inferred from individual psychology, much less from heredity; it must be studied directly and is the principal subject of sociology. It absorbs individuals into its life, conforming them to its requirements and at the same time developing their individuality. There is no general opposition between the individual and the social whole; they are complementary and work together to carry on the historical organism.[2]

---

methodology was expressed in a number of essays, the chief of which is "The Roots of Social Knowledge"; these have been collected under the title *Sociological Theory and Social Research* (New York: Henry Holt, 1930). For a collection of essays on Cooley, see Albert J. Reiss, Jr., ed., *Cooley and Sociological Analysis* (Ann Arbor: University of Michigan Press, 1968).

[2] "Reflections on Herbert Spencer," *Sociological Theory and Social Research,* p. 273.

Charles Horton Cooley (1864–1929)

While the socioculturalism suggested by this statement connects Cooley's criticism of Spencer with Durkheim's, Cooley's methodology was considerably different from Durkheim's. Cooley's basic epistemological assumption was that natural science and social science deal with different orders of phenomena and that each has its appropriate method for obtaining knowledge. The fields of natural and social science are so different that neither the substantive nor the methodological principles of natural science can be used in social science except as analogies or auxiliaries. The difficulty in amalgamating the two fields, he said, lies in the fact that while spatial knowledge, or the measurement of one material thing in terms of another, is validated by nature with the human mind merely acting as a mediator, the phenomenon studied by social science is the human mind itself. The product of the slow and intricate process of evolution, the human mind (which

Cooley called the *mental-social complex* to distinguish it from individual-istic-psychological interpretations), cannot be identified with the rest of nature. Though much of the human mind expresses itself in "standardized acts" and is therefore subject to behavioristic-quantitative analysis, there is a portion left over, Cooley insisted, that is creative, willful, and idio-matic. Since the mental-social complex is suffused with meaning, a statistical analysis of its external expressions cannot capture the ethical and aesthetic components lying beneath overt behavior.

Cooley's methodology was foreshadowed early by what is perhaps his most explicit formal definition of the subject matter of sociology.

> The imaginations which people have of one another are the *solid facts* of society, and that to observe and interpret these must be a chief aim of sociology. I do not mean merely that society must be studied *by* the imagination—that is true of all investigations in their higher reaches—but that the *object* of study is primarily an imaginative idea or group of ideas in the mind, that we have to imagine imaginations. The intimate grasp of any social fact will be found to require that we divine what men think of one another.[3]

The method for analyzing this unique subject matter is similar to the process that produces it in the first place, the process of socialization. Just as individuals develop their distinctively human selves through sympathetic interaction with others, said Cooley, the social scientist gains knowledge of the individual and society by using the same process. Though Cooley used a number of different terms to characterize this method, such as *introspection, sympathetic participation,* and *imaginative reconstruction,* he liked most to think of it as a process of *dramatic perception* in which the observer artistically visualizes the inner life of individuals. It was a method, he believed, that could yield rich cumulative results even though it could not provide the prediction characteristic of the experimental "spatial sci-ences." Despite this deficiency, Cooley argued, sociology cannot accept either the methods or the principles of physics, biology, or psychology. Its subject matter does not consist of repetitive processes like that of physics, it evolves on a different time scale than biology, and it cannot be reduced to psychology. In short, Cooley strongly suggested that sociology is a "cultural" rather than a natural science.

Qualitative Empiricism

Cooley's emphasis on qualitative analysis, on the need to recognize that social relationships and behavior contain meanings or values, did not imply

---

[3] *Human Nature and the Social Order,* p. 121f.

that he wanted to transform social science into moral philosophy. Indeed, his rejection of the mathematical methods of the spatial sciences was a plea for a more vital and effective sociological empiricism. His criticism of the statistical approach in social science rested on two grounds: the need for a more precise method to get at the complex, subjective nature of social facts, and the necessity for a more dynamic method to capture the novel or qualitative developments characteristic of social life.

Cooley's empiricism can be seen in other ways. He made a plea for more intensive, limited types of studies, neither too narrow nor too broad, so that sociology could supersede its formative stage of "provisional generalization" and escape the epithet "arm-chair sociology." To this end, he was quite prepared to use any method in addition to dramatic perception that would yield knowledge: statistics, case study or life history, psychiatry or personal interviews, biograms, photo-phonographic records, or literary description. Indeed, Cooley emphasized the need to avoid any one-method, "particularistic" approach and the need to adapt methods to the complex organic nature of social phenomena.

Despite Cooley's genuine commitment to empiricism, he was outside the main current that was developing in American sociology, which sought to adopt both the epistemological assumptions and the quantitative-empirical methods of natural science. For Cooley, however, the main avenue to knowledge was through qualitative analysis. Only the process of subjective dramatization, he felt, was capable of revealing the symbolic structure that formed the unique subject matter of sociology. Cooley did share, however, the main metaphysical goal of both natural and social science—the search for unitary knowledge. Ultimately, he was sure that a human nature existed and that with a little patience and diligence, one could capture the mental-social complex of humanity and thus indicate its main structure and process and its meaning and direction.

The heavily functional quality of Cooley's thought—that is, his characteristic emphasis on judging ideas and values in terms of their relationship to each other, stressing especially adaptation and control—connects Cooley with the general current of American pragmatism. In Cooley's epistemology, as in pragmatism in general, there is little emphasis on reason; the criterion for knowledge is not so much truth as control and adjustment. There is no objective, timeless order of phenomena that corresponds to the structure of the human mind; what exist rather are spontaneously creative life processes. Thus, Cooley's pragmatism could insist that it was not possible or even desirable to judge knowledge by the criterion of certainty or prediction.

However, there are similarities in Cooley's thought with the empirical temper of the Enlightenment. Knowledge still comes from "observation and thought" in fruitful interplay; there is no a priori method, but rather method comes from research itself; and somehow the general mass of phenomena contains law—in Cooley's case, evolutionary law. Also, Cooley's epistemology rested on the need to employ an inventory of qualitative categories and on the assumption that ideas, facts, and values are all part of a seamless web of natural existence. The source of these ideas is never indicated clearly—there was certainly no suggestion that it stemmed from any Kantian-like concept formation. For Cooley, knowledge was simply an evolutionary product developed along with other products to help human beings adjust to and control the conditions of life.

For all his emphasis on the organic structure of phenomena and on the need to come to grips with it in its totality, Cooley did not consciously strive for systematic or general theory. He was more an ad hoc, eclectic empiricist willing to let knowledge come from whence it came and willing to forego the security of a single avenue to truth. Perhaps his work can best be called a literary, artistic empiricism. Like the novelist or artist, Cooley insisted that the nuances and meanings of life could be captured only through a dramatic, selective presentation of materials. His strength as a scientist lay in his sensitivity to concrete details, in his willingness to resort to imaginative conceptualization, and in his insistence that facts exist only in terms of a multicausal, seamless, organic process. His weakness lay in his inability to separate values from science, ideas from facts. Ultimately, he could not resist the temptation to simplify social analysis by thinking of social facts in the same way one thinks of other natural facts—thereby merging the two orders of phenomena that he himself had labored so hard to separate.

SUBSTANTIVE WORK

Cooley's substantive work is best characterized as an attempt to develop an institutional explanation of human nature. Though Cooley was too deeply immersed in the characteristic thought forms of naturalistic positivism to escape from them completely, his work holds a special significance for Anglo-American sociology precisely to the extent that he avoided naturalistic, especially psychological, explanations of human behavior.

The Social Basis of Human Behavior

At variance with most of his forebears in Anglo-American thought, Cooley deliberately rejected the idea that the individual is a self-explanatory entity and that society is a derivative of individual needs and desires. Human nature, he argued, is neither a hereditary structure nor a fixed set of traits; its outstanding characteristic is its "teachability." All that is distinctively human, Cooley insisted, stems not from fixed traits or imperative urges but

from the "indeterminate character of human heredity." In short, it is false
to think of the individual and society as separate entities.

> A separate individual is an abstraction unknown to experience,
> and so likewise is society when regarded as something apart from
> individuals. The real thing is Human Life, which may be con-
> sidered either in an individual aspect or in a social, that is to say a
> general, aspect; but is always, as a matter of fact, both individual
> and general. In other words, "society" and "individuals" do not
> denote separable phenomena, but are simply collective and dis-
> tributive aspects of the same thing. . . [4]

Individuals acquire a self only through contact with others, especially as
they interpret or imagine the judgments passed on them by others. In
Cooley's famous words, the self is a "reflected or looking-glass self." It takes
shape in terms of the "general course of history, by the particular development of nations, classes, and professions, and other conditions of this sort."
As a matter of fact, Cooley asserted, "even those ideas that are most generally associated or colored with the 'my' feeling, such as one's idea of his
visible person, of his name, his family, his intimate friends, his property,
and so on, are not universally so associated, but may be separated from the
self by peculiar social conditions." [5]

Social Structure: Primary and Secondary Aspects

In his last two books, *Social Organization* and *Social Process,* Cooley
turned to a more detailed analysis of the relationships he had identified
as the subject matter of sociology, paying special attention to the distinction
between primary and secondary relations. The result was a rich addition to
Anglo-American sociology, though, here again many of the insights and
much of the flavor of his substantive work ran parallel to developments in
continental European sociology.

Cooley's emphasis on personal interaction or primary relationships is perhaps the best known though not the most important part of his work.
Along with Simmel, Cooley saw in ordinary behavior a fertile field for
sociological analysis. Cooley located the formative force that molds and sustains the individual in primary groups or "intimate face-to-face association
and cooperation"—the family, the playground, and the neighborhood community. However, these were for Cooley as much the expression of human
nature as they were its master. Despite his awareness of the role of social
conditioning and his pioneer contribution to the theory of group behavior,

---

[4] *Human Nature and the Social Order,* p. 36f.
[5] For these views and quotations, see *Human Nature and the Social Order,* pp.
183–185.

Cooley was convinced that human nature was pretty much the same throughout the world. Therefore, primary groups were also much the same everywhere since they expressed the permanent needs of human nature. Indeed, Cooley saw the entire structure and development of society, in its most simple terms, as the fuller expression not of individuals but of human nature over time.

Cooley's references to human nature contained two opposing emphases. On the one hand, he tended to define human nature as a set of vague unstructured dispositions having no concrete existence apart from social stimulation and discipline. On the other, he tended to give human nature concrete content. He suggested a long list of attributes that are universally present in human nature: honor, goods, children, courage, generosity, success, personal freedom, the right to labor, the right to property, the right to open competition, religion, and self-expression—which itself includes emulation, ambition, activity for its own sake, love of workmanship and creation, the impulse to assert one's individuality, and the desire to serve the social whole.

Cooley's concept of primary groups had a large bearing on his overall theory. Without much explanation, he argued that secondary institutions, which emerge from primary groups, somehow constitute a deep threat to primary values or what he also called "human-nature values." Indeed, one of the organizing themes of his work was the belief that secondary institutions were somehow artificial and lifeless and in perpetual tension with the creative, life-giving impulses in human nature. Cooley's use of the terms *primary* and *secondary*, therefore, implied not only a temporal and causal priority in the processes of evolution and socialization, but a priority in moral worth as well.

Cooley's distinction between primary and secondary aspects of social phenomena was a basic theme in all his works despite the fact that he never developed the distinction systematically. As a running contrast, however, it afforded him many insights into the nature of social structure. Sometimes he focused this contrast as a difference between *personal* and *impersonal* behavior, terms which distinguished between the interaction of whole persons and the interaction of segments of persons. The contrast between types of interaction was part of his deeper insight into the main trend of modern social development, the trend toward rationality. This trend, Cooley observed, has developed the functionally segmented individual and has drawn him into voluntary associations and specialized institutions. It is the same trend that has arranged populations into classes rather than castes. In short, rationality "nucleates" both groups and individuals and imposes specialized and sometimes contradictory behavior on them. Cooley saw clearly, in other words, that the structure of groups in modern society (with its growing demand for rational, functional performance) is based on a division of function, not of persons, and on a growing complexity of social obligations.

Out of his overall perspective Cooley developed an acute insight into the nature of individualism. He distinguished between the individuality of "isolation," which he identified with rural life, and the individuality of "choice," which he identified with modern society, especially urban life. Along the way he clearly stated his preference for the latter because it made life "rational and free instead of local and accidental." Cooley also observed that the contrast with the past is not confined to intellectual life; emotional life has changed for the better as well, having become more diverse, more refined, milder, and more uniformly spread throughout society.

Cooley's distinction between primary and secondary aspects of social phenomena was part of his characteristic tendency to think of society as an organic functional whole composed of more limited, functional subsystems; he could then pose the problem of social analysis in terms of how each subsystem worked in relation to each of the others and to the whole. By framing this approach in terms of institutions and by not taking the operation and integration of institutions for granted, Cooley developed a functional approach reminiscent of Durkheim and Weber. Again in terms somewhat similar to Durkheim's criticism of Spencer's utilitarianism, Cooley rejected the claim that the economy is an autonomous system composed of the actions of autonomous, rational individuals whose overall effects are automatically beneficial to society. On the contrary, the economy is deeply dependent on other social values for its successful functioning, and its consequences are often detrimental to social life. Far from deserving a special status, Cooley argued, the economy should be thought of as a subsystem operating along with other subsystems and evaluated in terms of how well it performs its special social task and how well it mixes with the different values of other subsystems. This approach by Cooley places him among the pioneers of institutional economics at the change of the century.

Despite the brilliance of Cooley's critique of laissez faire economics, the high point of his sociology was his contribution to the understanding of social stratification.[6] Whereas many of the earlier sociological treatments of social stratification, for example by Saint-Simon, Comte, Sumner, and Pareto, had been avowedly ideological and crudely psychological, Cooley (along with Max Weber) saw inequality as a social phenomenon and maintained a healthy separation between his analysis and his ideological preferences. The similarity with Weber went even further than method; without

---

[6] For Cooley's extended discussion of social stratification, see *Social Organization*, pt. 4; for additional comments, see *Social Process*, chaps. 8, 24.

using the same terms, Cooley shared many of Weber's conclusions about social stratification. He was aware, for example, that the phenomenon of inequality could be interpreted according to two principles, *inheritance* and *competition* (terms that correspond to Weber's *status* and *class*), and that each principle brings into effect a general type of stratification, *caste* and *class*. Cooley was also aware that these types could blend into a number of combinations: for example, he noted that even in the American class system, the one most free of caste, inheritance is a powerful force.

Cooley's grasp of the nature of social stratification included an insight into the multiple dimensions or "lines of division" that characterize inequality. Though he failed to develop this line of attack systematically, he distinguished three separate dimensions of inequality in the class system: occupation, income, and "culture." This distinction notwithstanding, the basic question about a class system can be reduced to a question of wealth, inherited or acquired. In addition to providing material benefits, Cooley observed, wealth also gives social power through prestige and politics. Lack of wealth means a lack of social power and can turn equality of opportunity into an empty formality. Thus, in analyzing the process that perpetuates the upper class, Cooley did not fail to make a related analysis of the "vicious circle" that minimizes the life chances of the poor.

Throughout his analysis of the dominant role of wealth, however, Cooley never forgot that the structure of a class system differs fundamentally from that of a caste system. Despite the strong tendency in the American class system toward inherited inequality, which sets up a strong pressure to merge the "lines of division," the class system always keeps separate the various dimensions of inequality. Under the class system, the individual more likely than not has different statuses in the various dimensions of inequality. Therefore, Cooley insisted, income and occupation are separate and neither is identical with "culture." In developing and using this analytical framework, Cooley derived a number of important insights into the overall dynamics of social stratification. He saw, for example, that equality of opportunity is incompatible with the structure of the family; that birth rates can be correlated with class membership; that class mobility tends to promote social stability; and that class conflict is obviated by the interlacing of class statuses.

Cooley's overall judgment about the American class system was optimistic. Despite the vicious circle that makes a mockery of equal opportunity and despite the evidence of sharp class cleavage, he was convinced that the United States was moving toward an ever-more functional and just system of inequality. The mixture of statuses, the fact that capital and labor were tied together by investment, habits of thrift, economic interdependence, and the absence of a caste tradition—all worked, he felt, to turn classes into functional parties and class conflict into an impersonal struggle of ideas and issues. As such, all classes are forced to appeal to common principles and must avoid being identified as selfish, partisan groups. On this basis, and on the basis of his faith in the power of education, Cooley concluded that the United States would never see the social cleavage characteristic of inequality in Europe and elsewhere.

Social Process: The Organic-Evolutionary Nature of Society

Though the organic-evolutionary concept of social phenomena was fundamental to Cooley's work from the beginning, it received its greatest emphasis and elaboration in his last major work, *Social Process* (1918). His opening paragraph states the theme of the book:

> We see around us in the world of men an onward movement of life. There seems to be a vital impulse, of unknown origin, that tends to work ahead in innumerable directions and manners, each continuous with something of the same sort in the past. The whole thing appears to be a kind of growth, and we might add that it is an *adaptive* growth meaning by this that the forms of life we see—men, associations of men, traditions, institutions, conventions, theories, ideals—are not separate or independent, but that the growth of each takes place in contact and interaction with that of others. Thus any one phase of the movement may be regarded as a series of adaptations to other phases.[7]

Cooley was never very explicit about what it is that evolves, but his general position is unmistakable. Cooley's thought structure is permeated by the characteristic views and preferences of philosophical idealism; for him that which evolves is essentially mind. He saw a vast reservoir of unformed mental energy that assumes forms as human beings strive to satisfy their needs. The concrete forms of adjustment are themselves part of a gigantic process of adaptation that is evolutionary in nature. Thus, the evolutionary process is fundamentally an enlargement of consciousness, a growing actualization of mind. Social evolution, which at any given time is nothing more than the sum total of realized mental relationships between individuals, is characterized by the growth of rationality, that is by a more conscious adaptation to life's conditions.

Cooley had hoped in his multicausal, organic theory to avoid all forms of monistic explanation, ideal as well as material. However laudable in inten-

[7] *Social Process,* p. 3.

tion, this theory remained unsatisfactory in execution. Cooley invariably referred to ideal factors whenever he attempted to explain anything, and ultimately he gave up the idea of causation altogether. That is, he found it impossible to explain the movement of history except through unverified assertions, the chief of which was that social development is an unconscious but lawful growth of rationality. Cooley went to considerable trouble to refute the belief in the autonomous, utilitarian, rational individual. In a related way, while insisting that society is everywhere characterized by functional processes, Cooley warned against characterizing it as consciously rational or purposive. "I make frequent use of this word function to mean an activity which furthers some general interest of the social group. It differs from 'purpose' in not necessarily implying intention." [8]

He argued even more forcefully that ". . . it is quite plain that the social development of the past has been mostly blind and without human intention." [9] Evolution must be seen as a process of "unintentional adaptation," a blind but effective process of ever-more rational adjustment that goes on not only behind the backs of human beings but even against their will. It is a process that works according to what Cooley called the *tentative method,* that is, in a groping, experimental manner. The functional forms produced by the tentative method cannot be foreseen; they can be known only after they are established. Finally, he argued that progress is a matter of faith, not of demonstration, adding that "there is something rank and groping about human life, like the growth of plants in the dark: If you peer intently into it you can make out weird shapes, the expression of forces as yet inchoate and obscure; but the growth is toward the light." [10] This language, which is characteristic of Cooley's general view of social evolution, illustrates the blatant way in which he fell back on natural-science models to analyze and explain social phenomena.

Social evolution for Cooley was an ever-more functional development of humanity's symbolic faculties, a process, oddly enough, that emerged from deep, unconscious teleological tendencies in human nature. For Cooley, individuals, groups, and institutions are not rational or conscious in and of themselves. However, somehow the eternal upward struggle of life or mind is at once functionally adaptive and progressively moral. Somewhere in the bosom of humanity lie forces that somehow manifest themselves as ever-more functional psychic structures. This emphasis on the rationality of the life process connects Cooley with the similar emphasis in Spencer and Ward,

[8] *Social Organization,* p. 239n.
[9] *Social Organization,* p. 398.
[10] For these views and quotations, see *Social Process,* chaps. 1, 2, 34.

and it also contains an element that connects him with the entire range of sociological theory: the belief in a hidden logic that explains error and evil and guarantees that beneath the diversity and malfunctioning of society there is a process at once lawful and beneficent.

CONCLUSION

The Sociocultural Promise Unfulfilled

Cooley's main contribution to the development of American sociology was to shift its attention from individual psychology and biology to social institutions and processes. In doing this he not only made insightful criticisms of biopsychological and atomistic interpretations of society. He also insisted that subjectivity, which formed a large and important part of the subject matter of social science, could be known only if the sociologist used a method appropriate to this order of phenomena. However, while he gave priority to the method of dramatic perception or understanding, Cooley readily acknowledged that social phenomena were complex enough to admit many methods of investigation. Thus he displayed a genuine commitment to empiricism, not simply because he advocated a plurality of methods but because he recognized the difficulty of gaining knowledge about social phenomena. Therefore, his argument that social phenomena can be divorced from both the methodological and the substantive principles of natural science stemmed from a sincere commitment to empiricism, and not from a desire to preserve moral phenomena from scientific scrutiny. The upshot of Cooley's work was to provide American sociology with a new awareness of methodological problems and to give it some new and lasting insights into the institutional and group nature of human behavior.

Cooley's shortcomings must also be noted. His methodology of dramatic perception, for example, lacked the scientific rigor that Weber had given his similar method of *verstehen*. By not embedding either his methods or his conclusions in a philosophy clearly separating reason, fact, and value, Cooley left the door open to the worst abuses of qualitative reasoning. This failure led him to a metaphysical or substantialist position that ultimately contradicted even his own insistence that the realms of human nature and physical nature be kept separate. Again and again he verged on a genuine sociocultural positivism, which posits culture and society as the unique subject matter of sociology and clearly separates them from the substantive or methodological principles of psychology, biology, or any other natural science. Each time, Cooley failed to realize the promise of his own insights. His main frame of reference focused rather on the relation between a given human nature and an evolving institutional order, an order that stemmed from and then somehow came into opposition to the given and thus unexplained nature of human beings.

The rich promise of Cooley's institutional approach was vitiated from the start by a startling inconsistency in his thought, his belief that the permanent needs of human nature form the structure of primary groups and, ultimately, of society in general. This view was deeply inconsistent with Cooley's quite different belief that society is a progressive organization of the unstructured capacities of human nature. By positing a human nature with attributes apparent to common sense, Cooley decided by fiat the very thing that social science must decide, the nature of human nature. In locating the attributes of human nature in primary groups, he also introduced a deep bias against secondary institutions by depicting them as antithetical to the needs and values of primary groups and thus of human nature. On the whole, and despite a number of contrary remarks, Cooley's characteristic approach was to identify the person, the individual, creativity, progress, and morals with the primary aspects of society, and formalism, mechanism, depersonalization, and stultification with secondary structures, especially economic institutions and political bureaucracies. At the heart of Cooley's approach, therefore, was the belief that individual human nature and what he called "human-nature values" were in perpetual tension with all institutions, especially those of a secondary nature. In the final analysis, this outlook prevented him from garnering the full fruits of the functional-sociocultural approach he had developed so carefully. He failed, in other words, to acquire the deep insight into society that Max Weber had obtained with a similar approach. To have done so, he would have had to abandon the idea of a substantive human nature in favor of a thoroughgoing institutional approach.

Thus, Cooley never realized the theoretical importance of his own insight into the sociocultural sources of human behavior. His assumption that the values associated with individualism and progress were latent in human nature and that they would manifest themselves under the inexorable promptings of evolution introduced major deficiencies into his understanding of historical evolution. He never appreciated, for example, the importance of the secondary institutions of state and economy in the development of the self, liberty, and equality. He never understood that the values associated with primary groups, especially the family, are far more compatible with static, communal social systems than with dynamic, individualistic societies. His analysis of social stratification identified inheritance or family with caste inequality and recognized that equality of opportunity was antagonistic to family structure. His analysis failed, however, to interpret the emergence of class inequality in sociocultural terms. It also overlooked the fact that secondary institutions and the class system associated with them had been highly instrumental in developing individuals and in allowing them to escape from the stultifying confines of institutions based on birth. Instead, Cooley everywhere assumed that the modern class system came into being to satisfy the basic attributes of human nature, that behind its development lay the activity of "naturally ambitious young men," and that the structure of social stratification would eventually reflect the natural diversity and inequality among human beings.

Perhaps the most regrettable aspect of Cooley's thought was his failure to recognize the importance of his own insight into the way that structures of behavior could be separated from social functions—that different combinations of values and statuses could be equally effective socially. This insight, however, succumbed to his pervasive belief that structure and function were ultimately connected by an all-determinative pattern of evolution.

Although Cooley's empirical orientation and his definition of the subject matter of sociology is similar to that of sociocultural positivism, he must be classified as a naturalistic positivist. As I have noted, the sociocultural theorists were not uniform in their definition of either the method or the subject matter of sociology. Durkheim and Pareto, for example, felt that the methodology of science was universal and that there was no need for sociology to develop any distinctive methods. Under such a view there is a great temptation to reduce sociocultural process to natural process. Despite his rich and profound contribution to sociocultural positivism, even Durkheim ended by viewing the social realm as a natural process.

The other major methodological outlook in sociocultural positivism is that the unique subject matter of human behavior requires a special method. In Vico and Max Weber, this perspective led to the methodology of understanding in which observers attempt to duplicate in their own minds and hearts the subjective, inner lives of acting individuals. One of the main arguments for this method is that human behavior is so various and plastic that the static models of natural-science methodology are inappropriate and misleading. But perhaps the major argument is the belief that human behavior is inescapably subjective, involving meaning and choice—in short, it is a moral realm.

The diversity, changeableness, and moral nature of human behavior does not necessarily mean that the monistic goal of Western rationalism was ruled out by the sociocultural approach. In Vico the method of understanding was compatible with the idea of truth (though in Weber it emerged from a philosophical position that denied the possibility of truth). In Cooley's case, the methodology of understanding was combined with a belief in truth, or rather with the related but contradictory belief in a universal moral law that emerged from a lawful process of evolution. Unlike Vico's concept of evolution, Cooley's was natural not sociocultural. Though his view of social evolution was similar to Vico's in that it had fixed limits and a fixed direction, it differed fundamentally in that its processes were similar to those of animal and plant life. Since Cooley himself had rejected the identification of social and natural phenomena, this form of naturalism formed a giant contradiction in his work. Again and again he argued against identifying social and biological evolution and against using biological or psychological models in social analysis. Society, he insisted, sprang not from the psychological traits of individuals, but from the unstructured psychic capacities of humanity. His distinction between a fixed and a malleable human nature, together with his insistence that social phenomena be separated from biology and physics, brought Cooley to the edge, but only the edge, of a genuine sociocultural interpretation of behavior.

In the final analysis, Cooley's explanation rested on a biologically inspired idealism. For Cooley, there existed something called life, an inchoate fund of consciousness that inexorably shapes itself according to a lawful if somewhat untidy scheme of evolution. His thought is another variation of the philosophical idealism characteristic of so much of sociological positivism. However, regardless of the nature of his major principle, Cooley's attempt to derive a substantialist principle from empirical investigation ran him afoul of the liberal dilemma, which caused him, like so many other sociologists, to make wide use of the idea of a hidden logic. In the final analysis, Cooley's theory amounted to a belief that the mind evolves to satisfy its needs, thereby producing an evolutionary process that brings about changes in human needs and the conditions under which they can be satisfied. Somewhere in the course of evolution the mind is able to produce knowledge about an empirical social order composed of unconsciously produced consciousness. In this way mind becomes social science as it gains awareness of the moral truth in human nature—a moral truth that is always present in human beings but that expresses itself through the blind and often immoral process of evolution.

Cooley as a Liberal Apologist

Ideologically, Cooley's sociological theory is easily identified as liberal in character. This is most apparent in his identification of human nature with the right to personal freedom, property, and opportunity and in his claim that human beings are intrinsically motivated by success, competition, workmanship, and creativity. Cooley's thought is everywhere informed by the major assumption of liberalism— that there exists apart from society a human nature, composed of relatively equal individuals, whose main characteristic is ego assertion. Cooley's concept of the individual, of course, was appreciably different from the early tradition of liberal thought. Ego assertion for the early liberals was a rational, utilitarian endeavor, and the individual was seen, by and large, as a self-sufficient entity. For Cooley, however, the individual was primarily a sociable, emotional creature who needs a vital, quasi-religious ethical and aesthetic fellowship.

Cooley's work belongs, therefore, to late liberalism, to the new phase of liberal social theory that emerged during the late-nineteenth century to reinterpret the theoretical basis of capitalist society. To this end he made penetrating criticisms of laissez faire economics, the American class system, and American society in general. The common theme of all his criticism was that the impersonal mechanism of secondary institutions constituted a deep threat to personal existence, to elementary moral decencies.

With such a position, Cooley could not very well uphold the sort of individualism that marked the thought of Sumner. Instead, he sought to protect individuals by defining them as the highest product of an inexorable, evolutionary process and by using the forms of interaction and values characteristic of primary groups as the criteria with which to judge society at large. In rejecting the idea of the rational, autonomous individual, Cooley was careful to transfer the rationality of the individual to evolution—a rationality that stemmed not from conscious calculation, social planning, or human control over social forces, but from the hidden logic or élan vital of the life process.

Nowhere is Cooley's liberalism so apparent as in his characteristic confusion between individual psychology and individualism—between the "voluntaristic nominalism" that dissolved society into self-propelled atoms and his argument that personality is a reflection of society. His thought expressed the deep American nostalgia for rural small-town life, a nostalgia that found full expression in early-twentieth-century sociology. In many ways Cooley's thought exemplified the distinctive impact of the American Midwest on sociology and politics. Ultimately, Cooley resolved the conflict between his early-liberal and late-liberal leanings by developing the theory of symbolic interaction. For Cooley, individuals became real as they engage in interaction with fellow human beings. Primary interaction is best because it is closest to the fundamental longings and predispositions of human nature. Cooley's emphasis on the social origins of individual personality is basically a focus on consciousness or symbolic process and growth emerging from the relations between individuals. As such, the focus on symbolic interaction is a distinctive product of American liberalism. It presupposes that America has already achieved a relatively classless society of autonomous individuals and that behavior and society reflect individual needs and attributes; and it sees the satisfaction of human beings and the protection of their rights in individually scaled social relationships (primary groups, small-town communities). All this is consistent with the American liberal emphasis on the primacy of ideological or symbolic causation.[11]

The evolutionary-organic focus allowed Cooley to think of society in terms of its ability to make pragmatic adjustments to new conditions, a point of view that again connects him with the late-liberal mentality. This perspective gave him an institutional, social-structure approach unique in American sociology. However, despite his new approach and his heavy criticism of American society, Cooley could never bring himself to see the United States without some kind of cosmic underpinning; he could not think of it as simply a historical society. On the contrary, American society for Cooley suffered not from intrinsic failings or contradictions in its normative or institutional structures, but from the fact that its institutions were in a state of evolutionary transition. Like Durkheim before him and others after him, Cooley identified a series of major problems and then explained them away by saying that they were temporary features of a maturing social system.

Cooley's failure to develop a genuine institutional approach can be explained in another way. If society is a natural process with a given direction, then it is not amenable to large-scale human control. Its processes and structures are natural, not sociocultural or historical, and there is therefore no special urgency about locating a specific hierarchy of causes to which problems can be referred. Ironically, Cooley's theory of causation was weak because he identified too many causes. His causal theory was undoubtedly inspired by his immersion in perhaps the purest example of a liberal social system, the American social structure with its supposed plurality of autonomous groups and actors. True to liberal thought in general, these essentially uncaused actors and groups eliminated the question of power from Cooley's mind and led him to accept the idea of a built-in functional harmony.

> We must remember [he tells us] that although large wholes are, as a rule, much inferior to individuals in explicit consciousness and purpose, they are capable of rational structure and action of a somewhat mechanical sort far transcending that of the individual mind. This is because of the vast scope and indefinite duration they may have, which enables them to store up and systematize the work of innumerable persons, as a nation does, or even an industrial corporation. A large whole may and usually does display in its activity a kind of rationality or adaptation of means to ends

---

[11] Symbolic interaction received a fuller expression as a philosophy and a social psychology in the work of Cooley's friend, George Herbert Mead (1863–1931). Of Mead's various works, the most relevant for sociology is *Mind, Self, and Society*, ed. Charles W. Morris (Chicago: University of Chicago Press, 1934), available in paperback.

which, as a whole, was never planned or purposed by anybody, but is the involuntary result of innumerable special endeavors.[12]

In Cooley's case, social integration came not from the natural law of classical liberal economic or political theory, but from evolution. However, though the integrative process was different, it had the same capacity for using conflict and competition to serve social functions and to produce social unity without explicit social control.

Evolution also inspired Cooley's instrumental empiricism and gave him his organic view of society; this overall perspective alerted him to the way in which American institutions were falling short of American standards, and perhaps more importantly, falling short of America's needs as a social system. While this made Cooley into a pragmatic reformer and placed him in the mainstream of the great age of reform, his empirical pragmatic temperament was also a heavy-footed liberal conservatism. Cooley not only accepted the basic beliefs and values of preindustrial America, but he also espoused a theory that made it difficult to construct or envisage alternate models of society. His thought was almost completely devoid of comparison, containing almost no contrast between modern and feudal society or between folk and developed societies. Finally, by defining human nature as primarily emotional and by locating rationality in unconscious evolutionary processes, he effectively barred reason and morality from transcending the given.

Oddly enough, and despite his focus on society and evolution, it is only the individual who had real existence for Cooley. Liberal in this respect, Cooley also expressed an optimistic faith in progress, a naive faith in the power of the unlettered masses to stimulate and select good leaders, a preference for intellectual and moral processes as opposed to governmental action, a strong tendency to reduce economic and other power structures to symbolic interaction between individuals, and a belief in the natural resiliency and harmony of liberal institutions. All that America needed, Cooley believed, was a better application and coordination of the values and beliefs it already had. To this end, he was quite prepared to admit a large measure of deliberate reform—despite his belief that adjustment ultimately comes not from human beings but from evolution. The late-liberal reform mentality is everywhere in his work: second thoughts about laissez faire; a wider acceptance of political solutions; a greater appreciation of the value of intellectual diversity; and his frank acknowledgement that values cannot be defined absolutely but must succumb to compromise and be judged by the criterion of effectiveness. Cooley's late-liberal mentality is perhaps most evident in his definition of society as an organic set of functional groups and institutions in need of more explicit coordination and his belief that the

[12] *Social Organization,* p. 369f.

capacities and loyalties of individuals could be developed only within the context of a viable social system.

Despite his late-liberal mentality, Cooley placed the main burden of reform on evolution. He never became a sociologistic or culturalistic reformer—that is, he never separated human nature from society in order to focus on the sociocultural structure that creates human nature, behavior, and social problems. True to the liberal tradition, Cooley believed that human nature exists prior to society as a substantive principle and that human nature not only creates society but contains a latent energy that always finds itself in tension with outmoded institutions.

Cooley's focus on subjectivity is in keeping with the developing sociocultural outlook, and his emphasis on the importance and the rationality of the passions links him to the main thrust of modern social science. That he was able to explain the structure of human passions and mental forms in terms of an accumulated heritage of responses to natural and social conditions marks the measure of his success in avoiding the pitfall of biopsychological naturalistic positivism. However, to the extent that he ultimately reduced this heritage to a universal law of development stemming from human nature, he not only succumbed to biopsychological naturalism, but to a metaphysical or monistic positivism that was out of keeping with both his own insights and the new phase of modern science from which these insights had been derived.

Chapter 20
William Isaac Thomas (1863–1947)

While similar in many respects to Cooley, W. I. Thomas stands much closer to the mainstream of twentieth-century American sociology. The similarities with Cooley's thought are relatively easy to identify. Both thinkers were anxious to leave the era of armchair sociology and orient sociology toward empirical research; both emphasized the need to limit research to small, well-defined areas and to develop and employ a variety of methodological procedures; both were predisposed to think of human beings and society as adjustive mechanisms; and both recognized the threat to social control posed by rapid social change and strongly urged that scientific knowledge about human behavior be expanded to counter this threat. Finally, Thomas, like Cooley, insisted that subjectivity was an integral part of scientific knowledge and that all knowledge about human behavior must be based on the relation between individual human nature and the institutional or social context in which it unfolded.

On the whole, however, Thomas's work was quite different from Cooley's. Basically, Thomas was committed to a much more hard-bitten scientific outlook than Cooley, an outlook much closer to the spirit of the natural sciences. Thomas never accepted the literary, qualitative, subjective empiricism of Cooley and never advanced a general theory of social structure and process as Cooley had done. Indeed, most of Thomas's substantive contribution to sociology lay in his methodological work. His methodological orientation made him the most influential of all the early-twentieth-century sociologists in promoting and directing the development of pluralistic positivism in the United States. His writings [1] reflect the main concerns and

---

[1] In addition to many books, Thomas wrote a large number of articles and reports, some of which were never published. Edmund H. Volkart's *Social Behavior and Personality: Contributions of W. I. Thomas to Theory and Social Research* (New York: Social Science Research Council, 1951) provides a quick if uncritical review of Thomas's long career, as well as extensive selections from his writings, many of them from unpublished works. Another selection from Thomas's work is provided by Morris Janowitz, ed., *W. I. Thomas on Social Organization and*

methods in American sociology after World War I, and they directly stimulated much of the creative work of this period.

PHILOSOPHY AND METHOD

Thomas's career illustrates the important, even predominant, role that
methodology has played in twentieth-century sociology. His overall me-
thology underwent modifications in response to his conviction that methodology is not an end in itself but must follow the nature of subject matter
and research problems. The main source of Thomas's methodology is the
classic Methodological Note that opens the *Polish Peasant*.[2] One of the
central features of this note is its insistence that the realm of subjectivity
is an important part of the data of social science. However, Thomas never
transformed his interest in subjectivity into a methodological principle. Unlike Vico, Weber, and Cooley, he does not belong to the methodological
school of understanding. Indeed, in what must obviously have been a reference to Cooley, Thomas began his criticism of what he called the "common
sense" or "practical" school of sociology by rejecting, first of all, its assumption that one can generalize about society on the basis of one's own empirical, subjective acquaintance with social reality.

According to Thomas, "practical" sociology has never become a truly
scientific social theory because of a number of methodological fallacies:
methods that begin with a distinction between the normal and abnormal,
that begin moralistically or with an assertion of values; methods that arti-
ficially and arbitrarily treat facts in isolation from the total life of society;
and the related methods that assume that human beings react in the same
way to the same influences or that they spontaneously profit in a uniform
way from given conditions. The general cause of all these fallacies, said
Thomas, has been the compelling need for social theorists to meet the

---

Social Personality (Chicago: University of Chicago Press, 1966), also in paperback. With a few exceptions, my analysis of Thomas's work will be based on his
three major works: in collaboration with Florian Znaniecki, *The Polish Peasant
in Europe and America*, 5 vols. (Boston: Richard G. Badger, 1918–1920), 2nd
ed., 2 vols., content unchanged (New York: Alfred A. Knopf, 1927); reissued by
Dover, 1958); in collaboration with Dorothy Swaine Thomas, *The Child in
America* (New York: Alfred A. Knopf, 1928); and *Primitive Behavior: An Introduction to the Social Sciences* (New York: McGraw-Hill, 1937).
[2] References to the *Polish Peasant* will be to the second edition published by
Knopf in 1928 and reissued by Dover in 1958. I shall refer to this book as
Thomas's, but it should not be forgotten that it had a co-author, Florian Znaniecki
(1882–1958), a distinguished sociologist in his own right. Indeed, this book is so
uncharacteristic of Thomas's work in general that Znaniecki's role in it may be
larger than is generally suspected. In any case, the *Polish Peasant*, in both its
methodology and its substantive theory, contains a sustained conceptual sophistication that is absent from Thomas's other work.

W. I. Thomas (1863–1947)

exigencies of day-to-day life. However, he warned, while the ultimate test of theory is practice, one must not let practice control theory. Success in the world of practical affairs must wait until science has provided "a large body of secure and objective knowledge capable of being applied to any situation, whether foreseen or unexpected." To acquire this body of knowledge, one must avoid the fallacies endemic to the "planless empiricism" of "practical" sociology, and the only way to do this is to treat science or theory as an end in itself.

Nomothetic Social Science

In outlining his methodology, Thomas set forth a lengthy and formal series of propositions about the procedures and objectives of social science. The two fundamental practical problems of social theory, he asserted, have always been: "(1) the problem of the dependence of the individual upon social organization and culture and (2) the problem of the dependence of social organization and culture upon the individual." These problems pose two types of data for social theory, "values," the objective cultural elements of social life, and "attitudes," the subjective characteristics of individuals.

"By a social value we understand any datum having an empirical content accessible to the members of some social group and a meaning with regard to which it is or may be an object of activity. Thus, a foodstuff, an instrument, a coin, a piece of pottery, a university, a myth, a scientific theory are social values." [3]

It is apparent that in defining *value*, Thomas was employing the concept of culture that was to gain almost universal acceptance in twentieth-century American social science. All these elements, arranged to illustrate the continuum from material (or "sensual") culture to nonmaterial (or "imaginary") culture, have no value, he said, except as they are defined by society to have meaning for human activity. Once defined, these elements become attitudes as well as values.

Thomas was careful not to explain an attitude in psychological terms, and he was just as careful to define psychology, social psychology, and sociology as distinct disciplines. Psychology probes for the natural states or processes of psychic phenomena; social psychology is concerned with attitudes, or the way in which "social values" are absorbed by or influence the life of the individual; and sociology focuses on cultural "rules," which in controlling behavior crystallize into "social institutions" and, in their totality, comprise "social organization." Taken together, social psychology and sociology make up the field of social theory.

Social theory, Thomas continued, can become scientific only to the extent that it provides a satisfactory causal explanation of its phenomena. If it is to provide a basis for social control, social theory must explain both stability and change, or social "becoming"; and it must establish laws, not approximations or probabilities. Unless this is recognized, Thomas insisted, social theory will be at a loss to explain why the same value can produce different effects on individuals, or why the same attitude can be provoked by a large variety of values. Even a uniform response to values needs to be explained, Thomas warned, unless one is willing to assume that the social conditions that produced it have an original natural status. On the other hand, if one goes to the other extreme and attempts to explain a change in values or social organization on the basis of individual acts or attitudes, one must

[3] *Polish Peasant,* 1:21.

face the fact that every change or novelty appears unique, and thus inexplicable. Accordingly,

> The fundamental methodological principle of both social psychology and sociology—the principle without which they can never reach a scientific explanation—is therefore the following one:
>
> *The cause of a social or individual phenomenon is never another social or individual phenomenon alone, but always a combination of a social and an individual phenomenon.*
>
> Or, in more exact terms: *"The cause of a value or of an attitude is never an attitude or a value alone, but always a combination of an attitude and a value."* [4]

From the footnote accompanying this principle, it is clear that Thomas was aware that he was dismissing Durkheim's theory of causation. Durkheim had defined the subject matter of sociology as social facts, or what would nowadays be called culture and interaction, and had found the cause of a social fact in a preceding social fact—a point of view that assumes that individual consciousness and behavior is not only a reflection of cultural codes and social processes, but a fairly exact reflection. In asserting a contrary position, Thomas was not simply introducing a psychological explanation into sociology. His primary motive was to obtain a higher level of precision than the gross-probability rates on which Durkheim had been forced to rely. Thomas wanted to tackle the full range of human behavior, no matter how diverse or unique. This meant that the behavior of individuals qua individuals had to be explained and that the scientist could not be satisfied with rates about the behavior of average individuals. Whereas Durkheim had been content to explain only large-scale social-system change and diversity, Thomas wanted science to explain individual behavior as well.

Human Documents

Thomas's interest in the subjective aspect of social reality led to a methodological innovation of considerable importance, the use of what at various times he called *human,* or *personal,* or *behavior* documents. The documents themselves varied. In the first volume of the *Polish Peasant,* Thomas examined personal letters. In the second volume, he used documents from newspapers and the records of courts, social agencies, and churches. Later in the volume, he used another type of document, personal life records, which according to Thomas "constitute the *perfect* type of sociolgical material."

---

[4] *Ibid.,* 1:44 (the emphasis is Thomas's).

The Situation and the Four Wishes

The Methodological Note to the *Polish Peasant* also contains Thomas's famous concepts of the *situation* and *four wishes*. Asserting his faith in the power of social science to achieve conscious control over every reach of social phenomena, Thomas introduced two ideas that are relevant not to the derivation but the application of scientific laws. The first stems from the fact that practical problems never conform exactly to generalizations, a fact that makes it necessary to think of "every concrete activity as the solution of a situation." It is desirable, Thomas asserted, from the standpoints of social evolution, hedonism, morals, and efficiency, that situations be defined and activities controlled through conscious individual reflection. To satisfy this or any other social goal, said Thomas, one must assume that it is possible to

> . . . find in the individual attitudes which cannot avoid response to the class of stimulations which society is able to apply to him. And apparently we do find this disposition. Every individual has a vast variety of wishes which can be satisfied only by his incorporation in a society. Among his general patterns of wishes we may enumerate: (1) the desire for new experience, for fresh stimulations; (2) the desire for recognition, including, for example, sexual response and general social appreciation, and secured by devices ranging from the display of ornaments to the demonstration of worth through scientific attainment; (3) the desire for mastery, or the "will to power," exemplified by ownership, domestic tyranny, political despotism, based on the instinct of hate, but capable of being sublimated to laudable ambition; (4) the desire for security, based on the instinct of fear and exemplified negatively by the wretchedness of the individual in perpetual solitude or under social taboo.[5]

Ideal Personality Types

To obviate the need to investigate each and every individual, Thomas advocated the use of ideal personality types. True to his earlier separation of individual psychology from social psychology, he made it clear that his three personality types, the *philistine*, the *bohemian*, and the *creative man*, have nothing to do with the original drives of human nature or what he called *temperament*. These types represent three general ways in which society develops personality to suit its needs: the philistine emerges from a settled scheme of society, the bohemian is a philistine trying to use the attitudes of a settled social world in a period of change, and the creative

[5] *Ibid.*, 1:72f.

man is one who has been given the attitudes that allow the creative man to redefine the changing world of social situations creatively.

However, almost immediately Thomas's sociocultural definition of behavior shaded off into contradiction and ambiguity. Individuals are not the product of society, said Thomas, but have the power to modify it according to their "wishes" or "tendencies" (not according to their "character," which is based on socially acquired attitudes). Of special importance to Thomas for understanding behavior were the two "universal traits" of *curiosity* and *fear,* which can also be called the "desire for new experience" and the "desire for stability." The alternation of these two fundamental tendencies is the principle that governs personal evolution.[6] Indeed, said Thomas, there is

> no pre-existing harmony whatever between the individual and the social factors of personal evolution, and the fundamental tendencies of the individual are always in some disaccordance with the fundamental tendencies of social control. Personal evolution is always a struggle between the individual and society—a struggle for self-expression on the part of the individual, for his subjection on the part of society— and it is in the total course of this struggle that the personality—not as a static "essence," but as a dynamic, continually evolving set of activities—manifests and constructs itself.[7]

These two wishes are also the source of social development, for only individuals, depending on whether their temperament disposes them toward new experience or toward stability, can ever be the source of new definitions and new schemes of social organization.

There are two other wishes, however, the "desire for response" and the "desire for recognition," that are not in tension with society—indeed, they actively promote social ends.

> The desire for response is the common socio-psychological element of all those attitudes by which an individual tends to adapt himself to the attitudes of other individuals—affection, friendship, sexual love, humility, personal subordination and imitation, flattery, admirative attachment of inferior to superior, etc.[8]

The second wish promotes social ends in another way:

> The desire for recognition is the common element of all those attitudes by which the individual tends to impose the positive

---

[6] *Ibid.,* 2:1858–1861. Note the similarity of Thomas's "fundamental tendencies" with Pareto's residues I and II (instinct for combinations; group-persistences).
[7] *Ibid.,* 2:1861f.
[8] *Ibid.,* 2:1882.

appreciation of his personality upon the group by adapting his activities to the social standards of valuation recognized by the group. It is found, more or less connected with other attitudes, in showing-off, pride, honor, feeling of self-righteousness, protection of inferiors, snobbishness, cabotinism, vanity, ambition, etc.[9]

Thomas identified these two classes of wishes, which refer to basic biopsychological drives and instrumental egotism, not as "temperamental tendencies" but as "fundamental social attitudes." He identified the first as *"emotional"* morality, which produces social cohesion at the primary-group level; the second is "rational" morality and produces social cohesion at the societal-group level.

The desire for response and the desire for recognition do not manifest themselves rigidly or concretely; they are altered by the development of complex society. In an advanced society, said Thomas, they are not only used to promote other activities and values, but they are often opposed to each other.

Thomas never resolved the ambiguity and contradiction in his analysis of the relation between psychology and sociology. He was somewhat aware that the four classes of wishes could be shaped into a variety of behavior structures and that identical social functions could be fulfilled by various forms of behavior; however, unlike Durkheim, he never followed up on this strategic insight and therefore never escaped from the grip of the biopsychological tradition.

The Merger of Theory and Practice

The Methodological Note that prefaced the *Polish Peasant* fairly explicitly separated theory, or pure knowledge, and practice, or applied knowledge. In this respect, Thomas's methodology was quite ahistorical; it emphasized the need to emancipate social science from the "planless empiricism" characteristic of thinkers engaged in coping with practical affairs; and suggested strongly that there were intrinsic formal procedures that the social scientist could use to overcome the shapeless magnitude of the empirical world. In the Methodological Note, Thomas not only sharply separated the intellectual problems associated with theory from those of practice, but he limited the data of social science in an ahistorical fashion. The

---

[9] *Ibid.*, 2:1883. These two wishes, it should be noted, are a reformulation of Thomas's earlier list in 1:73. The "desire for recognition" is here narrowed to include much of what was formerly the "desire for mastery," and a new term, "response," is used to characterize the need for sexual, personal, and family gratifications.

empirical world, he said, should be dealt with through ideal or representative cases—a method that assumed that formal or logical analysis would be more efficient and at the same time would protect the scientist against bias and arbitrariness. Finally, social science should study only "actual civilized" societies, postponing the study of historical or ethnographic data until it had a body of conclusions that would make such study fruitful and objective.

Thomas's uneasiness with his methodological position was reflected in a continuous series of writings about methodology. The crux of his final position appeared as early as 1928 in *The Child in America,* which he wrote with his wife, Dorothy Swaine Thomas. In Part III, Thomas canvassed a broad range of social-science research under what he called the psychometric, personality testing, psychiatric, physiological-morphological, and sociological approaches to human behavior. Thomas concluded that the "behavioristic" or "situational" approach is the most promising method in social science. He even went so far as to describe the development of American sociology as the gradual replacement of the psychological-physiological approach by the situational or behavioristic approach. Sociology has contributed to this approach by analyzing situations more complex than the home and the school, situations such as "neighborhoods, communities, geographical localities, containing a great variety and disparity of values and stimulations—playgrounds, libraries, settlements, boys' clubs, moving pictures, dance halls, cabarets, gang organizations, etc." In recounting the work of sociologists such as Park, Burgess, Thrasher, and Zorbaugh in enlarging the concept of situation and in providing the larger context for understanding the family and the school, Thomas also provided, incidentally, an insight into the large role played by the Department of Sociology of the University of Chicago in the development of empirical sociology in the United States.[10]

Behavioristic Sociology

The concluding chapter of *The Child in America* is arranged around two distinctive emphases. The first is the "behavioristic" approach, which Thomas distinguished sharply from Watsonian behaviorism. Obviously showing the influence of physiological and psychiatric psychology on social science during the 1920s, Thomas affirmed the importance of original nature, especially the natural drives of hunger and sex, in understanding behavior. However, his major emphasis was elsewhere, on social or learned behavior, and he cautioned social scientists against explaining behavior

[10] For a short informative history of this phase of American sociology, see Robert E. L. Faris, *Chicago Sociology, 1920–1932* (San Francisco: Chandler Publishing Co., 1967).

by simply multiplying instincts. The behavioristic explanation, he declared, ignores the question of original nature.

Thomas's second emphasis was on his new concept of science. Science is still a search for prediction and control, he said, but it cannot establish "complete" causation or general laws, only "limited laws." The social scientist, who deals with data far more complex than those of the natural sciences, cannot establish as many limited laws as the natural scientist. However, while the social scientist cannot establish laws, said Thomas, he or she can make "inferences," and while the social scientist cannot obtain complete causation, he or she can obtain an adequate causal explanation. In pursuing this more limited definition of science, the social scientist must still use subjective data, for unlike the school of behaviorism, the behavioristic approach is searching for "behavior expressions," not "behavior mechanisms." The behavior document, even though biased and subjective, supplies a necessary ingredient in the causal process, for "if men define situations as real, they are real in their consequences." However, statistics, not behavior documents, will supply inferences, for statistics, along with control groups, is the nearest that social science can come to the experimental method. Here Thomas was reflecting the influence of the quantitative sociology that had developed strongly at Columbia University under Franklin H. Giddings (1855–1931) and had spread to the University of Chicago (stimulated by William F. Ogburn's move from Columbia to Chicago in 1927) and elsewhere from the 1920s on.

In his later work Thomas substituted the concept of *situation* for the similar attitude-value scheme. One of the advantages of this later formulation was that it allowed Thomas to see interaction or social relationships as a causal factor while retaining the idea of cultural or normative causation. The attempt to distinguish conceptually between society and culture is an important theme running through most of pluralistic positivism. Though Thomas's awareness of this distinction was limited,[11] it serves to connect his thought with Durkheim, Weber, and Cooley, and with later American

[11] Two other references to this distinction may be found in *The Child in America*, pp. 506, 572. For evidence that Thomas was not overly clear or overly interested in the distinction between interaction and its normative content, see his article, "The Relation of Research to the Social Process," in W. F. D. Swann *et al.*, *Essays on Research in the Social Sciences* (Washington: The Brookings Institution, 1931), p. 176f., where he used the term *social relationship* to refer to both interaction and norms, and *Primitive Behavior*, p. 1, where he said, ". . . the social sciences are fundamentally concerned with relationships between individuals and individuals, individuals and groups, and groups and other groups. Language, gossip, customs, codes, institutions, organizations, governments, professions, etc., are concerned with the mediation of these relationships," but then goes on to ignore the distinction in the remainder of the book. On the whole, it cannot be said that Thomas profited much from the brilliant work in anthropology that emerged at the University of Chicago during the 1920s and 1930s.

sociologists such as Sorokin and Parsons who adopted and elaborated the idea that meaningful action is the core subject matter of sociology, and made this distinction a central part of their work. Basically, Thomas's contributions to the development of sociocultural positivism were to single out the concept of situation as the most strategic way to analyze the deep complexity of human behavior, and to call for a more precise delineation of situational variables as the most pressing task facing empirical social research.

Ad Hoc Empiricism

Thomas made a number of important modifications in his methodology in the years following the *Polish Peasant*, anticipating in almost all respects Herbert Blumer's classic criticism of that book.[12] These modifications, however, are not so deep-seated as they appear at first sight. The shifts from formal qualitative analysis to quantitative analysis and from "laws" to "probability-inferences," however important, in no way meant that Thomas abandoned the search for certainty, prediction, or nomothetic knowledge. His rejection of the concept of four wishes did not mean that he gave up the idea of an original human nature—it merely expressed his belief that human nature must be found empirically. While his shift in position cleared up some of the ambiguity in his use of psychology, it failed to establish the relevance of psychology to sociology or even to social psychology.

The shifts in Thomas's thought have a deeper meaning, however, if viewed in a wider context. They represent a shift away from a methodology in which empirical investigation is balanced by formal or conceptual analysis (with the avowed purpose of obtaining theory, or conceptualizing the interconnected laws about the allegedly universal features of behavior that exist beneath the complexity and uniqueness of practice or empirical life). Instead, Thomas moved toward a frankly stated, informal, ad hoc empiricism in which theory, both as methodology and as substantive conclusion, is derived from and subordinated to practice.

The conceptual shapelessness of Thomas's final approach to behavior may be illustrated in a number of ways. The idea of the situation, which in the *Polish Peasant* had been developed to translate theory into practice, was now employed to obtain theory. The realm of practice, which in the *Polish Peasant* had been identified with the "planless empiricism" responsible for

---

[12] Herbert Blumer, *Critiques of Research in the Social Sciences: 1,* "An Appraisal of Thomas's and Znaniecki's 'The Polish Peasant in Europe and America' " (New York: Social Science Research Council, 1939). For a summary of the critique (and appreciation), see pp. 69–81; for Thomas's rejoinder and acknowledgment, in which he presented almost a summary of his last chapter from *The Child in America,* see pp. 82–87.

contaminating "practical sociology," was now, via the concept of situation, the source of basic knowledge about behavior. Related to this change of orientation was Thomas's growing unconcern with total social-structure analysis and his growing interest in problems for their own sake. As Cooley had done before him, Thomas capped his new orientation by calling for intensive studies of limited areas.

Thomas's new orientation toward subjective factors is also revealing. In his earlier work, he believed it possible, through the use of formally derived types, to transcend the idiosyncratic nature of subjective factors and thus turn them into a source of rational or transhistorical knowledge. In his later work, Thomas saw the subjective realm as too complex and too filled with error and evil to generalize about. Despite the unreliability of such data, however, it was still real and therefore had to be accepted and studied.

Perhaps the most revealing contrast between Thomas's earlier and his later methodology is his flirtation with epistemological serendipity, that is, with a faith that a process of hidden logic is efficacious at the methodological level. In a letter to Robert Park,[13] Thomas explicitly rejected formal methodology.

> It is my experience [he writes] that formal methodological studies are relatively unprofitable. They have tended to represent the standpoint developed in philosophy and the history of philosophy. It is my impression that progress in method is made from point to point by setting up objectives, employing certain techniques, then resetting the problems with the introduction of still other objectives and the modification of techniques.

This approach, Thomas went on, which is standard practice in the natural sciences, has at last been adopted by the social sciences and has led to considerable success. Social science has now realized the need, he concluded,

> . . . to move from point to point without necessarily any formidable attempt to rationalize and generalize the process. It is only, in fact, so far as sociology is concerned, since we abandoned the search for standardized methods based largely on the work of dead men, that we have made the beginnings which I have indicated.

In his last book, *Primitive Behavior,* Thomas gave renewed emphasis to the comparative method, but unlike in the *Polish Peasant,* where he gave priority to the study of present-day civilized societies, he now plunged into a wide examination of data from primitive cultures, in effect rejecting his

---

[13] Reprinted in Herbert Blumer, *An Appraisal of Thomas and Znaniecki's 'The Polish Peasant in Europe and America,'* pp. 166–167.

earlier injunction against the study of such cultures, and for the most part, ignoring his own warning against taking facts out of context. His renewed interest in comparative study did not imply a change in basic orientation, however. The "central problem in the general life process" was still adjustment, and Thomas's comparative analysis was an effort to improve his understanding of adjustment processes. He again displayed a strong cultural approach to behavior and a continued use of psychological items, and he retained his master concept for relating psychology to culture, *the definition of the situation*. Thomas departed from his own advice against studying primitive cultures because he now considered it sound scientific procedure to attack the problems of maladjustment indirectly, even by delving into seemingly irrelevant situations.

In adopting a comparative cultural approach in which the definition of the situation is the key to understanding adjustment, Thomas explicitly rejected evolutionary, racial, and geographic-economic explanations. The major theme of *Primitive Behavior* is the variety of ways in which primitive people define situations pertaining to such things as kinship, incest, religion, sex, prestige, government, and law. There are two interesting things about Thomas's analysis: aside from the loose thematic structure provided by his interest in the relativity of situational definitions, the book contains no cumulative structure, summaries, or concluding chapter—that is, there is no attempt to generalize from or about the data or to extract either explanation or significance from it. His analysis represents the ultimate nadir of ad hoc empiricism, the sheer amassing of data without conceptual decision or order in the hope that a pattern will emerge of itself, or at the very least that a process of serendipitous stimulation will take place as a reward for diligence and interest. As such, *Primitive Behavior* forms a logical climax to Thomas's substantive work, in which he found it more and more difficult to say anything after his early books and easier and easier to advocate research.

Despite Thomas's behaviorist orientation and his emphasis on cultural relativism, he was still ambiguous about the relation of psychology to sociology. Though his main explanation for behavior was cultural, especially in the last chapter where he rejected a racial explanation for the seemingly bizarre and unsophisticated behavior of primitive people, Thomas still hedged and asserted the importance of biology and psychology. Ironically, his study contains an enormous mass of evidence pointing to a strictly sociocultural explanation of behavior. Methodologically, it contains the major insight for developing a Durkheimian functionalism. As was seen in the *Polish Peasant*, Thomas was well aware that personality and social needs can be satisfied in a variety of ways. Thomas, however, never seriously explored the implications of this insight. He was unable, in short, to separate behavior structure from psychological structure or to separate behavior structure from psychological or social function. He never abandoned the view that social deviation and social change stem primarily from antisocial drives in the individual or from inadequate socialization. His commitment to American individualism was too strong for him to see that social science must explain individualism itself; nor could he recognize that an industrial society creates internal pressures for change by placing a high value on certain forms of innovation and creativity. He never came to see, in other words, that individualism is the by-product of industrial society, not its precondition, and that social deviation is more likely to stem from the inculcation of contradictory values than from inadequate socialization.

Thomas's oscillation between a social-forces or psychological approach and a genuine sociological approach continued to the end of his career. For all his awareness of the causal role of values, or culture or history, and for all his emphasis on behavioristic explanation, Thomas could not extricate himself from the major presupposition of American liberalism—that individuals, whether understood according to natural law or to psychology, are autonomous agents who impart their characteristics to society. It was this presupposition that prompted Thomas to frame the data of sociology in terms of the relation between the individual and society, thereby defining the individual not as a problem to be explained but as a "given" or datum of social science. It was an orientation that for all its emphasis on culture is best described as pluralistic naturalistic positivism.

SUBSTANTIVE WORK

Aside from maintaining a measure of expository uniformity, there is little reason for devoting a separate section to Thomas's substantive work. Most of Thomas's creative energies were absorbed with methodology, and his important and influential work in this field comprises his major substantive contribution to sociology. Thomas exhibited great interest in substantive questions, but curiously his work after the *Polish Peasant* contains few concrete assertions or conclusions about the nature of society or its substructures and processes. In part, this reflected his healthy reluctance to engage in verbal or a priori investigations of social phenomena. However, the same empiricism turned him away from his earlier interest in substantive questions and made him devote more and more time to methodology. His substantive interests became limited in scope, and largely devoted to studies involving deviant behavior; Thomas, however, nowhere brought these studies together as part of a general theory of social disorganization. A brief comparison of his major substantive work, the *Polish Peasant,* with his later work bears out my contention that in substantive theory as well as in methodology, Thomas more and more abandoned formal systematic analysis for a shapeless, ad hoc empiricism, adopting, in effect, the "planless empiricism" that he had castigated in the Methodological Note.

The Sociocultural Universe of the Polish Peasant

My analysis of the *Polish Peasant* will be brief for a number of reasons. For one thing, there is considerable doubt about how much of the substantive work in this book is Thomas's and how much is Znaniecki's. Secondly, while the *Polish Peasant* is a classic attempt to derive sociological concepts from empirical materials (materials of a special sort, it will be remembered), and a first-rate, pioneering example of sociocultural analysis in American sociology, the work contains little that is new when compared with earlier work in pluralistic positivism. As an institutional analysis, it avoids psychological or rigidly naturalistic evolutionary explanations and deserves its reputation as a landmark in sociological theory. However, since the approach is familiar, I shall note only features that are new or of special interest.

The primary goal of the work is to provide a monographic study of Polish society through a focus on its peasantry. To this end, it examines the primary-group organization and the processes of social change, disorganization, and reconstruction in Polish peasant society. Attention is also given to the Polish-American community and finally to the processes of demoralization that community suffered at the hands of the alien structure of industrial America. Throughout, there is a running contrast between a primary-group society and a rational or individualistic society, together with the related ideas of social disorganization and social reconstruction. In keeping with his main objective, which was to provide an empirical study of an "actual civilized society" as a step toward future generalizations about human behavior, Thomas focused primarily on the concrete structure of Polish peasant society and gave little attention to the problem of developing higher level abstractions about social-system types that apprehend a variety of empirical types. The work makes no attempt to search the literature of sociology for relevant conceptual developments. If Thomas had been more familiar with this type of approach, he might have been prompted to search for the universals in his data. And it might have prevented him from putting forth the standard liberal interpretation of social development, the identification of the goal of history with individualism, voluntarism, and differentiated private and public groups, and might also have prevented him from assuming that there are intrinsic processes in the impersonal economic society that insure social harmony and rational cooperation.[14] While Thomas was acutely aware of the conflict between "individual efficiency" and a "stable social organization," and while he recognized that the bulk of modern populations are not functioning at peak efficiency (an awareness characteristic of the late-liberal mentality), he continued to assume

---

[14] The general acceptance of liberal society is implicit in the far-ranging social analysis and commentary to be found in the *Polish Peasant*, vol. 2, pt. 4, Introduction; also see chap. 5, "Cooperative Institutions," in pt. 2, sec. 2 in this connection.

that spontaneous tendencies in the individual, supplemented by the social processes of "conventionalization" and "sublimation," [15] would effectively coordinate the diversity and conflict of modern society. Thomas even implied that if the individual were given some training and some opportunity, society need not fear the full expression of individualism.

The problem of social instability is a deep and pervasive theme in the literature of sociology. Like many of the theorists before him, Thomas recognized the threat to social unity posed by the values of individualism and rationality. For the most part, however, Thomas did not derive the concept of social disorganization from an analysis of modern society, nor did he ever apply it to modern society. For him, the values of individualism and rationality were problems only for the primary-group society. Like Durkheim, Thomas was convinced that the problems of modern society were transitional, and that they would be corrected as the values of society developed more fully.

Despite the ideological nature of the *Polish Peasant*, there is no denying that it is a valuable and unique monograph about a social system different enough from the main line of Western development to contain enormous interest for sociologists, especially those interested in comparative social analysis. In addition, it has several features that deserve special mention. The sections on the peasant family and marriage are the finest analysis of a particular type of family system in the literature I have canvassed. The section on economic life is also one of the finest analyses of its kind, both for its technical knowledge and for the skill with which it shows how economic behavior is embedded, often in a subordinate fashion, in other institutions in the undifferentiated Primary or Communal society and how the emergence of a distinct economic mentality shatters this unity. It is unfortunate that Thomas failed to follow through and see that in the society of individualism and rationality, social relations become embedded in economic relations, often to their detriment.

Thomas's Later Work: The Focus on Social Problems

After the *Polish Peasant*, Thomas came to view social phenomena less in terms of the structure, dynamics, and problems of sociocultural universes,

---

[15] To conventionalize attitudes is to delimit their application to appropriate circumstances, thus permitting a wide range of diverse and contradictory attitudes to exist side by side in harmony. The same term, it will be remembered, was used by Sumner in *Folkways* to identify the same social process. The principle of sublimation insures that base attitudes will be rendered either harmless or socially useful by directing them to situations endowed with elements of social sacredness.

and more in terms of limited and precisely definable problems. In his next work, he explored processes at work in the Americanization of the immigrant.[16] While his analysis is a useful account of the cultural differences among America's various immigrant groups, its primary purpose was not to elicit new knowledge, but to improve the process of assimilation through the spread of old knowledge.

Thomas's next work, *The Unadjusted Girl*,[17] is a study of the sources and types of female sexual deviation, especially prostitution. The general method and ideas are familiar: the four wishes, human documents, and the definition of the situation through the interplay of attitude and value are all employed within a framework of social change. By this time, Thomas's earlier interest in social change—or, as he called it, social "becoming," the combination of stability and change—had itself changed. His interest in the laws of change at the social-system level had been transformed into an interest in studying and ameliorating the consequences of change within the emerging, ripening society of individualism. Actually, this book is another example of the ad hoc, qualitative, almost journalistic approach that characterized all of Thomas's works except the *Polish Peasant*.

In all his later writings, with the exception of his last work, *Primitive Behavior*, Thomas devoted himself to the same substantive theme, social problems. Even his last book, which was devoted to understanding the variety of ways in which human beings define situations, grew out of Thomas's belief that social problems result from false or outmoded definitions of the situation. Whether Thomas focused on immigration, prostitution, delinquency and crime, emotional disturbance, unrealized capacity, the individual's wishes, the creative unconscious,[18] or the decline of primary

[16] Robert E. Park and Herbert A. Miller, *Old World Traits Transplanted* (New York: Harper, 1921). Though Thomas's name does not appear on the title page, it is now generally accepted that he wrote most of the book, something quite apparent from its style, methods, concepts, and even illustrations.

[17] Boston: Little, Brown, 1924; available as a Harper paperback.

[18] Though Thomas was highly critical of Freud and his followers, his work was nevertheless influenced by some aspects of Freudian psychology. For example, one can interpret the four wishes and the process of sublimation in this sense. For an extended attempt to extract useful sociological insights from the psychoanalytic tradition, see Thomas's article "The Configurations of Personality" in C. M. Child et al., *The Unconscious: A Symposium* (New York: Alfred A. Knopf, 1927), chap. 6, where he posited the existence of an "unconscious" force or "creative imagination" and called for research to determine its relation to social and historical contexts. It should be noted that Thomas's earlier book, *Sex and Society* (Chicago: University of Chicago Press, 1907) was merely an attempt to show that sexual differences have important social consequences. Thus, while it reflected the general interest in human passions that is such a marked feature of post-Renaissance and especially post-Enlightenment intellectual life, it bears little relation to Freudianism.

norms and the rise of new values as the cause of the above problems, his main organizing idea was always the definition of the situation. It is regrettable that he made no attempt to write a general treatise on social disorganization or to catalog systematically the variety of personal and social maladjustments in an industrial social system. Instead, he assumed throughout his work that since the underlying process of social change is fundamentally sound, the sociologist's chief function is to obtain knowledge for purposes of reform so that the process of change can be speeded over its troublesome transitional stage. All this is to say, of course, that Thomas belongs to the later phase of liberalism during which sociology ceased being the critical, revolutionary instrument of the middle class and assumed as its chief practical and ideological function the defense and stabilization of capitalism.

The Social-Action Orientation

Despite its shortcomings, Thomas's work contains important suggestions about the proper focus of sociological analysis, suggestions that were given extended elaboration by his successors in American sociology. His earlier definition of sociology in the *Polish Peasant* as the study of "rules" and his emphasis on the individual as an actor oriented toward "values" bespoke not only an awareness of the importance of cultural prescriptions or norms in producing and maintaining social order, but an awareness of the essentially moral nature of human behavior. For Thomas, human behavior emerged from the decisions that the voluntary subject makes among alternative courses of meaningful action. This orientation made Thomas, along with Cooley, one of the earliest figures in the American *social-action* orientation, the broad school of thought that has come to dominate American sociology.

In his later work, probably due to his familiarity with Cooley's thought, Thomas also became somewhat aware of the importance of interaction and the need to think of the interplay of egos as part of the subject matter of sociology. In his later career, Thomas came to think of the situational environment as partly institutional (mores, values, norms) and partly interactional (social relationships). These were fleeting insights, but they prepared the way for the large-scale attempt in American sociology to focus on sociocultural structures as distinct from psychology and to define sociology as the study of interaction and value complexes. Thus, the major figures who rose to prominence during the 1920s and 1930s in American sociology, for example Florian Znaniecki, Robert M. MacIver, Pitirim Sorokin, Howard Becker, and Talcott Parsons, all shared the social-action orientation in varying degrees. These figures consciously sought to build a sociocultural positivism as an alternative to naturalistic positivism, or, in Thomas's words, they rejected behaviorism for a behavioristic approach.

CONCLUSION

Thomas as an Ahistorical Pragmatist

In analyzing the emergence of pluralistic positivism at the end of the nine-teenth century, I pointed to the fundamental unity between its European and American expressions: the common acceptance of the need to subord-inate theory to fact, the view of human reason as a research instrumentality rather than as a substance, and the definition of the subject matter of soci-ology as moral rather than natural. Thomas's thought emerged within the American version of pluralistic positivism, the pragmatic tradition. Like the pragmatists, he reduced reason to method and found the existence and validity of phenomena in activities and consequences. His contribution to empirical social science was a healthy corrective to the monistic methodology and substantive theory of his predecessors in American sociology. The enormous influence of his brand of empiricism, however, did not rest on this ground alone. Of equal importance was the sociocultural flavor he imparted to social-science analysis, insisting that the realm of values (mores, norms, institutions) and their internalization by human actors constitute legitimate and important focuses of sociological attention. In this sense, he continued and elaborated Sumner's sociology, both by advocating a radical empiricism and by seeing the importance of mores or cultural norms and values as a subject matter for sociology. In asserting the importance of norms, values, and human subjectivity, Thomas was also similar to Cooley. Thomas's work, however, exerted a wider influence than Cooley's because it contained little of Cooley's subjective methodology and avoided Cooley's easy, value-laden generalizations about human nature and social processes.

Thomas's orientation toward value analysis also enabled him to bring about a closer working liaison between cultural anthropology and sociology. Com-bined with empiricism, his cultural orientation helped to produce the be-havioristic or social psychology that has been so influential in twentieth-century social science. Finally, his characteristic American emphasis on the analysis of the relation between the individual and society meant that he did not neglect psychological aspects in his sociology. In particular, he helped to transmit the psychological work of Ivan Pavlov (1849–1936), John B. Watson (1878–1958), and Sigmund Freud (1856–1939) into sociology.

Indeed, Thomas's psychological approach was so strong that it prevented him from becoming a genuine sociocultural positivist. Although he had identified subjectivity as the factor that separates social science from natural science, and although he had qualms about using psychic mechanisms to explain behavior, Thomas always assumed that individuals are autonomous agents or actors animated by forces within themselves, and that these forces are always in tension with the cultural forces of social control. Despite the powerful forces of experience, in other words, individuals still act under their own power. Even when they make mistakes and misdefine situations, they are giving evidence of their freedom and creativity. The scientist, however, cannot only act, but think; with the growth of a sound method, the scientist will think ever more validly. With the combined efforts of the mass of individuals and the social scientist, society will eventually act rationally—that is, it will successfully and continuously adjust itself to changing conditions. Here, of course, is the pragmatic or nominalistic voluntarism so congenial to the American tradition, a perspective that in Thomas not only establishes the existence of freedom and truth but also effects a reconciliation between them.

Though Thomas abandoned the formally stated methodology and goals of nomothetic or systematic theory, he never abandoned the goal of truth in favor of a historical approach. He was historical only in the sense that he directed his attention to the facts of the tangible world. One of the most important features of pluralistic positivism is its commitment to finding a transhistorical empirical method. Thomas's work was enormously influential in directing American sociology toward an ahistorical definition of itself. The intrinsically ahistorical nature of sociology had been obscured from its beginnings by its commitment to progress and to pseudoevolutionary and evolutionary theory. As an ideological instrument, the general idea of evolution was ideally suited to the needs of liberalism—it provided a metaphysical basis by which to justify change, even revolutionary change, and at the same time it served admirably to defend the status quo, since the shortcomings of liberal society could be attributed to a cosmic process lying outside human control. Evolutionary theory had its limitations, however, for it could also be used against liberalism—as it was by Marx. Thus, once the theory of evolution had served its historic function of justifying the emergence and consolidation of capitalism, it was either subtly transformed or abandoned. Thomas was one of the first in American sociology to abandon it as a substantive principle, rejecting in the *Polish Peasant* the commitment to evolution that he had expressed in one of his earliest books, *Source Book for Social Origins.*[19]

Thomas's work represents the emancipation from conscious evolutionary theory by American sociology that was also seen in the thought of the Continental pluralistic positivists. Thomas also made an abortive effort in the *Polish Peasant* to turn social change into an intellectual problem, paralleling in this respect the far more important work by Durkheim and Weber. However, Thomas could never seriously develop his early interest in social change because the main bent of his thought was directed toward finding the universal laws of social phenomena. For him, the goal of social science

[19] Chicago: University of Chicago Press, 1909.

was the derivation of general laws from the multiplicity of data, the acquisition of nomothetic knowledge as opposed to the idiographic knowledge supplied by history. In this respect, Thomas's thought bears a fundamental kinship with the ahistorical definition of sociology found in the later Durkheim and in Pareto and Simmel. However, unlike the Continental pluralistic positivists, Thomas, like American sociology in general, never had to worry about the intrinsic stability of the society in which he lived, something that makes his ideological commitment to liberalism at one and the same time clearer and more deceptive.

Thomas and Liberal Ideology

The relationship between Thomas's sociological theory and the sociophilosophical structure of liberalism is not difficult to establish. His assumption that the individual is a basic entity or datum of social science and that one must explore the relation of this individual to other individuals is fundamental to liberal philosophy and social organization. The existence and potency of the individual human organism are not self-evident matters, however; indeed, one of the basic tasks of scientific analysis is to explain the nature of individualism, not to take it for granted by assuming that it represents the natural, bedrock structure of the original nature of human beings.

In a way, Thomas did try to explain the individual. Like many others in the post-Enlightenment world, he defined the individual not as a spiritual or mental but as a biopsychic substance. As the dominant orientation in sociology, especially in the Anglo-American countries, this view not only individualized human nature, but defined it as spontaneous and creative, well suited to the needs of an expanding industrial system. With this view of human nature, it is no longer necessary to know what the mental substance reason is; rather, it is important to know how psychic forces work in and through the medium of experience. If one can establish definite laws of learning and activity, one has then acquired not only an epistemology but an entire concept of human and social nature. The liberal concern with explaining the individual, however, goes only so far, for it rarely raises the question of whether or not the individual is a scientific category, that is, a causal agent—it is simply assumed that the answer to this question is yes. This assumption is endemic to the whole range of liberalism and particularly pervasive in the United States.

The deeply instrumental cast that Thomas gave to reason, knowledge, and values also bears a fundamental kinship to the this-worldly orientation and optimism of American pragmatism, the purest version of late-liberal philosophy. The practical bent in Thomas's thought was similar to liberal philosophy in another respect—it was combined with a metaphysical urge to uncover the invariable structure of phenomena. This is true of Thomas's early interest in nomothetic sociology and true of his later work in which he settled for "probability-inferences." It is not surprising, therefore, that Thomas was involved in the liberal dilemma. The problem of trying to relate and identify theory with fact caused Thomas uneasiness throughout his career, though, of course, he never stated the problem in formal philosophical terms. In the end, he sought escape by developing a radical empiricism, but he succeeded only in deconceptualizing sociology and directing it in ways fatal to science. Underlying his emphasis on intensive, limited studies is the assumption, nourished by an unwarranted faith in the power of the hidden logic of serendipity, that the sheer accumulation of data will somehow cohere into ever-larger patterns and will ultimately reveal the full structure of social reality. Such an approach, however, is the enemy of abstraction and historical awareness.

This criticism of Thomas's work is not directed at empiricism in general, but at ad hoc empiricism, at the research orientation that unwittingly smuggles assumptions into science to turn it into a disguised a priorism. Such a view feels that the total structural framework within which research is taking place need not be spelled out. It ignores the chief problem of empiricism in social science, the fact that there may exist not a unitary structure of social phenomena, but an irreducible diversity of empirical structures, or, in Weberian terms, a diversity of moral possibilities.

In turning his attention from the full range of social and historical phenomena, therefore, Thomas's ad hoc empiricism did more than make his science flat-footed; it turned it into ideology, into a defense of a particular social system. His absorption with immediately given social phenomena and his preference for "actual" civilized societies made it appear, of course, that the facts of the present are somehow more important, natural, and strategic than the facts of the past. Even his interest in the diversity produced by social change was never a genuine interest in social-system change but always a teleological view that accepted liberal society as the terminal stage of social history. By losing interest in social-system contrast and contact, Thomas also lent support to the idea that liberal society was a self-sufficient substantive entity containing its own explanation.

Perhaps the most revealing way in which Thomas's thought is ideological is his radical subordination of theory to practice. Thomas's almost exclusive concern with social problems after the *Polish Peasant* rested on the assumption that knowledge about problems could be obtained by viewing each problem in terms of its immediate variables. This assumed that there was an underlying objective structure of social and psychic phenomena and that knowledge about segments of it would eventually connect with knowledge about other segments to reveal the entire structure. Thus Thomas (forgetting his own warning against this practice in the Methodological Note) not only rejected the need for a formally stated methodology but conducted his research as if social problems were understandable apart from the social system from which they emerged.

What Thomas did, in effect, was to take for granted the legitimacy of the historical power structure of the United States and to locate the cause of social problems either in the individual or in the inadequacy of socialization. It was his individual-versus-society or subjective-versus-objective formulation that prevented him from seeing that the major cause of problems (as well as of behavior in general) lies within the complex value-norm and institutional structure of liberal society. Though his empirical investigations made him aware that many seemingly normal groups of individuals from good backgrounds exhibit deviant behavior, it did not alert him to the vast sociological insight contained in such data: perhaps it was the very absorption of American values that caused trouble; perhaps the ultimate cause of social problems lay in the incongruity of America's institutional and value system; perhaps, therefore, one should investigate the way in which various value combinations impinged upon and affected the behavior of differently located individuals or groups within a given social structure.

Like most of twentieth-century American social science, Thomas was a late liberal. He was aware that in large part the free and responsible individual had to be created through institutional management. Of course, this approach is deeply conservative since it accepts the basic institutional structure of liberalism, demanding not structural reform but only an improvement of existing institutions—most characteristically, a call for a more even distribution of opportunities. In its more extreme form, the narrow and unimaginative ad hoc empiricism of much of American social science, even when it exhibits a sophisticated awareness of the role of experience in controlling behavior, is, in reality, a disguised a priorism in which the historically produced values and experiences of American society become intrinsic to human nature and society.

One can think of the redefinition of reason in the United States at the turn of the century in terms of the changing needs of American society. With the onset of rapid industralization, Americans found reason increasingly less relevant, and there emerged a broad demand in field after field for a more empirically based mode of thought. By reducing reason to practical reason, that is, by defining reason as a method for solving problems, human rationality was harnessed to social reform. However, the ideological nature of pragmatic social thought, whether inside or outside sociology, is still apparent; for in solving problems and criticizing concrete inadequacies, the basic structural features of American institutions were not changed, but in fact acquired added sanctity because of their supposed flexibility and vitality.

Thomas's interest in values and his insistence that social science deal with the actor contains another ideological aspect. After Vico and Montesquieu, the pluralistic positivists were the first to give prime recognition to the role of values in producing social integration and stability; however, the social role of values and norms plays an important part in all sociology. While the early tradition in sociology was certain that science could establish socially needed values, it did not wait for society to accomplish this task. Condorcet, for example, accepted the tradition of natural rights, and Saint-Simon and Comte felt obliged to tack onto their theory a morality derived from a manufactured religion. Most theorists, however, in gaining insight into the role of values in establishing social cohesion, invariably saw the social advantage of *existing* values no matter how erroneous or evil. Again and again, in Vico, Montesquieu, Spencer, Sumner, Ward, Pareto, and less so in Durkheim, Simmel, Weber, and Cooley, sociology found utility in almost every practice, value, or belief. Most guilty of this, of course, were the monistic evolutionary theorists, although the pluralistic positivists came to the same insight via other paths. Only Durkheim and Weber, like Montesquieu before them, were able to raise the insight into the seemingly endless utility of error and evil into an intellectual problem and avoid seeing the history of error and evil as a teleological pattern that had its terminal in liberal society. Though they too succumbed to liberal ideology in the end, at least they saw the difficulty of producing a general theory of society in the face of the functional success of diverse patterns of behavior.

In Thomas's case, we have yet another variation of the ideological use of nonrational factors. Thomas accepted and legitimated error and evil in two ways. First, he focused on subjective factors, which, however false or biased, have real consequences. Since science deals with consequences and cannot pass on values, the social scientist must take subjectivity as a basic datum. Second, Thomas had a strong tendency to interpret deviant subjectivity in terms of an irrepressible original human nature. This was especially true of his attempt to introduce the rudiments of Freudian psychology into sociology, the ideological upshot of which was to distract attention from liberal institutions as the source of error and evil and to focus it on the individual—in effect refurbishing the Protestant-bourgeois ethic with Freudian psychology.

Thomas's empiricism, therefore, whether it focused on methodology or on subject matter, was substantialist. Even when he emphasized, as he did in the Methodological Note and elsewhere, that the scientist must focus on action (or activities or relations) and even when he warned against looking for essences or mechanisms, he never fully grasped the import of his own injunction. Doing so could have led him to a form of scientific empiricism that seeks knowledge strictly in terms of social relationships, the content of which comes not from the set structure of human nature but from the functional needs and requirements of human coexistence. It could also have led him to a historical perspective that recognizes neither universal essences nor universal relational structures. However, Thomas was too much of an American to adopt either an up-to-date empiricism or a radical historical position. As an American, he enjoyed an intellectual climate highly conducive to empirical science. The dynamics of a frontier society had transformed the liberal urge for world mastery from its rationalistic orientation into pragmatism. In this development the empirical philosophy of American liberalism derived a large measure of support from the antirational particularism and religious historicism of Protestantism. However, these empirical currents were based on a belief in an ultimate reality, the existence of which was never questioned. It was the substantialism inherent in this intellectual atmosphere, especially its belief in the reality of the individual, that made it difficult for Americans, Thomas included, to adopt either a strictly sociocultural or a strictly historical perspective.

Therefore, when Thomas claimed that science must content itself with "limited laws," what he really meant was that the way to general or systematic theory was through the accumulation of results from small-scale empirical research. Thomas's ahistorical empiricism had a corollary that is characteristic of much of contemporary sociology. His bias against history as a method and as subject matter was matched by an indifference to the history of social science. Whereas many of the early sociologists had sought to find their scientific bearings by studying and criticizing the work of their predecessors, Thomas simply dismissed the intellectual past except for a few casual references to Cooley, Sumner, and Durkheim.

In the final analysis, Thomas's work amounted to an identification of social reality with the structure of liberal society. In adopting the actor-situation scheme as his key idea, he not only kept intact the individualism of liberal society, but he invariably assumed that the structure of situations, either as norms or as modes of interaction, was valid and that what was needed for social stability and vitality was to remove situational vestiges of a previous era and to help the individual correctly apprehend and adjust to the true structure of society. As such, Thomas's thought was perfectly suited to helping liberalism move from one settled scheme of things to another without jeopardizing or even examining its basic institutions.

Chapter 21
Pitirim Sorokin (1889–1968)

Pitirim Sorokin was born in Russia of a peasant mother and artisan father. His life was an incredible series of personal hardships, including imprisonment by both czarist and Communist governments. In 1923 he emigrated to the United States and had a considerable impact on the development of American sociology. After six unusually creative years at the University of Minnesota, he was offered Harvard University's first chair in sociology and administered its new department of sociology between 1931 and 1942. Harvard's quick rise to prominence in sociology was due in no small measure to this remarkable scholar.

Sorokin's work demonstrates very clearly the diversity of thought known as pluralistic sociocultural positivism. Like his predecessors and many of his contemporaries in sociocultural positivism, Sorokin viewed culture and interaction as the subject matter of social science and claimed an empirical validity for his theory of human behavior. However, Sorokin's spirited critique of radical empiricism and his equally spirited assertion of the role of theory in methodology and of the moral nature of social phenomena eventually took him beyond the boundaries of science. In the end, his theory of society reverted to teleological rationalism, and for all his insistence on human uniqueness, he became, ironically enough, thoroughly naturalistic.

PHILOSOPHY AND METHOD

Sorokin's philosophical orientation is his integral theory of truth and reality.[1] According to Sorokin, there are three systems of truth, the truths of faith, of reason, and of the senses. A true philosophical position must accept the validity of all three.

---

[1] Despite Sorokin's far-flung writings and varied contributions to sociology, I shall refer chiefly to his magnum opus, *Social and Cultural Dynamics,* 4 vols. (New York: American Book Co., 1937–1941); rev. and abridged, 1 vol. (Boston: Porter

449

Pitirim Sorokin (1889–1968)

Causal and Logico-Meaningful Methods

Order can be brought into the conglomeration of cultural events, objects, and values, claimed Sorokin, by discerning within them two different kinds of unity. The first is the causal or functional unity which is obtained by establishing the existence of

---

Sargent, 1957). The abridged edition has two advantages: it is more easily available and, since it was prepared by Sorokin, represents his thought twenty years after the original publication date; henceforth cited as *Dynamics*.

No critical evaluation of Sorokin's work exists. Analysis of various aspects of his thought are contained in Philip J. Allen, ed., *Pitirim A. Sorokin in Review* (Durham, N.C.: Duke University Press, 1963). A clear but uncritical description of his work is F. R. Cowell's *Values in Human Society: The Contributions of Pitirim A. Sorokin to Sociology* (Boston: Porter Sargent, 1970).

> . . . *tangible, noticeable, testifiable, direct interdependence (mutual or one-sided) of the variables or parts upon one another and upon the whole system.* If variation A is always followed by B (under the same conditions and in a large enough number of cases so that mere chance is eliminated), we say that they are functionally related. *This means that any cultural synthesis is to be regarded as functional, when on the one hand, the elimination of one of its important elements perceptibly influences the rest of the synthesis in its functions (and usually in its structure); and when, on the other hand, the separate element, being transposed to a quite different combination, either cannot exist in it or has to undergo a profound modification to become a part of it.*[2]

The second level of cultural integration is the logico-meaningful. To obtain this unity, one must use

> . . . the logical laws of identity, contradiction, consistency: and it is these laws of logic which must be employed to discover whether any synthesis is or is not *logico-meaningful.* Side by side with such logical laws in the narrow sense, the broader principles of "keeping," of internal consistency, must also be used to determine the existence of this higher unity, or the lack of it. These are the principles expressed in the terms "consistent style," "consistent and harmonious whole," in contradistinction to "inconsistent mingling of styles," "hodgepodge," "clashing" patterns of forms, and they apply especially to the examination of artistic creation. Many such superlative unities cannot be described in analytical verbal terms; they are just felt as such, but this in no way makes their unity questionable.[3]

The crucial variable in the logico-meaningful method is the system of truth on which a culture is based. Cultures exhibit two basic attitudes about the nature of reality. At one pole is the view that the ultimate reality is supersenate, and at the other, that it is sensory. Once a culture becomes relatively integrated, all its parts will reflect its fundamental attitude toward reality.

Types of Culture Mentality

According to Sorokin, there are two integrated pure types of culture:

> We can begin by distinguishing two profoundly different types of the integrated culture. Each has its own mentality; its own system of truth and knowledge; its own philosophy and *Weltanschauung*; its own type of religion and standards of "holiness";

[2] *Dynamics,* p. 5f. (All emphases in this and subsequent quotations are Sorokin's.)
[3] *Ibid.,* p. 8.

452 PLURALISTIC POSITIVISM IN THE UNITED STATES

its own system of right and wrong; its own forms of art and literature; its own mores, laws, code of conduct; its own predominant forms of social relationships; its own economic and political organization; and finally, its own type of *human personality*, with a peculiar mentality and conduct. The values which correspond to one another throughout these cultures are irreconcilably at variance in their nature; but within each culture all the values fit closely together, belong to one another logically, often functionally.

Of these two systems one may be termed *Ideational* culture, the other *Sensate*. And as these names characterize the cultures as a whole, so do they indicate the nature of each of the component parts.

Ideational culture can be characterized under four headings:

(1) Reality is perceived as nonsensate and nonmaterial, everlasting Being (*Sein*); (2) the needs and ends are mainly spiritual; (3) the extent of their satisfaction is the largest, and the level, highest; (4) the method of their fulfillment or realization is self-imposed minimization or elimination of most of the physical needs, and to the greatest possible extent.

Within Ideational culture there are two subclasses, the *ascetic ideational*, in which there is a radical rejection of the sensate world, and the *active ideational*, in which an attempt is made to transform the sensate world in the light of spiritual values.

As opposed to the Ideational,

. . . the Sensate mentality views reality as only that which is presented to the sense organs. It does not seek or believe in any supersensory reality; at the most, in its diluted form, it assumes an agnostic attitude toward the entire world beyond the senses. The Sensate reality is thought of as a Becoming, Process, Change, Flux, Evolution, Progress, Transformation. Its needs and aims are mainly physical, and maximum satisfaction is sought of these needs. The method of realizing them is not that of a modification within the human individuals composing the culture, but a modification or exploitation of the external world. In brief, the Sensate culture is the opposite of the Ideational in its major premises.

Within the Sensate culture there are three subclasses, the *active*, the *passive*, and the *cynical sensate* culture mentalities. The active sensate mentality seeks to modify the external world, the passive is parasitic toward the external world, and the cynical seeks to gratify its physical needs and pleasures through a hypocritical use of ideational attitudes.

All cultures are mixtures of the Ideational and the Sensate. There is only one integrated mixed type, the Idealistic culture mentality.

> Quantitatively it represents a more or less balanced unification of Ideational and Sensate, with, however, a predominance of the Ideational elements. Qualitatively it synthesizes the premises of both types into one inwardly consistent and harmonious unity. For it reality is many-sided, with the aspects of everlasting Being and ever-changing Becoming of the spiritual and the material. Its needs and ends are both spiritual and material, with the material, however, subordinated to the spiritual. The methods for their realization involve both the modification of the self and the transformation of the external sensate world: in other words, it gives *sum cuique* to the Ideational and the Sensate.[4]

The Concept of Creative Recurrence

Sociocultural phenomena, Sorokin observed, can be classified as either unique or recurring. The unique or unicist view of cultural and social phenomena claims that history is never repeated and that no two cultural objects or values are ever the same. This is false, said Sorokin, because

> the great symphony of social life is "scored" for a countless number of separate processes, each proceeding in a wavelike manner and recurring in space, in time, in both space and time, periodically or nonperiodically, after long or short intervals. Briefly, or for an extensive time, in the same or in several social systems, a process moves in a certain quantitative or qualitative or spatial direction, or in all these directions, reaches its "point of saturation," and then often reverses its movements. Economic processes fluctuate endlessly between prosperity and depression, enrichment and poverty; vital processes between births, deaths, marriages, divorces; all undergo their "ups and downs," which sometimes become monotonously uniform. Crime and licentiousness, religion and irreligion, social stability and revolt, recur endlessly. Social systems—associations, organizations, institutions—forever repeat the processes of recruiting, change, dismissal of their members, orig-

---

[4] The preceding quotations appear in *Dynamics,* pp. 24–28f.

inate, grow, and dissolve. And so it goes with almost all social phenomena and process.[5]

Sorokin argued that sociocultural phenomena, which are always recurrent, may be linear in some of their aspects and for a time, but never unilinear. The most adequate depiction of the process inherent in sociocultural phenomena lies within one type of recurrent process, the cyclical. Rejecting both completely and relatively cyclical processes, Sorokin identified a valid third type, the variably or creatively recurrent pattern of cyclical process.

Sorokin stressed three corollaries that flow from his concept of *creative recurrence*. First, one can satisfy both the unicist and the cyclical points of view by seeing social processes as "ever new variations of old themes." Second, there is at work within social processes the principle of limits: "Processes go on for some time without any appreciable change in their direction, but sooner or later the trend reaches its limit, and then the process turns aside into a new path." Third, there is the ". . . principle of immanent causation or the self-regulation of sociocultural processes. According to this principle, when the unit is integrated the change in the direction of the process is caused not only and not so much by the interference of external forces but by the inner forces of the process itself and by the nature of its unit." [6]

The Concept of Immanent Causation

The major rival of Sorokin's theory of immanent causation is the "externalistic theory of change," or "environmentalism," in which the causal-functional method is applied not to the problem of unity, but to the problem of explaining change. The main assumption of this theory is that something is to be explained in terms of something else. The reason for a change in a family system, for example, is to be found in some factor or cause external to the family. However, said Sorokin, such an approach is useless because it leads to an infinite regression, to a metaphysical solution in a prime mover, to a belief in the immanent vitality of one of the factors, or to the intellectual trick of trying to produce something out of nothing. The only theory that satisfactorily explains change in a culture and its subsystems is that ". . . *it and its subsystems—be they painting, sculpture, architecture, music, science, philosophy, law, religion, mores, forms of social, political, and economic organizations*—change because each of these is a going concern, and bears in itself the reason of its change." [7]

The main fallacy in the externalistic or causal-functional explanation of change is that it lacks the principle of limit. It is utterly fallacious to assume

[5] *Ibid.*, p. 57.
[6] The three corollaries are described in *Dynamics*, pp. 63–64.
[7] *Ibid.*, p. 638f.

an unlimited validity to the causal relationships discerned among social variables. The same applies to sociocultural change; there are definite limits to the possible forms that organic, inorganic, and superorganic systems can assume. Even in the more variable superorganic realm, there are a set number of types of economic organization, family and marriage forms, political organizations, religious and artistic forms, philosophical systems, and theories and codes of ethics and law. Similarly, there are only a few main types of society and of sociocultural systems and processes.

The principle of immanent causation and the principle of limits explain the existence and behavior of the three main types of integrated sociocultural supersystems, the Ideational, Idealistic, and Sensate. The limited possibilities inherent in the superorganic realm can be reduced to these three supersystems. However, because the immanent theory of causation decrees that life is a "relentless becoming," all three must undergo change—rising, growing, ripening, and then declining. Further, because of the principle of limits, the superrhythm that these cultural systems exhibit has the sequence Sensate-Ideational-Idealistic. That is—and coming full circle to Sorokin's original proposition—the ultimate unification and understanding of all sociocultural phenomena lies in the fact that no system ever embodies the integral theory of truth, which is a combination of the truth of faith, reason, and senses. Rather, each develops as a one-sided version of truth and therefore succumbs to its own ideological inadequacy. For this reason sociocultural phenomena "trendlessly fluctuate," exhibiting both a restless creativity and an "eternal return."

The Modalities of Interaction

Since sociocultural phenomena can also be studied as social relationships, it is necessary to classify the various types of social interaction. Social relations can be thought of as factual behavior and as evaluative behavior. The mentality (or "color" or "qualification") that an actor or observer attaches to a relationship must be included, for otherwise the interaction has no meaning.

In any social group, as distinct from a conglomerate of individuals, there is a network of recurrent interactions that produces an interdependence between the behavior and the psychology of its members. The nature of any existing modality of interaction can be analyzed according to six criteria. These criteria are concerned with whether or not a given form of interaction

1. is one-sided or two-sided;

2. has limited or universal extensity;

3. has high or low intensity;

4. is durable and continuous;

5. is directed towards solidarity, antagonism or a mixture of these two;

6. is organized or unorganized.

By combining the above types, a further unification of social relationships can be made. Three basic types, the *familistic,* the *contractual,* and the *compulsory,* can be found in every "human universe." On the basis of all these classifications, one can analyze any sociocultural configuration in terms of the "proportion and quality" of each of these relationships.

SUBSTANTIVE WORK

Sorokin's substantive work is largely contained in his philosophy and method. Indeed, so carefully has he outlined the principles that will guide his research that his conclusions about the nature of social phenomena are almost explicitly set forth in his methodology. Despite his elaborate philosophical approach to human behavior, however, Sorokin explicitly claimed that his theory is scientific. His principles are to be judged by how well they bring order out of chaos and by how well they fit and represent the broadest and most significant range of facts. For expository purposes I shall divide his substantive findings into two parts, his analysis of cultural and social universes, and his attempt to achieve a cognitive unification of all sociocultural phenomena.

Sociocultural Universes

Sorokin, with the aid of a research team, amassed an enormous amount of data in an effort to establish the indisputable existence of universes in the superorganic realm. I shall make no attempt to present or to analyze his findings in detail; the material is best savored in the original. According to Sorokin, the empirical record reveals three cultural and social structures. In Greece, from approximately the twelfth to the fifth century B.C., an Ideational culture held sway; from the fifth through the fourth century B.C., an Idealistic culture was in the ascendency; and from the third century B.C. to approximately the third century A.D., a Sensate culture established its supremacy. Then the sequence repeated itself: from the end of the Greco-Roman Sensate era until the tenth century A.D., another Ideational culture emerges, followed by an Idealistic culture between the eleventh and fourteenth centuries, and then by a Sensate culture between the fifteenth and twentieth centuries.

These epochs do not result, argued Sorokin, from imposing abstractions on the record; they exist because abstractions have been verified by the record. Through a painstaking examination of biographies, art forms, philosophical output, and ethical and legal norms, the empirical record clearly establishes the existence of these unitary structures of culture. The vast chaos of cultural elements falls into place on both the causal-functional and logico-meaningful levels; each epoch receives its overall unity in terms of the type of truth that it has selected from the full spectrum of integral truth. In regard to social structure, there is a correlation between the system of truth and the prevailing type of interaction: in the Ideational culture, familistic relationships predominate; in the Idealistic culture, familistic relationships still prevail but there is a strong mixture of contractual and compulsory relationships; and in the Sensate culture, the prevailing structure of interaction is contractual. Finally, there is a correlation between the system of truth and the modal personality type of any given epoch.

The Unification of All Sociocultural Phenomena

Basic to Sorokin's empirical work was his attempt to derive a unified theory of sociocultural phenomena. The empirical record, he claimed, reveals not only the existence of interdependent structural unities but the validity of the integral theory of truth, the principle of immanent change, and the principle of limits as well. That is, the empirical record remains unintelligible unless ordered by the foregoing principles. Thus, no sociocultural universe is complete in itself—nor is it, in fact, a universe in any ultimate sense. Viewed from the perspective of the integral theory of truth, each epoch is parochial and becomes intelligible only in terms of the full record. The truth of the matter, in terms of both logic and the record, is that human beings and their works are best defined in terms of all three systems of culture. No one system is valid in itself, and therefore a trendless oscillation between all three superforms is intrinsic to the nature of the superorganic realm. The sequence through which Western populations have two times traveled is not necessarily the only order of succession. However, despite variations in order and in the "tempo and sharpness of the mutations from one type to another," recurrence there will be. Every cultural type is plagued by the "nemesis" of its one-sided version of truth. The more a cultural system succeeds, the more it fails, and each of its achievements merely prepares the way for the next system, and so on in endless oscillation. The uniformity of this static change from one supersystem to another can be expressed in terms of "crisis-catharsis-charisma-resurrection," a process that has begun again in the contemporary Sensate culture. At the beginning of the twentieth century, said Sorokin, the Sensate epoch entered the *cynical Sensate* phase of its existence. Values have become relative, centering themselves around the gratification of the senses, and human beings have come to see themselves as mechanical, biological, or chemical complexes. The only absolute is the *carpe diem* attitude. Cultural production has succumbed to colossalism and syncretism. The empirical record reveals that compulsory relations have increased in all Western nations and are slowly undermining contractualism. "This trend is universal in all the Western countries, no matter what concrete form it assumes in each—Communist, Fascist, Hitlerite, Labor Government, Socialist, Rooseveltian, Eisenhower's, or other." [8]

The crisis can also be seen in the increased amount of war, a phenomenon that always accompanies a transitional period. Already a strong reaction to an overripe Sensate age can be discerned in art, science, biology, psychology, the social sciences, philosophy, religion, ethics, and politics. The result, said Sorokin, is that

> ...we are seemingly between two epochs: the dying Sensate culture of our magnificent yesterday, and coming Ideational or Idealistic culture of the creative tomorrow. We are living, thinking, acting at the end of a brilliant six-hundred-year-long Sensate day. The oblique rays of the sun still illumine the glory of the passing epoch. But the light is fading, and in the deepening shadows it becomes more and more difficult to see clearly and to orient ourselves safely in the confusions of the twilight. The night of the transitory period begins to loom before us and the coming generations, perhaps with their nightmares, frightening shadows, and heartrending horrors. Beyond it, however, the dawn of a new great Ideational or Idealistic culture is probably waiting to greet the men of the future.[9]

CONCLUSION

The Retreat from Science

Sorokin's theory of society must receive credit on a number of grounds. He looked beyond the small-scale research characteristic of the sociology of his day and boldly set his sights on understanding sociocultural phenomena in the widest possible terms—as a total system displaying essential characteristics. In tackling his objective, he had no established methods to fall back on other than traditional philosophy of history models, and he developed and improvised methodological tools to suit his needs. Perhaps his strongest suit was classification, and he developed a useful repertory of analytical distinctions. In particular, his rigorous distinction between culture and society (and personality) and his classification of interaction types introduced a much-needed measure of conceptual precision into sociological theory. Throughout, he sought to support his statements empirically, especially through quantitative analysis. Using a research team he amassed

---

[8] *Ibid.*, p. 460.
[9] *Dynamics*, p. 625.

mountains of data, especially in the realms of art, intellectual life, and politics. Using experts who were checked against one another he subjected the data to what is today called *content analysis* to reveal patterns as they appear to objective observers and as they appear in the subjectivity of the actors themselves. Characteristically, he always tied his empirical-quantitative-causal approach to qualitative analysis, especially his insistence on the master concept of system and logico-meaningful integration.

As a synthesis of sociocultural phenomena, however, Sorokin's work is a contribution to sociological theory only in a negative manner—an unfortunate reminder that sociology can consort with philosophy only at its peril and that any such alliance, unless contracted on sociology's terms, can only dilute the bloodline of scientific social thought. Despite the elaborate sociological nomenclature and the enormous amounts of empirical material, Sorokin's theory of culture and social dynamics is not really sociology at all. Indeed, because of Sorokin's wide acquaintance with the tradition of sociological theory,[10] his own theory must be viewed as a repudiation of the basic presuppositions of scientific social theory.

The distinctly new intellectual perspective that sociology introduced into Western social thought was that a scientific understanding of sociocultural phenomena could be obtained only by applying to the existential world a precise set of analytical ideas free from logical or moral bias. Whatever its penchant for ideas, a sociological theory must be based on the world of facts. Sorokin's work, despite its colossal compilation of factual material, is not really animated by the empirical spirit at all; it is animated by ideas, not facts. Sorokin was not trying to reassert the role of theory in empirical investigation—something that always needs to be done. It is one thing to say that scientific fruit can be borne only from the interplay of ideas and facts, and quite another to say, as in effect Sorokin did, that only ideas produce the truth of science. In short, it is one thing to say that ideas and logic must be used to structure facts, and quite another to impose ideas and logic on facts.

Sorokin's basic approach can be criticized on another level. He not only faked the separation of logic and facts in order to give logic a greater autonomy in the formation of truth, but he also faked the separation among logic, facts, and values. His elaborate and insistent distinction between

---

[10] Sorokin wrote three major descriptive analyses of the various types of sociological theory: *Contemporary Sociological Theory* (New York: Harper & Row, 1928); *Social Philosophies in an Age of Crisis* (Boston: Beacon Press, 1950), available as a Dover paperback as *Modern Historical and Social Philosophies;* and *Sociological Theories of Today* (New York: Harper & Row, 1966).

causal-functional and externalistic analysis, on the one hand, and logico-meaningful and immanent causation, on the other, was not made to separate the operations of the mind, the heart, and the realm of facts. It was not made to indicate the need to use one approach for the study of empirical uniformities and another for the study of the world of subjectivity. The separation was for quite an opposite purpose—to assert the supremacy of logic and values over facts and to establish a connection between them that would validate the original logic and values with which the analysis was begun. It was a pseudo-*verstehen* approach designed to lend scientific plausibility to a philosophical theory of human culture. Weber, on the other hand, in constructing and using his *verstehen* approach, was careful to insist that his value-ideas were only instruments for illuminating problems and unearthing empirical uniformities, and that ideas were always separate from but dependent on facts. Weber was also careful to point out that the analysis of subjective states, however necessary to the social scientist, gave neither the method nor the results any special validity apart from its basis in fact.

Sorokin's attempt to base a blatant a priorism on an intensive examination of the empirical record, while standing partly in but mostly outside the discipline of sociology, involved him in numerous difficulties. His thought, despite its penchant for logicality, is strangely shapeless; it has a suppleness that is not subtlety and a rigidity that is not logic. It is actually a dogmatic eclecticism, in its own way an illustration of the truth of faith, in which the world blends into an all-embracing vision. Since everything is useful in establishing truth, one can use first Aristotelian logic, then Hegelian logic; first spirit, then matter; first biology, then psychology; first logic, then facts. Since no special procedure, carefully outlined and tested by results, is necessary, these approaches and arguments can be introduced wherever they are most convenient. Since nothing was alien to Sorokin's vision, he was free to criticize dogmatically all the misguided thinkers who have struggled to decide *which* structure of argument is best suited to the tasks of philosophy and social thought.

Sorokin's eclecticism has two derivative faults, a tendency toward concept-mongering and an elasticity of expression that robs words of their power to evoke concrete images. If the nature of sociology were defined as a systematic rummaging of the empirical world, Sorokin would have gloried in the complexity and contingency he unearthed. However, such challenges are neither intelligible not congenial to an a priori idealist. Instead, he made up out of whole cloth verbal clothing to cover the nakedness of all the exceptions and singularities that stubbornly pop up in the phenomena of history—thus his constant reference to subclasses, subtypes, and mixed forms. When the manufacture of concepts was not suitable, then he utilized verbal rubber bands to encompass disparate phenomena—the truth of faith, for example, includes not only faith but mysticism, intuition, divine inspiration, pure meditation, ecstasy, and trance. Similarly, he consistently referred to the phenomena of history in phrases that underscored his verbal skill rather than his sense of the illogicality, contrariness, and irony that may reside in phenomena—such phrases, for example, as "eternal return," "trendless fluctuations," "creatively recurrent," "ever-new and ever-old."

His pseudoempirical approach is also apparent in his consistent habit of slanting comparisons. Invariably the Ideational and Idealistic cultures are represented by their best values or in terms of their successes, while the Sensate is represented by its worst values or it failures. Sorokin's tendency to compare the best in one with the worst in the other, the ideal with the actual, is bound to repel even a sympathetic reader.[11]

Finally, Sorokin's theory of causation is thoroughly inadequate. The repudiation of the sociological tradition is nowhere better illustrated than in his rejection of the "externalistic" theory of causation. The scientific as opposed to the philosophic understanding of social and cultural phenomena requires that the explanation of a cultural element or social process be found in factors external to the thing itself. The focal point for causal analysis lies in relationships between variables, and not in the nature or the essence of the variables themselves. Sorokin's causal theory is similar to Pareto's in that both theorists end up by saying that things happen because they happen.[12] However, Pareto at least tried to locate the springs of action in the sentiments of individuals. Sorokin merely said that sociocultural systems change because of their inherent nature, which is no explanation at all and a flagrant repudiation of the entire tradition of social science.

Sorokin's a priorism amounted to roundabout reasoning that shortcircuited explanation and even simple description. He gave a statement of principles before his investigation and then proved the validity of the principles by canvassing the facts. Not only does theory precede fact, but there is no indication that he regarded an idea as a hypothesis to be either verified or rejected. It is apparent that an approach like Sorokin's can prove anything; his own material, for example, can easily be fitted into a liberal or a Marxian framework by altering the organizing concepts. Despite his graphs and statistics, Sorokin was really engaged in philosophical discourse, and a

---

[11] See, for example, *Dynamics,* pp. 24–39.
[12] It is interesting to note that of all the theorists Sorokin covered in his *Contemporary Sociological Theories,* he treated Pareto with the most sympathy and respect.

critique of his work in terms of empirical adequacy is almost beside the point. Nonetheless, it is important to show how deficient in empirical insight his Integralist approach is. He operated on such a high level of abstraction that he overlooked empirical structures of major importance. Whereas other sociologists have been culture-bound and parochial, he was universalistic to a fault. He roamed so high above history that he was blinded to the historical individuality of social structures.

At the heart of Sorokin's failure to see the stubborn and nagging problem posed by the uniqueness of sociocultural phenomena lies his dismissal of the unicist approach. He argued that the unicist approach is wrong, first because there are a limited number of social functions that must always be provided for, and, second, because these can be served in only a limited number of ways. It is of great empirical importance to observe, however—as Durkheim did for example—that the same social functions can be served by a great variety of cultural values and social processes. Societies can receive their unity, for example, from either homogeneous or heterogeneous interaction, just as cultural integration can come from either homogeneous or heterogeneous values.

It is surely of empirical importance to point out that nationalism is a unique occurrence; that noblesse oblige may be verbally attractive but oftentimes oppressive and degrading in fact; that contractualism may be impersonal and dehumanizing but that it also promotes liberty, equality, and justice through its very unconcern with personal categorization; that relations in familistic families may be stultifying and degrading as well as warm and uplifting; that the sensualism of the Sensate culture may find its justifying counterpart in what may be the healthiest sexual relations in history; that the vaunted innocence of the Ideational culture may contain, in fact, a great deal of sexual stupidity, crassness, hypocrisy, and mechanicalness; or that some religions are rational and some magical, and some closer to the Sensate world view than to the Ideational. It is true that in regard to this latter point Sorokin disinguished beween ascetic and active ideational types—terms whose meanings correspond exactly to Weber's distinction between exemplary and emissary types of religion—but he explored neither the qualitative nor the quantitative significance of this distinction. Nowhere is this failure better exemplified than in his declaration that self-discipline is a phenomenon identified with the Ideational culture, and license, with the Sensate.[13] Sorokin overlooked the fact that Weber used the same distinction to point up the way in which Protestantism, as an emissary type of religion, helped to provide the necessary mental and moral atmosphere for the rise of capitalism (Sensate culture), and that it did so through an unprecedented regimentation of the individual. He also overlooked Durkheim's

[13] *Dynamics*, pp. 27–28, 31, 37.

insight that the Organic social structure, with its advanced division of labor, leads to an intensive development of both intellecual skills and moral responsibilities within the individual. Finally, Sorokin overlooked Durkheim's critique of Spencer, in which he showed that contractualism does not mean the emergence of the free ego but the emergence of a new moral, political, legal, and economic framework within which the free ego is developed and kept socially responsible.

In general, Sorokin failed to see that the egoistic values of liberal society (Sensate culture) have been matched by massive controls ranging from the authority of the state to the authority of the conscience. Sorokin's inability to see the uniqueness of historical social structures is best illustrated at this level. His equation of the modern Sensate period with the Greco-Roman Sensate period (or of the medieval Idealistic period with fifth-century Athens and of the medieval Ideational period with Homeric Greece) is thoroughly misleading and blinded him to some of the essential empirical features of modern society. For example, when he said that the rise of the strong state under fascism, communism, or New Dealism is the growth of compulsory, totalitarian relations, he missed Weber's great insight that the growth of the strong state can be intrinsically related to the growth of liberty, equality, and justice. He overlooked not only the empirical differences between the liberal democracies and the totalitarian nations, but the fact that a given cultural value or social process may have different consequences and serve different functions in different sociocultural contexts.

Sorokin's charge that sexuality is an objectionable feature of the Sensate mentality is not only unsociological in its introduction of a value judgment, but it is empirically faulty. Far from being sexually incontinent, the Sensate culture has made an unprecedented attempt to inhibit the sexual and sensual gratifications of its populations in theory as well as in practice. In a two-pronged offensive, Puritanism and capitalism, each for its own reasons, have exacted a denial and deferment of sensual gratification that is unique in the annals of human culture. By centering society in the free individual, the Protestant-bourgeois ethic has tried to provide the built-in controls that make individualism functional to social existence. Even if it were possible to prove an increased incidence of sensuality during the Sensate period, this would not necessarily refute the point. A drastic control of sensuality and a drastic increase of sensuality may be logical opposites, but are empirically compatible and true if one remembers that a vast quantitative development of human potentiality has taken place during the Sensate era.

Even when passing moral judgment, Sorokin missed the meaning of modern sensuality because he was unable to see an act or value in terms of the cultural context in which it takes place. The same sensual act or value may have one meaning in the Greco-Roman Sensate period and quite another in the contemporary Sensate period. Sensuality, instead of being condemned out of hand, must be seen as intrinsically related to other values. Sorokin failed to see this because the Sensate period had but one value for him, the glorification of sensual experience. Surely, however, it would be more accurate and balanced to characterize the modern Sensate period as the first attempt to base society on a value system that emphasizes both discipline and spontaneity, authority and freedom, the public good and the private advantage. Surely the sensuality to which Sorokin objected derives from the attempt to place moral and intellectual decisions on a new basis, the conscious acceptance of the consequences of personal acts—which is the source of modern individualism with its heightened sense of personal worth. It is the attempt to make the free individual a *social* type that has required a new definition of human nature, which in addition to glorifying the senses has introduced the notion of personal responsibility. This is surely a unique achievement in both aim and fact and provides a totally new context for understanding not only sensuality but all the cultural and social elements of the modern period.

In the same way, Sorokin's classification of cultures according to their adherence to absolute or to relative values (a classification that corresponds exactly to Weber's ethic of absolute ends and ethic of responsibility) misses the point that what is logical may not be empirical. In keeping with its desire to master physical and social existence, the modern world has certainly introduced a rational and moral relativity to its political and economic activities. However, it has also introduced a stringent universalism, a substantialism, if you will, into its moral and social norms. It has destroyed the moral and social particularism of the Ideational world, which also had absolute and relative values, and has substituted a new absolutism and a new relativism. Far from introducing moral relativism, the modern world has attempted to install the moral imperatives of the Decalogue into the conscience of all individuals. Far from freeing social practice from the anchorage of truth and morality, it has made a continuous attempt to find a metaphysical base for its political and economic structures. Finally, in social thought, sociological theory has again and again sought to find the absolute law of the social universe.

Sorokin's failure to understand the nature of modern society was due to a deep-seated propensity to think of social phenomena in terms of logical either-or categories. Not only did he tend to think in terms of a limited set of integrated types of culture, but he recognized only one type of integration. For Sorokin, integration came from a partial, one-sided view of reality that leads to a homogeneous cultural and social structure. He failed to see that integration in the modern period is based on a considerable amount of pluralism, and that differences and conflict can be as much a source of unity and stability as can consensus and harmony. His failure to grasp the nature of modern society contains a touch of irony. His own theory of integral truth is itself a kind of philosophical pluralism. If he had not taken it so literally and logically, he might have seen that "truth" is an amazingly complex and probably inexhaustible mixture of uniformities, and that for the empiricist all things are possible and all things are true. He might have seen that the Sensate period is at bottom an attempt to realize the integral theory of truth. Instead of lopsidedly characterizing it as containing only the truth of the senses, he might have come to see it as a mighty attempt to mix the richest collection of values in the history of human culture. Indeed, the Sensate period has sought to promote material values for their own sake, and for the social and moral betterment of humanity as well. It has done so through the use of logic and empiricism and has sought to place material achievements in the service of a set of absolute moral values. Its material achievements have been purchased in the coin of work, honesty, good faith, and gratification postponement. Rarely has it failed to assert that its values and beliefs are anchored in the morality and rationality of the universe itself. As such, its failures stem not so much from the falseness of its values as from the extravagance of its goals, not from the parochialism of its values but from its attempt to achieve the deepest and most comprehensive set of values in human history. Its failures must be judged in these terms and not in terms of an outmoded logic or nostalgia for an outmoded and idealized past.

Sorokin as a Teleological Rationalist

Though Sorokin borrowed much from Weber, he unfortunately failed to embrace Weber's central insight that both the statics and the dynamics of cultural and social phenomena must be explained in terms of the empirical intersection of values on the individual's personality. However, to have done so would have introduced an element of historical thought into Sorokin's perspective. Ultimately his thought must be labeled as a form of substantialism, a teleological rationalism that, ironically enough, is closer to naturalistic positivism than to the ideational view he prefers and the integralist theory he professes. The basic presupposition of his approach is that human culture is to be viewed as an external spectacle of data and that the task of thought is to capture its structure. He denied the existence of the liberal dilemma in the same way Pareto did, by denying that anything new ever takes place. Like Pareto before him, he claimed that all cultures are basically nonrational since all are based on an inadequate definition of truth. However, this left no room for the explanation of the novelty represented by his own integral theory of truth. He would claim, of course, that the theory is not new, but has always existed. Certainly, however, its realization makes for a qualitative historical experience and changes the nature of anyone who accepts it. To see this, however, is to acknowledge that human nature is intimately involved in the process of history. To see it is to introduce novelty into sociocultural phenomena and to suggest that truth and values are embedded in historical experience. Whether historical experience is intelligible as a total unit, or whether it can be understood only as a series of segmental cultural structures containing no sequence of development, made no difference to Sorokin. Either viewpoint was repugnant to the presuppositions of his world view, since both are based on the assumption that the infinitude of experience is the proper locus of the sociologist's attention.

Chapter 22
Talcott Parsons (b. 1902)

The reaction against radical empiricism in Sorokin's work is also found in the work of Talcott Parsons, America's leading contemporary theorist. Sorokin and Parsons have other things in common besides a distaste for radical empiricism: both are European in education and orientation; both tend to view sociology as the analysis of social relationships and cultural products; and both are well informed on the work of their predecessors in sociology. Despite these similarities, a profound gulf separates their work, a gulf that corresponds to the difference between philosophy and science. Sorokin, in the final analysis, is a teleological rationalist. Parsons, on the other hand, however much he criticizes empiricism and upholds the role of reason in sociological theory is ultimately a hard-bitten scientist anxious to keep social science as close to natural science as possible. Sorokin's and Parsons's attitudes toward the tradition of sociology are also strikingly different. While Sorokin dismissed the general sociological tradition, approving only selected aspects of it, Parsons feels that sociology has had a cumulative and valid development, and, after achieving a major breakthrough in the later part of the nineteenth century, has had a continuous advance. Unlike Sorokin, who at bottom was opposed to science, Parsons is deeply committed to playing a role in the development of a genuine science of human behavior.

PHILOSOPHY AND METHOD

Parsons's work is best viewed as being almost entirely methodological in nature. His work falls into two parts: one, epistemology, which I shall discuss under the heading of "Philosophy and Method," and two, his general theory of society, which is among other things a codification of strategic empirical research, a design to facilitate research, and a gigantic hypothesis awaiting verification. This aspect of his work will be discussed under "Substantive Work."

Talcott Parsons (b. 1902)

Parsons's only extended discussion of the epistemological foundations of sociology is in his first major work, *The Structure of Social Action* [1], in which he developed what he called *analytical realism*. This point of view, despite changes in nomenclature (he now calls it *structural-functional*

---

[1] New York: McGraw-Hill, 1937; reprinted, New York: Free Press, 1949; available in paperback, 2 vols.—henceforth cited as *S.S.A.* Two essays, "The Present Position and Prospects of Systematic Theory in Sociology" (1945) and "The Prospects of Sociological Theory" (1950), both in *Essays in Sociological Theory*, rev. ed. (New York: Free Press, 1954, also in paperback), chaps. 11 and 17, contain shorter and less detailed versions of Parsons's epistemological thought. Parsons's only other important statement on methodology is in Talcott Parsons and Edward Shils, eds., *Toward a General Theory of Action* (Cambridge: Harvard University Press, 1951; reprinted as a Harper & Row paperback, 1962), pt. 1, chap. 1—henceforth cited at *T.G.T.A.*

analysis, or simply *functional analysis*) and despite various stages of development, has remained the same throughout his long and creative career.[2]

Theory as an Independent Methodological Variable

The key to understanding Parsons's unique contribution to sociological theory is his lifelong concern with "theory." In his difficult and influential book, *The Structure of Social Action,* Parsons asserted that the widespread achievement in social science at the end of the nineteenth century was due to a theoretical reorientation that allowed theorists not only to see new facts but to see old facts in a new way. From the theoretical creativity displayed by such thinkers as Durkheim, Pareto, Weber, and the economist Alfred Marshall, Parsons argued, there emerged a novel concept of social science, one based on the master conclusion that there is a sharp distinction between the sciences of nature and the sciences of (social) action.

Unlike the sciences of nature, said Parsons, the action sciences deal with the realm of interaction and values. The outstanding characteristic of moral and material values is scarcity; accordingly, human action is a ceaseless process of decision making about scarce values and alternate courses of conduct. The distinction between the sciences of nature and the sciences of action (almost identical to my distinction between naturalistic and sociocultural sociology) had its greatest development in Germany. However, the German variant of this distinction on the whole led to the definition of social science as a branch of philosophy; Parsons keeps social science as close to natural science as possible. Despite its distinctive subject matter, Parsons argued, social science still aims at the same type of conclusions and uses the same general method as natural science. Nevertheless, there is a distinction between the two great branches of science, a distinction blurred in the first instance, said Parsons, by the false empiricist methodology that dominated social science until the late nineteenth century.

The Rejection of Radical Empiricism

Unlike Sorokin, whose rejection of "positivism" was really a rejection of science, Parsons rejects only what he believes is a false definition of science,

---

[2] There is no easy-to-read commentary or overview of Parsons's thought. Two collections of useful, if somewhat advanced, essays on various aspects of his sociology are Max Black, ed., *The Social Theories of Talcott Parsons: A Critical Examination* (Englewood Cliffs, N.J.: Prentice-Hall, 1961); and Herman Turk and Richard L. Simpson, eds., *Institutions and Social Exchange: The Sociologies of Talcott Parsons and George C. Homans* (Indianapolis: Bobbs-Merrill, 1971). Fuller treatments are William Mitchell, *Sociological Analysis and Politics: The Theories of Talcott Parsons* (Englewood Cliffs, N.J.: Prentice-Hall, 1967); Alvin W. Gouldner, *The Coming Crisis of Western Sociology* (New York: Basic Books, 1970), pt. 2; and Harold J. Bershady, *Ideology and Social Knowledge* (Great Britain: Basil Blackwell, 1973).

the radical-empirical tradition that seeks to explain human behavior in terms of "heredity," or biopsychic forces, and "environment," or geography and climate. By saying that science is unable to gain knowledge about the symbolic world of values and the psychic relationships that make up human interaction, the radical-empirical tradition, Parsons feels, denies that these values and relationships exist and tends to make a scientifically untenable unification of the human and the natural worlds. Far from being too subjective, diverse, and ephemeral to be useful, as the radical empiricists claim, sociocultural phenomena are highly structured and thus amenable to scientfic analysis. However, he argues, the empiricist methodologies—and he identifies three distinct types—cannot capture these structures. Their common characteristic and fault is

> . . . the *identification* of the meanings of the concrete specific propositions of a given science, theoretical or empirical, with the scientifically knowable totality of the external reality to which they refer. They maintain, that is, that there is an immediate correspondence between *concrete* experienceable reality and scientific propositions, and only in so far as this exists can there be valid knowledge. In other words, they deny the legitimacy of theoretical abstraction.[3]

Parsons refers to the first and most important of the invalid empiricisms in sociology as *positivistic empiricism,* or the process of reifying or giving substantiality to concepts. This refers to the general attempt to understand and explain the totality of social phenomena in terms of a single general theoretical system derived from natural science. The other two types of empiricism deny the validity of general theoretical concepts. *Particularistic empiricism* states ". . . that the only objective knowledge is that of the details of concrete things and events. It is impossible to establish causal relationships between them which are analyzable in terms of general concepts. They can only be observed and described, and placed in temporal sequence."

The third type of empiricism, *intuitionist empiricism,*

> . . . permits a conceptual element in social science, but maintains that this can be only of an individualizing character; it must formulate the unique individuality of a concrete phenomenon, such as a person or a culture complex. Any attempt to break down this phenomenon into elements that can be subsumed under general categories of any sort destroys this individuality and leads not to valid knowledge but to a caricature of reality.[4]

---

[3] S.S.A., p. 23.
[4] These quotations may be found in S.S.A., pp. 728, 729. On the next page Parsons also rejects Max Weber's contention that scientific concepts are not reflections of reality but "useful fictions."

All these forms of empiricism deny the human mind an autonomous and creative role in the formation of knowledge. They either structure what the mind will see in terms of a monopolistic scheme derived from a different subject area (as in positivistic empiricism, which accepts the validity of general concepts), or they reduce the mind to either intuition or experience (in which both deny the validity of general concepts). In Weber's case, he gave the mind a creative role to play but only within an epistemology that denies the validity of general concepts.

In opposition to these views, Parsons asserts two things. First, he states the methodological need for theory as an independent variable, or the need to attack phenomena with a plurality of conceptual schemes suitable to the nature of a given subject matter. Second, he asserts the epistemological validity of general concepts, the existence of an objective transhistorical external reality independent of but accessible to the human mind. Parsons called his point of view *analytical realism.*

Despite Parsons's insistence on the role of theory, he is not a deductive rationalist—ultimately, theory must be verified by fact in accordance with the general canons of science. Further, despite his emphasis on the creative role of the mind and his insistence on the unique nature of social phenomena, he makes no attempt to develop a historical or *verstehen* approach to human behavior. For Parsons, social phenomena are similar in structure, not content, to phenomena in the sciences of nature; that is, they are lawful, and as such can be attacked by the same methodology used in natural science.

It is clear that Parsons is squarely in the scientific (empirical or positive) tradition. If by science one means the belief in an objective phenomenal world accessible to the human mind, then science is synonymous with any term that designates the unique characteristic of Western symbolic culture. Further, if one specifies that the oustanding characteristic of the post-Enlightenment period has been the revolutionary shift to some variation of empiricism, then Parsons's insistence that concepts and theoretical systems must ultimately be verified empirically identifies him as a positivist—as one who is in line with the general scientific climate of his age. And, it should also be clear that Parsons is a pluralistic sociocultural positivist.

The distinctive feature of Parsons's epistemological and substantive work, therefore, lies in his rejection of "positivism," the tradition in sociology that I have labeled naturalistic positivism. It lies in his attempt to reassert the true nature of scientific thinking, which was validated, he believes, not only by the methodological implications contained in the new substantive consensus that emerged in sociology and economics from the 1880s on, but also by the development of natural science itself. Not only did the sociological empiricists erroneously apply the valid substantive principles of physics or biology to social phenomena; they were also mistaken in thinking that theory had played no role in the formation of these principles.

The Structure and Function of an Empirical-Theoretical Science

Underlying Parsons's methodology is the firm belief that one always perceives facts in terms of ideas or perceptual schemes. Once it is recognized that facts do not speak for themselves, the position of theory in science will take on its true meaning. Theorists will then see that they can use theoretical structures to identify problems and formulate hypotheses; to describe accurately and sort out the known from the unknown; to identify significant data as opposed to trivial or irrelevant data; to control bias; and, finally, to accumulate and codify knowledge—that is, to reformulate existing knowledge to bring otherwise discrete data under general headings.[5]

For Parsons, a science is not mature until it passes the stage of ad hoc empiricism and develops rational knowledge, or logically closed structures of abstraction that denote and explain significant slices of the phenomenal world. Because of this, Parsons has insisted that theory always means a system of ideas, ideas that are logically connected and internally consistent rather than discursive, elegant, or dramatic. Such systems should not be confused with empirically closed systems. It is incumbent on the scientist to develop theoretical structures independent of empirical verification. To do this one must distinguish between types of theory or conceptualization. Accordingly, Parsons devotes considerable attention to the problem of identifying the elements that go into a theoretical system. In *The Structure of Social Action*,[6] he identified three levels of conceptualization:

1. frame of reference (anchorage in fact, loosely structured axioms);

2. unit or part concepts (structural elements leading to empirical generalizations);

3. analytical elements (abstraction across diverse phenomena and the identification of variables).

In *Toward a General Theory of Action*[7] there is a similar classification of the elements that make up a general theory. A theory may be judged to be systematic according to level of generality and complexity; by degree of "closure" or logical consistency; and by its progress through the four levels

---

[5] S.S.A., pt. 1, chap. 1. Writing in 1951 (in *T.G.T.A.*, p. 3f), Parsons stated simply that the functions of theory are codification, research, and control of bias.
[6] Pp. 27–42.
[7] Pp. 49–52.

of systematization. These levels are distinguished in terms of their remoteness from the ultimate goals of science: ad hoc classificatory schemes (descriptive frame of reference); categorical systems (unit or part, structural analysis); theoretical systems (analytical elements); and, finally, the ultimate goal of science, empirical-theoretical systems or verified theories that give a high order of prediction about the behavior of empirical variables.

Theorizing, for Parsons, must always be done in conjunction with data. However, if theory without data is sterile and empty, so too, he would argue, data without theory are not merely distorted and disconnected but impossible.

Theoretical Pluralism and Unified Theory

It is apparent that Parsons's general orientation is astride the tradition of pluralistic sociocultural positivism. Like the major figures in this tradition, he recognizes the need for a sharp distinction between the subject matter of natural and social science, and he is very much concerned with the problem of developing a methodology to get at the unique subject matter of social science. The human mind, for Parsons, while probably incapable of exhausting the objective empirical world, is capable of creating logical structures that can bring significant slices of that world into relief. Even in the social sciences, said Parsons, the theory of action is just one of many ways of slicing into the phenomena of human behavior. Nonetheless, it is still the most important and promising approach to social phenomena. It is widely accepted and fits well with empirical research. What it most needs is refinement, extension, and unification. Up to now, each of the disciplines of action has developed a particular perceptual scheme based on particular assumptions, problems, and data, and each in its own way has struggled to develop a theory, a coherent set of ideas describing and explaining significant reaches of the social world. The convergence in modern social science now makes it possible, Parsons feels, to classify these disciplines in terms of the various emergent properties of the general action frame of reference:

> Economics (rationality),
>
> Political Science (coercive rationality or power relationships),
>
> Sociology (common-value integration),
>
> Psychology (personality clearly distinguished from biology on the one hand and social personality on the other).[8]

Parsons refers to the disciplines of action as analytical sciences, as distinguished from the merely empirical or historical-action sciences, and he separates them from culture as well as from nature. (At this time in his

[8] S.S.A., pp. 757–775.

career he felt culture was composed of "eternal" phenomena devoid of spatiality and temporality and therefore lacking in those qualities that define a scientific discipline.)

All three systems, however, nature, action, and culture, still form "parts of a consistent whole of objective knowledge." Despite his opposition to natural-istic sociology, Parsons has not rejected the possibility that there might be significant relations between the realm of nature and the realms of action and culture—a possibility to which he has devoted more and more interest as his career has progressed. His main interest, of course, has always cen-tered on the problem of unifying the various analytical sciences of action. In *Toward a General Theory of Action* [9] Parsons spelled out somewhat more fully what this unification means. He adopted a threefold division of the science of action: personality, society, and culture, represented by the disciplines of psychology, sociology, and anthropology. His main goals were to standardize the terms in these fields, to identify overlapping insights, and to take social science from its present level of ad hoc classification and use of ·categorical schemes to the next level of science, the development of a genuine theoretical structure. With the validation of this theoretical struc-ture, or its transformation into an empirical-theoretical system, social science would reach maturity as a science.

Parsons has not restricted his efforts at integration to these fields, however. Working within the functional framework, which is the focal point of his mature thought, he has also made systematic efforts to incorporate economics and political science into a unified theory of action. The final outcome of this effort to integrate the social sciences will be analyzed as his substantive work.

Another aspect of Parsons's concept of scientific method and social science will serve as a summary of his philosophy and method. It has already been emphasized that Parsons views social science as a valid, autonomous, and cumulative tradition. He sees his own work as, first, a codification of the basic action frame of reference that emerged inchoately between the 1880s and the 1920s, and, second, as an extension of the action frame of reference into a closed theoretical system. All this he sees as a preliminary to the final stage of empirical verification, or the attainment of an empirical-theoretical science. The closed theoretical system, therefore, must be thought of as a vast hypothesis, which, while it fits the empirical world at important points, must still be verified. Of some importance is Parsons's view that something called *immanent rational causation* [10] is at work in science, which

---

[9] Pp. 238ff.
[10] S.S.A., pp. 5, 12f., 14, 26f.; Parsons said (p. 5) he used the word *immanent* essentially the same way as Sorokin used it.

testifies to the autonomy of theory in the life of science. As proof of the ability of science to transcend history and to live a life of its own, he cites the fact that the four theorists whose work he discussed in *The Structure of Social Action*, coming from different social and national backgrounds and with different temperaments, all arrived at the same general theory of action.

Parsons's general position bears a deep kinship to Western rationalism. It bespeaks a faith that human reason can provide the criteria for sorting out the deceptions and trivialities from the substantive structure of the empirical world and thus lead theorists to the primary rather than the secondary qualities in phenomena. More particularly, Parsons's general epistemology stands squarely in the tradition of the French Enlightenment. Like the Enlightenment, he separates reason from phenomena and transforms it into a tool adequate for the acquisition, but not the creation, of knowledge. Like the Enlightenment, he sees reason as a tool that is applicable to all phenomena, natural and moral. Again like the Enlightenment, Parsons believes that, while reason finds itself by interacting with phenomena, it is nevertheless an autonomous agency. However, unlike the original faith of the Enlightenment, Parsons's thought reflects the growing self-consciousness of contemporary science and its growing awareness of the complexities and problems in the relation between reason and phenomena. Reason is now a plurality of structures and operations, which somehow manages to fit delimited and perhaps unique empirical structures but may never fit the universe at large.

Parsons's defense of theory in methodology rests on the assumption that science does not proceed by empirical observation alone. Rather, it starts with a comprehensive, interconnected frame of reference derived from axioms about phenomena and then proceeds to analysis—that is, a systematic, selective process of abstraction. Only in this way can one proceed economically, observe truly, and build a cumulative body of rational knowledge, knowledge that is not merely empirical (a term that in Parsons's usage means disconnected), unrelated knowledge. Theory, for Parsons, is at once an independent variable in the acquisition of knowledge, and the form such knowledge must some day take if it is to be theoretically scientific and not merely empirically scientific.

SUBSTANTIVE WORK

The starting point of Parsons's substantive work is the descriptive frame of reference containing the axiomatic foundations of the theory of action. Since his theory represents a lifelong attempt to exhaust the logical implications of low-order generalizations, I must say a word about them before I analyze the theoretical structure he has deduced from them.

The Action Frame of Reference and Its Components

At the heart of what Parsons means by the action frame of reference is the distinction between the science of nature and the science of action. The latter has a moral rather than a natural subject matter because human behavior is necessarily a choice-making process. Human beings are intrinsically caught up in a problematic world of scarcity and alternatives. To do justice to the moral nature of human behavior, social science postulates three basic components: an actor (individual or collectivity), social situations or objects (other actors and collectivities), and cultural objects (especially the normative order). Each is studied as an independent variable and as interdependent with the others, all within the assumption that human behavior is fundamentally a process of choosing between scarce or conflicting goals. In analyzing these components and the relationships among them, Parsons divides responses to situations and problems into cognitive, cathectic, and evaluative responses. In relationships between actors, there is the added dimension of complementarity—the element of mutuality or interaction.

These distinctions cannot be empirically distinguished. For example, interaction is not ad hoc and random, but highly structured by beliefs and emotions supplied and sanctioned by culture. Despite this empirical interpenetration, each of the three components of action is an autonomous structure. According to Parsons, there are three great systems of action: personality, society, and culture.

The Three Systems of Action: Personality, Culture, and Society

One of Parsons's crucial assumptions is that there are three separate but related aspects of reality, three ultimate but related sets of data or variables: the personality system (biological energies plus socially acquired "need-dispositions"),[11] the cultural system (composed of belief or cognitive, emotional or cathectic, and moral or evaluative subsystems), and the social system (interaction). For Parsons, these three aspects of reality are interdependent but also independent—they cannot be reduced one to the other or to any other factor.

Although Parsons recognizes the cultural and social basis of personality, he has refused to define human nature as a noncausal structure unrelated to human behavior. Though he is aware that this was Durkheim's and Weber's

---

[11] For a time Parsons divided the personality into personality and organism, thus deriving four systems of action. He now feels that the organism is not a system of action but part of its environment; see his essay, "The Present Status of 'Structural-Functional' Theory in Sociology," in Lewis A. Coser, ed., *The Idea of Social Structure: Papers in Honor of Robert K. Merton* (New York: Harcourt Brace Jovanovich, 1975), p. 81, n. 17.

view—which helped to orient sociology away from psychology and toward the study of interaction and culture—Parsons has insisted that some aspects of human behavior are biopsychic in nature. In his recent works he has done this mostly in Freudian terms, though throughout his career he has always been careful to avoid attributing any specific causal connection between biopsychic nature and human behavior. The cultural system, for Parsons, consists of "ideal" elements only and contains three analytically distinguishable subsystems that he labels *cognitive, cathectic,* and *evaluative.*[12] As an analytically distinct variable, the social system consists of the types and levels of interaction. The elemental concepts for analyzing interaction are *status, role,* and *collectivity.*

It is primarily from this locus of subject matter that Parsons has worked his way out in search of a unified theory of action. Before I analyze the first climax to which his thought took him, the pattern-variables synthesis, it is well to remember that Parsons's grand objective is to spell out the main structural and dynamic properties and points of articulation among all three systems of action. His problem, in short, is to develop a language that will allow him to speak logically about all three systems at the same time with due regard for levels of complexity and generality and for empirical soundness.

The Pattern Variables and the Social-System Types

The action frame of reference postulates that no relation between an actor and a situation is determinate because an actor is always confronted by choices between alternatives. The concept of *pattern variables,* which Parsons derived from this postulate, is an attempt to supply a logically exhaustive list of action dilemmas on the highest possible level of abstraction. In his own words:

> A pattern variable is a dichotomy, one side of which must be chosen by an actor before the meaning of a situation is determinate for him, and thus before he can act with respect to that situation. We maintain that there are only five *basic* pattern variables (that is, pattern variables deriving directly from the frame of reference of the theory of action) and that, in the sense that they are *all* of the pattern variables which so derive, they constitute a system. . . . They are:
>
> 1. Affectivity—Affective neutrality [The Gratification-Discipline Dilemma]

[12] In his latest writings he has added a fourth subsystem, the "ultimacy of the grounds of belief."

2. Self-orientation—Collectivity-orientation [The Private vs. Collective Interest Dilemma]

3. Universalism—Particularism [The Choice Between Types of Value-Orientation Standard]

4. Ascription—Achievement [The Choice Between "Modalities" of the Social Object]

5. Specificity—Diffuseness [The Definition of Scope of Interest in the Object]

The first concerns the problem of whether or not evaluation is to take place in a given situation. The second concerns the primacy of moral standards in an evaluative procedure. The third concerns the relative primacy of cognitive and cathectic standards. The fourth concerns the seeing of objects as quality or performance complexes. The fifth concerns the scope of significance of the object.[13]

The pattern variables do not form a synthesis merely because they exhaust the logical possibilities of interaction. Their importance as integrative concepts, Parsons and his collaborators have recognized, is that they are ways of talking about personality and culture as well as about society. This fundamental insight constitutes a major breakthrough in social science, Parsons felt, because it is now in

. . . a position not merely to assert that a combination of independence and interdependence must be recognized, but to state on a certain level precisely in what this consists. We know just what we mean by the institutionalization of patterns of culture, and by the sense in which the structure of the social system is and is not an embodiment of a set of such patterns. We know certain of the most fundamental elements of personality as a system of action and its interrelations with the social system. We know that they *both* go back to the fundamental processes of interaction between actors, that in this one sense personality is just as much a "social" phenomenon as is the social system. We know certain fundamental relations between the institutionalization and the internalization of culture. Above all, perhaps, we know that the fundamental *common sector* of personalities and social systems consists in the value-patterns which define role-expectations. The

---

[13] *T.G.T.A.*, p. 77f. The bracketed material accompanying the above list represents alternate ways of stating the pattern variables; taken from Parsons, *The Social System* (New York: The Free Press, 1951; available in paperback), p. 67—henceforth cited as *S.S.* Note that the first three pattern variables are modes of orientation and the last two refer to object situations.

motivational structures thus organized are units *both* of personality as a system and of the social system in which the actor participates; they are need-dispositions of the personality and they are role-expectations of the social system. This is the key to the "transformation formula" between the two systems of personality and social system. It is maintained that, in spite of the many brilliant insights bearing this relationship, especially in the works of Durkheim and of Freud, in terms which are both precise and highly generalized this set of relationships has never been so clearly understood before. This fundamental relationship between need-dispositions of the personality, role-expectations of the social system and internalized-institutionalized value-patterns of the culture, is the fundamental nodal point of the *organization* of systems of action. It is the point at which both the interdependence and the independence from each other of personality, social system, and culture focus. If the nature of this organization is not clearly understood and formulated with theoretical precision, confusion on this fundamental subject will inevitably spread in all directions and poison the whole theory of action. It is a new level of clarity about this fundamental phenomenon, which more than any other factor has made the present level of analytical refinement of the theory of the social system possible.[14]

Using two of the pattern variables, universalism-particularism and ascription-achievement, Parsons derived a set of four social-system types:

1. Universalistic-Achievement (modern Western industrial societies);

2. Universalistic-Ascription (Imperial and Nazi Germany and to some extent Soviet Russia);

3. Particularistic-Achievement (Imperial China);

4. Particularistic-Ascriptive (primitive kin-locality societies, Spanish-American societies)[15]

From an overall perspective, the pattern-variables synthesis enabled Parsons to deal conceptually with behavior from the smallest units to total social structures. However, it still left him with a plurality of theoretical types, and true to his commitment to systematic theory he reformulated the pattern variables in an attempt to achieve a more general, unitary statement about human behavior. The key to this reorganization came when he realized that

[14] S.S., p. 540f.
[15] S.S., pp. 180–200; it should be noted that Parsons regarded this scheme of types of society as a tentative sketch and that he specifically mentioned that it fails to take transitional types into account.

the three systems of action could be reformulated in terms of the logic of functional analysis.

The Emergence of Functionalism

The concept of function has always played an important part in Parsons's thought. In an essay written in 1945, for example, Parsons said this about the "all-important concept of function":

> The significance of the concept of function implies the conception of the empirical system as a "going concern." Its structure is that system of determinate patterns which empirical observation shows, within certain limits, "tend to be maintained" or on a somewhat more dynamic version "tend to develop" according to an empirically constant pattern (e.g., the pattern of growth of a young organism).
>
> Functional significance in this context is inherently teleological. A process or set of conditions either "contributes" to the maintenance (or development) of the system or it is "dysfunctional" in that it detracts from the integration, effectiveness, etc., of the system. It is thus the functional reference of all particular conditions and processes *to the state of the total system as a going concern* which provides the logical equivalent of simultaneous equations in a fully developed system of analytical theory. This appears to be the only way in which dynamic *inter*dependence of variable factors in a system can be explicitly analyzed without the technical tools of mathematics and the operational and empirical prerequisites of their employment.[16]

Parsons's early thought did not give either emphasis or elaboration to the concept of function. However, his unique capacity for collaborating with his fellow social scientists led him to a new awareness of its possibilities. His major theoretical reformulation began when he realized that the pattern variables (minus one), which he had formulated with Edward Shils, were the same as the four system-problems formulated by Robert F. Bales in his small-group work.[17] In consequence, Parsons and Shils, in collaboration with Bales, made a concerted effort to explore this and other coincidences and correspondences in their work.[18] Using Bales's four functional dimensions, the integrative, expressive, instrumental and adaptive, as the main

---

[16] Talcott Parsons, *Essays in Sociological Theory*, rev. ed. (New York: Free Press, 1954), p. 217f.
[17] *Interaction Process Analysis* (Cambridge, Mass.: Addison-Wesley Publishing Co., 1950).
[18] Some of the other prospects for synthesis were Parsons's work in the theory of deviance, therapy, and symbolism.

synthesizing framework, the first fruits of this collaboration emerged as the *Working Papers in the Theory of Action*.[19]

Since the *Working Papers*, Parsons, again often in collaboration with others, has gone on to develop the functional approach and apply it to different areas and disciplines: family [20]; the relation between economy and society [21]; education, economics, and politics [22]; and psychology.[23] By the late 1950s, Parsons's functionalism had matured enough for him to put forth a tentative and somewhat sketchy summary of a unified functional theory of behavior.

The Unified Functional Approach to Society, Culture, and Personality

In discussing Parsons's unified functional theory of behavior, I shall focus on his theory of the social system [24] and say only a word or two about his theory of culture and personality. While I shall stress the innovations in Parsons's later writings, there is a large measure of continuity with previous work. Parsons himself stresses this continuity and identifies it with what he feels are certain elements of consensus in the field of sociology itself. He specifically mentions the following areas of agreement: the applicability of scientific method to social phenomena (this method includes an awareness that science uses selective analytical abstraction and the concept of system or the "logical integration of generalized propositions"), and the action frame of reference (the recognition that there exists an independent socio-cultural realm).[25]

The Social System

In developing his paradigm for the analysis of social systems, Parsons stated at the outset that

[19] New York: Free Press, 1953, especially chap. 3.
[20] Talcott Parsons and Robert F. Bales, et al., *Family, Socialization and Inter-action Process* (New York: Free Press, 1955). The terms and general meanings of the four functional dimensions that Parsons uses in his mature theory first appear in this book: pattern-maintenance, goal-attainment, adaptation, and integration.
[21] Talcott Parsons and Neil Smelser, *Economy and Society* (New York: Free Press, 1956), available in paperback.
[22] Talcott Parsons, "General Theory in Sociology," in Robert K. Merton et al., eds., *Sociology Today* (New York: Basic Books, 1959); Talcott Parsons, " 'Voting' and the Equilibrium of the American Political System," in Eugene Burdick and Arthur J. Brodbeck, eds., *American Voting Behavior* (New York: Free Press, 1959).
[23] Talcott Parsons, "An Approach to Psychological Theory in Terms of the Theory of Action," in Sigmund Koch, ed., *Psychology: A Study of a Science*, 6 vols. (New York: McGraw-Hill, 1959–1963), 3: 612–711.
[24] His mature theory may be found in "An Outline of the Social System," in Talcott Parsons et al., eds., *Theories of Society*, 2 vols. (New York: Free Press, 1961), 1: 30–79.
[25] "Outline of the Social System," pp. 31–33.

> . . . the concept of interpenetration implies that, however impor-
> tant *logical* closure may be as a theoretical ideal, *empirically* social
> systems are conceived as *open* systems, engaged in complicated
> processes of interchange with environing systems. The environing
> systems include, in this case, cultural and personality systems, the
> behavioral and other subsystems of the organism, and, through the
> organism, the physical environment. The same logic applies in-
> ternally to social systems, conceived as differentiated and seg-
> mented into a plurality of subsystems, each of which must be
> treated analytically as an open system interchanging with environ-
> ing subsystems of the large system.[26]

A set of phenomena remains a system, Parsons continues, as long as it shows
stability and patterning and maintains a boundary between itself and other
systems. In any general methodological paradigm, Parsons insists, the concept of *structure* comes first. In using it, one abstracts those features that
show constancy over given time periods, that is, one identifies recurrent
behavior or institutionalized patterns of normative culture. When the reference point is the relation between the constancy of a social system (which is
always problematical) and its environment (organisms, personalities, cultural systems), one is talking about functional categories.

Parsons outlined two other basic analytical sorters; the first of these is the
use of concepts concerned with *dynamic modes of analysis.* Here one must
distinguish sharply between equilibrating processes and structural or total
social-system change. The second analytic device is the use of concepts that
focus on what Parsons calls the *hierarchy of relations of control:* cultural
system over social system; social systems over the personalities of participating individuals; personality over behavioral organism, the latter being the
point of contact between the general system of action, on the one hand,
and the physical organism and the physical environment on the other.
The concept of function links structural and dynamic modes of analysis. All
social systems, Parsons feels, from the smallest to the largest collectivity
called society, can best be thought of as engaged in solving the four fundamental functional problems of pattern-maintenance, goal-attainment, adaptation, and integration. Because of their importance for Parsons's mature
thought, each of these functions deserves a separate word.

1. The function of pattern-maintenance: the need to preserve the value
system, something that is done through the mechanisms that articulate the
value system with the belief system and that socialize individuals and reduce
and reconcile strains in their commitments.

[26] Ibid., p. 36.

2. The function of goal-attainment: the fact that a given social system has a system of goals arranged in some order of relative urgency—"goal-attainment becomes a problem in so far as there arises some discrepancy between the inertial tendencies of the system and its 'needs' resulting from interchange with the situation."

3. The function of adaptation: closely allied to goals (or ends) is the function of providing "facilities" (or means). Given a plurality of goals, the question of "cost" arises. As an aid in calculating costs and achieving flexibility in the allocation of facilities, there is a prime adaptive need to provide "disposable facilities independent of their relevance to any particular goal."

4. The function of integration: with a plurality of subsystems, a total or inclusive system can exist only if the problem of integration is solved. This "concerns the mutual adjustments of these 'units' or subsystems from the point of view of their 'contributions' to the effective functioning of the system as a whole. This, in turn, concerns their relation to the pattern-maintenance problem, as well as to the external situation through processes of goal-attainment and adaptation." [27]

Parsons developed his functional paradigm further by adding the concepts needed for social-system analysis: *role, collectivity, value,* and *norm.* He was now ready to discuss three analytically distinct foci of sociological analysis: one, the structure of complex systems; two, the dynamics of social equilibrium; and three, the problem of structural change. There is no need to do more than to outline the new features in each of these areas and to indicate where Parsons feels sociological theory now stands—which Parsons tends to identify with his own thought. Sociological theory, Parsons argues, has advanced furthest in its analysis of the structure of complex systems, somewhat less far in its analysis of social equilibrium, and has made relatively little progress in the area of structural change. Not unexpectedly, Parsons devotes most of his attention to structural and equilibrium analysis. Significantly, he stresses not only the tentativeness of his overall theory of the social system, but the fact that it will remain incomplete until a satisfactory analysis of structural change is achieved.

Societies exist as total collectivities if they have a common institutionalized value system, a set of legal norms that are ultimately binding, and if they can cope successfully with their external relations. However, complex societies must also specialize behavior into subsystems, and values into norms.

---

[27] These explanations of the four functional problems are derived from the discussion in "Outline of the Social System," pp. 38–41. Two things should be noted: one, the four functional problems exist for each subsystem as well as for the total social system, and, two, the responsibility for these functions (from the standpoint of the total system) does not rest with any one institution. Thus the family, education, and religion, for example, all contribute to pattern-maintenance.

> To approach the structural analysis of the subsystem organization
> of a society, we must refer to the appropriate exigencies of both
> the societal system itself, and its various subsystems. The primary
> overall-principle is that of differentiation in relation to functional
> exigency; this is the master concept for the analysis of social
> structure.[28]

The fundamental process at work in the development of modern industrial
society, said Parsons, is a trend from functionally diffused structures toward
functionally specific structures with a clear-cut hierarchy of social duties.
The trend is accompanied by a growing abstractness about the nature
and functions of the two major societal resources, physical facilities and
human services. In a complex society, there is a need to turn physical
resources, goods, and human services into "disposable facilities." There is
a need, in other words, to alienate structures and norms from diffused
ascriptive patterns and definitions and to make them at once functionally
concrete and flexible. This is accomplished on the social level by the
development of occupational statuses (and the related development of
bureaucracy), which sharply separates incumbents from family and other
statuses. On the normative level, it is done by developing the ideas of
contract, private property, money, market, leadership, authority, and power.
On a more abstract level, one can identify another set of norms that contributes to the overall functioning of the system. Though contradictory,
these norms are sufficiently vague to prevent immediate trouble. They include such things as economic rationality (efficiency); the ethical obligation
to do one's duty toward others; collective loyalty and self-sacrifice; equity
as a guiding principle in law; and the patient's welfare in medicine. In
summary, Parsons identified three processes of adjustment or equilibrium in
modern society that do not exist in an ascriptive society: norms are stated
in abstract terms to allow for particular adjustments; there is a predisposition
toward accepting the redefinition of norms through legislation or interpretation; and there is a recognition that the internal structure of either an
individual or a subsystem can and must be modified as circumstances
demand.

At this point Parsons's structural analysis shades off into an analysis of the
dynamics of equilibrium and of structural change. His strong distinction between equilibrium and structural-change analysis should help to dispel the
criticism that his theoretical orientation is inherently static. He takes great
pains, moreover, to point out that the priority given to structural analysis
in social science and in his own work stems from the logical necessity of

---

[28] "Outline of the Social System," p. 44.

establishing first what it is that changes. He expressly disavows a preference for this emphasis and denies identifying it with the true nature of society. This is not surprising considering that the problematic nature of social order is intrinsic to Parsons's entire approach.

In developing his analysis of the dynamics of social equilibrium, Parsons exhibits the same flair for imaginative abstraction that has always characterized his work. Relying primarily on the conceptual models employed by economic theory, but also on some ideas borrowed from political science, he searches for common elements and processes in otherwise dissimilar phenomena. For example, adopting the input-output model of economic theory, Parsons reasons that there must be cognate input categories for each of the other primary subsystems resulting in ultimate outputs.[29] Parsons cautions that in thinking of social phenomena in terms of input-output categories, one must remember that, sociologically speaking, one is referring to rights over or ways of controlling physical objects or physical behavior, not to the entities themselves. To analyze inputs and outputs properly, one must also identify stages of resource processing (generation of resources; allocation to operative units; and utilization), with special emphasis on the mechanisms that control resource processing (money, markets, and power). Parsons concluded his equilibrium analysis by saying that ". . . the social system as a whole and its internal processes should, in regard to behavior, be considered as a complex set of cybernetic controlling mechanisms—not just one governor, but a complex series of them." [30]

A quite different problem is involved when dealing with change on the structural level. Structural change takes place, said Parsons, when the boundaries between the social system and the other systems of action (personality, organism, culture) break down and a new pattern of relations is established. In analyzing boundary breakdown one must distinguish between factors exogenous to the social system and those endogenous. Exogenous sources of change include genetic changes in organisms or in the distribution of genetic characteristics in a population, culture (values, religion), physical environment as mediated by culture (science), and foreign relations. Endogenous sources of change involve the identification of "strain," the "tendency to disequilibrium in the input-output balance between two or more units of the system."

In adopting a multicausal approach to social phenomena (in order to avoid a teleological bias), one must be careful, Parsons warned, to avoid becoming eclectic. One must carefully identify factors and relate them to the hierarchy

29 "Outline of the Social System," p. 61.
30 "Outline of the Social System," p. 70.

of control in order to determine impact. Throughout, one must be alert to disturbances that result from deficient or excessive input at given points.[31]

Parsons concluded his analysis of structural change by distinguishing between the various types of process encountered at this level. He warned that more is involved than the mere emergence of a new situation presenting rational advantages for changing an actor's behavior. If structural change is to take place, the forces of change must also affect the nonrational layer of personality in which values are embedded. Once the factors of change impinge at this level, they produce anxiety, utopianism, and widespread possibilities for deviance. One of the basic processes leading to structural change is structural differentiation, especially the differentiation between family and occupation. The classic case is in Great Britain, where a widespread change in the structure of behavior took place at the end of the eighteenth and beginning of the nineteenth century in keeping with the established value system. In analyzing the process of change in the cultural system, Parsons concluded, one must distinguish between change in which the social and cultural systems interact (along with charismatic personalities) to produce widespread propensity to change, and change that comes from outside the society and is imposed through colonialism or diffusion.[32]

The Cultural System

In his theory of culture [33] Parsons has introduced a number of changes that significantly modify his earlier view of culture as a system of "eternal objects." For him, culture is now clearly a system of action. His master category for analyzing culture is *meaning*, and his major frame of reference distinguishes between cultural forms concerned with the "meaning of *objects* oriented *to*" (cognitive and cathectic) and the "meanings of *orientation by* actors" (evaluative and the ultimate basis or grounding of meanings). The first pair of cultural dimensions, cognitive and cathectic, is engaged in solving the functional problems of adaptation and goal-attainment, and the second pair, evaluative and ultimate grounding of meanings, is involved in solving the functional problems of integration and pattern-maintenance.[34]

Each of these four cultural dimensions can be understood in terms of a fourfold series of levels of generality or abstraction,[35] and each is related to

---

[31] Parsons's capacity for abstraction allows him to give some interesting examples of excessive input: Keynes's thesis about oversaving and unemployment, Durkheim's generalization about the positive relation between economic prosperity and rates of suicide, and the destructive effects of maternal overprotection.

[32] "Outline of the Social System," pp. 74–79.

[33] For Parsons's analysis of culture see his Introduction to pt. 4, "Culture and the Social System," in Talcott Parsons et al., eds., *Theories of Society*, 2 vols. (New York: Free Press, 1961), 2: 963–993—henceforth cited as "Culture."

[34] Ibid., pp. 963–964; 982 ff.

[35] Ibid., pp. 965–971.

the others. Whereas in Parsons's earlier thought the cognitive and the cathectic dimensions of culture came under the general control of the evaluative dimension, he now identifies a fourth dimension, ultimacy of the grounds of meanings. The highest level of generality within the "ultimacy" dimension, religio-philosophic conceptions of ultimate reality, is the "point at which cognition, cathexis and evaluation merge, because they are all somehow modes of differentiation from a common matrix." [36]

When analyzing the relationship between culture and society, Parsons continues, one must note the central place of evaluation and the vital need for institutionalization, that is, the internalization of values and their careful specification for relevant situations. Values, as bases for interaction, range from the general to the particular, they have the property of "sharedness," and they undergo cumulative development.[37]

Parsons's belief that culture is cumulative is a major departure from his earlier concept of culture as composed of "eternal objects." He now feels that if there is to be a realistic concept of social evolution, it must be demonstrated that value systems evolve. Accordingly, he now takes the position that ". . . the general analysis of cultural systems provides foundation for the view that a principle of cumulative development is inherent in the nature of cultural systems as a whole, and not only of their empirically cognitive components and subsystems." [38] This development, Parsons feels, consists fundamentally of a growth in abstraction, a progressive upgrading of value systems through the fourfold series of "levels of generality" parallel to that of systems of empirical knowledge.

Alongside Parsons's view of society, this new perspective provides an overview of his mature theory. Each of the two systems of action, the social system and the cultural system, contains a process of functional differentiation leading to structures of interaction and values that are at once more concrete and general, more empirical and abstract, more relevant to human needs and yet sufficiently nonpractical to avoid the stagnation of traditionalism. Society, Parsons is saying, like sociology, needs a high order of achievement in abstraction if it is to avoid the dysfunctions inherent in the acceptance of the empirically given. What Parsons strongly suggests, especially in his discussion of the sociology of knowledge,[39] is that the capacity of both society and culture to achieve a functional mastery over nature and human nature through abstraction is real. Even the sociology of knowledge, with its widespread recognition of the historical basis of behavior and social thought, though important in some respects, does not militate against this

[36] Ibid., p. 971.
[37] Ibid., pp. 980–981.
[38] Ibid., pp. 988.
[39] Ibid., pp. 988–993.

capacity to achieve objective knowledge. What Parsons is saying, basically, is that an inherent process of objectivity or ascendance toward generality or rationality is at work in society and culture (and thus in that portion of culture called sociology and social science) and that each by remaining autonomous and interpenetrating with the other makes the movement toward objectivity possible.

The Personality System

Parsons has reworked his "psychological" theory, which for a time defined the organism and the personality as two distinct systems of action, to bring it into line with his functional theory of society and culture.[40]

From the standpoint of general theory and for locating Parsons's overall approach in the spectrum of American sociology, the most important aspect of his theory of psychology is that while he insists on the independent existence of organism and personality, he carefully avoids attributing to either one structures that correlate with overt behavior. The organism, for example, is defined as a fourfold set of "facilities," which conceived functionally can be thought of as inputs to the psychological (personality) system. These consist of (1) motivational energy; (2) perceptual or cognitive capacity; (3) "performance" or "response" capacity, or the capacity to utilize the structures of the organism, notably the skeletal-muscular structures; and (4) the mechanisms that integrate these facilities with each other and the needs of the psychological system, especially the pleasure mechanism.[41]

In turn, four categories of outputs from the personality to the organism act as both controls and facilities:

1. motive force to increase instrumental performance;

2. directional output or the control of organic facilities by the motivational structures of the psychological system;

3. expectation component or attitudinal set, the "expectation" that organic interests will be served by "going along" with the psychological system; and

4. "organic security," or the stability of the whole relationship between organic and psychological systems.[42]

Finally, there are the input-output relations or boundary interchanges between the personality-organic system taken as a whole and the social and

---

[40] In Talcott Parsons, "An Approach to Psychological Theory in Terms of the Theory of Action," in Sigmund Koch, ed., *Psychology: A Study of a Science,* 6 vols. (New York: McGraw-Hill, 1959–1963), 3: 612–711; henceforth cited as "Psychology."
[41] "Psychology," p. 647f.
[42] Ibid., p. 648f.

cultural systems. Whereas the psychological-organic boundary relation is an exchange of facilities, the relation between the psychological-organic system and the social-object system is an exchange of rewards. Furthermore, the relation between the psychological-organic system and the cultural system is a process of integration and stabilization in which cultural values legitimate and regulate psychological activity in return for which the psychological system supplies "motivational commitment."

According to Parsons, the key to understanding the relations among the three [43] great branches of the general theory of action is the process of internalization in which the personality is structured in terms of internalized social-object systems and internalized value-norm systems. The discovery of the process of internalization by such figures as Durkheim, Mead, Piaget, and especially Freud is one of the most important events in modern psychology.

Therefore, despite Parsons's insistence on the independent existence of the organism and the personality, he studiously avoids attributing to them any necessary or specific consequences for behavior. Throughout, he views the organic-psychic structure as a facility. It is here that Parsons's commitment to sociocultural sociology and his departure from the psychological tradition of Anglo-American sociology stands out most clearly. It is almost as if he were trying to spell out Durkheim's profound epigram that psychology does not cause society, but simply makes it possible.

The Evolutionary Synthesis

In his later career Parsons has explicitly adopted an evolutionary solution to the problem of general theory (or the liberal dilemma). His thought has always contained tendencies in this direction, but in two recent books [44] evolution has emerged (somewhat abruptly) as the main organizing principle. Evidently responding to criticisms of loose ends in his previous work, Parsons now claims to see an evolutionary pattern in the record of human behavior, and he has put forth adaptive capacity as the master standard by which to judge history. Judged by this standard, modern society is superior to all previous systems. It has evolved a "generalized adaptive capacity" based on differentiated subsystems (which specialize in the performance of

---

[43] Parsons no longer views the organism as a system of action but as part of its environment; see above, "The Three Systems of Action: Personality, Culture, and Society."
[44] *Societies: Evolutionary and Comparative Perspectives* (Englewood Cliffs, N.J.: Prentice-Hall, 1966), also in paperback; and *The System of Modern Societies* (Englewood Cliffs, N.J.: Prentice-Hall, 1971), also in paperback. These two books are really one, the first dealing with premodern social systems and the second with modern society as a system of societies.

social functions) and a universalistic culture (the "generalization of value systems"). The distinctive growth of a universalistic culture is also a separation of culture from society (interaction structures and processes), something that permits a full inclusion of all members of society into its workings: general values can be specified for particular tasks; abstract citizenship allows any and all individuals to perform specialized duties (the adaptive upgrading of societal members).

There are three distinct stages of adaptive capacity and advance, the primitive, the intermediate, and the modern, each with subtypes and phases. The historical record contains directionality in that it exhibits a growth in "generalized adaptive capacity." The modern system is now undergoing a maturation process, having increasingly institutionalized its values. It is a final stage of social evolution in that Parsons envisages no postmodern society. (Contemporary society will take a century or more to reach its full development, he claims, and after that, the future is unknowable.) Modern society is really a system of societies—a concept, Parsons feels, that, together with the advances in social action theory, differentiates his evolutionary theory from its cruder nineteenth-century anticipations.

One of the most significant aspects of Parsons's evolutionary focus is the self-conscious and defensive way in which he hedges on all the basic problems of behavioral analysis. Adaptive capacity, he tells us, it not necessarily the paramount object of human value. It is also possible that a "postmodern" system may emerge someday from origins outside the West. Further, modern society may become more universalistic and come to absorb cultural elements from the world over. Nonetheless, the salience of adaptive factors describes "the way human society is" and points to a process that links human behavior with the evolution of other living systems.

Even more significant are the difficulties Parsons encounters whenever he leaves his abstract scheme of functional adaptation (which presumably can be applied to any society in the service of any combination of values) and analyzes a concrete example of modern society, the United States. Parsons's immersion in the basic stereotypes of liberalism—American late liberalism for the most part—is evident throughout. Ascription has declined; equality of opportunity is distinctive and real; law is the central control and adaptive mechanism; bureaucracy is important but the trend is toward associationalism; society is deeply pluralistic; the old laissez faire capitalism of the nineteenth century is dead; property has given way to occupation; and occupations are filled by merit as determined by education. Education holds a special significance for Parsons. It is the third revolution of modern times, with the French Revolution in politics and the Industrial Revolution in economics the first two. I shall discuss aspects of these statements when I consider Parsons as a liberal apologist. At this point I must note that his analysis has a curious vagueness and unreality, going far deeper than his wide use of high-level abstractions.

Specifically, Parsons is vague about and almost studiously avoids all the problems of power. Second, his fluid, stretched out, fluctuating, cybernetic, maturating "societal community" is never stated as a problem. Despite perfunctory references to poverty, racism, the strains of the educational revolution, and the possibility of war, Parsons sees little significance in the large number of social problems in contemporary society, their apparent intractability, and the wide departure in actual behavior from the generalized value system. Certainly he shows no concern about economic concentration; the trend toward an intertwined economy and state; the massive power of class over education, law, politics, government, and associational structures (voluntary organizations, professional societies); the fact that women, racial minorities, the working class, and the poor do not (and perhaps cannot) effectively participate in contemporary society; the anomie (identity problems, widespread deviance) inherent in using universalistic values in a deeply unequal class society;[45] the conflict characterizing the modern system of industrial societies; and the possibility that much of the order among modern industrial societies stems from a common interest in dominating the nonindustrial portions of the globe.

Perhaps the most devastating criticism of Parsons's evolutionary theory is that he is probably wrong in saying that modern society has greater adaptive capacity than previous societies—putting value judgments aside, primitive society is probably the best adapted of all societies.

CONCLUSION

Parsons and the Sociocultural Tradition

Unlike many of his predecessors in sociology, Parsons thinks of himself as part of a fully established, if somewhat inchoate, social science tradition. The locus of this tradition lies squarely within the sociocultural perspective. Of special importance is the fact that Parsons has effectively broken with the psychological or naturalistic orientation of American sociology, which is not surprising given his immersion in European sociology. One is especially struck by the fact that except for a few casual references Parsons has not referred to or acknowledged the influence of any of his predecessors in American sociology, while he freely acknowledges an enormous debt to European sociologists. However, while much of his orientation is derived

---

[45] In this regard see Robert K. Merton's classic analysis, "Social Structure and Anomie," *American Sociological Review* 3 (October 1938): 672–682; widely reprinted.

from a careful study of the history of social and sociological theory, he has seen the writings of the past not as history, but as a mixed heritage of valid and invalid insights, techniques, and findings. As such he has devoted much of his time trying to extract the valid elements from this tradition and fuse them into a coherent foundation for the social sciences.

Fundamental to understanding Parsons's contribution to sociology is the special meaning he has given the word *theory*. Parsons has neither contributed an original view of human nature and society nor has he conducted any empirical research, and yet his reputation is secure because of his bold attempt to organize and integrate the complex tradition of modern social science in terms of a carefully thought out philosophy of science. While this has led him to insist on the role of theory in science in order to avoid the superficialities of naive empiricism, he has never advocated deduction as a process of verification. He has argued quite cogently that the history of science has been the interplay of theory and fact and that since one always observes fact in terms of a theoretical framework, one should do so deliberately and consistently. He has insisted, in short, on the need to see all the sciences as rational disciplines, as disciplines that use logic both as a working structure of axioms and hypotheses in research and as the form the results of that research must take.

For all of Parsons's support of theory, he is still acutely aware of the problematic relation between reason and phenomena. This aspect of his thought is doubly interesting since it helps to link his sociology with other currents in liberal intellectual culture and, of course, with liberal society itself. Thus, one can say that Parsons's awareness of the problematic relation between reason and phenomena is derived from the problematic nature of liberal civilization itself. There is more than a touch of similarity between the problem of social order that looms so large in liberal social theory, including Parsons's thought, and the epistemological problem of relating theory to data. Given the dynamic and problem-ridden character of liberal society, it is not surprising that liberal theorists from Hobbes on have been obsessed within the problem of order and that late-liberal theorists have rebelled against the deductive, static approach to human behavior in favor of a more inductive, open-ended view. In line with the development of pluralistic positivism in general, Parsons's attack on positivism and on idealistic emanationism can be thought of as an attempt to free late-liberal thought from the presuppositions of early-liberal social science. Ironically, for all of Parsons's respect for the role of reason in science, his attack on positivism and idealism amounts to a relatively severe limitation of the power of reason. For example, he rejects the positivist claim that one can totally grasp the external structure of phenomena. Such a view, based on the presupposition that there is a finished order of social reality, is out of keeping with the intellectual requirements of a fluid, complex industrial social system. The limitation of reason can also be seen in Parsons's rejection of idealism's claim that ideas are ultimately the only efficacious forces in human life. In other words, Parsons's attacks on metaphysical positivism and idealism are attacks on two concepts of science or reason that are relatively useless to a dynamic, earthbound social system faced with an ever-novel array of problems.

In substituting the view that there is an interplay between theory and fact, however, Parsons runs squarely into the liberal dilemma. His solution to this problem (which he does not confront directly or formally) is that somehow the use of theory is a sufficient safeguard against the distortions of experience and empirical investigation. It was theory, he believes, that led social science to the scientific breakthrough of the late nineteenth century, and he strongly implies that it will be theory (in interplay with fact) that will continue to keep sociology a science. Why this breakthrough took place at this particular time does not seem to interest Parsons, largely because his thought contains an ultimate solution to the liberal dilemma, the idea of "immanent causation." This idea has never left his thought, though the term used to express it does not appear after *The Structure of Social Action*. In this book, Parsons explicitly expressed his belief in an immanent or inherent development in science, one that stems from the "logical exigencies of theoretical systems in close mutual interrelations with observations of empirical fact and general statements embodying these facts," or from the "immanent tendency of reason to a rational integration of experience as a whole." [46] In short, despite the problem of relating reason and phenomena, Parsons is suggesting that there is an intrinsic connection between them and that somehow the immanent tendency of reason is powerful enough to overcome the handicaps associated with a scientist's location in time and space. To support his view, Parsons cites the example of the four theorists whose work he analyzed in *The Structure of Social Action*. Though they came from very different backgrounds, Parsons points out, they all arrived at basically similar conclusions. In a way strongly suggestive of laissez faire economic theory, Parsons is here arguing that individuals with different backgrounds and different motives can contribute, both manifestly and latently, to a valid, cumulative tradition of scientific truth.[47]

This line of argument takes Parsons considerably beyond the claim that he is extracting elements from the past with which to construct a theory; it implicates him in the view that modern social science is the result of an

[46] For these and other expressions of this belief, see S.S.A., pp. 5, 12f., 14, 26f.
[47] I should note that in my judgment Parsons has made serious mistakes in his interpretations of the thought of Durkheim, Pareto, and Weber; see pages 278, 287–288, 293–295, 346–347, 378n, 380n.

inherent self-explanatory and self-validating process of scientific development. Not unexpectedly, Parsons has gradually combined this position with the view that sociocultural systems are also governed by an inherent process of rationalization to form an explicit evolutionary theory.

To understand this development in Parsons's thought more fully, one must go back to his rejection of the early-liberal utilitarian view that rationality consists of successful goal seeking by individuals and that this process forms the only sociological reality. Such a view, Parsons feels, cannot explain social integration. Under the influence of sociocultural sociology, especially that of Max Weber, Parsons has posited instead that the realms of interaction and values are the true sociological reality.

The influence of Weber on Parsons is quite apparent. Like Weber, Parsons stresses religion as the prime expression of the fundamental values that stabilize human existence and produce the various types of social systems. Parsons has no qualms in using Weber's emphasis on religion to help explain the process of rationalization. However, Parsons's belief that sociology can achieve systematic, unified, general theory ultimately connects him not with Weber, but with Durkheim and the main line of development in sociological theory.[48] This is apparent in his last essays and books, where he reveals a commitment to what can only be called a teleological-evolutionary view of sociocultural phenomena—a view that in its general overtones is quite reminiscent of eighteenth- and nineteenth-century sociology. Unlike in his earlier work where Parsons seemed to be constructing a hypothesis to meet the necessities of a well-informed logic, he is now advancing a conclusion allegedly based on the empirical record. The thematic backbone of his recent writings is the quite explicit thesis that since the Middle Ages modern society has evolved toward an ever-more rational form.[49] Belief and moral structures as well as corresponding behavior structures have become more abstract and more empirical, more general and universal and yet more dynamically suitable to the needs of time and place. Of special interest is Parsons's general suggestion that social science has also evolved toward rationality (which Parsons tends to equate with the theory of

---

[48] Parsons has consistently said that Weber's thought was converging with the main line of development in sociology—the latest instance being his review of Reinhard Bendix and Guenther Roth, *Scholarship and Partianship: Essays on Max Weber* (Berkeley: University of California Press, 1971) in *Contemporary Sociology* 1 (May 1972): 203.

[49] The same point is sketched somewhat tentatively in *The Social System*, pp. 496–503. However, in this earlier attempt to posit an inherently rational directionality to sociocultural systems, Parsons clearly stated that he was not directly stating an empirical generalization. His reason for positing directionality was to meet the needs of scientific theory, that is, to provide a logical construct that explicitly denies random or haphazard movements and occurrences in the phenomena being studied.

action), abandoning its earlier attempt to define human nature and society once and for all via radical empiricism, especially positivism, and idealistic emanationism.

Parsons's emphasis on the open-ended nature of society does not prevent him, however, from identifying the present structure of society as the terminal stage of social development. In this regard, there are striking similarities between his theory and those of his predecessors in sociology. Though he emphasizes that the starting point of social theory is the problematic nature of social order, Parsons does not see modern society itself as a problem. Rather, he tends to define social instability and social deviance either as transitional problems or as lags in the knowledge of social processes. This perspective, especially when combined with his emphasis on theory, commits him to a view that rational-scientific knowledge is possible before the empirical structures being depicted have congealed into their final form. Like Comte's teleological theory, Parsons seems to be suggesting that the evolution of science or mind is an autonomous causal process that precedes social evolution and that it will emerge prior to society to guide it into its preordained structure. However, Parsons knows his history of social theory too well to present this evolutionary-functional orientation as a cleanly stated systematic theory. His theoretical statements have always hedged against substantialism, almost as if Parsons were deliberately avoiding the liberal dilemma. In *The Structure of Social Action,* for example, while asserting that theory and phenomena are connectable, he also emphasized that it is extremely difficult to make a valid connection between them and that perhaps this can never be done. As a further hedge against substantialism, he has also insisted that his theory of action is simply one limited way of looking at phenomena, and that his "approach is not yet a logico-deductive system, but rather a temporal and historical series of contributions toward the development of such a system." [50] At one point in his mature functional theory, he has hedged even further by stating rather explicitly that he was confining himself to complex industrial systems. His commitment to evolutionary theory, however, has limited his options, and his ability to hedge has disappeared.

Parsons as a Late-Liberal Apologist

Parsons's careful qualification of his work suggests that there is in his thought a nonsubstantialist strain running counter to the main orientation. From this perspective his thought can be interpreted as a late-liberal contribution to liberal democracy's problem-solving store of weapons. Parsons's

[50] Talcott Parsons, "The Point of View of the Author," in Max Black, ed., *The Social Theories of Talcott Parsons* (Englewood Cliffs, N.J.: Prentice-Hall, 1961), p. 321.

functionalism, in other words, can be considered as a systematic way to
think about a specific historical type of society and its problems. Parsons
stresses the need to focus on all levels of behavior and the relations among
them, on the interdependence of phenomena, and the need to think in terms
of the operation of the total social system. This emphasis can be thought of as
part of the late-liberal recognition that the atomism of early-liberal theory
and its assumption that social functions are performed by the natural,
harmonious, laissez faire economy and representative government are out of
keeping with reality. Though his orientation still aims at systematic theory,
Parsons strongly suggests that theory must serve practical social ends and
that social order must be created, not found.

From this perspective Parsons's critique of early-liberal theory for its neglect
of ends, his insistence on the intrinsic decision-making nature of human
action operating within a world of scarcity, his emphasis on control mechanisms and priority-determining processes (especially evaluation), his attempt
to pinpoint responsibilities for functions without giving precise definitions of
structures or empirical content, and his attempt to visualize society as a
dynamic cybernetic system—all bespeak his conscious and unconscious concern for a problem-ridden industrial society facing an ambiguous and
uncertain future.

In this regard, Parsons's typically late-liberal economic views are highly
instructive. The natural economy of early liberalism was thought to perform
many social functions besides providing material sustenance. Once late-
liberal theorists realized that such an economy did not exist, they were
compelled to rethink the problem of social functions, especially to reinterpret the relation between political institutions, once the domain of nonrationality, and the economic sector, once the mainspring of rational existence.
Parsons's thought is part of this late-liberal trend. He has tried to spell out
the functions needed for social survival and to assign in a general way the
responsibility for these functions to structures of behavior and norms. In
particular, he has redefined political institutions in a way quite different
from that of early-liberal thought—not only can political phenomena, including the exercise of power, be analyzed scientifically, but they make a
vital and positive contribution to the functional health of society. Of special
importance is the central role that Parsons assigns to law.

Parsons's concept of psychology also fits the needs of late-liberal social theory.
Gone is the early-liberal concept of human nature as a set of fixed biopsychic
structures. Psychology, now formulated in terms of input-output categories,
is conceived as a set of undefined "disposable facilities" adaptable to the
specialized and changing needs of social existence. As such, psychology or
human nature is now a receptacle capable of being socialized in highly
specialized ways, no longer the source of behavior but the medium through
which it takes place. A similar view, it will be remembered, emerged

throughout sociocultural sociology as part of the late-liberal need to emancipate industrial capitalism from fixed structures of all kinds. Of special interest is Parsons's use of Freudian theory, not to emphasize the autonomy of the individual nor to locate the springs of human action inside the individual, but to explain the way in which the organism acquires its deep commitments and attachments to social objects (parents) and cultural values (ego and superego).

For all his emphasis on theory, Parsons is a deeply empirical thinker; he is aware of the brute, complex world of experience and is eager to conquer it with a carefully worked out system of thought. He no longer assumes, as so many social theorists before him, that thought can prescribe a tightly linked hierarchy of explanation and value. His functionalism attempts to separate science and values even while it affirms values as its subject matter. To become genuinely historical and nonsubstantialist, Parsonian theory would need only a wholehearted acceptance of the notion that social order is always a problem, that societies have no inherently valid structures, and that one must also look beyond the assumptions of a given sociocultural system for solutions to the problems of order and scarcity.

The two contradictory emphases in Parsons's work can now be stated more explicitly; first, the belief that a theory of functional imperatives and processes applicable to all empirical contents can be constructed, and second, the contary belief that a theory is always historically circumscribed. Each orientation plays a large part in Parsons's thought, and together they represent, of course, another way of stating the liberal dilemma. The idea of history, or rather the problem of history, is implicit throughout Parsons's work. It leads to a healthy insistence that empirical contexts are crucial for understanding human behavior, that social science deals with relational phenomena, and that one must employ a multicausal approach. For all his emphasis on the need to build a theory that is ultimately free of empirical content, Parsons has always emphasized that such a theory is "free" because it has successfully explained all relevant facts. Indeed, he has emphasized the difficulty of developing conceptual schemes that do justice to the full range of phenomena.

It is this healthy historical point of view that has made Parsons refrain from formulating a closed and rigid general theory. Oddly enough, he has been criticized for being static, for emphasizing equilibrium, for taking the action out of the theory of action. One can see quite the opposite, however, if one looks at his theory from the perspective we have just outlined. His rejection of metaphysical, naturalistic positivism amounts to a rejection of any view that defines social phenomena as a constant, recurring natural process. He has substituted a more dynamic functional view that defines human beings as intrinsically moral or historical beings, as beings involved in a never-ending process of decision making and problem solving. In short, there is a deep inhibition in his thought that prevents him from undertaking a Durkheimian search for a universally valid functional theory. Instead, he qualifies his work by constantly suggesting that his theory is artificial though logical, selective but not arbitrary, and valid but only one of many ways of looking at social phenomena. Viewed from this perspective, Parsons's thought contains a deep pragmatic bias—here, he seems to be saying, is the world of problems faced by modern society and here is a conceptual scheme that permits both low- and high-level analyses of these problems. As such, his theory can be interpreted as an extremely sophisticated and perhaps fruitful statement of the problems faced by mature capitalism. It is almost as if his self-consciousness about the deep epistemological problems in the empiricist view of science has made him consciously practical and ideological—that is, has prevented him from believing that capitalism is rooted in the nature of things.

It would be misleading, of course, not to emphasize that Parsons's main goal is still a unified theory of behavior. His distinctive evolutionary-functional approach is yet another chapter in the functionalism that has become the dominant feature of postmedieval natural and social science. As I showed earlier, functionalism was profoundly transformed by the advent of industrialization and by the important biological discoveries of the nineteenth century. In general, this transformation saw fact substituted for reason, and life for logic—that is, it saw the reduction of mind to activity. In the United States this transformation took form as pragmatism in philosophy, behaviorism in psychology, and neonaturalistic positivism in sociology. It is within this climate that Parsons has built his distinctive version of pluralistic sociocultural positivism. In doing so, he has been profoundly influenced by biological thinking, especially in his use of the functional approach and his recognition of the importance of nonrational factors in human behavior. He has nonetheless avoided the American penchant for biopsychological sociology and has developed a pluralism in methodology that recognizes the need for diverse methods to capture a diverse subject matter. Finally, despite the "nominalism" that pervades his thinking, Parsons has not lost sight of the main goal of sociology. He is still in search of the underlying lawfulness that allegedly exists in human interaction, human beliefs and values, and in the relation of these to human biopsychic nature, other living organisms, and the geographical environment. His earlier equivocal steps in this direction [51] have now settled into an unconvincing unitary scheme that explicitly likens society to the functioning and evolution of biological

---

[51] For a detailed analysis of Parsons's earlier journey toward naturalism and a unitary (monistic) positivism, see John Furley Scott, "The Changing Foundations of the Parsonian Action Scheme," *American Sociological Review* 28 (October 1963):716–735.

organisms.[52] If, however, any part of the goal of explaining law in human behavior is ever reached, it will in no small measure be due to Parsons's life-long attempt to give the ad hoc empirical tradition in sociology the direction, breadth, and consistency of general theory.

[52] Talcott Parsons, "The Present Status of Structural-Functional Theory in Sociology," in Lewis A. Coser, ed., *The Idea of Social Structure: Papers in Honor of Robert K. Merton* (New York: Harcourt Brace Jovanovich, 1975), pp. 67–83.

PART VI
Summary and Application

Chapter 23
The General Character of Sociology

The general purpose of this study has been to present an accurate and faithful picture of the thought of representative sociologists and to gain a fresh perspective on the nature of sociology. In Part VI I shall summarize my findings about the general character of sociology (Chapter 23) and use them to order the various theories and trends in current sociology (Chapter 24).

THE MAIN LINE OF DEVELOPMENT

The Emergence of Pluralistic Sociocultural Positivism

The main line of development in sociology, considered either as intellectual history (that is, in terms of the relationship among ideas) or as history (that is, as the relationship among ideas and all other sociocultural factors), is clear enough in its broad outlines. The beginnings of modern social science are evident in the seventeenth century when the major presuppositions of Western intellectual life underwent a revolutionary transformation from the teleological to the mathematical world view. Abandoning qualitative reasoning and its search for essences, though still animated by the deductive tradition, social science found the wellsprings of both its methodology and its substantive principles in geometry and physics, especially mechanics. The intimate relationship between natural science and social science (natural philosophy and moral philosophy in the premodern period), which is a main feature of Western intellectual culture, is readily discernible during this century. Centuries of intellectual labor were climaxed as Western intellectuals dissolved all existence into indivisible particles, the particles of physics finding their social-science counterpart in the human particles of society.

Seventeenth-century developments were soon followed by an even more profound intellectual revolution. Without abandoning the mechanistic outlook of the Age of Genius, the Enlightenment produced a revolution in the West's intellectual orientation when it adopted an empirical epistemology.

Though the outlook of the Enlightenment is best characterized as rational-empirical, Western intellectual culture underwent a momentous transformation when it accepted the idea that the phenomenal world is lawful and thus directly accessible to human reason. Of transcendent importance was the related assumption that human nature as a whole—that is, the passions as well as the mind—is lawful and therefore rational and good. The general cause of these epistemological developments was the technological-economic revolution—itself partially explainable, of course, in terms of intellectual and moral variables—that occurred between 1200 and 1800. Economic expansion created the individual as well as the empirical mind; the early modern period could identify the individual as real, as a causal being and a viable social unit. More generally, it was the growth of calculable control over the material environment, through machinery in conjunction with a rational philosophical tradition, that led to the Newtonian world view in natural science and to the assumption in social science that human behavior could be viewed in the same mechanistic way. The climax to these related economic, intellectual, and moral developments came in the eighteenth century, when some form of social Newtonianism established itself in the lead countries of the West, in England, France, and in what was to become a main offshoot of European culture, the United States.

After the Enlightenment, the natural and social sciences developed apace as the entire range of Western intellectual life acquired a new confidence in the possibilities of an empirical science, a confidence born of liberal society's growing ability to cope with the empirical social and natural worlds. Despite the continuity and unity of Western intellectual life after the Enlightenment, it is important to distinguish the empirical-rational stage of intellectual culture of the nineteenth century from the more deductive or rational-empirical orientation of the eighteenth century. In my analysis of the history of sociological theory, I used this distinction to identify a transition period (the maturing tradition) between the age of monistic sociology and the contemporary empirical age of pluralistic positivism.

Discoveries in natural science were the most dramatic and influential events in the intellectual culture of the nineteenth century. Anglo-American sociology was especially influenced by the Darwinian theory of evolution, though only Darwin's empirical-functional method had a lasting impact.[1] Out of the ferment of nineteenth-century intellectual life came a gradual recognition that while the scientific method was common to both natural

---

[1] Though the application to human history of Darwin's specific explanation of evolution (natural selection) and the literal equation of biological and social evolution have been discredited, an unscientific faith in some kind of natural social evolution or progress is still pronounced among lay people and sociologists as well. For one of the ablest defenders of the neo-evolutionary perspective, see Gerhard Lenski, "History and Social Change," *American Journal of Sociology* 82 (November 1976): 548–564.

and social science, it had to be adapted to the unique subject matter of given disciplines. In sociology proper, the attempt to understand human behavior in terms of the laws of physical or biological nature was gradually abandoned in favor of a social and cultural definition of behavior, a view no less revolutionary than the adoption of the empirical-functional methodology. Hand in hand, these two developments gave rise to the now dominant orientation in sociology, pluralistic sociocultural positivism.

A Succession of Substantialisms

In analyzing the development of sociological theory, I stressed the relationship between sociological theory and the metaphysical or substantialist tradition of the West. I concluded that one of the most important and most neglected aspects of the study of sociological theory has been the deep metaphysical or substantialist basis of general, systematic, or unified sociological theory. Of course no one should overlook the enormously important scientific function that this metaphysical tradition performed—it allowed Western theorists to escape from the bondage to fact that is so characteristic of non-Western populations. Thanks to the continuing vitality of Greek rationalism, sociology has been able to affirm the existence of universal uniformities or causal principles while acknowledging the empirical diversity and temporality of human behavior. Regardless of important differences, all periods of Western thought have continued the basic premise of Greek idealism, that facts do not exist except in terms of mental structures. With the rise of empiricism in the eighteenth century, and the destruction of the belief in a mental substance (or mind or reason), the deductive phase of idealism ended. Henceforth sociologists struggled to maintain the role of mental structures in the formation of knowledge; that is, they grappled, wittingly or unwittingly, with the liberal dilemma. While sociologists have overwhelmingly affirmed the role of theory in social science, they have varied widely in their definition of the nature of mental images and structures and the role they play in the acquisition of knowledge. From this perspective, one can discern a number of variations on this substantialist theme in the methodological and substantive theories that have dominated sociology, and these variations are intimately connected with similar variations in the history of philosophy.

The standpoint from which I analyzed and classified sociologists is the belief that mental images and structures are derived from experience and can never be true in any metaphysical or universal sense. This perspective, derived from Hume and embodied fully in sociology only in the work of Max Weber, asserts that while theory cannot substantiate fact, neither can fact substantiate theory. Whether theorists assert the role of the mind or deny it, they must still use a priori assumptions, which, disguised or not, are nevertheless arbitrary. One can, of course, assert that a fruitful and creative relationship between theory and fact can be established—an intellectual assumption born of a dynamic industrial system that cannot define either the world of nature or human nature by a static logic or a parochial "empiricism." However, one is still asserting some anchorage, be it the creative mind, a transhistorical methodological paradigm, or an immanent process yielding a cumulative body of valid knowledge; and one is ignoring the fact that the relation between theory and fact is carried on within a specific sociocultural tradition. Not only is theory (logic, concepts, system of concepts) itself a sociocultural fact and therefore subject to historical conditioning, but theory inherently selects and arranges other facts according to historically determined assumptions and problems. Sociology has never been able to distinguish and validate a distinction between primary and secondary facts or variables on a universal basis, though there have been widespread ad hoc, arbitrary, or unwitting attempts. Sociology cannot do what natural science had done because it cannot as yet assume universal causation, fixed or dynamic. Sociology deals, at least for the time being, with an order of facts that need not be what it is; therefore, it cannot assume a given structure of phenomena. It has no data, only facts—historical facts in Weber's sense of the term, a moral realm as immune from scientific as from philosophic definition and apprehension.

Just as theory (as methodology) has undergone various stages of substantialist belief (deductive-empirical, mathematical-qualitative, monist-pluralist), so, too, the definition of fact has gone through various phases of substantialism. In the struggle to identify fact, to distinguish between phenomena and epiphenomena, one must be wary of the assumption that science is embarked upon the rescue of reality from ignorance and superstition. If there is anything certain about the history of the subject matter of sociology, it is that sociologists have looked at the world in terms of the problems created by the various types and phases of liberal social development.

During the initial stage of sociological theory, there developed a revolutionary assumption that human passions were lawful and that biopsychic structures were the central reality behind human behavior. In the course of the nineteenth century, a reaction to the age of biopsychology set in and attention focused on society and culture as the central reality behind behavior. Though a minority position at first, the new sociocultural emphasis rested on the revolutionary assumption that no easy correlation exists between human nature and human behavior. According to the new perspective, the individual qua individual is neither a structured nor a causal being. The individual as a social actor, however, exhibits lawful behavior. If one is to understand the causes and laws of human behavior, one must study personality (socially created psychology), social structure (interaction), and cultural structure (definitions or meanings that create reality and energize social action). The focus on sociocultural structure has not led to relativism, however. The overwhelming assumption behind contemporary sociology is

that whether one focuses on psychology in relation to sociocultural structure, on sociocultural structure alone, or on personality, society, and culture
(as either a functional or a dialectical system), one is dealing with an ultimate
substance, with an underlying uniformity whose structure is expressible in
rational terms (unified, systematic, or general theory).

In tracing the succession of substantialisms that constitute sociology, therefore, this study has done more than merely analyze the struggle to overcome
biopsychological substantialism—it has also focused on the problem of substantialism itself. Throughout, I have questioned the assumption that a
rational theory of human behavior is possible and have suggested that a
more appropriate goal for sociological theory is the management of humanity's historical fortunes. It must also be stated that of all the systematic
theories, the contemporary school of functionalism, especially the work of
Talcott Parsons, represents a promising beginning toward a unified theory
of behavior—provided it can be disentangled from its association with liberal
society. In any case, I shall raise the matter of functionalism and substantialism in Chapter 24, when I review the impressive methodological achievements of recent decades. The problem of metaphysics must be raised in the
context of contemporary methodology because of the widespread teleological
conviction that sociology has at last made a breakthrough in achieving a
transhistorical methodology. This view is the chief bearer in current sociology of the substantialist tradition.

THE SOCIOLOGY OF SOCIOLOGY

Social Power and the Development of Sociology

One must look to the social matrix in which sociology developed for a deeper
understanding of its history and nature. To view sociology as an immanent
process of scientific development is to turn effect into cause and to founder
on the liberal dilemma. For one thing, science is a derived phenomenon; for
another, its power and nature, like all historical causes, vary with historical
circumstance. It was the emergence of an unfamiliar and increasingly complex and dynamic urban-industrial society that prompted theorists to see
human and physical nature in empirical terms and to adopt a sociocultural
outlook. To put the matter more precisely, a maturing capitalist society
forced theorists to confront problems not handled by previous theorists. One
must avoid attributing empiricism to human nature. To do so is to commit
the anthropomorphic sin of reading into human nature qualities or attributes
that are the emergents of sociohistorical circumstances. Pluralistic positivism
arose because it was needed by the main power groups of a maturing
capitalist society.[2] Despite an almost obsessive concern about its origins,

[2] See "The Advent of Organized Empirical Social Research," in Chapter 13.

development, and identity, sociology has failed to explain itself. By and large, the explanation offered by successive sociologists (for example, Comte, Sumner, Ward, Cooley, Sorokin, Parsons) has relied on teleology: sociology arose and flourished because it was in the nature of things that sociology would rise and flourish. Recent attempts by sociologists to understand sociology have not gone much further despite their claim that they were pursuing the sociology of sociology.[3] The reason for the failure to explain sociology lies in the kind of thinking found in Thomas S. Kuhn's widely influential *The Structure of Scientific Revolutions*,[4] a work purporting to be a sociology of natural science but which is almost devoid of sociology. In an otherwise useful book, S. N. Eisenstadt also fails to shed much new light on the origins and development of sociology.[5] Like most failures in the sociology of sociology, Eisenstadt's analysis assumes that ideas cause not only themselves but social developments; accordingly, he concentrates his effort at understanding the development of sociology by focusing on the relation between sociological theory and various other symbolic specialties, and on the relation between sociology and the sociological community.

Sociological theory cannot be fully understood unless it is placed in a genuinely historical or sociocultural context. The general definition of the human being as a psychological reality that established itself during the seventeenth and eighteenth centuries takes on its full meaning only when it is related to the crystallizing capitalist society. The shift from the eighteenth-century rationalist definition of the individual to the nineteenth-century emphasis on the biological attributes of individuals, or the shift from social Newtonianism to social Darwinism, reflected a shift from a rural-commercial to an urban-industrial economy. The main ideological function of sociology during this transition was to provide values and beliefs that would facilitate and legitimate rapid capital formation and at the same time justify the hardships and inequality that could now, with the defeat or absence of feudalism, only be associated with and attributed to liberal society. To a large extent this was accomplished by refurbishing the Protestant-bourgeois ethic and laissez faire economics with Darwinian elements.

Toward the end of the nineteenth century, sociology changed in response to the new conditions and problems of a maturing industrial economy. American sociology revived the psychological emphasis—always an important

[3] For example, Robert W. Friedrichs, *A Sociology of Sociology* (New York: Free Press, 1970); Nicholas C. Mullins with the assistance of Carolyn J. Mullins, *Theories and Theory Groups in Contemporary American Sociology* (New York: Harper & Row, 1973); and George Ritzer, *Sociology: A Multiple Paradigm Science* (Boston: Allyn and Bacon, 1975).
[4] Rev. ed., Chicago: University of Chicago Press, 1970; originally published in 1962.
[5] With Miriam Curelaru, *The Form of Sociology—Paradigms and Crises* (New York: John Wiley, 1976).

component of liberal thought—and defined human beings more in terms of intelligence, will, purpose, and gregariousness, and less as blind, impulsive, biological organisms. This development ("telesis" in Ward, symbolic consciousness in Cooley, "consciousness of kind" in Giddings, "definition of the situation" in Thomas) reflected "the need to prepare" the American population for a new and more demanding occupational structure and for the novel array of social problems emerging from the hectic pace of industrialization, urbanization, and immigration. In a larger sense, renewed emphasis on individual rationality reflected the need in the United States to prepare its population to assume new roles in the interdependent and complex social system crystallizing around the new industrial structure and its intensively specialized division of labor. The new orientation of American sociology also included a growing emphasis on the sociocultural, group sources of human character and behavior, an orientation that came from the need to justify governmental and social engineering to insure up-to-date relations among character, intellect, family, polity, and economy.

Of some importance in the adjustment of American sociology to the newly emerging urban-industrial system was the social problems-social policy focus it adopted from the first decades of the twentieth century on. Sociology's new emphasis on problem-solving concepts, methods, and data was matched throughout American professional-intellectual culture: by the pragmatism of James and Dewey in philosophy; by the stress on liberal arts, intelligence, adjustment, and group learning in education; by the functional view of law in jurisprudence; by the social gospel in Protestantism; by Veblen's institutional view in economics; and by populism and progressivism in politics. The latent function of this mighty and creative interest in problem solving and reform through an informed, involved public was to help make American society work without questioning its fundamental structure. The empirical method and practice that accompanied this movement also tended to focus attention on limited aspects of society, to ask types of questions that lent themselves to available research techniques and data, to turn moral-political issues into technical-administrative questions, and to divert attention from alternative models of society.

The development of American sociology reflects the changing structure of the American economy and society from the Civil War on, in essence a transformation from a rural, small-town, small-scale economy and society to an urban-industrial-corporate, large-scale economy and society. During this period the ethnic and racial composition of the American population was altered through immigration and the displacement of millions of blacks from the Southern countryside into Northern and Western urban centers. Despite opposition from a property-oriented Supreme Court, a more explicitly directive central government emerged, made necessary by an increasingly centralized economy producing a wide array of national problems and conflicts. Further, America's emergence as an economic power was reflected in an extensive involvement of American economic groups, and thus the national government, with foreign nations and areas.

Many early sociologists had rural, small-town, religious backgrounds and tended to champion small-town, Protestant, early-liberal values and beliefs. This strand of sociology remained influential until World War II, long after the advent of an urban-industrial-corporate society. (Much of the influence of these sociologists came from the textbooks they wrote.)[6] However, as America changed after World War I, so did its sociology. Carey has identified and compared four sets of sociologists: the *founders* of sociology, members of the American Sociological Association between 1906 and 1918; *second-generation* sociology, roughly between World War I and the Great Depression; the *Chicago School,* a part of the second generation; and the *social pathologists,* a small part of the first two generations, so labeled by C. Wright Mills. Second-generation sociologists, especially their cutting edge, the Chicago School,

> . . . were less likely to have come from New England and more
> likely to have been born in cities and descended from more recent
> migrants. Their fathers were members of newly emerging profes-
> sions rather than clergymen. The limited data presented here
> suggest that they were more likely to be from new, aspiring
> groups, marginal ones, not the sons and daughters of the upper
> class. Finally, they were less religious than the larger sample and
> further to the left politically, and they had a higher proportion of
> women in their ranks than was common in the 1920s.[7]

Of considerable importance for the entire tone of twentieth-century American sociology was the incorporation of the Chicago School into the newly emerging late-liberal reform movement, itself a reflection of centralizing movements in the economy, government, education, and the academic world. The Chicago School displayed all the basic themes of the late-liberal reform mentality: emphasis on scientific research, especially on concrete problems; the use of Darwinian concepts to understand and explain social problems (the ecological-urban approach); and a theoretical stance that saw problems as by-products of a transitional age. In politics the Chicago School adopted the main themes of the new urban reformers: a strong executive, nonpartisanship, and the separation of administration and politics, with an emphasis on efficient, honest government. Hand in hand with the

---

[6] C. Wright Mills, "The Professional Ideology of Social Pathologists," *American Journal of Sociology* 49 (September 1943): 165–180.
[7] James T. Carey, *Sociology and Public Affairs: The Chicago School* (Beverly Hills, Cal.: Sage, 1975), p. 49f.

strong commitment to a scientific sociology, the strong antipolitical orientation (separation of facts and values) of the Chicago School and of sociologists in general was a definite political stance whether understood or not.
Also worthy of note was the growing reliance of the Chicago School—and of
sociology in general—on sponsorship by impersonal corporate bodies. Increasingly the offspring of members of the new bureaucratic professions,
their own professional lives anchored in bureaucratized educational settings
and with ties to other corporate bodies, sociologists were deeply implicated
in the maturing liberal social system.[8]

In this development sociology, along with other disciplines, tended to associate the interests, values, and capabilities of middle- and upper-class individuals and groups with the universal needs and attributes of society.[9]
Also contributing to this point of view was the pervasive morality of
progress that had emerged during the eighteenth century as the liberal
"solution" to the liberal dilemma. The net result of the reformist, gradualist
approach to the problems of an urban-industrial society was to hide society
from view, especially through its pervasive assumption that the errors and
evils of capitalism were transitional in nature and that their disappearance
could be speeded by research. In addition to all these developments was an
extensive acceptance of the functionality of error and evil, and a growing
professionalization in sociology and its establishment as an academically
oriented discipline. The idea of progress supplied a legitimate way for
liberal society to postpone the main issues of industrialization, especially the
question of whether an industrial society is really possible, and if so, how.
Finally, the idea of progress to a large extent allowed liberal society to
institutionalize an indefinite postponement not merely of life, but of a
rationally examined life.

That sociological theory developed as the scientific wing of liberal social
thought cannot be doubted. From its inception, and despite its contrasting
phases of development, sociological theory has maintained and furthered
the main intellectual and moral elements that make up liberal society: individualism, secularism, science, naturalism, the belief in the lawfulness, goodness, and utility of the passions, private property, the exchange economy—

---

[8] For a careful analysis of the development of sociology during the early decades
of pre-World War II America, see James T. Carey, *Sociology and Public Affairs:
The Chicago School* (Beverly Hills, Cal.: Sage, 1975), especially chaps. 2 and 5.
For the late-liberal sociology of Albion Small, the managerial genius who started
and established the Chicago School, see Vernon K. Dibble, *The Legacy of
Albion Small* (Chicago: University of Chicago Press, 1975).
[9] A striking example, made more interesting because of the use of quantitative-
empirical research methods, is the strong bias in family research that equated the
middle-class family with normality; in this regard see Veronica Stolte Heiskanen,
"The Myth of the Middle-Class Family in American Family Sociology," *American
Sociologist* 6 (February 1971): 14–18.

and the belief that a society composed of these elements is the terminal of social evolution. During the formative period of sociology, its main ideological, intellectual, and moral function was to further the revolutionary rise of the middle class by undermining feudal ideas and values, and by installing and legitimatizing the ideals and interests of the bourgeoisie. In its later and present period, sociology has became increasingly concerned with the internal problems of a maturing capitalist society. As a consequence, it has contributed greatly to the development of the late-liberal mentality, a mentality that has come to see the roots of behavior in social existence. In the process of contributing to the understanding and control of a mature capitalist society, sociology turned its critical weapons against the new enemy, socialism. Significantly, an explicit critique of socialism is one of the key similarities to be found in the thought of Comte, Spencer, Sumner, Durkheim, Simmel, Pareto, Weber, Cooley, and Parsons, and many other sociologists.

Sociology as History: The Rationality of Eternal Youth

In developing this historical perspective on sociological theory, I have made every effort to avoid the fallacy that depreciates something by pointing to its humble origins, or that unthinkingly equates the nature of something with its history. I have also tried to avoid debunking sociology through the use of philosophical or moral categories. The main thesis of this study, that sociology, whatever else it is, is intimately connected with the rise, development, and nature of liberal society, has been argued in terms of the methods and standards of sociology itself. Looking back, the reader will see that the main assumptions informing this study were derived from the contemporary phase of sociological theory, pluralistic sociocultural positivism. My use of the term *history* corresponds closely to the main orientation in this tradition, namely, the belief that human behavior is an emanation of social structure (interaction) and culture—that is, the reality created by human activities guided and energized by previous activities. I have assumed that sociological theorizing is simply another form of human behavior and as such is subject to analysis in the same way and by the same methods as any other type of behavior. Along with careful textual analyses of individual theorists, I have provided a broad categorization of the sociocultural conditions associated with the rise and development of sociological theory. I emphasized the continuity between the ancient, medieval, and modern periods, placing special stress on the enormous influence of the Greek metaphysical tradition and the Judaic-Christian moral and religious tradition on the rise of modern natural and social science. I also stressed the consequences of the various stages of technology on social relationships being careful throughout to stress the reciprocal and multiple influences of ideas, values, technologies, and economic, political, and social relationships. Throughout, I have identified sociological theory as the thoughtway expressing the intellectual and moral needs of first a nascent and then a triumphant capitalism. I also stressed that important national variations in the development of liberal society were matched by variations in the development of sociology.

While I have tried to present faithful pictures of each of the main types of sociological theory, I have also made it clear that I regard Max Weber's theory as the most adequate explanation of the scientific problem presented by the diversity and temporality of human behavior. Following Weber, I stressed that there is no way to relate biology or psychology (that is, human nature) to human behavior. Indeed, it would seem, to paraphrase Durkheim, that human nature exists only in the sense that it makes behavior possible. This is not to suggest that society exists in any universal or metaphysical sense. This study assumes that metaphysical craving stems from anxieties induced by historical scarcity. That is, metaphysics is the way in which dominant groups allege necessity in human affairs, turn historical problems into logical questions, and deflect attention from social power and alternative ways of doing things. This is true of agrarian metaphysics (the deductive tradition) and of industrial metaphysics (the inductive tradition)—the empirical tradition in sociology should be thought of as John Dewey thought of British empiricism, as a "disguised *apriorism.*"

Finally I stressed Weber's point that the social sciences have eternal youth, that is, they can achieve knowledge only in terms of the assumptions and problems of their day. The only choice open to social scientists is between being historical consciously (or problem-oriented) and being unconsciously historical (ideological). Ironically, the destruction of reason as substance, which is implicit in Weber's view, is probably the best way, if one is consciously historical, to achieve the autonomy and power of the human mind that is central to Western idealism.

Sociology as Science: The Rationality of Age and Consensus

Whatever criticisms can be made of sociology's claims as a science, it would be less than fair not to note its gains toward achieving its cherished goal of a science of human behavior.[10] Indeed, it has been the critical awareness of the failures and exaggerations marking the history of sociology that has made sociologists more sober and self-conscious about the nature of their discipline. Above all, they have enlarged their time perspective and have come to see themselves as part of a vast, even worldwide, cross-disciplinary

---

[10] I am indebted for some of the ideas and classifications in this section to the excellent review of methodology by John C. McKinney, "Methodology, Procedures, and Techniques," in Howard Becker and Alvin Boskoff, eds., *Modern Sociological Theory* (New York: Holt, Rinehart, and Winston, 1957), pp. 186–235.

division of scientific labor.[11] In at least a partial sense, they have come to view not only human behavior as social, but sociology itself as a social phenomenon requiring cooperative effort, institutional and financial support, professional ethics and organization, and a congenial intellectual and political climate. Despite their recognition of the social context and nature of sociology, however, sociologists have not given up the transhistorical goal of a science of human behavior. They have simply altered their strategy and postponed the search for substantive principles until they can acquire a valid set of methodological principles and a large enough body of validated knowledge. It is only in a limited sense, therefore, that one can speak of the historical awareness of contemporary sociology. A feeling has developed both that social science has had a cumulative development, rather than a miraculous breakthrough, and that it must now settle down to a long-term process of research and analysis.[12]

The record since the last decades of the nineteenth century reveals an impressive achievement in methodology that includes a broad agreement on many methodological principles. Perhaps sociology's most important methodological achievement has been its success in applying mathematics to social phenomena. Sociology has helped, at least in a partial sense, to substantiate in the realm of social phenomena the Western belief in a correspondence between the logical structures of the human mind and the phenomenal structures of physical and human nature. Overshadowed during the seventeenth century by the revolutionary but abortive attempt to analyze human nature in terms of geometry, the mathematics of statistics, as developed by Pascal and Fermat and first applied to social phenomena by Petty

---

[11] The first formal international organization in sociology, the International Institute of Sociology, was established in 1893 and predates most national associations. A rival, more empirically oriented organization, the International Sociological Association, was created after World War II under UNESCO auspices. For background and an inquiry into the functions of international associations, see Paul F. Lazarsfeld and Ruth Leeds, "International Sociology as a Sociological Problem, "*American Sociological Review* 27 (October 1962): 732–741.

For a sense of how "sociology" has developed in the major regions of the world and in many specific types of countries (First, Second, and Third Worlds), see Jerzy J. Wiatr, ed., *The State of Sociology in Eastern Europe Today* (Carbondale, Ill.: Southern Illinois University Press, 1971); and Raj P. Monan and Don Martindale, eds., *Handbook of Contemporary Developments in World Sociology* (Westport, Conn.: Greenwood Press, 1975). In surveying international developments one should keep firmly in mind not only the possibility of an objective, transnational sociology, but the fact that empirical research is compatible with, indeed a vital need of, all developed and developing countries regardless of their system of social power.

[12] This is as true of statistical neopositivists (naturalistic positivists) like George A. Lundberg and Paul F. Lazarsfeld (1901–1976) as it is of a grand theorist like Talcott Parsons who espouses the methodological validity of abstract thought in general. (For a brief discussion of neopositive theories, see below.) Two major figures who reject the cumulative perspective but for very different reasons are Pitirim Sorokin and C. Wright Mills (for a further reference to Mills as a member of an antiestablishment branch of sociology, see below).

and Graunt, has developed into the major logical tool of modern social-science research. The heroic age of quantitative social science occurred in the nineteenth and early twentieth century. The mathematical work of this period, which includes the work of Laplace, Quetelet, LePlay, Booth, Galton, Pearson, Hobhouse, and Giddings, marks the acceptance and consolidation of quantitative methods in sociology. As an outgrowth of this creative period in quantitative sociology, there has been a steady increase in the development of mathematical logic and its application to social phenomena in conjunction with and in response to felt research needs. In the twentieth century, a number of important research projects have been undertaken and expressed in terms of statistical methods, especially in the United States.[13]

Along with the striking success and refinement of the statistical method, there have been important refinements in experimental, typological, historical, and case methods. Of the greatest importance, however, is that these various approaches to social phenomena are no longer viewed as intellectual enemies but as supplements forming a many-pronged tool with which to unravel the complexity of the empirical world. A pragmatic formalism, or a readiness to use any method that yields knowledge, has emerged from this general perspective. There is the growing realization that there is no necessary logical or methodological antagonism between quantitative and qualitative approaches to social phenomena. Thanks to the insistence of such theorists as Znaniecki, Sorokin, Becker, MacIver, Parsons, and Mills, all of whom have argued the methodological merits of nonmathematical abstract thought, sociologists have come to see a logical continuum between quantitative and qualitative methods rather than dichotomy or incompatibility. As a result, there is a general agreement that a plurality of approaches is needed if the variegated realm of social phenomena is to be reduced to law. Out of the various schools that have competed for supremacy, ranging from neopositivism to the philosophical-moral-historical schools, has come a general recognition that the mind is no passive instrument simply recording the outer world, but an active energy that perceives the world in terms of "ideas." [14] Thus sociology has remained true to the traditional epistemology

---

[13] While the United States contributed little to the pioneering stage of developing and applying mathematics to social phenomena, its enthusiastic adoption and refinement of the quantitative approach is well known. Perhaps the first major figure in American sociology to advocate a quantitative sociology was Franklin H. Giddings (1855–1931) whose first work in this regard, *Inductive Sociology*, was published in 1901.

[14] It is interesting to note that there is some similarity in this regard between the so-called soft scientists stemming from Kantianism (for example, Georg Simmel and Max Weber), functional theorists (Robert K. Merton, Talcott Parsons), the neopositivists (George Lundberg), phenomenological sociologists (Alfred Schutz), and ethnomethodologists (Aaron Cicourel). All are aware of the way in which assumptions or language control the observation of, if not actually create, the world of fact.

of Western idealism, especially the variant formulated by the Age of Enlightenment.

Despite this broad agreement, there is still considerable disagreement and misunderstanding in contemporary sociology. The characterization of types of theory with outmoded stereotypes is partly to blame. Disagreement is also due partly to the way in which diversity in a small number of elements in a methodology can render a theory quite different from another theory that shares all the other elements. It also stems from the lack of institutionalized exchange and cross-examination within the discipline.[15] Finally, there is, of course, genuine disagreement on the philosophical level. To point to these disagreements is not to suggest that agreement is either possible or desirable. One of the chief functions of a history of sociological theory is to alert readers to the ease with which intellectual fads, schools, or styles of thought come into prominence and to stimulate a measure of critical detachment from (as well as appreciation of) the full range of claims that have been made for current theories. It would probably be helpful, however, if one could itemize and classify the constituent elements in theories so that incidental misunderstandings and disagreements could be separated from fundamental divergencies.[16]

No discussion of the problem of validity through age and consensus should end without expressing some reservations about the trend toward mathematical sociology that has made such headway in twentieth-century American sociology. It is not surprising, as we have already indicated, to learn that the United States is the classic land of quantitative sociology. The American belief and value system accords easily with an ahistorical, mathematical social science. Given the belief that the United States is a revealed society that has removed the artificial distinctions of birth and custom and

[15] A relatively recent and useful development are routine exchanges between authors and critics in journals, as well as the practice of book-review articles and symposiums. An example of an extremely useful type of publication, which has also been missing from most of the history of sociological theory, is *The Social Theories of Talcott Parsons*, ed. Max Black (Englewood Cliffs, N.J.: Prentice-Hall, 1961). This type of book, written while a sociologist is alive, allows a number of scholars to examine a theorist's work and permits the theorist to reply to criticisms, all within the conventions of scholarship.

[16] For example, Howard Becker (b. 1899) and C. Wright Mills share a common distaste for mathematical sociology and agree on the need for a wide measure of qualitative thinking in sociology—yet despite this agreement, a difficult-to-define difference exists between them, one based perhaps on a disagreement about the possibility of truth or perhaps on a difference in moral temperament. Both theorists, on the other hand, share with both Parsons and Sorokin a distaste for empirical mathematical sociology, and yet the differences become even more pronounced among the four. Other examples of similarity and yet wide divergence of approach can be cited: Vico and Lundberg both emphasize the importance of linguistic forms in social science and tend to see human beings as doers rather than thinkers, and yet are worlds apart in their basic orientaton—as are Condorcet and Lazarsfeld, both of whom have advocated the application of mathematics to the analysis of human behavior.

based itself on the natural individual, it is no wonder that American social scientists take it as axiomatic that they are studying something pristine and not merely historical. However, the same nagging question remains: While it is true that widespread statistical uniformities exist in human behavior, are these natural in any sense, whether biological, psychological, psychosocial, or sociocultural; or are they historical uniformities, behavior temporarily structured by unique conditions (social power) and thus unrelatable to human nature, other times, or other places? To try to establish uniformities as either emanations of human nature or as the final stage of human development is, of course, a legitimate task for social science. However, to do so without acknowledging or removing the scientific obstacles that stand in the way is to engage in ideology. One must agree with C. Wright Mills that much of American sociology is, wittingly or unwittingly, ideological, that it accepts the basic structure of capitalist society even as it criticizes or proposes reforms. With few exceptions, its concept of power is liberal—it ignores power, thinks of it as a self-negating pluralistic structure, or conceptualizes it in terms of the natural individual, on the one hand, and the power of the group, on the other, and studies the reciprocal, multicausal relation between them. One should be aware, of course, that the multicausal approach is not just more up-to-date than metaphysical monistic approaches; in social science the empirical mentality can easily be a defense of the given, a way in which the prestige of science is used to give ontological status to historical variables. The extent and significance of a plurality of groups must be carefully related to social differentiation and power and not assumed to be a natural system. In other words, the relevance of a multiplicity of groups for democracy and for the responsible exercise of power cannot be taken for granted.[17]

The multicausal, empirical approach to behavior, therefore, is not necessarily an objective intellectual process—it is an important device of a diversified and conflict-prone power structure, and as such may contain deep biases in favor of the status quo. The very act of scientific selection, definition, and analysis is political and moral in nature, not only because scientific action requires a rich legacy of sociocultural achievement, but because the scientist exercises choice, whether consciously or unconsciously. Thus, American sociologists are deeply biased in favor of the values and the ideas of individualism, liberty, equality, science, technological growth, civil rights, and, with some qualifications, in favor of private property, the idea of progress, the private corporation, and the market economy. To assume that vast and important amounts of social phenomena are somehow self-evidently natural is to add the power of sociology to the power of society and give a particular world view an unfair advantage over its rivals. All this goes quite beyond the naive, naturalistic empiricism that takes the world as given, the

[17] C. Wright Mills is one of the few sociologists to raise this issue.

culturally conditioned mind that busily tries to peel away the epiphenomena of culture in search of the natural human being but succeeds only in finding the attributes it has placed there itself. Such naiveté has been successfully attacked by all of America's major theorists. The issue raised here involves the degree of self-consciousness of American sociology, its ability to distinguish between the certainty of persuasion and conviction and the certainty of scientific validity. This distinction is difficult to establish not simply because of the influence of Cartesian philosophy on the modern temper. It is well known that an exquisite sense of certainty can develop as easily about the validity of such things as slavery, witch burning, head hunting, the truth of the Decalogue, and the rightness of private property as it can about the boiling point of water, the existence of germs, or the orbit of the earth.

The inevitable political nature of sociology, which will be examined again below, can be seen in a different light. If one remembers that all societies have significant illegitimate elements, variously called exploitation, privilege, oligarchy, ignorance, superstition, racism, sexism, and so on, then symbolic culture cannot avoid taking sides in the relations between tops and bottoms, oppressors and oppressed, exploiters and victims. To a considerable extent professionalism is a liberal method for easing the conscience of overdogs and perpetuating the myth of a consensus society based on knowledge, justice, and reform. In short, to practice sociology is just as political as voting, lobbying, executing or repressing deviants, writing an editorial, giving a sermon, or attending kindergarten, college, or medical school.

Chapter 24
Contemporary Orientations in Sociology

This concluding chapter classifies contemporary orientations in sociology from a variety of standpoints to gain a sense of their unities and particularities. Like all conceptual schemes, typologies cannot capture phenomena completely or precisely; accordingly, my approach is instrumental and tentative.

THREE TYPOLOGIES IN SEARCH OF REALITY

Sociological theories can be classified in numerous ways.[1] My analysis of contemporary orientations in sociology will utilize three typologies or criteria, each illuminating an important pattern in the hurly-burly of current sociological theory. The first scheme arranges theories according to their scientific orientation. The second analyzes specific positions within one of these orientations, the now dominant empirical or pluralistic approach. Finally, the third classification analyzes theories according to political-moral criteria. In typing orientations, it should be understood that a theory may be other than what a theorist thinks it is, and that parts of it may fall into different categories. Readers will also notice that the logics underlying these various typologies were used in my analysis of the history and nature of sociological theory, and as such, helped create my findings.

VARIETIES OF SCIENTIFIC ORIENTATION

Three basic scientific positions can be identified in sociology: monistic, pluralistic, and historical.

---

[1] For a useful review of existing typologies and a valuable one of his own, see Helmut R. Wagner, "Types of Sociological Theory," *American Sociological Review* 28 (October 1963): 735–742.

Monistic Sociology

Monistic positivists rely on a single method (mostly deduction even when they claim to be inductive) to unite all orders of phenomena from inanimate to animate, from the natural to the moral. In this latter respect, one must distinguish between two tendencies within sociological monism. The first, exemplified by Condorcet and Comte, views human behavior as an order of phenomena separate from the rest of nature, in which mind is the basic evolving reality. The second tendency, seen in the work of Saint-Simon and Spencer, unites social and natural phenomena into one objective structure and process subject to the same laws. In both subpositions, however, sociological theory is modeled on the alleged methods of natural science.

Pluralistic Sociology

A second basic position in sociology is pluralistic positivism, a more empirically oriented approach that accepts a variety of methods with which to establish knowledge. Pluralist sociology also has divisions based on differences in the definition of subject matter. The modal view defines human behavior as different from natural behavior primarily because of its subjective component. Despite this difference, the modal tradition hews as close to natural science as possible and is oriented toward a unified theory of the distinctive human world, and perhaps of the human and natural worlds at some future date. The ultimate goals of science in both monistic and pluralistic sociologies, however, are identical—the theoretical unification of phenomena, control through prediction, and presumably a scientifically based guide to the moral life.[2]

Historical Sociology

The third basic position in sociology claims that neither science nor any other mode of thought can produce truth or virtue. The human condition is essentially moral and political—that is, historical. This position should not be confused with grand unitary theories of historical development, for example, those of Karl Marx, Oswald Spengler (1880–1936),[3] or Arnold Toynbee (1889–1975).[4] The historical view is exemplified in the work of Montesquieu and Max Weber. Science, according to this view, cannot unify the particularities of time and place. Human beings and sociologists are essentially moral creatures, decision makers in a world of scarcity and uncertain alternatives. The main function of science is to assist the human actor in making value decisions and in devising means to realize values

---

[2] Variations in pluralistic sociology will be analyzed and classified in more detail shortly.

[3] *The Decline of the West*, 2 vols., trans. Charles F. Atkinson (New York: Alfred A. Knopf, 1926–1928).

[4] *A Study of History*, 12 vols. (London: Oxford University Press, 1935–1961).

with the clear understanding that values are neither derived from nor validated by science.

VARIETIES OF PLURALISTIC SOCIOLOGY

I have identified the pluralistic approach as modal in contemporary sociology and have sought to identify points of view within it. The dominant pluralistic positivist tradition uses a wide assortment of empirical methods ranging from mathematics to participant observation and from rigorously detailed paradigms to ad hoc interpretation to get at a wide range of subject matter defined (by the vast majority, for the time being at least) as uniquely human.

Symbolic Interaction-Exchange Theories

The largest segment of pluralist sociology is probably made up of sociologists who focus on the interaction between the biopsychic organism and the social environment—other biopsychic organisms, groups, situations, statuses and roles, socially defined relationships, culture. Broadly speaking, this tradition assumes that subjectivity is a knowable phenomenon, though most of it avoids the *verstehen* tradition—that is, it does not stress or use subjectivity as a method. While sharing a broad kinship with the German tradition of subjective idealism (Kant, Dilthey, Rickert, Windelband, and Husserl in philosophy; Simmel and Max Weber in sociology), this aspect of contemporary American sociology is similar to the symbolic interaction orientation found in W. I. Thomas.

In addition to Thomas (and Cooley), the symbolic interaction tradition has been developed by Robert M. MacIver (1882–1970)[5] and Herbert Blumer (b. 1900)[6] and is widely accepted largely because it accords well with American-style liberalism. An important offshoot of this tradition is exchange theory, which ranges from the psychologically oriented theory of George Homans (b. 1910)[7] to the more sociocultural theory of Peter M. Blau (b. 1918).[8] All in all, the American subjective interactionist-exchange tradition, especially its commitment to an "individual in relation to society" model of analysis, enjoys widespread support both in the work of theorists and in textbooks.[9]

[5] See his *Social Causation* (New York: Ginn, 1942; slightly rev. ed. in paperback, 1964), especially chaps. 10–13.
[6] *Symbolic Interactionism; Perspectives and Methods* (Englewood Cliffs, N.J.: Prentice-Hall, 1969).
[7] *The Human Group* (New York: Harcourt Brace Jovanovich, 1950); *Social Behavior: Its Elementary Forms* (New York: Harcourt Brace Jovanovich, 1961); *The Nature of Social Science* (New York: Harcourt Brace Jovanovich, 1967).
[8] *Exchange and Power in Social Life* (New York: John Wiley, 1964).
[9] For a comparison of the British "individualistic orientation," exemplified in exchange theory by George Homans, with Lévi-Strauss's French "collectivist orientation," see Peter P. Ekeh, *Social Exchange Theory: The Two Traditions* (Cambridge, Mass.: Harvard University Press, 1974).

Functionalist Theories

All theories that inquire into how things work are functional or scientifically oriented theories. Functionalist theories as such are broadly similar, therefore, to the symbolic interactionist-exchange theories I have just reviewed. Besides a common commitment to science, the main similarity is a focus on social action, or the view that sees behavior as a world of meaning (subjectivity) as well as a world of overt movements. Functionalists are somewhat different from symbolic interactionists and exchange theorists, however, in that they tend to focus more on sociocultural variables and on the operation of overall social systems, avoiding biopsychological variables as much as possible. The functionalists trace their ancestry to the major scientific transformation of the nineteenth century, the transformation of reason into method (or structure into function), as expressed in sociology in the work of Durkheim, Simmel, Pareto, Weber, and others.[10]

In addition to Talcott Parsons, the major figures in this tradition in the United States are Robert K. Merton (b. 1910), Kingsley Davis (b. 1908), Robin M. Williams (b. 1914), Lewis Coser (b. 1913), and Marion Levy, Jr. (b. 1918).[11] The British sociologist John Rex,[12] who is difficult to classify (that is, eminently sensible and politically-morally concerned), is represented both here and in the political-moral typology (see footnote 46). Ralf Dahrendorf (b. 1929)[13] is a notable German representative of this general orientation.

An extended discussion of functionalism is not necessary since I have devoted considerable attention to its ancestry and to its major contemporary exponent, Talcott Parsons. While some critics have argued that functionalism is biased in favor of social integration and has a static orientation, some of

---

[10] Other influences are the classical economists, utilitarianism, Karl Marx, and the social anthropologists, most notably Bronislaw Malinowski, *A Scientific Theory of Culture* (Chapel Hill, N.C.: University of North Carolina Press, 1944) and *Magic, Science, and Religion and Other Essays* (New York: Free Press, 1948); S. F. Nadel, *Foundations of Social Anthropology* (New York: Free Press, 1951); and A. R. Radcliffe-Brown, *Structure and Function in Primitive Society* (New York: Free Press, 1952).

[11] Robert K. Merton, *Social Theory and Social Structure*, enl. ed. (New York: Free Press, 1968); Kingsley Davis, *Human Society* (New York: Macmillan, 1948) and "The Myth of Functional Analysis as a Special Method in Sociology and Anthropology," *American Sociological Review* 25 (December 1959): 757–772; Robin M. Williams, *American Society: A Sociological Interpretation*, 3rd ed. (New York: Alfred A. Knopf, 1970); Lewis Coser, *The Functions of Social Conflict* (New York: Free Press, 1954) and *Continuities in the Study of Social Conflict* (New York: Free Press, 1967); and Marion Levy, Jr., *The Structure of Society* (Princeton, N.J.: Princeton University Press, 1952).

[12] *Discovering Sociology: Studies in Sociological Theory and Method* (Boston: Routledge and Kegan Paul, 1973).

[13] *Class and Class Conflict in Industrial Society* (Stanford, Cal.: Stanford University Press, 1957) and *Essays in the Theory of Society* (Stanford, Cal.: Stanford University Press, 1968).

the more notable work within the functional orientation has stressed the role of conflict in making society work.[14] (It is clear that Parsons is not a "static" theorist with a lopsided emphasis on consensus.)

Phenomenological-Ethnomethodological Sociologies

Phenomenological sociology and a related subtype called *ethnomethodological sociology* are distinct forms of pluralist theory. This general orientation has some elements that readers will recognize, but because I have not explicitly discussed a representative theorist from this orientation I shall outline it somewhat more fully than the symbolic interaction-exchange and functionalist theories. The phenomenological and ethnomethodological sociologies are diverse and only parts of them belong in the empirical scientific tradition. The most noticeable feature of this group of theorists is its self-conscious opposition to mainstream sociology on philosophical grounds. Though the philosophical basis of this movement is diverse, it draws its inspiration largely from German idealism (mostly Kant, but Hegel too) and tends to be based on the traditional German insistence that there is a real and unbridgeable distinction between the moral and natural sciences. Philosophers who have influenced phenomenological and ethnomethodological sociologies include such figures as Soren Kierkegaard (1813–1855), Martin Heidegger (1889–1976), Karl Jaspers (1883–1969), Edmund Husserl (1859–1938), Alfred Schutz (1899–1959), Jean-Paul Sartre (b. 1905), and Maurice Merleau-Ponty (1908–1961).[15]

In its study of human behavior phenomenology stresses subjectivity both as a method and as a subject matter. In a broad way, therefore, phenomenological sociology is related to the sociological tradition that assumes that subjectivity can be rendered scientific as a subject matter (Vico, Durkheim,

---

[14] The main conflict functionalists, Coser, Dahrendorf, and Gouldner, have drawn on Simmel's and Marx's ideas on conflict (and the perspective that views society as a dialectical process) to augment the functional outlook. Merton's focus on dysfunction, alternate institutions, anomie, and ambivalence have also played an important role in steering sociology away from teleology, ideology, and naive consensus functionalism. Another notable contribution to conflict functionalism within the tradition of evolutionary liberalism is Gerhard Lenski, *Power and Privilege: A Theory of Social Stratification* (New York: McGraw-Hill, 1966).

[15] Of these, Alfred Schutz and Maurice Merleau-Ponty have exerted direct influence on sociology by spelling out the implications of their philosophy for social science. For good introductions to their work, see Alfred Schutz, *The Phenomenology of the Social World,* trans. George Walsh and Frederick Lehnert (Chicago: Northwestern University Press, 1967) and Alden L. Fisher, ed., *The Essential Writings of Merleau-Ponty* (New York: Harcourt Brace Jovanovich paperback, 1969). For a general analysis of existentialism and a comparison with Durkheim, see Edward A. Tiryakian, *Sociologism and Existentialism* (Englewood Cliffs, N.J.: Prentice Hall paperback, 1962). For some useful philosophical materials in this area, see the two collections edited by Maurice Natanson, *Philosophy of the Social Sciences* (New York: Random House, 1963) and *Phenomenology and Social Reality* (The Hague: Martinus Nijhoff, 1970) as well as Dorothy Emmet and Alasdair MacIntyre, eds., *Sociological Theory and Philosophical Analysis*

Pareto, Weber, Cooley, Thomas, Sorokin, Parsons) and can be used as a method (Vico, Weber, Cooley). This tradition, however, has a strong scientific and sociocultural orientation, while phenomenological sociology tends to have a philosophical and biopsychological orientation. In this sense, it shares much of the outlook of biopsychic naturalistic positivism. It tends to locate the energy or impulse of behavior inside individuals, and it stresses voluntarism as a distinctive aspect of human nature—derived both from the German tradition of idealism, which separates human nature and culture from nature; and from the biopsychic tradition that sees the cause of behavior in the inner, natural promptings of human beings. Seen from this perspective, the individual is the basic reality; society is secondary, an epiphenomenon, in the last analysis simply other individuals. More specifically, phenomenological sociology eschews the role of detached observer and seeks to analyze behavior from the standpoint of the actor. Its philosophical basis in phenomenology and existentialism stresses the reality of immediate experience and calls for a depiction and analysis of subjective states. Thus it tends to deny the validity of any spectator theory of knowledge in which an observer tries to conceptualize an external world. Individuals are seen as coping with a complex, threatening and ambiguous world, as egos busily trying to create a world of meaning, as harassed actors trying to repair the world's damage to their self-esteem. In this sense phenomenological sociology stresses the "definition of the situation" approach found in W. I. Thomas and the symbolic interactionist paradigm that is such a distinctive feature of American sociology.

Another central theme in phenomenological sociology is the essential ambiguity of the world. Lay individuals are seen as coping with a problematic world while the trained intellect is asked to reflect on the nature of immediate perception and to trace the relationships established by intuition and consciousness. This stress on meaninglessness is reminiscent of Max Weber (who exerted a heavy influence on Alfred Schutz), but whereas Weber derived his position from science, much of phenomenological sociology seeks to absorb science into a subjectivist social philosophy.

Another theme in phenomenological sociology is a concern with ordinary, everyday life. Of course, Western intellectual-moral culture has always been concerned with everyday life. Some intellectuals have sought to transcend it through thought, others through piety, and still others through refinement and privilege. A concern with understanding and mastering everyday existence (rather than transcending it) is implicit in the general current of

---

(New York: Macmillan, 1970), also in paperback. For the basic features of phenomenological sociology as seen through the eyes of a variety of English and American practitioners, see Paul Filmer et al., *New Directions in Sociological Theory* (London: Collier-Macmillan, 1972) and George Psathas, ed., *Phenomenological Sociology: Issues and Applications* (New York: John Wiley, 1973).

empiricism from the eighteenth century on. In sociology proper, a focus on everyday existence is found in LePlay, Spencer, Mayhew, and Booth, and, of course, in Simmel, Cooley, and Thomas. Certainly the social-problems approach in general and the social-problems-ecological approach of the Chicago School were deeply involved with everyday life. Phenomenological sociology is similar to the foregoing traditions, but in addition it stresses the need to empathize with the subjects under scrutiny, a process that allegedly humanizes both the studier and those studied.

Perhaps the major assumption behind phenomenological sociology is that human beings, not society or sociologists, construct the actions that make up society; behavior and whatever behavioral laws exist have their source in the subjective imperatives and creations of the human psyche.[16] The focus on how individuals construct their social life in everyday encounters (a theme exemplified best in Erving Goffman's work) is especially pronounced in ethnomethodology.[17]

Instead of assuming, as many social scientists do, that there is an external social and cultural world, ethnomethodologists argue that society is simply the methods actors use in their ceaseless reformulation of conventional norms and values and in their endless negotiations about the meanings and outcomes of their various activities. Ethnomethodology is the study of the deeper, hidden world of these methods—literally, a study of the methods used by people to create order and meaning out of their everyday behavior.

Ethnomethodologists correctly point to the dangers of reification (regarding society as a thing) and stress the need to focus on actors actually engaged

---

[16] Perhaps the most widely known figure in this form of sociology is Erving Goffman, whose basic writings are: *The Presentation of Self in Everyday Life* (Garden City, N.Y.: Doubleday paperback, 1959); *Asylums* (Garden City, N.Y.: Doubleday paperback, 1961); *Encounters* (Indianapolis: Bobbs-Merrill paperback, 1961); *Behavior in Public Places* (New York: Free Press, 1963, also in paperback); *Stigma: Notes on the Management of a Spoiled Identity* (Englewood Cliffs, N.J.: Prentice-Hall paperback, 1963); and *Frame Analysis: An Essay on the Organization of Experience* (New York: Harper & Row, 1974, also in paperback). Other figures include Peter L. Berger, *An Invitation to Sociology* (Garden City, N.Y.: Doubleday paperback, 1963); Peter L. Berger and Thomas Luckmann, *The Social Construction of Reality* (Garden City, N.Y.: Doubleday, 1966, also in paperback); Burkart Holzner, *Reality Construction in Society* (Cambridge, Mass.: Schenkman, 1968, rev. ed., paperback, 1971); Stanford M. Lyman and Marvin B. Scott, *A Sociology of the Absurd* (New York: Appleton-Century-Crofts, 1970, also in paperback); Jack D. Douglas, *American Social Order: Social Rules in a Pluralistic Society* (New York: Free Press paperback, 1971).

[17] Some of the main figures in this sociology are Harold Garfinkel, *Studies in Ethnomethodology* (Englewood Cliffs, N.J.: Prentice-Hall, 1967); Aaron V. Cicourel, *Method and Measurement in Sociology* (New York: Free Press, 1964) and *Cognitive Sociology: Language and Meaning in Social Interaction* (New York: Free Press, 1974); and Hugh Mehan and Houston Wood, *The Reality of Ethnomethodology* (New York: John Wiley, 1975).

in behavior. Only by observing real individuals in action can the hidden assumptions that underlie, facilitate, and constitute successful interaction be seen. Far from following culture patterns like robots, argue ethno-methodologists, people adjust and trim general norms and values to suit the exigencies of situations, and they are able to explain what they have done only after they have done it. Perhaps above all, ethnomethodologists exhibit a healthy nominalism and skepticism. They stress, not the study of alleged objective social order (or what is said and believed about it), but the *methods* people, including social scientists, use for creating the appearance that beliefs and values are orderly, predictable, responsibility enforcing, and real—that is, that a society exists. Some of these methods have been mentioned: individuals creatively tailor cultural conventions to suit situa-tions, and when their creations are questioned they creatively rationalize in terms of the conventions. Given the ethnomethodological focus on indi-viduals, it is understandable that in searching for the deeper forces, or hidden rules, behind successful interaction, these theorists have tended to stress linguistic analysis.

The elements that make up ethnomethodology are not new—every major strand has a long ancestry in social science. Max Weber, for example, stressed the need for understanding the subjective meanings in human inter-action, while cautioning against the use of biopsychological explanations. The concern with subjectivity actually has a long history and has many variations that anticipate ethnomethodology. Many, including Durkheim, Pareto, Weber, and Sumner, have pointed to the deep nonrational forces in human behavior and to the unconscious understandings that constitute, clog, or lubricate behavior. Many, such as Weber, W. I. Thomas, and Parsons, have focused on processes for translating general cultural prescriptions into concrete behavior.

In blending these and other ingredients, ethnomethodology claims to have a perspective that is totally different from conventional sociologies. It is not, it claims, merely another body of concepts about an alleged external reality, nor is it a better method for studying behavior. What people call scientific sociology, it seems to be saying, is merely the method by which sociologists persuade one another that society exists; ethnomethodology knows better.

Unfortunately, it is not exactly clear what it is that ethnomethodology knows. Often bordering on solipsism—the belief that only the self exists and that the self can know only itself—ethnomethodology nonetheless asserts that a substantive force exists that makes society possible. This force appears to reside in the biopsychic entity called the individual, and access to it appears possible primarily through an analysis of language in action. How-ever, is this a new position, or has an elaborate facade been constructed to create the appearance of something new? Isn't ethnomethodology's image of society, as a collection of insecure, struggling actors who negotiate their existence, modeled on Adam Smith and the concept of a market society? Has ethnomethodology advanced cogent reasons for resurrecting the long-since-discredited biopsychological explanation of behavior? Significantly, ethnomethodology seems to flourish only in the United States and somewhat in England, that is, in societies with a pronounced early liberal flavor. Furthermore, it seems to have taken deepest root in a frontier region, the West Coast of North America, where individualist explanations appear especially plausible. To try to conceive the world as actors see and experience it is certainly a worthwhile, indeed indispensable, part of the sociological task. However, to restrict oneself to this task is to direct sociology only to the shadows on the cave's wall. Perhaps the first things to ask of ethnomethodologists is to say what they mean; to relate what they are doing to the literature and practice of sociology; to give order to their own behavior, which appears technically faulty as science, ad hoc and trivial in its choice of subject matter, and tedious in the telling. It may be that ethnomethodology is more ordinary than it thinks and that like ordinary people it will be able to explain what it has done after it is finished.

Randall Collins has made an ambitious attempt to synthesize ethnomethodology and phenomenology (especially Goffman) and the main traditions of liberal and radical functionalism (Durkheim, Weber, and Marx) in terms of a conflict paradigm.[18] This effort, however, only serves to highlight the early-liberal bias and superfluousness of ethnomethodology. Using the wholesome nominalism of ethnomethodology, Collins argues against reified concepts such as society, group, and institution in favor of the "real world of causal agents," interacting individuals. However, Durkheim, Weber, and Marx made the same point while emphatically warning against biopsychical explanations. Collins fails to relate ethnomethodology to these theorists largely because he cannot escape the assumption that individuals are the cause of their own behavior.

Collins develops an interesting theme in which he interprets society as ritual encounters among individuals maximizing their self-interest. He does this by blending Durkheim's explanation of the generation of social bonds through ritual interaction with Goffman's focus on identity management by selves. However, Collins fails to enter Durkheim's world fully or to give reasons for not doing so. After all, Durkheim's sociocultural outlook explained not only social bonds but the creation of the self as well. The same is true of Collins's ad hoc borrowings from Marx and Weber. Their contributions can be fully appreciated, evaluated, and used only after one

---

[18] Randall Collins, with a contribution by Joan Annett, *Conflict Sociology: Toward an Explanatory Science* (New York: Academic Press, 1975).

recognizes that, like Durkheim, they dispensed with biology and psychology in their analysis of human behavior. Thus, the ideas of these theorists remain undigested and unconnected with Collins's main assumption that individuals (mostly white middle-class males are assumed) come equipped with basic self-enhancing interests and motives—an early-liberal outlook reminiscent of such theorists as Hobbes, Malthus, and Sumner.[19]

Had Collins dispensed with the distorting imagery of society as a collection of individuals, he might have focused more squarely on power relations and not overlooked economic power. (Incidentally, Collins cannot use Weber to argue against Marx's focus on economics since both agreed on the primacy of economic factors in modern society.) Instead, Collins's main theme is that individuals struggle for something vaguely referred to as status or deference.

For some unexplained reason Collins abruptly abandons his healthy ethno-methodological skepticism in his concluding chapter, where he suddenly announces that "it is possible to detach oneself from the social pressures of conventionally organized illusions blocking the way to a social science." It is possible, in other words, to institute a community of scholars who compete only in terms of intellectual resources and norms. In addition, he says, sociology after much ideology and travail has now come of age and is slowly becoming a science—presumably along the lines laid down by Collins. Thus the liberal dilemma is solved by being ignored.

Despite its virtues, especially its Simmel-like empiricism, much of the phenomenological-ethnomethodological perspective is obscure and cultist and tends toward the trivial. It employs many old insights and ideas, often giving the appearance of having just discovered them, and coins neologisms without shame. Its concern with everyday, ordinary life often borders on self-abasement and provides readers with little understanding of or leverage against power structures. Whether its view that the world is meaningless and absurd is an invitation to reorder the world, or a contemporary form of cynicism and world acceptance is not clear. Certainly its interest in the psychological processes of everyman-woman and its tendency to accept them as substantive reality no more understands the reality of power or the sociocultural sources of psychological processes than the similar orientation in, say, Pareto and in the neopositivists, for example Lundberg. Perhaps

---

[19] Collins's outlook is similar to the early-liberal view of human nature found in Gerhard Lenski, *Power and Privilege: A Theory of Social Stratification* (New York: John Wiley, 1966). Collins refers approvingly to Lenski in a number of instances.

the most immediate problem faced by phenomenologists and ethnomethodologists in gaining acceptance is convincing outsiders that it is worth the effort to master their special jargon and their often turgid and precious prose.

Phenomenological-ethnometholodical sociology is similar in some respects to the subjective interactionist-exchange tradition, especially in its psychological, voluntaristic emphases and in its commitment to an "individual in relation to society" model of analysis. It should be noted, however, that the scientific credentials of the phenomenological-ethnomethodological orientation are somewhat in question.[20] Above all, it should be noted that phenomenological-ethnomethodological sociology is even more removed than the remainder of sociology from the central question of social theory: *By what process and for what reasons are human beings assigned to hearth and home, to field, factory, and office, to superordinate and subordinate statuses, and by what process and for what reasons are the benefits of social life distributed?* The answers to this question lie in the analysis of institutions and social power, and much of sociology notwithstanding, have little direct relationship with the nature of human beings.

Neopositive Theories

Another subtype within pluralistic positivism is neopositivism, or radical positivism, a movement that reached its high point during the second quarter of the twentieth century but that seems to have lost impetus. In considerable measure, it has waned because many of its elements have been absorbed by the general current of sociology. While neopositivism is a distinctive theory, it has many roots in past sociology. Like the thought of Saint-Simon, Comte, and others, it equates knowledge and human well-being with science. As in the thought of Hume and Weber, it denies that science can validate values. Like the thought of Sumner, it professes a radical nominalism, rejects recourse to concepts or values in science, and rejects the reality of subjectivity in general. Like the thought of Condorcet, Laplace, Quetelet, LePlay, Hobhouse, and Giddings, neopositivism advocates a quantitative sociology, though in a much more radical sense. It sees the establishment of quantitative laws as the essence of sociology and to this end sees all reality *as that which is measured by scientific measuring devices* (operationalism). Finally like the thought of Saint-Simon, Spencer, and

---

[20] Despite the influence on this movement of logical positivism (for example, Carnap, Wittgenstein, Moore, Russell, Popper). It should be noted that Erving Goffman explicitly separates his work from the "core matters of sociology—social organization and social structure" (*Frame Analysis: An Essay on the Organization of Experience*, p. 13).

others, neopositivism makes every attempt to model social science on natural science. A similar position in philosophy is known as logical positivism.

The heart of the neopositive approach is embodied in the work of George A. Lundberg (1895–1966), who advocated neopositivism in a number of publications,[21] and also in a work by his colleague Stuart C. Dodd (b. 1900).[22] However, neither Lundberg nor other members of this orientation have gone much beyond the stage of advocacy. Nevertheless, much of the neopositive orientation has been absorbed into sociology, especially its stress on mathematics. While not necessarily due to the influence of the neopositivists, the employment of mathematics and the development of mathematical units and procedures with which to analyze social behavior have gained wide acceptance in many subject areas and are now a part of many different orientations.

VARIETIES OF IDEOLOGICAL SOCIOLOGY

The third and perhaps most important classification of sociological theories is based on political and moral criteria. Regardless of their scientific orientation or their definition of subject matter, theories have political and moral consequences.

The Relation Between Social Theory and Politics

Many have noted that there are associations between types of theory (philosophy and method and substantive image of society) and types of politics (how public power should be organized, what values the state should serve, what stance one should take toward the state and society).[23] Too often the

---

[21] *Foundations of Sociology* (New York: McKay, 1964), originally published in 1939; *Social Research*, 2nd ed. (Westport, Conn.: Greenwood, 1968), originally published in 1942; *Can Science Save Us?*, 2nd ed. (New York: David McKay paperback, 1961), originally published in 1947; and *Sociology*, 2nd ed. (New York: Harper & Row, 1958). Two students of Giddings, William F. Ogburn (1886–1959) and F. Stuart Chapin (1888–1974), did much to pioneer and establish a quantitative empirical approach to social phenomena.

[22] *Dimensions of Society* (New York: Macmillan, 1942).

[23] For example, Don Martindale, *The Nature and Types of Sociological Theory* (Boston: Houghton Mifflin, 1960), pp. 76–77, 122; Werner Stark, *The Sociology of Knowledge* (London: Routledge and Kegan Paul, 1958), pp. 44ff., and *The Fundamental Forms of Social Thought* (New York: Fordham University Press, 1963), p. 8f.; Hermann Strasser, *The Normative Structure of Sociology: Conservative and Emancipatory Themes in Social Thought* (Boston: Routledge and Kegan Paul, 1976), chap. 1. Needless to say, many of the theorists of the sociology of knowledge (for example Karl Marx, Max Scheler, Karl Mannheim) have concerned themselves with the political implications of theoretical orientations.

analysis of the relation between social theory and politics has been animated by the substantialist tradition. Analysts have been disposed toward finding universal truths or generalizations between given theoretical stances and politics. In truth, the idea of a fixed relation between type of social theory and type of politics is far from certain. In the meantime the many known associations between theory and politics are valuable even if they are historical, that is, temporal and diverse in their causation and effects. To fully appreciate these associations one must remember that theories do not actually have any power—the belief in ideological causation is itself a substantialist and ideological premise of Western rationalism. Ideas are efficacious only when they are backed by power, only when they suit existential conditions and values.

Though many have commented that idealism is associated with conservatism, few have spelled out the reasons. Presumably philosophical idealism and social theories based on it have been elitist from Plato on in that they invariably claim the ability and/or the achievement of thinking for only the few. Furthermore, idealist thinkers invariably posit an objective, fixed social world that allegedly corresponds to the distribution of abilities in human populations. This general stance accords well with the interests of those intellectual elite who fail to acknowledge that mental abilities stem from education and the other advantages of property. It is also true that those who posit the reality of society tend to stress order, stability, hierarchy, and unity through consensus. However, commentators rarely point out that this basic model of society can vary in content as among, for example, Plato, Saint Thomas, Maistre, Comte, Pareto, Cooley, Stalin, Sorokin, Parsons. There is no greater evidence of the tyranny (and fertility) of Greek thought than the persistence through many diverse historical periods of the basic model of society and politics found in Plato's *Republic*. In citing the conservatism of idealist social theory, few commentators have pointed out that when an idealist theory is evaluated in its historic context, it can be both conservative and revolutionary. For example, Plato and Comte both proposed societal forms going far beyond the society they were living in.

In contrast thinkers who stress the validity of knowledge acquired through experience tend to be more democratic, as, for example, Democritos, the philosophes, and the American pragmatists. It is also true that those who take a nominalist view of society or who emphasize conflict and exploitation as basic features of society, or who suffer from conflict and exploitation tend to be progressive, to stress the autonomy and/or equality of individuals, or to assert the sovereignty of the people: examples are elements in the thought of many of the Sophists, the monarchomachs, Hobbes, Locke, Rousseau, Gracchus Babeuf (1760–1797), Sumner, Ward, and Marx. However, nominalism can also be supremely conservative and even reactionary as, for example, elements in the thought of Sumner and the powerful American tradition of "voluntary nominalism."

Thus, epistemologies can to some extent be associated with political orientations: deduction with conservative, elitist idealism and induction with individualism and equality. However, deduction can also be progressive and critical as witness Plato, who used teleological deduction to transcend the ascriptive society of his day; the monarchomachs, who used natural-law arguments against royal absolutism; Hobbes, who used mathematical deduction to erase feudalism, and many others. Though, on the other hand, the empirical or nominalist outlook, especially one that stresses the validity of ordinary experience, is often associated with democratic, progressive politics and with a critical stance toward social institutions, it is no guarantee of progressive politics. While empiricism was critical and progressive during the French Enlightenment and during the rise of liberal reformism and socialist social theory, it can now be thought of as part of established liberal and socialist societies, with the latent function of helping to manage and stabilize existing systems of privilege and exploitation.

Another pervasive and in my view misleading assumption in assessing the relation between theory and politics is the belief that science is nonpartisan, neutral, and nonpolitical, and that a sharp distinction should be maintained between the history of a discipline and its coming of age. Thus one should distinguish between the history of sociology, and its half-understood struggles through the compromises of time and place, and "systematic" sociology, or consciously objective, empirical sociological theory.[24]

As opposed to most views of the relation between theory and politics, my typology is based on the premise that no social system has a self-evident intellectual, moral, or political claim on scientists. All societies are historical power structures disguised in garbs of spurious or problematic legitimacy—custom, magic, religion, birth, progress, achievement, science, the people, representative government, people's democracy. From this point of view,

---

[24] For examples see Howard Becker, "Vitalizing Sociological Theory," *American Sociological Review* 19 (August 1954): 377–388; Robert K. Merton, "On the History and Systematics of Sociological Theory," *Social Theory and Social Structure*, enl. ed., (New York: Free Press, 1968), chap. 1; reprinted in R. K. Merton, *On Theoretical Sociology* (New York: Free Press paperback, 1967), chap. 1. Merton's argument that functional analysis in sociology can be politically neutral may be found in his essay, "Manifest and Latent Functions," chap. 3 in each of the above titles. A random sample of members (1973–1974) of the American Sociological Association revealed considerable support for propositions attesting the value of the history of sociology, but a majority (57 percent) agreed that "an important distinction must be maintained between the *history* of sociological theory and the construction of currently acceptable sociological theory"; for the above analysis see Robert Alun Jones and Sidney Kronus, "Professional Sociologists and the History of Sociology: A Survey of Recent Opinion," *Journal of the History of the Behavioral Sciences* 12 (1976): 3–13.

sociologists must ask themselves: What is the structure of power of my own society? How well does my society function when judged by its own values and beliefs? What are the possibilities revealed by history for alternative institutions and values?

In this section, theorists are classified as to whether or not they view the central skills of social and sociological theory in political and moral terms. Theories will be judged by whether or not they are aware of the social consequences of practicing given forms of social theory and whether or not they stress the need for social theorists to translate imaginatively all behavior, whether of everyday life or the worlds of high finance, diplomacy, race track, brothel, or medicine, into political and moral problems. The central sociological skill is the ability to relate behavior (voting, going to school, suffering, being unemployed, being mentally ill, doing sociology, and so on) to power, the ability to see the facts of behavior as necessary or unnecessary, useful or harmful reflections of social power. Exactly what are the functions of society's norms and values? Do things work as society's leaders claim, or are social facts methods of domination? Who benefits from philosophies of individualism, constitutionalism, competition, efficiency or equal opportunity, and how are these philosophies used as instruments of domination, privilege, and exploitation? Does free education free people, or is it a new form of domination? Are representative government and constitutionalism substitutes for democracy? Do elections control power, or do they hide it even as it is being expressed? Is an urban-industrial society really possible, and if so, how is it possible?

The basic stance for classification by political and moral criteria is derived from Max Weber's sociology, though of course there are many other contributors both in and out of sociology. Perhaps the crucial insight underlying this typology is that beyond the rudimentary folk systems, human society is essentially a mélange of contradictory values, practices, and beliefs held together by verbal magic, ad hoc compromise, exploitation, oppression, repression, and/or waste, and that therefore no general theory of society is possible. It follows that the social scientist is first and foremost an evaluative or moral being who analyzes the world in terms of value problems. Values come not from biology, psychology, reason, patriotism, or empirical analysis, but from experience—and, for the aware sociologist, from self-conscious, reflected-upon experience. The sociologist is always aware of the moral-political consequences of his or her actions and keeps the following question at the forefront of consciousness: Should I remain content with the status quo, should I try to reform society (that is, try to make it function better according to its own lights), or should I seek to transform the present power structure into something better?

The following classification of sociology in political-moral terms uses the term *establishment sociologists* to describe theorists who unwittingly accept the status quo, or liberal society. Theorists who more or less consciously support existing society are called *conservative (liberal) humanists;* and those who want fundamental changes in the system of society are called *radical humanists.*

Establishment Sociology

The basic assumption behind this classification is that sociology, once a revolutionary movement (1700–1850 in England and France; later in Germany), has become a part of the symbolic establishment of capitalism. Establishment sociology refers to the practices, concepts, and values in sociology that unwittingly support liberal society. Theorists and theories under this heading include elements from a wide variety of types: consensus functionalism, conflict functionalism, symbolic interaction, labeling theory, phenomenological theory, ethnomethodology, small-group theory, and so on. (Some of the theories that fall under this heading have elements that will be categorized shortly as radical and conservative.) A theory, it should be understood, can have consequences unintended by its advocates—this book, for example, hopes to politicize sociology (within the limits of science), but may well provoke a reaction toward apolitical detachment.

The main characteristic of most establishment theories is a faith in the validity of sociology as presently conducted: broadly empirical, employing a variety of methods, avoiding value judgments and political questions, confident that the piecemeal accumulation of knowledge is sound because the methods and broad orientation of sociology are sound, and hopeful, since science is a unity, that a reconciliation among competing positions will be achieved eventually. In short, establishment sociology believes that rationality through age and consensus is possible—a belief derived from the pervasive sociocultural atmosphere that assumes that liberal society itself has or can achieve rationality through age and consensus. Establishment sociology, in other words, is part and parcel of the political morality of evolutionary liberalism.

Establishment sociology promotes the status quo in a variety of ways:

1. By discussing human beings and their associations abstractly. This creates the impression that one is dealing with human nature and the universal problems and predicaments of human beings rather than with the time- and culture-bound features and troubles of capitalism. By turning social processes into natural processes (reification), establishment sociology neglects and obscures the concrete power relations that create and constitute society and its problems.

2. By its detached analysis of the functions served by error and evil, a pronounced theme in sociology from its inception.

3. By its value-neutral stance, which in effect endorses existing values and power relations.

4. By its technocratic faith in the beneficence of science, education, knowledge, and ideas.

5. By its failure to understand that material and moral scarcity, the twin pillars of all historical societies including liberal society, are social creations and indispensable to the maintenance of outmoded institutions.

6. By its tendency to claim or assume that all societies, including liberal society, are based on consensus.

7. By uncritically assuming that liberal society is evolving or is capable of evolving toward its own ideals.

Broadly speaking, establishment sociologists in the United States are either unaware of or indifferent to the essential historicity of all institutions, including American institutions. Though rarely discussed openly, it is taken for granted that human nature has been released by American society, thus making a science of human nature possible. Whether it uses quantitative or qualitative methods; whether it focuses on total social systems, small groups, or everyday life; whether it is sociocultural in orientation or prefers to analyze psychological, intersubjective phenomena the main effect of establishment sociology is to turn history into reality and provide power with legitimacy.

Though intellectually diverse, the vast bulk of American sociologies are unified by their acceptance of liberal society. The essentially conservative effect of establishment American sociology should not be obscured by the limited pluralism found within it nor by the critical, reformist late-liberal mentality displayed by most of its adherents. Thinking contains tensions and branchings that are often difficult to control—nevertheless the outstanding characteristic of sociological thinking is its basic containment within the liberal spectrum. The empiricism of establishment sociology, derived from the need for empirical knowledge on the part of business, political, and other leaders of liberal society, has misled sociologists into thinking that the facts of American society are universal facts and that the empirical method guarantees detachment and rational adjustment. Even among the numerous sociologists who are aware of the sociocultural nature of behavior and the relativity of culture, it cannot be said that the basic presuppositions of liberalism are ever questioned: Bill of Rights, representative government, private property, the nuclear family, technological and economic growth, economic concentration, free education, eventual integration and justice for minorities, and so on.

A basic support for the status quo is the adoption by establishment sociology of a value-neutral approach as an integral part of the definition of science. Value neutrality is not only a key aspect of the professional ethic of sociology but is found throughout liberal society in a variety of forms: the allegedly neutral market economy, the allegedly responsible corporation guided by well-educated managers, the private-profit banking and utility businesses hiding behind the label "public," and the vast, tax-exempt voluntary sector, including private colleges and universities, allegedly serving the public. Value neutrality is an outcome, of course, of the need of a dynamic "lead" society to escape a rigid, absolute, and diffused normative system, and as such can be traced back to William of Occam. However, it also serves to disguise differential power, the conflict of interest among the various segments of society, and the value-laden power processes that create and allocate scarce resources.

Establishment sociology's approach to social problems is not easy to depict in brief. Establishment sociology widely assumes that society causes problems, though this insight is rarely developed systematically.[25] By and large, the net result is to create the impression that the United States is a sound society with a variety of solvable problems. As Liazos and others have pointed out, there is little focus on problems in relation to power, or on powerholders at the upper levels. Most attention goes to lower-level deviants while those who make the rules and create the other conditions of deviance (such as unemployment), along with upper-level deviants (such as white collar criminals), are overlooked. Attention on power is focused almost exclusively on lower- or middle-level agents of social control: police officers, social workers, teachers, penologists, and so on.[26]

From the standpoint of a politically oriented sociology, social problems result from policies adopted by powerful groups to solve their own problems. By definition, those who have many problems have less power than those who have few problems, and those who cannot solve their problems are powerless. Unemployment and its attendant pathologies, for example, must be linked to the problems of inflation faced by business leaders and government officials—problems that such groups characteristically solve through deliberately created unemployment among the weak and less strong. Rape, to take another example, can be related to the values and norms of dominant groups. It can be argued that rape is a normal outcome of values and norms that generate male aggressiveness (masculinity) and female dependence (feminity), and values and norms that turn sexuality into a commodity within a general context that encourages the acquisition by all of all forms of commodities but makes it difficult for many to acquire them. Rape (and crime and deviance in general) can also be thought of as political acts by disoriented people who cannot focus their suffering or despair on the holders of power. There is no need to cite more examples of a politicized sociology

[25] Perhaps the best treatment of social problems within a framework emphasizing the social nature of social problems is Robert K. Merton and Robert Nisbet, eds., *Contemporary Social Problems,* 4th ed. (New York: Harcourt Brace Jovanovich, 1976).
[26] Alexander Liazos, "The Poverty of the Sociology of Deviance: Nuts, Sluts, and Preverts [sic], *Social Problems* 20 (Summer 1972): 103–120.

except to note that the general problem-solving, problem-creating process as depicted and practiced by establishment sociology is obscured by mythologies of universalism, competition, achievement, equal opportunity, and progress.

The establishment mentality is found throughout sociology. Perhaps the most obviously conservative, depoliticizing orientation is the concern for everyday life (whether deviant or not) found largely among phenomenological and ethnomethological sociologists.[27] Ethnomethodologists in particular (but also practitioners of the modal social problems approach) tend to transform the consequences of power into a fixed feature of the human condition. Sociology certainly needs to know what happens in mental institutions, prisons, back alleys, race tracks, pool halls, and so on, but it makes a world of difference if such knowledge is presented within a political-moral framework, or as stable manifestations of human passion and psychology. Sociology must certainly be a humane science and empathize with the victims of power at all levels of society, but it must also be careful not to equate the results of power with the nature of human beings nor to take these results as the brute, thought-controlling facts of life.

An indictment of establishment sociology can also be mounted in terms of its failure to anticipate social problems. The empirical approach need not doom sociology to an after-the-fact type of analysis. There is no epistemological reason why sociology cannot develop a comprehensive analysis of social problems oriented toward prediction and control, including a concept of liberal society itself as a problem. However, the absorption of establishment sociology in the mores of liberalism (progress, individualism, private property, specialization, economic growth, psychologism, biologism, racism, sexism, nationalism, and so on) has prevented it from anticipating problems (and led it to misdefine them), and has perhaps led to a pattern of systematic bias. Out of many examples, two will suffice: establishment sociology has paid almost no attention to the single most important aspect of a capitalist society, capital formation, and it has only begun to realize that the nation-state is no more a self-sufficient unit of study than individuals or groups.

Some sociologists, for example, Sorokin, have focused on broad types of sociocultural systems in an orientation similar to Toynbee, Spengler, Weber,

---

[27] Evidently responding to criticism, Goffman acknowledges that his focus on how individuals deal with their experience has "marked political implications, and that these are conservative ones. The analysis developed does not catch at the differences between the advantaged and disadvantaged classes and can be said to direct attention away from such matters. I think that is true. I can only suggest that he who would combat false consciousness and awaken people to their true interests has much to do, because the sleep is very deep. And I do not intend here to provide a lullaby but merely to sneak in and watch the way the people snore" (*Frame Analysis*, p. 14).

Marx, Spencer, Comte, Saint-Simon, Condorcet, Montesquieu, and Vico. However, the modal emphasis in sociology ever since theory and empirical research were fused at the end of the last century has been "society," the alleged self-sufficient unit of study. This orientation among theorists and researchers was augmented by the common textbook practice of assuming that the ultimate entity was something called *society,* or, more broadly, *types* of society. Indeed, American textbooks rarely gave full-bodied analyses of American society, but spent a great deal of time talking about sociology's methods and ideas. The abstract, universalist approach in which sociological ideas are illustrated by materials drawn from all over the world and from various aspects of American society has the net effect of hiding the particular nature of sociology, American society, and "society." For a considerable period the only general sociology text that focused on the particular nature of the overall American social system was Robin Williams's *American Society: A Sociological Interpretation.*[28] In the 1970s, such a focus has become more common in both introductory and advanced texts.

Sociology has always been aware of other societies or cultures in both a temporal and spatial sense. Vico and Montesquieu made pioneering contributions in the areas of history and comparative anthropology, and the influence of these modes of thought on sociology grew in the nineteenth and twentieth centuries. The relativizing influence on sociology of historical and comparative analysis did not bring the validity of liberalism into question, however (except in the isolated case of Max Weber). Its major effect probably was to help create and subsequently stabilize liberal society by loosening allegiance to obsolete elements, by pointing out the utility of error and evil, and by identifying the isolated society as an ultimate substance. There is little doubt that the one-world mentality, awareness of international interdependence, and concern for population growth, environmental pollution, resource depletion, and so on have all been part of sociology's orientation. None of these developments, however, have altered the basic belief in the ultimate substance called society, which by and large means the nation-state. Even the nation-state has been identified with the alleged homogeneous British and American examples, overlooking the world's more prevalent multiethnic societies. Even the comparative approach was largely oriented toward finding universals, world similarities, and functional processes.

To a large extent, the concern with the entire globe had the same hidden agenda as the concern with what went on in the street gang, factory, or voting booth: to uphold and substantiate an ahistorical, metaphysical

---

[28] 3rd ed. (New York: Alfred A. Knopf, 1970, originally published in 1951).

definition of the nature of knowledge.[29] A beginning toward a genuine redefinition of the subject matter of sociology to include various societies is discernible in Talcott Parsons's focus on the "system of societies." [30] But Parsons's focus is vitiated by his unitary evolutionary framework and by his continued assumption that the liberal nation-states are self-sufficient entities.

The idea that societies interpenetrate as parts of larger systems, culminating in imperialism, has received various intellectual expression. Karl Deutsch has identified a variety of theories of imperialism: folk theories (biologic-instinctive, demographic-Malthusian, geographic-strategic, cultural organi-cism, or the people as a psychological entity), which today command little respect; conservative theories (Jules Ferry, Disraeli, Rhodes, Kipling), which advocated imperial expansion to provide economic stability at home; liberal theories (John Hobson and Norman Angell), which argued that im-perialism was unnecessary and stood in the way of competition; a socio-logical/psychological theory (associated with Joseph Schumpeter), which argued that imperialism was learned behavior and thus not inevitable; and Marxian theories of imperialism (especially those of Lenin, Johan Galtung, and Samir Amin), which argue that capitalist economies necessarily reach outward to develop colonies to support themselves (with some arguing that imperialist nations weaken themselves by investing abroad and others argu-ing that they strengthen themselves by creating dependent, complementary colonial economies and societies).[31]

Perhaps the first systematic analysis of imperialism to influence sociology is Immanuel Wallerstein's *The Modern World-System: Capitalist Agriculture and the Origins of the European World-Economy in the Sixteenth Century*.[32] Wallerstein assumes that the internal development of society is greatly affected by international relations and that the modern world is unique be-cause it has abandoned empire as a method of domination in favor of economic specialization in which some societies dominate others through technological as well as military and political superiority, and through imperialist mechanisms such as colonies and free markets. More precisely,

[29] For a valuable criticism of a parochial sociology and a call for transcending the nation-state (but largely from within a universalist orientation), see Wilbert E. Moore, "Global Sociology: The World as a Singular System," *American Journal of Sociology* 71 (March 1966): 475–482.

[30] *The System of Modern Societies* (Englewood, N.J.: Prentice-Hall, 1971).

[31] For an extremely valuable analysis of these theories including the fine shades of meaning that our summary has obscured, see Karl W. Deutsch, "Theories of Imperialism and Neocolonialism," in Steven J. Rosen and James R. Kurth, eds., *Testing Theories of Economic Imperialism* (Lexington, Mass.: D.C. Heath, 1974), chap. 2.

[32] New York: Academic Press, 1974; first of four projected volumes on the world system of societies; winner of the American Sociological Association's 1975 Sorokin Award (given to the publication that makes an outstanding contribution to the progress of sociology).

the modern capitalist world system has evolved into a uniquely dynamic relation among societies because political and economic institutions have been separated. In the imperialism of empire, contiguous territories are absorbed into one political-military-legal-administrative-moral-religious unit, and economic relations take the form of tribute and taxation (both in forms that discourage production). Eventually all grievances and conflicts become focused on the state, and a top-heavy civil and military bureaucracy adds to the general stagnation and contributes to the eventual dissolution. By separating economics and politics, the imperialism of the capitalist world economy keeps down the costs of domination, diffuses conflict, and allows economic variables full sway. The result is that core societies (in which a strong state develops to service the capitalist economy) specialize in finance, trade, and manufacturing, giving them an exploitative economic advantage over staple producing areas. Not only does surplus flow into the core states, but the nonmanufacturing areas begin to specialize in agriculture and their internal structures eventually develop (the development of underdevelopment)[33] to complement the emerging international division of labor.

A genuine global sociology, therefore, undermines the substantialism of the national state, or society, by pointing to the permeability of national boundaries and to the indispensable roles of domestic and international processes in creating and maintaining each other. Its insights may well extend to an awareness that liberalism is a unique Western outcome of a nonrepeatable capitalist development and that its contemporary relevance for humanity is problematic. Indeed, given the failure of liberal society to realize its own ideals of equal opportunity, equal justice, and the elimination of poverty, and its voracious appetite for the world's scarce resources, the relevance of liberalism for liberal society itself may well have become problematic.

One of sociology's most important insights, the power of occupation over behavior, sheds considerable light on the historical development of establishment sociology. In this context, there are three significant facts about sociology: one, the typical sociologist is an academic; two, sociologists tend

---

[33] In this respect Wallerstein's work builds on the revisionist wing of Marxist imperialist theory. For two pioneering essays, see Paul A. Baran "On the Political Economy of Backwardness," *Manchester School of Economics and Social Studies* (January 1952), reprinted in Robert I. Rhodes, ed., *Imperialism and Underdevelopment: A Reader* (New York: Monthly Review Press, 1970), pp. 285–301; and Andre Gunder Frank, "The Development of Underdevelopment," *Monthly Review* (September 1966), reprinted in Andre Gunder Frank, *Latin America: Underdevelopment or Revolution: Essays on the Development of Underdevelopment and the Immediate Enemy* (New York: Monthly Review Press, 1969), pp. 3–17. Lenin felt that the imperialist export of capital to colonies would eventually weaken the mother countries and transform colonies into vigorous industrial powers. The revisionist wing argues that imperialism creates dependent natons mired in a state of relative underdevelopment.

to think of themselves as professionals; and three, abortive efforts have even been made to develop the profession of applied sociologist.[34]

1. Professionalism in the modern era is the marriage of occupation with science and as such involves the avoidance of value judgments and politics. To a large extent professionalism is synonomous with technocracy, the liberal faith that science can solve all problems and that society can perfect itself by doing more of the same.

2. Academic life offers secure and well-paid employment and is undoubtedly a factor in fostering attitudes of objectivity, balance, and nonpartisanship—and the political naiveté so often characteristic of such attitudes.

3. Teachers deal with dependent, captive audiences.

4. A centralized, elitist system of higher education, such as in England and France, will provide a different academic environment from that of the decentralized mass system in the United States and of the decentralized elite system of Germany. It is not surprising, for example, that a wide variety of perspectives and influences could become established in American sociology. One can even speculate that reformism came out of less developed, economically exploited regions of the United States (for example, the Midwest) and that new perspectives such as ethnomethodology are more easily developed in frontier states such as California than in more traditionalized states such as Massachusetts.

5. As a new discipline sociology had to fight for its place in the academic spectrum, and its sense of identity, approach, and subject matter were correspondingly narrowed.

Sociologists have many overlapping group memberships in the academic, economic, professional, family, religious, and political worlds, which also exercise influence over the way they conduct their professional affairs. Sociologists are members of the upper-middle class by education, income, occupation, and prestige, and they are deeply embedded in the rationalizing, reformist ethos of Corporate America. Indeed, many of their activities and concerns have spearheaded the modernization of the American class system as it shifts from the old entrepreneurial class to the new salaried middle class and from the era of rugged self-sufficiency to the welfare-bureaucratic stage of mature capitalism.[35] In any case, it is known that social scientists tend to be more "late liberal" than their colleagues in the natural sciences

---

[34] For valuable background material, see Morris Janowitz, "Professionalization of Sociology," *American Journal of Sociology* 78 (July 1972): 105–135.
[35] In this latter connection, see Alvin W. Gouldner, "The Sociologist as Partisan: Sociology and the Welfare State," *American Sociologist* 3 (May 1968): 103–116; widely reprinted.

and humanities, and that sociologists tend to be more "late liberal" than their fellow social scientists.[36]

The foregoing is a loose characterization of modal, establishment sociology and can serve as a general norm to measure countertendencies and deviations. It is not possible to say with any precision if there is more or less diversity in sociology today than in the past. Many interpreters of the history of sociology tend to see a trend toward consensus—or at least they think consensus is desirable and possible—[37] while others define sociology as a multiparadigm science, that is, an immature science lacking a unified image of its subject matter.[38]

It is not easy to decide whether or not sociology is becoming more unified. If it is, it is difficult to interpret its meaning—it may reflect the needs of or the stabilization of capitalism, or it may simply be another delusion in the West's age-old longing for unity and certainty.

Whatever unity developed in American sociology in the period between 1920 and 1960 may have been a reaction to the uses of social science, scientific knowledge, and technology under fascist and communist dictatorships, and to the apparent inadequacy of normative liberalism to forestall or counter the Great Depression. One can reasonably conjecture that many sociologists reacted to these historical events by putting their faith in the idea of a pure, nonpolitical social science.

The apparent diversity in American sociology may also be a temporary phenomenon caused by the upward mobility of non-Protestant groups into sociology and by a new array of social problems, both stemming from the unprecedented rate and type of economic growth in the post–1945 period. A heightened awareness of institutional malfunctioning also emerged from the war on poverty and from America's ambivalent and divisive involvement

---

[36] Seymour M. Lipset and Everett C. Ladd, Jr., "The Politics of American Sociologists," *American Journal of Sociology* 78 (July 1972): 67–104.

[37] For example, Nicholas S. Timasheff and George A. Theodorson, *Sociological Theory: Its Nature and Growth*, 4th ed., (New York: Random House, 1976; first published in 1955); Don Martindale, *The Nature and Types of Sociological Theory* (Boston: Houghton Mifflin, 1960); Alvin Boskoff, *The Mosaic of Sociological Theory* (New York: Thomas Y. Crowell, 1972); and S. N. Eisenstadt with Miriam Curelaru, *The Form of Sociology—Paradigms and Crises* (New York: John Wiley, 1976). As I shall discuss below, others see a trend away from consensus in sociology.

[38] See, for example, Irving M. Zeitlin, *Rethinking Sociology: A Critique of Contemporary Theory* (Englewood Cliffs, N.J.: Prentice-Hall, 1973); Nicholas C. Mullins with the assistance of Carolyn J. Mullins, *Theories and Theory Groups in Contemporary American Sociology* (New York: Harper & Row, 1973); Jonathan H. Turner, *The Structure of Sociological Theory* (Homewood, Illinois: Dorsey, 1974); and George Ritzer, *Sociology: A Multiple Paradigm Science* (Boston: Allyn and Bacon, 1975).

in the Vietnam war. On the other hand, it may be that the thoughtways and values of American liberalism contain too many preindustrial vestiges and that an advanced urban-industrial America, lacking an up-to-date symbolic legitimation, may continue to spawn considerable symbolic diversity and tension. It may also be that a multitude of noisy but weak and ineffectual critiques of modal sociology and liberalism may provide a false sense of diversity, dynamism, and relevance and thus, ironically, help to legitimate a status quo allegedly based on dynamic pluralism.

Whether establishment sociology is too narrow and ingrown, a sterile debate within and about a "one-dimensional society," cannot be said with scientific certainty. Whether its institutionalization in Academe (and government and business) will lead to mandarin routinization is similarly uncertain. Notwithstanding a faith in "socially unattached intellectuals," the establishment of a radical caucus within the American Sociological Association, calls for sociology to become a "skin trade," or longings for the alleged "ideational" past, there is much to be said for Saint-Simon's insight that the modern West was fortunate that its values and interests were carried by classes that grew up outside the feudal system. Given the comprehensive grip of a directed capitalism, a functional equivalent of an autonomous and creative social class may well be in order. A partial step in this direction might be a professional requirement that all sociologists work during the summer as night porters, migratory laborers, bedpan emptiers, or assembly-line workers. On the other hand, if this were possible, power would not be a problem and sociology would not need protection against co-optation—indeed, it would probably not be needed at all.

Radical Humanism

A diverse lot of sociologists who are critical of the basic outlook in sociology can be identified under the general heading of radical humanism.[39] Never very numerous in American sociology, radical theorists have a negative view of establishment sociology because of its acceptance of the basic

---

[39] Two pioneer figures in this tradition are Robert S. Lynd (1892–1970) and C. Wright Mills (1916–1962). Lynd, who with his wife Helen pioneered the empirical study of the American community—Middletown (New York: Harcourt Brace Jovanovich, 1929) and Middletown in Transition (New York: Harcourt Brace Jovanovich, 1937)—expressed his radical humanism and commitment to social democracy in left-wing magazines and in his teaching. His Knowledge For What? The Place of Social Science in American Culture (Princeton, N.J.: Princeton University Press, 1939, also in paperback) stands as an unanswered indictment of social science. Mills's work includes The New Men of Power (New York: Harcourt Brace Jovanovitch, 1948); White Collar (New York: Oxford University Press, 1953, also in paperback); and The Power Elite (New York: Oxford University Press, 1956, also in paperback). His formal quarrel with establishment sociology was expressed in "The Professional Ideology of Social Pathologists," American Journal of Sociology 49 (September 1943): 165–180 and in The Sociological Imagination (New York: Oxford University Press, 1959, also in paperback).

presuppositions of capitalism. Thus they tend to regard the objective, value-neutral stance of mainstream sociology as ideological. Theorists of this orientation tend to promote the idea that social scientists should be politically and morally committed to a better, more equal and democratic, order of things and people.

The category of radical humanism arbitrarily excludes "orthodox" Marxists. It does, however, focus on Marxists who consider themselves to be sociologists.[40] Indeed, Marxism is the major influence and component of radical humanism or "radical sociology." Other influences stem from the classic sociological tradition, especially Max Weber, from Darwin and Freud, and from existentialism and phenomenology. Two features of radical humanism are noteworthy: it is largely a blend of a number of creative currents, and it has grown up outside of sociology.[41]

Some of the major figures who have promoted self-consciousness (often political and radical) in sociology are Karl Mannheim (1893–1947),[42] Herbert Marcuse (b. 1898),[43] Barrington Moore, Jr. (b. 1913),[44] Alvin W.

[40] It is interesting to note that the American Sociological Association's Section on Marxist Sociology was first organized in 1975.

[41] For an analysis of the relation between Durkheim and existentialism, see Edward A. Tiryakian, *Sociologism and Existentialism: Two Perspectives on the Individual and Society* (Englewood Cliffs, N.J.: Prentice-Hall paperback, 1962). On the relation between Marxism and French existentialism, see Raymond Aron, *Marxism and the Existentialists* (New York: Harper & Row, 1969). For the relation between Marxism and phenomenology, see Fred R. Dallmayr, "Phenomenology and Marxism: A Salute to Enzo Paci," in George Psathas, ed., *Phenomenological Sociology: Issues and Applications* (New York: John Wiley, 1973), pp. 305–356. For a tightly argued analysis of the relations among Marxism, phenomenology and sociology, see Barry Smart, *Sociology, Phenomenology and Marxian Analysis: A Critical Discussion of the Theory and Practice of a Science of Society* (Boston: Routledge and Kegan Paul, 1976). For a history of the varied perspectives (within a loose Marxian framework) of the Frankfurt School, see Martin Jay, *The Dialectical Imagination: A History of the Frankfurt School and the Institute of Social Research, 1923–1950* (London: Heinemann, 1973).

[42] Mannheim's major work is *Ideology and Utopia: An Introduction to the Sociology of Knowledge,* trans. Louis Wirth and Edward Shils (New York: Harcourt Brace Jovanovich, 1936, originally published 1929). Other works are *Man and Society in an Age of Reconstruction* (New York: Harcourt Brace Jovanovich, 1940) and *Freedom, Power, and Democratic Planning* (Boston: Routledge and Kegan Paul, 1951). Selections from his work are in Kurt H. Wolff, ed. *From Karl Mannheim* (New York: Oxford University Press, 1971). Mannheim's career illustrates the perils of classificatory knowledge: his later thought exhibits a tendency toward the right.

[43] Marcuse is a distinguished interpreter of Hegel, Marx, and Freud. His works include *Reason and Revolution; Hegel and the Rise of Social Theory* (New York: Oxford University Press, 1941, also in paperback) and *Eros and Civilization* (Boston: Beacon Press, 1955, also in paperback). Marcuse has expressed his views of industrial society and contemporary social science in a number of writings, most notably *One-Dimensional Man* (Boston: Beacon Press, 1964, also in paperback).

[44] For Moore's comments on contemporary society and its social science, see his *Political Power and Social Theory* (Cambridge, Mass.: Harvard University Press, 1958, also in paperback).

Gouldner (b. 1920),[45] T. B. Bottomore (b. 1920), and John Rex.[46] Both Marxist and phenomenological branches of radical humanism have gained a measure of acceptance within sociology.[47] However, the success of American liberalism in limiting the definition of social science to liberal disciplines (sociology, political science, economics, psychology, history) has by and large curtailed the influence of Marxism in the United States. (Its relative lack of influence also stems from the nature of American society, which has provided uncongenial soil for socialist movements or ideas.) The relevance of Marx for social science has gone largely unnoticed in sociology because of sociology's preoccupation with issues inside liberal establishment sociology. There is some evidence that the Marxist orientation is growing in American social science, which suggests that American society may have become more amenable to analysis by Marxian ideas.

Conservative Liberal Humanism

The category *conservative liberal humanists* refers to sociologists who consciously defend liberal society. These theorists are difficult to define—like radical humanists, they show a basic antipathy to the use of natural

---

[45] For a sampling of Gouldner's theoretical work see his collection of essays, *For Sociology: Renewal and Critique in Sociology Today* (London: Allen Lane, 1973). Gouldner has finished two volumes in what is to be a series of studies of Western intellectual life: *Enter Plato; Classical Greece and the Origins of Social Theory* (New York: Basic Books, 1965; also in paperback, 2 vols., separate titles) and *The Coming Crisis of Western Sociology* (New York: Basic Books, 1970, also in paperback). His latest work, evidently intended as part of larger works in this series, is *The Dialectic of Ideology and Technology: The Origins, Grammar, and Future of Ideology* (New York: Seabury Press, 1976).

[46] T. B. Bottomore, *Critics of Society: Radical Thought in North America* (New York: Pantheon Books, 1969) and *Sociology as Social Criticism* (New York: Pantheon Books, 1974); John Rex, *Sociology and the Demystification of the Modern World* (London: Routledge & Kegan Paul, 1974).

[47] For a history, see Jack L. Roach, "The Radical Sociology Movement: A Short History and Commentary," *American Sociologist* 5 (August 1970): 224–233. Examples of this perspective are now widely available in a series of readers and special journal issues: Irving Louis Horowitz, ed., *The New Sociology: Essays in Social Science and Social Theory in Honor of C. Wright Mills* (New York: Oxford University Press, 1964; also in paperback); Kurt H. Wolff and Barrington Moore, Jr., eds., *The Critical Spirit: Essays in Honor of Herbert Marcuse* (Boston: Beacon Press, 1967, also in paperback); Larry T. Reynolds and Janice M. Reynolds, eds., *The Sociology of Sociology* (New York: David McKay paperback, 1970); "Some Radical Perspectives in Sociology," *Sociological Inquiry* 40 (Winter 1970); David Horowitz, ed., *Radical Sociology* (San Francisco: Canfield Press paperback, 1971); J. David Colfax, ed., *Radical Sociology* (New York: Basic Books, 1971, also in paperback). Other works include: John O'Neill, *Sociology As a Skin Trade* (London: Heinemann, 1972; also a Harper paperback); Dick Atkinson, *Orthodox Consensus and Radical Alternative* (New York: Basic Books, 1972); Herman Schwendinger and Julia R. Schwendinger, *The Sociologists of the Chair: A Radical Analysis of the Formative Years of North American Sociology, 1883–1922* (New York: Basic Books, 1974); and Hermann Strasser, *The Normative Structure of Sociology: Conservative and Emancipatory Themes in Social Thought* (Boston: Routledge and Kegan Paul, 1976).

science as a model for social science and a concern for political and moral issues. The distinguished sociologist and political theorist Robert M. MacIver did much to legitimate this point of view in the second quarter of the century.[48] A leading contemporary exponent is Robert Nisbet (b. 1913), whose work contains a basic ambivalence toward the French Enlightenment and the general current of liberalism. Sociology, he claims (in my judgment erroneously), has always been aware of the profoundly negative consequences of industrialization and urbanization. Nisbet's vague unhappiness with contemporary society is matched by a criticism of social science—he has no faith in the possibility either of radically transforming society or of achieving a science of human behavior. All in all, it is a curious and not always reliable blend of intellectual history and philosophy in the manner of an Oxford don.[49] Other figures whose works have fairly explicit conservative liberal political overtones and who are committed to writing for the educated lay public are Daniel Bell (b. 1919),[50] Nathan Glazer (b. 1923),[51] and Seymour Martin Lipset (b. 1922).[52] It is useful to note that Talcott Parsons has declared himself a New Deal Democrat in response to criticisms that his thought is conservative. Like Parsons, the above figures are conservative in the sense that they debate the issues of and advocate reforms for a society whose validity they take for granted. There is a characteristic concern among many conservative liberal humanists that the masses, with the help of government, are getting too much equality. Another concern,

---

[48] *Community* (New York: Macmillan, 1928); *Social Causation* (Boston: Ginn, 1942); *The Web of Government* (New York: Macmillan, 1947); *Society; An Introductory Analysis* with Charles H. Page (New York: Rinehart, 1949).

[49] Robert Nisbet, *The Quest for Community* (New York: Oxford University Press, 1953), reissued in paperback as *Community and Power; The Sociological Tradition* (New York: Basic Books, 1966); *Social Change and History* (New York: Oxford University Press, 1969, also in paperback); *The Social Philosophers: Community and Conflict in Western Thought* (New York: Thomas Y. Crowell, 1973); and *Twilight of Authority* (New York: Oxford University Press, 1976).

[50] See his *The End of Ideology: On the Exhaustion of Political Ideas in the Fifties*, rev. ed. (New York: Collier paperback, 1962); *The Coming of Postindustrial Society* (New York: Basic Books, 1973, also in paperback); and *The Cultural Contradictions of Capitalism* (New York: Basic Books, 1976).

[51] See his (with Daniel Patrick Moynihan) *Beyond the Melting Pot: The Negroes, Puerto Ricans, Jews, Italians, and Irish of New York City*, 2nd ed. (Cambridge, Mass.: M.I.T. Press, 1970) and *Affirmative Discrimination: Ethnic Inequality and Public Policy* (New York: Basic Books, 1976).

[52] A leader in the field of political sociology, Lipset has exchanged the socialism of his early career for *democratic elitism* (liberal democracy). See his *Political Man* (Garden City, N.Y.: Doubleday, 1960), *The First New Nation* (New York: Basic Books, 1963), and *Revolution and Counter-revolution* (New York: Basic Books, 1968). In view of Lipset's former commitment to socialism and his specialty, political sociology, it is curious that he does not understand that from a radical-left position, a liberal is a conservative whether he is an early liberal or a late liberal; see, for example, S. M. Lipset and E. C. Ladd, Jr. "The Politics of American Scientists," *American Journal of Sociology* 78 (July 1972): 67–104, in which it is argued that sociology is not conservative since sociologists, including Talcott Parsons, are late liberals.

also found in the later career of Karl Mannheim and reminiscent of Sorokin, is that modern culture is excessively egoistic and hedonistic.

Conservative liberal humanism is a minority position in sociology. However, a majority of sociologists reflect this position unwittingly in their practice of sociology or express late-liberal positions on public issues in their roles outside sociology.

FUNCTIONAL ANALYSIS: OBJECTIVITY IN A MEANINGLESS DIVERSITY

Though I described the overall development of methodology in terms of the contrasting concepts of monistic and pluralistic positivism, I have chosen the more familiar term *functional analysis* for my concluding section. To understand the complex, ever-shifting functional orientation, one should think of it in the first instance as simply a synonym for science.[53] Viewed in broad historical perspective, functional analysis represents the scientific spirit of Western culture. Though it may render the term excessively elastic, it is of some value to note that the word *function* is not out of place in the teleological-deductive age (600 B.C.–1500 A.D.), in the mathematical-deductive age (1500–1800), nor, of course, in the contemporary empirical-functional age.

My main interest is with the meaning of functionalism in post-Renaissance and especially in post-nineteenth-century social science. Thus, it must also be understood that there are two sharply different functional positions, the ancient-medieval, rooted in the teleological world view, and the modern, rooted in the mathematical-deductive and the empirical phases of modern science. Despite differences, both stages of modern science share an aversion to interpreting the world in terms of essences and inherent purposes, preferring to dissolve the phenomenal world into relationships between variables. The key philosophical idea behind modern functionalism, therefore, is that something is to be known by something else—that is, that knowledge comes from knowing the relationships between variables. As it emerges in the empirical phase of modern science, this key perspective fastens on the problem of identifying cause-effect relationships in the phenomenal world itself.

The pioneers of the empirical-functional perspective in sociology were Vico and Montesquieu—both pioneered the collection and organization of

---

[53] Kingsley Davis, "The Myth of Functional Analysis as a Special Method in Sociology and Anthropology," *American Sociological Review* 24 (December 1959): 757–772; available as Bobbs-Merrill reprint S-567.

empirical data as variables and put moral evaluation aside as they searched for the network of social causation amidst clearly identified variables. With the growth of empirical social science in the eighteenth century, theorists struggled to explain the seemingly irreducible diversity and temporality of human behavior. Functional theory was greatly advanced by the developmental or teleological-evolutionary framework that French theorists adopted to unify the data of human behavior. Thus the work of Condorcet, Saint-Simon, and Comte represents a genuine attempt to relate variables in terms of categories of time and place. It was not until the impact of the scientific theory of evolution, however, that functionalism in sociology began to slough off the teleological spirit of French evolutionary thought and again take on the empiricism and moral neutrality so characteristic of the work of Vico and Montesquieu. The work of Herbert Spencer, therefore, marks a significant advance in functional methodology even though his contribution was embedded in one of the last great statements of monistic naturalistic positivism. Thanks largely to the influence of Darwinism, the nineteenth century developed a genuinely empirical and relatively complete and self-conscious functionalism. By the end of the century the major contours and insights of empirical functional analysis were fully established, aided above all by the biological theory of evolution. Basic to the impact of biological thought was its assumption that empirical research could yield knowledge, especially if conducted within the framework provided by the model of a functional survival system. Both Sumner and Ward, for example, displayed this functional mentality throughout their work. Both thinkers developed important insights in functional terms, though Sumner's ability to think in sociocultural terms allowed him to develop the more lasting ideas about survival structures, such concepts as antagonistic cooperation, in-group and out-group, mores, folkways, and conventionalization.

Functionalism was also influenced by another evolutionary thought structure, the Hegelian-Marxian tradition. Indeed Hegel's philosophy is a source of inspiration for modern social science that is much neglected, though there is, of course, the conventional acknowledgment of his influence on Marx. The Hegelian idea that reason undergoes qualitative change in conjunction with qualitative changes in the structure of society is fundamental to the functional mentality. As for Marx, the importance of his contribution to functional analysis should not be overlooked simply because I have defined the substance of his thought as lying outside the tradition of liberalism and sociology. It was Marx's identification of sociocultural variables, of course, and his attempt to identify the functional or causal relations among them that constitutes his widely influential contribution to the development of social science and the late-liberal functional mentality. Marx's similarity with liberal thought on this score goes even deeper. Using Hegel's liberal social theory and dialectical logic, Marx also developed one of the key insights in contemporary sociocultural sociology, the concept of latent function, or the recognition that there exist functional structures operating beyond or below the consciousness of actors.

The emergence of sociocultural sociology was enormously important to the development of functionalism because it established the assumption that the diversity and temporality of human behavior and the full range of human symbolic and material existence could be explained without the teleological bias inherent in evolutionary social thought. Pareto applied the functional mentality of mechanics to human nonrationality, while Simmel sought to understand behavior as a function of interaction situations. Of even more importance was Weber's mode of functional analysis, which explicitly discarded the psychological explanation of behavior in favor of a view that saw behavior as a function of multicausal sociocultural systems. However, Weber's return to the socioculturalism of Montesquieu and Vico contained an explicit repudiation of the substantialism of the positivist tradition in sociology, both naturalistic and sociocultural, and it remained for Durkheim to supply the functional orientation that dominates contemporary sociology. Like Weber's, Durkheim's contribution to functionalism rose from his insistence that sociocultural elements and not psychology form the central subject matter of sociology. Unlike Weber, of course, Durkheim did not abandon the belief in systematic theory. In effect, he took the sociocultural tradition and wedded it to the idea of a positive rational science of human behavior.

The revolutionary discovery in sociocultural positivism that sociocultural forces (technology, morals, warfare, class conflict, myths, and so on), regardless of their nonrational origin or nature, are nevertheless lawful and thus subject to scientific analysis is as important for understanding the nature of sociological theory and functionalism as it is for understanding the nature of society. With the growing recognition of the role of nonscientific elements in furthering the aims of science, theorists came to see and insist on the role of abstraction in empirical investigation. With the recognition of the complexity and seemingly unpredictable pattern of causation in social life, sociologists refined their methods and concepts in an effort more adequately to grasp and explain the origins, functions, and ironic complexities of social existence.

Of all the theorists who recognized the role of irony in human life, only Weber gave it a central place in his thought, using it to define the nature of social science as well as of society. His recognition of the pervasive force of irony in human affairs enabled him to avoid the teleological bias that still infects most functional thought, an avoidance based on the conviction that historical forces can produce only historical sciences.[54] This is not to say that sociologists have not regarded the existence of the unpredictable, the accidental, or the spontaneous as challenges to systematic theory. A great deal of attention to problems, conflict, and deviant behavior has also been characteristic of the development of sociology. Many of the great creative theoretical advances in sociology have stemmed from a desire to explain the seemingly inexplicable. Combined with these advances, however, there has also developed a somewhat optimistic faith that everything is for the best, that either factors produce functional consequences or they are transitionally disruptive, awaiting only the passage of time or the hand of the reformer. It is this faith that led to the widespread resort to what I have called *hidden logic*, a prescientific vestige that runs throughout the teleological, the Newtonian, and the Darwinian phases of social science development. It renders suspect the thought of one thinker after another and connects the entire tradition of sociology with the nonscientific liberal faith in a natural process of harmony and progress.

It is of some importance, therefore, not to overlook the possible ideological function served by functionalism. The functional view of behavior that emerged in late-nineteenth-century sociology is part of late-liberal society's need to think of the individual less as a given structure with fixed rights, needs, and duties, and more as an adaptable, malleable, decision-making actor in a world of scarcity and complex, plausible alternatives. Along with this redefinition of the individual, which stemmed from widespread experience with the functional differentiation of a maturing industrial society, there also came a redefinition of sociology's method—a more explicit empirical-functional viewpoint, one that transformed reason into method. Such a viewpoint made reason a more serviceable tool for an advanced industrial society and helped liberal society tackle its problems more effectively. However, it also served an ideological purpose in that it blurred the idea that there are standards outside liberal society to which disputes about practices, beliefs, and values can be referred. The ideological function of the new functional mentality, the acceptance of the given, lies precisely in the belief that science can exist without moral or political consequences. The acceptance of the given is also found in the widespread attempt by sociologists to identify the latent (often positive) functions of error and evil and to postulate the existence of a hidden logic that assures social integration and adjustment. It is found as well in the complacent acceptance of the idea of

[54] For an opposite view, see Robert K. Merton, *Social Theory and Social Structure,* enl. ed. (New York: Free Press, 1968), chap. 3; this chapter is also available in paperback in Robert K. Merton's *On Theoretical Sociology* (New York: Free Press paperback, 1967), chap. 3. Merton's analysis is a valuable codification of the elements of functional analysis and an attempt to purge the functional approach of the vestiges of teleology ("the three erroneous postulates") that cling to it and to show that functionalism need not exhibit ideological bias.

multiple causation. At one level, multiple causation can be interpreted as an acceptance of the diverse, internal substructures of what may be a unique historical society; at another, even less sophisticated level, it can be interpreted as psychologistic, in effect an acceptance of the entire multitude of individuals as causes.

It is here, of course, that empiricism, with its stress on particulars, tangibles, observables, and the reality of the sensory world, tends to obliterate abstract thought and coincides with the liberal trend toward practicality—the (unintentional) conservative belief that the only way to master the incredibly complex natural and social worlds is to deal with problems on a piecemeal basis. Functionalism in sociology does not, of course, explicitly identify the structure of liberal industrial society as possibly a unique and unnecessary power structure and the ultimate cause of all social problems. Thus, one is led to think of it as having two sets of functions: the manifest functions of obtaining unified theory and of making society work, and the latent functions of disguising conflict, exploitation, and waste, and safeguarding the privileges of those who benefit from power arrangements, both legitimate and illegitimate.

Despite its ideological nature, functionalism has permeated twentieth-century science, including sociology, and has grown in refinement and sophistication. It has done so not only because it contains the overall appreciation of theory and fact that marks the Age of Empiricism, but because it promises to merge the logical rigor, comprehensiveness, and exactitude of the statistical, experimental, and systems theories; the disciplined imagination of the typological method; the empirical richness of the historical method; and the sense of organic purity of the case method. As such it holds exciting promise as a unified methodology, one that can relate sociology to its sister disciplines in social and natural science and perhaps transcend the limits of vulgar empiricism and solve or bypass the liberal dilemma. In short, functional analysis may be pregnant with the promise of Western social science, a unified theory of human behavior.

It is always possible, however (reflecting a perhaps sounder concept of science), that functionalism will eventually be divorced from substantive theory, and thus from its identification with liberal society, and become a tool for human beings to use in managing their historical, value-laden affairs. The social world would still be regarded as lawful, not in the sense of logic or as in the behavior of lizards, but lawful in the sense of the normative or the instituted. Social facts would be seen, as in Vico, as human creations fashioned to implement a hierarchy of values. Existing material and moral scarcity would be seen as historically induced because of social power. Henceforth, social power would no longer create unnecessary scarcity, falsely justified as the permanent attributes of society and human nature. Instead society would seek abundance and equity through a historically relevant division of social labor, and social power would be restricted solely to the management and equitable sharing of unavoidably scarce goods and services. Given the fact that all human beings; provided they are liberated from class, ethnic, racist, and sexist determination, can probably drive trucks, compute flow charts, or complete medical school, a content-less cosmology could well emerge to replace the mythological structures of prescientific social science—human nature, sex, race, nation, unified theory, society, evolution, achievement ethic; free world, economic growth, progress, democratic elitism, and so on. Functional analysis might well become a nonideological promoter of a genuinely problematic or moral diversity, a help in ending the babel of substantialist sociology and its subservience to unvalidated social power. If the history of sociology is any guide, however, these mythological structures, including substantialist sociology, will continue to thrive as long as the power structures they serve thrive.

Name Index

Abel, Theodore, 308 n, 355 n
Abelard, Peter, 27 n
Abrams, Philip, 174 n, 250 n, 253
Achilles, 74
Adam, 169 n
Aiken, Henry D., 151 n
Alexander, Samuel, 22, 258 n
Allen, Philip J., 450 n
Amin, Samir, 539
Andreski, Stanislav, 128 n
Angell, Norman, 539
Annett, Joan, 527 n
Aquinas, Saint Thomas, 26, 27, 37–38, 39, 149, 152, 167, 188, 333, 531
Aristotle, 21, 24, 25, 32–36, 38, 39, 79, 92, 97, 123, 147, 188, 324, 333, 350
Arnold, E. Vernon, 37 n
Aron, Raymond, 355 n, 544 n
Atkinson, Charles F., 520 n
Atkinson, Dick, 545 n
Austin, John, 171, 396

Babeuf, Gracchus, 531 ,
Bacon, Francis, 45, 48, 54, 117
Bagehot, Walter, 171
Baker, Keith Michael, 101 n
Bales, Robert F., 480, 481 n
Balzac, Honoré de, 145 n
Baran, Paul A., 540 n
Barber, Bernard, 23 n
Barker, Sir Ernest, 32 n, 35 n, 324 n
Barnes, H. E., 293 n
Barrès, Maurice, 236 n, 237
Bayle, Pierre, 105, 329
Beard, Charles A., 6, 171, 395
Becker, Carl, 29, 50
Becker, Howard, 441, 513 n, 515, 516 n, 532 n
Beetham, David, 355 n
Bell, Daniel, 546
Ben-David, Joseph, 23 n
Bendix, Reinhard, 305 n, 355 n, 378 n, 494 n

Benoit-Smullyan, Emile, 293 n
Bentham, Jeremy, 396
Berger, Peter, 525 n
Bergin, Thomas G., 67 n
Bergson, Henri, 22, 25 n, 171, 258 n
Berkeley, George, 22, 53
Berlin, Isaiah, 65 n
Berman, Marshall, 86 n
Bernstein, Eduard, 246
Bershady, Harold J., 469 n
Bichat, Marie François Xavier, 122, 209
Bigongiari, Dino, 38 n
Birnbaum, Norman, 373 n
Black, Max, 469 n, 495 n, 516 n
Blau, Peter, 521
Blumer, Herbert, 434, 435 n, 521
Bodin, Jean, 41, 42
Boltzmann, Ludwig, 260
Bolyai, János, 171, 265
Bonald, Louis (Vicomte de), 124, 146, 147, 171, 188, 236, 301, 319
Bonaparte, Napoleon, 255
Bongiorno, Andrew, 135 n, 328
Booth, Charles, 263, 264 n, 515, 525
Boskoff, Alvin, 513 n, 542 n
Bossuet, Bishop Jacques, 55, 82
Bottomore, T. B., 242 n, 545
Box, Steven, 23 n
Bridges, J. H., 134 n, 135 n
Brodbeck, Arthur J., 481 n
Bryson, Gladys, 47 n, 48 n, 58 n
Buffon, Georges, 31, 175
Bukharin, Nikolai I., 246 n
Burckhardt, Jacob, 378 n
Burdick, Eugene, 481 n
Burgess, Ernest W., 432
Burke, Edmund, 124 n, 147, 156, 252, 301
Burtt, E. A., 28
Bushman, William C., 237 n

Calvin, Jean, 398
Carey, James T., 510, 511 n
Carlyle, Thomas, 237

Subject Index